PERSONAL FINANCE

Dr. Edward R. Willett
CHAIRMAN
DEPARTMENT OF FINANCE
AND INSURANCE

Northeastern University

CHARLES E. MERRILL BOOKS, INC.
COLUMBUS, OHIO

Preface

An awareness of financial responsibilities will enable the reader to avoid mistakes that often are costly. PERSONAL FINANCE offers new information that will guide him through possible problem areas, and will enable him to budget the expenditure of his assets wisely. Each financial question faced by the individual can be solved intelligently only *if* he realizes the importance of the problem, the alternative solutions, and the experiences of others exposed to similar situations.

This book attempts to bring to practical reality the theory of efficient personal finance so that the reader has a better grasp of this very common, yet sometimes confusing, area which confronts us all. The logical organization of this book should enable the reader to understand all of the topics necessary to make him a better personal manager. "Earning a Living," "Budgeting," "Where to Put Your Savings," and "Borrowing" can be considered as general areas of personal finance that everyone has to know so that their liabilities do not exceed their assets. The following chapters deal with more specific financial decisions such as a purchase of a home, of life insurance and health insurance, property and casualty insurance, effective social security, pensions and annuities, and, of course, income taxes. Two unique chapters cover in great detail the very important areas of buying an automobile and college costs. Since these two areas are becoming more important in every generation, wise financial planning will always lead to a successful realization of these goals if foresight has been exercised.

The third section of chapters covers investment possibilities, both in the stock market and in mutual funds, so

iii 149207

that an individual can see increased financial gain other than just from his salary. Chapter 17 thoroughly covers the details of starting your own business, while the last chapter deals with estate planning, covering the final disposition of assets acquired during a person's lifetime.

For this book to be interesting, up-to-date, and practical, it was imperative that the author use forms, tables, and quotations relating to actual existing conditions. The amount of information available in the personal finance field was considerable. National associations cited in the text were generous in providing necessary information. Individual banks, insurance companies, finance companies, business firms, and the publishers freely permitted the use of specific examples and quotations. Special thanks is due the Riggs National Bank of Washington, D.C., which suggested and provided a check drawn by Frances Scott Key.

Special acknowledgements are due to Professors Golemne, Armen, Scioletti, Jackson, and Mr. Fitzgerald of Northeastern University for rendering advice in the areas in which they specialize. Additional thanks are due to Mr. Thomas C. Edwards, Vice-President of TIAA-CREF, who gave freely of his time and energy.

The rapidity with which laws, regulations and conditions change must of necessity outdate certain specific information before it is published. For any errors or omissions present, in spite of the time and services offered by the experts, the author claims sole responsibility.

E. Willett

Boston, Massachusetts
March, 1964

Table of Contents

Chapter 1

EARNING A LIVING

Everyone is interested in earning a living. And did you know that, as a college graduate, you may have an earnings potential of $1,000,000.00?

Table 1–1 shows comparative lifetime income estimates for the years 1949, 1956 and 1958. Note the progressive increase in the amounts, and the 1958 average for males who have completed four or more years of college.

According to current statistics, a person 25 years of age has forty productive, income-producing years ahead of him. The below figures were unbelievable forty years ago, and no one then would have predicted the income levels that were reached in 1958. We should consider, however, the predictions that were made: World War I was the war to end all wars. It didn't. Scientists estimated that an atomic explosion might be produced by the year 2,000. Scientists accomplished it in 1945. Forecasts of future events are often inaccurate. However, if the income levels in our economy continue to rise in the

Table 1–1

LIFETIME INCOME (EARNINGS) BASED ON ARITHMETIC MEANS FOR MALES 18 AND OVER, BY YEARS OF SCHOOL COMPLETED, FOR THE UNITED STATES: 1949, 1956 AND 1958[1]

Years of School Completed	Estimated Lifetime Income		
	1949	1956	1958
Elementary: Total	$113,330	$154,593	$154,114
Less than 8 years	98,222	132,736	129,764
8 years	132,683	180,857	181,695
High School: 1 to 3 years	152,068	205,277	211,193
4 years	185,279	253,631	257,557
College: 1 to 3 years	209,282	291,581	315,504
4 years or more	296,377	405,698	435,242

next forty years as they have during the past forty, the lifetime earnings potential of a person now 25 years of age, and a college graduate, is at least $1,000,000.00, and this figure may prove to be conservative.

Whether your income will be above, below, or equal to the average, depends primarily upon your choice of occupation and your ability to manage money.

CHOICE OF OCCUPATION

Planning your future and choosing your occupation should be done while you are young and have maximum freedom of choice. Chart 1–1 illustrates the reasons why. Note that the "Opportunity for Employment" curve shows the period of opportunity for employment

---

[1] Herman P. Miller, "Annual and Lifetime Income In Relation to Education: 1939–1959." *The American Economic Review*, December 1960, p. 981.

steadily rises between the ages of 20 and 35, and that the period of preparation for a lifetime career is from age 20 to 30. The greatest opportunity for employment occurs between ages 30 and 55, while the opportunity for employment curve reaches a peak earlier in life than the lifetime earnings peak.

Consider one or more occupations you have reason to believe you would enjoy. Few people are either happy or successful in an occupation selected solely for its financial rewards. Of course, the selections must also enable the individual to earn enough to establish a satisfactory standard of living.

There are wide differences between individual standards of living. This decision, too, is personal, and should be based upon what it takes to make you happy. A person working for relatively low pay for a charitable organization, for example, might enjoy a very gratifying sense of happiness and success, and be completely miserable as an industrial tycoon. Set your own standard, then study the opportunities available to you in the fields of your choice.

MANAGING YOUR MONEY

Most people must learn to live on the money they earn. This takes constant budgeting and planning. The ease or difficulty with which financial problems are met and solved is directly proportionate to the skill with which the individual manages his income.

A large income doesn't eliminate the need for good management. Many persons with comfortable incomes find themselves unprepared to meet emergencies and fail entirely to provide for their retirement. They never accumulate enough capital to do the things they want to do, and frequently borrow excessively against future earnings. They live from day to day, spending money when they have it, and using their credit when they don't. This type of person helps neither himself nor the society in which he lives.

The person who learns to manage his money develops a happy, healthy outlook early in life, takes an interest in his future, accepts responsibility, and utilizes his talents to the utmost.

MEETING COMPETITION

For most people, there is more than one specific job that seems attractive. Inasmuch as it is obviously easier to enter a field in which there is a shortage of labor than one in which there is an oversupply, some research is required to learn all you can about your competition.

Chart 1–1

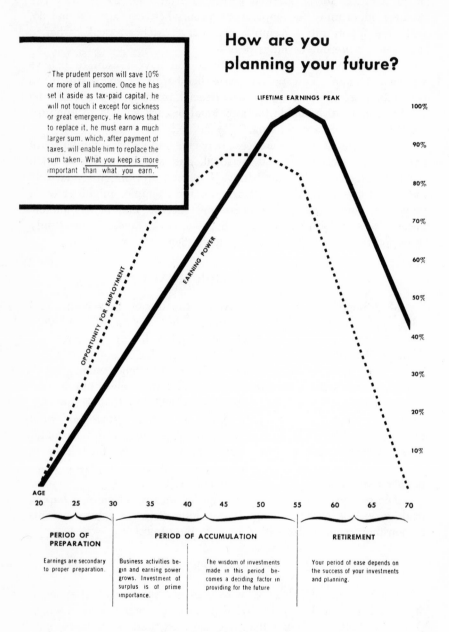

How are you planning your future?

"The prudent person will save 10% or more of all income. Once he has set it aside as tax-paid capital, he will not touch it except for sickness or great emergency. He knows that to replace it, he must earn a much larger sum, which, after payment of taxes, will enable him to replace the sum taken. What you keep is more important than what you earn."

LIFETIME EARNINGS PEAK

100%
90%
80%
70%
60%
50%
40%
30%
20%
10%

OPPORTUNITY FOR EMPLOYMENT

EARNING POWER

AGE
20   25   30   35   40   45   50   55   60   65   70

PERIOD OF PREPARATION	PERIOD OF ACCUMULATION	RETIREMENT
Earnings are secondary to proper preparation.	Business activities begin and earning power grows. Investment of surplus is of prime importance. / The wisdom of investments made in this period becomes a deciding factor in providing for the future	Your period of ease depends on the success of your investments and planning.

Source: *All You Need to Know about Mutual Funds. . .*, New York: Lee Higginson Corporation, p. 20.

How many others are looking for jobs in your areas of interest? Who are they?

Table 1–2 indicates the changes that are going to take place in the labor force between 1960 and 1970. Examine this table carefully and note the following:

1. The "under 25" age group shows the greatest increase. (Persons under 14 are not included in the labor force.)
2. The 25–34 year old age group shows the least increase.
3. The 35–44 year old age group shows a decline. This is usually considered the key group in the work force, as they are relatively young, and experienced.
4. The "over 45" age group shows the second largest increase.

All of this indicates that young people will face a very competitive situation in the next ten years, but that opportunities for advancement will be excellent.

Table 1–2

CHANGES IN THE NUMBER & AGE DISTRIBUTION OF PEOPLE IN THE LABOR FORCE, 1960–1970

Age Group	Number in labor force		Proportion in labor force		Change 1960 to 1970	
	1960 (millions)	1970 (millions)	1960 (percent)	1970 (percent)	(millions)	(percent)
All workers	73.6	87.1	100.0	100.0	+13.5	+18.3
Under 25 years	13.8	20.2	18.7	23.2	+ 6.4	+46.0
25–34 years	15.3	17.1	20.8	19.6	+ 1.8	+12.0
35–44 years	16.6	16.4	22.6	18.8	— 0.2	— 1.0
45 years and over	27.9	33.4	37.9	35.4	+ 5.5	+20.0

Source: "Occupational Outlook Handbook," United States Department of Labor, 1961 Edition, p. 15.

It might seem paradoxical that the number of workers in the labor force under 25 is increasing, while a higher percentage of persons under 25 are staying in school longer. The reason is that the total number in this age group is increasing. The birth rate rose in 1945, at the end of World War II, and has continued to rise ever since. In 1955, 2.2 million reached the age of 18. By 1965, 3.8 million will reach this age each year through 1970.

Referring again to Table 1–2, women should be aware of the fact that of the total increase of 13.5 million in the labor force, about half will be women. The usual pattern for them is to start work or college at 17 or 18, work or study for three or four years, and then marry. The majority of those who are working continue to work until the first baby arrives, then leave the labor market until their youngest child is old enough for school. They re-enter the market at this time, along with those who went to college, married, had children, and are entering the market for the first time. Statistically, they are now in their mid-thirties, and tend to stay in the market until they reach 65.

Not all women follow this pattern, of course. Some continue working while their children are young; others never re-enter the market; and still others, approximately one in ten, remain single and work about the same length of time as the men.

Table 1–3 indicates how long women can expect to hold jobs. Too often they assume that choosing an occupation is something for boys to do, but not for girls. The table shows that this is not true. The pattern presented in the table indicates that even women who get married and have children can expect to work about 27 years during their lives. They would be wise to select a career just as carefully as do boys, so that these 27 years will be both pleasant and rewarding.

Table 1–3

WOMEN'S WORK-LIFE EXPECTANCY

	Number of Years
Single	40
Married—no children	31
Married—with children	27

CAREERS AVAILABLE

In estimating future employment and job opportunities, the Bureau of Labor Statistics makes certain assumptions: [2]

---

[2] "Occupational Outlook Handbook," United States Department of Labor, Bureau of Labor Statistics, 1961 Edition, pp. 5–6.

1. that high levels of economic activity and employment will be maintained over the long run, even though there may be temporary recessions;
2. that there will be no major war, but, that the defense program will continue at about the current level;
3. that scientific and technical advances will continue;
4. that the institutions and fundamental economic structure of the United States will not change significantly.

History indicates that wars and other catastrophes do occur. If they do, of course, estimates will prove to be incorrect. Young people, however, couldn't plan without assumptions such as these to build on.

What jobs will be available is a question which is more difficult to estimate than the size and structure of the labor force. The number of males that will reach 18 in 1970 can be estimated quite easily. If you know the number of males 8 years old in 1960, all you have to do is subtract the number expected to die before reaching 18. While the answer won't be perfect, the estimate will be reasonably accurate.

Jobs are a different story. What jobs are available depends to a considerable degree on the four assumptions: that the economy maintains high levels of economic activity and employment; that there is no major war; that the institutions and economic structure of the United States stay the same; that scientific and technical advances will continue. How fast will the advances continue?

Mr. James E. Webb, Administrator, National Aeronautics and Space Administration, stated it this way:[3]

> Let me state it in terms you have heard before:
> Change, and the accelerating rate of change, will be the dominant features of your existence.
> Change means different things to different people. To some it means an uncomfortable uprooting of a settled existence. To others it may mean disillusionment and despair. To still others — and this is the group in which you can place yourselves — it means progress and opportunity.

Mr. Webb presented an interesting contrast by comparing the progress made in the time from King Solomon to George Washington with the progress made from Washington's time to the present. Both King Solomon and George Washington wore homespun clothing, used

---

[3] James E. Webb, "Science and Technology—Keys to Economic Progress," Address, June 17, 1962, Northeastern University, Boston, Mass., p. 5.

oil lamps, heated their homes with wood, and traveled in horse-drawn vehicles. Compare this, covering a period of almost 3,000 years, with the progress made in the period since Washington, just a little over 165 years.

Any estimate of jobs, any description of jobs, must be predicated upon the assumption that great changes can and will take place during the next forty or fifty years. Due in large part to the great increase in emphasis on research since World War II, scientific advances are made more rapidly, and affect our way of life more quickly, than ever before.

Table 1–4 lists some of the occupations in which the U.S. Department of Labor's 1961 Occupational Outlook Handbook estimates there will be employment opportunities during the period 1960–1970. This handbook, published about every two years, is one of the most thorough sources available. Reference to it is highly recommended for anyone interested in job opportunities. The researcher will find that some of the occupations listed in Table 1–4 are believed to offer opportunities beyond the 1960–1970 period.

Table 1–4[4]

Occupations Offering Employment Opportunities — 1960–1970

Accountants	Ceramic Engineers
Actuaries	Chemical Engineers
Aeronautical Engineers	Chemists
Air Conditioning Mechanics	Civil Engineers
Air Traffic Controllers	Clerical Workers
Agricultural Engineers	Clergy
Anthropologists	College Professors
Appliance Servicemen	Construction Electricians
Architects	Construction Machinery Operators
Astronomers	
Automobile Mechanics	Dancing Teachers
	Dental Hygienists
Barbers	Dental Laboratory Technicians
Beauty Operators	Dentists
Biophysicists	Diesel Mechanics
Bookkeeping Workers	Dieticians
Business Machine Servicemen	Draftsmen
Carpenters	Economists
Cement Masons	Electrical Engineers

---

[4] "Occupational Outlook Handbook," U.S. Department of Labor, 1961 Edition.

Electronic Computer Operating
  Personnel

Foresters

Geophysicists

Home Economists

Industrial Engineers
Industrial Machinery Repairmen
Instrument Machinery Repairmen
Industrial Traffic Managers

Lawyers
Librarians
Life Insurance Agents
Lithographic Craftsmen

Machinists
Maintenance Electricians
Market Research Workers
Mathematicians
Mechanical Engineers
Medical X-Ray Technicians
Medical Technologists
Metallurgists
Meteorologists
Microbiologists
Music Teachers

Nurses (Registered Prof. and Practical)

Occupational Therapists
Office Machine Operators
Optometrists

Pharmacists

Pharmacologists
Physicians
Physical Therapists
Physicists
Physiologists
Phytopathologists
Plumbers
Podiatrists
Political Scientists
Pressmen
Programmers
Property & Casualty Insurance Agents
  & Brokers
Psychologists
Public Relations Workers
Purchasing Agents

Refrigeration Mechanics

Salesmen & Saleswomen
School Counselors
Secretaries
Sheet Metal Workers
Singing Teachers
Social Workers
Statisticians
Stenographers
Stewardesses

Teachers
Tool & Die Makers
Truck Drivers (over-the-road)
Typists

Veterinarians

How can there be so many job opportunities when the United States is constantly facing the problem of unemployment? One reason is that there are oversupplies of workers in some fields and undersupplies in others. Many of the occupations in the table have extreme personnel shortages today and, according to the Department of Labor, are expected to have serious shortages for some years in the future (in teaching, for example). Other fields have more workers than demand requires. It is important that you carefully scrutinize your choice of occupation in the light of supply and demand.

The selection of an occupation must be considered in two parts. First, what type of work do you prefer, and second, what industry do you think offers the most opportunities? You may, for example, want to be an accountant. Next, do you want to be an accountant in the aero-space industry or in the insurance industry? According to the Occupational Handbook, employment in construction and finance industries will grow far more rapidly than the average. On the other hand, employment in agriculture is expected to decline substantially.

IMPORTANCE OF EDUCATION

Why bother with a high school diploma? Why go to college? One good reason is because, on the average, the further you go the higher your lifetime earnings will be. Refer again to Table 1–1. As you can see, the estimated lifetime earnings in 1958 for a male who had less than eight years of school was $129,764, and for one completing four years or more of college the figure was $435,242, more than three times as much.

Estimated lifetime earnings are higher at each succeeding educational level. The estimate for those completing eight years of elementary school is more than that for those completing less. The estimate for those completing high school is higher than for those just completing eight years of elementary school, and the figure for those completing four years of college is higher than for those just completing high school.

These estimates are based on average arithmetic means for males in the United States. Many make much less than these amounts, and many, much more. College graduates vary from the unsuccessful to the outstanding. Furthermore, these estimates do not mean that all college graduates will make more than all high school graduates, etc. Unfortunately, education sometimes is desired simply for prestige value, and some individuals who are not good students are forced to go to college by their well meaning parents. They are miserable and unsuccessful, not only because they are forced to continue their education, but also because they may never do the particular type of work they enjoy the most. There are very definitely non-college graduates who earn a much higher income than most college graduates.

It is more and more essential, however, for young people to continue their education. The most rapidly growing occupations are those requiring the most education and trained skills.

It is a fact of life that the competition is much greater today among non-college graduates than ever before, and that the averages favor the person with more education. It is unfortunate that estimates indicate that there will be 7½ million school dropouts between 1960 and 1970, and that 2½ million of those won't complete the eighth grade. These young people face an increasingly competitive situation. In 1961, about 41 percent of the high school graduates were enrolled in college (see Table 1–5), and this percentage will probably increase. The total number of bachelors and masters degrees and doctorates is expected to about double between 1959 and 1970.

Table 1–5[5]

COLLEGE ENROLLMENT AND LABOR FORCE STATUS OF JUNE 1961 HIGH SCHOOL GRADUATES IN THE CIVILIAN NONINSTITUTIONAL POPULATION, OCTOBER 1961

[Thousands of persons 16 to 24 years of age]

College enrollment status, sex, color, and marital status of women	Civilian noninsti-tutional population		Civilian labor force		Not in labor force
	Num-ber	Percent	Num-ber	Percent of population	
BOTH SEXES					
Total	1,763	100.0	924	52.4	839
White	1,612	91.4	839	52.0	773
Nonwhite	151	8.6	85	56.3	66
Enrolled in college	847	48.0	194	22.9	653
Full time	801	45.4	159	19.8	642
Part time	46	2.6	36	(1)	11
Not enrolled in college	916	52.0	730	79.7	186
In special schools	141	8.0	63	44.7	78
MALE					
Total	790	100.0	417	52.8	373
Enrolled in college	445	56.3	120	27.0	325
Not enrolled in college	345	43.7	297	86.1	48
FEMALE					
Total	973	100.0	507	52.1	466
Enrolled in college	402	41.3	74	18.4	328
Not enrolled in college	571	58.7	433	75.8	138
Single	482	49.5	392	81.3	90
Married and other marital status[2]	89	9.1	41	(1)	48

[1] Percent not shown where base is less than 100,000.
[2] Includes widowed, divorced, and separated women.
Note: Because of rounding, sums of individual items may not equal totals.

[5] Jacob Schiffman, "Employment of High School Graduates and Dropouts in 1961," *Monthly Labor Review,* U.S. Dept. of Labor, May 1962, Vol. 85, No. 5, p. 503.

Education, however, cannot be looked at just from a financial point of view. Examine the job opportunities in Table 1–4. Those jobs requiring the most education are usually considered the most desirable. The working conditions are better, the work is more satisfying, etc. Furthermore, the broadening nature of a college education helps one to get more out of life and to be a better citizen.

Business, too, has become more and more involved in education. It is estimated that about 17 billion dollars a year will be spent by business on formal and informal training programs. This represents an investment of $1.00 for every $3.00 allocated for education in our school system, including public and private, elementary and secondary schools, and colleges.[6]

Today, education is more important than ever as a key to the better jobs and the higher incomes. The more education, the greater the opportunities for both a satisfying lifetime career and a high income. Eventually, it may become necessary to continue studying throughout your business life, either in formal business-sponsored programs or informally on your own. Business, government, life in general, is not only changing at a rapidly accelerating pace, but is becoming more complex.

FINDING A JOB

Once you have decided on a career and have satisfied the necessary requirements in terms of education, you still have to get a job. This is the point where many people fail completely.

Job hunting is not simple. There are many helpful techniques which will teach prospective employees what to do and how to do it, and also what not to do. All available counseling services should be considered, and the many federal, state, and local programs investigated.

This subject cannot be adequately covered in this text, and no attempt has been made to do justice to it. It is impossible, however, to leave the subject of incomes and occupations without emphasizing the fact that job finding is a problem which requires time and effort; and it is hoped that this brief discussion will be a spur to prod people, young people especially, to give serious thought to the subject, and to be aware of the tremendous opportunities offered by the world

---

[6] "Education By Business," *Business in Brief*, New York: The Chase Manhattan Bank, No. 47, Nov.-Dec., 1962.

in which they live. If each person is to realize his full potential, opportunities must be recognized and plans carefully made.

From this point on, we will be concerned only with the many financial problems facing the individual and his family. Failure to deal adequately with these problems has brought frustration and unhappiness to many. Careful financial planning and an intelligent approach to financial problems can contribute greatly to a happy and satisfying life.

Questions

1. Why should an individual be concerned with the number of workers across the country working in his particular job title?

2. Explain the "Earnings Curve"—Chart 1-1, page 4, showing how this curve is logical. Give reasons.

3. What are three (3) key considerations in choosing a career?

4. During the next 10 years, there will be a shortage of individuals in the 35-45 age bracket (the most productive years). What effect will this have on the labor market?

5. Women should not choose a career carefully, since they will marry in the future and eventually leave the job in which they are working. Discuss.

6. What jobs will show tremendous "growth" potential during the next 10 years? Why?

7. Should your child be a harness-maker, if this is the field he chooses as a career? Discuss.

8. You should force your children to go to college, since college graduates earn more income than dropouts. Discuss.

9. Choose a career that offers the greatest financial rewards. Discuss.

10. Can you think of any industries that should show a decline during the next decade? Name one industry and explain, logically, why you expect it to decline.

Problems

1. Sam Katz is 26 years old. His annual earned income is $7200 per year. He is married, with one child. His long-range goal is to retire at age 62 and devote the rest of his life to his principal hobby; painting. What is Katz's potential worth.

2. Ben and Jack went to high school together. Ben was a "dropout," leaving high school at age 16 to enter the high paying construction business as a laborer. Jack managed to scrimp and save enough money to pay his way through college. After graduation, Jack accepts a job paying $480 per month. One day he meets Ben and the two exchange greetings. Ben states that he is now construction boss, earning $520 per month. Which individual should earn the most income in the future and why?

3. Tom is faced with a problem. He has just completed four years of college. During these years he has barely made ends meet. Now he is faced with an important decision. Shall he accept a job in business now, at an attractive salary, or shall he pursue his master's degree in business? Advise.

4. Stewart Stoler is a machinist. He has worked on the same machine for 30 years. His main job consists of running this machine and maintaining it. He takes pride in his work and jeers at fellow employees who are constantly discussing the effects of automation on their jobs. One day he discovers that automation has replaced him, and he is now unemployed. How could he have avoided this catastrophe?

5. Peter McCabe, age 53, is enjoying his peak earning years. Friends, older than he, have warned him about a sudden drop in income as he gets older. If Peter does not choose to retire at age 65, might he still experience a drop in income? Explain.

Selected Readings

Calvert, Robert Jr. and Steele, John E., *Planning Your Career*, McGraw-Hill Book Co., Inc., New York, N.Y., 1963

Lowen, Walter, *You and Your Job*, Collier Books, division of The Crowell-Collier Publishing Co., New York, N.Y., 1962

Markets of the Sixties, by the Editors of Fortune, Harper & Brothers, New York, N.Y., Copyright 1958, 1959, 1960 by Time, Inc.

Miller, Herman P., *Annual and Lifetime Income in Relation to Education: 1939-1959*, The American Economic Review, December 1960, p. 981

"Occupational Outlook Handbook," United States Department of Labor, Washington, D.C., (most recent edition)

Pitt, Galvin A., assisted by Smith, Richard W., *The Twenty-Minute Lifetime*, Prentice-Hall Inc., Englewood Cliffs, N.J., 1959

Winter, Elmer, *A Woman's Guide to Earning a Good Living*, Simon and Schuster, New York, N.Y., 1961

"Your Job & Your Future," *Changing Times, The Kiplinger Magazine,* The Kiplinger Washington Editors, Washington, D.C.

Chapter **2**

BUDGETING

When Mr. John S. Stormont was 15, he lived in Chelsea, Mass., and made 25¢ each week on his paper route. He earned this tremendous sum because his paper route was extremely long. By careful planning, he made this serve him well. Take Saturday, for example. Saturday afternoon is customarily a time when young people enjoy themselves, and John was no exception. He allotted 10¢ to Saturday and enjoyed himself immensely. The 10¢ went for the following, presented in the order of their purchase:

1. "Belly-wash" soda
   (without cream)   1¢
2. Two cigarettes   1¢
3. "Hoky-poky" ice cream cone
   (tablespoon size)   1¢
4. Handful of broken candy wafers   1¢
5. Movies
   (Until 6 P. M. when young people were ejected)   5¢
6. Grab-bag of candy   1¢
                                                                     ——

   Total   10¢

While John's Saturday left much to be desired nutritionally, he certainly did enjoy himself. The year was 1914.[1]

Things have changed considerably since 1914. Today, a Saturday like this would cost $1 or more; but on the other hand, 15 year old paper boys now make considerably more than 25¢ per week. Many of them make between $6 and $10 per week, depending on their route and tips. Notice that while the cost of the Saturday has increased about 10 times, the earnings of the paper boys are about 30 times higher. The same type of change has affected everyone. Prices have gone up considerably since 1914 in the United States, but income has climbed even more rapidly. This means that the average person, like the average paper boy, is much better off today in terms of "real income" (what he can buy with his money).

Why then is it so difficult for the average person to live on his income? One reason is that so many more things are available today. Take the paper boy, for example. Consider the things he may chose today. He may want a transistor radio, skis, microscope, or telescope; he may want to go into the city to visit the science museum or to see a professional sporting event; he probably wants to go to the weekly teen-age dance and go out afterwards for a sandwich; and he may already be considering the possibility of saving enough cash to buy his own car. These are only a few of the things that were not considered by boys his age in 1914, partly because some of these hadn't been invented (like transistor radios), while others were available only to the sons of the extremely wealthy. It is clear then that a boy must pay more for the same things now that he would have purchased in 1914, he must save more for the same dreams, and that the number of things available to him has increased.

---

[1] Mr. John S. Stormont has for many years owned and operated the Ox-Bow Pet Shop in Wakefield, Mass., and appears to be in the best of health in spite of his Saturday diet as a youth.

Because of the number of decisions he must make, the boy of today is no better off, in fact he may be worse off, than the boy in 1914. This is true for all of us. How we should spend our money is more of a problem today because the choices keep increasing. In 1914 we wouldn't have had to decide between the purchase of a new automobile, a new television, a summer cottage, a swimming pool, an electronic organ, another telephone, etc. Either these things would not have been invented or would have been completely out of our financial reach.

How this decision-making problem is handled determines, to a considerable degree, personal and family happiness. Two families may be of the same size, have the same income, and live in the same neighborhood; yet one family may live comfortably and enjoy life, while the other never seems to be able to get ahead and is always debt ridden. Why the difference? The unfortunate family often rationalizes by saying, "it's the breaks" or, "we've had tough luck." This can happen, of course. A family can be so stricken by constant sickness and disaster that they can never be financially solvent. Usually, however, this is not the case. Usually, the difference is that the happy family plans its spending, while the other lives from day to day and never plans ahead.

Is this a problem women as well as men should worry about? Definitely yes, for two reasons. This is true, first, because no family planning can ever be successful without the cooperation of every member of the family. Financial planning is a matter requiring total family participation. This means that husband and wife should work out such a plan together and be primarily responsible for its success or failure, while including the children in some of the planning. The earlier the children learn how to plan ahead, the better. The sooner they learn that all things are not immediately available when asked for, the better for them and their family. This isn't to suggest that they should know the family's income and the details of family financial problems. It does mean, however, that permitting them to share in the effort to save for something new that the family wants is good training for the future. The understanding that such things cannot be purchased on the spur of the moment, but require advance planning, hard work, and saving, can do a great deal to make them better citizens and happier persons when they grow up. Family financial planning is good training.

Another reason why this is a problem women should consider is because women have such an important role in the American family's financial picture. While men earn the largest percentage of family income, women control the spending of the largest part of the family income. Furthermore, due partly to their longer life expectancy, women own a large percentage of the nation's private wealth, and are beneficiaries of a large percentage of all life insurance policies.

BUDGETS

A plan for managing money is called a budget. Every single person and every family should have one. First, though, it might be a good idea to take inventory to see how things stand today. One possible inventory form is presented on Table 2–1. Once this is completed, you will know exactly where you or the family stand financially today. Furthermore, estimating your total wealth next year will permit a comparison between next year's actual inventory and this estimate. This will tell whether your financial condition is improving as expected. Setting a goal for age 65 gives a long-range objective. This goal will be the amount needed for your retirement and as an estate for your heirs.

Next, establish other goals. If you are married, this should be a family affair. Decide what things are needed or wanted this year, next year, and in the more distant future. Collective family planning is absolutely necessary, as any plan to achieve such goals can only be successful if everyone works together. Remember that goals are not achieved immediately. Time and patience are needed as well as money.

Establishing goals is especially important for newly married couples. This is the time when it is particularly necessary to realize that, in one sense, the race for financial success often seems to go to the tortoise and not to the hare. Many couples try to start their married lives with everything, and end up with nothing. Others, much wiser, start frugally and end up with everything they could hope for.

Now that an inventory has been taken and goals established, it is time to construct a budget, a plan for managing money. Fundamentally, this is very simple, involving three basic steps:

1. Estimate income for the next year.
2. Estimate expenses for the next year.
3. Balance the two, either by cutting estimated expenses or placing any surplus income in some form of savings.

Table 2-1
YOUR PERSONAL INVENTORY
ASSETS

SAVINGS ACCOUNTS	Present Value	Total		Present Value	Total
			TOTAL OF 1st COLUMN	_____	
BANK	_____		REAL ESTATE		
SAVINGS BANK	_____		HOUSE	_____	
SAVINGS AND LOAN	_____		GARAGE	_____	
CO-OPERATIVE BANK	_____		LAND	_____	
CREDIT UNIONS	_____		OTHER	_____	
OTHER	_____			TOTAL	_____
CASH VALUE OF LIFE INSURANCE	_____		VALUE OF AUTOMOBILE(S)	_____	
BONDS	_____		VALUE OF OTHER MEANS OF LOCOMOTION	_____	
COMMON AND PREFERRED STOCK	_____			TOTAL	_____
OTHER INVESTMENTS	_____		MISCELLANEOUS ASSETS		
PENSIONS	_____		BOOKS	_____	
OTHER	_____		HOBBIES	_____	
	TOTAL	_____	OTHER	_____	
HOUSEHOLD			CASH ON HAND		
FURNITURE, RUGS, ETC.	_____		POCKETBOOK	_____	
JEWELRY, SILVERWARE, ETC.	_____		"PIGGY BANK"	_____	
LINEN, CLOTHES, FURS, ETC.	_____		CHECKING ACCOUNT	_____	
				TOTAL	_____
OTHER	_____		ADD ALL TOTALS IN EACH CATEGORY TO GET TOTAL ASSETS		_____
	TOTAL	_____			

LIABILITIES

MORTGAGE ON REAL ESTATE	Owed	Total		Owed	Total
	_____		TOTAL OF 1st COLUMN		_____
INSTALLMENT LOANS			FINANCE COMPANY	_____	
BANK	_____		CLOTHING	_____	
CAR	_____		OTHER	_____	
FURNITURE	_____			TOTAL	_____
TAXES	_____		ADD ALL TOTALS IN EACH CATEGORY TO GET TOTAL LIABILITIES		_____
	TOTAL	_____			

SUBTRACT TOTAL LIABILITIES FROM TOTAL ASSETS

TOTAL ASSETS _____

TOTAL LIABILITIES _____

YOUR TOTAL WEALTH _____

What do you estimate your total wealth a year hence? _____

What is your goal for age 65? _____

Do the results please you? If not, start today on a program that will insure greater pleasure the next time you take this inventory!

How? Spend less than you earn, and put the surplus into the savings plan of your choice.

Source: The National Thrift Committee, Chicago, Illinois.

Making Estimates

Actually, of course, the task is over-simplified. Making a budget isn't quite that easy. A certain amount of work is necessary. To make this work easier, many organizations publish complete budget books. An example of these is one published by the Security First National Bank of Los Angeles, California. The first part of the book contains monthly forms to use for a household budget. There are 31 lines under each category so that entries may be made each day of the month. This form is presented on page 22. At the bottom of the page is the amount budgeted for the month for each expense, so that it may later be compared with the amount actually spent.

A "Budget Control Summary" is presented on pages 23–24. Monthly totals for each expense and the amount budgeted are entered on this form. There are two columns for each month, one for "Budget" and one for "Actual." At the far right are columns used to enter annual totals. This enables a person to see how his budget plan has actually worked for an entire year. Expenses which have been under or over the estimates can easily be spotted by comparing the actual with the budget figures.

A complete and self-explanatory plan for managing a family's money has been prepared by the Institute of Life Insurance and is presented on pages 26–27. This requires converting income and expenses to weekly figures. It is an extremely complete and useful method.

Making budget estimates requires family conferences and records. If no records of past spending are available, check-stubs may serve. If nothing is available it will be necessary to keep careful and detailed records for a short time for use in building a budget. A form that might be used for this purpose is presented in Chart 2-2.

Remember, too, that it is best to underestimate income and over-estimate expenses. It is an unfortunate fact of life that income often seems to be less than expected and expenses more than anticipated. This is why an "Emergency Fund" (as presented in *The Family Money Manager*) is so important. It is impossible to predict all expenses that may occur.

What happens if expenses exceed income? This means a complete re-examination of estimated expenses. First, consider the fixed expenses. Can fuel bills be reduced? Are windows and doors weather stripped? Has the heating system been checked recently? Can automobile insurance be reduced? Can insurance costs be reduced by making payments annually instead of monthly? How about amounts

HOUSEHOLD BUDGET

MONTH OF ____

	FOOD Groceries Dairy Items Beverages Meals Away From Home	HOUSING Mortgage or Rent • Utilities Insurance Taxes • Repairs Furnishings	CLOTHING Purchases Laundry & Cleaning Alterations	MEDICAL Doctors Dentists • Drugs Health Insurance	TRANS-PORTATION Car Expenses Insurance Fares • Parking License	RECREATION & ADVANCEMENT Schools • Tuition Lessons • Dues Vacation Recreation	GIFTS & CONTRIBU-TIONS Church Charities Personal Gifts	PERSONAL ALLOWANCES	OTHER EXPENSES Life Insurance Income Taxes Not Withheld	SAVINGS Savings Deposits Investments	TOTAL	INCOME After Deductions: Income Tax, Social Security, Etc.
	25%-35%	18%-30%	7%-12%	5%-7%	8%-12%	3%-5%	2%-10%	5%-8%	4%-6%	5%-15%		
1												
2												
3												
4												
5												
6												
7												
8												
9												
10												
11												
12												
13												
14												
15												
16												
17												
18												
19												
20												
21												
22												
23												
24												
25												
26												
27												
28												
29												
30												
31												
TOTAL SPENT												
AMOUNT BUDGETED												

BUDGET CONTROL SUMMARY

	JANUARY		FEBRUARY		MARCH		APRIL		MAY	
	BUDGET	ACTUAL	BUDGET	ACTUAL	BUDGET	ACTUAL	BUDGET	ACTUAL	BUDGET	ACTUAL
GROSS INCOME—Salary, wages, interest, dividends, and other income										
LESS: Income tax, Social Security, and other deductions from pay										
EQUALS: "SPENDABLE INCOME"										
FOOD—Including meals away from home, beverages										
HOUSING										
Mortgage payment or rent										
Property taxes										
Fire insurance										
Maintenance and repairs										
Household supplies, cleaning										
Home furnishings—furniture, appliances, dishes, linens										
Utilities—water, electricity, gas, telephone										
CLOTHING—Including laundry, cleaning, alterations & repairs, materials & supplies										
MEDICAL—Doctor, dentist, hospital, medical insurance, drugs and supplies										
TRANSPORTATION										
Car payment										
Auto insurance										
Auto registration & license										
Other auto expense—gas, oil, tires, repairs										
Public transportation										
RECREATION & ADVANCEMENT										
Annual vacation expenses										
Tuition, school expenses										
Other—newspapers, magazines, books, movies,										
toys, hobbies, music lessons, baby sitters										
PERSONAL ALLOWANCES—Barber & beauty shop services, cosmetics, pocket money										
GIFTS & CONTRIBUTIONS—Christmas, birthday, wedding gifts, church, Community Chest										
OTHER EXPENSES										
Life insurance										
Federal income tax, other than amounts withheld										
State income tax										
Other										
SAVINGS—Including investments										
TOTAL BUDGET (Compare with "Spendable Income" as above)										

23

	JUNE		JULY		AUGUST		SEPTEMBER		OCTOBER		NOVEMBER		DECEMBER		TOTAL	
	BUDGET	ACTUAL	BUDGET	ACTUAL	BUDGET	ACTUAL	BUDGET	ACTUAL	BUDGET	ACTUAL	BUDGET	ACTUAL	BUDGET	ACTUAL	BUDGET	ACTUAL

planned for Christmas and birthday gifts, annual subscriptions, needed repairs and equipment for the home, or a planned vacation? Can these be reduced?

How about reducing weekly living costs? Careful planning and wise buying can do a great deal to reduce the cost of food, household operations, car expenses, lunches, clothing, recreation, etc. Shop at the right time; retail stores usually reduce prices on certain items at particular times of the year, as indicated in Table 2-2. Plan in advance

Chart 2-2

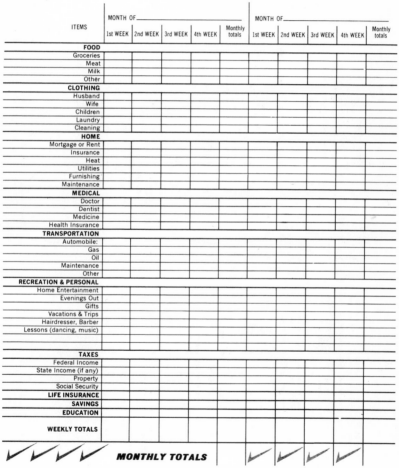

Source: "Your Family Budget Planner," reproduced, Courtesy of John Hancock Mutual Life Insurance Company, Boston, Massachusetts.

INCOME

Write down in this chart all the cash you expect to receive in the next 12 months. If your income is from wages or salary, include only your "take-home" cash pay. If it is from a business, farm or trade, make the best estimate you can.

Don't forget to include any extra cash income you may receive — interest or dividends from bonds and other investments, money which the children may turn into the family, rent you may get from property you own.

Add up your figures, divide by 52, and you will know what your average weekly income will be for the next 12 months. This is the money your family has to spend and save.

(Remember, you don't have to put your budget on a week-to-week basis unless you want to. If a twice-a-month budget is more desirable, divide by 24 all through your Money Manager whenever it says to divide by 52. If you want a monthly budget, divide by 12.)

FIXED EXPENSES AND OBLIGATIONS

The secret of the Money Manager is this: it allows you to "save ahead" to meet fixed expenses and obligations, so when they come due you will have enough money to pay them.

Here, under Step 2, write down what these fixed expenses and obligations are in your household — rent or mortgage payments, life insurance premiums, taxes other than payroll taxes, church contributions, installment payments and so on. Indicate in what months these outlays will come due.

If you *know* you are going to have a big fuel bill in October or a clothing bill for the children in the Spring or some expensive dentist work for Johnny in the winter, write down these expenses. But *don't* try to guess all your doubtful future expenses, for you'll find it's too difficult. Put down only the major expenses and obligations which you can estimate pretty closely in advance.

Add up all your items, divide by 52, and you will have your *weekly set-aside*. This money goes into a special fund every pay-day. When your fixed expenses and obligations come due later on, they will be paid out of this fund.

---

1 — ESTIMATE OF OUR TOTAL CASH INCOME

Annual Wages or Income from Farm or Business....................
Interest or Dividends from Bonds and Investments.................
Income from Other Members of Family............................
Other Income ....

Total ANNUAL Income....................................... $ _____ a year
Total WEEKLY Income (Divide Annual Income by 52)........ $ _____ a week

This is the money which we have to spend and save during the next 52 weeks.
Enter the amount in the "Family Balance Sheet" at the bottom of the page.

2 — ESTIMATE OF OUR FIXED EXPENSES AND OBLIGATIONS

	JAN.	FEB.	MAR.	APRIL	MAY	JUNE	JULY	AUG.	SEPT.	OCT.	NOV.	DEC.	Total 12 Months
FAMILY HOUSING													
Rent, Mortgage Payt.													
Major Fuel Bills													
Other													
FAMILY PROTECTION													
Life Insurance													
Other Insurance													
OUR FAMILY IN THE COMMUNITY													
Church													
Donations													
FAMILY DEBTS AND OBLIGATIONS													
Installments													
Other Debts													
TAXES AND LICENSES													
Taxes													
Licenses													
OTHER MAJOR ITEMS													

This is the Money We Shall Put in a Special Fund Every Week to Meet
Future Expenses and Obligations. Enter it on the "Family Balance Sheet"

Total for the Year _____
OUR WEEKLY SET ASIDE (Divide by 52) _____

ESTIMATE OF OUR WEEKLY LIVING ALLOWANCE

MOTHER'S EXPENDITURES	HOW MUCH A WEEK?
Food	
Household Operation	
Laundry	
TOTAL (Enter Here)	

PERSONAL ALLOWANCES, Minor Articles of Clothing, Cigarettes, Ice Cream Cones, Etc.	HOW MUCH A WEEK?
Father	
Mother	
Others in Family	
TOTAL (Enter Here)	

FATHER'S EXPENDITURES	
Car Operation	
Lunches	
TOTAL (Enter Here)	

OTHER ITEMS AND MISCELLANEOUS

TOTAL (Enter Here)

FAMILY EXPENSES	
Clothing	
Recreation	
Ordinary Medical and Drug Store	
TOTAL (Enter Here)	

OUR WEEKLY ESTIMATE FOR LIVING EXPENSES

This is the amount we shall pay ourselves every week and try to make last until the next week begins. Enter it on the "Balance Sheet."

OUR FAMILY "BALANCE SHEET"

OUR WEEKLY INCOME IS................................(Step 1)
OUR WEEKLY SET-ASIDES AMOUNT TO...............(Step 2)
OUR EMERGENCY FUND...............................(Step 3)
OUR WEEKLY LIVING ALLOWANCE IS..............(Step 4)
AND THIS IS WHAT'S LEFT FOR REGULAR SAVINGS.

ESTIMATE OF OUR EMERGENCY FUND

To meet unexpected expenses we shall put aside each payday...... $

Enter in "Balance Sheet" below.
This fund will be allowed to accumulate until it reaches $_____
after which we shall pay into it merely enough to keep it at that level.

Courtesy of Institute of Life Insurance, New York.

3

4

EMERGENCY FUND

One of the most important steps, if your Money Manager is to work smoothly, is to provide for an emergency fund.

There are two kinds of savings. Regular family savings is for long-range projects — family security, the children's education, a new house or a new television set or a good vacation. Emergency "set-asides" are something else — it's money you put aside every week to help meet unexpected emergencies or to help you buy things you simply must buy, but haven't provided for.

It is a nice, comfortable feeling to have a lot of extra money left over after you have paid all your bills and met all your other expenses. But most families don't have a lot of extra money. After all, there are other things more important than extra money — good diet and good housing and adequate clothing and the other things which spell out a warm, happy, healthy family life.

But you will need something for an emergency fund all the same, if your Money Manager is going to work properly. You can't estimate in advance all your future expenses; you can't know how much or how little you may have to pay for things like doctor bills and repairs for the car six months or a year in advance. By putting money every week into your emergency fund you will be building up a fund which will help meet these unexpected bills when they come due. So, at this point, set up a *definite* amount which will be placed each pay day in your emergency fund.

An emergency fund should never be allowed to grow too big. When it reaches two or three months' income, put the extra money into regular savings or into something else your family wants and needs.

WEEKLY LIVING ALLOWANCES

How much does it cost you and your family to live? Unless you have kept family books over a period of years you won't be able to tell to the penny. But if you have been moderately careful in the past, you will be able to make a pretty good estimate. Here, under Step 4, is the place to do it.

Exactly how you divide your living expenses into different classifications is up to you. Here, in this chart, they are divided into six sections — how much Mother needs to run the house, how much Father needs to go to and from work, how much the family needs for such items as clothes and ordinary doctor bills, recreation, and how much everybody in the family needs for incidental expenses and allowances. But there are extra lines in the chart for you to use if you want to divide things another way.

There won't be anything final in these estimates of yours — after a month or two, you and your family will probably want to come back and rework everything, according to the lessons you will have learned under your new Money Manager.

Now, you are ready to add all your estimates and find your total expenditures. When you subtract these from your total income have you anything left? If so, this amount may be placed in your regular savings account, in savings bonds or other investments.

27

Table 2-2

SHOPPING CALENDAR

JANUARY	FEBRUARY
shoes, clothing, white goods—sheets, cases, blankets, towels—furs, small appliances and sports equipment, store-wide clearance, Christmas cards and decorations.	furniture, rugs, mattresses, china, glassware, housewares, curtains, women's coats and notions.
MARCH	**APRIL**
housewares, spring apparel, luggage.	women's dresses, millinery, men's and boys' clothing.
MAY	**JUNE**
white goods, television, soaps and cleaning aids, lingerie, handbags.	women's dresses, television, refrigerators, fabrics, rug cleaning, lumber, storm windows and screens.
JULY	**AUGUST**
shoes, clothing, hosiery, bathing suits, refrigerators, washing machines, toiletries, floor coverings, furniture, garden supplies, used cars.	furniture, tires, coats and furs, curtains, garden and lawn equipment, paint, hardware, cameras, camping equipment, white goods.
SEPTEMBER	**OCTOBER**
clothing, back-to-school specials, housewares, fabrics.	cars, coats and lingerie.
NOVEMBER	**DECEMBER**
women's coats and dresses, blankets and fabrics.	toys and gift items after December 21, women's and girls' coats and men's and boys' winter suits and coats in late December.

Source: Taken from "Money Management, Your Shopping Dollar," published by Money Management Institute of Household Finance Corporation, Chicago, Illinois, p. 24.

to take advantage of annual sales. "It has been estimated that the woman who knows what she wants, the sources of supply, and how much she should pay for the quality she desires, will be able to get up to 30 per cent more for her money than the woman who buys haphazardly, carelessly, or with the idea of getting such-and-such because so-and-so has it." [2]

Read the excellent information available. The United States Government Printing Office has many pamphlets helpful to the house-wife and homeowner. Magazines such as "Good Housekeeping," "Better Homes and Gardens," "Kiplinger's Changing Times," etc., have excellent articles to help along these lines. The Money Management Institute of Household Finance Corporation publishes a Money Management Library available for very small cost, which contains booklets extremely helpful to people interested in learning how to spend their money wisely. Some of the larger banks and insurance companies have helpful booklets available. These are only some of the sources of information available to those interested in learning how to spend less and get more for their money.

Record Keeping

Some record keeping is necessary in any budget. How detailed these records are depends on the individual. Some people like to keep detailed records, while others prefer them to be as brief as possible. Many variations of forms are available. Two of these are presented in Tables 2-3 and 2-4. Notice that there is a space at the top of each form for the estimate made for each item. This makes it possible to compare the amount actually spent for each item with the amount planned. Undoubtedly, adjustments will have to be made. No budget is ever perfectly constructed the first time. Furthermore, a budget should be carefully re-examined each year. Family expenses vary as life goes on and as the number and age of its members changes.

Most bills are due monthly. For this reason many people prefer to estimate their expenses and keep records on a monthly basis. This is a matter of personal preference. One thing is definite, however, no one should try to keep track of every penny used, or make budgeting a big project. A budget is supposed to help make living more com-fortable. This cannot be accomplished by putting the budget and the family in a straightjacket.

---

[2] "On Making Ends Meet," *The Royal Bank of Canada Monthly Letter,* Montreal, Canada, Vol. 38, No. 11, May, 1961, p. 4.

Table 2-3

WHERE DOES THE MONEY GO?				A Guide for Regular Saving —				BUDGET AND	

Estimates for the Month $									

Date	TOTAL INCOME	PAYROLL Deductions	SPEND-ABLE INCOME	EXPEN-DITURES	MUST PAYMENTS ★				
					SAVINGS	FIXED EXPENSES	HOUSING	Operating Household	FOOD	CLOTHING
	Salary Commissions Interest Dividends Other	Income Tax Social Security Savings Bonds Other	or "Take-home Pay"	Daily or Weekly Totals	Savings Account Savings Bonds	Income Tax (Estimate & State) Life Insurance Other	Rent/or Taxes Interest Repairs/ Insurance, etc.	Gas, Heat Phone, Water Electricity Laundry Service Equipment	All Food Milk Meals Out	Wearing Apparel Cleaning Pressing For Entire Family
1										
2										
3										
4										
5										
6										
7										
8										
9										
10										
11										
12										
13										
14										
15										
16										
17										
18										
19										
20										
21										
22										
23										
24										
25										
26										
27										
28										
29										
30										
31										
TOTAL										
BALANCE—Subtract total for each column from Estimate for Month (see above)										

BALANCE OR RESERVE: The estimate made for certain items (for example: Clothing, Medical, Education) will not be spent each month. However, a definite sum should be allowed for these things, and the amount not spent can be added to the estimate for the next month — or, better yet, set aside as a Reserve Fund in your Savings Account. A record of the use to which this is put can be kept separately.

EXPENSE RECORD

— and for Wise Spending

For Month of...........................19......

LIVING EXPENSES							MEMORANDA
PERSONAL		ADVANCEMENT					
Carfare, Taxi, Papers Barber, Hairdresser, Other — Personal Allowances		Medical	Education Books	Clubs Gifts	Car		
Husband	Wife, Children	Doctor Dentist Drugs	Magazines Recreation Vacation	Contributions Church			
						1	
						2	
						3	
						4	
						5	
						6	
						7	
						8	
						9	
						10	
						11	
						12	
						13	
						14	
						15	
						16	
						17	
						18	
						19	
						20	
						21	
						22	
						23	
						24	
						25	
						26	
						27	
						28	
						29	
						30	
						31	

★ **MUST PAYMENTS — Savings and Fixed Expenses —**
Each month set aside in a Savings Account a definite amount as a Cash Reserve and Emergency Fund.
Also, estimate Fixed Expenses for the year: Income Tax (Estimate of amount not withheld and State Tax) — Life Insurance — Payment and Taxes on home (if owned and not under Housing) — and any other fixed payments. Take 1/12 of the total and each month deposit this amount in a Special Savings Account so there will be money on hand to meet these payments as they come due.

Source: Courtesy Union Dime Savings Bank of New York.

Table 2-4

MONTHLY BUDGET RECORD

Expense Record for the Month of _____

FOOD			HOUSE OPERATION			ADVANCEMENT			SHELTER			TRANSPORTATION		
Allowance $			Allowance $			Allowance $			Allowance $			Allowance $		
FOOD: Groceries, meat, milk, vegetables, eggs, fruit, etc., cost of lunches and all meals out.			HOUSE OPERATION: Fuel, light, gas, telephone, water, household help, baby sitter, gardener, laundry, household supplies, equipment, furniture, draperies, linen, etc.			ADVANCEMENT: Health, education, recreation, vacation expense, newspapers, magazines, books, hobbies, dues, membership fees, charity, personal allowances, etc.			SHELTER: Rent or payment on home, real estate taxes, repairs and property improvement, fire insurance.			TRANSPORTATION: Carfare, automobile payments, insurance, repairs, tires, gas, oil and depreciation on car.		
Date	ITEM	AMOUNT	Date	ITEM	AMOUNT	Date	ITEM	AMOUNT	Date	ITEM	AMOUNT	Date	ITEM	AMOUNT
1														
2														
3														
4														
5														
6														
7														
8														
9														
10														
11														
12														
13										TOTAL			TOTAL	
14									CLOTHING			SAVINGS		
15									Allowance $			Allowance $		
16									CLOTHING: Clothing for all members of family, dry cleaning, repairs, pressing, miscellaneous accessories.			SAVINGS: Savings accounts, life insurance premiums, Savings Bonds, principal on mortgage payments, Social Security payments, stocks and other securities.		
17														
18														
19									Date	ITEM	AMOUNT	Date	ITEM	AMOUNT
20														
21														
22														
23														
24														
25														
26														
27														
28														
29														
30														
31														
	TOTAL			TOTAL			TOTAL			TOTAL			TOTAL	

EXPENSE SUMMARY		INCOME		
ITEM	AMOUNT	Date	SOURCE	AMOUNT
Food				
House Operation				
Advancement				
Shelter				
Transportation				
EXPENSES: TOTAL				
SAVINGS				
TOTAL		TOTAL INCOME		

MONTHLY BUDGET RECORD

This monthly budget record has been prepared for use with your Pacific First Federal Family Budget Guide. The proper budgeting of your income is the first step toward financial security and happiness.

• ❖ •

Additional forms may be obtained from the nearest friendly office of

Pacific First Federal Savings and Loan Association
A MUTUAL SAVINGS INSTITUTION

BELLINGHAM · SEATTLE · TACOMA · LONGVIEW · PORTLAND · EUGENE

Source: Pacific First Federal Savings and Loan Assoc., Tacoma, Wash.

Guidelines

Before considering what guidelines to follow, it must be emphasized that there is no such thing as a standard budget. Individual
needs and tastes differ. Some prefer to spend more on automobiles,
while others prefer symphony records. Some prefer to spend a considerable amount on liquor, while others prefer a hobby such as "ham"
radio or stamp collecting. A budget cannot and should not change
a person. It cannot tell a person what to spend. In fact, if a person
expects to use a budget to remold his or his family's personality or
living habits, the budget plan will probably fail. A budget can only
help a family avoid spending more than it has, and to achieve certain
long-range goals which it has selected.

It is, however, helpful and interesting to at least consider what
others spend for different things. Table 2-5, A and B, indicates what
families in eleven large cities in the United States actually spent for
different items in 1960. Table A is interesting because it shows money
amounts, but Table B is more helpful. This presents the expenditures
as percentages of the total amount spent for current consumption.
This can be used for comparison. What percentage of your budget
is planned for each of these? How does this percentage compare with
that of the average family in these cities?

These tables must be used with care. Only a relatively small
number of families were sampled in each city. Yet the tables are
interesting for comparison purposes and can serve as rough examples
of spending patterns.

Several things have been discovered in studies such as these.
One is that as family income rises the percentage spent for food and
clothing usually declines. Another is that the percentage of income
spent for clothing is usually higher at the higher income levels
during any given year; but that the over-all percentage spent for
clothing has decreased as incomes, generally, have risen. These facts
indicate another reason why your spending pattern won't conform
to the average; the percentages spent on different items vary, depending on family income.

A budget for a family with a take-home pay of $9,696 a year is
presented in Table 2-6. Comparative figures are presented in Table
2-7. Percentages that may be used as guides were presented in the
monthly budget form on page 22. A. Mr. Ernest Messenger of the
Pacific First Federal Savings and Loan Association has developed a
"Family Budget Guide" in the form of a slide rule, as pictured on

Table 2-5

A — Average Expenditures Per Family in Eleven Cities, 1960

Item	Atlanta, Ga.	Boston, Mass.	Chicago, Ill.	Detroit, Mich.	Indianapolis, Indiana	New York, N.Y.	Philadelphia, Penn.	Pittsburgh, Penn.	San Francisco, Calif.	Seattle, Wash.	Washington, D.C.
Expenditures for current consumption	$5,118	$6,045	$6,156	$5,599	$4,902	$6,336	$5,667	$5,486	$5,705	$5,877	$5,813
Food and beverages	1,226	1,571	1,611	1,503	1,279	1,762	1,581	1,472	1,534	1,543	1,455
Tobacco	89	106	102	98	95	118	109	100	78	98	84
Housing, total	1,534	1,837	1,872	1,506	1,540	1,928	1,583	1,481	1,657	1,756	1,871
Shelter, fuel, light, refrigeration and water	853	1,212	1,224	954	960	1,223	944	932	1,002	1,055	1,217
Household operations	356	363	340	242	322	387	357	255	347	345	370
Housefurnishings and equipment	307	261	305	294	258	317	278	293	301	348	282
Cl thing, materials, services	563	605	633	601	489	694	575	598	523	583	605
Personal care	165	161	180	156	148	157	166	148	151	156	164
Medical care	308	321	376	367	282	431	309	346	393	399	339
Recreation	199	214	231	193	195	228	227	220	282	282	223
Reading and education	105	220	115	104	115	132	181	123	118	127	119
Automobile purchase and operation	757	730	787	870	585	529	700	745	737	655	658
Other transportation	77	100	149	87	79	178	102	120	119	132	157
Other expenditures	97	180	100	113	95	179	134	134	113	146	138
Gifts and contributions	299	366	266	269	236	412	376	357	402	356	317
Personal insurance	328	348	347	330	321	341	322	350	332	368	457

B — Percentage Distribution

Item	Atlanta, Ga.	Boston, Mass.	Chicago, Ill.	Detroit, Mich.	Indianapolis, Indiana	New York, N.Y.	Philadelphia, Penn.	Pittsburgh, Penn.	San Francisco, Calif.	Seattle, Wash.	Washington, D.C.
Expenditures for current consumption	100.0	100.0	100.0	100.0	100.0	100.0	100.0	100.0	100.0	100.0	100.0
Food and beverages	24.0	26.0	26.2	26.9	26.1	27.8	27.9	26.8	26.9	26.3	25.0
Tobacco	1.7	1.8	1.7	1.8	1.9	1.9	1.9	1.8	1.4	1.7	1.4
Housing, total	30.0	30.4	30.4	26.9	31.5	30.4	27.9	27.0	29.0	29.9	32.2
Shelter, fuel, light, refrigeration and water	16.7	20.1	19.9	17.1	19.6	19.3	16.7	17.0	17.6	17.9	20.9
Household operations	7.0	6.0	5.5	4.3	6.6	6.1	6.3	4.6	6.1	5.9	6.4
Housefurnishings and equipment	6.0	4.3	5.0	5.3	5.3	5.0	4.9	5.3	5.3	5.9	4.9
Clothing, materials, services	11.0	10.0	10.3	10.7	10.0	11.0	10.1	10.9	9.2	9.9	10.4
Personal care	3.2	2.7	2.9	2.8	3.0	2.5	2.9	2.7	2.6	2.7	2.8
Medical care	6.0	5.3	6.1	6.6	5.8	6.8	5.5	6.3	6.9	6.8	5.8
Recreation	3.9	3.5	3.8	3.4	4.0	3.6	4.1	4.0	4.9	4.8	3.8
Reading and education	2.1	3.6	1.9	1.9	2.3	2.1	3.2	2.2	2.1	2.2	2.0
Automobile purchase and operation	14.8	12.1	12.8	15.5	11.9	8.3	12.4	13.6	12.9	11.1	11.3
Other transportation	1.5	1.7	2.4	1.6	1.6	2.8	1.8	2.2	2.1	2.2	2.7
Other expenditures	1.9	3.0	1.6	2.0	1.9	2.8	2.4	2.4	2.0	2.5	2.4

Source: Bureau of Labor Statistics.

34

Table 2-6

One family's budget . . .

the big picture[3]

Here's the master budget worked out by one
family . . . two adults, two children . . . no income but the breadwinner's salary . . . take-home
pay $9,696 a year.

This budget won't fit your family, so don't try
to use it. You need to figure out your own, using
your own income and your own experience with
expenses.

But do look this over for inspiration. It shows
how simple a year's financial plan can be yet still
provide practical guidelines for spending and saving.

fixed expenses	per month	per year
mortgage	$115	$1,380
savings account	50	600
life insurance	35	420
taxes	45	540
personal allowances		
Jim	60	720
Sally	30	360
Dot	10	120
Little Jim	5	60
church, charities	20	240
variable expenses		
food and household operations	200	2,400
clothing	35	420
medical and dental	25	300
car upkeep and repair	15	180
house upkeep and repair	30	360
fuel	30	360
light	8	96
water	5	60
recreation, entertainment	25	300
accumulating funds		
Christmas	15	180
vacation	25	300
new furniture	25	300
total	$808	$9,696

[3] "Family Budget: Make It New for '63," *Changing Times, The Kiplinger Magazine,* The Kiplinger Washington Editors, Inc., Washington, D.C., Jan. 1963, p. 10.

Table 2-7[4]

BUDGET ESTIMATES

Spending Category	Range (According to Percentage of Spendable Income*)	Your Estimate
Food	15 – 40%	_____
Clothing	8 – 15%	_____
Housing	15 – 30%	_____
Household Operation	5 – 15%	_____
Furnishings & Equipment	4 – 9%	_____
Fuel	3 – 8%	_____
Transportation	8 – 15%	_____
Medical & Dental	2 – 10%	_____
Education & Recreation	2 – 10%	_____
Personal Care	2 – 6%	_____
Gifts & Contributions	2 – 10%	_____
Dues & Subscriptions	0 – 6%	_____

*Spendable income is gross income less payroll deductions and all Federal and state income taxes.

page 38. This makes it easy to find budget guides for families of from two to five persons having incomes of from $300 to $1,400 per month. Another slide rule has been developed by the National Consumer Finance Association for use with their "Divided Responsibility Family Budget Plan." This presents data for families of from two to five having incomes of from $250 to $1,100 per month. This is pictured on page 37.

OTHER HINTS

Obviously, there is a wealth of information available concerning budgeting. It is evident that everyone in the field of finance believes that a financial plan is essential for the average family. Two points to remember though are (1) not to try to make your budget fit some standard and (2) not to become discouraged and give up too soon.

Saving

One item often mistreated in a budget is the item of saving. Many people treat saving as a "leftover." After they estimate all of their expenses they consider the remainder to be saving. For many

---

[4] "Personal Money Management," Savings Division, by permission of The American Bankers Association, New York, N.Y., 1962, p. 17.

Educational Services Division
NATIONAL CONSUMER FINANCE ASSOCIATION
1000 Sixteenth Street, N.W., Washington 6, D. C.

Slide Guide — DIVIDED RESPONSIBILITY FAMILY BUDGET PLAN

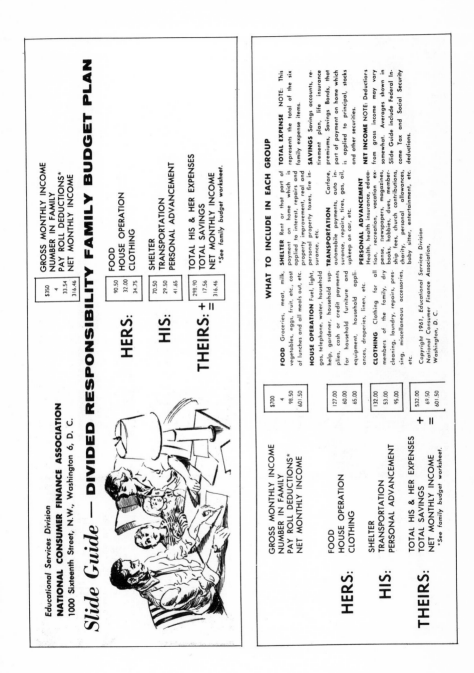

GROSS MONTHLY INCOME		$350
NUMBER IN FAMILY		4
PAY ROLL DEDUCTIONS*		33.54
NET MONTHLY INCOME		316.46

HERS:
FOOD	90.50
HOUSE OPERATION	32.00
CLOTHING	34.75

HIS:
SHELTER	70.50
TRANSPORTATION	29.50
PERSONAL ADVANCEMENT	41.65

THEIRS: +
=
TOTAL HIS & HER EXPENSES	298.90
TOTAL SAVINGS	17.56
NET MONTHLY INCOME	316.46

*See family budget worksheet.

GROSS MONTHLY INCOME		$700
NUMBER IN FAMILY		4
PAY ROLL DEDUCTIONS*		98.50
NET MONTHLY INCOME		601.50

HERS:
FOOD	127.00
HOUSE OPERATION	60.00
CLOTHING	65.00

HIS:
SHELTER	132.00
TRANSPORTATION	53.00
PERSONAL ADVANCEMENT	95.00

THEIRS: +
=
TOTAL HIS & HER EXPENSES	532.00
TOTAL SAVINGS	69.50
NET MONTHLY INCOME	601.50

*See family budget worksheet.

WHAT TO INCLUDE IN EACH GROUP

FOOD Groceries, meat, milk, vegetables, eggs, fruit, etc.; cost of lunches and all meals out, etc.

HOUSE OPERATION Fuel, light, gas, telephone, water, household help, gardener, household supplies, cash or credit payments for household furniture and equipment, household appliances, draperies, linen, etc.

CLOTHING Clothing for all members of the family, dry cleaning, laundry, repairs, pressing, miscellaneous accessories, etc.

SHELTER Rent or that part of payment on home which is applied to interest, repairs and property improvement, real and personal property taxes, fire insurance, etc.

TRANSPORTATION Carfare, automobile payments, auto insurance, repairs, tires, gas, oil, upkeep on car, etc.

PERSONAL ADVANCEMENT Health, health insurance, education, recreation, vacation expense, newspapers, magazines, books, hobbies, dues, membership fees, church contributions, charity, personal allowances, baby sitter, entertainment, etc.

TOTAL EXPENSE NOTE: This represents the total of the six family expense items.

SAVINGS Savings accounts, retirement plan, life insurance premiums, Savings Bonds, that part of payment on home which is applied to principal, stocks and other securities.

NET INCOME NOTE: Deductions from gross income may vary somewhat. Averages shown in Slide Guide include Federal Income Tax and Social Security deductions.

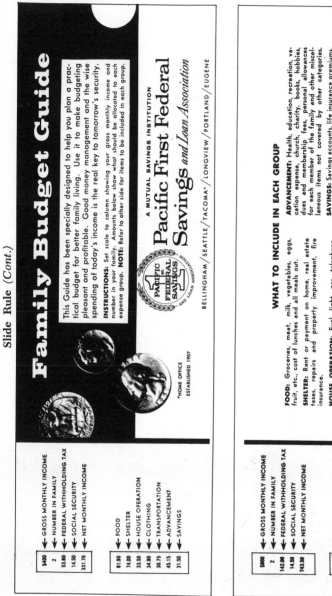

Family Budget Guide

This Guide has been specially designed to help you plan a practical budget for better family living. Use it to make budgeting pleasant and profitable. Good money management and the wise spending of today's income is the real key to tomorrow's security.

INSTRUCTIONS: Set scale to column showing your gross monthly income and number in your family. Amounts below show what should be allocated to each expense group. **NOTE:** Refer to other side for items to be included in each group.

A MUTUAL SAVINGS INSTITUTION

Pacific First Federal
Savings *and Loan Association*

*HOME OFFICE
ESTABLISHED 1907

BELLINGHAM/SEATTLE/TACOMA*/LONGVIEW/PORTLAND/EUGENE

GROSS MONTHLY INCOME	$400
NUMBER IN FAMILY	2
FEDERAL WITHHOLDING TAX	53.80
SOCIAL SECURITY	14.50
NET MONTHLY INCOME	331.70
FOOD	81.90
SHELTER	74.00
HOUSE OPERATION	33.50
CLOTHING	34.90
TRANSPORTATION	30.75
ADVANCEMENT	45.15
SAVINGS	31.50

WHAT TO INCLUDE IN EACH GROUP

FOOD: Groceries, meat, milk, vegetables, eggs, fruit, etc., cost of lunches and all meals out.

SHELTER: Rent or payment on home, real estate taxes, repairs and property improvement, fire insurance.

HOUSE OPERATION: Fuel, light, gas, telephone, water, household help, baby sitter, gardener, laundry, household supplies, equipment, furniture, draperies, linen, etc.

CLOTHING: Clothing for all members of family, dry cleaning, repairs, pressing, miscellaneous accessories.

TRANSPORTATION: Carfare, automobile payments, insurance, repairs, tires, gas, oil and depreciation on car.

ADVANCEMENT: Health, education, recreation, vacation expense, church, charity, books, hobbies, dues and membership fees, personal allowances for each member of the family and other miscellaneous items not covered by other categories.

SAVINGS: Savings accounts, life insurance premiums, Savings Bonds, principal on mortgage payments, Social Security payments, stocks and other securities.

NOTE: The figures given have been carefully compiled from the best possible private and Government sources and apply to the average family. It must be remembered, however, that individual family requirements may differ and if so, slightly different allocations to the various groups may be necessary to fit your specific family problem.

Source: Pacific First Federal Savings and Loan Assoc., Tacoma, Wash.

GROSS MONTHLY INCOME	$900
NUMBER IN FAMILY	2
FEDERAL WITHHOLDING TAX	142.90
SOCIAL SECURITY	14.50
NET MONTHLY INCOME	743.50
FOOD	116.75
SHELTER	159.50
HOUSE OPERATION	73.75
CLOTHING	77.35
TRANSPORTATION	65.00
ADVANCEMENT	141.15
SAVINGS	110.00

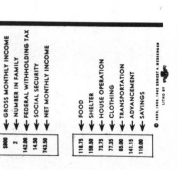

© 1955, 1956, 1958 ROBERT A. BESSERER
LITHO BY

people this means that nothing is ever available for saving. Now it is true that if a family has an extremely low income, saving is impossible. It is also true, however, that many families with incomes more than adequate to meet their needs never save because of this tendency to overlook the importance of saving.

Saving should be one of the first planned uses of a person's or family's income, not the last. If any money is left over at the end of the month it should be added to the original amount set aside for saving. A family's wealth, like that of a nation, can only be increased by saving, by spending less than is earned. Personal and family futures depend to a great extent on this ability to save. There are many methods that may be used. In the next chapter, the selection of a place to keep liquid savings, a bank, savings and loan association, credit union, etc., will be considered. In other chapters, buying a home, insurance, stocks, or mutual funds, investing in your own business, etc., all forms of saving will be carefully examined. How much should be saved and the form of saving will depend on the individual and the family. Furthermore, the amount and form of savings will vary as individuals and families change.

"While your situation may differ from that of others, the following stages are characteristic.

The Young Person. The young person may be primarily interested in investing in himself in the form of education and/or training for a job or profession. In obtaining a part-time or full-time job, he most likely will become eligible for participation in social security. In many jobs, he will be contributing to a pension fund and insurance. If marriage is being considered, the development of a life insurance program and savings to establish a home may be important.

The Beginning Family. After marriage, savings and investments may not change much from those in pre-marriage if either the husband or the wife is continuing education. If both are working, saving may be for furnishing a home or starting an investment program. Young families also strive to save some of their income for future needs, recognizing that demands on income will increase as the family grows.

The Growing Family. With the arrival of children, family needs expand and expenses continue to increase until education of children is completed. Money is distributed differently than before. The insurance program should place emphasis on maximum protection. Money is required for investment in durable

goods and possibly in home ownership. Depending on the size
of income and the demands on it, savings may be limited during
this period.

The Contracting Family. Savings and investment objectives
change decidedly as children leave home to marry or to take
jobs, and as parents are no longer responsible for children's
support. Major expenditures may be for furniture replacement,
for new wardrobes and for greater emphasis on recreation. This
is the time to concentrate on living satisfactorily both now and
in retirement years.

Retirement Years. Parents may be living on savings and the
returns on investments made during their lifetime. Social security,
pensions, annuities, and income-producing investments may provide for the expenses of one or both parents for the remainder
of their lives. The degree of enjoyment at this stage is greatly
influenced by the quality of financial planning through all preceding stages of the family cycle.

Unattached Adults. These persons have different savings and investment objectives than those of married people, because they
usually do not have the same financial responsibilities. Their
objectives for saving and investing may be to live effectively in
the present as well as in the future. They, too, need to evaluate
their objectives as changes occur in their pattern of living."[5]

Budget Helps

Some find budgeting easy, others find it difficult. In some families
the husband is primarily responsible for the budget, while in others it
is the wife's job. Some families use a checking account as a budget
help. Checks are drawn for the specific purpose and amount planned
in the budget. Stubs make good records. Other families convert
income to cash and place the cash in a number of envelopes labeled
with the names of the different expenses, such as "food," "heat,"
"clothing," etc. Whatever system works for you is the "best" system.

Two or three hints may help in budgeting at all ages. Don't
let anyone dictate how to spend your money. You know your
ambitions; what you have to do is sit down with pencil and paper
and devise the means whereby the money you have, and what
you reasonably expect to get, will achieve what you want.

[5] Taken from "Money Management, Your Savings and Investment Dollar,"
Published by the Money Management Institute of Household Finance Corporation,
Chicago, Illinois, 1961, pp. 3–4.

Don't be influenced by your parents' scale of living. They have been many years in reaching that point, and it is witless to think that you can start out from there, basing your starting scale of living on their attained goal. Be independent of neighbours' and friends' standards of living. Build your own plan to fit your own combination of desires and income.[6]

Borrowing

Borrowing, discussed in some detail in Chapter 5, has a very definite place in a family's financial plan. It must, however, be intelligent borrowing. Many people overload the family budget with installment payments. Buying on the installment plan to the extent that the family is in debt over its head has been one reason why many people never become financially stable. To make a budget work, it must be remembered that payments on installment or charge account purchases have a first claim on income. A person should be certain, before buying in this manner, that money will be available when the bill is due.

If a family is already heavily in debt, the unpaid bills should be listed, spending should be reduced to a minimum, and immediate plans should be made to systematically reduce the debt. It may be that creditors will be more lenient in demanding payment if a careful budget can be presented indicating a definite plan for paying debts.

SUMMARY

It's true that money isn't everything, but the fact must be faced that money is important. Most people need it for economic security and to share in the many material things available to make their lives more enjoyable. Earning all one can, spending it wisely, and giving generously, should help achieve a happy life. Remember, too, that you can't please everyone.

If a man runs after money, he's money mad; if he keeps it, he's a miser; if he spends it, he's a playboy; if he doesn't get it, he's a ne'er-do-well; if he gets it without working, he's a parasite; if he doesn't try to get it, he lacks ambition; and if he accumulates it after a lifetime of hard work, he's a fool who never got anything out of life.[7]

[6] "Planning Personal Financial Stability," *The Royal Bank of Canada Monthly Letter*, Montreal, Canada, December 1953, p. 4.

[7] "Personal Money Management," Savings Division, by permission of The American Bankers Association in collaboration with Dr. Jerome B. Cohen, 1962, p. 1.

Questions

1. Women should not be concerned with budgeting because men earn the income and should manage it. Comment.
2. List the steps involved in establishing a budget.
3. How can an individual reduce clothing expenditures?
4. List 10 expenses that could be considered "fixed expenses" for the average family.
5. List 10 expenses that could be classified as "variable expenses" for the average family.
6. What records should be kept when using a budget?
7. How can you "control" a budget?
8. Should children be taught financial planning?
9. How can using a budget save you money?
10. How much money per month should an individual spend on housing?

Problems

1. Jim Allen has spent 3 weeks doing research on budgeting. He has read books, articles, surveys and statistics from various sources. After much detailed work he has established budget figures for the "average" family based on all the readings he has done. He now has the percentage of income that an average family might spend on food, clothing, shelter, etc. But at this point, Jim is ready to quit. Comment on his approach to budgeting.
2. Anthony Burch is married, with no children. His wife does not work. They have been unable to save money regularly. Anthony says to you, his friend, "The money is there, all right, but it just seems to be spent before we can save any." He asks you to criticize the budget he has been using for the last 2 years. Comment on his budget, based on the following:

Monthly Income			$610
Monthly Expenses			

Fixed

Mortgage Payment & Real Estate Taxes	100		
Utilities	55		
Life Insurance Premiums	50		
Other Insurance Premiums	25		
Total	230	230	

Variable

House Equipment and Repairs	20		
Food	100		
Entertainment	50		
Automobile expense	25		
Medical	20		
Contributions	30		
Total	245	245	

Past Unpaid Bills

–0– Pays bills on time-never late			
Monthly allowances	100		
Clothing	35		
Other	135	135	
Grand Total			$610

In your comment, show Anthony how he can save $50 per month regularly. What good points can you see from this budget? What bad points?

3. Zachary Scott is 26, single, and happy-go-lucky. He maintains that he has no need for a budget because, "it wouldn't work anyhow." He has a tendency to live off next week's income. How would you convince him that a budget could aid him?

4. Cassidy King owns the following:
A 1963 "Corvair" automobile—valued at $2500. He pays $55 a month and owes the bank a balance of $2100. He has a savings account with $50 deposited and owns 3 co-operative bank shares valued at $60. He has $15 of cash value in his life insurance, but he has borrowed $10 of this recently. He owns $1000 in stock, $500 in bonds, and has an outboard motor valued at $600. Being single, his only other financial debt consists of a $200 bank loan (to pay for the boat), taxes due of $50, and an installment balance of $60 due at a local clothing store. What is King's net worth (total wealth) based on the above figures?

5. Theodore Ripley is stymied. He has checked and rechecked his budget figures carefully, but cannot make income—expenses. He now must face the fact that expenses will exceed income for the next two months. He needs money badly.

What form of borrowing would you recommend?

Selected Readings

"Budget Ideas for Youth," The National Thrift Committee, Inc., 121 West Wacker Drive, Chicago 1, Illinois

"Facts You Should Know About Budgeting," Association of Better Business Bureaus, 405 Lexington Ave., New York 17, New York (or local Better Business Bureau)

"Guiding Family Spending," Information Office, U.S. Dept. of Agriculture, Washington 25, D.C. (Misc. Publication No. 661)

"How to Get the Most Out of Your Income," Life Insurance Agency Management Association, Hartford 5, Connecticut, 1959

Money Management Library, Money Management Institute, Household Finance Corp., Prudential Plaza, Chicago 1, Illinois

"Personal Money Management," Savings Division, The American Bankers Association, New York, N.Y., 1962

Shiras, Sylvia, *Budgets Are What You Make Them*, The National Thrift Committee, 121 West Wacker Drive, Chicago, Illinois

"The ABC's, How to Keep Your Money From Dribbling Away," *Better Homes & Gardens*, 1716 Locust Street, Des Moines 3, Iowa, October 1962, pp. 8, 10, 13, 16, 18, 21, 23

Chapter **3**

WHERE TO PUT
YOUR SAVINGS

Wilshire Boulevard extends 15.6 miles from downtown Los Angeles to the ocean. Along this route at the beginning of 1963, there were offices of 47 banks and 18 savings and loan associations, four in each mile.[1] Things have certainly changed since Robert Morris founded the country's first bank in 1781.

---

[1] For a complete account see Hal Morris, "Wilshire Boulevard—Major Finance Row," Burroughs *Clearing House,* February, 1963, p. 42.

The importance of savings was emphasized in the chapter on budgeting. How should savings be handled? There are people who still bury their money in a tin can under a rock, located only by memory or on a hidden map with a large X. They remember the thousands of bank failures in the early 1930's and are afraid this will happen again. They are living in a dream world, in a past that cannot return.

There are many ways of saving. Insurance, investing in stocks and bonds, buying mutual funds, buying a home, are forms of saving which will be fully covered in later chapters. In this chapter, our concern is with the media most people class together under the general heading of "banks." These are places in which a person deposits savings, receives interest on the deposited money, and withdraws the cash, plus interest, when it is needed. The five most common of these are commercial banks, savings and loan associations, mutual savings banks, credit unions, and postal savings. Chart 3-1 shows the relative importance of these in terms of their share of total personal savings in the United States.

Chart 3-1

Where Personal Savings Accounts Are Kept in Financial Institutions — 1962

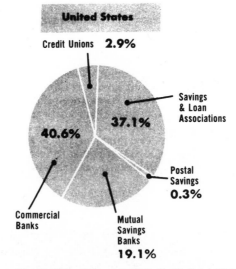

Source: "Credit Union Yearbook," 1963, Credit Union National Association, Madison, Wisconsin, p. 10.

The popularity of these different media varies in different sections of the country. Table 3-1 indicates the relative percentage of savings

on deposit in each media in different sections of the country. Notice
the importance of mutual savings banks in New England and the
Middle Atlantic States; while in all other sections of the country,
commercial banks and savings associations were the most popular.

Table 3-1[2]

SAVINGS IN SELECTED MEDIA, BY REGIONS

Region	Savings Associations 12/31/61	Mutual Savings Banks 12/31/61	Commercial Banks (Time Dep.) 6/30/61	Credit Unions 12/31/60	Postal Savings 6/30/61	Total
		Percentage Distribution				
New England	19.2%	62.8%	15.2%	2.7%	0.1%	100.0%
Middle Atlantic	20.3	46.3	32.2	1.0	0.2	100.0
East North Central	48.3	0.3	47.1	3.6	0.7	100.0
West North Central	47.8	2.9	44.7	3.8	0.8	100.0
South Atlantic*	57.5	4.2	35.4	2.4	0.5	100.0
South Central	48.5	....	46.7	4.3	0.5	100.0
Mountain	45.8	....	49.0	4.7	0.5	100.0
Pacific +	47.5	1.7	47.5	3.1	0.2	100.0
ENTIRE U.S.	37.9%	20.5%	38.6%	2.6%	0.4%	100.0%

* Includes Puerto Rico and the Virgin Islands.
+ Includes Guam.

INSTITUTIONAL COMPARISON

What are these different savings media? Due to the fact that
postal savings deposits have been declining since 1947, only the other
four media will be examined. This examination will consider only
institutional characteristics. Questions concerning the ability of the
commercial banking system to create money, the effect of each media
on the over-all economy of the country and similar matters, must be
left to texts on economics, money, and banking. The goal here is to
examine the mechanics of the media with regard to their relative
safety from the viewpoint of the savers.

Commercial Banks

Commercial banks are different from all other savings media in
that the largest part of the money which the public has deposited is

[2] "Personal Income and Savings," *Savings and Loan Fact Book, 1962*,
published by the United States Savings and Loan League, Chicago, Illinois,
1962, p. 15.

in the form of demand deposits, or checking accounts. A customary
practice in the United States is to pay bills by check. These demand
deposits represent most of the nation's money supply.

These banks are the chief suppliers of short term credit. In
recent years, they have evidenced an increased interest in mortgages,
due, in part, to the increase in savings deposits relative to demand
deposits; and they now make business, commercial, and mortgage
loans, invest in federal, state, and municipal securities, make loans
to farmers, etc.

> Today's commercial banking system consists of about
> 13,000 banks, located in approximately the same number of com-
> munities. While the number of banks has shown a slight down-
> ward trend in recent years, the number of bank offices has risen
> through the increase in branch operations.
>
> Modern commercial banks have roots which go more deeply
> into the nation's past than most sectors of business. More than
> 3,000 of our banks trace their origins back beyond 1900. Among
> these are nearly four hundred which date from before 1860.
> More than half of New England's banks have been in operation
> for a century or more. The First Pennsylvania Banking and Trust
> Company traces its ancestry to the country's first bank, the Bank
> of North America, which opened in 1782. Chase Manhattan
> is the successor to the Manhattan Company, the charter for
> which was obtained in 1799 by Aaron Burr, on promise of pro-
> viding water supply to New York City.[3]

The largest banks in the United States are listed in Table 3-2.
Commercial banks are owned by stockholders and may operate either
under a national or a state charter. This is known as the "dual banking
system." The Comptroller of the Currency supervises banks operating
under a national charter while state banking authorities supervise
those operating under state charters. Chart 3-2 on page 50 indicates
the total number of commercial banks in the United States and the
division of this number between national and state chartered.

The central bank system in the United States is the Federal
Reserve System, composed of twelve Federal Reserve Banks. These
are bankers' banks, and are primarily responsible for national monetary policy.

All nationally chartered commercial banks must be members of
this Federal Reserve System. State chartered banks may be if they

---

[3] Paul B. Trescott, *Financing American Enterprise, The Story of Commercial
Banking,* Harper & Row, Publishers, New York, Copyright © 1963 by The
American Bankers Association, p. 12.

Table 3-2⁴

DEPOSIT-EARNINGS TRENDS IN U.S. BANKS WITH $1 BILLION DEPOSITS

	Deposits		Earnings				
	Dec. 31, 1962	Dec. 31, 1961	Dec. 31, 1962	Per Share	Dec. 31, 1961	Per Share	Per Cent Change*
1. Bank of America, San Francisco....	$12,095,965,067	$11,475,436,134	$83,126,716	2.92	$87,782,804	3.08	− 5.6
2. Chase Manhattan Bank, New York..	9,631,947,815	8,875,793,657	72,056,470	5.16	70,533,320	5.05	+ 2.2
3. First National City Bank, New York.	9,141,539,698	8,371,837,148	74,108,000	5.80	72,861,000	5.70	+ 1.7
4. Manufacturers Hanover Trust, N.Y..	5,674,454,983	5,521,092,564	39,411,859	3.36	41,570,950	3.55	− 5.2
5. Chemical Bank-N.Y. Trust, N.Y....	4,562,502,942	4,352,767,712	44,927,487	5.30	43,905,330	5.18	+ 2.3
6. Morgan Guaranty Trust, New York.	4,381,189,847	4,135,554,504	50,293,170	6.67	49,271,114	6.53	+ 2.1
7. Security First Nat'l, Los Angeles...	3,949,766,726	3,661,896,479	27,030,077	3.77	27,765,555	3.87	− 2.6
8. Continental Ill. B&T, Chicago......	3,542,054,783	3,312,740,739	34,292,211	9.88	34,014,586	9.80	+ 0.8
9. Bankers Trust Company, New York.	3,476,441,549	3,390,921,255	30,841,587	3.44	30,810,175	3.43	− 7.0
10. First National Bank, Chicago......	3,314,590,170	3,142,110,532	32,517,000	4.33	35,083,000	4.67	−10.8
11. Wells Fargo Bank, San Francisco..	2,941,295,037	2,711,983,914	16,846,487	3.39	18,699,974	3.79	—
12. United California Bank, Los Angeles.	2,389,192,914	2,136,977,951	12,530,363	2.44	11,690,645	2.49	+ 1.1
13. Irving Trust Company, New York...	2,354,058,849	2,266,363,240	16,588,156	3.00	16,407,556	2.97	− 2.3
14. National Bank of Detroit.........	2,178,777,742	1,983,726,737	16,845,151	4.68	17,235,646	4.79	+ 7.1
15. Mellon Nat'l B&T, Pittsburgh......	2,172,849,502	2,032,131,512	25,987,940	3.91	24,264,491	3.65	
16. Crocker-Anglo Nat'l, San Francisco.	2,134,493,140	1,953,841,066	16,488,693	2.50	16,456,684	2.49	—
17. First National Bank, Boston.......	1,692,445,725	1,730,321,865	21,987,000	5.50	21,941,000	5.49	—
18. Cleveland Trust Company.........	1,505,004,620	1,375,927,155	12,138,613	24.28	14,171,887	28.34	−14.4
19. First Penn B&T, Philadelphia......	1,268,679,496	1,216,724,547	10,141,419	1.98	10,005,022	1.95	+ 1.5
20. Republic National Bank, Dallas....	1,201,333,113	1,102,453,411	10,049,398	2.88	10,037,106	2.93	− 1.7
21. Philadelphia National Bank........	1,145,994,237	1,050,404,866	9,601,333	3.63	9,862,929	3.72	− 2.4
22. Seattle First National Bank........	1,117,227,269	1,055,740,737	9,962,821	3.64	9,540,243	3.77	− 3.4
23. Harris Trust & Savings, Chicago....	1,089,500,264	1,059,390,115	8,402,167	6.15	8,234,575	6.03	+ 2.0
24. First National Bank, Dallas........	1,054,850,075	972,230,820	8,753,796	2.74	7,802,201	2.62	+ 4.6
25. Franklin Nat'l Bank, Mineola, N.Y..	1,043,906,948	821,948,485	9,799,402	2.78	9,452,102	2.69	+ 3.7
26. Union Bank, Los Angeles.........	1,016,904,227	823,816,123	7,992,701	3.29	6,855,280	2.85	+15.4
27. First Nat'l of Oregon, Portland.....	1,002,158,198	932,499,010	6,256,456	3.46	6,755,583	3.73	− 7.4

*Per Share

⁴ Lester Mason, *Scanning the Annual Reports*, Burroughs Clearing House, Burroughs Corporation, February 1963, p. 33.

49

Chart 3-2

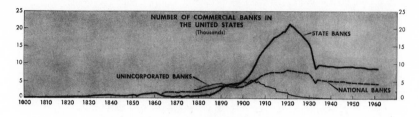

Source: "The Condition of Money and Credit," by permission of
Banking, the Official Journal of The American Bankers Association, February 1963, p. 35.

wish. Membership carries with it such privileges as check clearing
facilities, money packaging, loans to members, etc., but it also carries
the burden of strict supervision and examinations. Banks which are
members of the Federal Reserve System must have their accounts
insured by the Federal Deposit Insurance Corporation (FDIC); state
banks which are not members may have their accounts insured if
they so desire. Banks insured by the FDIC are subject to its regulations and examinations.

To summarize, four regulatory agencies control commercial banks:
the Comptroller of the Currency, the Federal Reserve System, the
Federal Deposit Insurance Corporation, and state banking authorities.
Table 3-3 indicates the distribution of supervisory powers among
these agencies. As almost all commercial banks are members of the
FDIC, the majority of them are subject to some federal regulation.

Savings and Loan Associations

A savings association may be defined as a locally owned
and privately managed savings and home financing institution.
As such, it accepts savings accounts from individuals and other
sources. These funds are invested principally in monthly payment
loans for the construction, purchase, or repair and modernization
of homes.[5]

Savings and loan associations invest most of their money in
mortgages. In many parts of the country these organizations are
more familiarly known as co-operative banks, building and loan associations, building associations, homestead associations, and savings

---

[5] Lawrence V. Conway, *Savings and Loan Principles,* American Savings and
Loan Institute Press, Chicago, Illinois, Second Edition, 1960, p. 17.

Table 3-3

DISTRIBUTION OF SUPERVISORY POWERS AMONG BANKING AUTHORITIES[a6]

	Exercised with Respect to			
Powers	National Banks	State Member Banks	State Nonmember Insured Banks	State Nonmember Noninsured Banks
Issuance of charters	CC	State	State	State
Approval of changes in name, changes in stock issues, etc.	CC	State FR	State FDIC	State
Authority to establish, change location of, and discontinue branches	CC	State FR	State FDIC	State
Admission to the Federal Reserve System	CC	FR		
Admission to deposit insurance	CC	FR	FDIC	
Authority to exercise trust powers	FR	State	State	State
Examinations	CC (FR) (FDIC)	State FR (FDIC)	State FDIC	State
Reports of condition	CC FR FDIC	State FR FDIC	State FDIC	State
Determination of reserve requirements	FR	State FR	State	State
Limitation of interest payments on deposits	FR	State FR	State FDIC	State
Receiver in case of insolvency	FDIC	State or FDIC	State or FDIC	State

ª Explanation of abbreviations used: "CC" for Comptroller of the Currency; "FR" for the Board of Governors and other officials of the Federal Reserve System; "FDIC" for Federal Deposit Insurance Corporation; and "State" for state supervisory authorities. Parentheses indicate that powers are not commonly exercised.

associations. Such associations were originally established to enable neighborhood groups to pool their savings and help members of the group finance their homes.

A dual banking system also exists in this banking category. These associations may be chartered and supervised by either state or federal governments. Those federally chartered are supervised by the Federal

ª From *Money and Banking*, Fourth Edition, by Raymond P. Kent, Copyright © 1961 Holt, Rinehart and Winston, Inc., p. 179. Reprinted by permission.

Home Loan Bank Board. While only a minority of the 6,358 savings and loan associations at the end of 1961 were federally chartered, 4,221 of them were insured by the Federal Savings and Loan Insurance Corporation.[7] As indicated by Chart 3-3 the insured savings and loan associations hold most of the total assets of all savings and loan associations. This does not include Massachusetts Cooperative Banks, which are insured by the Co-operative Central Bank of Massachusetts. Insured banks hold by far the great percentage of assets of all savings associations.

Established in 1932 to provide a central credit organization for the savings and loan business, the Federal Home Loan Bank System operates similarly, in this respect, to the Federal Reserve System. The expressed purposes of the Federal Home Loan Banks are to provide funds to meet unusual withdrawal demands, to provide seasonal fund requirements, and to make possible an additional source of long-term home financing funds.[8]

The majority of savings and loan associations are mutual institutions, owned by and operated for their members. When someone deposits money, he becomes a member and a shareholder. Some states permit the incorporation of savings associations, in which case they are owned by the stockholders.

Mutual Savings Banks

The dominant position of mutual savings banks in the New England area as of December 31, 1961, can be seen in Table 3-1. New England is followed closely by the Middle Atlantic States, but the position held by mutual savings banks in other sections of the country is relatively insignificant. Actually, mutual savings banks were even more heavily concentrated than these figures indicate. About three-fourths of them were located in Massachusetts, New York, and Connecticut, in that order. More than one-third were in Massachusetts alone; and New York had the largest percentage of the assets of all of the mutuals combined.

Due to the predominant position of mutual banks in Massachusetts, it seems justifiable to use the advertisement on page 54 as a refer-

[7] Statistics obtained from *Savings and Home Financing Source Book*, Federal Home Loan Bank Board, Washington, D.C., 1962, p. 5.

[8] *Savings and Loan Fact Book, 1962,* United States Savings and Loan League, Chicago, Illinois, 1962, p. 105.

Chart 3-3

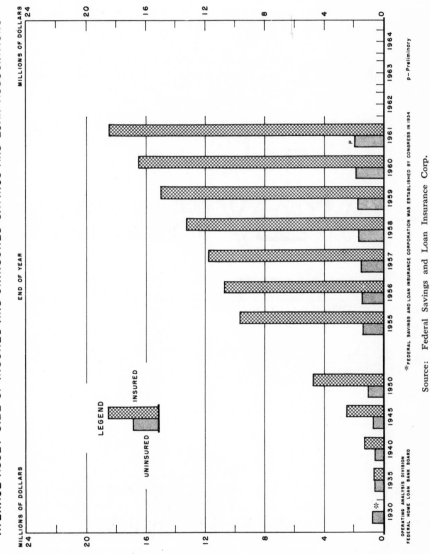

ALL SAVINGS AND LOAN ASSOCIATIONS

AVERAGE ASSET SIZE OF INSURED AND UNINSURED SAVINGS AND LOAN ASSOCIATIONS

END OF YEAR

MILLIONS OF DOLLARS

LEGEND

INSURED

UNINSURED

OPERATING ANALYSIS DIVISION
FEDERAL HOME LOAN BANK BOARD

*FEDERAL SAVINGS AND LOAN INSURANCE CORPORATION WAS ESTABLISHED BY CONGRESS IN 1934

p—Preliminary

Source: Federal Savings and Loan Insurance Corp.

ence. The statement in the first paragraph, concerning the long and successful experience of these institutions, applies generally wherever savings banks exist. Both the Provident Institution for Savings of Boston and the Saving Fund Society of Philadelphia (now the second largest mutual savings bank in the United States) were organized in 1816.

The second and third paragraphs in the advertisement explain, to some degree, why mutual savings banks were established and how they operate. The word "mutual" implies that they are owned by their

Mutual Savings Banks have established a 147 year unbroken record for safety, earnings and liquidity *unequaled by any other type of financial institution.* This unique record is the major reason why Mutual Savings Banks have earned the confidence of the people and why 3½ million in Massachusetts have made these banks first choice.

As specialists in savings, Mutual Savings Banks were primarily established to aid families by encouraging thrift, self-reliance and independence. Depositors know their money is insured in full and available whenever they want it. They know that dollars in Mutual Savings Banks do not fluctuate up and down as do the market values of stocks and bonds. They have learned that Mutual Savings Banks pay regular and generous dividends because they make sound investments, principally in home mortgages.

When you save at a Mutual Savings Bank, your money works only for you. Savings banks are owned solely by their depositors. After expenses have been paid and necessary reserves set aside for your protection, all earnings are credited to you and other depositors as interest on your savings.

That's why 2 out of 3 people prefer these banks for their savings accounts and why Mutual Savings Banks in this state are first in total savings dollars with $6½ billion entrusted to their care.

You will find Mutual Savings Banks are specialists in home financing, too. They know local conditions . . . and understand family budget problems. They make a sincere effort to arrange terms at favorable rates to fit your needs and your ability to pay. That is why 500,000 Massachusetts home owners prefer savings banks for their mortgages.

Your Mutual Savings Bank offers many practical ways of helping you save and borrow. You'll find they give all kinds of help to all kinds of people.

And most important, one of the 323 convenient offices is near where you live or work.

These plain facts are the reasons why so many people in Massachusetts prefer Mutual Savings Banks — and why a Mutual Savings Bank should be your first choice.

Look for this symbol

MUTUAL SAVINGS BANKS

Source: "The Savings Banker," Savings Banks Association of Massachusetts, January 1963, p. 5.

depositors and are operated for their benefit. Like savings and loan associations, they invest heavily in mortgages. Most state legislatures have carefully regulated the type of security which mutuals may buy and the loans which they may make.

At the present time, no mutual savings banks are federally chartered. It seems probable that they will push strongly for this right and the right, already granted by some states, to make consumer loans.

Almost all mutual savings banks are insured either by the Federal Deposit Insurance Corporation or by state insurance systems. New York has established the "Savings Bank Trust Company" to act as a central bank for mutuals in that state.

Credit Unions

While credit unions are still relatively small in terms of the percentage of total savings which they hold, they are rapidly growing. They are in operation in every state, and are becoming more and more important in the savings market and in the consumer loan market.

What a Credit Union Is [9]

A credit union is a group of people who agree to save their money together and to make loans to each other at low interest.

A credit union is organized by members of a particular group — for instance, people working for the same employer; people who belong to the same fraternal order, church, or labor union; or people who live in the same closely knit community. Membership is open to all in the group, regardless of race, color, or creed.

Credit unions are democratic. The members elect their own officers and committeemen and set policies for the credit union at the annual meeting.

The above quote lists some of the basic facts about credit unions. They are formed by groups wishing to pool their savings to make

---

[9] Excerpt from Form M-150 © 1961, Printed in U.S.A. by CUNA Supply Cooperative, an affiliate of the Credit Union National Association. Reproduced by permission of copyright holder.

loans to their members at low rates of interest. Credit unions can make loans only to their own members and to other credit unions. The Federal Credit Union Act regulates the amount that may be loaned to each member, and the amount and type of security required.

About half of all credit unions are federally chartered; the rest are state chartered. Federally chartered credit unions are supervised by the Bureau of Federal Credit Unions. This agency is affiliated with the Department of Health, Education, and Welfare. Although there are state insurance programs, there is no federal insurance coverage comparable to the F.D.I.C. or the F.S.L.I.C. A number of credit unions are liquidated each year. Usually, but not always, the depositors have received 100 percent of their money. Undoubtedly, some form of federal insurance will be initiated soon.

Credit unions hold an extremely important position in the consumer installment credit market, ranking third in total loans outstanding and having an excellent record with respect to average losses on personal loans. Part of this is due to the close personal relationship that exists between union members. Each knows that if he does not meet his loan obligation, he will be subject to the disapproval and judgment of his associates.

Credit unions have many attractive features. They are easy to organize. They are organized by groups having similar interests—workers in a plant, members of a union, members of a church, etc. Most of the work is done by unpaid members, and office space is often provided by the company. This keeps operating costs extremely low. Exemption from federal taxation is an important advantage. The successful unions have been able to lend money to members at reasonable rates and still pay excellent dividends.

Credit unions seem to have a large growth potential, but do have problems. Will they be provided with a federal insurance program? Will loan restrictions be relaxed so that increased savings deposits may be put to work profitably? Insurance would raise costs. Relaxing loan restrictions would increase income, but would change the credit union movement somewhat from its original purposes. In general, it would appear that future expansion and changes will mean that credit unions will grow to be progressively more like savings and loan associations.

COMPETITION

Chart 3-4 shows the growth rate of savings according to the type of institution in which the savings are placed. On this semilogarithmic

Chart 3-4

RATE OF GROWTH OF SELECTED SAVINGS
BY TYPE OR BY INSTITUTION
DECEMBER 31, 1950–1960

Semi-Logarithmic Scale

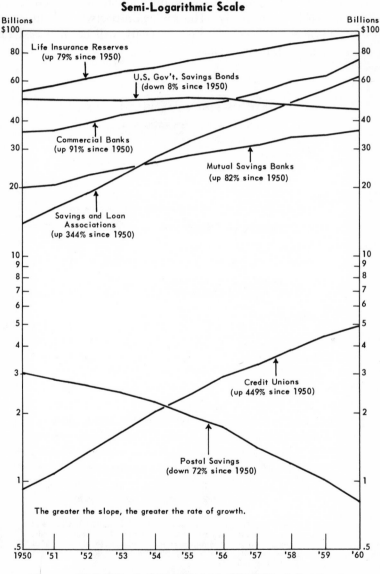

Billions $100

Life Insurance Reserves
(up 79% since 1950)

U.S. Gov't. Savings Bonds
(down 8% since 1950)

Commercial Banks
(up 91% since 1950)

Mutual Savings Banks
(up 82% since 1950)

Savings and Loan
Associations
(up 344% since 1950)

Credit Unions
(up 449% since 1950)

Postal Savings
(down 72% since 1950)

The greater the slope, the greater the rate of growth.

1950 '51 '52 '53 '54 '55 '56 '57 '58 '59 '60

Source: "Statistics on the Savings Market," (1961 Edition), Department
of Economics and Research, by permission of The American
Bankers Association, Chart 2, page 7.

scale, the steeper the line, the more rapid the percentage rate of change. Compare commercial banks, savings and loan associations, mutual savings banks and credit unions. During the time period covered, credit unions grew most rapidly, with savings and loan associations next. Commercial banks and mutual savings banks were third and fourth, respectively. The savings aspects of life insurance, fifth in rate of growth according to the chart, will be discussed fully in the chapter on Life Insurance.

Chart 3-5

GROWTH OF FINANCIAL INSTITUTIONS
(TOTAL ASSETS - - RATIO SCALE)

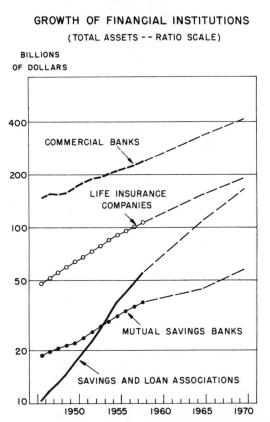

Source: "The Next Decade—and Its Opportunities for the Savings and Loan Business," United States Savings and Loan League, Chicago, Illinois, preliminary report prepared by the School of Business, Indiana University, Bloomington, Indiana, November 1, 1959, p. 26, Chart 9.

Terminology

Will these savings media continue their competitive struggle? Every indication is that they will, and that the competition will increase. Chart 3-5 shows not only how these savings media have grown during recent years, but also their potential growth to 1970, as forecast by the United States Savings and Loan League.

Savings organizations compete at every possible point. Consider terminology, for example. Words like "deposit" and "interest" are points of considerable controversy. Savings and loan associations have advertised extensively in their efforts to attract additional deposits.

> They have tried to make their savings accounts as liquid and safe as the deposit accounts in commercial and mutual savings banks. Indeed they have coveted the use of the word "deposit" in their advertising and promotion, while banks have just as vigorously lobbied against their access to this magic word. Most modern savings and loan associations have dropped or suppressed the "share" account terminology; they prefer to speak of "savings" accounts. While they cannot call the dividend payments on these accounts "interest," savings and loan managers seldom protest if customers make the mistake of using this phrase.[10]

Taxes

The effect of the federal income tax on the various media has caused a considerable furor in banking circles. For many years, commercial banks bore a much greater income tax burden than the others. The Revenue Act of 1962 changed this, and increased the tax responsibilities of the other banks.

The continued exemption of credit unions from federal income tax is the subject of sharp criticism by the other savings media. Table 3-4 presents the difference in the effect of the federal income tax on the four media in 1960. The comparison between the credit unions and the commercial banks is drastic, to say the least.

---

[10] Roland I. Robinson, (Ed.), Erwin W. Boehmler, Frank H. Gane, Loring C. Farwell, *Financial Institutions*, Richard D. Irwin, Inc., Homewood, Illinois, Third Edition, 1960, p. 552.

Table 3-4

AMOUNT OF FEDERAL INCOME TAX
PAID BY FOUR SAVINGS MEDIA
1960[11]

Institution	Div. and/or Int. Pd.	Fed. Income Taxes Paid
Savings & Loan Assns.	$2,040,000,000	$5 million
Mutual Savings Banks	$1,083,000,000	$1 million
Credit Unions	Net inc—$261 million	—0—
Commercial Banks	Div—$831,000,000 (after interest on dep.)	$1,300,000,000

Services

In terms of total customer services, commercial banks generally outperform their competitors. They offer checking accounts, foreign exchange departments, and many other services not provided by the others. These will be covered in the following chapter.

Table 3-5 illustrates the importance of these services when a choice has to be made between two media. The choice in this instance was made by the workers at Thomas & Betts Co., Inc., in Elizabeth, New Jersey. The table explains why they decided to use the services of the Elizabethport Banking Co., a commercial bank, instead of establishing a credit union.

Under today's competitive conditions, savings and loan associations are becoming keenly interested in the small loan market, and may become more and more competitive with commercial banks for this business. On the other hand, commercial banks are becoming more interested in mortgages and in providing fee services to their customers, to meet their increasing costs. Paying customers' bills, rendering accounting services, servicing mortgages, etc., for fees, are becoming important sources of income. More emphasis on these services can be expected as data processing equipment becomes more commonly used.

Rates

For many years commercial banks were at a disadvantage in competing for savings, in that the rate which they could pay on

---

[11] "Subversion of Competition," Reprinted from *Time Sales Financing*, published by the American Finance Conference, Inc., Chicago, Illinois, Vol. 27, No. 1, January-February 1963, p. 5.

Table 3-5

ELIZABETHPORT BANK ON-THE-JOB BANKING SERVICE	CREDIT UNIONS

Savings

4%	Low in initial period—then variable (depends on success in investing funds). Examples of present rates paid on savings by fully mature credit unions in our area:

	Singers	3.6%
	Simmons	3.75%
	Purolator	4.5%
	Phelps Dodge	4.0%

Loans

Interest—$5 per $100 per yr.	Interest—max. of 1% per month on
Auto loans—$4 per $100 per yr.	unpaid balance of all loans
Max. amt. on signature—$5,000	Max. amt. on signature—$750
Max. term—up to 5 yrs.	Max. term—up to 5 yrs.
Max. secured loan—unlimited	Max. secured loan—up to 10% of the total deposits on hand, otherwise no limit

Christmas Club and Vacation Club

Bank makes automatic deductions from paychecks	These services are not normally available through credit unions

Cost of Administration

Bank assumes responsibility for cost	On the average, credit unions pay out 40% of gross income for operating expenses

Loan and Savings Insurance

Not available unless there is strong desire on part of employees to provide it	Credit unions provide up to $10,000 insurance on loans and up to $2,000 on savings which will be paid to your beneficiary in the event of your death

Automatic Payroll Deduction

Available for: Regular savings plan Scheduled repayments against loans Christmas Club payments Vacation Club payments	Not normally available

Checking Accounts

E'port Bank will provide a checking account and a printed checkbook for each employee. One free check is allowed each payday and 10¢ is charged for each check used over this one	Not normally available

This comparison of the respective merits of on-the-job banking and credit unions, prepared by the Thomas & Betts workers' committee, played a major role in winning acceptance for the banking plan

Source: "Bank Bests Credit Union in Workers' Vote," by permission of *Banking*, the Official Journal of The American Bankers Association, New York, New York, March, 1963, p. 93.

savings deposits was strictly limited. This regulation was changed in 1962 and commercial banks were permitted to raise rates to 4 percent. This resulted in a substantial increase in commercial bank time deposits during 1962. The higher interest rates in turn produced problems due to the fact that they increased costs.

Interest rates vary considerably, both throughout the country and in specific areas. In the spring of 1963, annual rates paid by savings and loan associations varied from 3.5 per cent to 5 per cent, compounded semi-annually, plus 1 per cent additional on savings committed for a full year. In general, associations in the West were paying higher rates than those in the East.

Anyone considering saving by mail in an out-of-state bank to gain a higher interest rate should consider the move very carefully. Even the most efficient banks and the most intelligent people occasionally make errors; and straightening them out would certainly be easier if the bank was conveniently nearby. Income taxes should also be considered. Many states have reciprocal agreements to exempt the return earned on bank deposits from the state income tax, just as they exempt the return paid by the same organizations in their own state. If the out-of-state bank is in a non-reciprocating state, dividends or interest may be taxed. Of course, a lot depends on the rate differential, too. If rates in the depositor's area are only 3.5 per cent and he can realize 4.8 per cent in a sound West Coast bank, the out-of-state banking may be quite worthwhile.

Most amazing is the great difference that can exist between savings organizations in the same relatively small area. This situation offers an equality of convenience to the depositor. If one bank pays 3 per cent and another pays only 1½ per cent, a depositor of the first bank would obviously receive 100 per cent more return on his money. This difference has actually existed. Why, then, would anyone deposit money in the bank paying 1½ per cent? Often because they just didn't think about it. In Boston, Massachusetts, in the spring of 1963, one of the largest commercial banks in the city paid 3 per cent on savings, while another large commercial bank in the same city paid 4 per cent. Large savings and loan associations in the same city were paying 4¼ per cent. A person placing his savings in one of these savings and loan associations (and assuming that interest is calculated by the same method in all of the institutions) would receive almost 42 per cent more return on his money than he would receive from the bank paying 3 per cent.

WHERE TO PUT YOUR SAVINGS

How do you decide where to put *your* savings?

In deciding how and where to hold his savings, an individual will normally be governed by five considerations: (1) the safety of his funds, (2) the readiness with which the savings can be converted back into cash, (3) the ease and convenience of making the necessary transactions, (4) other services offered in conjunction with the savings facilities, (5) the rate of interest or other return received.[12]

This statement by The American Bankers Association sums up the things a person should consider in deciding where to place his savings.

Safety

Safety, here, is considered only in its narrowest sense. If a person deposits $1,000 in an account, can he get it back immediately when he wants it? The broader meaning of the term, its relation to purchasing power, etc., will be discussed later in considering whether or not a person should invest in common stocks.

Today, the subject of safety is closely tied to insurance. Insured funds are safer than uninsured. Even insured funds can be subdivided into those that are federally insured, state insured, or privately insured. It seems virtually impossible to imagine a situation in which accounts insured by either the Federal Deposit Insurance Corporation or the Federal Savings and Loan Insurance Corporation could ever be in serious jeopardy. This has nothing to do, really, with whether or not the reserves of these corporations are sufficient. Many believe that under extreme conditions, neither would have sufficient reserves. It seems, however, that if economic conditions became severe, Congress would certainly act to strengthen both corporations.

Both insure individual accounts up to $10,000. This can include several accounts in the same bank. A man might have an account in

---

[12] *The Commercial Banking Industry*, a monograph prepared for the Commission on Money and Credit by The American Bankers Association, Prentice-Hall, Inc., Englewood Cliffs, New Jersey, 1962, p. 80.

his name, he and his wife might have a joint account, etc. Each would be insured for the maximum. If a person has more than the amount that would be insured in any one bank, he can open an account in another, or in several others, to take advantage of the insurance protection.

State insurance is more difficult to assess than federal, as it differs in every state. In some states, the state sponsored fund is excellent. In Massachusetts, for example, the state sponsored fund insures mutual savings bank deposits 100 per cent.[13] In some states, savings institutions are required to be members of the state program. In others, membership is voluntary.

Some banks may be privately insured. These plans must be carefully considered before money is deposited. While there may be fifty varieties of insurance programs providing state insurance for a particular savings media, savings and loan institutions for example, there can be any number of private plans. In the past, many of these have proved to be inadequate. "A sound association that frankly admits it is not insured but that has a long record of success under the same management probably would be a safer bet than one that claims to be insured by some private insurance company."[14]

A person who deposits his savings in a federally insured account, or in an account insured under a good state program, seems to be in very little danger of losing his money. Money in an account insured by either a federal or good state program is much safer than it could ever be buried in the ground.

Credit unions must be evaluated on a different basis. They do not have the advantage of a federal insurance program, and should be evaluated by the competency of their management, the quality of their balance sheets, liquidity of assets, percentage of loans overdue, and adequacy of reserves. Credit unions are required by law to establish certain prescribed minimum reserves, and many voluntarily establish reserves higher than those required. Officials are bonded, loans and investments are restricted, etc. Any judgment concerning the safety of a credit union must be based, to a considerable degree, on the ability of its management and its history.

Readiness of Conversion

Legally, banks can require advance notice before a depositor withdraws funds from a savings account. Savings and loan associa-

---

[13] As of July 9, 1963, the limit under one ownership, whether in a single or joint account, is $30,000 exclusive of interest accumulations.

[14] "Rainy-day Money: Where to Put It Now," *Changing Times, The Kiplinger Magazine,* The Kiplinger Washington Editors, Inc., Washington, D.C., June 1962, p. 9.

tions can, in general, require the longest period of advance notice. Actually, few banks ever require notice except in an emergency, and then the notice is only a temporary measure. Savings deposits represent a highly liquid method of saving money.

Convenience and Services

Of course, the most convenient bank is the one nearest the depositor. Here, commercial banks have the advantage, because there are more of them. It is difficult, however, to separate convenience from service, as most depositors can choose from among several banks. If the institutions are comparable, in terms of safety and return (interest or dividends), a person's choice might well be influenced by the comparative services each offers. Here again, commercial banks usually have the advantage. In general, they offer the widest variety of services. A person quite often keeps his savings in a commercial bank because he has a checking account there, and it is convenient to take care of both accounts in one place.

As competition for the savers' dollars becomes more keen, competition between commercial banks increases. This competition usually is in the form of more varied services. Furthermore, savings and loan associations and mutual savings banks are expanding into areas which permit them to increase their services to depositors. Available services should be carefully considered when selecting a savings institution.

Return

Historically, commercial banks have been at a disadvantage with respect to the average rate of return paid on deposits. This is attributable, in part, to their heavy tax burden, legal restrictions on investments, and legal limits on the interest rates they are permitted to pay. In 1962, when they were permitted to increase interest rates, their increase in time deposits was greater than the gain made by either savings and loan institutions or mutual savings banks. It is quite likely, however, that savings and loan associations and mutual savings banks will regain the advantage previously enjoyed, by further increasing their rates.

Rates are important and should be carefully considered. Table 3-6 illustrates the difference between saving money at rates of 1½ per cent, 3 per cent, 4 per cent, 4¼ per cent and 4½ per cent. Let us assume a situation in which a person has a choice between two banks; both federally insured, both offering the same services, and both conveniently located. One offers 3 per cent on savings, while the other will pay 4 per cent. If this person follows a practice of savings regularly, as everyone should, and is able to deposit $20 each month in a savings account, the total amount in his account at the end of 20 years, at a 3 per cent rate would be $6,569.13, while the total amount in his account at the end of 20 years, at 4 per cent would be $7,332.80, a difference of almost $800.

Table 3-6

SAVINGS GROWTH TABLE [15]

*Savings of $20 made at the first
of each month**

YEARS	1½%	3%	4%	4¼%	4½%
1	241.95	243.92	245.23	245.56	245.89
2	487.55	495.20	500.36	501.66	502.96
3	736.85	754.09	765.81	768.76	771.73
4	989.89	1020.80	1041.97	1047.34	1052.74
5	1246.75	1295.56	1329.30	1337.88	1346.53
6	1507.48	1578.64	1628.23	1640.90	1653.69
7	1772.13	1870.27	1939.24	1956.94	1974.83
8	2040.76	2170.71	2262.81	2286.55	2310.58
9	2313.44	2480.24	2599.45	2630.32	2661.61
10	2590.23	2799.12	2949.70	2988.85	3028.62
11	2871.18	3127.64	3314.10	3362.78	3412.32
12	3156.37	3466.09	3693.21	3752.77	3813.49
13	3445.84	3814.77	4087.65	4159.52	4232.92
14	3739.68	4173.98	4498.02	4583.73	4671.42
15	4037.94	4544.06	4924.96	5026.17	5129.89
16	4340.69	4925.32	5369.16	5487.61	5609.22
17	4648.00	5318.10	5831.30	5968.86	6110.36
18	4959.93	5722.76	6312.12	6470.79	6634.30
19	5276.56	6139.64	6812.35	6994.28	7182.09
20	5597.96	6569.13	7332.80	7540.25	7754.80

*Additions earn dividends from the first day of each month. Dividends are compounded semi-annually.

A person should also consider the method of calculating interest used by a bank. Do deposits earn a return for an entire calendar quarter if they are deposited or withdrawn during the quarter? Are the returns compounded semi-annually, or quarterly? The answers to these questions will indicate which bank actually pays the highest return.

[15] Savings Growth Table, Financial Publishing Company, Boston, Massachusetts, 1954, pp. 7, 17, 25, 27 and 29.

SAVINGS BONDS

While savings bonds are different from the other media discussed in this chapter, they should be mentioned. Certainly, no investment can be safer, as they are based on the credit of the Federal Government. Two issues are of interest to the average investor, Series E and Series H bonds.

Series E bonds are appreciation bonds. They are issued for less than their face value and attain face value at maturity. A $100 bond, for example, is sold at $75, and can be redeemed at maturity for $100. The maturity date is 7 years and 9 months after the date of issue. If held to maturity, these bonds yield 3.75 per cent return.

Series H bonds are income bonds. They are purchased at face value, $1,000.00, and owners receive interest checks twice a year. The first check, in the amount of $8.00, is paid six months after the bond is purchased. This amount increases each six months to a total of $20 two years from date of purchase. It stays at $20 semi-annually for the remainder of a ten year period, until maturity. If the bond is held for the entire 10 years, the yield is 3.75 per cent.

Savings bonds are safe, convenient to purchase, and easy to sell. They may be purchased through payroll deduction plans in many companies, so that their purchase becomes relatively "painless." They do have certain disadvantages, which have caused them to lose some of their appeal since World War II: the return offered by other investments, including bank deposits, has surpassed the bond yield; many investors have become more interested in common stock investments (equities), as the threat of inflation increased; and, except for certain special situations, investors who are interested in the advantages offered by these bond investments are limited to a maximum of $10,000 per year.

At the present time, savings bonds are of much less interest to the small investor than they were in the past. Changes have been made from time to time in the rate of return offered, and it is entirely possible that the Treasury will seek further methods to make them more attractive. For this reason, savers should maintain an interest in announcements concerning changes in savings bond rates, maturities, etc. If their safety can be joined to a more attractive rate of return, savings bonds would be an extremely desirable and competitive savings media.

Questions

1. Commercial Banks differ from all other savings media in one respect. Explain.

2. Define:
   a. a commercial bank   c. a mutual savings bank
   b. a savings loan institution   d. a credit union

3. Four regulatory agencies control commercial banks. Discuss.

4. Compare the Federal Reserve System and the Federal Home Loan Bank System.

5. A dual banking system exists in both the commercial banking and savings and loan areas. Discuss.

6. Discuss the advantages and problems of credit unions.

7. List the considerations that should govern an individual's selection of a savings institution.

8. Discuss the question of "safety" that must be considered in selecting a savings institution.

9. Historically, commercial banks have been at a disadvantage in relation to the rate of return paid on deposits. Why?

10. Compare Series E bonds and Series H bonds.

Problems

1. List the savings institutions which John Shanfield might consider using for:
   a. Acquiring a home mortgage
   b. Opening a check account
   c. Borrowing $100

2. Jean Carthny has her savings in a local institution paying 4%. In the evening papers she discovers an advertisement by an out-of-state bank paying 5%. Should she change banks?

3. Mr. Symons has a checking account in a local bank. On opening a savings account he decides on this bank because first it is convenient, and second he believes all banks in a locality pay the same interest rate. Discuss Mr. Symons' reasoning.

4. Laura Frisby has a choice between two federally insured local savings institutions. **A** pays a return of 3% on savings, **B** pays 4%. She is about 40 years old and is saving for retirement. As the institution paying 3% is slightly nearer and her friend Georgette works there she selects **A**. After all she reasons a difference of 1% on savings of $20 per month is only 20¢ and is quite unimportant. Did she make the right choice?

5. John Ingraham lives in a metropolitan area. Every type of savings media is located in his area. How can he decide where to place his savings?

Selected Readings

The Commercial Banking Industry, Commission on Money and Credit, 1962, Prentice-Hall, Inc., Englewood Cliffs, New Jersey

Credit Union Yearbook, Credit Union National Association, Madison, Wisconsin, published annually

Conway, Lawrence V., *Savings and Loan Principles,* American Savings and Loan Institute Press, Chicago, Illinois, Second Edition, 1960

Ludtke, James B., *The American Financial System,* Allyn & Bacon, Boston, 1961

Robinson, Roland I., Editor, Boehmler, Erwin W., Gane, Frank H., Farwell, Loring C., *Financial Institutions,* Richard D. Irwin, Inc., Homewood, Illinois, Third Edition, 1960

Savings and Home Financing Source Book, Federal Home Loan Bank Board, Washington, D.C., Latest Edition

Trescott, Paul B., *Financing American Enterprise, The Story of Commercial Banking,* Harper & Row, Publishers, New York, N.Y., Copyright 1963 by The American Bankers Association

Chapter **4**

BANK SERVICES

Bank services increase in number and variety every year. Commercial banks are offering the widest diversification of services, but savings and loan associations and mutual savings banks are constantly adding to theirs, and it's becoming difficult to think of anything they don't do, or won't do, to service your needs with respect to money and valuables.

Many people do not avail themselves of the services offered because they are unaware of their availability. We can't begin to

cover them all in this chapter, but will consider those listed by the
Banking Education Committee of The American Bankers Association:

- Safeguarding Money and Valuables
  - —Safe deposit boxes for keeping important papers and
    valuables
  - —Checking accounts for individuals and businesses
  - —Savings accounts
- Transferring Funds
  - —Regular and special checking accounts
  - —Certified checks
  - —Official checks
  - —Travelers checks
  - —Money orders
  - —Bank drafts
  - —Telegraphic or cable transfers
- Making Loans
  - —Personal loans to meet emergencies
  - —Instalment loans to purchase a car or modernize a home
  - —Mortgage loans to buy a home
  - —Loans to businessmen and farmers
- Providing Trust Services
  - —Managing trusts and estates
  - —Providing financial and investment advice
- Supplying Other Services
  - —Providing currency and coin in denominations needed by
    the public
  - —Selling and redeeming U.S. Savings Bonds
  - —Preparing cash payrolls for local plants[1]

Even these services are so numerous that only the most outstanding, in terms of common usage, can be discussed.

SAFEGUARDING MONEY AND VALUABLES

According to television westerns, banks in the "old west" were
organized primarily to protect money by providing the townspeople
with a large vault. This storing of money is probably the oldest of
bank functions. Today, this is done through the provision of facilities
for safe deposit boxes, checking accounts, and savings accounts.

Safe Deposit Boxes

Safe deposit boxes are rented by bank customers to store money
and valuables. Banks use a double lock system. The customer is

---

[1] "Using Bank Services," Banking Education Committee, by permission of
The American Bankers Association, 1961, New York, New York, p. 6.

given a key to one lock and the bank keeps the key to the other. No safety deposit box can be opened until both locks are opened.

The customer's key is delivered to him in duplicate. If he loses one key, he still has the other. If he notifies the bank of the loss, the bank can change the lock and give him two new keys. If he loses both keys, the bank will have to drill the box open.

Keys are numbered. To enter a safety deposit box, a customer must have a key with the proper number, as registered with the bank. He must also permit the bank to compare his signature with that on the signature card kept by the bank.

> A banker in New Mexico tells this story. An Indian walked into the bank one day and asked for a loan of $300. "What security do you have?" the banker asked. "Two hundred horses," was the answer, and the loan was granted. Three months later, the Indian walked into the bank and peeled off $300 from a $2,500 bankroll. The banker eyed the bankroll and suggested to the Indian, "Why not let us take care of that money for you?" The Indian looked at the banker and asked: "How many horses you got?"
>
> Banks normally do not own horses, but bank facilities are excellent as a place to safeguard your money.[2]

Checking Accounts

The great percentage of all bills in this country are paid by check. A check is an order drawn on a bank by one of its depositors, authorizing the bank to pay funds out of the depositor's account to someone else. Certainly, checks are the most convenient method of making payments. The bank does all the bookkeeping, and once the checks have been endorsed by the payee and returned to the person writing the check, they offer proof of payment.

To open a checking account, a person must deposit money and supply the bank with a certain amount of personal information— address, place of birth, employer, etc. Next, a signature card must be completed. The bank then assigns an account number and gives the customer a passbook (or duplicate deposit ticket) as a receipt, and a checkbook. The account is now opened.

The signature card will be used to verify the signature on any check that might be questioned. Checking accounts may be opened individually, or jointly by two persons. A husband and wife, father

---

[2] "You and Your Bank: How Commercial Banks Help Farmers," by permission of The American Bankers Association, 1956, p. 6.

and son, business partners, etc., may open a joint account so that both parties may draw checks against it. In this case, both must provide the bank with their signatures on the signature card.

There are both advantages and disadvantages to joint accounts. Usually, they are set up with rights of survivorship, so that if one of the parties dies, the funds will go to the survivor. This makes a joint account convenient not only while both parties are living and drawing checks, but also if one dies. Both parties must be certain to record all deposits and withdrawals, to avoid confusing the records.

One possible disadvantage is that either party may withdraw all of the funds and leave the other holding an empty account. Such a situation might arise out of marital troubles. The one left with the empty account has no recourse. Despite this "calculated risk," joint accounts are widely used because of their convenience. Of course partners in joint accounts, business or marriage, should be selected with care.

Checking accounts are generally divided into two categories, regular and special. In a regular checking account, any charges made are related to the account balance and activity—the number of deposits made and checks drawn. If a person must write a large number of checks each month, and can do so and still maintain the minimum account balance prescribed by the bank, the regular checking account will usually be the most economical. In a special checking account, the charges are not related to the account balance and activity. While details of these accounts vary, the usual practice is for a person to pay so much per check—10¢, for example—plus some monthly maintenance charge. For people who draw a limited number of checks each month, special checking accounts are the most economical. If these people could maintain the necessary minimum deposit required for a regular checking account, they would be better off keeping just enough in their checking account to cover the few checks they write, and depositing the balance at interest.

Money may be deposited in a checking account either by taking it to the bank in person, or by mail. In either case, a deposit slip must be made out and submitted with the deposit. A sample deposit slip is presented on page 74. Note the basic information that must be provided:

1. The account number of the person making the deposit.
2. The name of the person who has the account.
3. The date.
4. The amounts deposited. These are separated into cash and checks, so that checks may be listed separately.

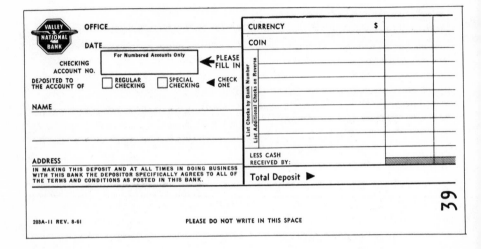

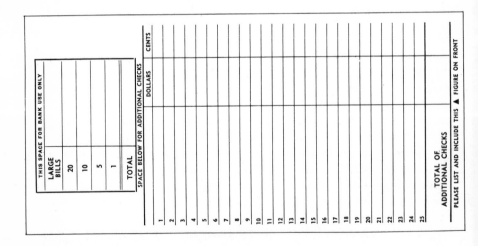

Source: Chase Manhattan Bank, New York, N.Y.

Periodically, usually at the end of each month, the bank will send a statement to each person or firm having a checking account. This is an accounting record of all deposits and check transactions for the period. All the checks drawn on the account and paid by the bank during the month will be returned with the statement. These are useful as receipts and, especially for important payments such as taxes, should be kept at least six years.

Receiving their monthly statement means the start of a task that, to many people, seems frustrating and complicated. It is called "reconciling." The whole idea is that the balance on the bank statement and the balance in the checkbook should agree.

Here is a good way to reconcile your records and the bank's:

1. See if you have received all checks charged to your account on the bank statement, then arrange them numerically or by date issued.
2. Reduce your checkbook stub balance by the amount of any bank service charges you have not previously recorded. Enter adjusted stub balance here. $ ....
3. Enter statement balance here. $ ....
4. Check each cancelled check against your checkbook stubs and make a list of all checks issued but not yet paid by the bank. Enter the total of these unpaid checks here. $ ....
5. Subtract item 4 from item 3. $ ....
6. Enter here any deposit in transit by mail or made later than the date of your statement. $ ....
7. Add items 5 and 6. This total should correspond to your stub balance (item 2).[3] $ ....

If you find that the figures do not agree, that your checkbook balance is more or less than that on the bank statement, check them again. While banks do occasionally make mistakes, it is far more likely that the mistake is yours.

Occasionally, after a check is made out the depositor will wish to stop the check. Perhaps there is the belief that the check has been lost, duplicated, or destroyed. Perhaps the depositor realizes the check was made out incorrectly, or shouldn't have been made out at all. If this happens, the stop payment notice must reach the bank before the check. If the check is cashed or certified, the stop payment order will be to no avail.

---

[3] "Using Bank Services," Banking Education Committee, by permission of The American Bankers Association, New York, N.Y., 1961, p. 17.

If a stop payment order is issued, if it appears that the check has been altered or that the signature might be forged, if the check has been postdated (dated in advance), or the figures and written amount do not agree, the bank will not honor a check. All of these precautions are, of course, for the protection of the depositor. There is one other reason why a bank will not honor a check, however, which a depositor can and should avoid—insufficient funds.

Generally, a check drawn against insufficient funds is the result of an error or oversight on the part of the depositor or the bank. Such cases are usually handled discreetly and in the best interests of the depositor. However, there are people, who, either through extreme carelessness or intent, continuously have checks returned marked "insufficient funds." This is a serious matter. The bank will levy a charge for each such check. Furthermore, if the situation occurs too frequently, the bank will no longer handle the depositor's account. Even more serious is the damage done to the depositor's credit standing. Creditors cannot possibly hold a customer in very high regard if the bank continually refuses to honor his checks.

A check may make many stops between the checkbook and the account on which it is drawn. Checks made out in one part of the country may go to pay bills in another. Checks drawn on a bank in one city may be deposited in another bank in that city, or in a suburb. It used to be possible to plan on this time lag. A person could make out checks for more money than he had in his account on the assumption that he would have several days to replenish the funds in the account before the checks would arrive at his bank. This is no longer true. With the use of magnetic ink systems and other processing innovations, the time needed to clear checks has been reduced considerably. The greater the advances in data processing, the shorter the time needed for check clearance. If both banks are located in the same city, messengers may take them to a local clearing house for exchange. If the banks are located in other cities, this clearing process may work through a "correspondent" bank in the other city, or through the Federal Reserve Bank. The Federal Reserve Banks serve as clearing houses for banks in their district, and are able to make settlements between districts through the Interdistrict Settlement Fund in Washington. A visitor visiting a Federal Reserve Bank in the late fifties or early sixties would have been impressed with the speed of check clearing. Those systems are now outmoded and the newer methods are even faster. The time that elapses between the drawing of a check by a depositor to pay a bill, its deposit in the creditor's bank, and its subtraction from the depositor's account, is becoming shorter and shorter. It may well be that as computer connections between banks increase, check clearing may be done almost instantaneously—a matter of a few hours at the most.

Of course, the most efficient clearing process imaginable cannot work until a check is deposited. If the person receiving the check simply keeps it, the clearing process can't even begin. How long may a check be held? Generally, a check is an obligation of the person drawing it for a period of six years, but it becomes "stale" after a certain period of time. In most states this is six months. After this time the bank may require proof that the person drawing the check still wants it paid.

Savings Accounts

Savings accounts pay interest; checking accounts do not. The importance of a return on savings was discussed in the preceding chapter. Every family should have a savings account. Any "extra" money in a checking account, returning no interest, is obviously a waste of the earning power of that money.

Money in a checking account can be withdrawn immediately. A checking account is a demand deposit. Savings accounts are time deposits, and banks can legally require a notice period—thirty days, for example—before a depositor may withdraw his money. This right is rarely exercised, however.

Many of the types of savings accounts that may be established are listed below.

Types of accounts [4]

1 Individual name . . . example, "John Doe."

2 Individual—Special Purpose Account . . . examples, "John Doe, Vacation," "John Doe, Home Purchase," "John Doe, Education."

3 Voluntary Trust . . . examples, "John Doe In Trust for James Doe." Can also be In Trust for non-profit organizations such as those engaged in religious, charitable, educational, philanthropic, or fraternal activities.

---

[4] First National City Bank, New York, New York.

4 Joint Account as Joint Tenants with rights of survivorship provided—2 or more names . . . example, "John Doe and/or Mrs. Mary Doe" (only one signature required for withdrawal).

5 Joint Account as Tenants in Common—with rights of survivorship provided jointly for the survivor(s) and the estate of the deceased—2 or more names . . . example, "John Jones and Harry Smith" (two or more signatures required on withdrawals or authorizations).

6 Society or Association Accounts (non-paid organizations including religious, charitable, educational, philanthropic, fraternal) . . . example, "The Jane Doe Foundation for Handicapped Children."

7 Landlord Trust Accounts (for security deposits received from tenants other than corporations organized for profit) . . . example, "John Doe as Trustee Under Section 233 Real Estate Property Law."

8 Estate Accounts—for Executors, Administrators, Trustees.

9 Fiduciary Accounts—Employee Thrift, Pension and Vacation plans. etc. Also for Guardians and Custodians of funds for minors or incompetent persons.

• These are illustrative examples and not intended to be all-inclusive. We will gladly discuss your particular needs for a special savings account.

The most common are the individual and joint accounts. To open a savings account, it is necessary to provide the bank with the same information—personal data, signature, etc.—as is necessary to open a checking account. A savings account deposit slip is presented later. Upon making the initial deposit, the depositor is assigned an account number and given a passbook with the date and amount of the deposit recorded. Each subsequent deposit and withdrawal will be entered in this passbook, and the total balance brought forward from one transaction to the next. A sample of the inside of such a passbook is presented on page 80. To withdraw funds, a withdrawal slip like the one on page 81 must be completed. Some banks require the passbook to be presented whenever a deposit or withdrawal is made; others no longer have this requirement, and periodically provide the depositor with a statement of all deposits and withdrawals, instead of entering the items in the passbook. In this case, the passbook is simply the depositor's own record of his transactions.

CHEMICAL BANK
NEW YORK
TRUST COMPANY

SAVINGS
ACCOUNT NO._____DATE_____19___
    FOR THE ACCOUNT OF

_____

_____

_____

CITY   ZONE   STATE
SUBJECT TO THE RULES AND REGULATIONS
OF THE SAVINGS DEPARTMENT.

	DOLLARS	CENTS
BILLS		
COIN		
CHECKS { Please List Each Check Separately		
Note Savings Account Number On Back Of Each Check.		
TOTAL ➡		

PLEASE ENDORSE ALL CHECKS

This space for Bank use only

Balance verified   New Balance

Teller _____ $

SAV 2 (7-62)   SEE OTHER SIDE FOR ADDITIONAL SERVICES

SAVINGS ACCOUNT DEPOSIT

Source: Chemical Bank, New York Trust Co.

BANKING PASSBOOK

ACCOUNT No._____	BRANCH AND NUMBER
Bank of America NATIONAL SAVINGS ASSOCIATION	
ALWAYS BRING THIS BOOK WITH YOU	ALWAYS FILL OUT A DEPOSIT TICKET

DATE	ENT. BY	WITHDRAWALS				DEPOSITS			BALANCE	

Source: Chase Manhattan Bank, New York, N.Y.

Writing Checks

The first important act in writing a check really does not concern the check itself—it is filling out the stub. These are a record of deposits and withdrawals. It is very easy to forget the stub if it isn't completed before the check is made out; and if it isn't completed, it is very easy to forget to whom the check was made out, and for how much. Indeed, it is suprisingly easy to forget that a check was made out. If there isn't a record of every check, the balance in the checking account will be wrong, and checks might eventually be returned "N.S.F." (not sufficient funds).

WITHDRAWAL

SAVINGS DEPARTMENT

ACCOUNT
NUMBER_____

DATE_____

RECEIVED FROM THE CHASE MANHATTAN BANK

DOLLARS	CENTS

_____DOLLARS

WHICH AMOUNT IS TO BE DEBITED TO ABOVE NUMBERED ACCOUNT

SIGNATURE_____

HAVE YOU CHANGED YOUR ADDRESS?

NEW
ADDRESS
ZONE NO.
STATE

PASSBOOK MUST BE PRESENTED WITH THIS WITHDRAWAL RECEIPT

B. SAV. 4 6-62

Source: The Chase Manhattan Bank, New York, New York.

An example of a check is presented on page 82. There are three parties to every check. First is the drawer, or maker, the person ordering the bank to pay. In the example, this is Francis Scott Key. Next is the payee, the person to whom the check is made out. In the example, this is a dry goods store. Third is the drawee, the one who is ordered to pay. The Riggs National Bank is the drawee in the example. Other important items on every check are the date, the check number, the amount in figures, and the amount in words.

The name of the drawer should correspond exactly with the name on the bank's signature card. Furthermore, signing the check is the last thing that should be done. If any of the other blanks have not been filled in, someone else could fill them in and the bank would naturally cash the check, as the signature would be legitimate.

The payee's name must be carefully filled in so that the name may not be altered. Probably the easiest name to alter is "Co.," the abbreviation for "Company." Thousands of names begin with "Co." It is quite easy for a check thief to add a few letters and then have it cashed. Care should be taken to begin the first name immediately after the words "Pay to the order of," to keep the first and last names close together, to avoid abbreviations like "Co.," and to fill in the remainder of the space with a wavy line.

A check should never be made out to "cash," unless the depositor is at the bank and wishes to withdraw money. Even then, it is safer for the depositor to make the check out to himself. A check made out to "Cash" may be cashed by anyone.

The drawee's name usually doesn't have to be filled in. The name of the bank always appears on checks provided the depositors. Only on those rare occasions when a person does not have his checkbook and must use a blank check, must this be written in.

The date on the check should be the date on which the check is drawn. Many people postdate checks—date them ahead. This is not a good idea. If the payee attempts to cash it early, the bank will refuse to honor it, and will return the check to the payee. The date is also important as evidence as to when payment was made, in case any controversy arises. It will also be used to determine when the check becomes "stale."

The check number helps in record keeping. It is easier to match checks against stubs (when they are returned by the bank with the statement) if the checks can be sorted out in numerical order. Furthermore, if a check is lost, or if the drawer wishes to stop payment, numbering makes it easier to identify. The simplest system is to number checks consecutively, starting with No. 1. People who make out many checks each year may prefer to start a new numerical series each year. They may number the first check each year with a "1" followed by the last two digits of the year. The first check in 1964 would be 164, the second 264, etc. Each depositor should select a system which is simple and meets his needs, and then stick with it.

Great care must be taken in entering both the amount of the check in figures and the amount in words. A bank will not cash a check if it has obviously been altered, but if the change has been cleverly made, the bank may not catch it. The person drawing the check should make alterations as difficult to make as possible. If any space is left between the dollar sign and the first number, another number may be inserted. If there is also space before the written amount, the same amount may be inserted there. For example:

$ 5^{67}

67

Five   100 ~~~~~~~~~~~~~ Dollars

May easily be changed to

$55^{67}

67

Fifty Five 100 ~~~~~~~~~~~~~ Dollars

The written amount should be as far to the left as possible in the space provided, and the remainder of the space should be filled in with a wavy line. If there is a difference between the amount of the check in figures and the amount in words, the amount in words generally governs, but many banks will refuse to cash a check under these circumstances.

Endorsements

A check must be endorsed before it can be cashed or deposited. The endorsement is the signature of the payee, and it passes his title to the check to another party. The three frequently used types of endorsement are presented on page 84.[5] The first is the blank endorsement. This is simply the signature of the payee. This enables anyone to cash the check. Blank endorsements should never be made unless the person is at the bank, and even then their use is questionable.

---

[5] "Using Bank Services," Banking Education Committee, by permission of The American Bankers Association, 1961 New York, New York, p. 15.

Checks have been lost between the desk or table on which the endorsement was made at the bank, and the cashier's window.

ENDORSEMENTS
This check was drawn to the order of John Smith, and
he passed it on by means of a—

blank endorsement
to Joseph Jones ⟶

who transferred it with
a special endorsement
to Alice Green ⟶

who signed a
restrictive endorsement
when depositing it
to her account ⟶

> *John Smith*
>
> *Pay to the order
> of Alice Green
> Joseph Jones*
>
> *For deposit only
> Alice Green*

The second is the special endorsement. This provides protection because it clearly specifies the payee. No one else could pick up the check and cash it.

The third is the restrictive endorsement. This restricts the use to which the check may be put. With a restrictive endorsement, only that specific use may be made of the check.

If the name on the face of the check is spelled wrong, the payee should first endorse the check just as the name appears on the face, then endorse it with his name correctly spelled.

Banks make every effort not to cash forged checks. If they do, it is their own money which they lose. A depositor rarely loses due to forgeries. Banks protect themselves by carrying forgery insurance.

Kinds of Checks

There are times when a check other than a personal check is preferable. A personal check may not be acceptable for transactions involving real estate, securities, contract bids, etc. In such cases, a personal check may be changed into a certified check. This means that the bank guarantees it to be good. The bank marks the check to indicate that it is certified, and immediately puts a hold on the account for the amount of the check. One disadvantage of the certified check is that the bank will keep the cancelled check and the drawer will not have the check as a receipt.

Another type of check is the cashier's or treasurer's check—depending on which bank official signs it. This is often used by a person who does not have a checking account and needs a check of unquestioned value. This check is drawn by the bank on itself, and is made payable to the payee you select. You pay the bank the amount of the check, plus a small fee. No cancelled check will be available as a receipt in this case either.

Registered checks, or bank money orders, can be purchased at the bank very reasonably. These provide a space for the sender's name, and a detachable stub or carbon duplicate which can be used as a receipt, and which has the same serial number as the check itself for identification purposes. Bank drafts are used to transfer large sums in this manner.

Travelers checks are a safe and convenient method of carrying funds while traveling. The most widely used are American Express

Source: American Express Company, New York, New York.

Company Travelers Cheques. They can be purchased at most banks for a small fee and are accepted almost anywhere in the world. A sample of such a check is presented on page 85.

The purchaser of travelers checks signs them twice, once in the presence of the bank official selling the checks when they are purchased, and a second time in the presence of the persons cashing them when they are cashed. The persons cashing the checks thus have the opportunity to compare the two signatures, to make certain they are alike. For larger sums than $500, a bank letter of credit is often used.

Most banks also have facilities for telegraphing or cabling funds. This is an advantage if it becomes necessary to transfer funds quickly from one part of the country to another, or overseas.

MAKING LOANS

Borrowing money seems to get easier and easier. It is only paying it back that becomes more difficult. Do you need money to meet medical bills, to pay for a college education, to buy a car? Loans for these and many other purposes can be obtained at the bank. This is the bank's business—lending money. They lend it as personal loans to individuals, to home buyers, to business firms, in fact to everyone who has a legitimate need and can meet the necessary requirements. Details of some of these loans will be presented in chapters specifically devoted to these subjects. Automobile loans will be covered in the chapter on Buying an Automobile, mortgage loans in the chapter on Buying a Home, and loans for a college education in the chapter on College Costs; and a comparison of banks and other sources of loans is presented in the chapter on Borrowing.

Procedure

The procedure for getting a bank loan is fairly standard. First you go to the loan department and tell them the amount you need and why. If, after investigation, the loan appears to be a desirable one for the bank to make, it will be approved by either the board of directors or a loan officer. Next, the borrower signs a promissory note and the money is given to him in cash or credited to his account.

Before the bank may make the loan, it is required by law to make certain that the loan is reasonably safe. It cannot tie up all of its funds in long term loans. Some of its loans must be fairly liquid—easily converted into cash. Finally, it must receive a reasonable rate of interest, as no one, not even banks, can afford to do business for nothing.

Promissory Notes

We have said that whenever money is borrowed from a bank a promissory note must be signed. An example of a promissory note is presented on page 88-89. This is an unconditional written promise to pay a definite amount of money to the order of the bank. It is signed by the maker, the person or firm borrowing the money. If it is a single-name note, it will be signed by only one person. If two parties are responsible for payment, both sign it, and it becomes two-name paper.

Notes are either secured or unsecured. If secured, the borrower must give the bank something of value (collateral) to hold. The securities most commonly used as collateral are life insurance, cash surrender values, a savings account passbook, marketable bonds, and listed stocks and bonds.

Promissory notes are negotiable instruments. Title to a note may pass from one person to another by endorsement.

Personal Loans

The excerpt from First National City Bank's pamphlet, presented below, describes personal loans. The bank will require information concerning the purpose of the loan, the time needed to repay it, the financial status of the borrower, etc., but once this information is made available, personal loans are quickly made to those meeting the bank's requirements.

> Every family occasionally experiences a special need for extra funds. The need may be unforeseen and immediate, as for emergency medical bills, or predictable in advance, as for educational costs, taxes, insurance premiums, or travel expenses.
>
> Your most practical answer may well be a personal loan— and your bank is probably the most practical source. Borrowing from your bank is less expensive than borrowing from most other sources. Bank rates are usually substantially lower. Dealing with your bank is also more personal and pleasant. Your banker is prepared to offer you sound financial counsel. That's part of his job.
>
> And don't, for goodness sake, feel that there is any stigma attached to borrowing. Since 1928, as a pioneer in the field,

$ _____

NEW YORK, N.Y., _____, 19 _____

On _____, 19 _____, *For Value Received, the undersigned,*

Promise To Pay To The Order of CHEMICAL BANK NEW YORK TRUST COMPANY

At its office at _____ *New York, N.Y.*

_____ DOLLARS

In the event of: default in payment of any liability to the holder hereof (however acquired), suspension or liquidation of usual business, calling of a meeting of creditors, assignment for the benefit of creditors, dissolution, bulk sale or notice thereof, mortgage or pledge, insolvency of any kind, attachment, distraint, levy, execution, judgment, death, application for or appointment of a receiver, filing of a voluntary or involuntary petition under any provision of the Bankruptcy Act or amendments thereto, of, by or against any Obligor (which term shall include each of the undersigned and each indorser or guarantor hereof) or any property or rights of any Obligor, failure of any Obligor, on request, to furnish any financial information, or to permit inspection of any books or records, any change in, or discovery with regard to, the condition or affairs of any Obligor which, in the holder's opinion, increases its credit risk, or if the holder for any other reason deems itself insecure—this note and all other liabilities,direct or contingent, of any Obligor to the holder (however acquired), shall become absolute, due and payable, without demand or notice. The holder shall have a lien on the deposit balances of any Obligor, and may at any time, without notice, apply the same to this note or such other liabilities, whether due or not. If an attorney is used to enforce or collect this note, an attorney's fee of 15% of principal and interest due shall be added hereto. Each Obligor waives trial by jury, and the right to interpose any counter-claims or set-offs of any kind in any litigation relating to this note or any of such other liabilities. The undersigned shall be jointly and severally liable hereon.

_____

_____

No. _____

LN. 211 (12—60)

88

The undersigned hereby (jointly and severally) guarantees to CHEMICAL BANK NEW YORK TRUST COMPANY its successors, indorsees and assigns, irrespective of the genuineness, validity or enforceability of the within note, the prompt payment thereof at maturity, by acceleration or otherwise, and agrees to be bound by and confirms the provisions of said note relating to liens on balances, attorney's fee and acceleration of maturities and agrees that, from time to time before or after maturity and without notice, said note may be renewed or extended, in whole or in part, the rate of interest thereon may be changed, the holder thereof need not affect any set-off, and may exchange, surrender or release, and need not sell, realize upon or conserve any collateral security, all without affecting or releasing the liability of the undersigned. The signature of the undersigned hereto is also an indorsement of said note. The undersigned waives protest, all notices to which the undersigned might otherwise be entitled, and the benefit of any extension of time conferred by any law now or hereafter in effect.

_____

Address_____

_____

Address_____

_____

Address_____

Source: Chemical Bank, New York Trust Company, New York, New York.

PERSONAL INSTALMENT NOTE   No. PI................
(For Discount)

$..   Calif.,........................, 19.......

FOR VALUE RECEIVED, the undersigned, jointly and severally, promise to pay, in lawful money of the United States of

America,   **Bank of America**   at its................................branch, in this city
to the order of   NATIONAL TRUST AND SAVINGS ASSOCIATION

....Dollars

in instalments as follows:................................Dollars ($................)........................, 19.......and

................equal successive................monthly instalments of................................, 19.......and............................Dollars

($................) beginning........................, 19.......and................
together with a delinquency charge on each instalment in default for 10 days in an amount equal to 5% of such instalment or
$5.00 whichever is less but not less than $1.00. This note is subject to all of the terms and provisions set forth on the reverse
hereof which are hereby specifically incorporated herein and agreed to.

Do not make any changes   Signatures:
or erasures in this note.

Complete Address:

1...
BORROWER

2...
CO-MAKER

3...
CO-MAKER

4...
CO-MAKER

5...
CO-MAKER

SPECIMEN

SPECIMEN

TPL-5X 5-62 (REV.)

90

First National City has made more than 10,000,000 personal loans to individuals. Personal credit, properly used, is a useful and sensible family tool. Tuition loans, for example, represent a wise investment in your children's future.

Your bank is glad to make credit available to you not as a favor, but as a straightforward matter of business.

First National City makes personal loans in amounts ranging from $50 to $5,000, repayable monthly over periods up to 36 months. Applications are processed usually within hours, whether you are a depositor or not. If you have an FNCB checking account, however, you can arrange to have us deduct your loan payment directly from your checking account each month, thus saving you the trouble of making individual payments.[6]

In making a personal loan, a bank usually requires the borrower to sign an installment note (see page 90). If the amount borrowed is $600 for one year at 6%, the borrower would sign a note for $636, and pay the bank $53 per month for twelve months. Sometimes the bank will want more than one person to be responsible for a personal loan, and will require a co-maker. This gives the bank added assurance that the loan will be paid.

Lines of Credit

One of the older types of credit available to business has been a "line of credit." Under this system, the bank permits a business to borrow up to some specified amount. The First National Bank of Boston was the first bank to establish such a plan for consumers. In 1955, it started the First Check-Credit Plan, and since then banks all over the country have started similar plans under a variety of names. The excerpt from a First National pamphlet, presented below, describes the First Check-Credit Plan.

What is
FIRST CHECK-CREDIT
?

Invented by The FIRST in 1955, *First* Check-Credit is still the newest way to borrow money — a revolving loan plan for mature, responsible people who value their privacy. *First* Check-Credit is very much like the line of credit we have extended for

[6] "What You Should Know About Bank Services and How to Use Them," *Reader's Digest*, First National City Bank, 1962, detachable advertisement, page 7.

many years to soundly-managed businesses. By putting it on a personal basis, we offer a truly business-like way for individuals and families to borrow money with the least red tape.

More than 35,000 people in and around Boston are now using this more convenient, more confidential way to borrow.

Here's how it works:

When you open your account, you and the Bank agree on an amount of money to be set aside for your use. This is your Maximum Credit. You can use part or all of this credit for anything you want, simply by writing out the checks we supply without charge. These are ordinary checks which you make out and sign just like any personal check.

The checks you draw become loans when we pay them. You pay back in regular monthly instalments equal to 1/12 or 1/24th of your Maximum Credit, according to which payment plan you choose. As you repay, you build your credit balance for future use.[7]

Applications for this type of loan are checked more carefully than those for regular loans, as this is a continuing line of credit. While the customer is asked to specify the monthly payment his budget can afford, the loan limit usually is about one month's income. Interest is charged only on the amount of credit actually being used at any time, plus a small fee for each check used. The amount the borrower must pay back is determined by the line of credit, not by the amount actually borrowed. For example, if a borrower has a $360 line of credit and a repayment period of twelve months, he must pay back $30 each month even if only $120 is actually used.

Revolving credit plans such as this are extremely convenient for borrowers. Money is available at any time, day or night, without going to the bank. Some banks, however, have found that such loans are almost too convenient, and have discovered that careful examination of the applicant's financial situation before granting the loan, and a periodic re-examination after the loan is granted, is necessary. Someone with an excellent credit rating today may be in financial difficulty tomorrow.

Business Loans

Banks have always been a source of money for business firms. Bank loans are used by firms both large and small.

---

[7] "First Check-Credit," The First National Bank of Boston, Boston, Mass., 1962, p. 1.

Consider a typical small business loan. Call this one "Who Helped Raise the Dough?" Paul Dean Arnold first learned about the baking business with National Biscuit Company. He decided that he wanted to produce the finest loaf of bread possible. So he went into business for himself. When demand began to overwhelm his tiny shop, Arnold found an abandoned plant in Port Chester, New York. It had three brick ovens which would cost about $3,500 to recondition. Arnold wished to borrow the money, but he lacked collateral. One day he and his wife went to a bank in a nearby city. They left a loaf of fresh bread on every desk and next day went back and had a talk with the president. They discussed their plans and hopes, their methods and techniques. Bank officials were impressed and the Arnolds were given a credit of $3,500 on their own signatures. It was only a beginning. Today the Arnolds have one of the finest companies in the industry.[8]

The most common type of business loan is for 30, 60, or 90 days, and may or may not be renewable at the end of that time. Beside these, many banks have flexible plans which provide relatively large sums of money for two or three years, and also make term loans to finance expensive new equipment for periods of five or ten years.

Among the many different kinds of loans made to business are:

1. Unsecured loans—for working capital.
2. Collateral loans—secured by marketable securities.
3. Commodity loans—for businesses with working capital largely in salable commodities.
4. Assigned accounts—for businesses with good accounts receivable for collateral.
5. Factoring—handling of accounts receivable for relatively large businesses.
6. Contract loans—to finance contracts including those a firm might have with the U.S. Government, secured by an assignment of the proceeds of the contract.

Agricultural Credit

Farming is becoming more and more technical. More equipment, chemicals, fertilizer, etc., are required each year. Farmers borrow from banks to purchase real estate and to finance current operations.

[8] "Using Bank Services," Banking Education Committee, by permission of The American Bankers Association, New York, New York, © 1961, p. 31.

The majority of farm borrowers need money for seasonal reasons. Many banks employ men who specialize in farm loans and also serve as counselors to help farmers meet their financial and general farm problems.

TRUSTEE SERVICES

Most people are familiar with the savings, checking account, and loan facilities of banks, but not as many are familiar with the many trust services provided. In those banks providing such services, the trust department often looks rather quiet compared to the other departments. Actually, their work is highly important to individuals, businesses, and the bank. People entrust billions of dollars to banks for them to manage.

Estate Services

Because banks provide experienced and trained specialists, they are often named as the executor or trustee under a will. They have many advantages over individual executors. One is that the bank will never get sick, or die. If a bank is named as trustee under a will, a person's estate will be managed as efficiently as possible to fulfil the desires expressed by the person making the will. This would mean that the beneficiaries could be assured of a regular income, that funds would be available for the education of the deceased's children, etc. Banks are also available to act as trustees of living trusts (trusts established while a person is still living), to act as trustee to handle the proceeds of insurance policies, to act as the guardian of estates of minor children, or to act as a conservator for the estates of incapacitated persons.

Custodian Services

As a custodian, a bank will take care of your securities. It will collect dividends and interest, handle all the necessary records, suggest investment changes, make certain that stock rights are not overlooked and that coupons are always clipped, and hundreds of other details. This may be done either on a complete service basis, in which case the bank performs every possible service in connection with a person's investment portfolio, or on a partial service basis, where it does everything but review the portfolio and recommend changes.

Stock Investment

Many banks will establish a person's portfolio for him by an arrangement under which he makes regular deposits in a special account. These savings earn interest while they are on deposit. When the money in the account reaches a certain amount, the bank will invest the money in securities. Each time the cash in the account reaches a specified amount, more securities will be purchased by the bank. Stocks purchased under such a plan are the property of the investor, and are not mixed with others. If the investor wishes, he can close his account and take out his stocks and any cash balance.

These are only a few of the services a trust department will perform for an individual. They will also act as trustee under a pension or profit-sharing plan, serve as administrator under health and welfare plans, and perform many other services. Many banks provide expert help in estate planning.

Corporate Trusts

Banks also provide many services of a trustee nature for business. Corporations with public stock issues must have a transfer agent and a registrar. The transfer agent maintains a record of the ownership of the various shares outstanding, and handles the bookkeeping involved in the transference of stock from one owner to another. The registrar makes certain that all outstanding stock is authorized—that stock is not over-issued.

Trustees must be appointed when a corporation issues bonds, and at least one of these trustees must be a bank or trust company. As a trustee, the bank watches out for the interests of the bondholders.

These examples only indicate the varied trust services made available by banks to business.

OTHER SERVICES

Banks perform many more services than the few that have been covered here. It might well be asked, "What is there that banks don't do?"

Christmas club accounts are made available at most banks. These, along with Vacation Clubs and all kinds of special purpose savings accounts, make it possible for a person to save for a particular goal. Drive-in windows make it possible to bank without getting out of your car. Mail service brings banking services to your nearest mailbox. Under automatic savings plans, banks will automatically deduct a specific amount from your checking account each month and place it in your savings account.

Banks have become more and more aggressive in securing accounts. One service which gains customers is the handling of a firm's payroll problems. Under this service, the bank pays the firm's employees each payday; and many of the employees find it convenient to keep their money in the bank handling the payroll.

In many areas banks will pay all of your bills. Customers give the bank their bill stubs and a check for the total amount, plus a small fee for each item to be paid. The bank then pays the bills.

Banks also provide many community services. According to an article in *Banking*, a bank in Manchester, New Hampshire, sponsored a mixed chorus at the state industrial school; one in New York gave a merit award for outstanding community service; another, in Wisconsin, provides a 10-passenger "courtesy car" for use by charitable and civic organizations; banks in Delaware started high school clubs for those interested in banking and business; a Denver bank has an Honor Award Club for young people who return lost items; one in Gastonia, North Carolina, started a public speaking course for presidents of local societies; and another, in Louisiana, made a good fishing area available to those who wanted to fish.[9]

It is pretty safe to say that whatever a person's needs may be in the general area of finance, his bank is more than apt to be able to handle it. Service is their business.

Questions

1. Explain the operation of the key and lock system used by most banks for their safety deposit boxes.

2. Compare a regular and special checking account.

3. A person with a checking account in a bank in Rhode Island can no longer draw a check on this account while visiting in California and

---

[9] John L. Cooley, "Banks are Good Neighbors," by permission of *Banking*, the Official Journal of The American Bankers Association, American Bankers Association, New York, New York, Feb. 1963, p. 45.

assume that the check will not reach his bank for any considerable period of time. Discuss.

4. Mr. Samuels received a check for $5.85 representing dividends on an investment in securities. He received the check eight months ago. Will he have any problem cashing the check today?

5. List seven types of savings accounts with a brief description.

6. State the suggested safeguards that a person should take when filling out a check to prevent any alteration.

7. Describe each of the following:
   a. Personal check
   b. Treasurer's check
   c. Registered checks
   d. Traveler's check

8. a. What is a promissory note?
   b. Why are they "negotiable instruments"?

9. Compare the following:
   a. Personal loan of $500
   b. A revolving credit plan at the bank for $500
   c. A business loan

10. Briefly describe the trustee services offered by banks.

Problems

1. Mrs. Phillips is a widow. She is retired, lives in an apartment. Her expenditures each month are few — usually rent, food, clothes, and telephone. Would you suggest she open a regular or a special checking account?

2. From a local bank acquire copies of each of the forms they have available discussed in this chapter. Compare them with those in the chapter.

3. Mr. Jones has a checking account in a local bank. His account balance at the beginning of the month was $285. During the month he made out the following checks:

    1. Hot Oil Company $ 25
    2. Indian Bank $120
    3. Indian Electric $ 10
    4. Foods Unlimited $150
    5. Church $ 15
    6. Super Gas Co. $ 20
    7. Monarch Auto Loans $ 50
    8. Southern Insurance Co. $ 15
    9. Solid Board Lumber Co. $ 35
  10. Speedy Repair Service $ 10
  11. Superior Mutual Fund $ 25
  12. Family Clothiers $ 30

On receiving his statement he finds that checks number 3, 5 and 11 have not yet been paid by the bank. His one deposit of $300 is recorded on the statement and there has been a service charge of $1.85. His stub balance is $80. The statement balance is $128.15. Reconcile these amounts.

4. Using a check obtained from a local bank, fill it in properly as if you had an account in that bank. (If you do have an account use John Doe as your signature.)

5. Prepare an example of each of the three types of endorsement and describe a situation in which they might be used.

Selected Readings

"Bank Terminology," The National Cash Register Company, Dayton, Ohio, 1962

Banking, the Official Journal of The American Bankers Association, American Bankers Association, New York, New York, published monthly

"Save Money on Your Checking Account," Changing Times, The Kiplinger Magazine, The Kiplinger Washington Editors, Inc., 1729 H St., N.W., Washington, D.C., 1 September 1962

"Using Bank Services," Banking Education Committee, The American Bankers Association, New York, New York, 1961

"You and Your Bank, How Commercial Banks Help Farmers," The American Bankers Association, New York, New York, 1956

"Your Bank and Its Services," The Chase Manhattan Bank, New York, N.Y.

Chapter **5**

BORROWING

CONSUMER CREDIT

This chapter concerns consumer credit.

Consumer credit may be defined as credit used by consumers to help finance the purchase of commodities and services for personal consumption or to refinance debts originally incurred for such purchases.[1]

Consumer loans are repayable within a short period of time, usually about two years, although they may run to five.

[1] Carl A. Dauten, "Financing the American Consumer," *Consumer Credit Monograph No. 1*, American Investment Company of Illinois, St. Louis, Missouri, 1956, Copyright © 1956 by Carl A. Dauten, p. 1.

Classification

One general way of classifying consumer credit is by the method of repayment. Single payment — noninstalment — credit is used for charge accounts and regular monthly bills such as oil, gas, doctor bills, etc., or a single payment cash loan. The second type—instalment credit—is used to repay a debt in a series of payments. One difference between the two is that a written legal contract is always necessary whenever instalment credit is used.

Instalment credit, itself, may be divided into two types. Let's assume someone wants to purchase a food freezer and pay for it over a period of time. One way of doing this would be to sign an instalment sales contract at the store where the freezer is purchased. Another way would be to borrow the money by getting an instalment cash loan, and then using it to buy the freezer.

Uses of Consumer Credit

Table 5-1 on page 101 indicates the major uses of consumer credit. This chapter will discuss all but the largest, automobile loans, which will be discussed in Chapter 6 on Buying an Automobile.

The second category given in the table, "Other Consumer Goods Paper," has to do primarily with the use of instalment sales contracts to purchase durable goods such as furniture and appliances. The third, "Repairs and Modernization Loans," concerns loans made to improve homes.

The next two columns, "Personal Loans" and "Single-Payment Loans," cover a much wider territory. Of these two, "Personal Loans" is by far the larger. These are used to refinance existing bills, or for medical expenses, automobiles, education, taxes, travel, or for just about any purpose imaginable.

Charge accounts are familiar to most Americans today. Everyone is accustomed to this method of shopping. Service credit is also familiar, but usually not by this name. It is the credit allowed by utilities, doctors, dentists, and others, who send their customers monthly bills.

WHY USE CREDIT?

The American attitude towards credit has changed considerably over the years. At one time, going into debt for any reason was looked

Table 5-1

TOTAL CREDIT
(In millions of dollars)

End of period	Total	Instalment					Noninstalment			
		Total	Automobile paper	Other consumer goods paper	Repair and modernization loans¹	Personal loans	Total	Single-payment loans	Charge accounts	Service credit
1939	7,222	4,503	1,497	1,620	298	1,088	2,719	787	1,414	518
1941	9,172	6,085	2,458	1,929	376	1,322	3,087	845	1,645	597
1945	5,665	2,462	455	816	182	1,009	3,203	746	1,612	845
1956	42,334	31,720	14,420	8,606	1,905	6,789	10,614	3,253	4,995	2,366
1957	44,970	33,867	15,340	8,844	2,101	7,582	11,103	3,364	5,146	2,593
1958	45,129	33,642	14,152	9,028	2,346	8,116	11,487	3,627	5,060	2,800
1959	51,542	39,245	16,420	10,630	2,809	9,386	12,297	4,129	5,104	3,064
1960	56,028	42,832	17,688	11,525	3,139	10,480	13,196	4,507	5,329	3,360
1961	57,678	43,527	17,223	11,857	3,191	11,256	14,151	5,136	5,324	3,691
1962	63,458	48,243	19,384	12,855	3,290	12,714	15,215	5,579	5,642	3,994
1962—Feb.	56,093	43,074	17,191	11,496	3,123	11,264	13,019	4,988	4,192	3,839
Mar.	56,275	43,211	17,348	11,407	3,113	11,343	13,064	5,146	4,074	3,844
Apr.	57,314	43,837	17,671	11,498	3,128	11,540	13,477	5,241	4,319	3,917
May	58,318	44,495	18,032	11,598	3,169	11,696	13,823	5,400	4,544	3,879
June	59,108	45,208	18,410	11,726	3,200	11,782	13,900	5,428	4,596	3,876
July	59,364	45,650	18,680	11,754	3,226	11,990	13,714	5,402	4,457	3,855
Aug.	60,003	46,204	18,933	11,824	3,260	12,187	13,799	5,469	4,491	3,839
Sept.	60,126	46,310	18,881	11,861	3,277	12,291	13,816	5,481	4,495	3,840
Oct.	60,626	46,722	19,083	11,986	3,289	12,364	13,904	5,442	4,663	3,799
Nov.	61,473	47,274	19,307	12,186	3,302	12,479	14,199	5,526	4,825	3,848
Dec.	63,458	48,243	19,384	12,855	3,290	12,714	15,215	5,579	5,642	3,994
1963—Jan.	r62,740	r48,130	19,426	r12,719	3,250	12,735	r14,610	5,511	r5,058	4,041
Feb.	62,219	48,025	19,503	12,511	3,221	12,790	14,194	5,545	4,496	4,153

¹ Holdings of financial institutions; holdings of retail outlets are included in other consumer goods paper.

r Revised.

NOTE.—Consumer credit estimates cover loans to individuals for household, family, and other personal expenditures, except real estate mortgage loans. The estimates include data for Alaska beginning with Jan. 1959 (except for instalment credit held by sales finance cos.), and for Hawaii beginning with Aug. 1959. For a description of the series see BULL., Apr. 1953. Back data are available upon request.

Source: Federal Reserve Bulletin, April, 1963, p. 524.

upon with considerable disfavor. Then, for a period of time, debt financing was given a sort of grudging acceptance. Today, at least 50 per cent of American families use some type of instalment credit. As far as going into debt is concerned, ask this question: How many Americans would own their own homes and automobiles today if they hadn't been able to go into debt (borrow) to do it?

Cash always has been, and still is, the least expensive way to buy. Then why use credit? There are several reasons. It enables you to buy without ready cash. It is convenient. It eliminates the necessity of carrying large amounts of cash (if you have it). Bills can be paid at the end of the month, which makes payment more convenient, particularly so if a person is paid only once or twice a month.

It can be used to meet financial emergencies. This is especially true for families with low incomes, who are unable to build up sufficient liquid reserves to meet unforeseen situations such as an accident or loss of a job.

It is used to buy higher-priced durable goods on time. The average consumer seldom has the cash to buy items such as a television set, a stereo, a new radio, a food freezer, or new furniture. Credit permits him to have more than he otherwise could afford.

It is used to pay old debts. Bills accumulate when the family wage earner suffers a cut in pay, or is sick, and credit may often solve the problem. Borrowing to consolidate debts will certainly not reduce or eliminate them. It will, however, make the payments easier to meet by spreading them out. If a family cuts its expenses and carefully budgets its income, smaller monthly payments for a longer period of time may solve their problems. It will enable them to pay their bills and keep their credit standing intact.

Sources of Credit

Table 5-2 indicates the various sources of credit. Each of them differs from the other. An examination of the types of credit offered by each of them will help you determine which one to use if the need arises. Table 5-3 A indicates types of credit offered by credit unions, consumer finance and other financial institutions presented in Table 5-2. Table 5-3 B indicates the sources of non-instalment credit.

Commercial Banks

As indicated by these tables, commercial banks are the largest single source of both instalment and non-instalment consumer credit,

Table 5-2

INSTALMENT CREDIT

(In millions of dollars)

End of period	Total	Financial institutions							Retail outlets					
		Total	Commercial banks	Sales finance cos.	Credit unions	Consumer finance [1]	Other [1]	Total	Department stores [2]	Furniture stores	Appliance stores	Automobile dealers [3]	Other
1939	4,503	3,065	1,079	1,197	132		657	1,438	354	439	183	123	339
1941	6,085	4,480	1,726	1,797	198		759	1,605	320	496	206	188	395
1945	2,462	1,776	745	300	102		629	686	131	240	17	28	270
1956	31,720	26,977	11,777	9,117	2,014	2,940	1,129	4,743	1,408	1,187	377	502	1,269
1957	33,867	29,200	12,843	9,609	2,429	3,124	1,195	4,668	1,393	1,210	361	478	1,226
1958	33,642	28,659	12,780	8,844	2,668	3,085	1,282	4,983	1,882	1,128	292	506	1,175
1959	39,245	33,570	15,227	10,319	3,280	3,337	1,407	5,676	2,292	1,225	310	481	1,368
1960	42,832	37,218	16,672	11,472	3,923	3,670	1,481	5,615	2,414	1,107	333	359	1,482
1961	43,527	37,935	17,008	11,273	4,330	3,799	1,525	5,595	2,421	1,058	293	342	1,481
1962	48,243	41,807	18,909	12,194	4,973	4,131	1,600	6,436	3,013	1,073	279	284	1,787
1962—Feb.	43,074	37,904	16,967	11,361	4,288	3,783	1,505	5,170	2,153	1,018	283	336	1,380
Mar.	43,211	37,995	17,062	11,283	4,333	3,795	1,522	5,216	2,227	998	278	330	1,383
Apr.	43,837	38,497	17,366	11,359	4,426	3,826	1,520	5,340	2,339	991	275	320	1,415
May	44,495	39,032	17,686	11,440	4,520	3,836	1,550	5,463	2,430	991	274	310	1,458
June	45,208	39,639	18,024	11,570	4,616	3,876	1,553	5,569	2,522	988	276	302	1,481
July	45,650	40,062	18,235	11,682	4,681	3,907	1,557	5,588	2,545	989	275	298	1,481
Aug.	46,204	40,537	18,427	11,796	4,783	3,948	1,583	5,667	2,609	999	275	296	1,488
Sept.	46,310	40,597	18,443	11,787	4,814	3,969	1,584	5,713	2,675	998	273	299	1,468
Oct.	46,722	40,896	18,613	11,860	4,874	3,974	1,575	5,826	2,737	1,002	273	298	1,516
Nov.	47,274	41,285	18,765	11,986	4,928	4,009	1,597	5,989	2,835	1,019	274	292	1,569
Dec.	48,243	41,807	18,909	12,194	4,973	4,131	1,600	6,436	3,013	1,073	279	284	1,787
1963—Jan.	48,130	42,317	18,981	12,681	4,939	4,134	1,582	5,813	2,478	1,049	275	272	1,739
Feb.	48,025	42,280	19,057	12,550	4,952	4,138	1,583	5,745	2,506	1,027	273	259	1,680

[1] Consumer finance cos. included with "other" financial institutions until Sept. 1950.
[2] Includes mail-order houses.
[3] Automobile paper only; other instalment credit held by automobile dealers is included with "other" retail outlets. See also Note to Table 5-1.

Source: Federal Reserve Bulletin, April, 1963 p. 524.

103

Table 5-3

A

INSTALMENT CREDIT HELD BY OTHER FINANCIAL INSTITUTIONS
(In millions of dollars)

End of period	Total	Automobile paper	Other consumer goods paper	Repair and modernization loans	Personal loans
1939	789	81	24	15	669
1941	957	122	36	14	785
1945	731	54	20	14	643
1956	6,083	954	624	404	4,101
1957	6,748	1,114	588	490	4,555
1958	7,035	1,152	565	595	4,723
1959	8,024	1,400	681	698	5,244
1960	9,074	1,665	771	800	5,837
1961	9,654	1,819	743	832	6,257
1962	10,704	2,077	769	882	6,976
1962—Feb.	9,576	1,801	729	814	6,232
Mar.	9,650	1,824	731	818	6,277
Apr.	9,772	1,862	732	820	6,358
May	9,906	1,895	736	837	6,438
June	10,045	1,934	746	844	6,521
July	10,145	1,962	749	849	6,585
Aug.	10,314	2,007	758	865	6,684
Sept.	10,367	2,018	758	870	6,721
Oct.	10,423	2,039	760	871	6,753
Nov.	10,534	2,058	760	881	6,835
Dec.	10,704	2,077	769	882	6,976
1963—Jan.	10,655	2,062	766	870	6,957
Feb.	10,673	2,069	763	865	6,976

NOTE—Institutions represented are consumer finance cos., credit unions, industrial loan cos., mutual savings banks, savings and loan assns., and other lending institutions holding consumer instalment loans. See NOTE to Table 5-1.

Source: Federal Reserve Bulletin, April, 1963, p. 525.

B

NONINSTALMENT CREDIT
(In millions of dollars)

End of period	Total	Single-payment loans		Charge accounts			Service credit
		Commercial banks	Other financial institutions	Department stores [1]	Other retail outlets	Credit cards [2]	
1939	2,719	625	162	236	1,178		518
1941	3,087	693	152	275	1,370		597
1945	3,203	674	72	290	1,322		845
1956	10,614	2,843	410	893	3,842	260	2,366
1957	11,103	2,937	427	876	3,953	317	2,593
1958	11,487	3,156	471	907	3,808	345	2,800
1959	12,297	3,582	547	958	3,753	393	3,064
1960	13,196	3,884	623	941	3,952	436	3,360
1961	14,151	4,413	723	948	3,907	469	3,691
1962	15,215	4,704	875	927	4,203	512	3,994
1962—Feb.	13,019	4,294	694	635	3,085	472	3,839
Mar.	13,064	4,391	755	594	3,025	455	3,844
Apr.	13,477	4,544	697	620	3,249	450	3,917
May	13,823	4,614	786	636	3,444	464	3,879
June	13,900	4,671	757	612	3,505	479	3,876
July	13,714	4,662	740	569	3,388	500	3,855
Aug.	13,799	4,657	812	570	3,394	527	3,839
Sept.	13,816	4,666	815	614	3,353	528	3,840
Oct.	13,904	4,662	780	638	3,507	518	3,799
Nov.	14,199	4,680	846	688	3,629	508	3,848
Dec.	15,215	4,704	875	927	4,203	512	3,994
1963—Jan.	r14,610	4,680	831	r775	3,759	524	4,041
Feb.	14,194	4,704	841	646	3,324	526	4,153

[1] Includes mail-order houses.
[2] Service station and misc. credit-card accounts and home-heating oil accounts.
See NOTE to Table 5-1.

despite the fact that they entered the field much later than other financial institutions. In 1934, the U. S. Government authorized the Federal Housing Administration to guarantee loans made by authorized lenders for home repair and modernization. This program gave the real "push" to the activities of commercial banks in the consumer credit field. Additional impetus was provided by The Bankers Association for Consumer Credit, formed in 1938. This organization later merged with the American Bankers Association. In the thirty years between 1933 and 1963, the number of banks making consumer loans grew from less than 250 to about 13,000.

What kinds of loans do commercial banks grant? Below are listed some of those available at one commercial bank. This list is representative of the variety available at almost all commercial banks.

AUTO LOANS	INSURANCE PREMIUM
EDUCATION LOANS	LOANS
BILL CONSOLIDATION	VACATION OR TRAVEL
LOANS	LOANS
BOAT LOANS	HOUSEHOLD LOANS
MEDICAL EXPENSE LOANS	MODERNIZATION LOANS
BUSINESS LOANS	MORTGAGE LOANS

READY-CREDIT

In February of 1963, these banks held a total of about 19 billion dollars of instalment credit paper. About 10 billion of this was in the form of automobile paper, roughly two-thirds of which was purchased by the banks from dealers, and about one-third of which represented loans made directly by the banks. Of the remaining 9 billion dollars, about 3 billion represented other consumer goods paper, about 2 billion was in repair and modernization loans, and about 4 billion was in personal loans.

A recent innovation in commercial bank consumer loans are the revolving check-credit plans first started by the First National Bank of Boston and described in Chapter 4, "Bank Services." While it is easy to keep a record of the purpose of certain types of loans, such as automobile, and repair and modernization loans, it is impossible to record the precise use of personal loans by any means, including the revolving check-credit plans.

Some of the money loaned by commercial banks is obtained from the investments of the owners and from retained earnings, but most of it comes from depositors.

Most commercial banks follow strict credit standards. Whether or not collateral is required depends upon the nature of the loan. Personal loans, for example, usually require only the signature of the borrower. Lower rates, however, are available on automobile loans, loans secured by securities or an insurance policy, or loans against a savings account passbook.

Banks have had a very low loss experience, due to a considerable degree, to the fact that they are stricter than credit unions, sales finance companies, or consumer finance companies, in approving borrowers. There is every reason to believe that consumer loans are a profitable business for commercial banks. Otherwise, they would not try so hard to attract more customers.

Sales Finance Companies

Sales finance companies are primarily engaged in buying instalment contracts from dealers. These contracts cover merchandise purchased by consumers from these dealers. Most automobiles and major household appliances are purchased in this manner. These companies also finance the retailer's wholesale purchases from the manufacturer.

As automobile financing will be reviewed in Chapter 6, let's discuss here the instalment credit purchase of a new television set from a local retailer. The consumer will sign a conditional sale contract, which will state the price of the television set, the down payment, the balance due (including finance charge) and the terms of payment; and will further recite that the buyer does not take title to the television set until the amount due is fully paid. Sometimes a separate note is signed for the unpaid balance.

In most cases, the retailer cannot wait a year or two for his money. He needs cash to buy more television sets. This is where the sales finance company enters the picture. The retailer will sell the sale contract to the finance company for cash, and the finance company will collect the instalments from the person who bought the television set.

Notice that the sales finance company is a third party in this procedure. The original agreement is between the buyer of the television set and the retailer. When the finance company buys the contract, it acquires title to the television set, and from that point on the buyer's credit relationship is with the finance company.

However, if the television set doesn't perform satisfactorily, he should see the retailer. While the credit relationship is between the buyer and the finance company, the television set relationship is between the buyer and the retailer. Remember the difference between these relationships. People often stop making payments, in protest of the unsatisfactory performance of their television set (or other appliance), and to "force" the retailer to do something about it. This disrupts the credit relationship, and "forces" the finance company to repossess the television set and sell it for the balance due. If the sale doesn't bring in enough cash to settle the balance, the person who failed to make the payments will be liable to the finance company for the difference.

Sales finance companies have several different plans available to finance goods such as television sets, refrigerators, etc. First, there is the full recourse plan. Under this plan, if the person buying the television set doesn't pay, the seller is responsible to the finance company for the unpaid balance. There are also limited recourse plans, which hold the seller fully responsible for the first few months, and then either reduce his responsibility or release him from further responsibility. However, under all these plans, the finance company retains the right to repossess the set and sue the buyer for any unpaid balance.

There are three types of instalment sale contracts used in the United States. The most common is the conditional sale contract described above. In some states, a chattel mortgage is used. This gives the seller the right to request the court to have the mortgaged goods sold for his benefit. In Pennsylvania, the bailment lease is used. Under this arrangement, the buyer actually hires the goods until the final payment is made. If payments are not made as agreed, the seller will simply take back his merchandise. Any payments made would belong to the seller, since they were actually payments to hire the merchandise.

Which kind of contract is used depends mainly on the laws of the particular state. All three kinds of contracts come to the same as far as their basic provisions are concerned. So we can refer to the document the buyer signs as simply the contract.

Basic provisions. — What are the main provisions which one may expect to find when he reads the contract?

1. The basic feature is that, although the instalment buyer gets immediate possession of the automobile or other goods, the creditor (the seller or financing institution) remains the legal owner of, or secures a lien on, the merchandise until the obligation has been paid in full.

2. The buyer also agrees that, until he has completed his instalment payments, he will not sell, remove, or encumber the merchandise without first getting the written consent of the creditor.

3. He further agrees that he will be responsible for any loss or damage which may occur to the merchandise. (For this reason the buyer arranges to have the insurance coverage needed during the time he is indebted on his instalment contract.)

4. Finally, the buyer agrees that if he fails to make his payments as promised, the creditor may either take back the merchandise or affirm the sale and hold the buyer liable for the full unpaid balance.

Other provisions. – A contract may have various other provisions. And there are a number of important questions to which the buyer should secure answers before he signs on the dotted line. Let us list them.

1. If he completes all of his payments before the final maturity of the contract, will he be refunded a fair part of the finance charge?

2. If he should be late in making an instalment payment, how much will he be charged as a default charge?

3. In the event that it becomes necessary for the creditor to consider repossessing the merchandise, will the buyer be given fair notice before action is taken?

4. In case the creditor should repossess the merchandise, how much are the repossession charges that the buyer would have to pay?

5. Just what security will the buyer be pledging if he signs the contract? That is to say, is he pledging as security for the instalment debt only the merchandise being purchased? Or does the contract give the creditor a claim against other merchandise previously purchased by the buyer?

6. Does it contain a wage assignment, giving the creditor a right to attach part of the buyer's wages if payments are not made as agreed?

7. Does the contract require the buyer to waive any valuable legal safeguards?

8. Finally, to whom will the buyer owe his instalment payments? Are they to be paid to the retailer, to one of the great

national sales finance companies, or to some other responsible institution? Or are they to be paid to some financing institution whose integrity is not known to the consumer?[2]

Whatever you do, be certain that you carefully read the contract, and ascertain that all information is fully presented, before you sign. The exhibit on page 110 indicates why.

Sales finance companies obtain a large proportion of the money they lend by borrowing. Long term loans are obtained from insurance companies, pension funds, etc., while short term loans are obtained from commercial banks. Some of their funds are obtained from their owners through the sale of stock.

Credit Unions

Credit unions make loans only to their members, and, for this group, they constitute a convenient loan source. These unions were described in Chapter 3, "Where to Save." Notice in Table 5-2 that the amount of instalment credit paper held by credit unions is considerably less than that held by either commercial banks or sales finance companies. They do offer excellent service to their members, but their loan volume is limited by the fact that they can offer their services only to members.

Like commercial banks, credit unions obtain funds from depositors; but, unlike commercial banks, the savings deposited by their members is their only source of funds other than borrowing, chiefly from other credit unions.

No security is required for small loans—only the signature of the borrower. Security is required, however, for larger loans. The security may be the signature of a co-endorser or a pledge of property. Most loans are repayable by instalments.

Consumer Finance Companies

Consumer finance companies specialize in personal cash loans. They differ from sales finance companies in their relation to the consumer. There are only two parties involved when a person borrows money from a consumer finance company—the borrower and the

---

[2] Clyde William Phelps, "Using Installment Credit," *Studies in Consumer Credit, No. 4,* Educational Division, Commercial Credit Company, Baltimore Maryland, Copyright, 1955, pp. 60–61.

HOW FINANCING COSTS CAN BE BOOSTED

1 *Padded prices* on merchandise.

2 *High-premium insurance charges* (especially. on cars).

3 *Other costs—service charges and fees.*

4 *No rebate* (or a short-rate rebate) for early payment.

"Packing" refers to the way inflated costs are usually hidden. It means lumping all finance, insurance, and other costs together in one sum.

Further costs may be provided in the contract. They become due if you miss payments, or if the merchandise is repossessed. You may be liable for penalty payments, or for the difference between the purchase price of the merchandise and its depreciated value. Repossession charges alone can add as much as ⅓ to the original amount owed, when court costs, warehouse bills, and other charges are tacked on.

DO NOT SIGN THE CONTRACT, UNLESS <u>ALL</u> OF THESE ARE ITEMIZED

1 Cash price, including tax.

2 Down payment.

3 Trade-in allowance.

4 Balance to be financed.

5 Insurance charges.

6 Any other costs: filing, recording, service charges.

7 Total purchase price.

8 Finance charge *in dollars*.

9 Total amount due in installments.

10 Number, amount, and time of payments.

NEVER SIGN A BLANK CONTRACT

(because excessive charges can be filled in later)

Source: "Finance Charges and How to Watch Them—," *Credit Union Yearbook, 1957,* Credit Union National Association, Madison, Wisconsin.

lender. There were three parties concerned in the transaction involving a sales finance company; the buyer of the merchandise, the person selling the merchandise, and the sales finance company.

In both the sales finance and consumer finance fields, a few large, highly respected companies dominate the field.

> In terms of both types of finance companies, in mid-1960, there were 20 companies each of which had consumer instalment credit outstanding (including automobile paper and other consumer goods paper) of $100,000,000 or over and there were 3,583 small companies each of which had less than $1,000,000 in outstanding consumer instalment credit.[3]

Consumer finance and sales finance companies obtain their funds from about the same sources, but consumer finance companies derive less from bank borrowing and commercial paper and more from long-term debt, capital, and surplus.

People most often use the services of a consumer finance company to tide them over a period of financial emergency. While the size of these loans has increased over the years, they can still be classified as primarily small loans—under $500.

Consumer finance companies used to loan money only when the loan was secured. The security consisted of either a co-maker or a chattel mortgage. The chattel mortgages were on assets such as furniture, automobiles, etc., and gave the lender the right to take possession of the security if the borrower did not pay his loan. Consumer finance companies have seldom actually taken possession of such security. After all, they don't want living room furniture, refrigerators, etc.; they want cash. It is much better for them to work out some refinancing arrangement which will enable the borrower to pay off his debt. During recent years, an increasing percentage of such loans have been made on the borrower's signature alone.

There are still instances when the finance company feels that some security is needed. In such cases, it requests a chattel mortgage on some of the borrower's assets, or requests him to sign a wage or salary assignment. The assignment will permit the lender to collect the debt from the borrower's employer, as a wage or salary deduction, if payment is not made.

While funds are available from other sources at lower rates, consumer finance companies manage to do an excellent business because they meet specific needs. They will, for example, loan to a person

---

[3] "1962 Finance Facts Yearbook," Educational Services Division, National Consumer Finance Association, Washington, D.C., p. 38.

whom a commercial bank would not consider a good risk, and they will lend money in very small amounts.

Other

The "other" category presented in Table 5-2 includes industrial loan companies, mutual savings banks, savings and loan associations, etc. Even when combined into one group, they are extremely small compared to the other sources of this type of credit.

Retail Outlets

One large section of Table 5-2 concerns different types of retail outlets, consisting primarily of department stores, furniture stores, appliance stores, and automobile dealers. In comparison to the other sources of instalment credit, they are individually quite small. As a group, they are slightly larger than credit unions, but much smaller than commercial banks and sales finance companies. It seems wise to include charge accounts as presented in Table 5-3 B, in this general discussion. While charge accounts are not a form of instalment credit, they are one of the general credit facilities provided by retail stores.

Retailers provide four types of credit:

1. Charge accounts
2. Budget accounts
3. Revolving charge accounts
4. Instalment sale credit

A charge account is a particular type of credit arrangement under which the purchaser promises to pay for the merchandise within a short time, usually a month. This is a great convenience, as it permits the buyer to pay for many small purchases in one lump sum, to order by phone without the problems of C.O.D., and to buy without cash.

One of the big problems of charge accounts is caused by the convenience they offer. A considerable amount of self-control is necessary to prevent their over-use. The fact that $50 will be due next month if a particular purchase is made today is often not considered in relation to the total amount that may be due as the result of purchases in other stores.

These accounts do not involve any specific payment for the privilege of charging purchases. There is no interest charge. Yet it is a mistake to assume that the credit is "free." While no separate charge is made, the cost is included in the purchase price of the goods. Think about the problems involved. A department store, for example, must maintain a credit department, buy and stock various credit forms, allocate office space, make investigations, suffer losses, and tie up its cash. All of these things cost money, and the customer pays the bill.

A budget account permits the extension of the "charge" privilege over a longer period of time, usually 3 to 6 months. Some extend the period as long as a year, and, if the purchaser pays within 90 days, do not charge any interest or service charge.

Revolving charge accounts are one of the newer types of retail credit. Under these plans, a customer is given a "line-of-credit." Let's suppose that the credit maximum is $300. The customer may then purchase merchandise up to the $300 maximum at any time. The retailer usually charges 1 to 1¼ per cent a month on the unpaid balance. (These same charges are often levied on regular charge accounts and budget accounts when they become past due.) Specific repayment amounts are usually stated in revolving charge account plans. If the customer charges $300, monthly payments of $30 might be required; while if the amount charged was only $100, only $10 per month might be requested. Under this type of plan, a customer may keep adding on to his charge account balance as long as it is less than the maximum. He might, for example, charge $300 worth of merchandise, make payments for several months, charge another $50, and so on, as long as he never exceeds $300.

Today, the merchandise offered by most department stores includes high priced items such as television or stereo sets, washing machines, air conditioners, etc. These would be difficult to pay for under one of the preceding charge plans. The fourth plan, installment sale credit, was created to meet this need. This plan involves a contractual arrangement. A conditional sale, lease, or chattel mortgage contract is almost always necessary. In effect, the purchaser signs a promissory note which states the monthly payments that must be made and, as security, the seller usually retains title to the goods, and the right to repossess them, until all of these payments have been made. An interest or finance charge is made when instalment sale credit is used.

Credit Cards and Service Credit

Credit cards have mushroomed in popularity in recent years. Some of these are all-purpose, in that they may be used for purchases of almost any type, at almost any place. Merchants bill the company issuing the credit card, and this company, in turn, bills the customer. Other credit cards are issued for specific purposes only, such as buying gasoline, oil, and other automotive needs. If they are handled with care, and not abused, credit cards are a great convenience. While there is a cost involved in using the general credit card, those issued for specific purposes usually do not involve any extra cost. A gasoline company credit card, for example, is furnished free after a person's credit is investigated and approved. It permits the customer to buy gasoline or other products at any of the company's many stations. At the end of each month, the customer receives one bill for all purchases, even though his purchases are made in different locations.

Service credit refers to those bills, such as utility bills and doctor bills, which are usually paid on a monthly basis. These bills are sent out at regular intervals and payment requested. If a dentist is visited on May 5, the customer may not be billed until May 31, and the payment may not be expected for another two weeks. This means that credit has actually been granted for a period of about six weeks. No interest charge is made for service credit, if the bill is paid promptly.

Insurance Loans

There are certain sources of credit not listed in Table 5-2. One of the most important of these is the insurance loan. Life insurance policies, other than term (see Chapter 9), have a cash surrender value. The life insurance company will make loans against this amount, or the cash surrender value may be used as security in obtaining loans from other sources. It is a very desirable loan from the viewpoint of both borrower and lender. It is attractive to the borrower because of its low cost, and attractive to the lender because no risk is involved, as the money can be collected by or from the insurance company without expense, if the borrower doesn't pay.

This type of loan is especially convenient when it is arranged directly with the insurance company. The company cannot force the borrower to pay the loan within any fixed time period, and as long as there is any cash value remaining, the company will simply add unpaid interest amounts to the balance of the debt. Unfortunately, many borrowers never repay such loans because they are so convenient, and when they die their obligations are deducted from the face value of their policies, leaving that much less for their heirs.

Other Loan Sources

Coverage of loan sources could not possibly be complete without some mention of pawnshops. These loans are made on the basis of saleable personal property. If someone wants to pawn a diamond ring, he will probably be able to borrow from 60 to 90 per cent of its auction value, and will be required to repay the loan within a stated period of time. Interest rates on such loans are usually quite high.

There are a few semi-philanthropic pawnshops. The most famous is The Provident Loan Society of New York. It was organized in 1894 and is a non-profit institution which distributes any net income to charity. It makes loans of large and small amounts, based upon the value of articles of personal property which are pledged and left in the custody of the society. The interest charge is 1 per cent per month on unpaid balances, and no payments are due for a year. If the borrower pays the interest, the loan may, at his request, be renewed for another year.

There are also remedial loan societies which make various types of loans, but these have considerably decreased in number in recent years. Some of them have dissolved, and others have become consumer finance companies.

WHAT DOES CREDIT COST?

No method of borrowing is free, but some methods and some sources are cheaper than others. Calculating the cost of borrowing is not simple. Very rarely is the stated rate of interest on a loan the actual rate that the consumer will pay. A 6 per cent stated rate on one loan might be cheaper than a 4 per cent stated rate on another, even though the amount borrowed and the time period are the same in both cases. It would depend upon the method used to repay the loan, the method used to calculate the interest rate, etc.

Consumers have a wide choice of sources. Should a new refrigerator be financed through a finance company, or paid for with money borrowed from a bank? Should a personal loan be obtained from a personal finance (consumer finance) company, a credit union, or a commercial bank? Even after the type of source has been selected, the problem of choice still remains. Suppose the decision is to take out a personal loan at a commercial bank. Which commercial bank should be selected?

Cost is not the only thing to consider. The terms of the contract, convenience, dependability, reputation of the lender for fairness, and many other things must be considered. Cost, however, is definitely a factor and an important one. How is it calculated?

Simple Percentage Method

Credit unions and consumer finance companies state their interest charge as a monthly percentage rate on the unpaid balance of the loan. Credit unions have a standard rate of 1 per cent per month, although the rates may be lower on occasion. Consumer finance company rates will vary according to state law. Let's suppose the law permits a rate of 3 per cent per month. You borrow $200 on May 1. At the end of May, you would owe interest of $6. Suppose you pay $50 of the principal on May 31. On June 30 you would then owe interest of $4.50 (3% of $150).

States which operate under the Uniform Small Loan Law do not permit consumer finance companies to levy fees, delinquency charges, or any other kind of extra payments. If the borrower misses an interest payment, it cannot be added to the principal balance, although he will have to pay interest on the deliquent amount. For this reason, the monthly rate quoted by a consumer finance company is the actual total rate. Most of these same rules apply to credit unions, although they are usually permitted to levy a delinquency charge.

The annual interest rate charged under this method can be calculated more easily than it can for any other method. It is simply twelve times the monthly rate. Thus the 1 per cent per month charged by a credit union is 12 per cent per year.

The calculation is not this simple when consumer finance company rates are examined, because most states require graduated rates. Under these laws, the larger the loan the smaller the interest rate that may be charged. For example, the law might state a maximum allowable interest charge of 2½ per cent on amounts up to $100, 2 per cent from $100 to $300, and ¾ per cent from $300 to $800. These rates would be applied to the unpaid principal balance of a loan each month, and the annual rate, in terms of percentage, would be twelve times the monthly rate, i.e., 30 per cent on the first $100, 24 per cent on the next $200, and 9 per cent on the next $500. But the annual interest rate on an $800 loan, for example, would be a composite of these, and would have to be computed.

Credit union loans are usually at the rate of 12 per cent per year, a lower rate than that charged by finance companies. This is due to their special advantages. One of these is their great tax advantage as compared to other lenders (discussed in Chapter 3). They also often receive office space and services free, or at nominal cost. They can, however, loan money only to their own members.

The "Add-On" Method

This method is extremely easy to compute. The interest on a loan is computed for the full amount for the full term, and added to the amount loaned. The sum is the total amount of the note. For example, if $100 is borrowed for one year at 5 per cent, the total amount of the note would be $105.

This is the method often used by commercial banks, sales finance companies, and companies selling merchandise on the instalment plan. It does not result in a "true" annual rate of interest like the simple percentage method.

A precise calculation of the "true interest" rate would require the use of compound interest formulas, and this would be quite complicated. There are two commonly used methods of approximating this rate.

The first method gives only an approximate answer, but it is extremely simple. If there are no other charges—if the interest rate is all-inclusive — and the loan is to be repaid in equal monthly instalments, the annual interest rate is about twice the add-on rate stated. Thus, if you borrow $100 at 5 per cent, to be paid back over the next year in equal monthly payments, the actual annual interest rate is about 10 per cent.

The constant ratio method of computing the actual annual interest rate is more complicated, but also more exact. One formula[4] suggested for this purpose is:

Interest rate =

$$\frac{2 \times (\text{no. of payment periods}^*) \times (\text{dollar cost of credit})}{(\text{Balance owed}) \times (\text{Number of payments} +1)}$$

*12 if repaying monthly; 52 if repaying weekly.

Using the example of $100 borrowed at 5 per cent, to be paid back over the next year in equal monthly payments ($8.75 each), the formula would be:

$$\text{Interest rate} = \frac{2 \times 12 \times \$5}{\$100 \times (12+1)} = \frac{\$120}{\$1300} = 9.2\%$$

---

[4] "How to Get the Most Out of Your Income," Life Insurance Agency Management Association, Hartford, Connecticut, 1959, p. 24.

The Discount Method

Commercial banks, sales finance companies, and instalment sellers sometimes deduct the interest in advance, and the borrower pays the face amount of the loan. For example, if $100 was loaned for one year at 5 per cent under this system, the borrower would actually receive $95 ($100 — $5). According to the constant ratio formula, if this was paid back in equal monthly instalments of $8.33 per month (plus 4¢ additional at some time during the year, as 12 × $8.33 is only $99.96), the formula would read:

$$\text{Interest rate} = \frac{2 \times 12 \times \$5}{\$95 \times (12+1)} = \frac{\$120}{\$1235} = 9.7\%$$

Notice that under this method, the annual interest rate is slightly higher than it is when the add-on method is used. This is something a borrower should notice when deciding where to take out a loan. If two banks both advertise loans at the same percentage rate, and one uses the add-on method while the other discounts, the actual interest rate will be higher on the second loan than on the first.

Summary

While these are not the only methods of calculating interest, they are the most commonly used. It is evident that the stated rate is not sufficient in itself. Borrowing $100 when interest is calculated by the simple interest method as 1 per cent per month is borrowing at a true annual rate of 12 per cent. The same amount borrowed at 6 per cent a year when the add-on method is used is borrowing at a true annual rate of a little less than 12 per cent (11.4 per cent), while using the discount method would mean a true annual rate of a little more than 12 per cent (12.1 per cent). A stated rate of 6 per cent per year may not be quite as inexpensive as it might appear, and a stated rate of 12 per cent may not be quite as expensive. The method used to calculate interest is important to the borrower.

DOLLAR COSTS

Borrowing Cash

So far, we have compared various methods of stating the interest charge on borrowed money. This is only part of the story. Before the annual rate of interest can be calculated, a person must make certain that *all* costs have been considered.

What other costs are there besides interest? Many banks charge an investigation fee. There may be a chattel mortgage fee. Is there a delinquency charge? Will interest be refunded if the loan is paid in advance? All of these things must be considered in calculating the "true interest" rate.

Suppose, for example, that money may be borrowed from two different sources. Both offer loans at the same 5 per cent interest rate, but source "A" charges a $3 additional fee. Using the formula, the following results are obtained for a $100 loan to be paid in one year in equal monthly instalments, when interest is calculated by the add-on method.

$$\text{Source A — Interest Rate} = \frac{2 \times 12 \times \$8}{\$100 \times (12+1)} = \frac{\$192}{\$1300} = 14.8\%$$

$$\text{Source B — Interest Rate} = \frac{2 \times 12 \times \$5}{\$100 \times (12+1)} = \frac{\$120}{\$1300} = 9.2\%$$

Obviously, added charges or fees can make quite a difference in the interest rate charged. If the loan was paid in advance and interest was not refunded, or if a penalty charge was levied for a late payment, the actual annual interest rate would rise sharply. A commonly used method of figuring rebates, if they are permitted, is presented in Table 5-4.

Table 5-4
THE "RULE OF 78"

Where the instalment payments are equal each month, the rebate is commonly figured by the Rule of 78, also known as "sum of the digits" method. The "78" is derived from the total number of instalment units outstanding month to month in a 12 month contract. For example, in a 12 month contract, 12 plus 11 plus 10-9-8-7-6-5-4-3-2-1 equals 78.

In the first month, you use 12/78ths of the total finance charge. In the second month an additional 11/78ths or a total of 23/78ths. In the sixth month 7/78ths or a total of 57/78ths. In the eleventh month you have used 77/78ths of the total finance charge. In any month when you pay off, the amount of the rebate would be the number of 78ths you had **not** used.

The following chart indicates more clearly how it is figured:

Length of Contract by Month	Portion of Finance Charge Used Each Month	Total portions of finance charge used month by month and due to the finance company
1	12/78ths	12/78ths
2	11/78ths	23/78ths
3	10/78ths	33/78ths
4	9/78ths	42/78ths
5	8/78ths	50/78ths
6	7/78ths	57/78ths
7	6/78ths	63/78ths
8	5/78ths	68/78ths
9	4/78ths	72/78ths
10	3/78ths	75/78ths
11	2/78ths	77/78ths
12	1/78th	78/78ths
—		
78		

For example, if the finance charge, after allowable deductions, is $82.50 and the account is paid off in six months, 57/78ths of the finance charge (57/78 x $82.50 = $60.28) would be due to the finance company. The difference (21/78ths) $82.50 — $60.28 = $22.22 would be payable as rebate.

Similarly, it is figured on contracts of different length, by sum of the digits, — six months contract 6 + 5 + 4 + 3 + 2 + 1 = 21, and if paid off in fourth month you owe the finance company 18/21sts of the finance charge and the rebate is the remainder or 3/21sts. For nine months, the method is similar in 45ths; for 15 months in 120ths; for 18 months in 171sts, etc. Tables similar to the above can be set up for any such period.[5]

Instalment Buying

How much does it really cost to buy on the instalment plan? Unfortunately, many people do not consider the cost of buying in this manner. They only consider — if anything — the size of the monthly payment that must be made, and whether or not they can meet it. Unfortunately, too, from the consumer's point of view, the cost of buying on the instalment plan is not usually as obvious as the cost of borrowing money.

There are many costs that may be involved in buying on the instalment plan. Examples of those that may be added on to the actual cost of the merchandise are finance and insurance charges. A

---

[5] Quoted from "Facts You Should Know About Your Credit," Educational Division, Better Business Bureau of Metropolitan Boston, Inc., 1962, p. 11.

minority of those selling on the instalment plan will add a "pack" onto the finance charge. This was indicated in the exhibit (p. 110). With a "pack," the seller charges a rate above the amount actually charged by the finance company or bank, and keeps the difference. In some instances, the seller may be receiving a "kickback." Banks and finance companies competing for the seller's finance business may have agreed to kickback — share the finance charge — to the seller. Both of these practices should be regulated by the state to protect the buyer.

Not only are there many costs that may be involved in buying on the instalment plan, but it is often difficult to uncover this charge.

Suppose, for example, a food freezer is offered under a combination plan which requires regular monthly payments for a fixed period of time, plus an agreement to regularly purchase frozen food to restock the freezer? How much is the actual finance cost? This is very difficult to calculate. The consumer must determine the purchase price of the freezer if purchased for cash. He must also find out whether frozen foods of comparable quality could be purchased elsewhere at lower prices. Any difference between the price of the freezer bought on time and the price of the freezer purchased for cash plus any extra cost of the frozen food must be considered as the cost of buying on the instalment plan.

Instalment credit charges may be represented in several ways. For example, the sign may say "NO CHARGE FOR CREDIT." Let's suppose this refers to a color television set on sale at $600. It can be purchased for $60 down and $45 per month for 12 months. In another store, the same model television set is available for $500 cash. How much did the credit cost? Using the constant-ratio formula:

$$\text{Interest rate} = \frac{2 \times 12 \times \$100}{\$540 \times (12 + 1)} = \frac{\$2,400}{\$7,020} = 34.2\%$$

Under these circumstances, "NO CHARGE FOR CREDIT" would certainly be misleading. You have to be certain, of course, that the exact same item is being compared, but this type of selling is quite common.

Another method of representing instalment credit is to state a down payment, plus a percentage charge on the balance. Suppose, for example, that a portable stereo is advertised for $190, $40 down and 6 per cent on the unpaid balance of $150. Payments are to be $6.36 per week for 25 weeks. Using the constant ratio formula:

$$\text{Interest rate} = \frac{2 \times 52 \times \$9}{\$150 \times (25 + 1)} = \frac{\$936}{\$3900} = 24\%.$$

Still another method is to state a down payment plus some flat charge. The stereo set in the above example might have been listed as $190, $40 down and the balance of $150, plus a flat charge of $9, to be paid off over 25 weeks. This would also amount to an annual interest rate of 24 per cent.

ACTUAL CREDIT COSTS

Table 5-5 on page 123 indicates the cost of borrowing money, and compares the cost of buying appliances by financing through the dealer vs. borrowing the money from a commercial bank and paying cash for the merchandise. As this is a combination of two individual studies, there is some difference between the amount financed through the dealer and that borrowed from a bank. The appliance to be financed through a dealer was an automatic washing machine. A balance of $200 was to be financed over a period of 12 months. To obtain the commercial bank rates, negotiations were carried on to borrow $500 on an unsecured instalment note, for a period of 18 months. The time of each study also was not precisely the same. Shopping contacts for the appliance were completed within a four month period in 1962, while the unsecured loan negotiations occurred between October, 1959 and October, 1960. While the two are not strictly comparable, the difference in the rates involved when the two sources of credit are compared indicates that, in the cities studied, it would have been better to borrow cash from a commercial bank and pay cash for the washing machine than to finance the appliance through the dealer.

The amount of this difference varies considerably between cities. The average finance rate charged by dealers in St. Louis was 16.7 per cent, while the average loan interest rate charged by commercial banks in that city was 16.1 per cent. New York appliance dealers, on the other hand, charged an average rate of 17.8 per cent, while New York commercial banks had an average rate of 9.1 per cent. In each case, the interest rate was converted to an annual interest rate.

Would it have been better to buy an appliance through a department store, discount house, or other appliance dealer? Table 5-6 compares these organizations. According to this table, department stores had the highest prices (the least discount from list) and the lowest finance rates, while discount houses had the lowest prices (the highest discount from list) and the highest finance rates. On an instalment purchase, then, these would tend to cancel each other out, so that the final price might be lower, or the same, in the department store as in the discount house.

Table 5-5

FINANCE CHARGES QUOTED BY APPLIANCE DEALERS AND BY
COMMERCIAL BANKS EXPRESSED IN SIMPLE ANNUAL INTEREST
(PER CENT) AND PRICES FOR APPLIANCES IN SELECTED CITIES[6]

City	Finance Rates at Dealers[1]		Prices[2]	Finance Rates at Commercial Banks[3]
	Mean[4]	Range[5]	Index (Chicago = 100)	Per Cent
Boston	19.0	12.9–20.4	104.6	10.8
Chicago	19.0	14.8–27.7	100.0	13.2
Cleveland	17.8	14.8–25.2	111.8	14.1
Denver	17.3	14.8–22.1	106.4	13.0
Detroit	19.3	14.8–22.2	104.9	12.5
New York	17.8	14.8–18.4	97.5	9.1
Pittsburgh	16.9	13.8–20.3	105.6	12.1
St. Louis	16.7	14.8–18.4	104.6	16.1
San Francisco	17.3	9.2–22.2	106.1	13.7

[1] A balance of $200 on an automatic washing machine was to be financed over twelve months.

[2] Prices were obtained at the same dealers that quoted finance charges.

[3] Averages weighted for each bank in sample by estimate of the total volume of "other instalment loans, for household, family, and other personal expenditures" in its portfolio as of December, 1959. "All Group" average based on estimates of total volume of such loans of each size class of banks.

[4] Means are unweighted arithmetic averages.

[5] Results based on actual negotiations for standardized unsecured cash instalment loans in period October, 1959, to October, 1960. Amount of loan was $500 and term 18 months. Rates include interest and other charges if any, for credit investigation and registration of loan and are quoted in form of simple interest at annual rate. Credit life insurance is not included. If charge quoted included credit life insurance automatically, an allowance of 40 cents per $100 of loan has been deducted.

[6] Data on appliance dealers from Allen F. Jung, "Charges for Appliance and Automobile Instalment Credit in Major Cities," *The Journal of Business,* The Graduate School of Business of the University of Chicago, Vol. XXXV, No. 4, October 1962, p. 388.

Data on commercial banks from Irving Schweiger and John S. McGee, "Chicago Banking," *The Journal of Business,* The Graduate School of Business of the University of Chicago, Vol. XXXIV, No. 3, July 1961, p. 261.

Table 5-6
FINANCE CHARGES EXPRESSED AS SIMPLE ANNUAL INTEREST (PER CENT)
AND DISCOUNTS FROM LIST PRICE EXPRESSED AS PER CENT QUOTED BY
APPLICABLE DEALERS BY TYPE OF OUTLET[*7]

(Number of Sample Dealers Quoting Finance Charges and Discounts
from List Price in Parentheses)

Type of Outlet	Finance Rates		Discounts from List Price	
	Mean	Range	Mean	Range
Department stores (31)	16.0	9.2–20.3	23.4	15.0–35.2
Discount houses (34)	20.0	15.5–27.7	28.2	14.6–36.5
Other appliance dealers (39)	17.9	13.8–22.2	24.1	7.5–33.5
All outlets (104)	18.0	9.2–27.7	25.3	7.5–36.5

° Means are unweighted arithmetic averages.

How about a comparison between the rates charged on a $500 unsecured loan by commercial banks and small loan companies in the same cities?

In each city studied, there were also substantial differences in the average rates charged by banks and small loan companies for a standard unsecured cash instalment loan by a borrower with standard characteristics. For a standard 18 month loan of $500, the citywide bank average ranged from a low of 9.1 per cent in New York City to a high of 16.1 per cent in St. Louis. For the identical loan, small loan companies in New York were lowest with an average of 23.7 per cent and were highest in Denver with 34.8 per cent. Chicago banks had an average charge of 13.2 per cent for this loan and Chicago small loan companies averaged 29.0 per cent.

In each city studied, the rate charged by small loan companies was at the legal maximum and was at least double the average rate charged by banks in the same city, with the exception of St. Louis where the bank rate was very high. It may be argued with some merit that small loan companies accept poorer risks than do banks and that a higher charge is necessary. What this study indicates, however, is that if a person of "bank quality" goes to a small loan company he will pay approximately double

[7] Allen F. Jung, "Charges for Appliance and Automobile Instalment Credit in Major Cities," *The Journal of Business,* The Graduate School of Business of the University of Chicago, The University of Chicago Press, Chicago, Illinois, October 1962, p. 389.

the bank rate. The small loan companies apparently have no mechanism, or do not choose to use one, of tailoring their rates to the quality of the individual risk as do insurance companies with respect to preferred risk automobile and life insurance.

The tremendous gap in rates between banks and small loan companies adds to the importance of bank lending behavior.

If banks will not lend in this fashion to the people in their community, the chief alternative is the small loan company at double the bank rate. Another alternative which has been growing in importance is the credit union, but this has not been available to the entire population.[8]

These comparisons must be considered as generalities. The study referred to indicates that there is considerable variation between banks within a city, according to the size of the bank and according to the age of the bank. Nevertheless, the difference in rates between the commercial bank and the small loan company is sizable.

Is this general situation true today? The following table illustrates a very limited sample of rates publicized by four different organizations in May of 1963, for loans of 12 months' duration.

Source	Net Amount of Loan	Monthly Payments	Total Payments	Constant Ratio Rate
New York commercial bank-personal loan	$571.50	$50.00	$600.00	9.2%
Canadian bank	500.00	43.83	525.96	9.6
Credit union	500.00	44.43 (ave.)	533.16	12.2 *
Kentucky finance co.	500.00	48.65	583.80	30.9

* Credit unions only indicate average monthly payments. Actual rate per year would be 12%.

On the basis of this very limited sample, the general relationships indicated by the study made during an earlier period still held true in 1963.

OTHER FACTORS

Based upon the discussion up to this point, the question might be asked, "Why would anyone borrow money from a small loan com-

[8] Irving Schweiger and John S. McGee, "Chicago Banking," *The Journal of Business,* The Graduate School of Business of the University of Chicago. The University of Chicago Press, Chicago, Illinois, July 1961, pp. 263-264.

pany, or finance the purchase of an appliance through a dealer? Why wouldn't everyone borrow from a commercial bank?" Two answers are: everyone can't, and there are other factors to consider besides interest rate and dollar cost.

1. Convenience.

   Financing is available through a dealer at the same time and place where the sale is made. Dealers and finance companies may be open more hours than commercial banks.

2. Promptness.

   If you are new in the neighborhood will it take one source some time to grant credit, while another will grant it promptly?

3. Courtesy.

   Who is most considerate of your time and welfare throughout the credit application procedure?

4. Flexibility.

   Are the loan contracts flexible? Which source offers the best choice (due date, number of payments, prepayment privileges, etc.)?

5. Service.

   Will the retailer handle any complaints about the merchandise more promptly if the purchaser owes him money?

These are just a few of the questions that must be asked before a source is selected. Remember, too, that not all commercial banks make personal unsecured loans, and some of them are not interested in loans below a minimum amount. Generally speaking, consumer loan companies will grant loans to people who might not be able to obtain them from a commercial bank.

Whether a person is buying a refrigerator, a television set, a stereo — anything — the price charged is only part of the story. The quality and extent of the service offered must be considered before a wise decision can be made as to whether to borrow the money or buy on the instalment plan. Paying a slightly higher rate, for example, to finance a purchase through a mail order house may well be worth the cost difference in the convenience offered. When a comparison is made of sources of cash loans, the same factors must be considered.

While quality and service might understandably affect the cost of a household appliance, it might be more difficult to understand just what affects the cost of credit. What are the costs of providing credit?

The costs of doing business, in this case, would include:

   a. Cost of the money loaned — that is, the interest on borrowed capital.

    b. Expense of investigating credit application.

    c. Collection costs,
        including such routine costs as:
            Sending out statements
            Receiving and recording payments
            Issuing receipts
        and such non-routine costs as:
            Following up on slow payers.

    d. Debt losses, including the extra collection costs involved in following up delinquent accounts, plus the total loss incurred when such debts are not paid and are ultimately written off.

    e. Overhead expenses, such as rent, salaries, taxes, etc.

All of these expenses are factors in determining the costs of consumer credit services.[9]

Consumer finance companies have higher costs of doing business than commercial banks or credit unions. In the first place, much of their money is borrowed, often from a commercial bank. They must have a separate office just to loan money, while in a commercial bank the personal loan department shares part of the overhead of the bank with the many other services the bank provides. If the consumer finance company accepts smaller loans and/or "riskier" loans than the commercial bank, its investigating expense, collection costs, and debt losses are likely to be higher.

These are some of the valid reasons for *some* difference in costs between the various sources of consumer credit. A consumer must consider the services offered as well as the cost.

THE LAW AND COMMERCIAL CREDIT

Public pressure is necessary to get good laws of any kind, and this is particularly true in the small loan field. Most agencies dealing in credit operate under government charter, license, or supervision. Commercial banks and savings and loan associations are under federal or state charter and supervision. Small loan companies and insurance companies are under state laws and supervision, as are consumer finance companies in many states.

If adequate small loan laws do not exist, or if a state establishes maximum small loan rates so low that legitimate companies cannot operate at a profit, the "loan shark" — present to some degree in every

---

[9] "Basic Principles in Family Money and Credit Management," Educational Services Division, National Consumer Finance Association, Washington, D.C., 1962, pp. 5-6.

state — really takes over. Their charges may exceed 1,000 per cent. Adequate small loan laws must include provisions concerning the maximum size loan that may be made, the maximum rate that may be charged, requirements for licensing, effective supervision, etc. All of these are necessary if a state is to have adequate legitimate sources of consumer credit.

Laws regulating consumer finance are also necessary. Adequate laws of this type usually state the basic facts which must be contained in a conditional sales contract, fix maximum charges and amounts that may be financed, and specify licensing requirements and the methods of supervision.

CREDIT INSURANCE

Credit life insurance has been available for many years, but has grown rapidly recently. This type of insurance insures the life of the borrower for* the amount of the unpaid balance, and is an excellent investment, well worth the slight additional charge.

Credit disability insurance is also available, and provides for payments on the loan if the borrower is ill or injured. This, however, is a much higher cost insurance than credit life. Many states also permit the loan company to sell property insurance on property pledged as security, but such insurance is usually subject to restrictions concerning the type of security, a minimum loan before such insurance may be sold, etc.

HOW TO GET CREDIT

Each applicant for consumer credit is judged in terms of three qualifications — sometimes referred to as "the three C's of credit." These are:

Character — the personal attributes of the individual which have a bearing on his performance as a borrower. These include honesty, sense of responsibility, trustworthiness, sound judgment.

Capacity — the financial ability of the individual to pay his obligations. Capacity is based on the job now held, the amount of money earned, the length of time he has been employed, and his prospects for continued employment.

---

* The insurance should be on the life of the one providing the money for the payment of the loan. If the wife is the borrower, insurance on her life will be of little value if the husband—the wage earner—should die.

Capital — the financial resources of the individual which can serve as collateral or security for the loan. This might be a home, a bank account, stocks and bonds, an automobile, other tangible property.[10]

Wealth isn't necessary, to have a good credit rating. In fact, many people with a high income have a poor credit rating. They are among those people who have a complete disregard for keeping their promises to pay their bills when due. Anyone who has ever had experience attempting to collect loans may well develop a rather unsympathetic attitude toward people, as a result of such experience. A number of people, when questioned as to why their bill was unpaid, replied with answers such as:

"I needed the money to go on a vacation."

"I'll pay when I get good and ready."

"What are you going to do about it?"

Is it difficult to believe? It happens. There are people who have a completely callous attitude toward credit. Don't be one of them. A good credit rating is an invaluable asset.

There are two main rules for preserving a good credit standing. The first is: *Buy only what you know you can pay for, and make payments promptly when they are due.*[11]

This seems obvious, yet for many it is a difficult rule to follow. Those who are unable to withstand the temptation of easy credit buy much more than they need, and soon find themselves unable to meet their payments.

The second rule for preserving a good credit standing is: *Act cooperatively toward your creditors if financial difficulties arise.*[12]

A creditor is not in business to repossess merchandise or to punish borrowers. They are in business to sell merchandise or to loan money. It is entirely possible that the best of borrowers will meet with financial difficulty. If a payment is expected to be late, the borrower should take the responsibility of letting the creditor know the facts. An explanation of the situation, and the borrower's plan to make the

---

[10] *Ibid.*, p. 7.

[11] Clyde William Phelps, "Using Instalment Credit," *Studies in Consumer Credit, No. 4*, Commercial Credit Company, Baltimore, Maryland, Copyright, 1955, Ninth Printing, 1962, p. 65.

[12] *Ibid,* p. 66.

missed payment, will impress the creditor favorably and permit both parties to work out some mutually satisfactory arrangement.

This second rule should also be considered when applying for a loan. Whether a person wants to borrow from a bank or consumer finance company, or finance a purchase through a dealer or sales finance company, he stands a better chance if he is cooperative. Loss ratios in the consumer finance field have been quite low, due in part to the credit investigation made by creditors. The borrower should be prepared and willing to answer all necessary questions when requesting the loan. A person who approaches a bank, for example, with a well thought out program, including his reasons for needing a loan, his ability to pay, credit references, etc., will impress the bank much more favorably than the person who simply asks for a loan because he needs money, and does very little to encourage the bank to lend it to him.

CONCLUSION

Everyone agrees that consumers should use credit wisely. Consumers use credit wisely when they *understand and do* three things: (1) use credit only when necessary or where the benefit justifies the cost and the risk involved, (2) assume no more debt than they can reasonably expect to repay out of their current level of income, and (3) hunt for the best credit bargain when they do use credit.[13]

Remember to do business only with well known reputable sources, carefully read all contracts, and check all figures before signing.

Questions

1. a. What is consumer credit?
   b. Differentiate between the two basic types of consumer credit when it is classified by the method of repayment.

---

[13] Wallace P. Mors, "Consumer Credit Facts For You," *Educational Pamphlet No. 1*, Bureau of Business Research, Western Reserve University, 1959, p. 29.

2. Cash is the least expensive way to buy. Why use credit?

3. Compare sales finance companies and consumer finance companies.

4. Describe three (3) of the types of credit provided by retailers.

5. A disadvantage of insurance loans is that they are too convenient. Explain.

6. What other costs besides interest should be included before calculating the annual interest rate by the constant ratio formula?

7. In comparing finance charges quoted by appliance dealers and commercial banks, it seems that the rate is affected both by where you live and the source you borrow from. Explain.

8. A person should find the source that offers money at the lowest annual rate and borrow only from that source. Discuss.

9. If consumer finance companies charge higher rates than commercial banks or credit unions, they must be making a greater profit. Is this true?

10. State the two rules for preserving a good credit standing.

Problems

1. Mr. Ward recently purchased a color television receiver from the "Clear Color TV Company." He and the retailer entered into a contractual arrangement permitting him to finance the purchase over a period of 18 months. The "Clear Color TV Company" then sold the contract to the Triple D finance company.
   a. Who will Mr. Ward make his payments to?
   b. What will happen if Mr. Ward becomes dissatisfied with his set and refuses to make payments until it is remedied?
   c. What will be the difference in the procedure if the plan is a full recourse plan as compared to a limited recourse plan if Mr. Ward doesn't pay?

2. Theresa Fitzgerald intends to buy an electric dishwasher. She is unable to pay cash and must finance the purchase. Two stores offer the machine at the same price. Both are willing to arrange for the

financing of the appliance with her. Both advertise that the interest rate on such credit is 5%. Theresa decides that either store might be suitable as the price and interest charges are the same. Furthermore, she does not enjoy reading legal documents, and, as both firms offer the same terms, she plans to simply make certain that the agreed upon price of the appliance is entered on the contract and then sign it. The salesman or office staff can then fill in the rest of the blanks and mail her copy. Is she right?

3. James Anthony wants to borrow $500 and pay it back in equal monthly instalments over a period of 18 months. Using the constant ratio formula, what is the annual interest rate if:
   a. A credit union charges ½% per month?
   b. A bank charges a stated rate of 6% and uses the add-on method.
   c. A bank charges a stated rate of 6% and uses the discount method.

4. The "Real Cool Food Co." is advertising a freezer deal. This is how it works. You pay nothing down and make payments of $31 a month for two years. The company will keep the freezer completely stocked with an agreed upon variety of "Real Cool" frozen foods over this two year period. These delicacies will be sold to you at the same price that the "Real Cool" foods are sold in food stores. The same freezer is available for $600 cash in a local appliance store. Is the "Real Cool's" offer a good deal?

5. Assume that you're going to borrow $600 and pay it back in 12 equal monthly instalments. What is the dollar cost of credit if:
   a. You borrow the money from a loan company and pay monthly instalments of $57.14?
   b. You borrow from a bank at 5% discounted?
   c. You borrow from a bank at 5% using the add-on method?

Selected Readings

"Basic Principles in Family Money and Credit Management," Educational Services Division, National Consumer Finance Association, Washington, D.C., 1962

Dauten, Carl A., "Financing the American Consumer," *Consumer Credit Monograph No. 1,* American Investment Company of Illinois, St. Louis, Missouri, 1956, Copyright 1956 by Carl A. Dauten

Dauten, Carl A., "The Consumer Finance Industry in a Dynamic Economy," *Consumer Credit Monograph No. 2*, American Investment Company of Illinois, St. Louis, Missouri, 1959, Copyright 1959 by Carl A. Dauten

"Facts You Should Know About Your Credit," Association of Better Business Bureaus, 405 Lexington Ave., New York 17, New York (or local Better Business Bureau)

"Finance Charges and How To Watch Them," Form M-106, Credit Union National Association, Madison, Wisconsin

"How to Get the Most Out of Your Income," Life Insurance Agency Management Association, Hartford, Connecticut, 1959

Mors, Wallace P., "Consumer Credit Facts for You," (Second Edition), *Educational Pamphlet No. 1*, Bureau of Business Research, Western Reserve University, 1959, available through Money Management Institute of Household Finance Corp., Prudential Plaza, Chicago 1, Illinois

Mors, Wallace P., "Small Loan Laws" (Thirteenth Edition), *Educational Pamphlet No. 2*, Bureau of Business Research, Western Reserve University, 1961

Phelps, Clyde William, "Using Instalment Credit," *Studies in Consumer Credit No. 4*, Educational Division, Commercial Credit Company, Baltimore, Maryland, Copyright 1955, Ninth Printing, 1962

Chapter **6**

BUYING AN AUTOMOBILE

Is buying an automobile a sufficiently important financial problem to merit a chapter in a text on personal finance? Certainly the amount of money involved is enough to make the expenditure important to the average family. For most families, it represents their largest expenditure for any one asset other than the purchase of a home. It also represents one of the largest expenses in a person's regular budget, i.e., operating costs, depreciation, maintenance and repair.

In 1961, 56.9 per cent of American housing units had one car, while 21.5 per cent had two or more.[1] In 1963, there were about 66 million passenger cars registered in the United States.

In the United States, car numbers tend to increase about one per cent for every 1½ to 2 per cent increase in per capita income. Anticipated increases in population and incomes during the Sixties could lift the U.S. car park from about 60 million in 1960 to 82 million by 1970. In Western Europe, where incomes are rising relatively faster than here, the pattern of growth should be similar to that in the United States during the Twenties, with car numbers likely to rise from 22 million in 1960 to 65 million by 1970. Subject in part to the development of a modern highway system, it is quite possible that by 1970 the world will have well over 180 million cars — almost twice as many as it has now.

If assumptions about population and income growth are realistic, car sales in the United States and Canada, where about 2 million cars are added to the car park every year, and where most new car sales are replacements, are likely to climb 3½ to 4 per cent annually over the decade, passing 9 million in 1965 and approaching 11 million in 1970. In Western Europe and in the remainder of the world, car sales may climb some 9 to 10 per cent annually — almost three times as fast as in the United States.[2]

The automobile plays an important role in the American family's financial picture, and the importance of this role will continue to increase, not only in the United States, but throughout the world.

WHAT CAR TO BUY

Over 3,000 car makes have appeared in the United States alone since the invention of the automobile. Relatively few of them are left. Table 6–1 indicates the leading makes of cars sold in 1963.

Because buying an automobile costs enough to make it a major purchase, a buyer should carefully consider every detail. Some people do this much more conscientiously than others. Some, in fact, go to extremes. A young man planning to buy his first car may study dealers' catalogues, charts, automobile books, etc., with a thoroughness rarely devoted to school work.

---

[1] For these statistics refer to "Automobile Facts & Figures," 1962 Edition, Automobile Manufacturers Association, Detroit, Michigan.

[2] "Automobiles Around the World," *Foreign Information Service Bulletin*, First National City Bank, New York, New York, December 1961, p. 7.

Ward's Automotive Reports
DETROIT, MICHIGAN

May 6, 1963

Table 6-1

*1963 MODEL YEAR U.S. CAR PRODUCTION BY $100 PRICE GROUPS
(Model Year through March 31, 1963)

$100 PRICE GROUPS	Chevrolet	Chevy II	Corvair	Pontiac	Tempest	Oldsmobile	F-85	Buick	Special	Ford Galaxie	Fairlane	Falcon	Thunderbird	Mercury Monterey	Meteor	Comet	Plymouth	Valiant	Dodge	Dart	Chrysler	Cadillac Lincoln Imperial	Rambler	Studebaker†	ALL CARS TOTAL Units	% Tot.
$1,601-$1,700																							15,780		15,780	0.35
1,701- 1,800		1,613	10,242									43,361						40,416					21,532	1,025	118,189	2.62
1,801- 1,900		40,322	21,756								11,848	61,563						5,237					11,945	10,350	208,294	4.62
1,901- 2,000		126,083			27,131						27,875	38,120				3,877		31,194		33,004			49,160	13,647	371,114	8.23
2,001- 2,100	85,154	189	109,612		7,423				26,489	19,106	43,537	14,737			2,416	12,269	31,089	22,997	21,659	23,137			60,449	8,386	474,931	10.53
2,101- 2,200	43,896	26,679			29,586		11,595			27,130	80,746	48,965			10,477	34,767	22,364	9,791	15,941	17,811			33,484	3,690	380,390	8.43
2,201- 2,300	94,637	33,629	24,977		9,910		18,370		29,664	22,518	5,040	10,667			15,872	9,760	25,220	4,212	7,301	6,286			26,652	2,068	336,805	7.47
2,301- 2,400	135,405			7,465			24,480		3,850	46,994	32,787	344			187	9,319	11,579		23,729	7,072			38,391	7,044	344,136	7.63
2,401- 2,500	312,272		6,838	39,579	10,333		2,156		1,623	197,190	20,483	198		14,131	5,964	4,763	32,041		22,876				27,830	2,851	687,017	15.23
2,501- 2,600	137,070			51,462			4,225	4,410	27,844	22,301	6,168			4,021	2,850	1,558	16,020		15,818				4,573	2,124	308,542	6.84
2,601- 2,700	81,276					58,160	6,227	36,048	6,543	35,600				35,700	1,253	480	13,165		12,764		28,568		3,639		289,218	6.39
2,701- 2,800	28,036			16,427		35,379	5,001	42,266		40,818				6,530					12,956		6,489		1,187		226,638	5.02
2,801- 2,900	8,277			27,611		15,407				11,443				11,093			2,379		2,672		5,646			3,019	85,364	1.89
2,901- 3,000				25,939		6,227		5,763		50,982							4,759		3,217						103,221	2.29
3,001- 3,100				32,228		29,788													927		8,006				70,949	1.57
3,101- 3,200				55,985		4,350		3,417		11,683											9,944				85,379	1.89
3,201- 3,300				3,431				2,368						4,107							1,854				11,760	0.26
3,301- 3,400						2,668								834											3,502	0.08
3,401- 3,500								18,825													2,612				21,437	0.48
3,501- 3,600						7,405		20,246						994											28,645	0.64
3,601- 3,700	5,311					15,615		13,383													11,208				45,517	1.01
3,701- 3,800						17,714		8,844													7,837				34,395	0.76
3,801- 3,900	6,522					16,750		31,539																	54,811	1.22
3,901- 4,000						8,573							33,699												42,272	0.94
4,001- 4,100													11,114											1,700	12,814	0.28
4,101- 4,200																									.....	
4,201- 4,300						2,850															843				3,693	0.08
4,301- 4,400																					927				927	0.02
4,401 & Over													4,515								337	140,858			145,710	3.23
Totals	937,856	228,515	173,445	260,127	84,383	220,886	72,054	187,129	96,013	485,765	228,484	217,955	49,328	77,410	39,019	76,793	158,616	113,847	139,860	87,310	84,271	140,858	294,622	55,904	4,510,450	100.00

†Estimated. *Based on factory list prices before excise tax, dealer handling charges and optional equipment installations. 1963 model year prices include deduction of heater prices for General Motors Corp. and Ford Motor Co. car lines to put industry-wide prices on an equal basis with entire 1962 model year. Source: Ward's Statistical Dept.

†Estimated

Source: "Ward's Automotive Reports, 1963."   Reprinted by permission.

136

While few people ever approach this degree of thoroughness a second time, it is always a mistake to buy simply on impulse. No one chapter would be sufficient to cover all details of price, make, and model, but some of the major points can be discussed. These are:

1. How much should you pay?
2. Should you buy a new or used car?
3. What body style is preferable?
4. What equipment should be purchased?
5. When to trade.

The answers to these questions depend upon the status and nature of the person asking the questions—his income, for example, and the emphasis he places upon looks and style. Some people don't particularly care what their car looks like; others spend countless hours polishing and adjusting. To one person, a car is "important," while to another, it is simply a means of transportation.

The choice of car depends upon the use it will be put to. Is the car to be primarily used for transportation to and from work, or for the wife to use running errands? Will it be used in business, or only as a family car? Will it be driven under "tough" or "easy" road and weather conditions? How many people will usually ride in it?

However, it is possible to give broad answers to these questions which are generally applicable, or to present information leading to specific decisions. These general answers and information should help a person plan the purchase of a car with a little more thought and understanding.

How Much Should You Pay?

What amount of money will your budget permit you to spend on an automobile? Each automobile manufacturer turns out several series of cars in different price ranges. The amount you can afford will determine which series merits further consideration.

Once make and series have been selected, the amount to be paid for a model in that series must be determined. The answer to this is, "Shop and Negotiate." Ask several dealers for their best deal on the model you have tentatively selected, and compare:

1. List the base price of the car being considered.
2. List the individual costs of extra equipment not included in the base price.
3. Add any taxes that must be paid.
4. Add these three to get the total cost.

5. Subtract the amount offered as a trade-in on your present car (if any).

6. Remainder is the amount that must be paid.

You might consider selling your present car yourself, rather than trading it in. This will mean that step 5 would now be a subtraction of the amount you expect to get from the sale of your car. Usually, the final amount that must be paid is less if you sell your own old car. In this case the dealer isn't left with another used car that must be sold and will usually make a quite worthwhile reduction in the price charged for the new car. While United States law requires the manufacturer's price—including the manufacturer's suggested retail price and the price of each item of optional equipment installed at the factory—to appear on the window of each new car, this "list" price is subject to bargaining. Again, even if you sell your own old car, a comparison should be made between several dealers to get the best deal.

Curiously, many people get completely wrapped up in trade-in values and do not properly consider the final amount that must be paid. They brag about the trade-in they got for the old jalopy. What possible difference can it make if one dealer will allow a trade-in of $1,500 while others will allow only $1,200, if other adjustments in the "list" price mean the net cost is the same, or even higher, when the car is purchased from the dealer offering the high trade-in? The buyer's chief concern should be the remainder that must be paid, not the trade-in value.

One word of caution should be injected. By all means buy an automobile where it can be purchased at the lowest cost, *but*—and this is a very important "but"—be certain to purchase the car from a reputable dealer. The dealer's reputation is a most important consideration when buying a car. Select a dealer who has the reputation of standing behind his guarantees and of providing competent service.

The subject of price cannot be brought to a close without some consideration of whether or not automobiles cost too much. Undoubtedly, automobile prices have gone up. In 1923, a Reo Speed Wagon could be purchased for $1,185 plus tax, and a new Chevrolet cost $680, f.o.b. Flint, Michigan.

American cars have been improved each year, perform better, and last longer than ever before. Few automobiles are traded in because they have worn out. The usual reasons are because the owner wants to keep up-to-date, or because the cost of maintaining the old car in "new car condition" is beginning to increase.

Prices have certainly increased, but not the relative cost. For example, at the prevailing rates of pay in 1930, the average U. S. worker worked 1,200 hours to earn the price of a low-priced car; while in 1960, the average U. S. worker worked only 1,136 hours to earn the price of the 1960 model of the same low-priced car.[3]

New Or Used Car?

About two used cars are purchased in the United States for every new one sold. Which would be the best buy for you? Again, a good part of the answer depends upon the individual's financial situation, the planned use of the car, etc. It is impossible to give general advice as to which is the best buy for each individual. Instead, let's discuss some of the merits of each type.

Very little needs to be said about the merits of a new car. The outstanding advantage, of course, is that it is new. It has the latest design and styling. It carries a warranty or owner-service policy which keeps maintenance costs to a minimum. It may need lubrication and oil changes less frequently than the older models.

Of course, a new car costs more. State excise taxes (if any) will be higher, as will insurance. Depreciation is a big cost factor. In the first two years, a new car may lose more than 50 per cent of its original value.

A used car will cost less from the standpoint of original price, depreciation, insurance, and taxes. While it is probable that maintenance costs will be higher than on a new car, there is no reason why they should be excessive if the purchase is carefully made. (See the rules presented below.) Again, the one basic rule to remember is to do business only with a reputable dealer.

Today's used cars are much better values than were those of a few years ago. New methods of treating metal, improvements in design, less frequent need for lubricating and oil change, improved interior fabrics, and many other changes which have been made in the new car market during the late 1950's and early 1960's, are now available on the used cars as these models are turned in. If the car is bought from a reliable dealer, is carefully examined as suggested in the first five rules on page 140, and is backed by a written guarantee, driving costs may be much less than expected.

---

[3] Statistics from "Are Car Prices Too High?," *The Buyer's Digest of New Car Facts for '60,* Ford Division of Ford Motor Company, 1960, p. 82.

Thinking of buying a used car?
HERE ARE 10 GOOD
RULES TO GO "BUY":

1. Drive it first! Two-thirds of all used car complaints to the Better Business Bureau are from people who never test-drove the used car before they bought it. The reputable dealer is happy to have you drive the car because he knows it's in proper running condition.

2. Check the speedometer reading! It's fairly easy to do. Grease and oil stickers may give you the clue. They record the mileage at which service has been performed. If the tires aren't the originals, high mileage is indicated. If arm rests, gas pedal, clutch and brake pedals show a lot more wear than speedometer indicates, then beware!

3. Note the steering wheel play! More than two inches of "free" play either way is too much.

4. Where there's smoke . . . ! Heavy, bluish exhaust smoke when you accelerate rapidly is a danger signal.

5. Sluggish pickup on a high mileage car *could* mean that the rings are ripe for replacement.

6. Let a mechanic see it! A good mechanic can spot serious defects you might miss. For example, he can tell normal exhaust smoke from smoke caused by heavy oil burning merely by *feeling it with his hand*.

7. Insist on a detailed, receipted bill with *all* the facts about your purchase.

8. A written guarantee (if there is a guarantee) should be in your hands when you close the deal.

9. Know what you're signing! On a financed purchase, be sure the contract is made out and read by you *before* you sign it! You should get a copy, too.

10. Shop for the dealer, not the car! An established dealer with a good reputation is your best bet. More than three-quarters of the used cars sold every year in the U.S.A. are sold through new car dealers! And for something extra special in used cars, your Ford Dealer has the answer. A-1. Every A-1 Used Car on his lot has been thoroughly inspected, reconditioned when necessary, road-tested and is ready for the road. The A-1 sign may save you money![4]

---

[4] "Buyer's Digest of New Car Facts for 1963," Ford Division of Ford Motor Company, Detroit, Michigan, 1963, p. 79.

A certain amount of common sense is as necessary in buying a used car as in making any purchase. Remember that a car which is "repossessed" is not necessarily any better or cheaper than any other car of the same age, make and model, that buying a wrecked car is a gamble, and that taxicabs have had extremely hard use. It is necessary to pay a "fair" price for a reasonably good used car. "Bargain prices" are not guarantees of good buys. Used car dealers, like everyone else, have to make money on a sale. They aren't in business just for the fun of it.

Today's new cars supposedly have a life expectancy of about 100,000 miles before the engine should need a major overhaul. When purchasing a used car, this might be considered as a guide as to its remaining life. The mileage appearing on the speedometer, however, should be accepted only as a very rough indication of the use the automobile has had. Two cars may both have gone 25,000 miles, and have had quite different use. One, used very carefully under ideal driving conditions, has many miles of service remaining; while the other, used under very hard conditions, may be badly worn. It will pay to look into the history of the ownership of the car. Not all used cars are turned in by little old ladies who used them only to drive to church on Sunday.

Body Type

Body type is also a matter of personal choice. Discussion will be limited to two general considerations:
1. Whether the car should be a sedan, convertible, hardtop, or station wagon.
2. Whether it should be a compact or standard size.

The first decision depends partly on a person's taste and partly on the use to which the car will be put. The information presented on Chart 6-1 indicates that the sedan is still, by far, the most popular car on the road. In 1961, 56 per cent of passenger car sales were sedans, 38.6 per cent four-door, and 17.6 per cent two-door. It is also to be noted that in each group the four-door car is more popular than the two-door.

The sedan undoubtedly has definite advantages as a family car. It is safer and more rigidly built than a hardtop or convertible, and will generally cost less than the equivalent car in hardtop, convertible, or station wagon style. The station wagon has its advantages, too, as a family car, in the extra room and seating capacity it offers. This advantage extends to salesmen, small businessmen, and anyone

Chart 6–1

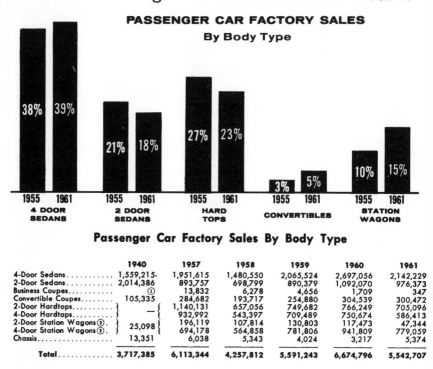

39% of Passenger Car Sales are 4-Door Sedans

PASSENGER CAR FACTORY SALES
By Body Type

38%	39%	21%	18%	27%	23%	3%	5%	10%	15%
1955	1961	1955	1961	1955	1961	1955	1961	1955	1961
4 DOOR SEDANS		2 DOOR SEDANS		HARD TOPS		CONVERTIBLES		STATION WAGONS	

Passenger Car Factory Sales By Body Type

	1940	1957	1958	1959	1960	1961
4-Door Sedans	1,559,215.	1,951,615	1,480,550	2,065,524	2,697,056	2,142,229
2-Door Sedans	2,014,386	893,757	698,799	890,379	1,092,070	976,373
Business Coupes	①	13,832	6,278	4,656	1,709	347
Convertible Coupes	105,335	284,682	193,717	254,880	304,539	300,472
2-Door Hardtops	—	1,140,131	657,056	749,682	766,249	705,096
4-Door Hardtops		932,992	543,397	709,489	750,674	586,413
2-Door Station Wagons②	25,098	196,119	107,814	130,803	117,473	47,344
4-Door Station Wagons②		694,178	564,858	781,806	941,809	779,059
Chassis	13,351	6,038	5,343	4,024	3,217	5,374
Total	3,717,385	6,113,344	4,257,812	5,591,243	6,674,796	5,542,707

① Business coupes sold in 1940 are included with 2-door sedans.

② Station wagons produced on commercial vehicle chassis are not included.

Source: "Automobile Facts & Figures, 1962 Edition," Automobile Manufacturers Association, Detroit, Michigan, p. 6.

else who needs plenty of room. A convertible, of course, is preferred by those who are interested in a sportier car. Evidently, convertibles are not as much in demand as other body types, and stand in fourth position among the basic body types available, in terms of factory sales.

Whether the car should be a compact or standard size car depends upon the relative importance of room and cost. A compact has less room than the standard size and costs less. However, a car should be selected which will give the buyer the combination of price, operating cost, ease of handling, and roominess which he prefers.

Equipment

A wide variety of equipment is available for installation on today's automobiles. Even in a text on Personal Finance, two of these merit further discussion.

The number of cylinders, for example, will affect both the original price of the car and the subsequent operating costs. The greater the number of cylinders, the higher the price and the higher the operating cost.

> Contrary to common belief, the number of cylinders by itself doesn't determine engine power. A six can be built big enough for a truck, a four-cylinder engine "hot" enough for the Indianapolis races. The power potential is determined basically by total *internal* volume of all cylinders, whatever their number, in cubic inches.
>
> The designer can enlarge the cubic capacity of an engine, and thereby its power, in two ways: by enlarging each cylinder in bore or in piston stroke, or by adding more cylinders. The second is the more desirable solution in passenger cars. It provides a smoother, quieter action along with greater efficiency.[5]

In selecting the number of cylinders, the decision must be based primarily on the proposed use of the car.

A similar decision must be made in choosing between a standard or automatic transmission. An automatic transmission does take slightly more power and therefore consumes more gas than a standard, but the difference can be reduced if the automatic transmission is properly used. Studies indicate that on certain makes of cars, letting up on the gas so the automatic will shift sooner, will mean a slower acceleration but an increase in gas economy. The great advantage of an automatic transmission is the amount of effort saved in heavy traffic. Its acceptance by the public is evident in the fact that the great majority of the major makes of cars sold have this type of transmission. In general, it has also been found that an automatic transmission requires less maintenance than a standard transmission.

Best Time to Trade

When is the best time to buy a new car and trade in the old one? In studies made concerning this question, 10,000 miles per year

---

[5] "Buyer's Digest of New Car Facts for '60," Ford Division of Ford Motor Company, Detroit, Michigan, p. 78.

has been assumed to be the number driven by the average American motorist. Exactly when a car should be traded depends upon how it has been used, and what you want. The proverbial little old lady, who only drives to church on Sunday, certainly can keep her car longer than a salesman who travels 2,000 miles a month. In addition to the longevity of the car, it is probable that her car will continue to perform well long after the salesman's car is worn out. 30,000 miles driven under ideal conditions will not be as hard on a car as 25,000 miles driven under difficult conditions. Normally speaking, it has been found that an automobile seems to reach a repair plateau at about 30,000 miles. Even the most carefully cared for automobile is subject to normal wear and tear.

> How much will it cost to correct this normal deterioration? Based on national averages, a car priced around $2,300 when new, if driven 15,000 miles a year, costs about $60 for maintenance the first year, about $112 in the second year.
>
> But the maintenance cost jumps suddenly to $180 in the third year, or beyond 30,000 miles of normal use. And it keeps on rising after that to a peak of $325 at 60,000 miles.[6]

In trading a car a balance should be struck between the cost of a new car and the decline in the value of the old one, as measured in terms of depreciation plus increasing maintenance costs. It is true that the trade-in value of a car depends partly on the mileage and condition of the car, but the primary factor is the car's age in model years. A low-priced new car depreciates more than 25 per cent the first year. The depreciation rate then declines to about 16 per cent the second year, and at the rate of three or four per cent a year thereafter.

Available sources indicate that the usual trade-in period is from two and one-half to three years.

> Our records indicate that a three year cycle is, with one exception, the most frequent. This exception is the "over 6 year" trade.
>
> Rambler experience of yearly trades as of November, 1962, was:

One year trades	7.6%
Two ″ ″	17.6%
Three ″ ″	18.1%
Four ″ ″	12.1%

---

[6] "Buyer's Digest of New Car Facts for '60," Ford Division of Ford Motor Company, Detroit, Michigan, p. 21.

Five	”	”	11.9%
Six	”	”	9.3%
Over Six		”	23.4%

Of course, this is *Rambler* experience, and the high in "over 6 years" may be, and probably is, due to buyers of new Ramblers at compact prices, who might otherwise have bought used cars.

Discounting the reasons for "over 6 year" trades on new cars, and concentrating on the 3 year trade cycle, this latter is considered the most economical period, as the depreciation on the trades, and the expense of obtaining new tires and mechanical repairs, makes them ready to trade at that time.[7]

The Ford Motor Company has had quite similar experiences, as indicated in Chart 6–2. Evidently, any time after 20,000 miles or 2½ years is the time to start to consider trading.

Chart 6–2

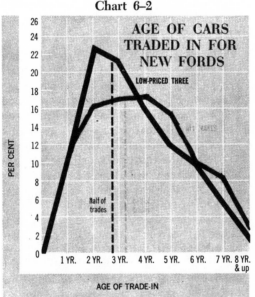

Chart shows trading peak in 2- and 3-year-old cars. Half of low-priced models are replaced before 2 years, 9 months of ownership, half of higher priced makes in another 6 months

Source: "Buyer's Digest of New Car Facts for '60," Ford Division of Ford Motor Company, Detroit, Michigan, p. 22.

---

[7] Letter from Mr. H. E. Cardoze, Jr., National Used Car Manager, American Motors Corporation, Detroit, Michigan, February 1963, p. 1.

Financing

Now we get to the subject most pertinent to the field of Personal Finance—financing the purchase of the automobile. In most cases, the expenditure will run from one to three thousand dollars. Paying cash is certainly the most economical method of purchasing a car, but the amount of cash needed forces the majority of us to buy the car on time. Automobile financing has been going on for some time. Since 1916, when the first advertisement for automobile financing appeared in the *Saturday Evening Post*, the importance of this industry has increased to the point where total automobile "paper" outstanding at the end of 1962 was 19.4 billion dollars.

According to the Federal Reserve Bulletin of May, 1963, the proportion of new-car sales financed on instalments was about 60 per cent. Commercial banks hold more automobile "paper" than any other loan source. In 1962, they held about 50 per cent of the outstanding automobile instalment sales contracts and notes, followed by sales finance companies with 38 per cent. The four most commonly used sources of financing, from the purchasers' point of view, are commercial banks, automobile dealers, insurance companies, and credit unions. Insurance company loans are available only to policy holders, and credit union loans only to members. Dealers commonly sell the instalment contracts they make to a bank or sales finance company, and the automobile purchaser pays the financing source directly.

Comparison between the two most commonly used financing sources, commercial banks and automobile dealers, give the edge to the banks, in terms of the cost of borrowing. Table 6–2 indicates the finance rates charged by these sources, as found in one study. Notice that in only one city, St. Louis, did a dealer quote a rate below the bank average; and even in that city the average dealer rate was 2.2 per cent higher than the average commercial bank rate.

Table 6–3 indicates the relationship between rates charged by Chevrolet and Ford dealers in certain cities. Two interesting facts are brought out by this table. One is that the average rate charged by both Chevrolet and Ford dealers was the same—12.3 per cent. The other is the interesting variations from city to city.

Chevrolet dealers varied from an average rate of 11.2 per cent at St. Louis to a rate of 13.8 per cent in San Francisco, while Ford dealers ranged from 11.8 per cent in Boston and

Table 6–2

FINANCE CHARGES QUOTED BY AUTOMOBILE DEALERS AND
COMMERCIAL BANKS EXPRESSED IN SIMPLE ANNUAL INTEREST (PER
CENT) AND PRICES FOR AUTOMOBILES IN CERTAIN SELECTED CITIES[a8]
(Number of Sample Dealers or Banks Quoting Charges in Parentheses)

| City | Automobiles[d] | | | |
| | Finance Rates at Dealers (Per Cent) | | Prices | Finance Rates at Commercial Banks[b] |
	Mean	Range	Index[c] (Chicago = 100)	(Per Cent)
Boston	12.2 (12)	9.7–15.8	104.7	9.0 (9)
Chicago	11.9 (22)	11.1–13.6	100.0	10.6 (59)
Cleveland	12.3 (16)	9.7–15.4	102.4	10.8 (8)
Denver	12.7 (12)	9.7–15.0	102.8	9.7 (15)
Detroit	11.9 (12)	11.7–13.6	100.3	11.6 (8)
New York	13.0 (12)	11.5–14.0	101.5	9.7 (32)
Pittsburgh	12.3 (11)	11.7–13.6	105.0	9.6 (10)
St. Louis	11.7 (15)	8.8–15.8	101.2	9.5 (14)
San Francisco	13.3 (11)	11.7–14.4	106.4	11.4 (8)

[a] Means are unweighted arithmetic averages except for mean rates at commercial banks which are weighted by estimated volume of loans of sample banks.
[b] See Irving Schweiger and John S. McGee, "Chicago Banking," *The Journal of Business* XXXIV, No. 3 (July, 1961), 259.
[c] Prices were obtained at the same dealers that quoted finance charges.
[d] Request was to finance a $1,500 balance on a new car to be financed over three years. The down-payment was to be over one-third of the price of a new car.

Detroit to 12.8 per cent in New York and San Francisco. The lowest rate quoted by a Chevrolet dealer was 8.8 per cent in St. Louis, and the highest rate was 15.8 quoted in Boston. For Ford, the dealers with the lowest finance charge quoted 9.7 per cent in Boston, Cleveland, Denver, and St. Louis, while the dealer with the highest charge, 15.8 per cent, was located in St. Louis. Average rates by cities varied only one point for Ford dealers, ranging from 11.8 per cent to 12.8 per cent, while city averages for Chevrolet differed 2.6 points, from 11.2 per cent to 13.8 per cent. All eight Chevrolet dealers in Cleveland quoted an identical rate of 11.9 per cent. Cities that averaged high or low

[8] Allen F. Jung, "Charges for Appliance and Automobile Instalment Credit in Major Cities," *The Journal of Business*, The Graduate School of Business of the University of Chicago, The University of Chicago Press, Chicago, Illinois, October 1962, p. 388.

rates for credit at Chevrolet dealers did not average high or low rates at Ford dealers. Chevrolet or Ford dealers that quoted above- or below-average finance charges in a given city did not quote above- or below- average prices.[9]

Table 6–3

FINANCE CHARGES QUOTED BY CHEVROLET AND FORD DEALERS IN SELECTED CITIES EXPRESSED AS SIMPLE ANNUAL INTEREST (PER CENT)*[10]
(Number of Sample Dealers Quoting Finance Charges in Parentheses)

City	Chevrolet Dealers		Ford Dealers	
	Mean	Range	Mean	Range
Boston	12.5 (6)	9.7–15.8	11.8 (6)	9.7–13.2
Chicago	11.9 (11)	11.7–12.6	11.9 (11)	11.1–13.6
Cleveland	11.9 (8)	11.9–11.9	12.7 (8)	9.7–15.4
Denver	13.2 (6)	11.7–13.8	12.1 (6)	9.7–15.0
Detroit	12.0 (6)	11.7–13.6	11.8 (6)	11.7–12.1
New York	13.2 (6)	11.5–13.8	12.8 (6)	11.7–14.0
Pittsburgh	12.0 (7)	11.7–13.6	12.7 (4)	11.7–13.6
St. Louis	11.2 (8)	8.8–14.8	12.3 (7)	9.7–15.8
San Francisco	13.8 (6)	13.6–14.4	12.8 (5)	11.7–14.0
All Cities	12.3 (64)	8.8–15.8	12.3 (59)	9.7–15.8

* Means are unweighted arithmetic averages.

Now these are the results of only one limited study, but evidently a person interested in purchasing a car should investigate the cost of bank loans in his community, as the results presented in Table 6–2 indicate that, *on the average,* they are cheaper. Remember two things, however: First, "on the average" doesn't mean "always"; second, financing an automobile through the dealer does offer a certain amount of convenience, in that the purchase of the car and its financing can be handled at one location.

Table 6–4 is an excellent means of comparing the cost of financing through the dealer with the costs of financing through other

---

[9] Allen F. Jung, "Charges for Appliance and Automobile Instalment Credit in Major Cities," *The Journal of Business,* The Graduate School of Business of the University of Chicago, The University of Chicago Press, Chicago, Ill., October 1962, p. 390.
[10] Allen F. Jung, "Charges for Appliance and Automobile Instalment Credit in Major Cities," *The Journal of Business,* The Graduate School of Business of the University of Chicago, The University of Chicago Press, Chicago, Ill., October 1962, p. 390.

sources. Every buyer should make such a comparison. In fact, it would be wise to compare several dealers and several banks in this respect. Costs vary considerably, even within one locality.

Table 6–4[11]

Facts You Need	Example	Dealer's Arrangement	Other Source
1) Total cost of the car including all extras and taxes	$3000.00		
2) Subtract down payment			
Trade-in allowance	$880		
Cash	328		
Total	1208.00		
3) Balance due	1792.00		
4) Insurance costs throughout contract period	208.00		
5) Total amount (principal to be financed)	2000.00		
6) Amount of monthly payments	$ 76.67		
7) Number of monthly payments	30		
8) Total amount of monthly payments	2300.10		
9) *Dollar Cost of Credit* (subtract principal from total amount of monthly payments)	$ 300.10		

Be certain to carefully read any contracts you are asked to sign when financing an automobile, and make certain that all information has been filled in.

Those who sign contracts in blank are making it easy for the unethical dealer to "pack" the account. For example, assume a *balance* of $300 is to be paid. The dealer will add the finance charge and the insurance premium, which may total $50. The customer may agree to pay off the $350 at $35 per month for 10 months. BUT, if the contract had been signed in blank, the unethical dealer could "pack" it by filling in the total of $500, $150 more for financing, insurance, etc., than in the first illustration. This concealed charge is the "pack" and is rebated to the dealer or split with the finance company.[12]

---

[11] Taken from "Money Management: Your Automobile Dollar," published by the Money Management Institute of Household Finance Corporation, Chicago, Illinois, 1963, p. 19.

[12] From "Facts You Should Know about Buying New or Used Cars," Better Business Bureau of Metropolitan Boston, Inc., Boston, Mass., 1963, p. 8.

The form presented on pages 152 and 153 is the conditional sale contract used by the General Motors Acceptance Corporation in the State of Massachusetts. Notice that the first sentence of this contract refers to terms and conditions "set forth below *and upon the reverse side hereof.*" The provisions on the reverse side set forth such things as the obligations of the buyer, the need for insurance on the vehicle and the procedure to be followed if such insurance is not carried by the purchaser, an explanation of delinquency charges, procedure in case the buyer defaults, etc. Obviously, such terms are important and should be read by the purchaser.

Notice, also, that the contract form warns the buyer not to sign the contract before reading, or if it contains any blank spaces. It then recites the buyer's rights. Such a contract, when completely filled in, contains complete and detailed information.

The availability of money affects financing rates, the length of contract, and the down payment required. If money is scarce, financing rates will be higher, the contract term shorter, and the required down payment larger. The reverse will be true when money is plentiful. In 1962 and 1963, the competition among lenders was keen, and terms were liberalized. There were some reductions in financing rates, and the average maturity on new car contracts rose, with a larger proportion of contracts written at the prevailing maximum term of 36 months. During the first quarter of 1963, approximately 75 per cent of the instalment sales contracts purchased from dealers by commercial banks and sales finance companies had a 36 month maturity, and a few new car contracts were for terms of 42 and 48 months. The prevailing maturity period on used-car loans was 24 months, but an increasing number were being made for 36 months.

Occasionally, "balloon" contracts are used in automobile financing. These call for a final instalment much larger than previous instalments. Except for special purposes, such as the financing of the purchase of a car by an automobile salesman, the use of such a contract is unwise. The charges paid by the purchaser are usually higher, and the difficulty of making the final "balloon" payment forces the purchaser to refinance the ballooned balance, with its attendant refinancing costs.

Banks discovered long ago that the likelihood of a borrower making regular payments is much greater if:

(1) the performance of the car is satisfactory;
(2) the dealer service is adequate;

(3) the current value of the automobile is more than the bal-
     ance owing;
(4) there is sufficient equity in the automobile to motivate him
     to make his payments; and
(5) the ability to pay is present.[13]

The importance of the first two items is obvious. A purchaser is
going to balk at paying for his car if it does not perform satisfactorily,
or if the dealer does not provide adequate service. Whether or not
this is legal is a moot point. Most conditional sales contracts specifically state that such considerations are not valid reasons for avoiding
payment. But, if the customer is dissatisfied enough, he will apply
pressure wherever possible in an effort to get an equitable adjustment,
and this means difficulty for the lender. To avoid such difficulties,
lenders give careful consideration to the responsibility and reputation
of the dealers from whom they purchase contract "paper."

The third and fourth items involve the equity the purchaser has
in the car. Both the lender and the borrower should be concerned
about the amount of this equity. If it is less than the amount owed,
the purchaser will be less interested in keeping up the payments,
particularly if any financial problems arise. If he defaults, the lender
will have a difficult time recovering his money. And a deficiency
judgment will certainly impair the borrower's credit standing.

The fifth item, the ability to pay, is discussed in the chapter on
"Borrowing," which explains the method of calculating the actual
costs of credit, and offers other information generally applicable to
borrowing for any purpose.

Driving Costs

How much does it cost to drive a car? Is it cheaper to use some
other form of transportation? Many studies have been made of
driving costs. Let's examine some of the results.

The form on page 154 is a handy means of calculating operating
costs on a specific car. Notice that the costs are broken down into
three parts: depreciation, fixed costs, and flexible costs.

---

[13] "Automobile Financing: Dealer Plan," Instalment Credit Committee, by
permission of The American Bankers Association, New York, New York, 1961,
p. 63.

CONDITIONAL SALE CONTRACT

Contract Number _____

The undersigned seller hereby sells, and the undersigned buyer or buyers, jointly and severally, hereby purchase(s), subject to the terms and conditions set forth below, **and upon the reverse side hereof,** the following property, delivery and acceptance of which in good order are hereby acknowledged by buyer, viz.::

DESCRIPTION OF PROPERTY

New or Used	Year Model	No. Cyl.	Make Trade Name	Body Type If Truck, Give Tonnage	Model Number or Series	Manufacturer's Serial No.	Motor No.

Optional Equipment or Accessories (Check, if included on car)

☐ Radio ☐ Automatic Trans. ☐ Power Steering ☐ Power Windows ☐ High H/P Engine (Describe) _____
☐ Tinted Glass ☐ 4 Speed Trans. ☐ Power Brakes ☐ Power Seats ☐ Air Conditioning

For a TOTAL TIME PRICE computed as follows:

1. CASH SALE PRICE (including accessories or extras, if any) - - - - - - - $ _____ (1)

2. TOTAL DOWN PAYMENT—consisting of $ _____ , $ _____ $ _____ (2)
   (Trade-In Allowance) (Cash) (Other Credits)

   DESCRIPTION OF TRADE-IN - Make _____ Model _____ Year _____

3. DIFFERENCE BETWEEN ITEMS 1 AND 2 - - - - - - - - - - - - - - - $ _____ (3)

*4a. COST OF REQUIRED CAR INSURANCE (Include this item if buyer has authorized seller to apply for this insurance) - - - $ _____ (4a)

**4b. CHARGE FOR CREDITOR INSURANCE ON LIFE OF BUYER (Include this item, if buyer has authorized seller to apply for the insurance) - $ _____ (4b)

4c. - $ _____ (4c)

5. RECORDING CHARGES, if any—Describe _____ - - - - - - - - - $ _____ (5)

6. PRINCIPAL BALANCE (Add items 3, 4a, 4b, 4c and 5) - - - - - - - - - $ _____ (6)

7. FINANCE CHARGE - $ _____ (7)

8. TIME (DEFERRED) BALANCE (Add items 6 and 7) - - - - - - - - - - - $ _____ (8)

9. TOTAL TIME PRICE (Add items 2 and 8) - - - - - - - - - - - - - - $ _____ (9)

The aforesaid Time (Deferred) Balance is payable at the seller's office designated below or at such office of any assignee as may be hereafter designated in _____ instalments of $ _____ , and on the same day of each successive month thereafter, or as indicated in space each, commencing _____ 19___, below. The final instalment shall equal the amount of time balance remaining due.

---

* Covering Accidental Physical Damage to the car as outlined below (check which applies) for a term of _____ months, and { including } optional coverage for Towing and Labor Costs, { excluding }
   ☐ Comprehensive Coverage { including } $ _____ Deductible Collision.
   ☐ Fire-Theft and Additional Coverage { excluding }
   Insurance settlement shall be based upon actual value of property at time of loss, not to exceed limits of liability set forth in the policy, and shall be payable to buyer, seller or seller's assignee, as interests may appear.

THE INSURANCE, IF ANY, REFERRED TO IN THIS CONTRACT DOES NOT INCLUDE COVERAGE FOR BODILY INJURY AND PROPERTY DAMAGE CAUSED TO OTHERS.

NOTICE TO BUYER: 1. Do not sign this contract before you read it or if it contains any blank space. 2. You
are entitled to an exact copy of the contract you signed. 3. Under the law, you have the following rights,
among others: (a) to pay off in advance the full amount due and to obtain a partial refund of the finance charge;
(b) to redeem the property if repossessed for a default; (c) to require, under certain conditions, a resale of
the property if repossessed.

Executed in quintuplicate, this _____ day of _____, 19 ____

_____ _____
(Do not date on Sunday)

A **Buyer Signs in Ink** ➤ _____ _____ _____ _____
(Street) (Town) (Postal Zone) (State)

B **Co-Buyer Signs in Ink** ➤ _____ _____ _____ _____
(Street) (Town) (Postal Zone) (State)

Seller Signs in Ink ➤ _____ By _____ _____
(Title) (Address)

Undersigned hereby acknowledges receipt from seller of a true, correct and complete copy of this conditional
sale contract at time of execution, and represents that the purchase of said property hereunder is (not)* for use only
for personal or family purposes. *Cross out if not applicable.

Buyer Signs _____ Co-Buyer Signs _____

Source: General Motors Acceptance Corporation.

153

ANNUAL COSTS OF OWNING AND OPERATING A CAR

	Estimated Figures Annual Mileage_____		Actual Figures Annual Mileage_____	
	Cost per year	Cost per mile	Cost per year	Cost per mile
1. Depreciation				
Fixed Costs				
2. Instalment Payments				
3. Insurance				
4. License Fees				
5. Garage Rent				
6. Total *Fixed Costs*				
Flexible Costs				
7. Gasoline				
8. Oil				
9. Tires				
10. Maintenance (including repairs)				
11. Miscellaneous				
12. Total *Flexible Costs*				
ANNUAL CAR COSTS (Total lines 1, 6, and 12)				
MONTHLY CAR COSTS For Depreciation (Divide amount in line 1 by 12 months)				
For Fixed Costs (Divide amount in line 6 by 12 months)				
For Flexible Costs (Divide amount in line 12 by 12 months)				
TOTAL MONTHLY COSTS				

Source: Taken from "Money Management: Your Automobile Dollar," published by the Money Management Institute of Household Finance Corp., Chicago, Ill., 1963, p. 27.

Depreciation

Very little can be added to what has been said about depreciation earlier in this chapter. There is no specific formula for calculating depreciation. It varies with the number of years the car is owned, with its appearance and condition, and with the make and price of the car on which the present car is traded. It is one of the most difficult costs to determine accurately, and 20 per cent per year is often used as a rough estimate.

Fixed Costs

The monthly instalment payment is a fixed cost until the contract is paid. Garage rent is a fixed cost. The amount depends upon the car owner's particular situation, and will vary according to the locality in which he lives. Insurance is a fixed cost. Chapter 11 should be read for a complete discussion of automobile insurance.

How much are these fixed costs? Table 6–5 gives an interesting compilation of such figures. Notice that comparisons can be made according to three variables. First, as the city and state headings indicate, a comparison can be made between different locations. Second, a comparison can be made between a medium size sedan and a compact, by comparing figures presented in the top half of the table for each city with those presented in the bottom half for the same city. Third, the effect of mileage can be seen by examining the breakdown according to mileage, presented at the bottom of each half of the table.

Fixed costs decrease, per mile, as the mileage increases. For example, the cost of a driver's license remains the same, regardless of the miles traveled. This, as you can see, is equally true of the contract payments, garage rent, insurance premiums, license fees, and taxes.

Before leaving fixed costs, a brief reminder might be helpful. Most of the taxes paid on automobile use are deductible from the owner's income tax. Table 6–6 is helpful in this connection. It indicates the amount that may be deducted for income tax purposes, (1) if the car is not used for business and (2) if the car is used for business. Also presented are various state charges, taxes, and fees, in effect in August of 1962. The "Tax Deduction Computer" applies to the federal income tax, and these rules can change, as can the specific state rates charged. For this reason, you should check federal tax laws and state rates annually.

Table 6–5

COST OF CAR OPERATION

ANNUAL FIXED CHARGES OF CAR OPERATION

CAR A - Medium size 4-door sedan. 8 cylinder motor. Cost $3800.00. Weight 4050 lbs. Used for business.

	Hartford, Conn.	Willimantic, Conn.	Lewiston, Maine	Boston, Mass.	Pittsfield, Mass.
Item 1. Insurance:					
Liability $10,000/$20,000 limits	$146.00	$ 72.00	$ 34.00	$ 185.15	$ 60.95
Property Damage	38.00	27.00	21.00	70.50	44.00
Fire & Theft (Comprehensive)	18.00	20.00	25.00	36.00	23.00
Collision ($50 deductible)	83.00	92.00	63.00	121.00	88.00
Item 2. Taxes:					
*Local taxes and sales tax, if any	55.00	59.00	46.55	103.95	103.95
Registration fee	10.00	10.00	15.00	6.00	6.00
Operator's license	3.00	3.00	2.00	2.50	2.50
Item 3. Depreciation @ 20 per cent	760.00	760.00	760.00	760.00	760.00
Item 4. **Maintenance and repairs	100.00	100.00	100.00	100.00	100.00
Total annual fixed charges	$ 1213.00	$ 1143.00	$ 1066.55	$ 1385.10	$ 1188.40
Cost per Day	$3.323	$3.132	$2.922	$3.795	$3.256

Cost Per Mile if Spread Over Indicated Annual Mileage (Includes 2.747¢ operating cost per mile.

For 5,000 miles annual mileage	27.007¢	25.607¢	24.078¢	30.449¢	26.515¢
For 10,000 " " "	14.877¢	14.177¢	13.412¢	16.598¢	14.631¢
For 15,000 " " "	10.834¢	10.367¢	9.857¢	11.981¢	10.670¢
For 20,000 " " "	8.812¢	8.462¢	8.080¢	9.672¢	8.689¢
For 25,000 " " "	7.599¢	7.319¢	7.013¢	8.287¢	7.501¢
For 30,000 " " "	6.790¢	6.557¢	6.302¢	7.364¢	6.708¢

*Local taxes include excise taxes and permit fees in Maine, Massachusetts, New Hampshire and local property taxes elsewhere.   Also included is the sales tax in Connecticut, Maine, Rhode Island and Vermont. Taxes are averaged over 5 years.

ANNUAL FIXED CHARGES OF CAR OPERATION

CAR B - Small (compact) 4-door sedan. 4 cylinder motor. Cost $2400.00. Weight 2470 lbs. Used for business.

	Hartford, Conn.	Willimantic, Conn.	Lewiston, Maine	Boston, Mass.	Pittsfield, Mass.
Item 1. Insurance:					
Liability $10,000/$20,000 limits	$131.40	$ 64.80	$ 31.00	$ 185.15	$60.95
Property Damage	34.20	24.30	19.00	70.50	44.00
Fire & Theft (Comprehensive)	12.00	13.00	16.00	24.00	15.00
Collision ($50 deductible)	55.00	62.00	42.00	90.00	65.00
Item 2. Taxes:					
*Local taxes and sales tax, if any	32.00	34.00	44.39	68.31	68.31
Registration fee	10.00	10.00	15.00	6.00	6.00
Operator's license	3.00	3.00	2.00	2.50	2.50
Item 3. Depreciation @ 20 per cent	480.00	480.00	480.00	480.00	480.00
**Item 4. **Maintenance and repairs	100.00	100.00	100.00	100.00	100.00
Total annual fixed charges	$ 857.60	$791.10	$ 749.39	$1026.46	$841.76
Cost per Day	$ 2.349	$ 2.167	$ 2.053	$2.812	$ 2.306

Cost Per Mile if Spread Over Indicated Annual Mileage (Includes 1.617¢ operating cost per mile.

For 5,000 miles annual mileage	18.769¢	17.439¢	16.605¢	22.146¢	18.452¢
For 10,000 " " "	10.193¢	9.528¢	9.111¢	11.882¢	10.035¢
For 15,000 " " "	7.334¢	6.891¢	6.613¢	8.460¢	7.229¢
For 20,000 " " "	5.905¢	5.572¢	5.364¢	6.749¢	5.826¢
For 25,000 " " "	5.047¢	4.781¢	4.614¢	5.723¢	4.984¢
For 30,000 " " "	4.476¢	4.254¢	4.115¢	5.039¢	4.423¢

*Local taxes include excise taxes and permit fees in Maine, Massachusetts, New Hampshire and local property taxes elsewhere. Also included is the sales tax in Connecticut, Maine, Rhode Island and Vermont. Taxes are averaged over 5 years.

No driver under 25. No accident record.

Manchester, N. H.	Newark, N. J.	Morristown, N. J.	Providence, R. I.	Westerly, R. I.	New York, N. Y.	Albany, N. Y.	Rutland, Vt.
$ 40.00	$ 132.00)	$ 66.00)	$ 105.70	$ 70.70	$ 204.00	$ 127.20	$ 58.00
22.00	)	)	38.00	26.00	39.00	36.00	28.00
21.00	36.00	21.00	33.00	33.00	45.00	20.00	23.00
38.00	117.00	75.00	135.00	81.00	135.00	83.00	81.00
32.20	0	0	56.00	52.00	23.00	10.00	22.00
15.50	25.00	25.00	17.00	17.00	28.50	28.50	32.00
2.00	3.00	3.00	4.00	4.00	1.00	1.00	2.50
760.00	760.00	760.00	760.00	760.00	760.00	760.00	760.00
100.00	100.00	100.00	100.00	100.00	100.00	100.00	100.00
$ 1030.70	$1173.00	$ 1050.00	$1248.70	$1143.70	$ 1335.50	$ 1165.70	$1106.50
$2.824	$3.214	$ 2.877	$ 3.421	$ 3.133	$3.659	$ 3.207	$ 3.194
23.361¢	26.207¢	23.747¢	27.721¢	25.621¢	29.457¢	26.061¢	24.877¢
13.054¢	14.477¢	13.247¢	15.234¢	14.184¢	16.102¢	14.404¢	13.812¢
9.618¢	10.567¢	9.747¢	11.071¢	10.371¢	11.650¢	10.517¢	10.124¢
7.900¢	8.612¢	7.997¢	8.990¢	8.466¢	9.424¢	8.575¢	8.279¢
6.870¢	7.439¢	6.947¢	7.741¢	7.322¢	8.089¢	7.410¢	7.173¢
6.183¢	6.657¢	6.247¢	6.909¢	6.559¢	7.199¢	6.633¢	6.435¢

**Replacements and repairs include such as battery, spark plugs, engine tune-up, etc.
The figure is an estimated average per year.

No driver under 25. No accident record.

Manchester, N. H.	Newark, N. J.	Morristown, N. J.	Providence, R. I.	Westerly, R. I.	New York, N. Y.	Albany, N. Y.	Rutland, Vt.
$ 40.00	$132.00)	$66.00)	$95.83	$ 64.23	$ 204.00	$ 127.20	$ 52.20
22.00	)	)	34.00	23.00	39.00	36.00	25.20
14.00	24.00	14.00	22.00	22.00	30.00	13.00	15.00
26.00	88.00	55.00	91.00	62.00	101.00	62.00	54.00
21.06	0	0	32.00	30.00	14.00	5.00	14.00
12.00	10.00	10.00	10.00	10.00	12.00	12.00	32.00
2.00	3.00	3.00	4.00	4.00	1.00	1.00	2.50
480.00	480.00	480.00	480.00	480.00	480.00	480.00	480.00
100.00	100.00	100.00	100.00	100.00	100.00	100.00	100.00
$717.06	$ 837.00	$ 728.00	$868.83	$795.23	$ 981.00	$ 836.20	$ 774.90
$ 1.964	$ 2.293	$ 1.994	$ 2.380	$2.179	$2.688	$ 2.291	$ 2.123
15.958¢	18.357¢	16.177¢	18.994¢	17.522¢	21.237¢	18.341¢	17.115¢
8.787¢	9.987¢	8.897¢	10.305¢	9.569¢	11.427¢	9.979¢	9.366¢
6.397¢	7.197¢	6.470¢	7.409¢	6.919¢	8.157¢	7.191¢	6.783¢
5.202¢	5.802¢	5.257¢	5.961¢	5.593¢	6.522¢	5.798¢	5.591¢
4.485¢	4.965¢	4.529¢	5.092¢	4.798¢	5.541¢	4.962¢	4.716¢
4.007¢	4.407¢	4.043¢	4.513¢	4.268¢	4.887¢	4.404¢	4.200¢

**Replacements and repairs include such as battery, spark plugs, engine tune-up, etc. The figure is an estimated average per year.

Source: Sidney S. Von Loesecke, "Cost of Car Operation, 1961," Automobile Legal Association, Boston, Massachusetts, pp. 2-3.

Table 6–6

TAX DEDUCTION COMPUTER

Jot down your deductible expenses in the spaces below and add them up. You may save money on April 15.

FAMILY CAR — NO BUSINESS USE*

Interest on car financing .... $_____

Casualty losses from accidents, theft, etc.,
    not recovered by insurance... _____

Taxes:
    Gasoline (____gal. x____tax/gal.).. _____
Registration fee... _____
Driver's license.. _____
Sales or use tax.. _____
Annual tax.. _____

                                                        TOTAL $_____

CAR USED FOR BUSINESS**

Operating costs (including gasoline, oil and lubrication, tires,
    washing, repairs, antifreeze, garaging, parking and road tolls)...... $_____
Title and inspection fees.. _____
Insurance .... _____
Depreciation... _____

                    TOTAL (incl. nonbusiness total) $_____

*Deduction for nonbusiness use may be claimed only if you itemize your deductions.
**If car is used for both business and pleasure, deductions for business use should be only
  that proportion of total mileage driven on business.

———

Source: "Buyer's Digest of New Car Facts for 1963," Ford Division of
          Ford Motor Company, Detroit, Michigan, p. 67.

Flexible Costs

The cost per mile, calculated in Table 6–5, was calculated by adding total annual fixed charges and a cost per mile figure obtained from the following table:

Table 6–7

OPERATING COST PER MILE [14]

	Car A	Car B
Gasoline	2.260¢*	1.156¢**
Grease every 1,000 miles	.150	.150
Oil change every 2,000 miles	.163	.163
Tire cost	.667	.533
	3.240¢	2.002¢

 * High test @ 33.9¢ per gallon
 ** Regular @ 28.9¢ per gallon

———

[14] Sidney S. Von Loesecke, "Cost of Car Operation, 1961," Automobile Legal Association, Boston, Massachusetts, p. 1.

Thus, for the medium size sedan in Hartford, Conn., the 29.748¢ per mile for an annual mileage of 5,000 miles was calculated by:

1. Multiplying 5,000 times 3.24 = $162.
2. Adding the $162 to the total annual fixed charges ($162 plus $1,325.40 equals $1,487.40).
3. Dividing this $1,487.40 by 5,000 miles.

Actually, maintenance could be considered either a fixed or a flexible cost. It is not a fixed total amount regardless of the number of miles traveled, as are garage costs and license fees. On the other hand, it does not remain the same per mile, as do gasoline and oil. This is why it was included under the general heading of flexible costs in the form suggested for use in keeping records of costs, while it is included under fixed charges in the table on Cost of Car Operation.

Maintenance costs can be separated into two categories. The cost of items such as battery and spark plugs can be estimated with some degree of accuracy, based upon manufacturers' life tests or suggested replacement periods. The cost of maintenance expenses such as repairs cannot be estimated as accurately, as they depend upon many variables. Some idea of the frequency with which such repairs are needed is indicated by the following table:

		1962		*1961*	
	Type Service	*Number*	*Per Cent*	*Number*	*Per Cent*
1.	Battery & Electrical	18,342,000	26.69	16,541,000	25.41
2.	Tire	12,768,000	18.58	12,746,000	19.58
3.	Ignition	9,992,000	14.54	8,795,000	13.51
4.	Tow and Wrecker	9,538,000	13.88	8,325,000	12.79
5.	Stuck (mud, snow)	3,697,000	5.38	4,316,000	6.63
6.	Starter	3,464,000	5.04	3,229,000	4.96
7.	Out of Gas	2,240,000	3.26	2,356,000	3.62
8.	Carburetor	1,691,000	2.46	2,044,000	3.14
9.	Gas Line	1,065,000	1.55	723,000	1.11
10.	Lock and Key	728,000	1.06	755,000	1.16
11.	Brakes	522,000	.76	963,000	1.48
12.	Lights	385,000	.56	176,000	.27
13.	All others	4,289,000	6.24	4,127,000	6.34
		68,721,000	100.00	65,096,000	100.00

Passenger cars registered 1962—65,077,000
Passenger cars registered 1961—62,596,000

Source: "Starting Troubles—Major Cause for Motoring Woes in 1962, AAA Reports," *AAA News Service,* a projection based on the reports from their affiliated clubs, American Automobile Association, Washington, D.C.

These figures were obtained by the American Automobile Association and are estimates for all passenger cars in the United States, based upon reports of garages under contract with the American Automobile Association to render emergency road service to its members.

Repair costs can be reduced by paying careful attention to the frequency of oil changes, the quality of oil used, the use of proper anti-freeze, wheel alignment, and other maintenance items. The few dollars saved by scrimping on such items may mean more dollars spent in the long run.

Savings can be realized, too, through proper tire care. Keeping them properly inflated, avoiding sudden stops and starts and cutting corners, avoiding the excessive use of brakes, and maintaining proper wheel alignment and balance can save money. Rotating tires also increases their length of life.

According to the Bureau of Public Roads, the average number of miles traveled by a passenger car in 1960 was 9,446. Average gasoline consumption was 661 gallons per car. Average miles traveled per gallon was 14.28.

Gasoline economy is measured by the cost per mile, not by the miles per gallon. The same number of miles per gallon in a car using regular gasoline is less expensive, per mile, than the same mileage in a car requiring premium gas.

Total Costs

Cost estimates will vary from year to year. In 1961, Mr. E. M. Cope, Chief of the Research Statistics Staff of the U.S. Department of Commerce, Bureau of Public Roads, and Mr. L. L. Liston, Head of the Motor Fuel and Registration Section, estimated total costs of a 1960 vehicle at 9.76 cents per mile.[15] In 1963, Mr. Cope estimated the costs at 10.1 cents a mile.[16] According to Mr. Cope, the general increase in prices in the United States during the two year span between the two studies accounts for most of the difference.[17]

It seems obvious, however, that in any year, lowest operating costs will be obtained by those drivers who keep their vehicles properly serviced, and adopt good driving habits.

---

[15] Edwin M. Cope and Laurence L. Liston, "A Discussion of Gasoline Tax Rates and Gasoline Consumption," *Highway Research Board Proceedings*, Vol. 40, 1961, p. 51.

[16] Edwin M. Cope, "The Price is Right," *American Road Builder*, American Road Builders Association, Washington, D.C., Feb. 1963, p. 4.

[17] Letter from Mr. Edwin M. Cope, March 7, 1963.

CONCLUSION & SUMMARY

When buying a car:
1. Know your dealers.
2. Know your needs.
3. Know what you can honestly afford. (Be practical!)
4. Shop for the best financing.
5. Select the car that best meets your needs and your pocketbook.
6. Select one or more reliable dealers, and rely upon their good judgment to find the car that is best for *you.*
7. *Don't* shop every used car lot for "bargains." Such buys are rarely bargains.
8. Think! Don't buy on impulse.

Questions

1. "The choice of a car depends on the use it will be put to." Discuss.

2. What specific information is necessary to compare prices quoted by several automobile dealers on the same make and model car?

3. The "net" amount you must pay for a new car will usually be less if you sell your old car yourself than if you trade it in on the new car. Why?

4. Compare the advantages of buying a new car with those of buying a used car.

5. How many years should an automobile be kept before trading it in?

6. How do finance rates charged by commercial banks compare with those charged when an automobile is financed through an automobile dealer?

7. Banks have found that, among other things, the likelihood of a borrower making regular payments on an automobile loan depends on the owner's equity in the car. Discuss.

8. Differentiate between the fixed and flexible costs of driving an automobile.

9. The cost of driving an automobile varies depending on the number of miles driven, the size of the car, and the city in which the car is garaged. Discuss.

10. Which driving costs are tax deductible:
    a. If a car is not used for business?
    b. If a car is used for business?

Problems

1. Mr. Andrews and Mr. Zilch have for many years purchased identical cars. Who gets the best deal has become a matter of considerable importance. In their most recent purchases, Mr. Andrews was given a trade-in of $2,000 on his old car and paid a balance in cash of $1,800. Mr. Zilch was given a trade-in of $1,700 on his old car and paid a balance of $1,700. Mr. Andrews claims that he got the best deal because he was given a higher trade-in on his old car. Mr. Zilch claims his deal was best because the new car will cost him $100 less in cash than Mr. Andrew's car. Who is right?

2. Mr. Buckley wants to buy a new car. He does not have a car to trade in. A local dealer who has been in business for many years and has an excellent reputation in the community quotes him a price of $3,300. In the Sunday paper, Mr. Buckley sees the following advertisement for the identical car.

> ### Cleaning out stock
> Automobile Agency—Mom's—Two brand new .... cars still on the lot. $3,150 takes one away. No money down. Five years to pay. Highest trade-in allowance. Take advantage of our money back four year warranty. Ask for Mom and have free coffee and doughnuts.

Mr. Buckley decides to buy at Mom's. His reasoning is that he can get the identical car for $150 less. Why not save the money — especially when the warranty is so generous? What do you think of his decision?

3. Sally is buying an $800 used car from the "Super Used Car Company." She is going to pay $300 down and the used car company has agreed to arrange financing for the remaining $500. She is in a

hurry and the salesman says to give him the $300 and sign the contract. He will fill in the blanks in the contract later to save time. Should she take his suggestion?

4. Using Table 6-5 explain how the cost per mile of 5.946 for driving a compact car an annual mileage of 20,000 miles in Morristown, New Jersey, was calculated.

5. Mr. Dennis wants to keep driving costs as low as possible. He plans to trade cars every three years. He decides to change oil once a year, use the least expensive oil, and spend no money on maintenance unless it is absolutely necessary. He reasons that as he only plans to keep the car three years it will last that long without "babying." Future troubles will be the new owner's problem. Is his reasoning correct?

Selected Readings

"Automobile Facts & Figures," published annually by the Automobile Manufacturers Association, Detroit, Michigan

"Buyer's Digest of New Car Facts," published annually by Ford Division, Ford Motor Co., Detroit, Michigan

"Buying New or Used Cars," Association of Better Business Bureaus, 405 Lexington Ave., New York 17, New York (or local Better Business Bureau)

"Care for Your Car for Safe Driving," Chrysler Corporation, Automotive Safety Engineering Office, Detroit, Michigan, 1963

Frome, Michael, *1001 Ways to Enjoy Your Car*, Popular Library, Inc., New York, N. Y., 1962

Jung, Allen F., "Charges for Appliance and Automobile Instalment Credit in Major Cities," *The Journal of Business*, The Graduate School of Business of the University of Chicago, The University of Chicago Press, Chicago, Illinois, October 1962

"Money Management: Your Automobile Dollar," Money Management Institute, Household Finance Corporation, Prudential Plaza, Chicago 1, Illinois

Von Loesecke, Sidney S., "Cost of Car Operation," American Legal Association, Boston, Mass., 1961

"Your Driving Costs," American Automobile Association, Washington, D.C., 1963-64 Edition

Chapter **7**

COLLEGE COSTS

It wasn't too many years ago, in the United States, that the highest educational objective was a high school diploma. A small percentage of the population went to college, and most of those were males. Today, things are quite different. In 1940, about 15 per cent of the 18-21 year olds went to college. By 1970, it is estimated that about 50 per cent will go to college. In 1960, total college enrollment was about 3,500,000; the estimate for 1970 is seven million.

164

The question that haunts many parents is whether or not their children will go to college. The answer is—

Yes . . .

> *If* they graduate from high school or preparatory school with something better than a "scrape-by" record.

> *If* they apply to the college or university that is right for them— aiming their sights (and their application forms) neither too high nor too low, but with an individuality and precision made possible by sound guidance both in school and in their homes.

> *If* America's colleges and universities can find the resources to carry out their plans to meet the huge demand for higher education that is certain to exist in this country for years to come.[1]

Going to College

There are many reasons why a person should go to college. Chapter I—Earning a Living—emphasized the financial advantages enjoyed by college graduates. Another reason is the personal satisfaction to be gained by making the most of one's abilities. The ability to broaden your knowledge, develop your talents, assume leadership, and increase your understanding of your fellow men, your nation, and the world, are all part of this intangible benefit of a college education.

A third reason is competition. If more and more young people are going to college, it becomes certain that a college degree is going to be a necessary "ticket" to job opportunities.

A fourth reason is technological development. More and more jobs are becoming so complicated that a great deal of training is necessary. An examination of job opportunities indicates that those which seem to be the "best," in terms of financial return and working conditions, require a college degree.

A fifth reason why many go to college is because of their parents' wishes. Able high school students often fail to appreciate the advantages of a college education. Their parents do, and can and should apply the necessary "push" to give their children the benefit of these advantages.

However, this "push" should be given very careful consideration by the parents. Before taking action, they should take inventory of

---

[1] "The College of Tomorrow," Editorial Projects for Education, Inc., Washington, D.C., Copyright © 1962, p. 1.

the child's aptitude for higher learning, and mental attitude toward going to college. There are young people who should not attend college because their interests are completely incompatible with a college education. To force such a person to attend college is to make his future less promising, not more so. His or her talents may lie in directions where a college degree is not necessary, and greater success, in every sense of the word, will probably be achieved if these talents are nurtured. Fortunately, the number of students who are forced to attend college when it isn't in their best interest, seems small.

A sixth reason is love of education. There is always a small group of intellectuals, too small perhaps, who attend college because they enjoy education. They love to study, and will probably study and learn in one way or another, for the rest of their lives.

A seventh reason is patriotism.

> Thinking men and women will continue to be the most important weapon in the arsenal of the free world.[2]

The need for rocket experts, mathematicians, physicists, doctors, and scientists in various fields, is obvious. Often forgotten, however, is the fact that teachers, business leaders, poets, are equally essential for a strong, free, productive country. The important need is for people who can "think," regardless of the field. While there seems to be considerable doubt that college can teach anyone how to think, it can help those with this ability to use it more efficiently, skillfully, and deeply.

What About You?

When deciding on a college career, your first step should be not to ask what the college can do for you but what you can do for the college. With the numbers of applicants increasing at a rapid rate, any one individual is certainly not going to be needed by a college simply to get his tuition payments. Why should the college accept you?

Basically, the answer boils down to ability. Colleges want "able" students, those who can grasp the education offered and benefit from it. A student who is unable to handle the material, and holds his classmates back, is a detriment.

Unfortunately, it is difficult to determine ability in advance. Inability to do so is certainly one reason for the large percentage of

---

[2] "Facing Facts About College Costs," The Prudential Insurance Company of America, 1960, p. 5.

those entering college who do not graduate. This inability to judge accurately is also the reason some able students are not admitted to colleges of their choice.

It would certainly be helpful if college applicants could be placed in a machine which would accurately measure their ability. On pushing a button, a light would flash under either "yes" or "no," and the prospective student would then either be admitted or not admitted. However, no such machine has been invented and no 100 per cent sure way exists to measure ability. Colleges place considerable reliance on high school grades, and your chances of being admitted into college are much better if grades are high. Class standing is also important.

Admission examinations supplement high school grades because school systems vary so greatly that complete reliance cannot be placed on grades alone. All A's in one school system might be the equivalent of all C's in another, and vice versa. It would be unfair to admit the student with all A's from an "easy marking" school system, and not admit the student with somewhat lower grades from a "tough marking" school system. Tests provide an opportunity to assess the applicants on a more equal basis.

High school grades and test scores are admittedly far from perfect indications of ability, but at least they are guides. Besides these, colleges rely upon recommendations from high school counselors and teachers, personal interviews, etc.

The point is, you must have something to offer before a college, faced with more applicants than it can handle, can afford to accept you. Each prospective student must examine his characteristics, abilities and interests, to determine whether or not he is really college material.

Selecting a College

If a person is a good student, there will be an opportunity to attend a choice of colleges. In general, the better the student, the greater the number of colleges from which he can choose.

Selecting a college because of its "prestige," or because your parents went there, is a poor way to make a selection. Searching for a list, or a person who can tell you which colleges are "good" and which are "bad," is futile. No such list exists, and no qualified person would be willing to make such a distinction. One college may be "good" for one person and "bad" for another.

The basic reason for going to college is to learn. The basic question, then, is, "Where can I learn what I want to know?" College curricula must be examined to find those which offer the courses wanted, and those which have the most competent faculties. Other factors which must be considered are:

1. The general reputation of the college. Do students go there for enjoyment or learning?
2. Its scholastic requirements. Are its standards so high that you don't have a chance of being accepted?
3. The available facilities. How are the libraries, laboratories, etc.?
4. The cost. While this shouldn't be the prime determinant, it must be considered.
5. Location. A decision must be made between living at home or away from home.

Now these aren't the only factors, but they are important ones. The answers, especially to the question of courses and faculty, are complicated. This is especially true in some fields. How do parents and students find out where the best physics, chemistry, or mathematics programs are given, for example? Some information can be gained by reading, but with the tremendous number of colleges to choose from, it can't provide the complete answer to the problem.

Thousands of rejection slips are mailed to young people each year. Many of these young people would have been cheerfully accepted if they had applied to a college which was either better suited to their needs and aptitude or had received fewer applications. The problem is matching the right college with the right person. This calls for considerable reliance upon high school guidance counselors, college and university admissions people, and college catalogues.

One factor which will probably gain increased importance is the nonprofit college application clearing house. At the present time, high school seniors and transfer students who have not been accepted by a college can get information from the College Admissions Center, 610 Church Street, Evanston, Illinois; the College Admissions Assistance Center, 41 East 65th Street, New York 21, New York 10021; or the Catholic College Information and Admissions Center, Assumption College, Worcester, Massachusetts. These centers have, for a small registration fee, done an excellent job of bringing students looking for colleges and colleges looking for students together.

Another word might well be said about the high school guidance counselor. The field of guidance counseling is relatively new, and guidance counselors vary in ability. However, a well trained person in this position can be an invaluable asset to the future of the students, and if his importance is appreciated, a community will make the same effort to acquire competent guidance counselors that it makes to acquire competent teachers.

COSTS

One thing is fairly certain—people just do not realize what a college education costs, until they are faced with the necessity of paying for it. Studies indicate that, on the average, those parents planning to send their children to college have saved a ridiculously small amount of money. As with any large expenditure of money, the further in advance it can be planned, the better. For this reason, it may be advisable to spend some time emphasizing the costs involved in a college education. If they are sufficiently emphasized, they may encourage people to plan ahead.

The Great Change

Parents fail to realize the costs involved possibly because costs have changed so radically since the parents went to college. Let's consider an average young man who is to enter college in 1970. He plans to attend the same college his father went to in 1945. In 1945, it cost his father $5,400 for tuition, fees, room and board, for four years at one of the nation's Ivy League colleges. In 1962, it would cost $10,660 to cover the same expenses at the same college for four years. This is an increase of almost 100 per cent in seventeen years. What will the cost be in 1970?

It is obviously impossible to quote figures for all of the colleges in the United States. The costs quoted in the above example were and are above average. The general relationship, however, is correct. One way, then, to make a rough estimate is to determine the cost of attending some specific college in the early 1960's, and increase this cost by 50 per cent for 1970 and by 100 per cent for 1980.

College costs in 1963 averaged a little more than $6,000 for four years. Estimates of these costs for 1970 go as high as $15,000 and by 1980, $20,000. Notice that these are averages. Costs vary considerably from college to college and, of course, no one can predict the future with perfect accuracy. Nevertheless, the general trend of college costs is clearly upward.

Costs Included

Actually, an estimate of $15,990 ($10,660 + 50%) for sending John to his father's college for four years would be too low. It would include only tuition, fees, room and board. A person will receive a rude awakening if these are the only costs included in such estimates.

The Budget Schedules form below may be used to compare the costs of attending three different colleges. Typical amounts allowed for personal expenses are presented at the left of the table.

— BUDGET SCHEDULES —

Use these check-lists to determine the approximate expenses you may expect to pay *for one year* at colleges of your choice. The figures arrived at multiplied by the number of years your child expects to remain in school will be your Education Fund Goal Amount.

		1st choice	2nd choice	3rd choice
Basic College Expenses	Name of school			
		(enter estimated expenses here)		
Tuition, fees				
Books, supplies				
Room, board				
Expenses (sub-total) ➡				

Studies show most students spend these amounts

Personal Expenses
(Items often overlooked when preparing a yearly college budget.)

($200)	Clothing			
(150)	Travel			
(150)	Recreation, entertainment			
(105)	Snacks, refreshments, etc.			
(75)	Health & grooming			
(65)	Dues and contributions			
(50)	Laundry			
(40)	Miscellaneous			

Personal Expenses sub-total ➡

Add Basic Expenses sub-total ➡

Total cost, one year of college

Education Fund Goal Amount

(Cost of one year of college X

number of school years)

Source: "Dollars for Scholars," The First National Bank of Boston, Boston, Mass., Copyright © 1962, p. 4.

Such estimates vary, of course, according to the individual, the location of the college, and the college itself. The cost of clothing, for example, will vary with the personal needs and tastes of each individual, as between urban colleges and campus colleges, those in cold climates and those in warm, and those attended primarily by students from moderate income families as compared to those attended primarily by students from high income families.

Most colleges are cooperative in providing information concerning Basic College Expenses, as called for at the top of the form. By adding these to estimated Personal Expenses, the cost of attending each college for one year is obtained. Multiplying this figure by the number of years will produce the total amount needed to cover the costs of a college education in each college. According to many colleges with tuitions of about $1,000 per year in 1962, a total amount of $10,000 per child should be planned for a four year education.

Cutting Costs

It is impossible for colleges to cut costs. Faculty salaries must be increased to attract competent teachers. Building and maintenance costs are constantly increasing, research facilities become increasingly expensive and expansive, new books are constantly required for the library, and administrative costs continue to rise. All expenditures are affected by rising costs in the economy as a whole.

Can students cut costs? The answer here is "maybe." Living at home and commuting to college saves a considerable amount of money, although it deprives the student of a part of the educational experience which most educators think is quite valuable. Attending a tax supported institution is usually less expensive than attending a private one. Attending a college with a co-operative plan of education, where students alternate periods of work and study, will permit the student to earn a considerable portion of education costs. All of these things will help, but the fact remains, costs are going to continue to rise, in all probability.

Not only are costs going to continue to rise, but tuitions are going to have to cover a larger portion of total college costs. Tax support, endowment income, and contributions are not increasing and probably will not increase as fast as the expenses of operating a college. Many people do not realize that tuitions have paid only a part of the cost of education. In many colleges, they have paid less than half. This means that other sources of income have made up the difference. There is little likelihood that these other sources will increase at any rate comparable to college costs.

PAYING THE BILL

Where are students and families to get money to meet the rising cost of college? The major sources are:

1. Parents
   a. From current income
   b. From savings
2. Students themselves
   a. From savings
   b. From current income
3. Scholarships
4. Loans

Parents

A considerable portion of the average college student's costs are undoubtedly going to have to be met by parents. In many cases, part of the money will have to come from current income. Very few families can spend an additional $1,000 or more out of their annual net income for four years, without feeling the pinch. This means that either other expenditures must be cut or family income increased. This may mean that the father may have to find extra work or that the mother may have to go to work. Obviously, the better method is to save money in advance to meet this need.

There are three primary ways of saving money to finance college costs. To be successful, all three must be started early. One of these is to invest in either common stocks, mutual funds, or bonds (see Chapters 14, 15 and 16). This savings plan should receive careful consideration if a person has adequate insurance and liquid savings. If stock prices rise during the sixties as rapidly as they rose during the fifties, equity investments will prove to be the best savings method of all. The only problem is the "if." What if they don't rise this rapidly, or even decline? For safety's sake, considerable reliance must be placed on more certain forms of savings.

Buying high grade corporate bonds yielding 4½ per cent or tax exempt municipal bonds at 3½ percent would require investing $520 per year for 16 years to establish a $10,000 fund for education. This method of investing is much more secure than equities.

Mutual funds have performed remarkably well during the past ten years. Whether they will continue to do so during the next ten, no one can state for certain. As relative safety, growth, and other comparative advantages vary from one type of fund to another, those

Table 7–1

STRAIGHT SAVINGS PROGRAM

For a:
FOUR YEAR
EDUCATION
PLAN*

With the:
FINAL PAYMENT
JANUARY OF FINAL
SCHOOL YEAR

USING the following chart and Goal Amounts, you can quickly approximate the monthly payment necessary to reach a given Goal Amount under the Straight Savings program. The top line of figures in the chart shows the *number* of months from the start of your program to the time the student will enter school. The second line shows, for each of the periods on the top line, the *number* of monthly payments needed to complete your entire program. The lower part of the chart shows the *amounts* of monthly payments required for the various terms and Goal Amounts.

In *all* Straight Savings programs you get back more than you pay because of the generous interest credited to your account on your payments as they accumulate.

Months Before School Begins	72	60	48	36	24	12
Total Number Monthly Payments**	113	101	89	77	65	53
Goal Amount	MONTHLY PAYMENTS					
$ 1,000	$ 8	$ 9	$ 11	$ 12	$ 15	★
2,000	17	19	22	25	30	★
3,000	26	29	33	38	46	★
4,000	35	39	44	51	61	$ 75
5,000	43	49	56	64	76	94
6,000	52	59	67	77	92	113
7,000	60	68	78	90	107	132
8,000	69	78	89	103	123	150
9,000	77	88	101	116	138	169
10,000	86	97	112	129	153	188
11,000	95	107	123	142	168	207
12,000	103	116	134	155	183	226
13,000	111	126	145	167	198	244
14,000	120	135	156	180	213	262
15,000	128	145	166	193	228	281

TO HELP YOU CALCULATE YOUR MONTHLY PAYMENT:

	1st Choice	2nd Choice	3rd Choice
Months before School Begins	_____	_____	_____
Total number Monthly Payments	_____	_____	_____
Goal amount	_____	_____	_____
Monthly payment (indicated above)	_____	_____	_____

* Charts are available for 3, 2 or 1 year of school at any office of *The* FIRST.
** To January of the fourth year of school.

Source: "Dollar for Scholars," The First National Bank of Boston, Boston, Mass., Copyright © 1962, p. 5.

Table 7–2

Reproduced, Courtesy of John Hancock Mutual Life Insurance Company, Boston, Mass.

interested in them as a form of saving for a college education should read Chapter 16.

A second method of saving is to accumulate money in the bank. Many banks have established savings programs similar to the one described in Table 7–1. The sooner the saving begins, the smaller the amount that must be set aside each month. For example, if $10,000 is needed, and a person started saving six years before college entrance, $86 per month must be saved.

Savings of $10 per week, deposited in a bank which pays 4½ per cent interest, compounded quarterly, will accumulate to a total of $10,000 in about 15 years.

A third method is to include the needed money for education in the family's life insurance program. This is more thoroughly discussed in Chapters 9 and 10. This method insures the availability of the necessary funds at the time they are needed, regardless of what happens to the income producer. As Table 7–2 indicates, this is an important advantage. Most insurance companies have plans which provide for regular payments for college expenses throughout the college years. Two large payments are made per year, to cover tuition, and smaller payments are made throughout the year to cover other expenses.

Parents who are in a high tax bracket should consult their lawyer, accountant, or local bank specializing in trust management. Important tax advantages are possible by the proper use of temporary trusts, but such trusts must run for a minimum number of years, so, again, it is necessary to plan early. Under such a plan, property is placed in a temporary trust for the benefit of the children. Income is distributed annually to the children, tax free, as long as it is less than their $600 income tax exemption. At the end of a specified period of time, the trust ends and the property returns to the parent.

Students

Many students manage to save a portion of their own college funds by working before entering college.

> *Students think early of college.* 29% of junior high school boys and 22% of girls were saving for an education. Among senior school boys, percentage jumped to 39% and among girls to 29%.[3]

---

[3] "Finance Facts," National Consumer Finance Association, Educational Services Division, Washington, D.C., November 1962, p. 1.

Some students postpone entering college for a year or two to obtain the necessary funds for college. Others earn money during vacations.

Working part-time while attending college is another possibility. How much of this can be done depends upon the individual, his college program, and the location of the college. Some individuals can work more than others and still get good grades, but too much part-time work will affect grades and prevent the student from getting the full benefit of his educational experience. Some college programs require more hours of study than others. If the college is located in a small community, job opportunities may well be insufficient to meet the needs of all the students interested. It is estimated that a reasonable amount of part-time work will pay the cost of the student's board.

Another method is to attend a college operating on a cooperative plan of education. Under such a plan, students alternate periods of work and periods of study. About 90 colleges in the United States permit students to follow some plan of alternating work and study. The largest cooperative education program in the country is at Northeastern University in Boston, Massachusetts, and this might well be used as an example. Here, the college program is five years. During their freshman year, students attend college full time. During their four upper class years they alternate periods of work and study, attending college for two ten week terms and one five week term and working for two ten week periods and one five week period, each year. This enables students to earn a considerable part of the costs of their college education. One department in the University is responsible for student placement and makes every effort to place them in positions in their selected field, such work contributing practical experience to their educational objectives. Other colleges have different periods of work and study, but operate in a similar manner. Among these are Antioch College in Ohio, Drexel Institute of Technology, the University of Cincinnati in Ohio, and the University of Detroit in Michigan.

Scholarships

Many parents assume their child may obtain a scholarship. It's a fair assumption. Their child may. However, there just aren't enough scholarships to go around, and the assumption should never be set down as a dollars and cents part of the financial planning.

The word "scholarship" is a little old-fashioned. The new term "grant" is much more accurate. "Scholarship" denotes an award made

Table 7-3

Summary of Applicants and Awards to Enrolled Freshmen for 313 Colleges Participating in the College Scholarship Service — by Region

Region	No. of Colleges			Total No. of Applicants for Freshman Class	No. of Applicants for Aid for Freshman Class	Total Fresh. Enroll.	Enrolled Freshmen Receiving Aid		No. of Fresh. Aid Applicants Enrld. Without Aid
	Private	Public	Total				No.	% Fresh. Enrold.	
New England	33	2	35	65,071	17,865	17,457	3,704	21.2%	2,327
Middle States	89	11	100	160,374	54,626	48,828	13,639	27.9%	8,143
Southern	33	7	40	41,083	9,113	16,671	4,256	25.5%	1,867
North Central	93	10	103	112,593	30,625	63,780	14,871	23.2%	9,825
Western	20	4	24	24,341	6,464	10,545	1,918	18.2%	1,197
Northwestern	8	3	11	11,612	3,463	8,100	1,228	15.2%	1,337
TOTAL	276	37	313	415,074	122,156	165,421	39,526	23.9%	24,696

Source: Summary Report of the College Scholarship Service Survey of Financial Aid Awards to 1962–63 Freshmen in 313 Colleges and Universities, prepared in mimeograph form by the College Scholarship Service, New York, N. Y., July 20, 1963, Table I, p. 2. Reprinted with the permission of the College Entrance Examination Board and the College Scholarship Service.

Table 7-4

Summary of Dollars Awarded by 313 Colleges by Type of Award

Type of Award	Dollars Awarded	Percent of Total Dollars Awarded
SCHOLARSHIPS	$14,713,861	61.5
JOBS	3,004,814	12.6
LOANS	6,187,976	25.9
TOTAL	$23,906,651	100.0

Source: Summary Report of the College Scholarship Service Survey of Financial Aid Awards to 1962–63 Freshmen in 313 Colleges and Universities, prepared in mimeograph form by the College Scholarship Service, New York, N. Y., July 20, 1963, Table III, p. 3. Reprinted with the permission of the College Entrance Examination Board and the College Scholarship Service.

on the basis of outstanding scholastic performance, while the typical scholarship today denotes a grant made on the basis of scholastic achievement and need. If one student gets a larger scholarship than another, the difference may be attributable to a difference in need, rather than to a difference in scholastic achievement.

Table 7–3 indicates several important points. Compare first the figure representing "Total No. of Applicants for Freshman Class" with those representing "Total Freshman Enrollment." This indicates the sizable number of applications who either are not accepted or are accepted but decide to attend another university. Next, look at the column indicating the "% of Enrolled Freshmen Receiving Aid." The average is 23.9%. Furthermore, "Aid" in this case doesn't mean just scholarships. Table 7–4 indicates the general breakdown of funds between scholarships, jobs, and loans.

Table 7–5 indicates the type of awards that are made, the percentage of each type made in different areas of the country, and the average amount awarded in dollars.

It should be realized, too, that scholarship funds are concentrated in colleges.

> Most college-controlled scholarship funds—altogether amount to approximately $100 million annually—are held by a small group of private colleges. Three percent of all colleges in the United States control more than one-third of all scholarship funds. Most of these institutions have high tuition charges, so that even with scholarship help the recipient may have to pay more at one of these schools than at a State or other lower cost educational institution.[4]

It is up to parents and students to do a considerable amount of research concerning scholarship availability. Besides need and scholastic ability, many scholarships have other requirements such as place of birth or residence, membership of the student or parent in some organization, etc. One scholarship, established by a will in 1962, makes money available to a person of a particular religious faith, who doesn't smoke or drink, who lives within a ten mile radius of a particular city, and who is acceptable to a specific college.

Colleges themselves are excellent sources of information of this type. In the United States, the Office of Education publishes a con-

---

[4] S. Norman Feingold, "Latest Information on Scholarships in the Space Age," *Occupational Outlook Quarterly*, Bureau of Labor Statistics, U.S. Department of Labor, Washington, D.C., September 1962, reprint, p. 2.

Table 7–5
Financial Aid Awards to Entering Freshmen in 1962 by Region

Type of Award	NEW ENGLAND (35 colleges)		MIDDLE STATES (100 colleges)		SOUTHERN (40 colleges)		NORTH CENTRAL (103 colleges)		WESTERN (24 colleges)		NORTHWESTERN (11 colleges)	
	Percent of Total Awards	Mean of Dollars Awarded	Percent of Total Awards	Mean of Dollars Awarded	Percent of Total Awards	Mean of Dollars Awarded	Percent of Total Awards	Mean of Dollars Awarded	Percent of Total Awards	Mean of Dollars Awarded	Percent of Total Awards	Mean of Dollars Awarded
1 SCHOLARSHIP (only)	50.9	$763	37.5	$673	44.9	$464	42.9	$431	51.6	$618	39.7	$344
2 JOB (only)	4.6	348	20.8	260	10.6	209	10.1	302	9.9	142	10.6	818
3 LOAN (only)	15.9	516	20.1	503	13.9	514	10.6	579	28.4	619	13.1	483
4 SCHOLARSHIP AND JOB	6.0	1,191	3.4	1,024	4.7	670	7.4	741	2.5	817	5.9	579
5 SCHOLARSHIP AND LOAN	12.0	1,258	8.1	1,140	10.6	905	12.8	735	5.8	1,377	13.1	752
6 SCHOLARSHIP AND JOB AND LOAN	6.3	1,767	4.9	1,291	5.3	1,268	8.7	836	.7	1,404	8.8	927
7 JOB AND LOAN	.6	727	1.2	797	1.9	813	1.3	641	.5	1,275	1.4	801
8 JOB-OPTION OF LOAN	...	...	.1	499	.5	726	.2	654	.4	531	...	817
9 LOAN-OPTION OF JOB	...	...	...	800	.4	725	.4	574	...	...	2.8	817
10 SCHOLARSHIP-OPTION OF JOB	.6	1,113	.5	1,464	.9	848	1.1	759	...	...	2.1	526
11 SCHOLARSHIP-OPTION OF LOAN	2.9	1,327	2.9	1,122	3.9	702	1.8	840	.1	663	2.5	699
12 SCHOLARSHIP AND JOB-OPTION OF LOAN	...	...	.3	1,259	1.1	1,354	1.3	1,118	.1	713	...	...
13 SCHOLARSHIP AND LOAN-OPTION OF JOB	.2	992	.2	1,575	1.3	1,333	1.4	897	...	...	...	...
TOTAL	100.0		100.0		100.0		100.0		100.0		100.0	

Source: Summary Report of the College Scholarship Service Survey of Financial Aid Awards to 1962–63 Freshmen in 313 Colleges and Universities, prepared in mimeograph form by the College Scholarship Service, New York, N. Y., July 20, 1963, Table X, p. 9. Reprinted with the permission of the College Entrance Examination Board and the College Scholarship Service.

siderable amount of such information. In Canada, similar information can be obtained from the Information Services Division, Dominion Bureau of Statistics, Ottawa, Ontario. There are also scholarship directories available. While the total number of scholarships available is much less than the number of persons wanting them, they are made available by so many different sources that some opportunities are not made use of because the sources are not known. Among the many sources providing such funds are: industries, labor unions, states, The War Orphans' Educational Assistance Act, veterans organizations, religious groups, fraternal organizations, military academies — West Point, Annapolis, the Coast Guard Academy, and the Air Force Academy — and individual scholarships such as the aforementioned scholarship established by a will.

Many business firms offer tuition-refund plans. Under such plans the business firm refunds a part or all of the tuition paid by an employee who is attending classes part-time, or in some cases, the tuition of the employee's children.

Inasmuch as scholarships are awarded primarily on the basis of scholastic ability and need, the comparative needs of the applicants must be measured. Many of the questions on the application forms are designed to do this. A family is expected to contribute some percentage of its income for a child's education. How much will depend upon such things as the total income and the number of children in the family. Each applicant's financial need is the difference between the total annual cost of attending a particular college and the amount the parents and applicant are able to provide.

Loans

Many authorities now believe that there will be, and should be, a change in the general public attitude toward paying for a college education. Indeed, to some extent, this change has already taken place. The expense is now being classified as long term rather than short, and money can be borrowed and paid back over a period of years.

There are several methods of borrowing. One method, for example, would be to refinance a home mortgage. If a family has lived in the home for some length of time, a new mortgage loan might provide the necessary funds. This would be cheaper than consumer loans, in terms of interest cost. Another inexpensive method of borrowing is to borrow on a life insurance policy. Various borrowing methods were discussed in Chapter 5.

A fairly recent method of borrowing is to participate in a deferred tuition plan. Many colleges permit tuition payments to be made in instalments, sometimes stretching over a period of years after graduation.

Usually, however, the custom is to borrow under one of the many loan plans specifically devised to finance college costs. One of these is to borrow through the college or university financial aid program. Interest rates, available amounts of money, and other details vary from one college to another.

Commercial banks have devised various loan plans. One interesting plan combines savings and loan features. When the plan begins, during high school or earlier, the plan involves simply time deposits. Funds are accumulated in the account and interest is paid on the amount deposited at the current savings interest rate. When the student enters college, the bank starts to make tuition payments. Interest payments continue as long as there is a savings balance in the account. When the money saved is used up, the bank's own funds are used. The borrower pays interest on the money actually loaned by the bank, and continues to make the same regular payments to the bank, as he did while building the savings fund, all during college years and for two years thereafter.[5] Under such a plan, college costs may be spread over a period of as long as twelve years.

Under most plans of this type, credit life insurance covers the outstanding balance of the loan. This usually means that if the father dies the life insurance will cover the money already advanced to the college by the lender. Under the "Dollars for Scholars" plan, however, the customer's life is insured for the entire goal amount (up to $10,000) as soon as he signs up for the plan and makes his first payments. The "goal amount" is the sum he has stated he will need to put his child through college. This is considerably better than the usual practice of insuring only the currently outstanding balance of the loan.

Pages 182, 183, and 184 contain a summary of provisions of selected state, private, and federal higher education assistance programs. These are commonly known as student loan guaranty plans. Usually, commercial banks have played a role in these plans as sponsors or supporters, and loans are usually made through a bank. It might seem that banks would be unwilling to provide services of this type when they have their own educational loan plans. Actually, however, the two plans are quite different. Under a loan guaranty plan, the

---

[5] See "Dollars for Scholars," The First National Bank of Boston, Boston, Massachusetts, 1962, for a description of such a plan.

| LENDING AGENCY | ELIGIBLE | MAXIMUM LOAN | | REPAYMENT PROVISIONS | | INTEREST RATE | | SECURITY | GUARANTY | GUARANTY FEE |
		ANNUAL	TOTAL [a]	START	MAX. TERM THEREAFTER	BEFORE GRADUATION [b]	AFTER GRADUATION [c]			
American Medical Association Education and Research Foundation— Guarantee Loan Program	Full-time students Medical students attending approved medical schools Interns and residents training in approved hospitals U. S. Nationals only	$1500	$10,000 (within seven year period)	Five months after completion of residency	Up to Ten Years	Maximum 5½% simple interest per year	3½% add-on per year	Student's signature Minors are eligible	100% of unpaid principal balance plus interest	None
National Defense Student Loan Program	Undergraduate and graduate students Full-time students U. S. Nationals only Enrolled in institution of higher education located in the U. S. or territories	$1000 per academic year or its equivalent	$5000	One year after ceases studies [d]	Ten Years [d]	None	3% simple interest per annum	Student's signature Oath of allegiance to U. S. Disclaimer affidavit Participating institution may require security or endorsement if the state law prohibits borrowers under 18 or 21 years of age to incur a binding obligation.	A $9 federal grant for every $1 contributed by participating college or university.	None

[a] All accumulated loans for educational purposes may not exceed $15,000.
[b] Before completion of training.
[c] After completion of training.
[d] Student borrowers who become full-time teachers in public elementary or secondary schools need not repay 10% of their loan plus interest for each academic year of teaching service, up to 50% of the loan.

LENDING AGENCY	ELIGIBLE	MAXIMUM LOAN		REPAYMENT PROVISIONS		INTEREST RATE		SECURITY	GUARANTY	GUARANTY FEE
		ANNUAL	TOTAL	START	MAX. TERM THEREAFTER	BEFORE GRADUATION	AFTER GRADUATION			
Massachusetts Higher Education Assistance Corporation—Higher Education Loan Plan	Sophomores, juniors, seniors and graduate students Enrolled in approved educational institution Residents of Massachusetts Full-time day and cooperative plan students	$500	$1500	Six months after graduation	Three Years	½ of 1% above prime rate; range—3½%-5½% simple interest per annum	$4.50 per $100 per annum	Student's signature Legally bound if under 21 years old Application approved by student's parent or guardian If married, spouse's signature required	80% of unpaid principal balance	½ of 1% per annum and $.50 per $100 per annum on the principal amounts of the original and renewal notes, respectively
New York Higher Education Assistance Corporation—Guaranty Loan Plan	Undergraduate and graduate students Accepted at approved educational institution Resident of New York State Full-time and part-time students	Full-time (Degree Course) $500-$1500 Part-time (Degree Course) $250-$750 Full-time (Other "Post-Secondary" Schools) Amount of tuition charge or $500, whichever is less	$7500 $3750 $1500	Last day of calendar month following month student completes studies or last day of calendar month student terminates study.	Six Years	6% simple interest per annum paid by NYHEAC	Maximum 6% simple interest—3% simple interest per annum paid by student and the difference assumed by NYHEAC	Student's signature Legally bound if under 21 years of age Acknowledged by parent or guardian	100% of loan balance	None
The Higher Education Assistance Foundation—Student's Loan Plan (Maine)	Sophomores, juniors, seniors and graduate students Enrolled in approved educational institution Resident of Maine	$500	$1500	Not later than six months after graduation	Three Years	4½% simple interest	$4.50 per $100 per annum	Student's signature Legally bound if 16 years of age or older	80% of loan balance	½ of 1% per annum and $.50 per $100 per annum on the principal amounts of the original and renewal notes, respectively

| LENDING AGENCY | ELIGIBLE | MAXIMUM LOAN | | REPAYMENT PROVISIONS | | INTEREST RATE | | SECURITY | GUARANTY | GUARANTY FEE |
		ANNUAL	TOTAL	START	MAX. TERM THEREAFTER	BEFORE GRADUATION	AFTER GRADUATION			
New Jersey Higher Education Assistance Authority— State Student Loan Program	Undergraduate and graduate students Accepted by or enrolled in approved educational institution Resident of New Jersey Full-time student	$500-$1000	$5000	Three months after graduation	Six Years	5% simple interest per annum	5% simple interest per annum	Student's signature Legally bound if 18 years or older Application approved by student's parent or guardian if under 21 years of age	90%-100% of balance owed (Depending on whether loan is guaranteed or insured)	½ of 1% of balance owed
State Education Assistance Authority (Virginia)	Undergraduate and graduate students Resident of Virginia Accepted at state supported educational institution Full-time student	$750	$3000	Six months after graduation or after leaves college; maximum maturity of original notes 4 years, 3 months	Four Years	4½% simple interest per annum	$5.00 per $100 per annum	Student's signature Legally bound if 16 years of age or older Consult parent or guardian	80% of loan balance	½ of 1% per annum and $.50 per $100 per annum of the principal amounts of the original and renewal notes, respectively
United Student Aid Funds— USA Funds	Sophomores, juniors, seniors and graduate students Resident of state where loan is applied for Attending approved educational institution Full-time student	$1000	$3000	Four months after graduation	Three Years	Maximum 6% simple interest per year	$3 per $100 per annum	Student's signature only Legally bound if under 21 years of age Acknowledged by parent	100% of balance owed	None

Source: "Financing Higher Education," *Special Bulletin No. 294*, Instalment Credit Committee, by permission of The American Bankers Association, New York, N.Y., March 1962, pp. 17, 18, 19.

loan is made to the student and no interest or principal payments are required until after the student leaves college. Under the typical bank plan, the loan is made to the parent of the student, and monthly payments start as soon as the loan is made.

This is by no means a complete list of loan programs. Many others make millions available each year for student loans. Again, parents and students must do a considerable amount of research, and solicit the help of high school guidance counselors, college and university representatives, and others who specialize in such services.

Borrowing in any form costs money. Saving in advance is obviously the cheapest method of financing a college education. Not only is interest cost avoided, but income is received on the money saved. The actual cost of borrowing under the various methods available can be determined and compared by the methods described in Chapter 5.

SUMMARY

Summarizing the preceding material might be helpful.

1. A college degree is becoming more and more important.
2. A college should be carefully selected on the basis of valid reasons.
3. It costs more to attend college than many people realize, and these costs are rising.
4. Colleges are faced with increasing costs, and there is no possibility that they will decrease in the foreseeable future.
5. Tuition payments are going to have to cover a larger portion of these rising college costs, as other sources of college income are not expected to increase rapidly enough.
6. Parents and students may obtain money to meet college costs from savings, current income, scholarships, or loans.
7. Financial aid available from colleges is not sufficient to cover a major portion of college expenses (as indicated in Table 7-5), and only a small percentage of students (23.9 per cent of freshmen was the average indicated in Table 7-3) actually receive this aid. Most colleges, in fact, operate with a student aid deficit; their student aid income is not enough to cover these costs.
8. Many loan plans are available and should be carefully investigated by parents and students needing funds to cover college expenses.
9. Young people planning to attend college, and their parents, must start their savings program early, make plans carefully,

and do a considerable amount of research into colleges available, financial aid possibilities, etc.

Questions

1. Will your children get into college?

2. "The first step in deciding on a college career should be not to ask what the college can do for you but what you can do for the college." Discuss.

3. List six (6) questions which you should ask in selecting a college.

4. Compare the three primary methods of saving money to finance college costs.

5. Discuss three (3) methods a student might use to earn money to help pay college costs.

6. "The most brilliant applicant to a college will get the largest scholarship." Is this true?

7. It is up to parents and students to do a considerable amount of research concerning scholarship availability. Why?

8. How is "financial need" determined?

9. What is the expected change in the general attitude toward paying for a college education?

10. What is the difference between a loan guaranty plan and the typical bank loan plan?

Problems

1. Joe is a high school junior. His grades are average and could be much better if he put more effort into his school work. Joe's attitude is

"Why study too much? You only live once—have fun. I know men who have retired with plenty of money who never went to college. Why should I bother to go to college? I'm just as smart as they were." What do you think of Joe's attitude?

2. Jean has applied to three colleges. All of them were well known, prestige universities. Her grades in high school were excellent and her college board scores were above average. All three colleges send her rejection slips. Jean is heartbroken. To her it looks like she might as well give up the idea of attending college. What should Jean do?

3. Mr. and Mrs. Carlson met while attending a midwestern four year liberal arts college about twenty years ago. Mr. Carlson was then attending college under one of the government veterans' programs which paid part of his expenses. They now have four children ages 6, 9, 11 and 13. They hope to send all four to the college they attended. Based on their own experience, Mr. and Mrs. Carlson estimate that it will cost them a total of about $20,000 to send all four children to college. This they believe will cover all college costs, including tuition, books, board and room, etc.
What do you think of their estimate?

4. Using the table "Straight Savings Program" on page 173, find the monthly payments that will have to be made if four years remain before a student will enter college and the Goal Amount is $10,000.

5. The Daughertys have a fine, intelligent son. He wants to go to college and he certainly is college material. There is, however, a major problem. They do not have enough money and certainly cannot hope to save enough before he graduates from high school. What would you suggest?

Selected Readings

Armsby, Henry H., *Cooperative Education in the United States*, (OE-50018), Department of Health, Education, and Welfare, Washington 25, D.C., March 1961

College Attendance Costs and Scholarships, Education Information Service (No. 12). The College Life Insurance Company of America, Indianapolis, Indiana, December 1960

Facing Facts About College Costs, The Prudential Insurance Company of America, 1960, Newark 1, N. J.

"Financing Higher Education," *Special Bulletin No. 294*, Instalment Credit Committee, The American Bankers Association, New York, N.Y., March 1962

Feingold, S. Norman, "Latest Information on Scholarships in the Space Age," *Occupational Outlook Quarterly*, Bureau of Labor Statistics, U.S. Department of Labor, September, 1962

Feingold, S. Norman, *Scholarships, Fellowships and Loans*, Bellman Publishing Company, Cambridge, Mass., Vol. III, 1955, Vol. IV, 1962

How About College?, American School Counselor Association, a Division of the American Personnel and Guidance Association, Washington, D.C., 1960

How About College Financing?, American School Counselor Association, a Division of the American Personnel and Guidance Association, Washington, D.C., 1961

The College of Tomorrow, Editorial Projects for Education, Inc., Washington, D.C., 1962

The Fundamentals of College Placement, The College Placement Council, Inc., Bethlehem, Penn., 1962

Chapter **8**

LIVING SPACE

Can you remember twenty years ago? Even ten? Remember the empty areas where houses have now been built? Many of these areas were considered by most people to be unsuitable for building. Today they are completely filled with homes. In more sparsely populated states wide areas of vacant land, even deserts, have now become housing developments.

In most parts of the country, the problem of living space continuously gets worse, never better. Why? There are many reasons.

One of these has been the increase in the popularity of single homes—due at least partially to such things as the increase in the real income of the American people and the increased availability of mortgage money. Another prominent reason is the increase in the population. Both of these are expected to continue. Consider for a moment the problems created by an increasing population. In less than 100 years—if it continues to increase at the rate of the past 10 years—the population of the United States should increase more than 10 times. Before then, the annual increase in the population will be as great as the present entire population of the country. Based on factors such as these, it appears that not only will the problem of finding living space continue to exist, but it will continue to get worse.

CHANGING NEEDS

There is no one final solution to the problem of living space for the individual. His needs change continuously through life.

Let's take Joe for an example. Once he was single. He lived happily in a room near the office. The room was relatively inexpensive and could be maintained with a minimum of effort. Eventually he left this state of freedom with its relative lack of problems and got married. Now his requirements changed. First he and his wife moved into an apartment. Next they managed to buy a small home. Soon they had their first child. Fortunately their home had an extra room for just such an event. Eventually they had seven children. The small home then seemed about to burst at the seams. While Joe and his wife managed for some years by adding two rooms, the problem became more acute as the children grew older. The older children needed room to study, and the younger ones needed room to play. Joe and his wife needed room to escape occasionally from the continuous activity of their large family. Fortunately Joe's income had increased over the years and to solve the problem he purchased a much larger home in the country. Everybody was quite happy in his new home, but not "forever after." Eventually the children grew up and went to college, to work, or got married. As they left home one by one the house seemed to expand in size. Soon, except for visits by their children and grandchildren, Joe and his wife were alone in a home much too large for them. They moved to an apartment. Joe's cycle was complete—from apartment, to house, to apartment.

Now everyone doesn't follow exactly this pattern. For one thing, everyone doesn't have seven children. Nevertheless, the general pattern is a common one. Family needs change as the family increases in number, grows older, and then decreases in number.

RENT OR OWN?

Which is best, to rent or buy? More than a million families per year become home owners, but this alone is not conclusive. In the first place, accurate information as to the number renting for the first time is not readily available. In the second place, even though evidence indicates the popularity of home owning, it doesn't prove that, from the viewpoint of personal finance, it is the "best" move to make.

Comparative Cost

Which is cheaper—owning or renting?

The question of whether it is cheaper to own or to rent deserves short shrift. Few people actually seek the answer; the nearest issue is a matching of the satisfactions of tenancy related to its cost against the satisfactions of homeownership related to its cost. An attempt at direct comparison of tenants' and owners' costs is fruitless for these reasons:

1. In real life the comparison is not between equivalent dwellings and thus not between equal services received.

2. The costs of different dwelling types are not comparable.

3. One of the largest costs of homeownership (depreciation) is not determinable without knowing the cost of acquisition and the proceeds from the sale at disposition. But the selling price will be strongly influenced by market conditions at time of sale, which is indeterminate.

4. In a changing housing market there are times when ownership is a better bargain, and there are other times when market conditions favor tenancy.[1]

Advantages of Owning

What are the advantages of owning a home? First, homes occupied by their owners tend to be located in better neighborhoods. There has been an increase in recent years of garden type apartments

---

[1] From Richard U. Ratcliff, *Real Estate Analysis*, Copyright 1961, McGraw-Hill Book Company, Inc., New York, N.Y., p. 188. Used by permission.

outside of the city, so this advantage isn't quite as outstanding as it used to be, but it still exists.

Another advantage of buying a home is its investment value. Instead of making monthly payments to a landlord, the homeowner builds an equity in his home. Not only is this a form of saving, but, historically, it has been a method of hedging against inflation. Real estate values have increased considerably over the years.

A third advantage is the tax status of homeowners. Tax laws permit them to deduct property taxes and mortgage interest. This gives a distinct advantage to the homeowner if he is compared with someone paying the same price to rent living space. Furthermore, the homeowner is permitted to make an investment which increases in value and not have to pay a capital gains tax, as long as he purchases a new home within one year after selling the old one.

A fourth advantage is more space. Usually a homeowner has more space, and more privacy, than a renter.

There are other advantages: personal contentment, better design, building an estate, opportunity for hobbies, etc., that make home-owning the choice of a large percentage of the population.

Disadvantages of Owning

In the face of such great advantages, why would anyone rent? For one thing, there are disadvantages to owning a home. Almost every homeowner reaches a point where he feels like a slave to his home. He can't go away on a vacation without worrying about storms, the plumbing, the lawn, and a thousand and one other things. While he is home a multitude of things need to be done. During the winter he has to shovel snow. As soon as the snow stops, lawn mowing seems to begin along with the invasion of the dandelions and the plague of ants.

Furthermore, owning a home is expensive. Adding a porch, building a playroom in the basement, etc. are all temptations that most homeowners succumb to. Painting, repairing the plumbing, resurfacing the driveway and other such problems are not tempta-tions—they are musts. Property taxes seem to always increase along with the cost of insurance, utility bills and other expenses.

Many people, in fact, would never be happy in a home of their own. They come from a long line of apartment dwellers. This is their way of life. They enjoy a kind of freedom and flexibility unknown to the home owner. They can move when their lease expires, and never have to worry about such problems as mowing the lawn and shoveling snow. They can travel free of the chains tying the homeowner to his property.

RENTING

A little over 60 per cent of the nation's households are home-owners and a little less than 40 per cent are tenants. Single persons, young married couples, and elderly persons find definite advantages in renting. Also included in the renter group are those who firmly believe that renting an apartment is the only way to live, and those who cannot commit themselves to the permanency of home ownership.

It is also true that in a cost comparison, many people decide that owning a home is no more expensive than renting, and later on find that this is not true. The original error is usually due to the fact that they overlook many of the costs involved in home-owning. Simply comparing the monthly rental that must be paid with the monthly principal and interest on a home may lead to an erroneous conclusion. Later, it is discovered that items such as property taxes, insurance, maintenance costs, utility expenses, etc., that enter into home-owning, were not considered. When they are included, renting becomes relatively much less expensive, and the home-owner might consider renting again.

Finding a Place to Rent

Where can a person obtain information concerning the availability of places to rent? There are several sources, including friends, rela-tives, classified ads, signs, and real estate agencies. If information is obtained from friends or classified ads, it is wise to telephone the first. This may save a time-consuming trip, as the rent, neighbor-hood, or other factors may prove to be undesirable from the renter's point of view. On the other hand, friends and real estate agencies can be told the price range, neighborhood, apartment size, etc., in which the renter is interested. Real estate agencies can, of course, really perform a service in this respect.

Selecting a Place to Rent

Many of the factors that must be considered in selecting a place to rent are the same as those that must be considered in buying a home. Location, for example, should be a primary consideration. It may sound "snobbish" to state that there are some neighborhoods a

CHECKLIST FOR

In looking at either apartments or houses to rent or buy, there are both general and specific points to consider (such as those included in the checklist below) to help you decide whether the facilities will meet your requirements. Answers to many of the questions can be found through careful inspection, trying out equipment and plumbing, and by asking questions of the occupant, owner, or other person in charge. Questions of a technical nature to which you would like the answers may require the help of an expert. *To use the checklist*, make a check opposite each point that is adequate for your needs, omitting

Exterior

- Is the character of the community:
  - to your liking? _____
  - convenient for your activities? _____
- Is the style of the dwelling:
  - attractive? _____
  - in keeping with others in the area? _____
- Is exterior construction in good condition? _____
- Are major views pleasant? _____
  - Is there sufficient:
  - daylight? _____
  - sunlight? _____
- If there is a yard, is it large enough for:
  - a play area? _____
  - outdoor living? _____
  - a garden? _____
- If it is a house, is it located to take best advantage of:
  - sun? _____
  - wind? _____
  - shade? _____
- Is property fenced in or enclosed with shrubs for children's safety? _____
- Are the dwellings far enough apart to provide the privacy you want on either side, as well as at the back of the house? _____
- Is yard landscaped, with lawn and shrubs in good condition? _____
- If there is a well instead of a public water system, are the following adequate:
  - depth of well? _____
  - quantity of water? _____
  - flow of water? _____
- If there is a septic tank instead of a municipal sewer system, is it:
  - adequate in size for your family? _____
  - properly installed? _____

- Are there improvements on the lot, such as:
  - sidewalks and streets? _____
  - grading? _____
  - utility connections? _____
- Are there parking facilities, such as:
  - a garage or carport? _____
  - 24-hour parking on street or in an alley? _____

Entrance

- Are entrances well lighted? _____
- Is there a side or rear entrance for deliveries? _____
- Is there an outside entrance for fuel deliveries? _____
- Is the entrance to inside hallway kept locked? _____
- Are there locked mailboxes? _____
- Are there facilities for accepting packages when you are away? _____
- Are hallways and stairways well lighted and clean? _____
- Is there elevator service that eliminates climbing steps to the apartment? _____
- Are there adequate fire escapes? _____

Interior

- Are the following in good condition:
  - windows and doors? _____
  - floors, walls, and ceilings? _____
  - roof and gutters? _____
  - porches, including railings? _____
  - steps? _____
- Is insulation adequate? _____
- Are walls and floors insulated against noise? _____
- Are electric outlets where you will need them for:
  - lamps? _____
  - radio and television? _____
  - large appliances? _____
  - small appliances? _____

person wouldn't live in, but this is not true. Some people aren't happy in a particular neighborhood, while others think it is ideal.

Consider George Donovan for a moment. He has a small business. He and his wife have always had an apartment in a particular section of a large city which many might consider "undesirable." The apartment houses are crowded together. Their neighbors are poor, and the sidewalk and street is the place where those living in the neighborhood spend a good portion of their time, and where the children play.

RENTING OR BUYING

those which do not apply to the property at which you are looking. Then evaluate the importance to you of the points you have left unchecked. You probably will not find any one location that will measure up to your standards in all respects, but if the features most important to you are included, perhaps you can afford to overlook the less important items. Applying this checklist to each house or apartment in which you are interested may give you a basis for making an intelligent decision, and may save you from dissatisfaction and unnecessary expense later on.

- Is the current adequate for all purposes and appliances? _____

- If there is a basement, is it:
  well ventilated and dry? _____
  well lighted? _____
  without hazards, such as low beams, exposed pipes and wires? _____

Equipment
- If needed, are the following provided for all windows:
  shades or blinds? _____
  storm windows? _____
  screens? _____

- Are the following adequate and in good condition:
  plumbing? _____
  heating unit? _____
  kitchen appliances? _____
  laundry appliances? _____
  water heater? _____
  Are all of the above operating satisfactorily? _____

- If needed, is there a place for storing:
  screens? _____
  storm windows and doors? _____
  outdoor furniture? _____
  garden and yard tools? _____

- Are there facilities for disposal of garbage, such as:
  an incinerator? _____
  disposer in kitchen sink? _____
  city garbage collection? _____

- Is there telephone service? _____
  Must you have a telephone installed? _____

- May you have an outside aerial for television? _____

- Is there a charge for plugging into a common aerial? _____

Arrangement of space
- Can the rooms be adapted to your needs? _____

- Are rooms and wall spaces large enough for your furniture? _____

- Is amount and arrangement of work space in kitchen satisfactory? _____

- Is there space for laundry purposes? _____

- Is placement of bathroom convenient to all areas of house? _____

- Are closets, cabinets, shelves and all other storage spaces adequate for your needs? _____

- Are windows well placed for satisfactory ventilation in all rooms? _____
  If not, are there fans or an air conditioning system? _____

Responsibility for maintenance when renting
- Is the person responsible for upkeep and taking care of complaints easy to get in touch with? _____
  Is he:
  the owner? _____
  an agent? _____
  a representative of a management firm? _____

- What maintenance costs are included in the rent, such as for:
  electricity? _____
  gas? _____
  water? _____
  telephone? _____
  repairs and replacement? _____
  decorating? _____

- If needed:
  will the landlord make repairs? _____
  decorate completely before you move in? _____

- Is window washing taken care of by the management? _____

- Are you offered a written lease? _____

Source: Taken from "Money Management, Your Shelter Dollar," published by the Money Management Institute of Household Finance Corporation, Chicago, Ill., Copyright 1957, reviewed and reprinted 1963, pp. 10-11.

George became moderately successful in his business, and he and his family moved to one of the new, more expensive, garden type apartments in the suburbs. The children had plenty of room to play, conditions were much less crowded, the neighbors were financially better off and, to many people, it would seem that George should have been extremely happy. He wasn't. He was miserable.

George had developed a way of living. He liked to drink a bottle of beer on his front steps and gossip with his neighbors. In the old neighborhood, this was quite acceptable. In the new neighborhood, the neighbors frowned on such habits. George likes to sit outside in his undershirt. This didn't go in the new neighborhood. He and his wife enjoyed the commotion and, to them, friendliness of constant close contact with their neighbors. In the new neighborhood, neighbors were friendly but distant. It wasn't long before George started to hunt for an apartment to rent in his old neighborhood. The moral is: everybody is different. It is up to each individual to determine the particular type of location he prefers.

In most cases, renting an apartment or a house means signing a lease. Be certain to do what you should do before signing any contract — *read it*. Make certain that both parties are aware of how long the lease will run, who bears the responsibility for maintenance and utilities, the exact amount of the rent, how much rent must be paid in advance, under what conditions the rent may be increased, how much notice is required before moving, subletting rights, etc. These details are of the utmost importance. Learning about some of the restrictions in a lease after signing it is too late. The time to raise questions and objections is before signing.

The checklist on pages 194 and 195 is useful for both renting or buying. Many of the items included apply to both, but some specifically refer to renting, such as those concerning locked mailboxes, facilities for accepting packages, the charge for plugging into a common TV aerial, and those included under the general heading, "Responsibility for maintenance when renting." Careful consideration of all these items before renting will help a person to make a wise selection.

One basic factor to consider, whether renting or buying, is how much you can afford. A person must carefully consider all of his expenses other than housing (and don't forget to include "savings" as an expense, as recommended in Chapter 2 on Budgeting). After obtaining this total, subtract it from income after taxes. The difference will be the amount that can be spent for housing. This, of course, will in itself establish limits as to the size apartment, neighborhood, etc. One general rule is that a person can afford about one week's pay each month for housing expenses.

OWNING A HOME

Many of the same problems are encountered in owning a home as in renting. The checklist on pages 194 and 195 is a good general reference in both cases. Some problems, however, take on added significance. The appearance of the neighborhood, congeniality of the neighbors, transportation facilities, accessibility to schools and other community services, restrictions, taxes and other similar factors must be more carefully considered in buying, because owning a home is a much more permanent commitment.

How Much to Spend

How much can a person afford to pay for a home? Many general rules are suggested. One is that a person should spend no more than 25 per cent of his income after taxes on housing. Another is that a person can afford to purchase a home which costs about 2½ times his annual income.

Basically, of course, the decision is an individual one, depending upon a family's assets, income, debts, plans for the family's future, and the sort of social life desired. General rules should not be considered as gospel. The greatest danger to successful home ownership is probably taking on more than a person can afford.

Once a person determines how much of a down payment he can make, and how much he can afford to spend for housing each month, the price of the house that may be purchased can be determined. Table 8–1 shows the relationship between the monthly (and annual) amounts to be spent on housing and the size of the mortgage, at various interest rates and for varying terms, that can be handled with this amount. Notice, for example, that $50 per month would be only enough to meet the payments on a $6,000 mortgage for 20 years at 5 per cent interest; and $200 per month would be sufficient to meet the payments on a $24,000 loan for 20 years at 5 per cent. Adding the amount of the mortgage he can afford to the down payment he can make will determine the total amount a person can pay for a home. If $5,000 is available for a down payment, and a person can afford to pay $100 per month, a $17,000 home could be considered (assuming mortgage loans are available for 20 years at 5 per cent).

While the size of the down payment is important, it should not take all available cash, as other initial costs will be incurred, such as appraisal fees, loan charges, mortgage recording, title search, repairs, and moving expenses. Also, from 1 to 5 per cent of the purchase price of the house should be budgeted for maintenance and upkeep each year. The exact amount, of course, will depend upon such factors as the age, size, condition, and construction of the house.

After all of these anticipated costs are considered, a contingency reserve should be established. Unforeseen costs will occur, such as

Table 8-1

INCOME FOR HOUSING		AT 5%			AT 5½%		
Monthly	Annual	10 yr.	15 yr.	20 yr.	10 yr.	15 yr.	20 yr.
$40	$480	$3,245	$4,140	$4,800	$3,180	$4,035	$4,615
50	600	4,055	5,170	6,000	3,975	5,040	5,770
60	720	4,865	6,205	7,200	4,770	6,050	6,920
80	960	6,485	8,275	9,600	6,360	8,070	9,230
100	1,200	8,110	10,345	12,000	7,950	10,085	11,540
125	1,500	10,135	12,930	15,000	9,935	12,605	14,425
150	1,800	12,160	15,520	18,000	11,920	15,125	17,310
175	2,100	14,190	18,105	21,000	13,910	17,650	20,190
200	2,400	16,215	20,690	24,000	15,895	20,170	23,075
225	2,700	18,245	23,275	27,000	17,880	22,690	25,960
250	3,000	20,270	25,860	30,000	19,870	25,210	28,845

		AT 6%			AT 6¼%		
		10 yr.	15 yr.	20 yr.	10 yr.	15 yr.	20 yr.
$40	$480	$3,115	$3,935	$4,485	$3,075	$3,870	$4,405
50	600	3,895	4,920	5,605	3,845	4,840	5,505
60	720	4,675	5,900	6,730	4,615	5,805	6,605
80	960	6,235	7,870	8,970	6,155	7,740	8,805
100	1,200	7,790	9,835	11,215	7,690	9,675	11,010
125	1,500	9,740	12,295	14,020	9,615	12,095	13,760
150	1,800	11,690	14,755	16,820	11,540	14,515	16,515
175	2,100	13,635	17,215	19,625	13,460	16,935	19,265
200	2,400	15,585	19,670	22,430	15,385	19,355	22,020
225	2,700	17,530	22,130	25,235	17,310	21,775	24,770
250	3,000	19,480	24,590	28,035	19,230	24,195	27,525

For all of above tables taxes have been estimated at $18 annually, insurance at $3 annually, for every $1,000 loaned on the home.

Source: "What You Should Know Before You Buy A Home," published by the United States Savings and Loan League, Chicago, Ill., 1962, p. 8.

emergency repairs, or tax increases, which make it advisable to hold some resources in reserve.

BUYING OR BUILDING

There are two ways to acquire a home: buy one that is already built, or build one. While the two methods are similar in many respects, there are important differences. In both cases, the buyer is faced with the question, "Just what is a good house?"

> A good house is one that is adequate for the size of the family and that provides a maximum amount of comfort for the dollars spent. It should be in keeping with the financial status of the family, suitable to their social outlook, and it should, as far as possible, anticipate changes in size and composition of the family.[2]

Buying an Existing Home

If the decision is to buy rather than to build, another question must be answered: Should the prospective homeowner buy a new house or an older one?

There are advantages in buying a new house. A housewife is certainly favorably impressed when everything is brand new. Often, when a new house is purchased, the buyer has the opportunity to select the interior decoration, to suggest basic landscaping ideas, and even to select the color of the exterior paint. Certainly a new home will have modern plumbing, heating, laundry and electric facilities, and appliances.

One inherent danger in selecting a new home is that the buyer may be so impressed by new paint and modern appliances that he will overlook more important items. In one very expensive new development, for example, all of the houses were equipped with automatic laundries and dishwashers. According to the comments of many of those visiting the model home, it seemed apparent that many buyers purchased homes in this development because of these appliances, and gave little thought to the more basic considerations, such as the materials used in the construction of the house. In this particular situation, the houses were poorly constructed, and many purchasers became quite dissatisfied after a few years. The appli-

---

[2] The Royal Bank of Canada, *Monthly Letter*, Montreal, Quebec, October 1955, p. 1.

ances, in fact, stood the test of time much better than the building materials used.

One basic rule to follow in buying anything, and it certainly is applicable to home buying, is to make certain that the seller is reputable. The new home should not be considered unless it was built by a reputable builder who will give a warranty against defects in materials and workmanship.

Older homes appeal to many people because they believe they get more for their money. This may be true, but a realistic price comparison between the older and newer homes should be carefully made.

In 1955, Ed purchased a new home for $12,500. A few months later, John purchased an older home for the same price. John boasted that he had received a lot more for his money because his house had nine rooms, while Ed's had only four and one-half, with an unfinished attic. To John, nine rooms for $12,500 was a much better buy than four and a half for $12,500.

Two years later, John was noticeably silent. The interior of the foundation of his home suddenly required considerable work, the outside badly needed a paint job, and a large part of the interior plumbing needed replacing. John wisely decided that his house wasn't worth the expenditure of such a large sum of money, sold the house at a loss, and moved to a new (and much smaller) one.

There are, however, excellent opportunities in older homes if the buyer carefully considers all factors. Older homes do tend to have more space, to be built with more substantial materials, to be located in established neighborhoods, to be on larger lots, and to have established lawns, trees and landscaping.

In buying an older home, a certain amount of work will undoubtedly have to be done. A prospective buyer should carefully estimate the amount of work required and its cost. Not only must basic components be carefully checked, such as the heating plant, wiring, plumbing, roof, basement, gutters, etc., but the question of updating must be considered. It would be unrealistic to consider only the price of the home plus basic repairs, if the members of the family are going to be dissatisfied with the older style facilities. Will the kitchen, for example, have to be remodeled? Will the interior need new wallpaper and paint? Are the ceilings in good condition? Is there enough closet space? Do the floors need repair or refinishing? Some of these repairs and improvements can be made gradually, while the house is being occupied, but this should be ascertained before, not after, the house is purchased.

CHECK LIST:

EXTERIOR

- [ ] Architecture ....
- [ ] House setting ....
- [ ] Orientation ....
- [ ] Plot grading ....
- [ ] Landscaping ....
- [ ] Walks, curbs, driveways ....
- [ ] Utilities ....

INTERIOR

- [ ] Layout ....
- [ ] Exposure ....
- [ ] Expansion potential ....
- [ ] Wall space ....
- [ ] Electric outlets ....
- [ ] Closets ....
- [ ] Entry ....
- [ ] Decoration ....
- [ ] Floors..
- [ ] Doors and windows ....

LIVING ROOM

- [ ] Size ....
- [ ] Wall Space.......................................
- [ ] Windows ....
- [ ] Electric outlets................................

DINING ROOM

- [ ] Dining capacity ....
- [ ] Serving convenience ....
- [ ] Windows ....
- [ ] Electric outlets................................

KITCHEN

- [ ] Sink location....................................
- [ ] Cabinet space ....
- [ ] Counter space ....
- [ ] Equipment space ....
- [ ] Electric outlets................................
- [ ] Exhaust fan......................................
- [ ] Floor covering..................................
- [ ] Service entry....................................

BEDROOMS

- [ ] Size ....
- [ ] Closet space ....
- [ ] Convenience to bath ....
- [ ] Windows ....
- [ ] Electric outlets ....

BATHS

- [ ] Number...
- [ ] Wall and floor tiling ....
- [ ] Towel bars ....
- [ ] Hamper space ....
- [ ] Safe electric outlet ....

LAUNDRY

- [ ] Location..
- [ ] Convenience ....
- [ ] Electric outlets ....
- [ ] Storage space ....

BASEMENT

- [ ] Dampness ....
- [ ] Heating plant ....
- [ ] Hot water unit ....
- [ ] Plumbing ....
- [ ] Electric power service.......................
- [ ] Playroom potential ....
- [ ] Workshop space ....
- [ ] Storage area ....

GARAGE

- [ ] Size ....
- [ ] Work area..
- [ ] Storage space ....
- [ ] Attached ....
- [ ] Detached ....
- [ ] Breezeway ....
- [ ] Covered access to house....................

Source: "The Home for You . . . and How to Select it," by Eugene M. Mortlock, President, First Federal Savings and Loan Association of New York, 1962, pp. 15-16.

The check list on page 201 lists some of the things that must be considered when buying a house, new or old. It assumes that a specific house is being considered, and indicates items which merit the buyer's attention. Even this is only a partial list, and does not include items such as insulation, weather-stripping, and other important features. But it is an excellent start, and other things will occur to you as you check it.

Expert Services

It never hurts to seek expert help when buying a home.

The first expert, and a very essential one, is a lawyer. One of the easiest ways to get into legal difficulty is to try to buy or build without the services of a lawyer. He is needed to check the title to the property, make certain that there are no outstanding tax liens or assessments, see that zoning laws and building regulations have been observed, examine the terms of the mortgage, etc. Again, this is only a partial list of what he can do for you. A lawyer will interpret the various legal documents involved, and acquaint you with your rights and obligations.

The second expert is the Realtor. He acts as a go-between and, for a commission, brings buyer and seller together. A Realtor knows what property is available, and can save both time and money for buyer and seller. Select the Realtor whom you believe to be best qualified to serve you. One may often be selected by local reputation, or on the advice of a local bank, or by your lawyer.

RELY ON YOUR REALTOR[3]

The term *Realtor* is the distinctive and exclusive designation for men and women within the membership of the National Association of Real Estate Boards. Every Realtor has pledged that he will abide by the Code of Ethics promulgated by the National Association, and has manifested that he is of good business character and that he is capable of properly caring for real estate matters entrusted to him.

How to Build

You may prefer to build, instead of to buy. By building, you can specify exactly what you want. You can either hire an architect to

---

[3] "Preferred Attention," National Institute of Real Estate Brokers of the National Association of Real Estate Boards, Chicago, Illinois, 1962.

design the house, buy stock plans, use a plan offered by a builder or real estate agency, or buy a prefabricated house. Architects or stock plans will, of course, provide a much greater selection of plans than the selection available from other sources.

If plans are carefully made and a site can be found, building can be less expensive than buying. The problem of finding a site at reasonable cost, however, increases every year. In 1963, site value on new homes had risen about 190 per cent above those of 1947. During the same period, housing construction costs rose about 50 per cent.

By all means, plan carefully when building a home. Avail yourself of an architect's services. A competent architect can plan a house which will meet the owner's needs today and in the future. He can offer advice on the selection of a site and on the selection of a builder. He will also supervise the construction of the home, if requested. Architectural fees vary considerably, but range from 8 to 15 per cent of the cost of the house. As an example, let's use 10 per cent. Would this mean adding $2,500 to a $25,000 home? Not necessarily. A competent architect may be able to design a lower cost home which will meet both the requirements and aesthetic interests of the owner, and save him money.

Many people select their own builder and forego the services of an architect. While this does save the architect's fee, it charges these persons with greater responsibility. It also means that they will have to make decisions which they may not be competent to make.

There are four main classes of home builders:

1. Operative or speculative builders who are engaged in constructing large or small scale housing developments for sale.

2. Custom builders who will originate a development, prepare plans for different types of houses, but will build houses only on order.

3. Contract builders who build houses under a contract agreement with the owner or the owner's architect.

4. The owner-builder who handles the construction of his own home by letting individual contracts. If sufficiently skilled, he may do a considerable part of the construction work himself.[4]

Let's consider each of these four briefly. A person who plans to build his own home obviously would not be interested in selecting an operative or speculative builder; nor would the builder be interested in him. He might be interested in selecting a custom builder, assuming the builder has a good reputation, an acceptable site, and a

---

[4] Stanley L. McMichael and Paul T. O'Keefe, *How to Finance Real Estate,* 2nd Ed., © 1953. Prentice-Hall, Inc., Englewood Cliffs, N.J., p. 250.

satisfactory basic plan. However, the selection would more logically be made from one of the last two categories, and the third category would probably be the safest. The basic consideration here is to select a contract builder in whom you can have complete confidence. He must be someone who has a reputation for building quality homes, and who can be trusted to follow plans and specifications.

The fourth class, where the prospective homeowner acts as his own contractor, may prove to be the least expensive under certain conditions, but imposes maximum responsibility upon the homeowner. If the owner has a comprehensive knowledge of home construction, is competent to select and supervise sub-contractors, and has sufficient time to devote to the job, he may save money. If he is personally skilled in one or more of the building trades, he can save money by doing some of the work himself.

Time is the essential ingredient, and time is money. A person acting as his own contractor all too often discovers this method of building to be the most expensive and the most frustrating of all methods. He should be absolutely certain that he has the necessary qualifications, and time, before starting such a project.

Following are the steps in building. Depending on a variety of factors there may be some variation in the order in which they occur.

- Choose an architect, if you plan to have one, or buy a house plan. In the latter case, select a builder.

- Look for a site.

- Have architect or builder check lot as to dimensions, suitability for a building site, including slope of land and depth of water level, to assure dry basement. Check improvements on lot—water, sewers, (storm and sanitary), electricity and gas, grading, sidewalks, streets, and alleys. Find out the cost if you must put in any such facilities.

- Check on zoning, building and electrical codes, and union practices in the locality where you plan to build.

- Have a lawyer prepare an offer to buy lot. Submit offer to the seller with ten percent of purchase price, subject to seller furnishing: (1) clear title, (2) survey of lot, and (3) proof that all back taxes and assessments have been paid.

- If offer is accepted, have lawyer handle balance of payment of total purchase price when all terms of offer have been fulfilled. Take title, with full ownership and a warranty deed. Have title insured and recorded, or get a Torrens title certificate.

- Visit several lending institutions to find out whether suitable financing is available for construction purposes.

- Have topographical survey made of lot.

- Have architect prepare house plan and specifications, or have purchased plan checked by a reliable builder or architect.

- Investigate and get bids from several builders—then determine total cost of house. If you have an architect, he will get bids.

- Have lawyer check terms of your contracts with architect and builder.

- Arrange financing—obtain firm commitment for loan from lending institution. Execute loan with lending institution that gave commitment.

- Sign a fixed-price contract with a builder or sub-contractors for construction of house when you are satisfied that the price and time schedule are right.

- Take out fire and liability insurance.

- Either you or the architect work with the builder in staking out the house. Inspect construction as building progresses. This should be done by you and the architect, if you have one.

- Make partial payments to builder according to terms of contract.

- Obtain *completion certificate* as your assurance that the house is satisfactorily completed. Lending institution must agree. Have builder, all supply people, and architect sign a waiver of all prior liens against the property.

- Obtain final payment of loan from lending institution to pay builder.[5]

Caution

Any discussion of buying or building a home cannot be complete without at least a brief warning concerning the dangers of buying

---

[5] Taken from "Money Management, Your Shelter Dollar," published by the Money Management Institute of Household Finance Corporation, Chicago, Ill. Copyright 1957, reviewed and reprinted 1963, pp. 22–23.

"sight unseen." In recent years, land promotions in Florida, Arizona, and other states, have attracted out-of-state buyers with the lure of fabulous land at unbelievably low prices. Some of these promotions are legitimate; some are not. In some instances, people have found that the fabulous land they purchased is located in the middle of a desert, a swamp, or some other inaccessible, unpopulated, and completely undesirable area. For this reason, many states warn the public not to buy property until they have seen it. This is a sound warning and should be heeded.

Remember, too, that even after seeing such land, a person should consider the same factors as are considered when buying any other piece of land. Title should be clear, utilities should be available, the neighborhood should be attractive, community services should be adequate.

FINANCING

Table 8-2 shows how mortgage debt has been increasing since 1946, and the expected amount of increase to 1970.

In the purchase and sale of a home, the prospective homeowner and the seller of the property sign a sales contract. Before signing this, the buyer should make certain that the contract contains a provision for the return of any deposit under certain conditions. Usually, this provision provides for the return of the buyer's earnest money deposit if he cannot obtain a desirable mortgage. As there are many other necessary provisions in such a contract, an attorney should examine it before the buyer signs.

Next, the buyer must find a financial institution from which he may obtain the required mortgage loan. The wisest practice is for the buyer to "shop" for a mortgage before signing a contract. This will enable him to get the lowest cost and the best terms. All other things being equal, it is usually best to do business locally. It is much more convenient, especially if some emergency arises.

The Mortgage

The mortgage consists of two principal legal documents—a note and a trust deed. They may be separate or combined into a single instrument. The note is a contract to repay the amount borrowed. The trust deed (or deed of trust) is a pledge of real estate as security.

In about one-third of the states, the mortgagee (lender) holds title to the land until the debt is paid. In the other two-thirds of the states, the mortgager retains title and gives the mortgagee a lien on

Table 8-2

RESIDENTIAL MORTGAGE DEBT OUTSTANDING, 1946-1970[6]

Year	Billions of Dollars
1946	28.1
1947	33.8
1948	39.6
1949	44.9
1950	53.6
1951	61.4
1952	68.9
1953	77.1
1954	87.3
1955	100.6
1956	112.1
1957	121.7
1958	134.0
1959	145.3
1960	157.2
1961	169.4
1962	182.4
1963	196.0
1964	210.2
1965	225.1
1966	240.6
1967	256.8
1968	273.8
1969	291.5
1970	310.0

NOTE: Figures for 1959 and after are estimates.

the property as security for the mortgage debt, which can be exercised if the debt is not paid.

Sources of Mortgages

At the end of 1961, about 41 percent of the mortgage debt for one- to four-family nonfarm homes was held by savings and loan

[6] "The Next Decade—and Its Opportunities for the Savings and Loan Business," a preliminary report prepared for the United States Savings and Loan League by the School of Business, Indiana University, Bloomington, Indiana, Nov. 1959, p. 20. Copyright 1959, published by the United States Savings and Loan League.

associations, which specialize in this area of financing. (Approximately 85 per cent of their assets are in the form of mortgage loans.) Other sources commonly used by homeowners are commercial banks, mutual savings banks, and life insurance companies.

Quite often, home owners are unable to understand why one bank will loan them money on a mortgage, while others will not. One reason is that the different sources have different legal restrictions and different historical backgrounds. The nature of savings and loan associations, commercial banks, and mutual savings banks, was discussed in Chapter 3. Consider some of the general characteristics and practices of these institutions in relation to mortgage loans, as of 1961.

1. Savings and loan associations were generally permitted by law to loan up to 80 per cent of the appraised value of the security. Rules affecting state chartered associations vary, but federally chartered associations must invest most of their assets in first mortgages on one- to four-family dwellings. Compared to other loan sources, they are willing to make higher risk loans (in relation to the value of the property to be mortgaged) in order to earn higher returns, and are authorized to charge any legal interest rate. They are also permitted to write mortgages for terms of up to thirty years.

2. Federally chartered commercial banks are limited by law to maximum conventional loans of two-thirds of the value of the property to be mortgaged and a maximum term of twenty years, on an amortized basis; and maximum conventional loans of 50% of value, and a maximum term of five years, on a non-amortized basis.

3. In recent years, mutual savings banks have become more competitive in the mortgage field by relaxing some of their policies. As they are state chartered, their limiting regulations vary. In general, they are limited to first mortgages, and have specific limitations on the maximum size loan, the total amount that may be loaned on first mortgages in relation to total assets, the loan-to-value ratio, etc.

4. Insurance company mortgages are usually limited to two-thirds of the appraised value of the security. The term may run to 30 years, and interest rates are usually low. Exact legal regulations on insurance companies differ according to the state granting their charter.

The above observations are, of necessity, very general in nature. The lending practices and privileges of individual institutions vary from one section of the country to another, and often within the same locality; laws and regulations change continually; and the mortgage market as a whole changes with fluctuations in the supply of and demand for mortgage money.

There are other sources of mortgages besides these better known, traditional ones. Of these, mortgage companies are the fastest growing. Their usual role is to provide funds to mortgagors (borrowers) and then sell the mortgages to insurance companies or banks. Mortgage funds are also occasionally provided by casualty insurance companies, endowment funds, pension and welfare funds, certain government agencies, state loan funds, and others. However, the usual sources are still the savings and loan associations, commercial banks, mutual savings banks, and life insurance companies.

Types of Loans

There are basically three types of mortgage loans available: the conventional loan, the VA loan and the FHA loan. The comparative popularity of each is indicated by the information presented in Table 8-3.

Table 8–3

ALL SAVINGS AND LOAN ASSOCIATIONS

MORTGAGE LOANS HELD BY TYPE OF LOAN

Millions of dollars

December 31	Type of Loan			Total Loans*	% Guaranteed or Insured to Total
	FHA Insured	VA Guaranteed	Conventional		
1948	$ 563	$ 2,397	$ 7,345	$10,305	28.7
1949	717	2,586	8,313	11,616	28.4
1950	848	2,973	9,836	13,657	28.0
1951	866	3,133	11,565	15,564	25.7
1952	904	3,394	14,098	18,396	23.4
1953	1,048	3,979	16,935	21,962	22.9
1954	1,170	4,709	20,229	26,108	22.5
1955	1,404	5,883	24,121	31,408	23.2
1956	1,486	6,643	27,600	35,729	22.8
1957	1,643	7,011	31,353	40,007	21.6
1958	2,206	7,077	36,344	45,627	20.3
1959	2,997	7,192	43,005	53,194	19.2
1960	3,524	7,222	49,324	60,070	17.9
1961ᵖ	4,167	7,152	57,514	68,833	16.4

* Less mortgage pledged shares thru 1957; included since that year.
ᵖ Preliminary.

[7] "Savings and Home Financing Chart Book 1962, No. 7," Operating Analysis Division, Federal Home Loan Bank Board, April 1962, p. 16a.

What is a conventional mortgage? Describing it negatively, it is a mortgage which is not insured or guaranteed by the government. The lender loans its own money at its own risk. The interest rate may be a little higher and the term a little shorter, but it does have many advantages. The lending institution can be more flexible in meeting the needs of the mortgagor, and a much shorter time is required to commit and process the loan. VA and FHA loans must meet certain government specifications and receive government approval. The conventional loan must meet only the requirements of the lender and need be approved only by the lender.

The percentage of government guaranteed or insured loans (FHA and VA) to the total loans held by savings and loan associations is indicated by the figures in the right hand column in Table 8–3. The percentage has declined over the years because savings and loan associations have placed greater emphasis on the conventional loan. Almost three-fourths of all mortgage loans made each year are now of the conventional type.

The VA loan is one guaranteed by the Veterans Administration of the United States Government. It is available only to veterans who served in the armed forces between September 16, 1940 and July 25, 1947 (World War II), or between June 27, 1950 and January 31, 1955 (the Korean War). World War II veterans lost their eligibility in 1960, but Korean veterans are eligible until January 31, 1965, unless the law should be changed.

The VA appraises the property to establish a reasonable value, and will not guarantee a loan for more than this amount. The term may be for 30 years, and the permissible interest rate has been raised from an original 4 percent to 5¼ percent in 1963. This is still below market rates, and lenders naturally favor conventional mortgages on which they can charge the higher rates. The VA does not place any upper limit on home loan mortgages, but will not guarantee any more than $7,500, or 60 percent of the loan, whichever is less. Many VA guaranteed home loans have been made for 100% of the purchase price of the property.

The VA guarantee is not insurance. It is simply a guarantee which covers almost all of the losses the lender might suffer, including principal, interest, foreclosure costs, etc. In almost every case, the guarantee has been sufficient to cover all losses. Mortgage companies have been the most frequent grantors of this type of mortgage in recent years.

A VA loan offers definite advantages to the borrower: the term of the loan can be longer, the down payment smaller, and it may be prepaid without penalty. If a person is eligible, these and other advantages of VA mortgages should be carefully considered.

The FHA (Federal Housing Administration) loan provides insurance protection to the lender. The mortgagor (borrower) must pay a premium (½ of 1 percent on the average outstanding balance of the loan in the current year) into a reserve fund. The entire loan is insured, and the FHA specifies the maximum amount that can be loaned, the maximum term allowed, and the down payment required. These specifications will vary according to factors such as whether the house exists or is to be built, the type of construction, its age if existent, whether it is a one, two, three or four family home, and the FHA appraised value. A loan will not qualify for FHA insurance if it fails to meet any of the FHA requirements.

Chief features of the FHA plan are—
(1) small down payments;
(2) reasonable financing charges;
(3) repayment of the loan in equal monthly installments that include not only interest and a part of the loan principal but also taxes and insurance;
(4) a long-term maturity for the loan in order that the monthly installment may be in an amount that the borrower can conveniently pay;
(5) a mortgage of standard quality that may be bought and sold in any part of the country, so that mortgage money may be made available where it is needed;
(6) elimination of second mortgages and of the need for periodic and expensive refinancing;
(7) encouragement of improvement in housing standards and conditions.[8]

As stated earlier, interest rates are fixed by law for both VA and FHA insured loans. When interest rates rise, these loans become less attractive to lenders, conventional loans become proportionately more attractive, and VA and FHA loan funds become very scarce.

Other features to look for are — Does the mortgage permit the borrower to adjust the original terms if he meets serious financial difficulties, such as a serious illness might bring? Does it permit the borrower to prepay his mortgage without a penalty? Does it have an "open-end", which will permit the borrower to increase the loan in the future without having to take out a new mortgage? Does it permit the borrower to finance anything else, such as appliances, under the mortgage?

---

[8] "FHA Facts for Home Buyers," Federal Housing Administration, Washington, D.C., 1959, p. 1.

VA and FHA laws and procedures have been changed from time to time. Interest rates on all three types of loans, especially the conventional, also change. For these reasons, it is essential that existing rules, regulations, and rates be investigated at the time a mortgage loan is applied for.

If the plan is to build a home rather than buy an existing one, a construction mortgage will be needed. Under this type of mortgage, the money is paid out to the person building the house, in instalments, as the work progresses. If the owner builds the home himself, or uses a general contractor, money is advanced directly to the owner.

On a conventional construction loan, there are commonly from three to six advances made at different stages of construction. The purpose of this arrangement is to make certain that the money advanced by the lender is actually used for labor and materials.

THE MORTGAGE FOR YOU

How does one go about taking out a mortgage, and how much should he apply for? Specific answers depend upon specific factors, such as the part of the country in which the borrower lives, his financial resources and obligations, and other pertinent considerations; but general answers to these questions can be given.

Pages 214 and 215 show a mortgage application. The person wishing to buy or build must apply for a loan just as he does whenever money is borrowed. Borrowers are required to evidence ability to meet their loan obligations before being approved. Because of the large amount of money involved in a mortgage loan, and the length of time it will be outstanding, more careful examination of the property and the borrower will be made than might be made for smaller, short term, loans.

Besides appraising the property to be mortgaged, the lender must make certain that there is a clear title. This requires a search of county and court records to be sure there are no title encumbrances. The condition of title can be evidenced in four ways. The two most common are, by an "abstract of title," which is a summary of the publicly recorded transactions that have occurred concerning this piece of property; and by "title insurance," which is issued by a title insurance company and assures both the mortgagee and mortgagor that their rights to the property, as shown in the title insurance policy, will be protected if such rights are ever questioned. Two other methods are, by use of a Torrens Certificate, which is issued by a governmental unit and evidences and registers title to real property;

and the certificate of title, in which an attorney certifies that he has examined the records and that, in his opinion, there appear to be no unsettled prior claims or liens.

The final step is the "closing." The Realtor, the seller of the property, the lender, the buyer, and their attorneys get together, and agree upon a closing statement, showing all prorations as debits and credits, and the net amount due the seller. The lender gives the buyer a check for the net proceeds of the mortgage loan. The buyer then endorses this over to the seller, and gives the seller a check for the balance of the net price due the seller. The seller then delivers to the buyer a warranty deed to the property, together with the evidence of title. Certain closing costs must also be paid by the buyer. These usually include an appraisal fee, legal fees, fees for title search and insurance, fees for recording the mortgage, and a charge by the lender for specific costs such as clerical work involved in making the loan.

Down Payment

The amount of the down payment required will differ between lending institutions. If the mortgage is VA or FHA, the down payment required may be smaller than if the loan is conventional.

The down payment should be as large as possible, but all available cash shouldn't be used for this purpose, as many other cash needs will arise.

The actual amount of the mortgage cannot be suggested, as it depends on specific factors. One general bit of sound advice, however, is to make it as small as possible. Obviously, the more you borrow, the greater will be the cost of borrowing and the larger the monthly payments.

Monthly Payments

The size of the monthly payment will depend upon four things: the amount of the down payment, the amount of the loan, the length of the loan, and the interest rate. Today, almost all mortgage loans are amortized. This means that the borrower pays fixed monthly instalments which include payments toward the principal of the loan and the interest. An example of this is presented in Table 8-4. At the beginning of the loan, the interest is the major portion of the monthly payment. As time passes and the outstanding loan balance becomes smaller, the interest payment becomes a smaller portion of the monthly payment and the principal payment a larger portion.

Name ....   Res. Telephone ....

Mailing Address ....   Bus. Telephone ....

City and State ....   Loan Number ....

Property Address ....   Term of Loan ....

City and State ....   Date ....

Application *for* Loan *from*

I (We) hereby apply for a first mortgage loan of $............to be repaid in installments of $............ per month to be applied first to interest and the balance to principal, and offer as security, a mortgage on the following described property:

LEGAL DESCRIPTION

....

....

Complete description of the buildings, including garages, etc.: Type, Structure, Heat, Rooms, Baths, etc.

....

....

....

....

Size of Lot ....   Last Tax Paid ....   General Assessments ....

Age of Building ....   When Remodeled ....   Cost of Repairs ....

When Purchased ....   Purchase Price ....   Construction Cost ....

State amount of the Original Mortgage, when made and balance due ....

....

....

Mortgage held by ....

Address ....Telephone ....

Other Liens ....

Judgments—Explain ....

Places of residence for past 7 years ....

....

PURPOSE OF LOAN ....

....

....

....

....

Where did you hear
about the Association? ....

PERSONAL

(Husband)
NAME ....Address ....

Age ....Married ....Children ....Ages ....

Employed by ....Address ....

Kind of Business ....Term of Employment ....

Position ....How Long ....Previous Position ....

Previous Employers ....Reason
for Change ....

....Reason
for Change ....

(Wife)
NAME ....Age ....

Employed by ....Address ....How Long ....

Merchant References

....Address ....

....Address ....

....Address ....

INCOME Salary ....Paid By ....

Wife ....Paid By ....

Children ....Paid By ....

Children ....Paid By ....

Rent ....

Other Sources ....

LIFE INSURANCE

Company	Amount	Purchased	Premium
....	....	....	....
....	....	....	....
....	....	....	....

Have you borrowed against policies? ....Amount ....

Other Obligations ....Amount ....

Installment Payments ....Nature ....Amount ....

Bank Account at ....Checking
Savings ....

Bank Account at ....Checking
Savings ....

Own Other Real Estate? ....Location..

Value ....Encumbrances ....

Personal Property (stocks, bonds, etc.) ....

The undersigned agree to furnish a complete and merchantable abstract of title or guarantee policy, continued so as to show said mortgage to be a first record lien, which shall remain in the hands of said Association together with all insurance policies and other recorded and necessary required securities for use of the lender until the said loan is paid.

Applicant further agrees to pay or reimburse the Association for the payment of all necessary expenses incurred for abstract, guarantee policy, Torrens title, recording charges, taxes due, unpaid interest, committee charges and fees, or other disbursements on said loan as authorized in the preceding paragraph or hereunder on said loan and attorney fees for examination of abstract, but if applicant at any time before completion decides that he does not wish the loan, he shall pay or reimburse the Association for payment of, only such expenses charged, fees, taxes and interest, as may have been incurred or paid up to the time notice of such decision has been given by applicant to the Association. All of such amounts may be deducted from any loan made the applicant (if not previously paid by applicant). Notwithstanding an agreement of the Association to make this loan, it is understood that the same may be rejected by the Association for falsity in any statement in this application or if, in the opinion of the Association, this applicant has an unsatisfactory credit reputation, or if the examination of title discloses unsatisfactory conditions which cannot, within a reasonable time, be perfected. In the event of such rejection, applicant agrees to pay, or reimburse the Association for the payment of, all of the above described fees and charges which have then been incurred or paid.

....(SEAL)   ....(SEAL)

Source: "The Story of Modern Home Financing," published by the United States Savings and Loan League, Chicago, Ill., 1957-58, Revised 1961, pp. 19-20.

Table 8-4

ILLUSTRATION OF MONTHLY
AMORTIZED LOAN PAYMENTS

Amount Borrowed: $10,000		Interest Rate: 6%		Term of Loan: 20 Years	
Time		Monthly Payment			Balance Due on Loan at End of Month
Years	Months	Total	Interest Portion	Principal Repayment	
0	1	$71.70	$50.00	$21.70	$9,978.30
0	2	71.70	49.90	21.80	9,956.50
0	3	71.70	49.80	21.90	9,934.60
3	1	71.70	45.70	26.00	9,120.40
3	2	71.70	45.60	26.10	9,094.30
3	3	71.70	45.50	26.20	9,068.10
10	1	71.70	32.20	39.50	6,404.10
10	2	71.70	32.00	39.70	6,364.40
15	1	71.70	18.40	53.30	3,635.60
18	1	71.70	8.00	63.70	1,530.60
19	10	71.70	.90	70.80	116.10
19	11	71.70	.60	71.10	45.00
Final Payment		45.20	.20	45.00	0.00

Source: "The Story of Modern Home Financing," published by the United States Savings and Loan League, Chicago, Illinois, 1957-58, Revised 1961, p. 17.

How important are the various factors affecting the size of the monthly payment? The down payment and the amount of the loan can be considered together as, given a particular piece of property selling at a specific price, it is obvious that the larger the down payment the smaller the loan, and vice versa. How much will the amount of the loan affect the monthly payments? Table 8-5 lists monthly payments which apply to an FHA loan and include principal, interest and mortgage insurance. As you can see, the monthly payment for a $10,000 loan for 20 years at 5¼ per cent would be $71.51, while the monthly payment on a $20,000 mortgage would be $143.02.

Table 8-5

Monthly Payment To Principal, Interest and Mortgage Insurance Premium and Total Monthly Payment At 5¼ Percent[9]

Term of Loan	$10,000			$15,000			$20,000		
	Principal and Interest	Mortgage Insurance Premium*	Total Monthly Payment	Principal and Interest	Mortgage Insurance Premium*	Total Monthly Payment	Principal and Interest	Mortgage Insurance Premium*	Total Monthly Payment
20 years	$ 67.40	$ 4.11	$ 71.51	$101.10	$ 6.17	$107.27	$134.80	$ 8.22	$143.02
25 "	60.00	4.13	64.13	90.00	6.19	96.19	120.00	8.26	128.26
30 "	55.30	4.14	59.44	82.95	6.21	89.16	110.60	8.28	118.88
35 "	52.10	4.15	56.25	78.15	6.22	84.37	104.20	8.29	112.49
**40 "	49.90	4.15	54.05	74.85	6.23	81.08			

Total Cost of Interest at 5¼ Percent and Total Mortgage Insurance Premiums

Term of Loan	$10,000 LOAN			$15,000 LOAN			$20,000 LOAN		
	Interest	Mortgage Insurance Premium	Total	Interest	Mortgage Insurance Premium	Total	Interest	Mortgage Insurance Premium	Total
20 years	$ 6,169	$ 588	$ 6,757	$ 9,254	$ 882	$10,136	$12,339	$1,175	$13,514
25 "	7,954	757	8,711	11,930	1,136	13,066	15,907	1,515	17,422
30 "	9,839	937	10,776	14,758	1,405	16,163	19,678	1,873	21,551
35 "	11,851	1,129	12,980	17,777	1,693	19,470	23,702	2,258	25,960
**40 "	13,931	1,327	15,258	20,896	1,990	22,886			

Taxes and hazard insurance are added to the monthly payments, but not shown in these charts.

* Monthly premium during first year of loan at the rate of ½% per annum on average outstanding balance during year.

** Maximum mortgage term 30 years or, if property was inspected by FHA or VA during construction, 35 years. On low-cost homes the 35-year term may be increased to not more than 40 years when authorized by FHA Commissioner.

[9] "FHA Financing for Home Purchases and Home Improvements," Federal Housing Administration, Washington, D.C., 1962, p. 3.

How about the length of the loan? Table 8-5 also indicates the effect of this factor. The monthly payment on a $10,000 loan at 5¼ per cent for 20 years would be $71.51, while the monthly payment for 40 years would be only $54.05.

The last factor was the interest rate. To illustrate the effect of this, let's assume a conventional loan of $10,000 and a term of 20 years, but allow the interest rate to vary. The following indicates how various interest rates would affect the monthly payments:

Interest Rate	Monthly Payments
5%	$66.00
5¼%	67.39
5½%	68.80
5¾%	70.20
6%	71.65

To sum up: the smaller the loan, the longer the term, and the lower the interest rate, the smaller the monthly payment.

A borrower should try to get the lowest possible rate and borrow only an amount that is absolutely necessary. The monthly payment could be reduced even further by increasing the length of the loan period, but, at this point, the goal should be to make monthly payments an amount which the borrower can carry without financial difficulty, not to attempt to reduce them to as small an amount as possible. The reason is that lengthening the time period increases the total interest cost.

Notice the bottom portion of Table 8-5. If a person borrowed $10,000 for a period of 20 years at 5¼%, the total interest cost would be $6,169; and for 40 years, the total cost would be $13,931. This is a difference of 126 per cent, while the difference in the size of the payments, $67.40 as against $49.90, is only 26 per cent. If the lower payment is not absolutely necessary, it would certainly be unwise to extend the term simply to reduce the monthly payments.

INSURANCE

If the property is mortgaged, a certain amount of hazard insurance will be required for the lender's protection. The best buy for the average homeowner is the "Homeowners" package type policy, described in Chapter 11. This is a policy covering most of the risks faced by a homeowner. In addition to this protection, "mortgage insurance" will solve the problem of paying off the mortgage if the income-producer should become disabled or die. Table 8-6 indicates the importance of this coverage. "Mortgage insurance" is discussed in Chapter 9 while disability problems are covered in Chapter 10.

Table 8-6

The CHANCE A MAN Takes

Age of Homeowner	Chance of death within 15 years	Chance of death within 20 years
25	1 in 30	1 in 18
30	1 in 20	1 in 12
35	1 in 13	1 in 7
40	1 in 8	1 in 5
45	1 in 6	1 in 3
50	1 in 4	1 in 2

where do mortgage payments come
from with Dad's regular earned
income GONE...

Source: "Mortgage Retirement Plan," New England Mutual Life Insurance Company, Boston, Mass., 1962, p. 3.

PROPERTY TAXES

In estimating the cost of owning a home, the enthusiastic prospective homeowner often underestimates the importance of property taxes. While the problem is much more acute in some locations than in others, there seems little likelihood that the costs of community services will do anything but continue to rise. Unless new methods of dealing with this problem of rising costs are discovered and put into effect, property owners will continue to bear an increasing tax burden. Table 8-7 illustrates the amount of this tax burden in one particular location. Taxes must play a role in any estimate of home-owning costs.

Table 8-7

MORTGAGE PAYMENTS AND TAXES
$16,750 Northwest Suburban Chicago Area Home
with a $15,000, 20-Year, 5 1/2% Mortgage

Monthly Payment	Town A	Town B	Town C
For Mortgage	$103.18	$103.18	$103.18
For Taxes:			
1952	14.69	10.82	12.02
1956	18.40	19.34	16.89
1961	25.97	27.73	31.54
Tax as % of Total Payment:			
1952	12.5%	9.5%	10.4%
1956	15.1	15.8	14.1
1962	20.1	21.2	23.4

Data: First Federal Savings, Des Plaines, Ill.

Source: "Quarterly Letter on Savings and Home Mortgage Lending," published by the United States Savings and Loan League, Chicago, Illinois, Sept. 1962, p. 3.

CONCLUSION

An estimate of needs and costs is necessary whether a person wishes to rent or to buy. Buying or building means additional problems, but home ownership is the accepted way of life for the majority of American families. Buying or building requires the same care, common sense, and business-like approach that are needed in any financial transaction. Careful attention to details, a willingness to face facts as to the home that a person can afford, and the expenditure of time and effort in shopping both for the home and the mortgage are prerequisites to happy home ownership.

Questions

1. The problem of living space continuously gets worse. Why?

2. Which is cheaper—owning or renting?

3. "Every family should own its home." Discuss.

4. List 10 of the steps in building a home.

5. Discuss the various things that should be checked by the borrower obtaining a mortgage.

6. List five factors that should be considered in selecting a place to rent or buy.

7. "The greatest danger to successful homeowning is probably taking on more than a person can afford." Discuss.

8. Compare the advantages of buying a new home with those of buying an older home.

9. Why may it be unwise to attempt to reduce monthly mortgage payments to as small an amount as possible?

10. Compare conventional, VA and FHA mortgage loans.

Problems

1. Tom and Jean are planning to get married. They are trying to decide where to live. Jean seems easy to please and has found several small apartment she feels would be suitable. Tom is more difficult. One he doesn't like because it is not large enough for the children they hope to have. Another doesn't have any place for a garden, etc.
   Who is right?

2. The Thompsons need a place to live. They have found an apartment which they can rent for $125 per month. The rent includes electricity

and heat. They have also found a suitable house which they could buy. Monthly payments on the house for principal, interest and taxes would be $90. They estimate electricity and heat would be about $35. Mr. Thompson decides to buy. His reasoning is that if they can afford to pay $125 month rent on an apartment they can afford to spend the same amount to buy their own home and have all of the advantages of home owning. Discuss.

3. Using Table 8-1, how much could a person pay for a home if he makes a $4,000 down payment and can afford monthly mortgage payments of:
   a. $100 and the mortgage is for 20 years at 6%.
   b. $225 and the mortgage is for 15 years at 5%.
   c. $80 and his mortgage is for 20 years at 5½%.

4. Mr. Penning is buying a home in a suburb of a large metropolitan area. He has visited two lending sources—one a savings and loan association and the other a mutual savings bank. He finds that the terms offered by this savings and loan association are better than those offered by this mutual savings bank. He makes two assumptions.
   1. The people at the mutual savings bank don't like him or their terms would be better.
   2. He is going to insist on an FHA loan. Discuss his decisions.

5. Using Table 8-5
   a. What would the monthly payment be on a $15,000 mortgage for 25 years at 5¼%?
   b. What would the monthly payment be on a $15,000 mortgage for 35 years at 5¼%?
   c. What would be the percentage increase in total interest costs of the 35 year mortgage as compared to the 25 year?
   d. What would be the percentage reduction in monthly payments on the 35 year mortgage as compared to the 25 year?

Selected Readings

McMichael, Stanley L. and O'Keefe, Paul T., *How to Finance Real Estate*, Prentice Hall, Inc., Englewood Cliffs, New Jersey, Second Edition, 1953
"Money Management: Your Shelter Dollar," Money Management Institute, Household Finance Corporation, Prudential Plaza, Chicago 1, Illinois

Mortlock, Eugene M., "The Home for You . . . and How to Select it," First Federal Savings and Loan Association of New York, New York, N.Y., 1962

Ratcliff, Richard W., *Real Estate Analysis*, McGraw-Hill Publishing Co., New York, N.Y., 1961

"The Story of Modern Home Financing," United States Savings and Loan League, Chicago, Illinois

"What You Should Know Before You Buy a Home," United States Savings and Loan League, Chicago, Illinois, 1962

Publications for homeowners published by:

Federal Housing Administration, Printing and Publications Section, Washington 25, D.C.

Housing and Home Finance Agency, Washington, D.C.

Small Homes Council, University of Illinois, Mumford House, Urbana, Illinois

Veterans Administration, Washington, D.C.

Chapter 9

LIFE INSURANCE

One very significant value will be lost with us when we are deceased. That is our earning power. The impact of this loss will be felt by those whose needs it met, unless, during our lifetime, we provide a means of replacing it. Insurance is one such means.

There are three events which can terminate earning power: death, disability, and retirement. Life and health insurance policies have been designed to replace the income of this lost earning power under each eventuality, and a good insurance program combines the various types of coverage to meet the needs of those who are dependent upon this income.

"Buy life insurance" is probably the most widely accepted financial advice given. Even mutual funds and brokerage firms selling common stocks, which both compete for every investment dollar, caution prospective investors to buy adequate life insurance before investing in equities.

By the end of 1962, there were 134 million policyholders in the United States, and $730 billion of life insurance in force. The average amount per family was $12,300.[1] This average should have been much higher. $12,300 is about two years of average family income. Insurance experts agree that a rough measure of the minimum amount needed by the average man is from four to five times his annual income before taxes. Other experts suggest a premium outlay of from 10 to 15 percent of a man's annual income before taxes.

Young people often find it difficult to recognize a need for life insurance. They are healthy and full of life, and the possibility of death seems quite remote. On an average, they have few dependents, and those that are single generally have none.

But life insurance offers more than death benefits. It is an investment, and the longer the investment is postponed, the more expensive it becomes. Every person has reason to plan for the future. Look at the problems presented in Table 9-1 and note particularly the results in the last column. The 39 failures failed to plan.

TYPES OF COMPANIES

Mutual and Stock

At the end of 1961, there were more than 1,450 "legal reserve" life insurance companies in the United States, with about $629 billion of life insurance in force. They are called "legal reserve" companies because of the strict legal requirements governing their reserves.

These may be either stock or mutual companies. If they are stock companies, they are owned by their stockholders, who share in the profits. Some of these companies issue non-participating policies, under which the policyholders do not share in the profits. Others issue participating policies under which the policyholders do share in the profits.

---

[1] Statistics from "Life Insurance Fact Book 1963," Institute of Life Insurance, New York, New York, pp. 5 and 11.

Table 9-1

A primer on the problems of life and living

HERE ARE 100 AMERICAN MEN

. . . all married, each 25 years old. They are a healthy group, all enjoying life and looking forward to a solid, satisfying future. When not pursuing their careers, each spends his time at home with the wife and children, busy in the yard, or puttering on a hobby. If you asked any one of them about life, he might complain mildly about bills but would admit that life looked rosy.

Age 35	Age 45	Age 55	Age 65	29 Widows	71 Survivors
—Here is the same group ten years later, at age 35.	—Ten years later, at age 45, this original group has shrunk to 95 men.	—Despite the advances of modern medical science, age begins to take a heavy toll by 55.	—At age 65, there are but 71 men left of the original 100.	—Of the group's 29 widows, two have remarried, one died in an auto accident and another— sorely pressed financially— ended her life with sleeping pills.	—Let's look at the 71 men and their lives:
Only 98 men made it through the decade.	The years saw one man die following a heart attack, one in an auto accident and a third from T.B.	Of the original group, there are 87 living men.	Fifteen men—husbands and fathers—died in the last decade of the following causes:	The remaining 25 widows depend for at least part of their support on their 47 children: the balance from public charity and Social Security.	—4 live on skid row as derelicts —2 are in jail —17 eke out a living on Social Security and relief —16 live with families or are supported in homes for the aged by their children —23 bolster their Social Security with small savings and company pensions —3 are wealthy —6 are fixed for life.
One man died in an auto accident and one of a heart attack.		The decade of their late forties and early fifties counted three deaths from accidents, three from heart trouble, one from coronary brain clot and one from cancer.	four from heart attacks, two from cancer, two from coronary brain clots, two from pneumonia and influenza, two from kidney trouble, one from suicide, one from diabetes and one in a homicide.		
One widow has remarried.	By now, four widows survive their husbands, and seven of the eight fatherless children are in school.	There are 12 widows, most of whom have virtually no opportunity for remarriage.		Most had life insurance benefits, but these funds were quickly dissipated on medical expenses.	They have incomes from real estate, stocks, bonds or savings, and life insurance and annuities.
The other has two children to support.			For the survivors, life ahead looks toward retirement or forced suspension from work and income.	Only three have lifetime incomes from life insurance and annuities.	—Thirty-nine of these 71 men did not plan to fail. They just failed to plan.
For the other 98, incomes have improved, many own their homes, nearly all are raising families and looking forward to many good years ahead.	For the widows, the possibility for remarriage are becoming remote.	Ten of the 12 depend upon at least part of their support from their children, who are just beginning married lives of their own.			The purpose of life insurance is to help these people plan.

Source: Occidental Life Insurance Company of California

226

Mutual companies have no stockholders. They are owned by the policyholders, and almost all of their policies are participating. At the end of each year the company sets part of its profits aside as reserves and distributes the entire balance to the policyholders in the form of dividends.

Dividends received from stock and mutual companies are not the same. Dividends received from stock companies represent a share of the profit that has been made on the capital invested. Dividends received from mutual companies are considered a return of that part of the premium paid by the policyholder which was not needed to meet claims or cover operating expenses. These dividends will vary according to the type of policy owned, the period the policy has been in force, and the policyholder's age.

There is very little difference in the methods of operation of stock and mutual companies. They pay similar taxes, issue the same types of policies, etc. Due to their large size, they are both operated by boards of directors and officers. Neither policyholders nor stockholders have much voice in determining company policies. There were 1,480 legal reserve companies in business in mid-1962. Of these, 1,322 were owned by stockholders and 158 were mutual companies. The mutual companies, generally older and larger than most of the stock companies, accounted for three-fifths of the total life insurance in force.[2]

Fraternal

Another type of company is the "fraternal" life company. At the end of 1961, $13.1 billion of fraternal life insurance was in force. These companies originally provided insurance for members of a particular lodge, society, or other fraternal organization. They are exempt from the taxes paid by legal reserve companies, including the federal income tax. They are not as stringently regulated, in terms of reserve requirements, as stock and mutual companies. They often write "open-end" policies, which permit them to change the coverage given by the policy by changing the organization's charter or by-laws. This is an advantage to the fraternal order, but a disadvantage to the policyholder if such a change reduces the effective coverage.

Savings Bank

In Massachusetts, New York, and Connecticut, mutual savings banks sell life insurance. They issue all of the usual forms of policies,

---

[2] Statistics from "Life Insurance Fact Book 1963," Institute of Life Insurance, New York, N.Y., 1963, pp. 97–98.

and sell them at a lower cost than most of those sold by legal reserve companies. These policies have early and liberal cash and loan values. Dividends have been paid on policies issued in Massachusetts every year since Savings Bank Life Insurance originated in that state, in 1907.

In all, there are about $1.5 billion in savings bank life insurance. Massachusetts, where the system is the oldest, had over $800 million in Savings Bank Insurance in force at the end of 1962.

This insurance was originally intended to provide the working man with an opportunity to buy low cost life insurance in small amounts. Primarily because banks are not permitted to employ insurance salesmen, their expenses are quite low.

It might be expected that such a system would seriously reduce the amount of insurance sold by regular legal reserve companies. The reserves behind Savings Bank Life Insurance are carefully regulated; their dividends, loan values, and cash values are liberal; they offer a wide variety of policies; and their costs to the purchaser are usually less. Yet sales of Savings Bank Life Insurance have not been startling. In the three states having this system, the insurance sold each year is only a fraction of that sold by the ordinary legal reserve insurance company.

If Savings Bank Life Insurance is such a good buy for most people —and it is—why isn't more of it sold? There are two reasons, and both have to do with the services of the salesman. In the first place, insurance salesmen perform a necessary and valuable service. Very few people know enough about insurance to plan their own program. A trained insurance agent is much more than a salesman. He can set up a proper insurance program, suggest when changes should be made in insurance coverage, assist in estate planning, and help the beneficiaries at a time when they may badly need such help.

In the second place, even those few people who might do without the services of an agent, either because they know quite a bit about insurance themselves or because someone who does is advising them, often do not buy the lowest cost coverage. Look at it this way. There are many people who do not vote in national elections. Even they will admit that they should. Why don't they? Well, if the laws are ever changed to permit someone to bring the ballot to them, show them where to place their mark, and lend them a pen, then these people will vote. The same is true of insurance. Even though almost everyone agrees that insurance is essential, and even though it is available for less money a short distance away at the savings bank, many people evidently will not make the effort to buy it. They want someone to bring the policy to the house, show them where to sign, and put the pen in their hand.

State Insurance

Wisconsin has a state owned insurance company which can issue policies of from $1,000 to $10,000 to residents of the state. There are no salesmen. Insurance policies are sold in the office of the state insurance commissioner. The Wisconsin State Life Fund has an extremely small percentage of the total life insurance business done in the state. Again, as in the case of Savings Bank Life Insurance, it seems that agents are needed to sell insurance.

Veteran's Insurance

At the present time, servicemen are not entitled to any special kind of government insurance. This has been true since 1956, when they were brought into the social security system. There is, however, a considerable amount of National Service Life Insurance and U.S. Government Life Insurance still in force, resulting from World Wars I and II and the Korean War. It totalled over $40 billion at the end of 1960. There is one small, but important, bit of advice that may be given to those now holding it. KEEP IT. No other insurance can compete with it in terms of cost. In fact, if, as a result of the pressure of various veteran's groups, there is ever a reopening of eligibility for this insurance, it would be wise for all who can to take advantage of the opportunity.

Conclusion

With the exception of less than $2 billion of insurance with assessment associations, burial societies, and mutual aid groups—an amount which doesn't change much from year to year—we have now examined the various sources of insurance. It is obvious that the most important, in terms of both total insurance in force and total sales each year, are the legal reserve mutual and stock companies.

TYPES OF POLICIES

Table 9-2 indicates some of the different types of insurance available. The three basic types of insurance contracts are term, straight life, and endowment. These are combined in various ways to produce a large number of different type coverages to meet different needs.

Table 9-2

What $100 A Year Will Buy†

(Starting at age 22)

	Annual Rate Per $1,000 of Insurance	Amount of Ins. $100 a Year Will Buy*	Cash Value at Age 65 Per $100 Annual Premium	Monthly Life Income at Age 65, Men (10 Years Certain)
1. Term (5 year renewable & convertible)	$ 5.80	$17,241	—	—
2. Term (10 year renewable & convertible)	7.00	14,286	—	—
3. Modified 5 (minimum policy $2,000)	11.88**			
	17.24***	5,800	$3,567	$22.47
4. Straight Life	14.85	6,734	4,141	26.09
5. Straight Life (with 20 year family income rider)	18.30	5,464	3,360	21.17
6. Straight Life (with 20 year family maintenance rider)	20.00	5,000	3,075	19.37
7. Life-Paid-Up-At-65	17.10	5,848	4,298	27.08
8. 20-Payment Life	26.75	3,738	2,747	17.31
9. Endowment at 65	19.60	5,102	5,102	32.14
10. 20-Year Endowment	47.05	2,125	—	—
11. Retirement Income At 65 (male)	27.15	3,683	6,095	38.40
12. Retirement Income At 65 (female)	29.85	3,350	6,265	39.47

* (Most policies are issued in $1,000 units or in multiples of $500)
** (1st year)
*** (Thereafter)
† While actual dollar amounts may change over the years as rates, etc., change, the *relative* positions of the various policies in terms of cost will stay the same.

Source: Jerome B. Cohen, *Decade of Decision*, prepared by Educational Division, Institute of Life Insurance, New York, N.Y., 1960, p. 26.

Term

Term insurance offers protection for a period of time stated in the policy—usually 5, 10, or 20 years—or to some stated age, such as 65. Premiums are low because it is limited coverage and does not build any cash value. However, term insurance will be the most expensive form in the long run for those who outlive the term of coverage.

There are certain instances when term insurance is advisable. Some of these are :

1. To supplement straight life insurance while the children are growing.
2. To cover a mortgage on the home—the popular mortgage term policy.
3. To provide protection when a person cannot afford the premium on straight life.
4. To protect the family or estate against temporary debts expected to be paid within a few years.
5. To protect a creditor against loss if death should occur before the debt is paid.

At the end of the contract period, a term policy ends. During this time, no cash value has been accumulated. If the policyholder wishes to renew his coverage, the premium will be higher.

Straight Life

The basic type of life insurance providing permanent protection is "straight life." This is a level premium insurance, and the cost doesn't change. The premium will stay the same until the policyholder dies.

Most people buy life insurance with two purposes in mind:

1. To protect their families against the loss of income they would suffer if the policyholder were to die.
2. To build up savings that can be used in an emergency, for a special purpose, or to supplement income after the policyholder's retirement.[3]

Straight life insurance can serve both of these purposes, primarily because it builds up a cash value and a loan value. After a certain period of time, a policyholder will receive cash if he cancels his policy, or he can borrow against it.

The level premium is developed on the principle of longevity. Using mortality tables which they have compiled, insurance companies can predict the number of policyholders that will die at each age. They establish premiums that will assure an income sufficient to cover all of the death claims that must be paid. This means that during the early years, a surplus will be accumulated. The extra money will be invested, and the return also used to pay off claims, thus reducing the policyholders' premiums. Besides paying death claims, the premium must also cover operating expenses and provide a

---

[3] "A Date With Your Future," *Money Management for the Young Adult,* Educational Division, Institute of Life Insurance, New York, New York, 1962, p. 20.

small amount to cover investment losses and other contingencies. An excellent example of this process is presented in Table 9-3 on page 233.

Chart 9-1 is an illustration of how a level premium compares with the increasing amounts that must be paid for term insurance. Notice the amount paid during the early years for the straight life policy in excess of the amount needed to meet death claims. As stated above, the extra money is invested and the return on the investment helps to pay part of the cost of the insurance. The total number of dollars a policyholder would pay over the entire period would be higher for the step-rate plan, because there is no reserve fund that may be used to earn interest and defray part of the cost of the insurance.

Chart 9-1

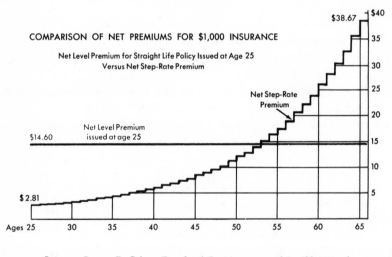

Source: Jerome B. Cohen, *Decade of Decision*, prepared by Educational Division, Institute of Life Insurance, New York, N.Y., 1960, p. 11.

Limited Payment Life

This also provides lifetime protection. The difference between limited payment life and the preceding straight life policy is that premiums are paid only during a limited time period. Naturally, the premiums are higher than under straight life, because they are paid over a shorter period of time. Because of these higher premiums, the cash and loan values of these policies increase faster than those of straight life policies.

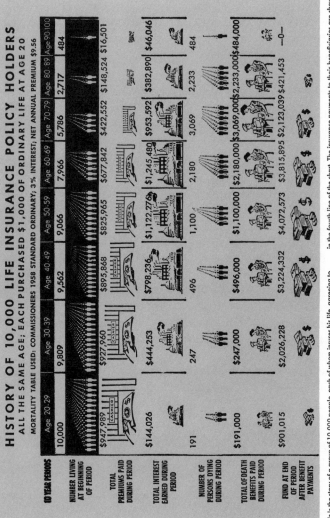

HISTORY OF 10,000 LIFE INSURANCE POLICY HOLDERS
ALL THE SAME AGE; EACH PURCHASED $1,000 OF ORDINARY LIFE AT AGE 20
MORTALITY TABLE USED: COMMISSIONERS 1958 STANDARD ORDINARY; 3% INTEREST; NET ANNUAL PREMIUM $9.56

10 YEAR PERIODS	Age 20-29	Age 30-39	Age 40-49	Age 50-59	Age 60-69	Age 70-79	Age 80-89	Age 90-100
NUMBER LIVING AT BEGINNING OF PERIOD	10,000	9,809	9,562	9,066	7,966	5,786	2,717	484
TOTAL PREMIUMS PAID DURING PERIOD	$947,989	$927,960	$895,868	$825,965	$677,842	$422,552	$148,524	$16,501
TOTAL INTEREST EARNED DURING PERIOD	$144,026	$444,253	$798,236	$1,122,276	$1,245,480	$953,592	$382,890	$46,046
NUMBER OF PERSONS DYING DURING PERIOD	191	247	496	1,100	2,180	3,069	2,233	484
TOTAL OF DEATH BENEFITS PAID DURING PERIOD	$191,000	$247,000	$496,000	$1,100,000	$2,180,000	$3,069,000	$2,233,000	$484,000
FUND AT END OF PERIOD AFTER BENEFIT PAYMENTS	$901,015	$2,026,228	$3,224,332	$4,072,573	$3,815,895	$2,123,039	$421,453	—0—

This is the story of a group of 10,000 people, each of whom insures his life, agreeing to pay the same premium each year as long as he lives. According to a standard mortality table, and assuming that 3% interest can be earned, the money needed to pay for this protection is $9.56 annually per person, without any allowance for operating expenses. The number living at the start of each ten year period, based on this mortality table, is illustrated in the first row. The total premiums paid for each ten year period are shown over the cashiers' windows. These premiums build up a fund from which all death benefits are paid. Until needed the fund is invested. The miniature cities illustrate the interest earnings, which also become part of the fund. Those who die in each period, according to the mortality table, are represented by the ranks of people in the fourth line of the chart. The insurance payments to their beneficiaries are shown by the postman delivering the insurance checks. The last line pictures the fund which is built up by premiums and interest earnings, and from which death benefits are paid. Since the fund disappears entirely when the last benefit is paid, it is evident that the "net" annual payments of $9.56 by each policyholder are just sufficient, with the aid of interest earnings, to pay all claims. In other words, total premiums paid of $4,863,201 plus total interest earned of $5,136,799 during the eighty years are just equal to the total benefit payments of $10,000,000 to the beneficiaries of all 10,000 policyholders. This chart shows why sizable assets are needed to meet policyholders' obligations.

Source: R. Wilfred Kelsey, *Handbook of Life Insurance*, Institute of Life Insurance, New York, N.Y., 1963, pp. 44-45.

A popular policy is the limited payment to age 65. Many people do not wish to continue paying premiums after retirement. This type of policy gives them protection and cash and loan values, and requires no premium payments after 65. Limited payment life policies for shorter periods, e.g., ten to twenty years, are not too popular as they require such high premiums that the extra money could more advantageously be used for either additional straight life insurance coverage, or other family needs.

Endowments

Endowment policies cover a specified period of time, and emphasize savings. If the policyholder dies during the specified period, the face amount of the policy is paid to the beneficiary. If the policyholder lives, he will be paid this amount at the end of the time period.

Endowment policies are much more expensive than straight life because of the emphasis on savings. For this reason, a person should carefully consider the relative importance of savings vs. protection when purchasing insurance. A great deal more protection can be purchased for the same amount of money if a straight life policy is purchased. Endowments are often used to save funds for some special financial goal, and should be approached with care. Taking out an endowment policy on a child's life to provide cash to cover college costs is unwise. If the father dies, the children might be hard-pressed to pay the premiums. It would be much wiser to carry extra insurance on the father's life during this period. Then, if he dies, the extra coverage will provide the cash necessary to cover the college costs. If he lives, it will have a cash and loan value.

Combinations

By combining term and straight life, or limited payment life and endowment insurance, a variety of coverages can be created to meet special needs. A few of these will be described.

One of the most popular combinations is the family income, or family protection, policy. This is a combination of straight life and decreasing term insurance.

A family income policy assures the family a regular monthly income for a specified number of years from the date of the policy, commencing as of the date the policyholder dies. If, for example, a 20 year family income policy was taken out in 1964, providing for a payment of $100 per month to the family in the event of the death of the policyholder during the 20 year term, the $100 per month would be paid from the date of death to 1984. If the policyholder dies in 1964, the payments would be made over a twenty year period. If the policyholder dies in 1983, payments would be made for just one year. This is the decreasing term part of the combined coverage. At the end of the twenty year period, the beneficiaries would receive the full amount of the straight life portion. If the insured lives, the policy becomes a straight life policy at the end of the twenty year period. Under a typical policy of this type, a small amount would be paid to the beneficiaries upon the death of the insured—let's say $750—to help cover funeral expenses, etc. The family would then receive the $100 per month for the remainder of the original twenty year period and, at the end of the period, would receive the face value of the straight life portion, perhaps $5,000. The actual amounts vary, of course, depending upon the specific policy purchased.

A family maintenance policy is similar to the family income policy, except that payments would continue for twenty years after the death of the insured instead of for just the balance of the original twenty year period. Again, the face value of the straight life portion of the combined policy would be paid to the beneficiaries when the monthly payments end.

Another combination of straight life and term insurance provides straight life insurance for the husband and term insurance for the wife and children. The wife is usually insured until her husband reaches 65, and the children until they reach some specified age, usually 21 to 25.

Another combination, the modified life policy, is especially attractive to newlyweds. It provides lifetime protection for those who are not yet financially able to pay for it. For the first few years, the premiums are lower than for a straight life policy, but more than for term. This is term insurance which can be switched to a straight life policy at the end of the term. The premiums then increase, but are not as high as the premiums would be on a straight life policy purchased at the later age.

A retirement policy combines life insurance with a life income of a specified amount per month. These are even more expensive than endowment policies, as the accumulated cash value must be greater than the face value of the policy, and must build up even faster than the endowment policy. If the policyholder should die before retirement, his beneficiary would receive the face amount or the cash value, whichever was higher.

Term and permanent insurance may serve as "mortgage insurance." Table 9-4 illustrates how the mortgage on a home may be covered by either term insurance, a combination of term and ordinary

Table 9–4

I. *Lowest Premium*
DECREASING TERM (15 units)
The amount of life insurance protection decreases
year by year as the amount of the mortgage grows
smaller.

$15,000, 20 Year Mortgage, Age 30

Annual premium	$ 73.35

20 Year Summary

premiums	$1,467.00
dividends	$ 363.30*
net cost	$1,103.70*

2. *Specially Designed*
COMBINATION PLAN
*(combining $6,000 Ordinary Life and 6 units of 15 year
Mortgage Rider)*
A Mortgage Rider providing a decreasing amount of
life insurance protection for the first part of the
mortgage period with a base of permanent insurance
and a growing cash value.

$15,000, 20 Year Mortgage, Age 30

Annual premium (First 15 years)	$ 149.52
(Thereafter	$ 121.32)

20 Year Summary

premiums	$2,849.40
accumulated dividends	$ 748.00*
cash value	$1,967.94

3. *The All-Permanent Plan*
ORDINARY LIFE ($15,000)
This plan uses permanent insurance to cover the
amount of the mortgage, at the same time building
sufficient cash value to pay off a 20-year mortgage in
a lump sum as much as 4 years ahead of schedule,
if so desired.

$15,000, 20 Year Mortgage, Age 30

Annual premium	$ 303.30

20 Year Summary

premiums	$6,066.00
accumulated dividends	$2,044.00*
cash value	$4,919.85

*Dividends are computed on the 1962 dividend scale and are
neither estimates nor guarantees for the future. A terminal dividend is payable upon surrender, lapse or death after at least
fifteen policy years, but only if declared by the company at
such time.

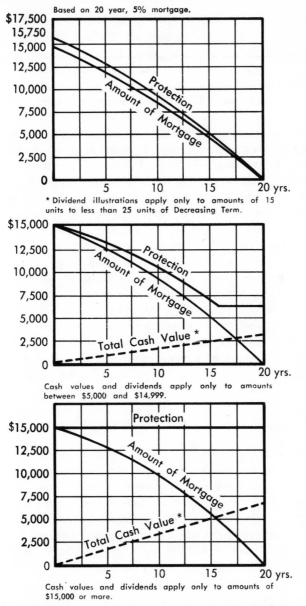

Based on 20 year, 5% mortgage.

* Dividend illustrations apply only to amounts of 15 units to less than 25 units of Decreasing Term.

Cash values and dividends apply only to amounts between $5,000 and $14,999.

Cash values and dividends apply only to amounts of $15,000 or more.

Naturally, the permanent insurance present in plans 2 and 3 has certain advantages not available in most term insurance plans. For example: there is a growing amount of cash value which, when the need for mortgage protection has passed, may be taken as cash or used to purchase paid-up insurance.

Source: *Three Ways to Insure a Mortgage,* New England Mutual Life Insurance Company, Boston, Massachusetts.

(straight) life, or by ordinary life alone. It is obvious that the annual premiums are highest on the ordinary life and lowest on term insurance, but that the ordinary life proves to be the least expensive over a twenty year period due to the accumulated dividends and cash value.

As Table 9-5 indicates, some types of insurance can be used for different purposes. This table presents the values offered by a 20 payment ordinary life policy. Note that if death occurred during the first year, the entire $15,000 face value of the policy would be needed to pay off the mortgage. If death occurred at the end of 20 years, only $1,093 would be needed to pay off the mortgage, and the remaining $13,907 would be available to pay costs of education, or to meet other costs. One policy, then, serves a number of purposes. Regarded in one light, it is "mortgage insurance," in another, it is "education insurance," and in another, it is simply "life insurance."

Most families have a mortgage and mortgage insurance policies are popular. How wise an investment is mortgage insurance? True, it will pay off the mortgage, upon the death of the insured, but is it always advisable for the widow to keep the house? Even with the mortgage paid, the house might be too expensive for her to support. The thousand and one little odd jobs the deceased used to do must now be done either by the widow or by hired help. Taxes, insurance, maintenance and repair expense will continue. It is likely that, in many cases, the premiums used to purchase mortgage insurance might more wisely have been used to purchase other types of insurance.

Group Insurance

Group life insurance has grown rapidly in the United States during the past 20 years. During 1962, the number of individual certificates outstanding rose by 2.3 million and the number of master contracts by 13,000. More than two out of three of the nation's civilian non-farm workers were covered. By the end of 1962, the amount in force in the United States reached a record total of 209.2 billion. There were 48 million individual certificates in force under 193,000 group life insurance master contracts.[4]

This type of insurance is sold under one master policy, on a group basis, to a business organization, labor union, professional group, an industry, etc. Usually, no medical examination is required. The insurance has no cash value, and is issued on a renewable term basis of one year. Sometimes, employees pay part of the cost, but the

---

[4] Statistics from "Life Insurance Fact Book 1963," Institute of Life Insurance, New York, N.Y., 1963, p. 27.

Table 9-5

How Your Life Insurance Does
DOUBLE DUTY
Based on $15,000 of Ordinary Life

**GUARANTEES THE MONEY
TO PAY OFF THE MORTGAGE***

**PROVIDES FUND FOR
COLLEGE OR OTHER NEEDS**

		AMOUNT OF LIFE INSURANCE		
Year	Amount of the mortgage	To pay mortgage	For other needs	Guaranteed cash value (For policy issued at age 30)
1	$15,000	$15,000	—	$ 66.60
2	14,525	14,525	$ 475	310.20
3	14,029	14,029	971	558.00
4	13,511	13,511	1,489	810.00
5	12,968	12,968	2,032	1,066.20
6	12,401	12,401	2,599	1,326.30
7	11,807	11,807	3,193	1,590.75
8	11,187	11,187	3,813	1,831.35
9	10,537	10,537	4,463	2,075.25
10	9,858	9,858	5,142	2,322.00
11	9,148	9,148	5,852	2,571.60
12	8,405	8,405	6,595	2,823.90
13	7,628	7,628	7,372	3,078.75
14	6,815	6,815	8,185	3,336.15
15	5,965	5,965	9,035	3,595.65
16	5,076	5,076	9,924	3,857.25
17	4,146	4,146	10,854	4,120.65
18	3,174	3,174	11,826	4,385.70
19	2,157	2,157	12,843	4,652.25
20	1,093	1,093	13,907	4,919.85

*Based on 20 year, 4½% mortgage.

Source: New England Mutual Life Insurance Company.

employer usually pays the full premium. Whether the employee pays part of the cost or not, group insurance is a valuable fringe benefit. The premium is lower than it would be if the same coverage was bought by an individual. Many policies contain a conversion clause, permitting an employee who leaves the group to convert his policy within a certain number of days to straight life or endowment insurance. The premium will then be higher, but the coverage will be broader. Most of these plans now provide some life insurance coverage after retirement.

Industrial Life Insurance

For the coverage it provides, industrial life insurance is the highest cost insurance sold. It is issued for small amounts, and the premiums are usually paid weekly to an agent who calls at the policyholder's home. Generally speaking, no medical examination is required. Because it provides insurance coverage in small amounts, to individual families unable to pay quarterly premiums, the policies are expensive to handle, and the premiums are much higher than for ordinary insurance.

Credit Life Insurance

One of the smallest but fastest growing types of insurance coverage is credit life insurance. This covers the balance of the debt due on a time-payment purchase, or a personal loan. Buying on the instalment plan has become a part of the American way of life. Credit life insurance means that the borrower's family will not be left with a debt if he should die, and also gives added assurance to the bank, finance company or retailer making the loan. This type of insurance has taken some of the risk out of consumer borrowing.

CONTRACTUAL PROVISIONS

Many people who buy life insurance read only the first page of their policy, if that. This gives them the name of the company, the face value of the policy, the name of the beneficiary (the one who will receive the proceeds if the insured dies), the name of the insured, and a few dates. There are many provisions on the following pages which are of importance to the insured and the beneficiary. Unfortunately, they are often written in language which discourages their reading by the average person. We can't possibly take up all of the provisions in this chapter, but certainly the more important deserve our attention.

Protective Clauses

There are many clauses included in an insurance contract which are primarily for the protection of the insured and the beneficiary. The incontestability clause, for example, makes it impossible for the insurance company to contest any statements made in the application for insurance, after a specified time. Even if the company can absolutely prove that the insured intended to mis-state material facts, or deliberately conceal them, nothing can be done after the specified time (usually two years) has elapsed. The company must pay the proceeds of the policy. This applies to all facts except the mis-statement of age. A person's age is the primary factor determining the premium rate that must be paid. If someone 35 says he is 25, for the purpose of getting a lower rate, his beneficiary would be entitled only to the amount of insurance his premiums would have purchased if his age had been correctly stated.

Most policies include a suicide clause, which stipulates that the insurance company will not pay if the insured dies by suicide during the first two years after the issuance of the contract. Occasionally, someone will take out a substantial amount of insurance and then commit suicide, thinking to benefit some beloved heirs. In these cases, the company's only obligation (during the first two years) is to return the premiums actually paid.

The grace period clause states that the policy will not lapse if the premium is paid within thirty-one days after payment becomes due. If the insured should die during this period, the premium will be deducted from the amount paid to the beneficiary.

If the premium is not paid during the grace period, the problem may be resolved under the reinstatement clause. This usually gives a person three to five years to reinstate the policy after it has lapsed. Reinstatement requires a special application and payment of all premiums in arrears, plus interest. The incontestability clause is reinstated, permitting the company to contest statements made in the policy for another period of time. The suicide clause is not reopened. Sometimes a new medical examination is required, sometimes not. This often depends on how long the policy has lapsed.

Too often, people assume that it will be less expensive to purchase a new policy than to reinstate the old one. A new policy means higher premiums because the insured is now older, there are new sales costs, etc. Normally, the wiser course is to take advantage of the reinstatement clause. A person should at least be aware of the clause, and carefully check the comparative costs of the two possibilities before buying a new policy.

The reinstatement clause is certainly helpful if a person is financially embarrassed and cannot pay his premiums. Another clause that helps out in such a situation is the loan clause. This permits the insured to borrow an amount equal to the cash surrender value of the policy. Usually, a policy doesn't have a cash value for one or two years, but after this time, the cash value, and therefore the loan value, grows year after year. If there is an automatic premium loan provision in the contract, it means that the company agrees to lend money to the insured automatically, to pay any premiums that may be overdue.

There are many advantages in this type of borrowing. It is true that interest must be paid on the amount borrowed, but the interest rate is usually relatively low. Remember, too, that the interest can be deducted in calculating federal income taxes. Furthermore, the insurance company cannot refuse to lend the money, cannot change the interest rate, and cannot demand repayment. This is true of any borrowing done by the insured on his policy, regardless of whether or not the money is used to pay premiums under an automatic premium loan provision, or for some other use. If anything should happen to the insured, the beneficiary will receive the face value of the policy less the loan and the accumulated interest. If at any time the loan, plus interest, equals or exceeds the cash value of the policy, the policy becomes invalid after the insured is properly notified.

Nonforfeiture Options

Earlier, it was stated that under any level term policy the premiums would be higher than necessary in the early years and lower than necessary in the later years. This extra amount paid in during the early years was invested by the company. It created a reserve, and a cash value. What happens to this cash value if, due to unfortunate financial circumstances, premium payments cannot be continued?

One option available in such circumstances is to take the accumulated cash value. This should be done only if there is a great need for cash. If the financial problems are expected to be temporary in nature, it would be better to borrow on the policy and pay the premiums.

Another option, which might be exercised if the financial problem is expected to be prolonged, is the extended term option. If this option is selected, the insured will use the cash value of his policy to purchase a term policy. This will provide the same insurance coverage as under the previous policy, for an extended period of time. How long a time will depend upon the insured's age at the time the level term policy lapsed, and its cash value. Assuming the same cash value, a young person can purchase $1,000 of term insurance for a longer period of time than an older person can, because his premium rate is lower.

A third option is to accept a reduced amount of paid-up insurance. While the insurance coverage would be smaller, no further payments would be necessary and the coverage would be permanent.

These three options are extremely beneficial to the insured. They mean that under no circumstance will he lose the cash value of his policy because he cannot afford to continue premium payments. Which one of the three is best, depends, of course, on individual circumstances. If at all possible, none of them should be used—the policy should be continued in force. If cash is desperately needed, the policyholder may be forced to take the accumulated cash value. If the need for cash isn't quite this desperate, and there is a need for a considerable amount of protection, (if the insured has young children, for example) the extended term option would be preferable. If neither cash nor maximum short-term protection is needed, the third option would be the wiser choice.

Dividend Options

Usually, a person buying a participating policy realizes that dividends will be earned, but quite often his decision as to what to do with them is not carefully thought out. Dividends amount to a considerable amount of money during the life of a policy, and merit careful consideration.

One possible choice is to take dividends in cash. This is an easy to understand possibility. The money can be used as the insured wishes. However, it may not be the wisest choice, and it is unfortunate that this choice is sometimes made only because it is the easiest to understand.

Another possibility is to use dividends to reduce the premium. This, of course, reduces the cost of insurance, and permits a person to carry greater coverage.

A third possibility is to apply dividends toward paying up the contract sooner. If they are used for this purpose, the dividends, plus the cash value, will eventually be enough to keep the insurance in force for the remainder of the insured's life, without additional premiums.

Notice that none of these three choices would increase the face value of the insurance, and therefore would not be of any advantage to the beneficiary. These three options are of benefit only to the insured.

A fourth possibility is to leave the dividends with the insurance company at interest. The company will guarantee the minimum interest rate that will be paid on these dividends.

A fifth choice is to use the dividends to buy paid-up additions. This is additional insurance which remains in force for life without any further premiums.

These last two options do benefit the beneficiary, as the total amount that will ultimately be received will be greater than the face value of the original policy. Purchasing paid-up additions is especially beneficial: no medical examination is required; the additions accrue a cash and loan value; the dividends are not taxable; and there are no sales charges.

Settlement Options

A certain amount of ready cash is needed at the time of death. How large should this amount be? If your life insurance coverage amounts to $30,000, would you want your beneficiary to receive it all in one lump? Many people would prefer to have such sums protected for future use. This can be done by selecting the proper settlement option.

The four most common settlement options are presented in Table 9-6. Under the first of these, the interest option, the money will be left with the company to earn interest. This is an extremely flexible option. It may permit the beneficiary to withdraw the money at any time, if the insured has given the beneficiary the right to make withdrawals. It gives the beneficiary time to decide which of the other options he would like to exercise. If the amount involved is large, the insured may elect not to give the beneficiary the right to withdraw the principal. The beneficiary, then, would receive only the interest. There is a perpetuity rule, however, which limits this last option so that a family can not collect such interest for eternity.

The second option guarantees payment of a certain amount of money periodically, until the money and the interest are used up.

Table 9-6

WHAT $10,000 WILL PROVIDE UNDER THE FOUR SETTLEMENT OPTIONS*[5]

OPTION	SETTLEMENT
THE INTEREST OPTION Money left at interest until the family asks for it.	At 2½% interest, $250 a year until the mortgage is withdrawn.
THE AMOUNT OPTION A regular income of as much money as you want, paid until money and interest are used up.	$100 a month for 9 years and 3 months, for example, or $200 a month for 4 years and 4 months.
THE TIME OPTION A monthly income to last as many years as you want, paid until money and interest are used up.	10 years income of $92 a month, for example, or 20 years income of $51 a month.
THE LIFETIME INCOME OPTION A regular income guaranteed for the person's lifetime.	$50 a month for life (for a woman 65 years old) $63 a month for life (for a man 65 years old)

* Interest figured at the guaranteed rate of 2½%. Companies will pay higher interest than this as earned.

The beneficiary is provided the opportunity of determining the amount of the payments.

The third, the time option, guarantees an income for a fixed period of time. This is just like the second option, except that instead of dividing the total amount of money, plus interest, by the amount the beneficiary wants to receive each month, the total amount of money, plus interest, is divided by a selected number of years or other units of time. This division determines the amount of the payments that will be made per year or other selected period of time.

The fourth option guarantees the beneficiary a lifetime income. Another name for this option is a life annuity. There are many variations of this. Suppose, for example, that your wife is the beneficiary and that she is left with two small children. If she should die, a straight life annuity would terminate with her death, and leave the children without income. It may be preferable to select an "instalments certain and life thereafter" annuity, which guarantees a con-

[5] Jerome Cohen, *Decade of Decision,* prepared by Educational Division, Institute of Life Insurance, New York, N.Y., 1960, p. 42.

tinuity of payments for a specified number of years. The payments would be smaller, but if the initial beneficiary should die during the specified time period, the payments would continue to be made to other named beneficiaries for the remainder of the time period.

Another variation of the annuity option is the joint and survivorship annuity. This guarantees that the income will continue as long as either one of two persons lives. This is especially desirable in endowment policies. In this case, the income would last as long as either of two persons (husband and wife, for example) lived. Annuities will be discussed at greater length in Chapter 13.

Riders

There are three "riders" available on most insurance policies: waiver of premium, disability, and double indemnity.

The waiver of premium rider is usually available on a life insurance policy for a very small extra fee. It provides that if the insured is unable to pay premiums, due to total and permanent disability, the plan will still be completed, i.e., the cash values, dividends, etc., will be exactly the same as if premiums were being paid. There is usually a six month waiting period before premiums are waived. This rider is well worth the slight extra cost.

The disability income rider provides a specified monthly income per $1,000 of the face amount of life insurance, if the insured becomes totally and permanently disabled. The income is guaranteed for as long as the disability continues. If it is available, and if the insured can afford the added cost, this rider is well worth considering.

The double-indemnity rider guarantees that the beneficiary will receive twice the face value of the policy if the insured dies from "accidental means." While this rider is extremely inexpensive, it is also quite restricted. "Accidental means" is not as all-inclusive as it sounds. For example, a patient who dies while having a tooth extracted might be said to have died by accident; but not by accidental means. There are many exclusions, such as murder, suicide, death resulting from military service, etc.

INSURANCE AS AN INVESTMENT

Why buy insurance? Why not use some other form of investment? What will insurance do for you that the others can't?

When you hear the word 'investment' what does it call to mind? The year-by-year accumulation of good property? Some degree of speculation, with an outside chance of great gain? Saving now for income in the future? Protection against 'rainy days' for yourself and your family?

Perhaps you think of all of these—perhaps part of them. Or perhaps you have some other concept. But—wouldn't you agree that property possessing the following characteristics is a 'good investment'?

IF YOU LIVE

A rate of return guaranteed over a long period of time
Automatic reinvestment of interest and dividends, with never a day of time lost
A guaranteed resale price at any time
Constant accumulation, not subject to current income taxes
Guaranteed income at retirement, with substantial tax advantages
Constant supervision by experts in the investment field
Guaranteed loan values available whenever the need to borrow arises

IF YOU DIE

A guaranteed lump sum or monthly income with decided tax advantages for your family
No probate delays or costs
Protection against claims of creditors
Unusual freedom from state death taxes

AND

A substantial estate created with your first deposit
Life insurance is just such an investment.[6]

Actually, life insurance companies handle and invest a person's money for him. It is true that if the stock market should continue to rise, and inflation continue, other investments might be worth more in twenty or thirty years. But what if the market doesn't continue to rise, and inflation doesn't continue? Life insurance *guarantees* a particular sum of money for a person's heirs, *immediately*. The principal, both in terms of the face value of the policy to be paid at death and the cash values from year to year, is perfectly secure. It is also always readily available, making the investment extremely liquid. For many years, life insurance companies have had an almost perfect

---

[6] "Life Insurance, Your Best Investment," reprinted by special arrangement with the Research and Review Service of America, Inc., Copyright MCMLVIII, Indianapolis, Indiana, p. 1.

record of solvency. The rate of return on cash invested in insurance can be quite satisfactory. Let's look at this return, which is realized in the event of the insured's untimely death:

Age when purchased	*Return on premium investment if death occurs in:[7]		
	5th Year	10th Year	20th Year
30	1108%	542%	269%
40	743%	347%	155%
50	464%	198%	70%

* Dividends based on the 1963 scale have been applied to reduce premiums and are not guaranteed.

Life insurance also has many tax advantages. The policyholder doesn't have to pay any income tax on the compound interest earned on that portion of his premiums which the insurance company invests, and which creates his cash value. The rate of taxable return on any other type of investment would have to be unusually good to equal this tax-exempt return, and would be highly improbable to attain if the policyholder was in a relatively high tax bracket. And when the policyholder dies, the proceeds of the policy paid to a beneficiary are not usually subject to the federal income tax.

The returns on life insurance investments may, in fact, *never* be taxed. For example, if a wife is beneficiary of her husband's insurance policy, and he dies, most states exempt the insurance money from inheritance taxes, and proper planning will keep federal estate and gift taxes to a minimum. (Inheritance and gift taxes are covered in greater detail in Chapter 18.)

If the wife decides to take the money in instalments, the money remaining with the company will continue to earn a return. Each instalment the wife receives will be composed of two parts: one, a portion of the face value of the policy, which would have been available to the wife if payment had been in one lump sum; two, the interest earned on the money remaining with the insurance company. The first portion is not taxable under the federal income tax law. The second part is, but there is a $1,000 annual exclusion, which permits a wife to receive this much interest every year without paying any income tax.

If the policyholder takes the money during his lifetime (under an endowment policy, for example) the general rule is that the money

[7] "Is Life Insurance a Good Investment Today?," Connecticut Mutual Life Insurance Company, Hartford, Connecticut, p. 8.

in excess of premiums paid will be treated like other income. There are, however, provisions in the income tax law which make it possible to reduce this tax considerably. If, for example, the money is taken as a guaranteed life income, the rather complicated tax regulations in effect provide that a sizable part of each annuity payment will be tax exempt, for the remainder of the annuitant's life.

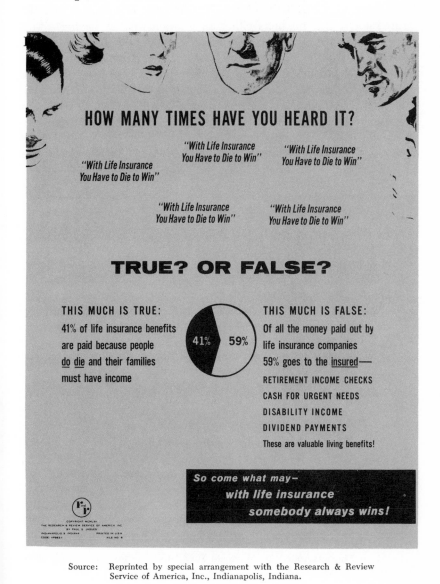

Source: Reprinted by special arrangement with the Research & Review Service of America, Inc., Indianapolis, Indiana.

One way of reducing inheritance and estate taxes is to reduce the size of a person's estate. This can be done by giving a life insurance policy to a person's heirs before death. What about the gift tax? Everyone has a $30,000 lifetime exemption before any gift taxes must be paid. Furthermore, $3,000 can be given to each of any number of people each year, free of the gift tax, and these gifts are in addition to the $30,000 lifetime exemption. This means that the insured could give his heirs either an insurance policy having a face value of up to $30,000, or an annual amount equal to the annual premium. In either case, the proceeds of the policy would not be part of the insured's estate, and therefore not subject to estate taxes.

Many people say that any consideration of life insurance as an investment is foolish, because you have to die to win. The facts presented on page 249 indicate that this is not true. Not only does life insurance have a definite investment value, but, in terms of total benefits paid, this investment value will most likely benefit the person insured.

WIFE INSURANCE

So far, the discussion has been largely about the husband — the wage earner. Now, let's consider the wife.

There are a number of sound reasons for insurance on the life of a married woman:
(1) When a wife dies, there is an immediate need for cash for funeral expenses as well as those in connection with her last illness.
(2) If the wife was working, there should be a fund to replace the loss of her earnings.
(3) If there is substantial jointly-held or individually owned property in the wife's name, there will be the need for a fund to clear her estate taxes and administration expenses.
(4) To hedge a possible loss of the estate tax marital deduction because of her prior death.
(5) To pay a housekeeper anywhere from $4,000 to $8,000 a year, if there are young children, to do what the wife did for free.[8]

Obviously, while the wage earner must be covered first, a wife has a definite monetary value and should be insured if possible.

---

[8] "How Much Is Your Wife Worth to You?," Institute for Business Planning, Inc., New York, N.Y., 1962, p. 2.

BUSINESS INSURANCE

Life insurance is definitely needed by the average family. It also meets many other needs. One of these is to insure the life of some "key man" in a business — the president of the company, the production manager, the foreman, or other "key" personnel. If the "key member" should die, the company might face a loss of customer confidence, a loss of business to competitors, etc. Among other things, "key man" insurance will provide cash to keep the business going, to carry out the insured person's plans, and to hire and train someone to take his place.

In the case of a sole proprietorship, such insurance can be used to provide funds for the proprietor's successor to purchase the interests the family of the present proprietor may have in the business. In such a case, the proprietor and the successor will enter into a business purchase agreement establishing a fair purchase price. Insurance on the proprietor's life will provide the necessary funds. A similar arrangement can be made in the case of a closely held corporation. An agreement between the corporation and the stockholders provides for the sale of the stock by the heirs to the corporation, and the corporation commits itself to buy. Each stockholder is insured by the corporation, and when a stockholder dies, the insurance payment is used to buy the stock.

In the case of a partnership, when one partner dies the partnership ends. What happens to the business? It can always be liquidated, but this usually means a loss to everyone concerned. The heirs could buy out the surviving partners, the surviving partners could take in the heirs as new partners, or the surviving partners could buy out the interest of the deceased partner. A partnership buy-and-sell agreement, with a proper insurance plan, can provide the surviving partners with enough money to keep the business going and to pay the deceased partner's heirs for his share of the business.

CHOOSING A SALESMAN

The life and health insurance business is large enough and complicated enough to merit the services of experts. This is where the life insurance agent comes in.

Prospective insurance buyers should select a life insurance agent carefully. A trained man is needed. There is obviously no advantage to doing business with an agent who knows little or nothing more than the buyer. The buyer should also select someone who appeals to him personally, as he will, or should, consult with him often in the future as the family grows and the buyer's financial condition changes.

Quite often, an insurance agent is selected because he is recommended by friends, is well known in the community, and has an excellent reputation. He is an obvious choice. Sometimes, however, the choice is not that easy. Many men may be available and apparently qualified, but none may be outstanding. One suggestion, under such circumstances, is to select a CLU. If a man has this designation, it means that he has passed a series of examinations given by the College of Life Underwriters. To pass these examinations, it is necessary for him to study a variety of subjects ranging from economics and accounting to estate planning, law, and taxation. This means not only that he has been trained, but that he is probably a career man who will be able to help build a sound program over the years.

CONCLUSIONS

The American Bankers' Association, in its booklet "Personal Money Management" presents a series of insurance suggestions which, to some degree, sum up the preceding discussion. They constitute an excellent summary to any consideration of life and health insurance.

1. If you have GI life insurance, keep it. The premiums are low, dividends high, and terms most attractive.
2. Concentrate life insurance on the family breadwinner—the working head of the family, usually the father.
3. Estimate your Social Security benefits—for yourself at retirement and for dependents at your death—and coordinate them with your insurance plan.
4. Find out about your employer's group life insurance protection for employees and integrate this coverage in your insurance plan.
5. If you live in Connecticut, Massachusetts, or New York, look into the possibilities of Savings Bank Life Insurance, available through many mutual savings banks.
6. Make every effort to pay your insurance premiums on an annual basis. You will save money.
7. Set up and follow your own "reminder system" for paying premiums when they become due.
8. Protect your insurance principal, and your beneficiaries, by finding out how your policies can pay off through settlement options other than lump-sum cash payment. If such options

are desirable in your case, select those that you feel will be best for your family.

9. Take advantage of conversion privileges in your policies if they are good for your particular situation, but be extremely careful about switching from one policy to another. It usually doesn't pay!

10. Review your policies regularly to make certain that you are taking advantage of policy provisions. Also, check your policies everytime your family's circumstances change—for example, a new child in the family.

11. Make sure your family knows where all of your insurance policies are kept.

12. Above all, consult an experienced life insurance agent for advice and guidance.[9]

Other important points the insured should consider in regard to his own policies are:

1. Is the beneficiary selection wording correct and up to date?

2. Is there an Automatic Premium Loan provision on all policies (except term)?

3. Is there a Common Disaster clause in all policies, directing the disposition of the proceeds if both husband and wife, for example, should die within 30 days of each other?

4. Are all policies "creditor proof"? Are clauses included which prevent creditors from in any way obtaining the cash value of the policy during the life of the insured, or the proceeds after death?

5. Can outstanding policy loans be repaid from current dividends?

Questions

1. What is meant by "the monetary value" of a human life?

2. Compare "mutual" and "stock" insurance companies.

3. a. Savings Bank Life Insurance, in those states where it is available, usually sells for less than that sold by the usual legal reserve company. Why?

---

[9] "Personal Money Management," Savings Division, by permission of The American Bankers Association, New York, N.Y., 1962, pp. 33–34.

b. If Savings Bank Life Insurance is such a good buy why isn't more of it sold?

4. Under what circumstances can term insurance be recommended?

5. Are the family maintenance and family income policies the same?

6. Describe four (4) protective clauses which are included in the usual insurance policy.

7. Compare the reinstatement clause and the nonforfeiture option.

8. What is the best way to utilize life insurance dividends?

9. Describe the "riders" available on most insurance policies.

10. What are some of the tax advantages of life insurance?

Problems

1. Joseph King, age 28, is married and has two children, one 2 and the other 3. He has set two main objectives in his life insurance planning:
   1. To provide for a minimum standard of living for his family in the event he dies prior to accumulating adequate funds.
   2. To retire at age 65 and not be dependent upon his children for support.

   After inquiring about life insurance he is faced with the problem of choosing one of the following:
   a. A retirement annuity contract (age 65)
   b. A thirty-payment life insurance contract
   c. A twenty-year family-income contract
   d. A ten year renewable term insurance contract
   e. An endowment maturing at age 65 contract

   Question
   1. Will any of the above contracts not be able to meet King's objectives. Why or why not?
   2. Which contract would you recommend and why?

2. "A" applied for a $10,000 life insurance policy. In the application he stated he was age 30, when in reality he was age 32. He also made several fraudulent mis-statements relative to his health in the application. The policy issued was standard. Three years later "A" dies. What

two clauses of the insurance contract would apply in the settlement of this death claim?

3. "C" is 24 years old, a college graduate, and recently married. He has just purchased a new home and made an application for "mortgage" insurance. His agent informed him that there are various plans of insurance available to insure a mortgage. What are 3 ways for "C" to insure his mortgage? Which would you recommend?

4. Mr. Adams wants to select a settlement option which will provide an education fund for his children. Which options should he consider?

5. Mr. Connors is about to purchase a $50,000 life insurance policy issued by a mutual company. He must come to some decision as to which dividend option to select. Which would you recommend?

Selected Readings

Greene, Mark R., *Risk & Insurance*, South-Western Publishing Co., Cincinnati 27, Ohio, 1962

"How Much & What Kind of Life Insurance Should I Own?", The Connecticut Mutual Life Insurance Co. of Hartford, Hartford, Connecticut, 1961

Maclean, Joseph B., *Life Insurance*, McGraw-Hill Publishing Co., New York, N.Y., Ninth Edition, 1962

Magee, John H., *General Insurance*, Richard D. Irwin, Inc., Homewood, Illinois, 1961

Mayerson, Allen L., *Introduction to Insurance*, The Macmillan Co., New York, N.Y., 1962

Mehr, Robt. I. and Cammack, Emerson, *Principles of Insurance*, Richard D. Irwin, Inc., Homewood, Illinois, 1961

Mowbray, Albert H. and Blanchard, Ralph H., *Insurance: Its Theory and Practice in the United States*, McGraw-Hill Publishing Co., New York, N.Y., 1961

Publications of the Institute of Life Insurance, 488 Madison Avenue, New York 22, N.Y.

Chapter 10

HEALTH INSURANCE

Life insurance certainly helps a person when he retires, or his heirs if he dies prematurely. But it is not designed to be of help in case of sickness or disability. Loss of income is loss of income, regardless of its cause. Sickness and disability sometimes create more financial hardships than death, because of the medical expenses which are added to the burden. This is where health insurance steps into the picture.

How important is health insurance? According to Chart 10–1 and Table 10–1, health costs are substantial enough to be worrisome, and are increasing steadily, year by year.

Chart 10–1

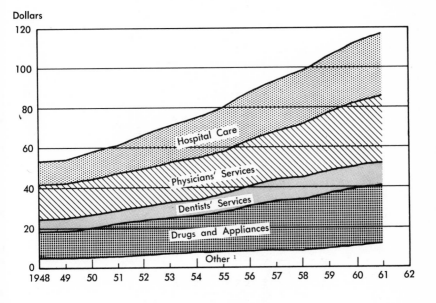

Dollars

Source: (See Table 10–1.)

More than 200 individuals are disabled in the United States every time the second hand sweeps around the face of the clock. It is a fact that for every one person disabled by accident, there are five or six disabled by sickness. It is almost inconceivable to realize that there are 28,100 people at work today who will not leave their beds to go to work tomorrow. Of these, 260 will be accidentally killed and another 355 will be permanently disabled, never again to work, never again to bring home a pay check. This year more than 8 million people will meet with an accident or become ill for the first time.

The financial losses that accompany illness and disability are equally staggering. The American Medical Association reports that more than 16 million patients are admitted to hospitals every year. That means one hospital admission every 1.9 seconds. The average hospital stay is more than 10 days, with one person in every 10 staying more than three weeks. As a matter of fact, the annual cost for treatment is almost 10 billion dollars, not counting lost income.

Table 10-1

Per capita private expenditures for medical care, 1948-61[1]

Type of expenditure	1948	1949	1950	1951	1952	1953	1954	1955	1956	1957	1958	1959	1960	1961
Total	$52.79	$53.74	$57.72	$62.08	$66.08	$70.70	$74.77	$79.52	$86.83	$92.66	$97.66	$104.86	$111.12	$116.60
Hospital care	11.63	12.21	14.15	15.45	16.97	18.64	19.91	20.64	23.62	25.07	26.38	27.70	29.78	32.16
Physicians' services	17.15	16.95	17.29	17.85	18.59	19.63	20.97	21.15	22.90	24.36	26.56	29.19	30.69	32.15
Dentists' services	6.20	6.23	6.40	6.60	7.16	7.91	8.84	9.29	9.83	10.32	10.79	10.75	11.11	11.46
Drugs and drug sundries	10.10	10.54	11.44	13.10	13.42	13.69	13.60	15.24	17.35	18.19	19.31	20.55	21.86	22.16
Eyeglasses and appliances	2.97	3.08	3.24	3.61	3.78	3.87	3.74	4.22	4.92	5.88	5.78	6.78	6.84	6.88
Other professional services	2.28	2.34	2.47	2.64	2.81	3.01	3.21	3.27	3.50	3.81	4.06	4.38	4.52	4.70
Nursing-home care	.69	.71	.73	.79	.82	.83	.88	.92	1.03	1.07	1.17	1.26	1.57	1.68
Health insurance, net cost	1.76	1.69	1.99	2.03	2.54	3.11	3.63	3.78	3.68	3.98	3.62	4.24	4.74	5.40

[1] Data related to civilian population as of July 1 of each year.

Source: "Private Medical Care Expenditures and Voluntary Health Insurance," *Social Security Bulletin*, 1948-61, Social Security Administration, U.S. Department of Health, Education, and Welfare, Washington, D.C., Volume 25, Number 12, December 1962, pp. 6-7.

Table 10-2

Average Costs of Specified Medical Services In 20 Large Cities in The United States 1961[1]

(Based on data collected primarily for calculation of Consumer Price Index not adjusted for comparability. Cost differences among cities may be due to variation in quality of service priced. Cost differences from time to time for a city may be due to changes in outlet sample, changes in service priced, and corrections.)

City	Hospital Daily Service Charge Per Day			Physician Services		Obstetrical Case		Surgical Fee		Dental Services
	Men's Pay Ward	Semi-private Room	Private Room	Office Visit	House Visit	Including Wasserman Test	Excluding Wasserman Test	Appendectomy	Tonsilectomy	Tooth Filling[2]
Atlanta	$13.38	$15.38	$18.25	$4.50	$7.83	$168.33	$ —	$166.67	$80.83	$4.83
Baltimore	19.12	20.50	24.25	4.41	6.00	—	180.45	145.83	66.67	4.20
Boston	26.62	29.88	33.50	4.85	6.22	200.83	—	158.33	75.83	5.17
Chicago	21.40	24.40	28.90	5.00	8.83	—	160.00	195.83	92.50	4.50
Cincinnati	12.00	19.00	21.88	4.11	6.28	110.00	159.38	160.42	75.00	4.00
Cleveland[3]	30.10	33.33	38.92	4.78	7.72	155.00	167.86	168.75	73.33	5.17
Detroit	21.75	23.75	28.38	4.56	8.18	148.93	187.50	155.00	67.08	5.25
Houston	11.38	14.25	18.00	4.44	9.65	161.88	185.00	177.08	68.33	5.50
Kansas City	14.86	16.92	20.05	4.28	8.06	186.88	150.00	150.42	72.50	4.58
Los Angeles	26.10	29.00	34.20	6.25	11.11	—	244.69	240.28	113.33	9.40
Minneapolis	23.15	25.35	28.55	4.22	7.56	130.42	—	170.83	70.83	4.67
New York[4]	23.20	26.40	32.60	5.85	8.68	224.07	162.50	206.17	91.88	5.75
Philadelphia	16.00	20.38	24.75	4.28	6.36	187.50	200.83	145.88	75.00	5.17
Pittsburgh	17.80	22.30	26.20	4.50	6.69	—	167.50	145.83	69.17	5.00
Portland, Ore.	23.06	25.56	27.94	4.75	8.88	156.67	171.67	185.42	67.00	6.58
Saint Louis	15.88	18.30	21.80	4.28	7.88	156.11	—	154.17	75.00	5.33
San Francisco	27.88	30.62	34.88	6.17	9.53	—	211.59	217.17	96.67	8.71
Scranton	12.00	15.50	19.67	3.58	5.00	—	117.50	170.83	59.17	4.00
Seattle	27.00	29.75	33.25	5.22	9.29	173.33	—	177.08	72.00	6.67
Washington, D.C.	19.12	21.00	26.00	5.21	7.82	225.00	207.27	145.42	70.00	7.50

[1] Data for the last month available of year.
[2] Amalgam, one surface.
[3] Combination of quotations from hospitals using Daily Service Charge and inclusive Rate Plans for men's ward, semi-private and private room.
[4] Combination of quotations from hospitals using Daily Service Charge and inclusive Rate Plans for men's ward rooms only.

Source: *Source Book of Health Insurance Data 1962*, Health Insurance Institute, New York, New York, 1962, p. 67.

The rapidly rising cost of medical treatment is another factor contributing to the need for adequate sickness and accident protection. The cost of such treatment has more than kept pace with the rising cost of living. In the past two decades hospital rates have increased 255 per cent, doctors' fees have increased 150 per cent, and the cost of drugs and prescriptions have risen 130 per cent.[1]

Health insurance offers five types of coverage:
1. Loss of income insurance
2. Major medical expense insurance
3. Hospital expense insurance
4. Surgical expense insurance
5. General medical expense insurance

Loss of Income Insurance

There is some disagreement among experts as to which health insurance coverage is of greater importance—loss of income, or major medical. Both are extremely important. Loss of income insurance is the oldest type. It may be taken out by an individual, or may be provided under a group policy. Let's suppose Sam Jones has a disabling accident. If he is covered by this type of policy, he will receive a stated weekly sum from the insurance company in accordance with the terms and conditions of his policy. Usually, the policy will stipulate that the accident must make it impossible for him to carry on his usual occupation, and that he will have to wait some period of time, at least a week or more, after his pay stops before he will start to receive payments. While lifetime benefit policies are available, most policies establish a maximum number of years for which benefits will be paid.

Under the above individual policy, Sam could receive benefits whether or not the accident was connected with his job. But if Sam is covered by a group policy and the accident happened on the job, he would probably not receive these benefits if the group was covered by Workmen's Compensation.

Most benefits are limited to a percentage (75%, for example) of a person's regular income. The reason is obvious. If a person could be insured for as much as, or more than, his regular income, it might

---

[1] "Accident and Sickness Insurance," Temporary Career Course Unit, Unit 11A, Aetna Life Insurance Company, Hartford, Conn., Revised 1961, pp. A–2 and A–3.

influence some people to take advantage of health and accident situations by unnecessarily prolonging recovery; or even going to the extreme of "faking" illness or accidental injuries.

In general, the period of time during which benefits will be paid is longer for accidents than it is for sickness. A policy providing benefits only in case of accident is much cheaper than one providing coverage for loss of income due to either accident or sickness. There are far fewer accident benefit claims than sickness benefit claims.

In buying a loss of income policy, a person should make certain that it is both non-cancellable and guaranteed renewable until retirement. Otherwise, an insurance company might refuse to renew the policy on some anniversary date, at a time when the policy would be of most value to the insured because of accident, sickness, or just general decline in health.

Major Medical Insurance

Most people can't afford to have every type of insurance; nor can they set aside enough money to meet every eventuality. (It would be nice to be insured against expenses of the common cold, for example, but it would be extremely expensive insurance.) In fact, most people can't afford to pay any more than relatively small medical bills out of their regular income. So the most important coverage for them, in addition to loss of income insurance, is major medical. This is sometimes called "catastrophe" insurance, and covers the cost of serious illness.

Major medical insurance is generally provided by a group policy, and the coverage often includes hospital and medical expense insurance. In such situations, the major medical policy is usually coordinate with other policies. The coverage is subject to a deductible amount, as it is designed to cover serious illness only. The size of the deduction can vary according to the wishes of the insured, and the premium is adjusted accordingly. When this policy is coordinated with other coverage for a group, this deductible is often set up so that the basic coverage (the part deducted) is provided by the other policies. Then the concept known as the "corridor" enters the picture. To make certain that the same coverage is not provided by more than one policy, there will be some amount—the corridor—between the basic policy and the major medical policy which the insured must pay himself. An example of such a coordinated plan is presented in Table 10-3.

Table 10–3[2]

	Total Charges	Covered By Base Plan*	Covered By Major Medical
Hospital Room and Board			
50 days @ $15 per day	$ 750	$350	$ 400
Other Hospital Charges:			
X-rays, blood tests, medicines, etc.	325	150	175
Registered Nurses—			
$15 per day for 20 days	300	—	300
Physicians' Fees	700	150	550
TOTALS	$2,075	$650	$1,425
Less Deductible of $100			−100
Balance Subject to Co-insurance			$1,325
Less Co-insurance at 20%			−265
Amount Paid by Major Medical			$1,060

SUMMARY

Paid by Base Plan*	$ 650
Paid by major medical	1,060
Paid by patient	365
TOTAL	$2,075

(*Hospital room and board and general medical expense)

Major medical policies will not cover all medical bills. The policy holder, in all cases, will have to pay part of them himself. A policy might, for example, pay 75% of all medical bills above the deductible. If total medical bills were $2,000 and the deductible was $300, the insurance company would pay 75% of $1,700, or $1,275, and the insured would pay $425. This is a necessary practice. As in the case of loss of income insurance, 100% coverage would lead to abusive practices, and questionable claims. If a person has to pay part of the bill, he will probably make some effort to keep expenses as low as possible.

Hospital Expense Insurance

Benefits from this type of policy pay all or part of hospital costs, including room and board and certain "extras." Room and board costs are usually met by some fixed rate payment. As an example, the

[2] Jerome Cohen, *Decade of Decision,* prepared by Educational Division, Institute of Life Insurance, New York, N.Y., 1960, p. 33.

policy might pay $20 per day for 90 days. Some policies provide coverage for a year or more; others provide full coverage for a speci- fied period and partial coverage for an additional period. The "extras" are other hospital costs such as oxygen, use of an operating room, etc. Most policies will cover these extras up to some multiple of the daily benefit. If, for example, the daily benefit is $20, the policy might cover such extras up to 10 times the daily benefit, or up to $200. Many of these policies also provide a fixed amount as a maternity benefit.

Surgical Expense Insurance

As the name indicates, the benefits from this insurance are to pay for surgical services. A schedule of fees is established, and benefits are paid according to the schedule. Fees vary with the severity of the operation. Inasmuch as it would be impossible to write a schedule that would include all operations, there is usually a clause in the policy stating that if an operation which is not listed is required, compensation will be determined by the amount specified in the list for an operation of equal severity.

People are often disappointed in their surgical coverage, simply because they do not understand it. Let's take Sally and Martha, for example. They have the same surgical insurance coverage, and both have an appendectomy. The operation costs Sally $100 and Martha $500 above the amount paid by the insurance company. Why didn't their insurance provide the same coverage? The answer is that it did. The same surgical fee, established by the schedule, was paid in both cases. The difference was in the total costs charged to each. They had different doctors, lived in different localities, and went to differ- ent hospitals. Doctors' fees and hospital charges vary considerably. The attention and medication each required might have been quite different. The point is, that the surgical insurance coverage was in no way to blame for the cost difference.

General Medical Expense Insurance

This is often considered to be the least important of the health insurance coverages, as it covers the small costs. Generally, these provide specified amounts for doctor's visits at home, at his office, or in the hospital. Usually, it is combined with some other type of health insurance under one policy.

When written in a policy providing surgical and hospital insur- ance, this type of insurance is extremely reasonable, and quite worthwhile. To attempt to cover office and home visits, however, is usually considered of little value, as the cost will be high compared to benefits. In case of serious illness, the patient would undoubtedly be hospitalized, and covered by the hospital insurance policy.

BLUE CROSS AND BLUE SHIELD

Insurance companies write almost all of the loss of income insurance. Other types of health insurance are offered by both life and casualty companies, and by Blue Cross and Blue Shield associations and other organizations.

Chart 10–2

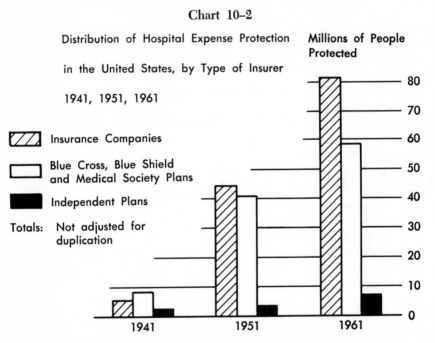

Distribution of Hospital Expense Protection in the United States, by Type of Insurer

1941, 1951, 1961

Millions of People Protected

Insurance Companies

Blue Cross, Blue Shield and Medical Society Plans

Independent Plans

Totals: Not adjusted for duplication

Source: *Source Book of Health Insurance Data 1962*, Health Insurance Institute, New York, New York, 1962, p. 12.

"The distinctive feature of Blue Cross and Blue Shield is that they are nonprofit, community enterprises, organized by the hospitals and doctors themselves to ease the burden of hospital and medical expense for families in the community."[3] Blue Cross plans provide

[3] Robert M. Cunningham, Jr., "The Story of Blue Shield," *Public Affairs Pamphlet No. 218*, Public Affairs Committee, Inc., National Association of Blue Shield Plans, Second Edition, Jan. 1961, p. 4.

benefits to cover hospital expenses. Blue Shield coverage pays doctors' bills. Blue Cross and Blue Shield do not make payments to subscribers. Blue Cross makes payments to the hospital directly, and Blue Shield to the doctor.

In most states, Blue Cross and Blue Shield plans are not considered to be mutual insurance corporations, as they are controlled by the hospitals and physicians and not by the subscribers. They are not even considered to be selling insurance, but medical services and hospital care.

Activities of the many Blue Cross plans in North America are coordinated by the Blue Cross Commission created by the American Hospital Association. Blue Shield plans are coordinated by the National Association of Blue Shield Plans. Chart 10-3 shows the growth that has taken place in Blue Cross membership, while Chart 10-4 shows the growth of Blue Shield plans.

Chart 10–3

Growth of Blue Cross membership in the U.S.

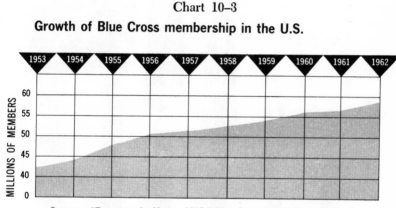

Source: "Report to the Nation 1962," Blue Cross Association, 840 North Lake Shore Drive, Chicago, Illinois, p. 3.

There are many different Blue Cross Plans, each having several types of contracts, and different rates and benefits. Basically, however, these plans provide service in semi-private hospital accommodations for a specified number of days per year, plus other hopsital services. The Blue Cross Commission operates an "Inter-Plan Service Benefit Bank" to cover subscribers while away from home, and the local Blue Cross Plan collects from the subscriber's "home" Plan.

Blue Shield Plans also vary considerably. Surgical fees vary according to local conditions. Most plans provide benefits for medical service to hospital patients, and a few pay for a physician's visits at home, or in his office, as well as at the hospital. The typical contract

Chart 10–4

growth of
Blue Shield
membership—

1950-1962

1950	1952	1954	1956	1958	1960	1962
16,629,596	24,670,701	31,489,023	38,802,846	42,575,256	47,084,988	50,904,714
MEMBERS	MEMBERS	MEMBERS	MEMBERS	MEMBERS	MEMBERS	MEMBERS

OVER 50 MILLION PEOPLE — more than one-fourth of the entire
population of the United States — were enrolled in Blue Shield Plans
at the end of 1962. Of this number, approximately 3.5 million persons
were age 65 or over. New York City, Washington, D.C., Boston, Cleveland and Detroit — as well as eight other large American cities — had
more than 40% of their populations covered by Blue Shield protection.

Courtesy of National Association of Blue Shield Plans, Chicago, Illinois.

provides surgical, obstetrical, anesthesia, in-hospital medical care, diagnostic x-ray, and radiation therapy benefits.

The coverage, rates, etc. offered by Blue Cross and Blue Shield vary considerably from one area of the country to another. One thing, however, seems quite clear; the general tendency is for these plans to broaden. Recent Master Medical Plans, for example, combine basic coverage, Prolonged Illness Certificate coverage, and additional benefits. The result is a policy which provides coverage over a long period of time for most of the surgical, medical and hospital expenses encountered by the average family, including benefits for oral surgery, maternity, mental and nervous conditions, electric shock treatments, etc.

TRAVEL ACCIDENT INSURANCE

One well known type of accident insurance policy is the kind sold at every airport. For multiples of 25¢, inserted in a coin-operated vending machine, a person can purchase various amounts of coverage. This is limited coverage, in that it provides only for accidents to the insured that occur during one specific airplane flight, and pays benefits only for certain specified losses, such as loss of life, hands, feet, or eyes. Coverage is also provided for some specific payment for medical expenses resulting from such an accident.

The value of such a policy depends upon how often a person travels. If a person travels frequently, travel insurance can be purchased on an annual basis much more cheaply than the one-trip type of policy. In travel insurance, as well as in other lines, the insurance tries to keep up-to-date. The Space Travel policy presented on page 268 may be a joke today, but who can tell how soon some such coverage will become a reality.

SUMMARY

Health insurance is available from a variety of sources. In addition to the coverage offered by regular insurance companies, Blue Cross, and Blue Shield, health insurance is offered by other non-profit organizations such as the Kaiser Foundation Health Plan in California and the Health Insurance Plan of Greater New York. About half of the people who have life insurance are covered under one of the non-profit plans.

Differences between policies in the health insurance field are extremely wide. There is also considerable price variation for the same type of policy providing the same benefits. It would be im-

SPACE TRAVEL ACCIDENT POLICY

Kemper Insurance

CHICAGO 40   U.S.A., EARTH

In consideration of the payment in premium prescribed, the Kemper Insurance organization, hereinafter called the company, insures the terrestrial person or persons known herein as the insured against all unearthly accidents.

NOTE: But not against whatever-on-earth can accidentally happen to him or her.

BENEFITS

PART I—ONE WAY TRIPS, FLIGHT LIGHT RETURNS

The company shall pay in accordance with the schedule listed below the sum set opposite the loss, providing that said losses occur within one Light Year from blast-off; and if insured de-spaces following payment, beneficiaries are bound to unearth said sum, plus the usual inflation.

One Way Trip . . . Ultimate Benefits;

Flight Light Returns (returning without all members) . . . Two-Stage Benefits

PARTIAL BENEFITS

If insured sustains injuries that are out of this world, the company shall pay for necessary expenses, but not ex-ORBIT-ant funds for treatment as follows:

1. Space-station emergency treatment.
2. Artificial wings, cloudhoppers for walking on air and other prosthetic devices for self-support.
3. Space helmets for those with heads in the clouds.

4. Ionine for ionospheric cuts.
5. Blow-in patches for SPUT-NICKS.

Provided said treatments (or equipment) are acquired within 90 heavenly days.

LIMITED LAND TRAVEL UNCOVERAGE

This policy shall not cover the insured while traveling on land or sea or underwater, except from hanger to space ship in space suits, zipped up.

MYSTERIOUS DISAPPEARANCE

Claims will be paid when disappeared person notifies us of his address, if latter is within the solar system.

EXCLUSIONS

1. Those pursuing the following occupations are not eligible:

Space cadets, TV or otherwise;
Space salesmen;
Cab drivers, with or without meteor;
Guides (for guided missiles);
Parachutists, with or without parachute;
Left Handed Pitchers.

Bronco busters;
Window washers;
High divers;
Hi-fliers;
Sopranos;

2. Accidents occurring while going up and down elevators will not be covered.

POLICY PROVISIONS

This policy will constitute the entire contract of insurance unless changes are approved by the company on a high level.

All claims shall be in writing and sent air mail.

The company may cancel at any time by notice in sky writing.

Reprinted with permission of Kemper Insurance, Chicago 40, Illinois.

possible to examine all of them. A person buying health insurance should carefully compare the costs and benefits of several different policies before making a selection.

There are certain points that should be carefully considered. Is the policy non-cancellable, and guaranteed renewable for life? Does it provide broad coverage or cover only certain specific (and perhaps rare) illnesses? Are all members of the family covered? If it is a group policy, what happens to the coverage if the insured retires?

Always purchase from a reputable insurer, and, in general, purchase the least expensive policy which gives the broadest possible coverage to all members of the family.

PROGRAMMING

The preceding information concerning life and health insurance should convince everyone that there is a wide variety of choices available. Actually, the choices are much more varied than those presented here. How much insurance should a person carry? What kind should he carry? These are questions that almost everyone asks at one time or another during his life. To answer them properly, a person should understand the many alternatives available, and create a plan meeting his specific needs. How much and what kind depend upon the number in the family, the income of the family, whether the family owns its own home, educational objectives, and many other things which vary with the individual person and family.

A complete insurance program combines life and health insurance into one over-all plan to meet all of the possible needs of the family. However, few people can afford complete coverage, and the money which can reasonably be invested in insurance should be invested in coverage designed to meet the most important needs. Planning an insurance program (programming) requires finding the answers to three questions:

1. What are your needs?
2. What coverage do you now have?
3. What additional insurance is required to meet your needs?

Needs

These seem like pretty simple questions. They aren't. Needs, for example, must be listed in order of importance, and none overlooked. Money is needed for many things, including:

1. Final expenses and medical care
2. Readjustment
3. The critical "family" period
4. The wife's later years
5. Retirement
6. Education
7. Mortgage redemption

The money needed for final expense is often called the "clean-up" fund. There are many more of these final expenses than might be imagined: doctor's bills, hospital bills, funeral expenses, cemetery lot, utility bills, loans, balances due on instalment purchases, etc. These bills must be paid immediately. What is the average total? Estimates run from $2,500 to $5,000 for the average family. Social security provides a maximum lump sum benefit of $255. Here we have a need for both life insurance and health insurance. Health insurance is needed to cover the medical expenses and life insurance to provide a lump sum for the other final expenses. Specifically, whole life and major medical insurance is needed.

When the family breadwinner dies, the family's income stops, and a readjustment is required. Even if the wife plans to work, it will take time to locate a job, make babysitting arrangements, etc. Social security will help in most cases, but more money will be needed for this readjustment period. There should be at least enough money to enable the family to live in its accustomed manner for at least one year after the wage earner's death or disability. Part of this money can be provided by selecting one of the annuity settlement options on an ordinary life policy. The total sum required might be provided by a combination of social security, income insurance, and ordinary insurance, under most programs.

While the family is young, a regular monthly income will be needed. Again, social security will help in this critical family period, but most wage earners would like to have enough insurance to provide enough money each month to meet living expenses until the youngest child reaches 18. How much insurance is needed obviously depends upon how old the children are, and the accustomed standard of living. One policy, the family income policy, is specifically designed to meet these needs. Disability income coverage of some type will be needed to cover loss of income due to sickness or accident, rather than death.

What income will the wife have after the children are grown up? It may be more difficult for her to get a job as she gets older, and she will not receive any social security benefits between the time the youngest child reaches 18 and she reaches 62. Even a small amount each month would be helpful. Remember that the possibilities of both death and disability must be considered. If a good disability income policy exists, it will provide an income either for life or until age 65. Either decreasing term, or straight life with a life annuity settlement option, will provide the needed income if the wage earner should die. Declining term insurance will, of course, be the least expensive, but straight life will accumulate a cash value which might be used for retirement purposes.

It takes money to retire comfortably. Cash or maturity values can be used to provide part of the needed income, as less insurance coverage will be needed after retirement. Somes types of permanent insurance will produce such values, as they combine protection and saving. Retirement income policies are, of course, specifically designed for this purpose. If a person has managed to save a fairly large sum of money, it would be worth his while to consider a single-premium, immediate annuity of the type discussed in Chapter 13. Medical insurance coverage will also be needed. It is an error to assume that expenses automatically decline with old age. Income, yes—expenses, never. Health expenses may very likely be higher, and more money will be wanted for travel and recreation.

The children's education should be provided for, in the event of the wage earner's disability or death. College becomes more and more important every year. Permanent insurance, with a waiver of premium rider, will build cash values. If the wage earner becomes disabled, this cash value can be used for education expenses. Health insurance, especially income insurance, will protect the children from the necessity of having to go to work immediately, to support the family or to pay hospital bills. There are many types of policies which can be used to provide money for educational purposes.

What Coverage Do You Have?

It is doubtful that you really know. So many types of coverage are provided by insurance that much of it is easily overlooked, or too complicated to estimate. The coverage easiest to remember is that provided by policies which the insured has purchased himself. Even in this case, careful analysis is necessary. Then there are the group insurance plans. Many people do not realize or appreciate the coverage provided under these plans. There is also government insurance. Not only do many veterans have National Service Life Insurance, but many are also entitled to disability pensions and hospital and medical benefits under various government laws. In many cases, survivors are entitled to pensions and death benefits. And last, but not least, there are social security benefits, workmen's compensation laws, and unemployment compensation. A person's insurance coverage is not simple to sum up. It can be complicated, and much more inclusive than many realize.

Additional Insurance

If present coverage is matched against needs, it will almost certainly be evident that certain of the needs are not now covered by insurance. These are the areas where additional insurance is needed. But take care of first things first. Most of us do not have money enough to provide complete protection for all needs. Make certain that the most important are covered first.

Questions

1. Loss of income insurance and major medical insurance are believed to be the most important types of health insurance. Why?

2. Major medical policies intentionally do not cover all medical bills. Explain.

3. a. Compare Blue Cross coverage with that of Blue Shield.
   b. What are some of the distinctive features of Blue Cross and Blue Shield Plans as compared with private insurance plans?

4. State the general rules that should be considered in purchasing health insurance?

5. What is "programming"?

6. In the preceding chapter the "monetary value" of a man was discussed. In this chapter the "needs" of heirs are considered. Compare the two approaches.

7. It is necessary to give special consideration to the insurance needs of a wife between the time the youngest child reaches 18 and she reaches 62. Why?

8. The same insurance policy might be considered as simply "life insurance," as "mortgage insurance," or as "education insurance." Explain.

9. What is the concept known as the "corridor" in major medical insurance?

10. Of what value to the purchaser of life or health insurance is the fact that the agent is a C.L.U.?

Problems

1. Mr. Johnson has an annual income of $9,000. He has been told by an insurance agent that there are five general types of health insurance, but he cannot, on his income, afford to purchase all five. He decides to purchase the most important type first and then, as his income grows, purchase the other types in order of their importance. In what order would you suggest that he purchase these policies?

2. Mr. Kennedy is considering the purchase of health insurance. He decides that general medical expenses insurance is the most important because it covers the smaller items of costs such as doctors' visits to the home, and these occur the most frequently. Is his reasoning valid?

3. Mr. Paulson has for many years operated quite successfully his own manufacturing business. In talking with one of his employees, Mr. Tompkins, he discovers that they both have identical surgical insurance policies with the same insurance company. By coincidence both are taken ill at the same time and have identical operations. While recuperating in the hospital Mr. Paulson discovers that the operation cost him $700 in out-of-pocket costs while Mr. Tompkins only had to pay $200—Mr. Paulson is quite incensed. Why didn't the insurance contract provide him with the same coverage as Mr. Tompkins?

4. Mr. Benton wants to be a conscientious husband and a good father to his children. He believes that to do so he must, among other things, carry sufficient insurance coverage. He believes that he must provide enough insurance to cover burial costs and the expense of "bringing up the children" until they are old enough to work. Assuming expense is no problem, will he provide sufficient insurance coverage if he proceeds according to his present plan?

5. Mr. Adams, Barnaby, and Saunders are partners in a very successful enterprise. They are concerned about the future of their families if

they should die. Mr. Adams suggests that he contact a good insurance agent. His idea is that he will have the insurance agent set up an insurance program for him. Mr. Barnaby and Mr. Saunders can use this plan and not have to contact an agent themselves until it is time to sign the necessary papers. Do you agree with Mr. Adams' plan?

Selected Readings

Angell, Frank Joseph, *Health Insurance,* The Ronald Press Co., New York, N.Y., 1963

Dickerson, O. D., *Health Insurance,* Richard D. Irwin, Inc., Homewood, Illinois, 1963

Follman, J. F., Jr., *Medical Care and Health Insurance,* Richard D. Irwin, Inc., Homewood, Illinois, 1963

Greene, Mark R., *Risk & Insurance,* South-Western Publishing Co., Cincinnati 27, Ohio, 1962

Mayerson, Allen L., *Introduction to Insurance,* The Macmillan Co., New York, N.Y., 1962

Publications of the Health Insurance Institute, 488 Madison Avenue, New York 22, N.Y.

"Your Health, Your Doctor and Your Pocketbook," reprinted from *Changing Times, The Kiplinger Magazine,* Washington 6, D.C., June 1961

Chapter **11**

PROPERTY AND CASUALTY INSURANCE

In one of the more remote parts of the world there is a religious sect which is literally afraid to move. One of its basic tenets is that no one should take the life of anyone or anything. "Anything," according to this group, includes animals, insects, and all other forms of animal life. If one of these people should walk, they might inadvertently kill an ant or some other insect. Therefore, they simply don't walk.

It is probably safe to say that the number of faithful followers of this particular cult in the United States is small enough to constitute a real "minority" group. Yet, if any of us allowed ourselves to think seriously about the consequences of moving around, the great majority of us might conclude that only in absolute immobility is there safety.

Let's take the Jones family on a particular Saturday. They get up, and the oldest daughter starts some ironing. Dad uses his new power mower to cut the grass. The younger children go out to play with their dog. One of the neighbor's children joins the family for lunch. In the afternoon, Mother goes shopping and Dad plays golf. In the evening, Mother uses her new pressure cooker to make a beef stew. After dinner, they watch television and then go to bed.

What could possibly happen to such a family on such an ordinary day? Let's imagine that this day is a very "unlucky" one. Mother, not quite awake, forgets to put water in the glass coffee percolator. It becomes red hot and shatters, and the red hot glass sears the linoleum on the kitchen floor. While the daughter is ironing, the telephone and door bell both ring at the same time, and in her excitement, daughter places the iron on the counter top, seriously scorching the finish. Dad's rotary power mower picks up a small stone and throws it forcefully enough to break a window in the neighbor's house. The dog, finally pushed beyond the limits of its endurance, bites one of the neighborhood children. The luncheon guest trips on a scatter-rug and breaks her wrist. Dad manages to hit a long drive straight to another golfer's head. In the preparation of the evening meal, the pressure cooker explodes, covering the entire area from ceiling to floor with beef stew. Finally, Dad does not properly extinguish a cigarette when he goes to bed, and a fire starts during the night. The family escapes, but the house is severely damaged.

If these things had actually happened, this family would have become involved in several lawsuits, in addition to suffering serious damage to their property. While few families ever have days this bad, only a very small fraction of the various misfortunes that might affect a family have been mentioned.

The most serious loss a family can have is the loss of the wage earner's power to earn an income. This can and should be covered by life and health insurance. There are, however, many other losses that might occur, some of them quite large, that should be insured against. This coverage is provided by property and casualty insurance.

HISTORY

At one time there were only three kinds of insurance available in the United States: marine, fire, and life. This made the insurance business a relatively uncomplicated one, but left many risks uninsurable, and others difficult for the average person to insure.

Chart 11–1 indicates the complexity of today's insurance coverage. The insurance business is no longer as simple is it used to be, and very few risks are uninsurable. Complete coverage is now much more readily available. Questions are frequently asked as to why different types of insurance are not sold as a package, and the answers, to some degree, are based on the historical development of the industry.

Marine

The first type of insurance to be sold in the United States was marine insurance. It is divided into two branches. One, called ocean marine insurance ("wet-marine"), is concerned with water transportation, while the other, called inland marine insurance ("dry-marine"), is concerned with transportation on land. In 1760, the London Coffee House in Philadelphia functioned in about the same manner as Lloyd's Coffee House in London, serving as a meeting place for underwriters and ship owners. The first company chartered to provide marine insurance coverage in the United States, with sufficient capital to accept large risks and compete with English insurers, was the Insurance Company of North America, founded in 1792.

Fire

The Philadelphia Contributionship for the Insurance of Houses from Loss by Fire, started with the support of Benjamin Franklin in 1752, was the first company in North America to provide fire coverage. This was followed by the Mutual Assurance Company for Insuring Houses from Loss by Fire in and near Philadelphia, more commonly known as the Green Tree Mutual. The Insurance Company of the State of Pennsylvania was organized in 1792, and was the first stock company organized specifically to write fire insurance. In 1794,

Chart 11-1

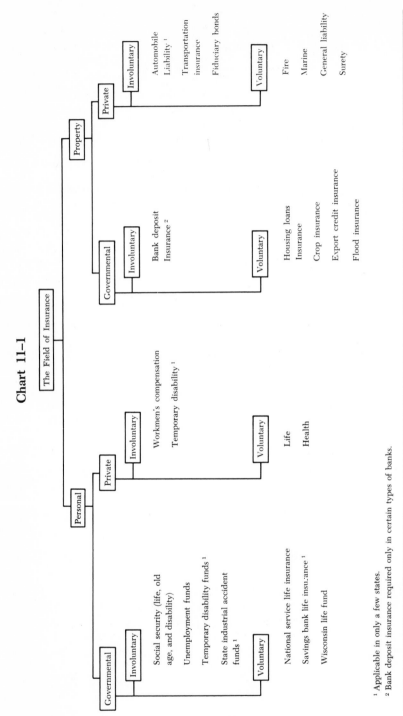

The Field of Insurance

Personal

Governmental

Involuntary

Social security (life, old age, and disability)
Unemployment funds
Temporary disability funds [1]
State industrial accident funds [1]

Voluntary

National service life insurance
Savings bank life insu:ance [1]
Wisconsin life fund

Private

Involuntary

Workmen's compensation
Temporary disability [1]

Voluntary

Life
Health

Property

Governmental

Involuntary

Bank deposit Insurance [2]

Voluntary

Housing loans Insurance
Crop insurance
Export credit insurance
Flood insurance

Private

Involuntary

Automobile Liability [1]
Transportation insurance
Fiduciary bonds

Voluntary

Fire
Marine
General liability
Surety

[1] Applicable in only a few states.
[2] Bank deposit insurance required only in certain types of banks.

Source: Mark R. Greene, *Risk and Insurance*, South-Western Publishing Co., Cincinnati, Ohio, 1962, p. 97. Reprinted by permission of South-Western Publishing Co.

the Insurance Company of North America entered the field, and was the first in this country to insure the contents of buildings as well as the buildings themselves.

Life

In 1759, the "Corporation for the Relief of Poor and Distressed Presbyterian Ministers and for the Poor and Distressed Widows and Children of Presbyterian Ministers" was formed to provide life insurance. The Insurance Company of North America was the first stock company to offer life insurance, but it issued only a few policies, and soon dropped out of this field. The Pennsylvania Company for Insurance on Lives and Granting Annuities was incorporated as the first company organized exclusively to issue life policies to the public, and wrote life insurance policies until 1872. The New England Mutual Life Insurance Company, chartered in 1835, was the first to be chartered, but didn't issue its first policy until 1844. The Mutual Life Insurance Company of New York wasn't chartered until 1842, but issued its first policy in 1843. These two mutual companies are the oldest existing commercial companies now writing life insurance.

Casualty Insurance

The Travelers Insurance Companies, founded in 1864, were the first in this country to sell accident insurance. Interest in accident insurance coverage was sparked by the invention of the railroad and injuries resulting from railroad accidents. The first policies sold by Travelers were travel policies.

Fidelity bonds, and burglary and theft insurance, were the next types of casualty coverage to enter the picture. Automobile insurance started in 1898, when an automobile liability policy was first written in the United States. Automobile insurance, and workmen's compensation insurance (which started in 1910), are the two largest classes of coverage written by casualty companies today.

Summary

The history of the insurance business is quite fascinating, but this text is not the proper place to thoroughly cover the topic. A minimum amount of history, however, is necessary as a background.

While marine and fire insurance companies were the first in the insurance field, they were not too interested in the newer areas of coverage. Casualty insurance became a separate industry, and, in many states, fire insurance companies were not allowed to write casualty coverage and casualty companies were not allowed to write fire coverage. It wasn't until the 1940's that this separation was generally realized to be unsatisfactory for both the insured and the insurance industry, and today, all states permit multiple-line underwriting. Multiple-line companies underwrite various types of property and liability insurance. Today, the insurance business is really divided into two parts—life and property—although there still are companies specializing in fire, marine, casualty, etc.

Even this two-part division may not last. There is considerable pressure to permit all-line underwriting. This is the underwriting of all types of insurance by one company, including life. There are both advantages and disadvantages to this possible development. One advantage is the obvious convenience to the purchaser of being able to buy all of his insurance in one package. An outstanding disadvantage is the difficulty of training agents to the degree that they are competent to advise customers in all areas of insurance. Life and property, individually, are enormous and complicated fields. Proper training in any one insurance field requires considerable study and time. To expect competence in all fields seems rather optimistic.

Life and Health insurance have been covered in Chapters 9 and 10. In this chapter, because this a book on Personal Finance, those areas of property and casualty insurance will be covered which are of most interest to the average person.

PROPERTY INSURANCE

The largest single investment most families make is the purchase of a home, and one of the largest financial losses that a family might suffer would be the destruction of its home by fire. Property insurance provides for reimbursement in the case of loss or damage to an insured's property, and specifies the risks that will be insured against. The limits of coverage are specified in the policy according to actual cash value, cost of repairs or replacement, and the face amount of the policy.

The most common type of property insurance is "fire." Other types protect against loss or damage due to windstorm, hail, smoke, explosion, riot, vehicles, falling aircraft, burglary, theft, etc.

Is fire insurance necessary?

> Every 31 seconds a fire breaks out in some city in the United States. Estimated fire losses in 1961 rose to an all-time high of 1.2 billion dollars.[1]

---

[1] "A Family Guide to Property & Liability Insurance," Educational Division, Insurance Information Institute, New York, N.Y., 1962, p. 7.

Today, every state has laws which stipulate a standard fire policy. This is very advantageous to the insured, as policies will be just as favorable from one company as another, minimum coverage must be provided, and small print cannot be used to covertly attempt to reduce the protection provided by the contract. Another advantage is that the Standard Fire Policy is well understood both by agents and by the courts. It must be used verbatim. The law does not allow any changes to be made except by endorsement, and these must not conflict with the terms of the policy itself. Insurance policies are never very interesting reading, but because this policy is standard, its clauses, exclusions, and conditions are important enough to merit some attention.

First Page

The first page of a Standard Fire Insurance Policy provides specific information including:
1. Name of the insuring company
2. Name and address of the insured
3. Amount of insurance provided
4. Applicable rate
5. Premium that must be paid
6. Perils insured against
7. Description and location of the property covered
8. Beginning and ending dates of the policy coverage
9. The name of the mortgagee, if any

Insuring Agreement

The insuring agreement is also on the first page, and states that the company insures the individual named in the policy against all direct loss by fire, lightning, and removal of property from the premises which are endangered by the perils insured against in the policy, except as otherwise provided in the policy. The amount of the coverage is also stated. The first sentence of the insuring agreement states that the consideration for the contract consists of two things:
1. Payment of the specified premium
2. Compliance with and acceptance of the provisions and stipulations in the contract

This means that the person insured must pay the premium and abide by the provisions and stipulations if he wants the contract to hold.

The inside page of the policy contains the various exclusions and conditions. They deserve careful attention.

Misrepresentation and Exclusions

First, it is stated that certain actions, such as the misrepresentation of a material fact, will void the policy. Next, certain exclusions are stated.

There are three general types of exclusions. The first is property such as currency and deeds. The second is perils which are not insured against, such as fires resulting from invasion or war. The third excludes certain types of losses, e.g., securities destroyed in a fire.

Losses Not Covered

The policy does not cover losses resulting from hazards which have been increased by any means within the control or knowledge of the insured. This means that a person can't change the character of the risk, by converting his business from furniture to munitions for example, and expect the building to still be protected by the same fire insurance policy.

The policy does not cover losses which occur after the property has been unoccupied for longer than sixty consecutive days. This is because the fire danger in a vacant building is greater than in an occupied building. Coverage by the policy will be suspended after the building has been vacant for 60 days, unless the insured obtains special permission from the insurance company.

The policy does not cover losses resulting from explosion or riot unless a fire results, in which case only the fire loss is covered.

Cancellation

Under certain circumstances, the policy may be canceled by either the person insured or by the insurance company. Neither need give any reason for cancellation. The policy carefully states the terms under which the company may cancel. It must give the insured a five day written notice of cancellation, and either return the unearned premium with the notice or include a statement that it will be returned. The policy remains in force during the five day notice period.

Mortgagee Relationship

Suppose a home is mortgaged for $15,000 and insured for $20,000. In case of total loss by fire, what could the owner of the property collect? The answer is, only up to the amount of his interest in the property, in this case $5,000. The policy contains provisions governing the relationship with any mortgagee named in the policy. This relationship is more specifically covered in the mortgage clause, which is part of the Dwelling and Contents Form usually attached to a home insurance policy. It stipulates the mortgagee's rights and obligations, including the right to receive any loss or damage payments according to his interest, even under adverse conditions such as property neglect or vacancy, foreclosure proceedings or notice of sale, change in title or ownership, or increase of the hazard.

Loss or damage payments are usually paid by check, made out jointly to the owner and the mortgagee. If the owner's coverage has been suspended, and the mortgagee was not aware of the change, the mortgagee will be paid and the insurance company will have a claim against the owner.

Pro-rata Liability

Sometimes a home is insured by several companies, either because the amount is so large that no one company will take the entire risk, or because the agent wants to spread the amount among several of the companies he represents, or because the insured wants to accommodate friends who are in the insurance business. A clause in the policy, the pro-rata liability clause, states that the company is not liable for a greater proportion of any loss than the proportion that the amount of the coverage its policy bears to the total insurance coverage. In other words, if its policy amounts to 25% of the total insurance coverage, the company will pay 25% of any loss that occurs. This will be true whether the other insurance is collectible or not.

Obligations of Insured

What you should do after a fire loss is presented below. This is also carefully stated in the individual policy. The insured has the following obligations:

1. To give immediate written notice to the company.
2. To protect the property from further damage.
3. To separate the damaged and undamaged personal property.
4. To put the property in the best possible order.
5. To furnish the company with a complete inventory of the destroyed, damaged, and undamaged property, showing quantities, costs, etc., in detail.

6. To provide the company with proof of loss within 60 days after the loss. This proof must contain all of the specific information stated in this clause in the policy.
7. To permit persons designated by the company to examine the property.
8. To submit to examinations, under oath, by persons designated by the company.
9. To produce books of account, bills, invoices, etc., for examintion if requested by the company.

Property Inventory

Furnishing a complete inventory is the most difficult thing for many people to do. As an experiment, try to think of all of the contents of just one room in your home. To help out, many fire insurance companies provide inventory forms. These can be filled out and filed away in a safe place. Then, if a fire does occur, the inventory will be readily available.

Claim Settlement

If the company and the insured cannot agree on the amount of a loss, the procedure that must be followed is stipulated in the policy. On the written demand of either party, each must select a competent and disinterested appraiser. The appraisers then select an umpire. If they can't agree, the umpire will be selected by the court. Differences between the appraisals will be submitted to the umpire, and arbitrated. The appraisers have nothing to do with determining whether or not the company is liable. Their only purpose is to determine the amount of the loss.

The company is given several options in the policy in regard to the treatment of property in case of a loss. It can, for example, take the property and pay the insured the agreed or appraised value, repair or rebuild it, or make a cash settlement. Usually, the cash settlement method is used. Notice that the choice is up to the company, not the insured. The person insured cannot abandon any property to the company.

Once the amount of loss is agreed upon or arbitrated, and all obligations of the policyholder have been fulfilled, the company must pay the claim within sixty days after the proof of loss is received. The policy also states that any suit or action on the policy must be started within twelve months after the loss.[2] If any third party is responsible for any part of the loss, the insured must assign the company the right of recovery. This is known as the "subrogation" clause.

Other Forms

This *Standard Fire Insurance Policy* is broad enough to cover all kinds of property—residential, business, real, and personal. To make it apply to one specific type of property, it is necessary to add additional forms. One of the most widely used is the *Dwelling and Contents Form*. This defines the property, and specifically states the various provisions concerning the insurance on the dwelling and its contents. It not only describes the dwelling and its contents, but also specifies a rental value which will be allowed by the company if the property should become untenable, for any period of time until it again becomes tenable. It also specifies the amount of coverage that will apply to cover household and personal property while it is away from the premises.

An *Extended Coverage Endorsement* extends the coverage to other perils. Only damage from fire and lightning are covered by the policy itself. This additional coverage extends the policy to include damage from wind storms, hail, explosion, riot, riot attending a strike, civil commotion, aircraft, vehicles, and certain kinds of smoke damage.

These are only two of many forms which may be attached to the Standard Fire Insurance Policy. While these are the most common, there are many others. Considerable space has been devoted to describing the provisions of the Standard Fire Insurance Policy because it is basic in all areas of fire insurance coverage. Endorsements, while they are important to the insured, are too numerous to be completely described in this text. Furthermore, the tendency today is for homeowners to obtain such coverage in a comprehensive "Homeowners Policy," which will be fully described later in this chapter.

Questions

Some of the seemingly simple provisions of a fire insurance policy cause the most difficulty. Just what, for example, is a fire? Are cigarette burns covered? How about the damage done by the red hot glass of a coffee percolater that the housewife neglected to fill with water? The answer depends upon exactly what happened. The courts

---

[2] In some states this rule is modified by state law.

have generally defined a fire to mean a burning that produces a visible light, or heat. Usually, cigarette ashes or red hot glass would char. No visible light would appear and very little heat would be generated. For this reason, these burns would not be covered. If any flame at all appears, the damage would be covered. In practice, there are so many borderline cases that each must be decided on its own merits. Often, the decision seems to depend upon the insurance company involved and the aggressiveness of the agent or the person insured.

The law also distinguishes between friendly and hostile fires. Damage caused by a friendly fire, one which has remained in the fireplace, stove, etc., where it belongs, is not covered. Damage from a hostile fire is covered. Let's suppose you arrive home on a cold winter evening and find that the fire in the fireplace has died down. Before taking off your outdoor clothes, you stir it up a bit. In the process, your hat falls in the fire. Because the fire is friendly, your hat would not be covered. If, however, a spark lands on a rug near the fireplace, the rug would be covered, as the fire is no longer where it is supposed to be, in the fireplace. Once it leaves the fireplace, it changes from a friendly fire to a hostile one.

Direct Loss

The insuring agreement clearly states that the coverage applies to "direct loss by fire or lightning." Indirect loss will not be covered. For example, if there is a fire in the neighbor's house, any damage done by firemen to your property would be covered by your insurance. Water damage might result if it was believed necessary to wet down your roof to prevent the fire from spreading. On the other hand, if a utility pole is struck by lightning, losses due to the lack of electric power will not be covered.

Actual Value

How much is the "actual cash value"? This is what the insuring agreement states the company will pay. This means the cost of replacement less depreciation. In a few states which have valued-policy laws, the company must pay the insured the full face value of the policy in case of total loss, regardless of the actual cash value of the building. Replacement-cost insurance is available at a higher premium, and is usually one of the agreements in the broad "Homeowners" type policy.

Coinsurance

Very rarely is there a total fire loss. Usually, only a small percentage of the property is actually damaged. For this reason, there is a temptation to underinsure property—insure it at less than full value. This is especially true in urban areas where there is adequate fire-fighting equipment. In the country, however, people usually feel that it is necessary to fully cover the value of their property, because of the greater likelihood of total loss. It would not be fair to provide insurance protection for the same cost to both those who underinsure and those who carry full insurance.

Because most losses are for less than full value, an insurance company can afford to provide insurance at lower rates for people who carry insurance equal to a large percentage of the actual value. Imagine, for example, an insurance company insuring one hundred $20,000 homes; total $2,000,000. Assume that during a year the total losses amounted to $3,200. If these homes were insured for only 40% of their value, a total of $800,000, the rate would have to be 40¢ per $100 to cover $3,200. If these homes were insured for 80% of their value—a total of $1,600,000 then the rate would only have to be 20¢ per $100 to cover the same amount.

The percentage of the value that must be insured to take advantage of the lower rate is stated by the insurer. This is called the "co-insurance clause." Suppose, for example, that there is an 80% "co-insurance clause" in the policy. This would mean that on a $20,000 home, the insured must carry $16,000 worth of insurance. If less insurance is carried, the insured would become a co-insurer with the insurance company. The insurance company would be required to pay only that percentage of any claim which the insurance coverage bears to the amount which should be carried. Suppose, for example, that the insurance is for $12,000 instead of $16,000. $12,000 divided by $16,000 is 75%. This means that in the event of any loss, the insurance company would only be obligated to pay 75% of the loss, up to the face value of the policy. The insured must pay the other 25%, and, of course, everything over $12,000.

Assignment

One difference between life insurance and property insurance is assignability. A life policy can be assigned, and used as collateral for a loan. Property insurance cannot be assigned. A fire insurance policy insures the owner of the property against losses due to fire. The property itself is not insured. The person taking out the insurance cannot assign it to someone else. If the property is sold, the insurance does not transfer to the new owner with the property. Such a transfer can only take place if permission is granted by the insurance company.

Insurable Interest

In property insurance, a person must have an insurable interest in the property at the time the loss occurs, to have a valid claim for damages. If he suffers some financial loss by virtue of having a loss against which he is insured, then he is said to have an insurable interest. It is obvious then, that anyone who owns something has an insurable interest in it. It may also exist without ownership. Creditors who hold property as security for loans they made, workmen who have a lien against property for work done, etc., have an insurable interest.

The insurable interest must exist at the time the loss occurs. Let's suppose a person is building a home. Fire insurance might be taken out when building starts, even though no house exists. Insurance will be issued as long as the builder will have an insurable interest if a loss should occur. On the other hand, if a person sells his home, but does not cancel his insurance, he would be unable to collect if a fire occurred, because his insurable interest ended with the sale of the house.

Warning

In the last dozen years, building costs have approximately doubled. The cost of appliances, home furnishings, etc., have also increased. Too many people do not consider these facts. It is amazing, in a way. They constantly complain about the rise in prices, and yet expect the same amount of fire insurance they purchased many years ago to be sufficient today. A home which sold for $5,000 in 1940, in many instances is worth $20,000 or more today. Yet many homeowners still have such homes insured for $5,000. Remember, as the dollar value of a home and its contents increases, fire insurance should also be increased. Existing coverage should be reviewed periodically.

PERSONAL LIABILITY INSURANCE

There are other causes of financial loss besides fire. This is true for everyone, but especially for homeowners. Consider the family used as an example at the beginning of this chapter. The rock thrown by the power mower, the neighbor bitten by the homeowner's dog, the golf ball which hit a player in the head—all of these things and hundreds of others can bring about legal claims which may cost large sums of money.

Personal liability insurance protects a person from such claims. Homeowners' liability insurance usually covers accidents either on the insured's property or away from it, which are caused by the actions of the insured or a member of his family. It will also pay legal costs when the insured is sued for damages which are payable under the policy.

There are various types of liability policies, but the one most commonly used by the general public is the Comprehensive Personal Liability (CPL) policy. This protects the insured by providing, among other things:

1. Very broad personal liability coverage.
   a. The policy reads "to pay on behalf of the insured all sums which the insured shall become legally obligated to pay as damages because of bodily injury, sickness or disease, sustained by any person, and as damages because of injury to or destruction of property, including the loss of use thereof."
   b. One limit, e.g., $10,000 or $25,000, applies to both the bodily injury and property damage coverage.
2. Broad coverage for bodily injury, sickness or disease caused by accident.
3. Nonliability physical damage to property coverage.
4. Coverage of the insured person named in the policy, his wife, children, other relatives living with him, persons legally responsible for animals and boats when an accident occurs, and employees operating farm equipment as part of their job.
5. Payment for defense in any suit alleging the liability of the insured, even if the suit is groundless, false, or fraudulent.

This is not true, however, of the medical payment and physical damage to property coverage. In these cases, no actual liability is required. This covers situations in which the insured feels a moral responsibility as well as those in which he is legally liable. Two examples will indicate the importance of this:

1. Mrs. Jones, the next door neighbor, visits the insured in his home. On entering the front door, she trips and breaks her wrist. The insurer will pay the medical bills, up to the policy limits, whether or not the insured is legally liable.
2. The insured's son is trying out for the school football team. He practices kicking one Saturday afternoon at home. A highly successful kick goes off course and through the neighbor's window. Again, the insurer will pay damages, whether or not the insured is legally liable.

If the insured or his family are responsible for personal injuries or property damage, either on or away from the insured's premises, this insurance will provide coverage. Furthermore, some damages are covered even if they are intentionally caused by any of the insured's children under 12.

These coverages are so broad they cover just about everything. However, there has to be some limit, and certain exclusions are listed in the policy. Some of these are:

1. Damage caused by automobiles driven by the insured or a member of his family, unless the automobile is on the insured's premises.
2. Boats over a specified length or with motors above a specified horsepower.
3. Swimming pools capable of being filled to a depth of more than 30 inches. (Notice that this says "capable of." The pool does not have to have this much water in it to be excluded.)
4. Business and professional activities of the insured.
5. Injuries to employees or servants in states where workmen's compensation insurance is required by law.
6. Damage or injury caused by aircraft.
7. Intentional sickness, injury, or destruction.
8. Destruction or damaging of property in the insured's care, custody, or control.
9. Liability the insured assumes by contract, except under certain specific conditions.

The insured does have certain obligations under a personal liability policy in addition to paying the premium. He must give written notice to the insurer of any occurrence. He must send all summonses, or notices of any claim or suit, to the company. He must cooperate with the company in its efforts to reach a settlement, or in its defense against a suit. This is important. Occasionally, the insured sympathizes with the claimant, but if he carries this sympathy too far, the insurer may claim "lack of cooperation," and the insured may end up paying the claim himself.

Any suit or claim is made by the company in the name of the insured. The insurer agrees only to make payments and settlements in the insured's name. The insurance company is never a co-defendant in a suit. The court action must in no way be prejudiced by the fact that insurance exists.

Even the most careful person can find himself the defendant in a suit charging negligence, and the monetary loss can be extreme. This makes liability insurance a "must." Furthermore, either because of an increase in public awareness, a decline in scruples, or inflation, there is a very definite tendency to sue for negligence with the slightest excuse. This tendency is further encouraged by the fact that settlements are becoming larger and larger. While the discussion here has concerned only personal liability insurance, there are many other types, such as medical malpractice insurance, comprehensive general liability, druggist's liability, etc. These are all written for specific purposes. It is well for a person to consider liability insurance which will cover all phases of his activities.

THE HOMEOWNERS POLICY

Due to the historical development of the insurance industry, as indicated at the beginning of this chapter, fire and casualty insurance were for some time sold by separate companies and under separate policies. This meant that to be completely protected against all perils, a homeowner had to carry more than one policy and often do business with more than one company. Many perils were not covered. Fire insurance on the home itself was the most commonly purchased, but liability and personal property coverage were usually insufficient.

It wasn't until the early 1950's that insurance policies offering various combinations of property and liability coverage started to appear. This is, then, a relatively new field, and the forms of policies presently available cannot be considered as permanent. Changes will undoubtedly continue to occur. Yet it is safe to say that, for home-owners, the general type of policy called the "Homeowners" policy is the best buy. There is only one policy to purchase and only one premium to pay. Also, because of the fact that many perils are packaged in the one policy, insurance companies are able to offer this broad coverage for much less (20 to 30 per cent less) than the individual coverages would cost if purchased separately.

Coverage Offered

Chart 11-2 indicates the coverage offered by three different forms of "Homeowners" policies. All three are the same as far as liability and property coverage is concerned, but they differ as to the number of perils covered.

Several different coverages are included under the general headings of "Liability Coverage" and "Property Coverage," and the amounts of coverage for each category are automatically determined. The only amount that the insured must determine is that applicable to the house itself.

Let us suppose that your house has been appraised and its replacement value set at $20,000, excluding land and underground items such as foundation and pipes. An inventory of your household contents indicates that their actual cash value is about $6,000. To receive full payment (replacement cost) for partial loss or damage to your dwelling under the homeowners policy, you need insure it for only 80 per cent of replacement value. You can, of course, insure to full value, $20,000, if you wish. Eighty per cent of $20,000, the assumed replacement value of your house, is $16,000, and it is the basis for determining the amount of other property coverages. In our example, the Broad Form of the homeowners policy will give you protection in the amounts shown below. Since personal liability insurance is automatically included in all homeowners policies, this coverage is shown also.

Property
Dwelling $16,000 (80% of full value)
Appurtenant Private Structures 1,600 (10% of dwelling)
Personal Property
(not otherwise covered) 6,400 (40% of dwelling)
Additional Living Expenses 3,200 (20% of dwelling)
Liability
Comprehensive Personal
Liability 25,000 (each occurrence)*
Medical Payments 500 (each person)
Physical Damage to Property
of others 250 (each occurrence)
May be increased* [3]

How much does this coverage cost?

Given on page 296 is a comparison of costs of the Standard, Broad, and Comprehensive Forms of the homeowners policy.

[3] "A Family Guide to Property & Liability Insurance," Educational Division, Insurance Information Institute, New York, N.Y., 1962, p. 15.

YOUR HOMEOWNERS POLICY

Summary of Coverage—Standard, Broad and Comprehensive Forms

PROPERTY COVERAGE	POLICY FORM	PERILS INSURED AGAINST	LIABILITY COVERAGE
Property coverages include:	**S T A N D A R D** (C O M)	1. fire and lightning 2. loss or damage to property removed from premises endangered by fire 3. windstorm or hail 4. explosion 5. riot, riot attending a strike, and civil commotion 6. aircraft	7. vehicles, if not owned or operated by an occupant of the premises 8. smoke or smudge caused by sudden, unusual, or faulty operations of a cooking or heating unit 9. vandalism and malicious mischief 10. theft 11. breaking of glass constituting a part of the building	**All members of the family have the following coverages:** 1. **Comprehensive Personal Liability** 2. **Medical Payments** 3. **Physical Damage to the Property of Others**
1. Dwelling 2. Private Structures 3. Personal Property 4. Additional Living Expense Property coverage is the same for all forms of a homeowners policy	**B R O A D** (P R) **H O M E** (E O) **A N D** (E N D) **S I V E** (S I V E)	12. falling objects 13. weight of ice, snow, or sleet 14. collapse of building or any part thereof 15. accidental discharge, leakage or overflow of water or steam from within a plumbing, heating, or air-conditioning system 16. sudden and accidental tearing asunder, cracking, burning, or bulging of a steam or hot water heating system **All perils except:** earthquake, landslide, flood, surface water, waves, tidal water or tidal wave, backing up of sewers, seepage, war, and nuclear radiation	17. sudden and accidental tearing asunder, cracking, burning, or bulging of appliances for heating water for domestic consumption 18. freezing of plumbing, heating and air-conditioning systems and domestic appliances 19. sudden and accidental injury to electrical appliances, devices, fixtures, and wiring. (TV picture tube not included)	Liability coverage is the same for all forms of a homeowners policy.

Source: "A Teacher's Guide to Patterns of Protection," Educational Division, Insurance Information Institute, New York, N.Y., 1963, p. 11.

Table 11-1

Comparison of New Homeowners Policies

1962 REVISIONS

(Coverage Descriptions Are General. Coverages Are Subject to Conditions of Policies.)

	Form 1 Standard Form	Form 2 Broad Form	Form 3 — Dwelling Special Form Combined With 4 — Residence Contents Broad Form	Form 4 Residence Contents Broad Form	Form 5 Comprehensive Form
ELIGIBLE DWELLING RISKS					
Owner occupied 1 or 2 family	Yes	Yes	Yes	Yes	Yes
Owner occupied 3 or 4 family	No	No	No	Yes	No
Tenant occupancy	No	No	No	Yes	No
Incidental office occupancy	Yes	Yes	Yes	Yes	Yes
COVERAGE FOR					
Dwelling	$8,000 min.; no max.	$8,000 min.; no max.	$8,000 min.; no max.	———	$15,000 min.; no max.
Related private structures	10% of dwelling limit but may be increased $5,000 min. by endorsement	10% of dwelling limit but may be increased $5,000 min. by endorsement	10% of dwelling limit but may be increased $5,000 min. by endorsement	———	10% of dwelling limit but may be increased $5,000 min. by endorsement
Seasonal (secondary) dwelling in same state					
Personal property on premises	40% of dwelling limit but may be increased or reduced to 30%	40% of dwelling limit but may be increased or reduced to 30%	40% of dwelling limit but may be increased or reduced to 30%	$4,000 minimum	50% of dwelling limit but may be increased
Personal property away from premises	10% of premises limit; min. of $1,000	10% of premises limit; min. of $1,000	10% of premises limit; min. of $1,000	10% of premises limit; min. of $1,000	Same as premises limit
Scheduled personal articles				Yes	Yes
Additional living expense	10% of dwelling limit	20% of dwelling limit	20% of dwelling limit	20% of unscheduled personal property limit	20% of dwelling limit
Trees, shrubs, lawns and plants	Yes	Yes	Yes	———	Yes
Replacement cost on buildings	Yes	Yes	Yes	———	Yes
Fire department service charge	Yes	Yes	Yes	Yes	Yes
PERILS COVERED					
Fire, lightning, windstorm, hail, riot, civil commotion, aircraft	Yes	Yes	Yes	Yes	Yes
Sonic boom	No, but $50 on glass	Yes	Yes	Yes	Yes
Explosion other than steam boiler	Yes	Yes	Yes	Yes	Yes
Explosion of steam boiler	No	Yes	Yes	Yes	Yes
Bursting of steam or hot water appliances and heating systems		Yes	Yes	Yes	Yes
Damage by vehicles to:					
Building	Yes, except by an occupant of the premises	Yes	Yes	Yes	Yes
Fences	No	Yes	Yes	———	Yes
Driveways	No	Yes, except by an occupant of the premises	Yes, except by an occupant of the premises	———	Yes
Walks	No	Yes, except by an occupant of the premises	Yes, except by an occupant of the premises	———	Yes
Lawns	Yes, except by an occupant of the premises	Yes, except by an occupant of the premises	Yes, except by an occupant of the premises	———	Yes, except by an occupant of the premises
Trees, shrubs, plants	Yes, except by an occupant of the premises	Yes, except by an occupant of the premises	Yes, except by an occupant of the premises	———	Yes, except by an occupant of the premises
Smoke: From industrial operations	No	No	No	No	No

Comparison of coverages (dwelling / homeowners forms)

Peril / Coverage	1	2	3	4	5	6
From heating or cooking unit					Yes	Yes
Vandalism and malicious mischief	Yes, except when vacant beyond 30 days	Yes, except when vacant beyond 30 days	Yes, except when vacant beyond 30 days	Yes, except when vacant beyond 30 days	Yes, except when vacant beyond 30 days	Yes, except when vacant beyond 30 days
Water:						
Surface water or flood	No	No	No	No	No	No, except personal property away from premises
Backing up of sewers or drains	No	No	No	No	No	Yes
Leakage from plumbing or heating systems	Yes, excluding repair to system	Yes, excluding repair to system	Yes, excluding repair to system	Yes, excluding repair to system	Yes, excluding repair to system	Yes
Rain through doors, windows, bad roof	No	No	No	Building but not contents	No	Yes
Freezing of plumbing, heating systems	No	Yes, except while vacant or unoccupied and heat not maintained or system drained	Yes, except while vacant or unoccupied and heat not maintained or system drained	Yes, except while vacant or unoccupied and heat not maintained or system drained	Yes, except while vacant or unoccupied and heat not maintained or system drained	Yes, except while vacant or unoccupied and heat not maintained or system drained
Falling objects, including trees	No, except from aircraft	Yes	Yes	Yes	Yes	Yes
Weight of ice, snow, sleet	No	Yes	Yes	Yes	Yes	Yes
Wind damage to trees, including debris removal	No	No	No	No	No	No
Collapse of building	No	Yes	Yes	Yes	Yes	Yes
Landslide	No	No	No	No	No	Yes
Earthquake	No, except by endorsement	No, except by endorsement	No, except by endorsement	No, except by endorsement	No	No
Personal property damage by pets	No	No	No, except by endorsement	No, except by endorsement	No, except by endorsement	Yes, pers. prop. only. Pers. prop. "yes." Dwelling by end. No
Residence glass breakage	Up to $50, except if vacant more than 30 days	Yes, except if vacant more than 30 days	Yes, except if vacant more than 30 days	Yes, except if vacant more than 30 days	—	Yes, except if vacant more than 30 days
Sudden and accidental injury to electrical appliances and fixtures	No	Yes	Yes	Yes	Yes	Yes
Theft:						
Of personal property	Yes	Yes	Yes	Yes	Yes	Yes
Mysterious disappearance	No	No	By endorsement	By endorsement	By endorsement	Yes
From unattended auto	No	No	By endorsement	By endorsement	By endorsement	Yes
Of building equipment, fixtures	Yes, except when under construction	Yes, except when under construction	Yes, except when under construction	Yes, except when under construction	Yes, except when under construction	Yes, except when under construction
Of property not integral part when dwelling under construction	No	No	No	No	No	No
Consequential loss to personal property	Yes, when temperature change is due to damage by insured peril in building at described location	Yes, when temperature change is due to damage by insured peril in building at described location	Yes, when temperature change is due to damage by insured peril in building at described location	Yes, when temperature change is due to damage by insured peril in building at described location	Yes, when temperature change is due to damage by insured peril in building at described location	Yes, when temperature change is due to damage by insured peril in building at described location
Wind and hail deductible	Yes—$50*	Yes—$50*	Yes—$50*	Yes—$50*	Yes—$50*	Yes—$100†
Other perils (except fire and lightning) deductible	Yes—$50*	Yes—$50*	Yes—$50*	Yes—$50* may be modified	Yes—$50* may be modified	Yes—$100†
Third party bodily injury and property damage claims	Yes—$25,000 basic	Yes—$25,000 basic	Yes—$25,000 basic	Yes—$25,000 basic	Yes—$25,000 basic	Yes—$25,000 basic
Fire legal liability	Yes	Yes	Yes	Yes	Yes	Yes
Medical payments	Yes—$500 basic	Yes—$500 basic	Yes—$500 basic	Yes—$500 basic	Yes—$500 basic	Yes—$500 basic
Physical damage to property	Yes—$250	Yes—$250	Yes—$250	Yes—$250	Yes—$250	Yes—$250

*Not applicable if loss exceeds $500. When loss is between $50 and $500, company pays 111% of loss in excess of $50. Deductibles may be eliminated entirely for extra charges (but on wind and hail only if State rules permit).

†Not applicable if loss exceeds $500. When loss is between $100 and $500, company pays 125% of loss in excess of $100. Deductibles may be reduced to $50 for extra charge but may not be eliminated.

Source: The Rough Notes Co., Inc., 1962.

295

These figures are based on a frame residence in a specific midwestern town in 1962. The replacement value of the dwelling, excluding land and underground values, is $20,000.

Coverage	Cost for 3 Years	
Standard Form (11 perils)	$136*	($ 3.78 a mo.)
Broad Form (19 perils)	174*	($ 4.83 a mo.)
Comprehensive Form ("all-risks")	361**	($10.03 a mo.)

*$50 deductible on Wind and Hail only.
**$100 deductible on all perils except fire and lightning. If loss is $500 or more, this deductible does not apply. [4]

The example presented is specific. The homeowner must buy a "package" and cannot select specific coverages, but because of the number of Homeowners' Forms— five were in common use in 1962 — and the modifications available, enough flexibility is provided to satisfy most homeowners and renters. (See pages 294 and 295.)

Standard Fire Policy

The Standard Fire Insurance Policy is part of each Homeowner Policy. This means that the statements made earlier in this chapter concerning the restrictions, exclusions, etc., contained in the Standard Policy are applicable here.

The determination of how much the company will pay in case of loss differs in two ways, under homeowners forms, from the method used in a fire insurance policy. First, deductible amounts are involved. Sometimes these are "disappearing" deductibles, in that they do not apply if the total loss is above a certain amount. For example, in the Comprehensive Form presented in the example on page 292, there was a $100 deductible on all perils except fire and lightning, but if the loss was $500 or more, the $100 would not be deducted. Secondly, under certain conditions the Homeowner Policy will pay the cost of replacement rather than cash value. Cash value means the cost of replacement less depreciation, so replacement cost is a more liberal coverage. Replacement cost is usually allowed only if the loss is less than a certain dollar amount and less than a specified percentage of the total amount of insurance.

Many who have a Homeowners Policy do not realize the amount of coverage provided, and fail to claim their full benefits. Remember the example of the dropping of the red hot glass on the linoleum, and the placing of a hot iron on a counter top? In neither of these cases was a fire created, in the sense in which it is legally defined. Yet both of these events were covered under a Homeowners Policy on property

---

[4] *Ibid*, p. 16.

COMPARE THE COST — COMPARE THE COVERAGE [5]

FOR YOUR	Perils Covered	YOUR PRESENT POLICIES Amount	3-Yr. Cost	HOMEOWNERS "A" Amount	3-Yr. Cost	HOMEOWNERS "B" Amount	3-Yr. Cost
HOME	Fire and Lightning						
	Windstorm, Hail, Explosion, Riot and Civil Commotion, Aircraft, Vehicles, Smoke, Removal						
	Building Glass Breakage			Limit of $50			
	Vandalism and Malicious Mischief						
	Water Escape, Rupture of Steam or Hot Water Heating Systems, Freezing, Falling Objects, Collapse, Weight of Ice, Snow or Sleet, Injury to Electrical Appliances			Not Applicable			
TREES, PLANTS AND SHRUBS	Fire and Other Perils (not Windstorm)			5% of Dwelling Amount Limit $250 Per Tree Plant or Shrub		5% of Dwelling Amount Limit $250 Per Tree Plant or Shrub	
CONTENTS	Fire and Lightning						
	Windstorm, Hail, Explosion, Riot and Civil Commotion, Aircraft, Vehicles, Smoke, Removal						
	Vandalism and Malicious Mischief						
	Water Escape, Rupture of Steam or Hot Water Heating Systems, Freezing, Falling Objects, Collapse, Weight of Ice, Snow or Sleet, Injury to Electrical Appliances			Not Applicable			
	Theft From Premises						
	Theft, World-Wide						
ADDITIONAL LIVING EXPENSE	All Perils covered by the Policy						
LIABILITY	Comprehensive Personal Liability						
	Medical Payments						
	Physical Damage to Property						

Number of present policies _____ or 1 Homeowners Policy with one premium to pay and one expiration date.

Three Year Premium _____

paid annually, the cost will be:

Prepaid $ _____
First Yr. $ _____
Second Yr. $ _____
Third Yr. $ _____

Prepaid $ _____

297

[5] "More and More Homeowners are Turning to Us . . .," Pamphlet H–509, Insurance Company of North America, Philadelphia, Pa., 1960.

in Stoneham, Massachusetts. Furthermore, this Homeowners Policy also covered the theft of a wallet, and the insured was paid the $25 contained in the wallet, the cost of renewing the automobile driver's license lost with the wallet, and the cost of the wallet itself.

To describe all of the specific perils covered by the Homeowners policy would require much more space than is available here. It should be sufficient to state that the coverages are extremely broad and home-owners should investigate both costs and coverages. More than likely each will find a policy well suited to his personal needs and budget.

Most policies, fire, casualty, personal property, and Homeowners, are written for a three year period. This was the period used in the cost comparison presented on page 296. These figures, however, are only examples. Insurance costs vary for many reasons. They will differ according to the construction of the building, e.g., whether it is frame or masonry, according to the location of the building, the water supply available for fire fighting, and other pertinent factors. Such factors cause considerable variation in the actual cost of such insurance. Chart 11-3 is useful for comparing the costs and coverage for a specific home.

AUTOMOBILE INSURANCE

Chart 11-4 indicates the six basic coverages included in the general category of "automobile insurance." It shows clearly to what persons and what property each coverage applies. An automobile owner should clearly understand the specific perils covered. Notice, referring to the chart, that:

1. Bodily injury liability applies to persons other than the insured.
2. Property damage liability applies to cars other than the insured's and to property other than cars.
3. Medical payments coverage applies to the insured, his family and other persons.
4. Comprehensive physical damage applies to the insured's car.
5. Collision applies to the insured's car.
6. Uninsured motorist protection applies to the insured and his family.

Bodily Injury and Property Damage Liability

Bodily injury liability insurance provides protection for the in-sured, his family, or anyone driving his car with his permission, in case his car injures or kills someone. The insured and his family are

Chart 11–4

AUTOMOBILE INSURANCE
A Summary Chart — Six Basic Coverages

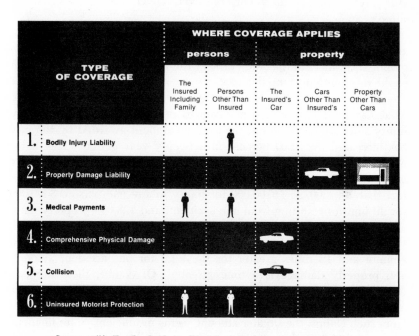

TYPE OF COVERAGE	WHERE COVERAGE APPLIES				
	persons		property		
	The Insured Including Family	Persons Other Than Insured	The Insured's Car	Cars Other Than Insured's	Property Other Than Cars
1. Bodily Injury Liability		●			
2. Property Damage Liability				●	●
3. Medical Payments	●	●			
4. Comprehensive Physical Damage			●		
5. Collision			●		
6. Uninsured Motorist Protection	●	●			

Source: "A Family Guide to Property & Liability Insurance," Educational Division, Insurance Information Institute, New York, N.Y., 1962, p. 32.

also protected while driving someone else's car, as long as they have the owner's permission. If the insured's car is being repaired and he borrows or rents one, he and his family will be protected while driving the substitute car.

This insurance further protects the insured against loss arising out of the death, bodily injury, sickness, or disease of any person or persons, when the insured is legally liable. The insurer also agrees to defend the insured against damage suits involving such claims, to pay court costs, attorney's fees, and other related costs.

This type of insurance is usually referred to as "ten, twenty," "twenty-five, fifty," etc. Using "ten, twenty" as an example, the figures indicate that the insurer will pay up to $10,000 for injury to any one person and up to $20,000 for all the injuries resulting from one accident, regardless of the number of persons injured.

Property damage liability insurance covers the same persons as bodily injury liability covers, and under the same conditions. If you hit another car, crash into someone's prize grape arbor, or damage someone's garage door, property damage liability insurance will provide protection. It does not, however, cover damages to the insured's car.

Bodily injury and property damage liability insurance are almost always sold together. They are the most important forms of automobile insurance, in that they protect the insured against perils which could result in substantial losses.

What limits should the average person carry? Consider, first, what has happened in recent years to decisions rendered in bodily injury suits. In many states, the average amount awarded by the jury has increased over 200 percent in a twenty year period. This is far more than the increase in the cost of living in the same period. There is no indication that this trend will reverse itself. Consider, also, the fact that 100/300/25 ($100,000 for injury to any one person, $300,000 for all injuries resulting from one accident, and $25,000 property damage liability) costs only slightly over one-third more than 10/20/5; yet the bodily injury coverage is 10 times greater for the single person amount and 15 times greater for the total for one accident amount, and property damage is 5 times greater. Of course, these are two extremes, one representing very low, and the other very high, coverage. Due to the possible losses an automobile owner might suffer from such claims, the smaller amount seems insufficient. State financial responsibility laws vary in the limits of liability coverage required, but in any event they only establish the minimum coverage that *must* be carried. If a motorist is involved in an accident and does not carry liability insurance, most states require that he either get such insurance or post bond if he wants to keep his license and registration.

Medical Payments

This coverage protects the insured and his family while riding in any car, as well as passengers and guests riding in the insured's car. There is no question of liability here, as protection is provided regardless of who is at fault in the accident. The limits of liability available are between $500 and $5,000 per person. These rates apply to each individual injured, so if there were five passengers, and the limit carried was $5,000, the total limit for costs resulting from one accident would be $25,000.

This insurance is relatively inexpensive and well worth the price. The costs of medical care have gone up considerably in recent years and are still rising. This means that sizable medical bills could result from an accident. Furthermore, guests are often reluctant to sue the driver, particularly if he is a friend or relative; and the driver may feel morally obligated even if he is not legally liable. Medical payments insurance will save both parties from embarrassment.

Comprehensive Physical Damage

This coverage protects the insured's car against most losses except collision, but does not include such things as wear and tear, mechanical failure, etc. It does cover vandalism and malicious mischief damage, glass breakage, theft of the car or any part of it, damage by fire, lightning, flood, windstorm, earthquake, falling objects, riot, and civil commotion. Some coverage is provided for damage to wearing apparel. It also provides for payments to the insured to reimburse him for transportation expenses incurred because his car has been stolen.

The importance of this type of insurance depends upon such things as where the car is parked and garaged. Anyone who frequently parks his car in one of the less desirable neighborhoods in town runs the risk of frequent damage, and would probably find such insurance worth carrying. He may find the cost higher than he expects because it varies according to risk exposure, losses paid in the insured's territory, the age of the car, and its original price.

The amount of malicious damage done is surprising. In early 1963, an individual parked a new convertible outside a bowling alley for about an hour. The bowling alley was located on a main route which was heavily travelled and well lit. On leaving the alley, the new car owner found that someone had walked on his convertible roof, slit it with a knife, and smashed in his radiator. Comprehensive physical damage insurance was a great comfort.

Even thievery has its surprising aspects. If the thief simply makes off with the entire car, the loss is quite definite and obvious. However, thieves often steal only the wheels, motor, radiator, drive shaft, or other parts. Thievery runs all the way from the complete car down to hub caps, in varying degrees of thoroughness. Comprehensive physical damage insurance provides protection, regardless of the percentage of the car stolen.

Collision Insurance

Collision insurance protects the insured against damage to his vehicle resulting from colliding with another car, a telephone pole, a stone wall, or any other object; and damage from upset. Inasmuch as the costs of repairing a new car are higher than the costs of repairing an old one, the cost of collision insurance is higher on the new car.

This type of insurance is usually sold with a deductible of $50 or $100. With a $50 deductible policy, the insured would pay the first $50 damages; and with a $100 deductible policy, the first $100 damages. The $50 deductible obviously offers the most coverage, but the difference in cost should be carefully considered. If, for example, the $50 deductible costs $15 more per year than the $100 deductible, the insured is paying $15 for $50 worth of insurance. This is extremely high cost coverage. It may even be found that the cost of this $50 additional coverage is more than $50.

A car does not have to be moving to have a collision, as defined under the terms of the policy. Let's assume you park your car at the curb on a main thoroughfare, and thoughtlessly open the door on the driver's side, into the path of an oncoming car. The car strikes the door, demolishing it. Your collision insurance would cover the damage done to your car.

Collision insurance also covers damage to your car resulting from accidents caused by others. While the other party may clearly be responsible for the accident and therefore liable for the damages, such claims are often difficult to settle. In fact, there may be no settlement if the other party does not carry property damage liability insurance.

The damage can be appraised and repaired much more quickly and expediently under your own collision insurance. You then subrogate your claim against the other party to your insurance company, and they sue, if they think it is worth while. If they win a judgment, and collect it, they may or may not return the deductible amount of your policy to you. This is a matter of company policy. Some do, and some don't.

Whether or not a particular accident is covered by comprehensive physical damage insurance or collision insurance is quite important to the insured. If it is covered by collision, he must pay the deductible of $50 or $100. If it is covered by comprehensive, there is no deductible to be paid.

Uninsured Motorist Protection

The cost of this coverage is extremely small and well worth the expense. It covers medical and hospital expenses in the event the uninsured motorist is legally liable for an accident resulting in injuries to yourself and others covered by your policy; or if one of you is injured by a hit-and-run driver. While the uninsured motorist may be sued and forced to pay, the time involved may be considerable and the money collected may be insufficient.

Insurance Rates

One of the most frequently heard complaints of automobile owners concerns the high cost of automobile insurance. The reason is the increased frequency and rising costs of accidents.

There are three basic reasons why automobile insurance rates change:

1. The number of traffic accidents.
2. The costs, following accidents, of repairing vehicles and providing medical care for people.
3. The awards provided by either claim settlements or court decisions.

Last year 38,000 persons died in traffic accidents alone, a decrease of about 2 per cent below 1960.

The toll of fatal and bodily injury traffic accidents as well as property damage accidents caused by automobiles last year reached the staggering total of 12,300,000, or double the figure for 1939.

In this tragic sum, 3,057,000 men, women, and children suffered personal injuries, a greater number than the combined populations of Colorado, Delaware, Nevada, New Hampshire, Vermont and Wyoming. Put another way, there were more than twice as many casualties in traffic accidents last year as in our Armed Services during all the years of World War I and World War II.

Every weekend was a catastrophe in 1961; almost one half the traffic disasters occurred on weekends. Death struck every nine minutes, and every ten seconds someone suffered injury in an automobile accident.

Economic losses from traffic accidents in the United States in 1961 totaled $7,900,000 compared with $7,600,000 in 1960.

In the years between 1939 and 1961, traffic accidents increased 107 per cent, and traffic injuries rose 154 per cent.[6]

While there is some variation between companies, automobile insurance rates are based primarily on the following factors:

1. The place of garaging
2. The use of the car
3. The age of the drivers
4. The year, make, and age of the automobile
5. The amount of insurance purchased

This is not the place to completely analyze each of these factors. There are, however, certain general basic facts that automobile owners should understand.

Let's immediately dispose of the fifth factor. It is obvious that the greater the coverage carried by the insured, the higher the cost.

All of the other factors are concerned with the dollar amount of claims. Some areas have more accidents than others. Insurance companies keep detailed statistics concerning accident experience. States are divided into territories; some states have many, others only a few. Each territory is assigned a rate according to the frequency of accidents. The premium rate used, depends upon where the car is garaged, not where the insured lives. Of course, a car usually is garaged where the insured lives, but this is not always the case.

Suppose someone living and garaging his car in Maine, travels to San Francisco. He becomes so intent on the beautiful scenery that he crashes into another car driven by a resident of the San Francisco area. It is important to realize that the accident claim is charged against the territory in which the car at fault is garaged, regardless of where the accident occurs.

Rates also vary according to whether or not the car is used for business or traveling to work. Chart 11–5 indicates the six classifications generally used. The first three, 1A, 1B, and 1C, and the last, 3, are used when there is no male driver under 25. The variation, here, is concerned with the use of the car. The more it is used, the higher the rate. Classifications 2A and 2C concern situations where there is a male driver under 25. Notice that these are the highest rate categories. The rate in 2C is more than three times the rate in 1A. This is because the cost of settling liability claims for drivers in the

---

[6] "Insurance Statistics 1962," Insurance Information Institute, New York, N.Y.

2C classification has been more than three times that for drivers in 1A, over a period of years.

Notice also that the higher rates for drivers under 25 apply to males. Girls under this age have had far fewer accidents than boys, and therefore no extra premium is charged in some areas, while in others the extra premium is less.

Chart 11–5

A COMPARISON OF LIABILITY RATES BY DRIVER CLASSIFICATIONS IN LARGE CITIES

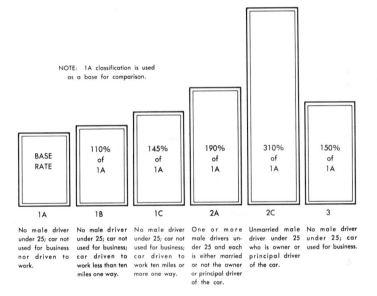

NOTE: 1A classification is used as a base for comparison.

1A	1B	1C	2A	2C	3
BASE RATE	110% of 1A	145% of 1A	190% of 1A	310% of 1A	150% of 1A
No male driver under 25; car not used for business nor driven to work.	No male driver under 25; car not used for business; car driven to work less than ten miles one way.	No male driver under 25; car not used for business; car driven to work ten miles or more one way.	One or more male drivers under 25 and each is either married or not the owner or principal driver of the car.	Unmarried male driver under 25 who is owner or principal driver of the car.	No male driver under 25; car used for business.

Source: "A Family Guide to Property & Liability Insurance," Educational Division, Insurance Information Institute, New York, N.Y., 1962, p. 29.

Comprehensive physical damage rates depend upon the year, make, and age of the vehicle insured, as well as upon the place of garaging. The newer and more expensive the car, the greater the possible loss that might be incurred.

There are various types of discounts available. In many states, safe driver discounts of 10, 15, or 20 percent are available if the insured and his family have not been involved in accidents or serious traffic law violations for a period of years. Driver education discounts are available, even in those states where an extra premium is charged for drivers under 25, when the driver, male or female, has successfully completed an acceptable driver education course. If a person owns more than one private passenger automobile, buys an economy-type "special automobile policy," or is classified as a farmer, discounts may be available. As these discounts are not available in all states, state regulations must be investigated before assuming that such discounts may be obtained. In those states where such discounts are not available, automobile owners should be concerned with the reason why. Reduced premiums for safe driving, for example, have saved drivers money in many states.

Selecting the Company

An insured should carefully compare the costs of automobile insurance offered by various companies. If two companies offer the same coverage for different costs, the one with the lowest cost would naturally appear to be the most attractive. There are, however, other things to consider besides cost. Some companies have a reputation for service; others do not. Some customarily pay legitimate claims promptly; others do not. Such factors must be carefully considered.

SUMMARY

This chapter has been concerned with those types of property and casualty insurance most important from the viewpoint of personal finance. There are many other types which have been mentioned here only briefly, or not at all. These include comprehensive general liability, burglary and theft, glass, and workmen's compensation, for example. Workmen's compensation insurance is important in that it provides medical care and weekly payments coverage for injured employees. It is, however, purchased by the employer, not the employee, and therefore there are no questions concerning what type of insurance to carry or how much, from the viewpoint of personal finance.

In buying property and casualty insurance, a competent insurance agent is just as important as in buying life and health insurance. The field is large and complicated. How can a "competent" agent be selected? One of the usual methods, of course, is to select an agent respected in the community. Quite often, no specific agent seems to be any more outstanding than any other. In such cases, it would be worth considering an agent who has a Certified Property and Casualty Underwriter (C.P.C.U.) designation. This means that he has passed examinations in various departments relevant to the general fields of property and casualty insurance. Passing the examinations means that he has spent a considerable amount of time studying these areas. Due to the time devoted to this effort, it probably also means that he has selected the field of property and casualty insurance as a career, and will be available for advice and assistance in the future.

Questions

1. Compare multiple line underwriting and all line underwriting.

2. What is included in the "insuring agreement" presented on the first page of the standard fire policy?

3. Describe two of the three types of losses not covered by the standard fire insurance policy.

4. How is the mortgagee protected in the standard fire insurance policy?

5. To be covered under a standard fire policy what is
   a. A "fire"?
   b. The difference between a "friendly" and a "hostile" fire?
   c. A "direct loss"?
   d. "Actual cash value?"

6. Explain the meaning of the term "insurable interest."

7. Under the Comprehensive Personal Liability policy coverage is provided regardless of whether or not the insured is actually liable in some cases but not in others. Explain.

8. Compare the coverage offered by standard, broad, and comprehensive homeowners policies.

9. List the six types of automobile insurance coverage and indicate to whom or what each applies.

10. Compare the coverage provided by comprehensive physical damage insurance and collision insurance.

Problems

1. Mr. Walsh has recently decided to take out fire insurance coverage on his home. He has paid his premium and believes that he is now protected against fire loss regardless of anything he may do because the company offered a contract and he paid his premium as consideration for the contract. Is he right?

2. John Anders owns a $40,000 home. He has purchased fire insurance policies from five companies as follows:

    Company A $ 4,000
    Company B   6,000
    Company C   7,200
    Company D   8,800
    Company E   14,000

    A fire partially destroys Mr. Anders' home. The total loss is $30,000. Company B above had gone out of business prior to the fire. How much coverage will the other companies provide?

3. Mrs. Flanders owns a home valued at $30,000. She purchases a standard fire insurance policy providing $20,400 coverage and containing an 80% coinsurance clause. What would happen if a fire caused the following losses:
    a. $30,000
    b. $ 3,000
    c. $24,000
    d. $20,400

4. Rex Dresser owns a home valued at $35,000. Which of the following would be covered by both a standard fire insurance policy and by a broad coverage homeowner policy, only by the homeowners policy, and by neither.
    a. Loss resulting from a fire started by lightning.
    b. Loss resulting from steam produced by hot water leaking from a dishwashing machine.
    c. Loss resulting from the explosion of fireworks when the use of the building was changed without the company's knowledge.
    d. Broken windows resulting from malicious mischief.

5. What might be the difference in the automobile insurance coverage you would suggest for the person owning a new $4,000 car compared to that you would suggest for the person owning an old, second-hand $500 car?

Selected Readings

Brainard, Calvin H., *Automobile Insurance,* Richard D. Irwin, Inc., Homewood, Illinois, 1961

Crane, Frederick G., "Automobile Insurance Rate Regulation," *Bureau of Business Research Monograph Number 105,* Bureau of Business Research, College of Commerce and Administration, The Ohio State University, Columbus, Ohio, 1962

Greene, Mark R., *Risk & Insurance,* South-Western Publishing Co., Cincinnati 27, Ohio, 1962

Magee, John H., *Property Insurance,* Richard D. Irwin, Inc., Homewood, Illinois, 1955

Mayerson, Allen L., *Introduction to Insurance,* The Macmillan Co., New York, N.Y., 1962

Mehr, Robert I. and Hedges, Bob A., *Risk Management in the Business Enterprise,* Richard D. Irwin, Inc., Homewood, Illinois, 1963

Publications of the Insurance Information Institute

Rodda, William H., *Inland Marine and Transportation Insurance,* Prentice-Hall, Inc., Englewood Cliffs, New Jersey, Second Edition, 1958

Schultz, Robert E. and Bardwell, Edward C., *Property Insurance,* Holt, Rinehart & Winston, Inc., New York, N.Y., 1959

Chapter **12**

INCOME TAXES

One score and nineteen years ago, our fathers brought forth upon this nation a new tax, conceived in desperation and dedicated to the proposition that all men are fair game. Now we are engaged in a great mass of calculations, testing whether that taxpayer or any taxpayer so confused and so impoverished can long endure. . . . We have come to dedicate a large portion of our income to a final resting place with those who here spend their lives that they may spend our money. It is altogether anguish and torture that we should do this. But in a legal sense we cannot evade, we cannot cheat, we cannot underestimate this tax. . . .

Our creditors will little note or long remember what we pay here, but the Bureau of Internal Revenue can never forget what we report here. It is for us, the taxpayers, rather to be devoted here to the tax return which the Government has thus far so nobly spent. It is rather for us to be dedicated to the great task remaining before us—that from these vanishing dollars we take increasing devotion to the few remaining . . . and that taxation of the people, by Congress, for the Government shall not cause the solvency to perish.[1]

The first sentence of this quotation needs updating. It has been more than two score years since the Sixteenth Amendment was ratified by the States in 1913. Actually, the first federal income tax law in the United States was enacted in 1861 to help pay for the Civil War.

It is difficult to believe that there was opposition to the Revenue Act of 1913, which established a normal tax of 1 per cent on personal incomes over $3,000 and a surtax of up to 6 per cent on incomes over $500,000. This is one aspect of the "good old days" most of us would enjoy today. In 1963, the normal rate on 1962 income was 20 per cent, and the combined normal and surtax rates (a maximum of 7 per cent in 1913) reached a maximum of 91 per cent on taxable individual incomes over $200,000—as much as 87 per cent of an individual's total taxable income. This is quite a change in a fifty year period. Table 12–1 indicates the tax "bite" in 1963.

The power to tax is the power to govern and regulate, to build or destroy. The American people have become increasingly aware of the role taxes play in determining whether the economy will face prosperity or recession, inflation or deflation, etc. These issues are argued regularly by our political parties. In addition, industry does everything possible to publicize its problems when taxes become extremely high, or when a proposed tax change seems onerous.

Generally, however, the people of the United States have accepted the federal income tax with mild protest. While there still is, and should be, a continuing and philosophical argument as to whether the current income tax is fair, equitable, etc., there is nearly universal agreement that it costs money to run a government; and that as these costs increase, income taxes will be increased to meet them. For example, income taxes collected over a period of eleven years during the Civil War era totalled 347 million dollars; while in the year 1962

[1] "New Gettysburg Address for the Embattled Taxpayer," *Chemical and Engineering News*, Washington, D.C., February, 1952, p. 848. Reprinted by permission.

Table 12–1
Tax Rate Schedule*[2]

If the taxable
income is:

Not over $2,000......................20% of the taxable income

Over	But not over				of excess over
$ 2,000 –	$ 4,000	. . .	.$	400, plus 22% –	$ 2,000
4,000 –	6,000	. . .		840, plus 26% –	4,000
6,000 –	8,000	. . .		1,360, plus 30% –	6,000
8,000 –	10,000	. . .		1,960, plus 34% –	8,000
10,000 –	12,000	. . .		2,640, plus 38% –	10,000
12,000 –	14,000	. . .		3,400, plus 43% –	12,000
14,000 –	16,000	. . .		4,260, plus 47% –	14,000
16,000 –	18,000	. . .		5,200, plus 50% –	16,000
18,000 –	20,000	. . .		6,200, plus 53% –	18,000
20,000 –	22,000	. . .		7,260, plus 56% –	20,000
22,000 –	26,000	. . .		8,380, plus 59% –	22,000
26,000 –	32,000	. . .		10,740, plus 62% –	26,000
32,000 –	38,000	. . .		14,460, plus 65% –	32,000
38,000 –	44,000	. . .		18,360, plus 69% –	38,000
44,000 –	50,000	. . .		22,500, plus 72% –	44,000
50,000 –	60,000	. . .		26,820, plus 75% –	50,000
60,000 –	70,000	. . .		34,320, plus 78% –	60,000
70,000 –	80,000	. . .		42,120, plus 81% –	70,000
80,000 –	90,000	. . .		50,220, plus 84% –	80,000
90,000 –	100,000	. . .		58,620, plus 87% –	90,000
100,000 –	150,000	. . .		67,320, plus 89% –	100,000
150,000 –	200,000	. . .		111,820, plus 90% –	150,000
200,000 –		. . .		156,820, plus 91% –	200,000

* For single taxpayers or married persons filing separate returns.

alone, the American people paid some 99.4 billion dollars to meet the increased costs of government.[3]

Fortunately, the income tax is relatively inexpensive to collect. In 1962, for example, the cost was approximately ½¢ for each dollar collected. American taxpayers have established a record, unequalled anywhere in the world, for paying taxes through self-assessment on tax returns, and through withholding; and the impressive total of 97% of the 1962 receipts was paid in this manner.

[2] Federal Income Tax Forms for 1962, p. 9.
[3] Mortimer M. Caplin, Commissioner of Internal Revenue, *A Personal Letter to Taxpayers:* Federal Income Tax Forms for 1962, U.S., Government Printing Office, p. 1.

PENALTIES

The success of the federal income tax might be attributed, in part, to the government's watchfulness, and insistence that it be paid. If you are late in filing your income tax return and have not been granted an extension, or do not have a reasonable excuse, you are subject to a civil penalty of 5 per cent of the net amount of the tax due, for each month (or fraction thereof) that you are late, up to a maximum of 25%. In addition to this, if you neglect to pay the tax entirely, or intentionally disregard the rules and regulations, without intent to defraud, you are guilty of a misdemeanor under the criminal provisions of the law, and subject to a maximum fine of $10,000.00, one year in prison, or both. Further, if you fail to file, with intent to defraud, you are subject to a civil penalty of 50% of the net amount of the tax due, and a criminal code penalty, for felony, of a maximum fine of $10,000.00, five years in prison, or both.

A person who wilfully makes out a tax form to help someone else evade the income tax, may be liable to a $5,000 fine, three years in prison, or both. It is also possible that the taxpayer and the person making out the return for him might both be charged with fraud, and both be penalized.

These penalties indicate the seriousness of any attempt to evade the tax. Actually, our government is cooperative, and willing to excuse the late filing of a return if there is a reasonable excuse, such as illness or misfortune, and if the taxpayer obtains permission for an extension of time from the District Director's office; but it will not tolerate deliberate attempts to evade the just payment of the tax.

WHO MUST FILE

Under the Internal Revenue Code of 1954, every resident of the United States must file an income tax return if his income is $600 or more ($1,200 or more if 65 years of age or over). This includes resident aliens as well as citizens, children as well as adults, and married people as well as single. The only limitation is that the person must be a resident. In general, an alien is considered a resident if he has no definite plan to return to another country, or if the purpose of his visit requires an extended stay in this country. Usually, an alien whose stay is limited by our immigration laws to a definite and temporary period of time, is not considered a resident. Citizens of the United States, with certain exceptions, must pay a tax on their income even if they are living in another country. There are, however, a few exemptions from this rule which should be investigated by the small group living abroad.

These minimums of $600 if under 65 and $1,200 if the person reaches 65 before the end of the taxable year, are so low that, in effect, almost everyone receiving an income must file a return. $600 a year is less than $12 per week. As prices and wages rise, it becomes more difficult to imagine any steady income totalling less than $600 per year. If a person does earn less than this, and an amount is withheld from his salary or wages for the payment of income tax, he must file a return to recover the amount withheld.

CHOICE OF FORMS

The government provides three different tax forms. A taxpayer must select the form which meets his own particular needs. They are:

1. *Form 1040*—Long form, which may be used regardless of the amount of income.
2. *Form 1040*—Short form, which may be used only if adjusted gross income is less than $5,000. The tax due is taken from a tax table, which provides for a standard 10% deduction to determine adjusted gross income.
3. *Form 1040A*, which may be used only if gross income is less than $10,000 and derived entirely from salaries or wages, dividends, and interest, not more than $200 of which may be from sources not subject to withholding tax.

Form 1040A is the most convenient form to use. It is a card form, and a taxpayer may either determine the tax from the tax table, or provide the other information requested and permit the Bureau of Internal Revenue to calculate his tax and send him a bill or a refund. However, the number of persons who are qualified to use it is diminishing each year, and the obvious advantage of itemizing deductions when they total more than the 10% permitted by 1040A or the 1040 short form, is bringing the long form 1040 more widely into use. This is a more complicated form, and presents more problems to the taxpayer, but its use is justified by the savings it effects.

CALCULATIONS

Attempting to explain the intricacies of the federal income tax is a major problem. The tax law is very complicated, and a great deal of study is necessary before a person qualifies as an expert. However, the government does a remarkably fine job of explaining the tax to the average person. It has prepared a well written, relatively simple explanation, and sends a copy free to anyone requesting it.

No single chapter explanation can possibly contain enough information to compete with entire books and courses on the subject. Also, due to the tax law changes which occur from year to year, no chapter can be as up-to-date as the explanation provided annually by the federal government. If there are drastic tax reforms, this problem becomes even greater.

The goal of this chapter, then, is to provide an explanation as to why certain regulations exist, rather than attempt to explain the details of their operation, and to suggest possible tax saving methods of reporting your income tax.

This approach also seems to have the merit of longevity. While basic changes may occur in tax rates during the next few years, it seems less likely that many changes will occur in the purposes of the regulations.

Generally, a taxpayer is required to proceed through a series of steps leading to taxable income:

Income	This includes all income in the broad sense of all receipts by the taxpayer.
Less: Exclusions	These are items included in the term income, above, which are not considered to be income for tax purposes.
Result: Gross Income	
Less: Deductions	These deductions are called deductions *for* adjusted gross income and generally include business expenses.
Result: Adjusted Gross Income	
Less: Deductions	Deductions in this class are called deductions *from* adjusted gross income and generally include certain personal expenses of the taxpayer.
Less: Exemptions	The taxpayer may here deduct $600 for himself, his wife and each of his dependents.
Result: Taxable Income	This is the figure to which the tax rates are applied and a tax computed.[4]

[4] Grant C. Shafer, *Elements of Federal Taxation,* Charles E. Merrill Books, Inc., Columbus, Ohio, 1961, pp. 5–6.

Let's follow these steps through to taxable income. While particular regulations and forms may change, these basic steps seem to be quite permanent.

Income

What type of income is taxable? If all income was taxable, tax forms would be quite simple. Actually, the law says that all income is taxable unless expressly exempted. While this may sound definite, the very fact that some types of income are expressly exempted complicates things.

Table 12-2 lists many types of taxable income. Some of these, such as income from extortion, involve very few taxpayers. Others, such as income from fellowships, interest on government bonds, etc., are sometimes incorrectly believed to be non-taxable.

Table 12-3 lists many types of income which are exempt from the income tax. If these are carefully examined, it will be seen that they represent either an exemption specifically granted by the government (such as interest on state and municipal obligations), a return of cost (such as annuity payments), or an income that has already been subjected to another tax (such as inheritances).

Neither of these lists is meant to be complete or definitive. Life insurance proceeds and sick pay, for example, are, under certain circumstances, partially taxable. Alimony, under certain conditions, may be exempt. However, the lists are complete enough to indicate the difference between the types of income which are taxable and those considered exempt.

Subtracting tax exempt income from total income gives gross income. This amount will appear on the federal tax form. Certain deductions from this amount are permitted by the government.

Deductions for Adjusted Gross Income

The first deductions permitted are called deductions *for* adjusted gross income. They are to determine what part of the gross income is subject to tax. The "for" indicates that they are used to find taxable gross income.

These deductions are, for the most part, business expenses. They also include expenses of an outside salesman, travel expenses, deductions which may be attributed to rents and royalties, the deduction of 50% of the excess of net long term capital gains over net short term capital losses, etc.

Table 12-2
TAXABLE INCOME

Alimony
Annuities—to the extent not a part of cost
Awards and prizes
Bonuses
Business income
Cancellation of a debt for consideration—e.g. work
Children's compensation
Compensation in form of property—not cash
Contest winnings
Estate and trust income
Illegal operations—income from swindling, extortion, etc.
Interest on corporate bonds, bank deposits, notes, etc.
Interest on obligations of the U.S. issued on or after
      March 1, 1941.
Jury duty fees
Military pay
Pensions, etc., to retired employees
Profit, if employee purchases property at less than fair market
      value—e.g. employee stock options
Receipt of accrued interest
Rents and royalties
Rewards
Scholarships and fellowships, if services are required of student
Tips

The calculation of adjusted gross income is important. It determines the maximum dollar amount of the deductions that may be taken for medical expenses, charitable contributions, and other allowable items which are figured on a percentage basis.

Deductions from Adjusted Gross Income

Once adjusted gross income is calculated, certain deductions *from* it are permitted. These include personal expenses such as medical expenses, charitable contributions, taxes, interest, etc. If a person does not wish to itemize these deductions, he is permitted to take a standard deduction of 10% of adjusted gross income. If the adjusted gross income figure is less than $5,000, the tax table may be used. The standard 10% deduction was taken when the tax figures in the table were calculated. If the adjusted gross income is over $5,000, the standard deduction for a married taxpayer filing separately is $500;

Table 12-3
EXEMPT INCOME

Accident and health insurance proceeds

Annuity payments—to the extent they are a return of cost

Board and lodging, if furnished to suit convenience of employer
    and accepted as a condition of employment

Casualty insurance proceeds

Dividends on a mutual life insurance policy

Gifts

Inheritances

Interest on obligations of U.S. possessions

Interest on state and municipal obligations

Life insurance proceeds paid due to death of insured

Mustering out pay

Payments to veterans

Payments for support of minor children

Personal or family rights damages—e.g. slander and libel

Proceeds of G.I. bills for education

Property damages

Railroad Retirement Act pensions

Scholarship and fellowship grants (unless teaching, research,
    etc., is required)

Sick pay

Social Security benefits

Unemployment insurance benefits

Workmen's compensation benefits

for all others, the standard deduction is 10% of the adjusted gross income or $1,000, whichever is smaller.

There are both advantages and disadvantages to using a standard deduction. Obviously, a standard deduction is easier to calculate than itemized deductions; but itemized deductions may add up to more than the standard, and result in less tax. For most people, it is wise to try both ways and find out which will result in the lowest tax.

Exemptions are established by legislative enactments, and may be changed by the legislature at any time. Suggestions favoring reductions in tax rates are generally accompanied by suggestions favoring the disallowance or modification of one or more of the allowable deductions.

Deductions *for* and *from* adjusted gross income are the most complicated part of the tax calculation. People with complicated problems should by all means hire an expert. It is up to the taxpayer to prove the legitimacy of his deductions—not up to the government to prove they are illegitimate; and if he can't prove it, the deduction will not be permitted.

Exemptions

Exemptions, in general, are quite easy to determine. The law allows an exemption of $600 for the taxpayer, and an additional $600 for each dependent. Taxpayers who are over 65, or blind, may deduct another $600. Thus a taxpayer who is over 65 and blind can deduct $1,800 as a personal exemption. These rules also apply to the taxpayer's spouse.

The most difficult problem in the exemption area concerns dependents. Who is a dependent? The tax law defines a dependent as one who does not file a joint return with a spouse, and meets certain requirements as to relationship, support and gross income. The extra exemptions for age and blindness do not apply to dependents.

Taxable Income

The resulting figure—after all deductions and exemptions—is taxable income. For most people, the largest source of income is from wages and salaries. The government makes payment easier by requiring employers to withhold taxes from wages, as the wages are paid. There has been considerable disagreement as to whether or not withholding is a good idea. Certainly, from the viewpoint of the employer, extra record-keeping is required, which results in extra costs. However, from the viewpoint of the taxpayer, withholding eases the pain considerably. Imagine paying the total tax on your income in one lump. If your taxable income was $8,000, could you pay $1,680 in one lump—the amount that would be owed by a married taxpayer filing a joint return in 1963? For that matter, if your taxable income was only $4,000, the amount due would have been $820; still enough to create a problem for most of us.

Many people even use the withholding tax as a form of forced saving, by requesting that more tax be withheld than is required. The overpayment is, of course, refunded when the annual tax return is submitted.

Taxpayers with income of over $200 from which a tax is not withheld, are required to file an estimated tax return and make tax payments quarterly. While there is no civil penalty for failing to file an estimate, there is a penalty of 6% per year on any underpayment.

Mr. Cushman Phillips says that he made a few hundred dollars more this year than last. He is complaining loudly to everyone that this put him in a higher tax bracket, which meant that his income after taxes was less this year. Next year, he is going to make certain that his income before taxes is less, so that he will have more left over after taxes.

Stories like this seem quite common. Usually they aren't true. The federal income tax is a "progressive" tax. The higher the income, the higher the percentage tax on the *additional* income. Table 12-1 is a copy of the tax rate schedule for single taxpayers and married persons filing separate returns. This table was presented in the booklet sent by the government to each taxpayer with tax forms 1040 and 1040A in 1963, and reflects the tax rates on 1962 income. It can be used as an example, even if the rates change, because the federal income tax will probably remain a "progressive" tax, regardless of any changes that may take place in rates.

The tax rate on the first $2,000 of taxable income was 20%; on the next $2,000, 22%. Accordingly, the tax on taxable income of $4,000 would be:

$$20\% \text{ of first } \$2,000 = \$400$$
$$22\% \text{ of next } \$2,000 = 440$$

Total Income and Tax $4,000 $840

Now let's say Mr. Phillips' taxable income was $4,000 last year, and is $6,000 this year. According to the table, Mr. Phillips' tax this year will still be 20% of the first $2,000 and 22% of the next $2,000, or $840, the amount he paid last year. The only change in his status is that he will pay an *additional* tax of 26% of the *additional* $2,000 taxable income he earned this year. This obviously does not reduce his total income after taxes to a lower total than he enjoyed last year.

EVASION AND AVOIDANCE

One obvious way to keep the income tax that a person must pay to a minimum is to calculate a low taxable income. There are two ways of doing this: by evasion, which is illegal, and by avoidance, which is legal.

Evasion means not reporting income which is taxable. In some groups, such as farmers, professional men, and independent businessmen, this act is difficult to trace. Some personal expenses may be hidden as business expenses, and cash receipts might not be reported. These techniques are, of course, illegal, and the taxpayer is flirting with the penalties of the law—a heavy fine, imprisonment, or both.

Tax avoidance, however, is another matter. The courts have established the right of every taxpayer to take advantage of every method of tax reduction permitted by law. They not only have held that such efforts are legal, but that they are neither immoral nor unpatriotic.

The possibility of tax avoidance exists with respect to all taxes, not just the federal income tax. It requires a knowledge of the tax laws, careful planning, and good management. Tax avoidance does not mean that you are not paying a tax liability; it means that the tax liability hasn't been permitted to arise in the first place.

TAX PLANNING

Tax planning requires a clear understanding of the tax laws. This enables a person to recognize the most favorable alternatives permitted by law, and the loopholes that exist. There are many techniques that may be used as part of a tax plan. Only a few, relating to the federal income tax, will be mentioned as examples. They are: sheltered income; deferred income; capital gains; tax exempt income; and charitable contributions.

Sheltered Income

Fred is an executive and works very hard at his job. The company forces him to accept certain things as a condition of employment: country club membership, group life insurance, meals and lodging, and a chauffeur driven limousine. He is also encouraged to use the company swimming pool, and is granted an option to buy 15,000 shares of the company's stock at less than market value.

All of these are, in a sense, part of Fred's income, and yet none of them are taxable. The company is extremely careful to make certain that the tax regulations are fully complied with. Take the limousine, for example. It is used strictly for business. Of course, the chauffeur picks Fred up every morning and takes him home every afternoon. This is an arrangement everyone would like, and if it is carefully controlled so that it meets tax regulations, the service is not considered income.

Many people react quite strongly to situations such as this. "Why should Fred get these things when I don't?" is a comment often heard. However, if our government decided to tax all fringe benefits as income, everyone would object. While it is true that very few are given the use of a chauffeur-driven limousine, most of us are given the benefits of group life insurance, company recreational facilities, etc. Many companies provide their employees with additional income by subsidizing a company cafeteria so that excellent meals can be obtained at extremely low cost. Should these fringe benefits be counted as income and taxed? Where should such a rule start, and where should it stop?

Fringe benefits are the most usual form of sheltered income. As it is difficult for industry today to find and keep competent executives, these benefits usually increase as a person advances in rank. The fact that they add tax free income to salaried income should be appreciated. This is especially true when a person in a middle or upper tax bracket has prospects of a promotion. A tax free fringe benefit might be preferable to an increase in income which is taxable at a high rate.

Deferred Income

In 1958, a leading television comedienne signed a contract with one of the networks. The network agreed to pay her a large sum of money over a period of twenty years, and she, in turn, agreed to appear in a certain number of spectaculars per year, for a period of five years.

Under this type of contract, the compensation period is much longer than the work period. The reason is that if the total sum was paid during a five year period, the tax would be much higher. Spread out over twenty years, the annual income is smaller and the tax is lower.

Another form of deferred income is that provided by company pension plans. If a plan meets the requirements of the tax laws, the employer may consider his payments a business expense, and employees don't have to recognize them as income until money is actually distributed to them. Employees usually do not receive a pension until they retire; and retirement usually reduces their income. This means that the tax on the money will be less than if the money had been taxed as additional income when it was originally put into the fund.

Capital Gains

A gain or loss from the sale or exchange of a capital asset is a "capital gain" or a "capital loss." A capital gain from the sale or exchange of a capital asset owned by the taxpayer for more than six months is called a "long-term capital gain." If the period of ownership does not exceed six months, the gain is "short-term capital gain." The same holding period is used to distinguish between "short-term" and "long-term" capital losses.[5]

The most common types of "capital assets" held by taxpayers are homes and securities. The distinction between long and short term gains and losses is important in both cases. In 1963, the highest tax rate on a long-term capital gain was 25 per cent. Actually, the calculation was a little more roundabout than this. The rule was:

1. First, find the long term gain.
2. Divide it by two.
3. Include half in gross income.
4. Limit the tax on this half to 50 per cent.

The highest possible tax on a long-term capital gain under these rules was 25 per cent (50 per cent of one-half of the gain). The actual tax for most taxpayers, all who were not yet in the 50 per cent bracket, would not only be less than 25 per cent, but would be less than the tax on their other income. For example, if a person was in an income bracket in which additional income would be taxed at 30 per cent, the capital gain would be taxed at only 15 per cent, because only half of the gain would be taxed.

Short-term capital gains, on the other hand, are taxed at the same rate as ordinary income. It is best, if possible, to time the sale of a capital asset so the profit will be considered a long-term, rather than a short-term, gain. This is more important as a person's total income increases. A person in a 91 per cent bracket would have to pay this rate on a short-term gain, but only 25 per cent on a long-term gain.

Both long-term and short-term losses may be deducted from ordinary income. The amount that may be deducted, however, is limited to $1,000. Chart 12-1 shows the various combinations of long-term and short-term gains and losses which might exist, and the treatment of each. Now these rules may change. In fact, one of the most frequently discussed changes in tax laws concerns the special treatment given to long-term capital gains. Like most issues, the situation

---

[5] William E. Dickerson and Leo D. Stone, *Federal Income Tax Fundamentals*, Wadsworth Publishing Company, Inc., San Francisco, 1961, p. 7–3.

Chart 12-1

WHICH OF THESE APPLIES
TO YOU?

It is possible for you to have any one of eight combinations of net gains and net losses. Locate the one that applies to you in the left column of the following table. The right column gives you the tax treatment for each, which is discussed in detail immediately after the table.

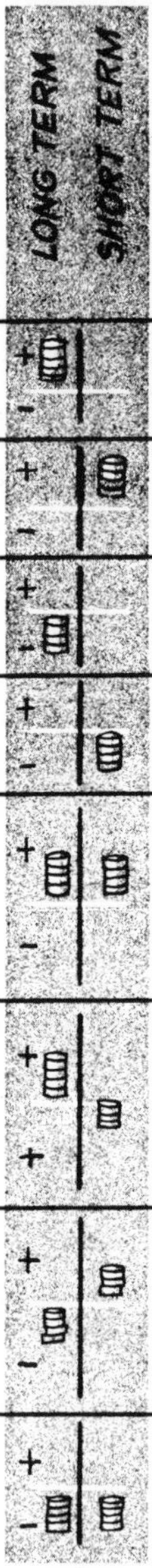

	If You Have This Combination of Net Capital Gains and Losses	This Tax Treatment Applies
+⊟ − (LONG TERM)	Net Long-Term Gains Only	Long-Term Capital Gain
+ ⊟ − (SHORT TERM)	Net Short-Term Gains Only	Short-Term Capital Gain
+ −⊟	Net Long-Term Losses Only	Capital Loss
+ −⊟	Net Short-Term Losses Only	Capital Loss
+⊟ ⊟ −	Net Long-Term Gain and Net Short-Term Gain	Long-Term Capital Gain for Net Long-Term Gain; Short-Term Capital Gain for the Net Short-Term Capital Gain
+⊟ ⊟ +	Net Long-Term Gain and Net Short-Term Loss	Long-Term Capital Gain for the Difference (if gain exceeds loss) Capital Loss for Difference (if loss exceeds gain)
+ ⊟ ⊟ −	Net Short-Term Gain and Net Long-Term Loss	Short-Term Capital Gain for the Difference (if gain exceeds loss) Capital Loss for Difference (if loss exceeds gain)
+ −⊟ ⊟	Net Long-Term Loss and Net Short-Term Loss	Capital Loss for the Total

Source: "Tax Saving Strategy for Investors," J. K. Lasser Tax Institute, New York, N. Y., MCMLVII, p. 4.

is not clear cut. There are arguments for removing the tax advantage, and other arguments for keeping or strengthening it. There is a good chance, however, that differential treatment will remain. It is wise to carefully consider the distinction in the treatment of long-term and short-term gains. Even under possible changes in tax laws, it is probable that such consideration will be profitable to the taxpayer.

Tax Exempt Income

Of the many types of tax exempt income, the type which can be used directly in tax planning is the income from state and municipal obligations. Taxpayers, especially those in high income brackets, gain a great advantage by investing in such securities. Even a person in the 50 per cent bracket would have to have an additional taxable income of $60 to equal, after taxes, a $30 return on a $1,000 municipal bond. In the 91 per cent bracket, his taxable income would have to be increased $333 to have $30 remaining after taxes.

As a person's income rises and, consequently, he enters higher tax brackets, investing money in municipal and state securities becomes more attractive. In most states, no state income tax is levied on income from investments in obligations of the state. This means that neither a federal nor a state income tax would have to be paid on this income. Certainly, this is quite an attraction to a person in even a moderately high bracket, and should be carefully considered.[6]

At election time, closing up this so-called tax loophole is usually mentioned. Yet it seems to be one of the most secure of the tax saving methods available to the tax planner. According to most tax authorities, the income from state and municipal obligations cannot be taxed, for constitutional reasons. Thus it will probably take more than mere legislation to remove the exemption. Table 12-4 indicates the importance of selecting tax exempt income.

Charitable Contributions

Deductions for contributions are taken by almost everyone. These include gifts to religious, charitable, educational, scientific, and other organizations, which are not operated for a personal profit and meet certain other requirements. And charitable contributions have certain other features which are not as commonly realized.

---

[6] Municipal bonds are discussed in Chapter 14.

Table 12-4
TABLES[7]

¶ 12,895

¶ 12,895.1 *How much is $1 of Additional Income Worth*

To get after tax value from

Tax free income — includes municipal bonds, life insurance return, special income earned abroad, etc.

Ordinary income — includes fully taxable bonds, wages and salary, net rental income, etc.

Capital gains — includes sales and exchange of capital items, dividends on stock where company has no earnings and profits, sales of depreciable business property, etc.

Dividends — includes ordinary dividends from domestic corporations to an individual. Remember there is also an exclusion of the first $50 of dividends.

Taxable Income Married, joint return	Single Person	Tax Free Income	Income Ordinary	Capital Gain	Dividend Income	Net of Capital Gain over Ordinary Income	Net of Capital Gain over Dividend Income
—	—	$1.00	$ .80	$.90	$.84	13%	7%
$ 4,000	$ 2,000	1.00	.78	.89	.82	14	9
8,000	4,000	1.00	.74	.87	.78	18	12
12,000	6,000	1.00	.70	.85	.74	21	15
16,000	8,000	1.00	.66	.83	.70	26	19
20,000	10,000	1.00	.62	.81	.66	31	23
24,000	12,000	1.00	.57	.785	.61	38	29
28,000	14,000	1.00	.53	.765	.57	44	34
32,000	16,000	1.00	.50	.75	.54	50	39
36,000	18,000	1.00	.47	.75	.51	60	47
40,000	20,000	1.00	.44	.75	.48	70	56
44,000	22,000	1.00	.41	.75	.45	83	67
52,000	26,000	1.00	.38	.75	.42	97	79
64,000	32,000	1.00	.35	.75	.39	114	92
76,000	38,000	1.00	.31	.75	.35	142	114
88,000	44,000	1.00	.28	.75	.32	168	134
100,000	50,000	1.00	.25	.75	.29	200	159
120,000	60,000	1.00	.22	.75	.26	241	188
140,000	70,000	1.00	.19	.75	.23	295	226
160,000	80,000	1.00	.16	.75	.20	369	275
180,000	90,000	1.00	.13	.75	.17	477	341
200,000	100,000	1.00	.11	.75	.15	582	400
300,000	150,000	1.00	.10	.75	.14	650	436
400,000	200,000	1.00	.09	.75	.13	733	477
1,259,000	629,500	1.00	.13	.75	.17	477	341

[7]Reprinted from William J. Casey, "Life Insurance Plans," by permission of the publisher, Institute for Business Planning, Inc., p. 12,824.6, New York, N.Y., 1962.

For example, Joe has a charity which he wants to help financially. He would like to make a large contribution, $120,000, but realizes that the law limits the amount which he may deduct to 20% (in some cases 30%) of his adjusted gross income. Is there some way he can make this large sum available to the charity and deduct the entire amount?

It is possible for him to lend the money to the charity, and cancel part of the loan each year as he determines how much he can deduct. He must have evidence of the loan, such as a note, but if it is done properly, he may give the charity the money it needs now, and not lose the opportunity to take the entire $120,000 contribution as a deduction. Of course, for most of us, such a generous contribution would not be entirely deductible due to the limit of 20% or 30% of a person's adjusted gross income. To deduct $120,000, a person would need an adjusted gross income of at least $400,000—a rather sizable amount.

If a person owns appreciated property, such as stocks that have gone up, it would be better to donate the property than to sell it and donate cash. If you sell it, there will be a tax on the capital gain. This will mean a smaller donation. If you donate the property, the entire market value can be deducted (up to the 20 or 30 percent limit) as a charitable contribution.

For extremely wealthy persons, the donation of appreciated property has offered even greater advantages. A great deal of publicity was given to this situation in the spring of 1963. According to the law, if an individual's total contributions plus income taxes paid in the current year and in eight out of ten of the preceding years, had exceeded 90% of his adjusted gross income, he could then deduct his entire contribution. According to the Treasury, certain multi-millionaires had annual incomes of several million dollars, and yet paid no income tax due to this feature of the tax law. They had donated securities which had appreciated greatly in value, then had deducted the entire market value of the securities from their adjusted gross income. The result was little or no tax liability.

The probability seems good that this section of the law will be revised in the near future, although its merits are debatable. Some say the unlimited deduction privilege has very little significance in encouraging contributions; others hold that it has great significance.

Both the tax laws affecting contributions and the nature of the contributions themselves, have changed over the years. Chart 12-2 on page 328 indicates some of the changes that took place between 1929 and 1960.

Chart 12-2

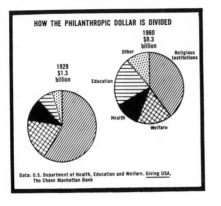

Organized philanthropy now runs to more than $10 billion a year. Individuals' contributions constitute four-fifths of this as they did in 1929. As a proportion of people's after-tax income, however, donations have increased from 1¼% to 2¼%. In addition, person-to-person gifts, some of which are philanthropic in nature, may amount to as much as organized giving.

Families on the lower end of the income scale provide the bulk of the donations. Of those who itemize their income tax, 60% of all giving was done by people with incomes under $10,000, and those with less than $5,000 gave the highest percentage of their incomes.

	contributions as a % of income	proportion of families itemizing
Under $5,000	4.6%	24%
$5,000-10,000	3.4%	58%
Over $10,000	3.8%	73%

The remaining contributions consisted of:
• Bequests which amount to 4½% of all philanthropy compared with 12% in 1929.
• Foundation grants which have risen from 5% to 7½% of the total.
• And corporate giving, the fastest growing, which supplies over 5% of all organized philanthropy compared with 2½% in 1929.

A forthcoming study by the National Bureau of Economic Research, preliminary results of which were published in **Philanthropy and Public Policy,** includes some government social welfare expenditures in the definition of philanthropy. According to this definition, American society now more than tithes: public and private philanthropy amounts to about 14% of GNP, up from 6% in 1929.

Source: "The Changing Role of Philanthropy," *Business in Brief,* The Chase Manhattan Bank, New York, N. Y., January-February 1963, pp. 6-7.

CONCLUSION

This discussion of taxes has been limited to the federal personal income tax. Nothing has been said about state income taxes, property taxes, sales taxes, corporate income taxes, inheritance taxes, gift taxes, automobile excise taxes, etc. Many of these will be discussed in other chapters, in connection with specific areas. Inheritance and gift taxes, for example, will be discussed in the chapter on Estate Planning.

The federal income tax deserves special treatment. Very few individuals in the United States escape its consequences each year. While state income taxes, sales taxes, etc., vary from state to state, the federal income tax is the same for everyone.

Certainly, this chapter would never make anyone a tax expert. The income tax is an extremely complicated affair. Unfortunately, people occasionally try to avoid the tax and end up evading it. When they find that avoidance is impossible, they "evade," in an attempt to escape paying what they owe. Although there is no proof, the instinct to escape, or to reduce, payment of the federal income tax probably leads more people to commit illegal acts than any other single cause. This is certainly unfortunate, both for the country and for the individual.

Tax planning should be considered by everyone, but, unless the situation is quite simple, few individuals should attempt to undertake this venture on their own.

> For complete and effective tax planning, the average citizen should seek the technical and professional advice of certified public accountants, attorneys, and certified life underwriters or others qualified by training and experience. Hearsay tricks and 'do-it-yourself' kits have no place in this intricate and important undertaking.[8]

Questions

1. Compare the penalties for not paying your income tax with and without intention to defraud.

---

[8] C. Aubrey Smith and Jim G. Ashburne, *Financial and Administrative Accounting*, McGraw-Hill Book Co., N.Y., 1960, p. 478.

2. Who must file an income tax return?

3. Explain the usual reasons why certain types of income are exempted from the income tax.

4. What is the difference between tax exempt income, a deduction for adjusted gross income and a deduction from adjusted gross income.

5. Using the tax table on page 312 how much must taxable income be before the tax rate on each additional dollar of income is 50%?

6. Differentiate between evasion and avoidance.

7. What would be the tax on a long term capital gain of $5,000 if a person was
   a. In the 75% bracket?
   b. " " 50% bracket?
   c. " " 30% bracket?

8. Distinguish between a short and long term capital gain.

9. Should you sell property on which you have made a capital gain before or after contributing it to charity? Explain.

10. a. What is "tax planning?"
    b. Who should undertake "tax planning?"

Problems

1. Who of the following would have to file an income tax return?
   a. A person receiving $100 per month as Social Security benefits.
   b. A six year old television star who earns $50,000 per year.
   c. A person over 65 who earns $1,000 per year working part time as a sales clerk.
   d. An alien who has applied for citizenship and earns $5,000 per year.

2. Assuming a $55,000 taxable income, use the tax table on page 312 to calculate:
   The amount of the tax on each part of this income so that the sum of the parts will equal the total tax due on the $55,000.

3. Before election politicians often make statements such as:

"We should eliminate all means of avoiding the income tax by closing existing loopholes." Present some of the problems involved in closing the following "loopholes."

a. Sheltered income
b. Deferred income
c. Capital gains
d. Tax exempt income
e. Charitable contributions

4. Using the following examples indicate the amount that for tax purposes would be treated as a short term capital gain, a short term capital loss, a long term capital gain, and a long term capital loss.

a. A sale of securities held four months resulting in a capital gain of $3,000.
b. A sale of securities held four months resulting in a capital gain of $3,000, and the sale of securities held two years resulting in a capital loss of $4,000.
c. A sale of securities held four months resulting in a capital loss of $3,000, and the sale of securities held two years resulting in a capital gain of $4,000.
d. A sale of securities held four months resulting in a capital gain of $3,000, and the sale of securities held two years resulting in a capital gain of $4,000.

5. Using the table on page 326 how much would $500 of additional income be worth after taxes if you were married and filing a joint return:

a. If you had a taxable income of $12,000 and the $500 was in tax free income.
b. If you had a taxable income of $12,000 and the $500 was a long term capital gain.
c. If you had a taxable income of $12,000 and the $500 was dividend income.
d. All of the above, except that your taxable income was $40,000.

Selected Readings

Dickerson, William E., and Stone, Leo D., *Federal Income Tax Fundamentals*, Wadsworth Publishing Co., Inc., San Francisco, California, 1961

Niswonger, C. Rollin, and Bower, James B., *Income Tax Procedure*, South-
Western Publishing Co., Cincinnati, Ohio, published annually
Publications of the J. K. Lasser Tax Institute, New York, N.Y.
Schafer, Grant C., *Elements of Federal Taxation*, Charles E. Merrill Books,
Inc., Columbus, Ohio, 1961
Smith, C. Aubrey and Ashburne, Jim G., *Financial and Administrative
Accounting*, McGraw-Hill Publishing Co., New York, N.Y., 1960

Chapter **13**

SOCIAL SECURITY, PENSIONS AND ANNUITIES

In the United States, age 65 is generally considered to be the age of retirement. Some voluntarily retire at this age; others are required to do so. A man used to be old at 65, and considered to have little life expectancy. This is no longer true. Life expectancy in the United States has increased fairly consistently, and today, in this country, people reaching retirement age still have many healthy, active years ahead. Longevity is still increasing, and, in the future, people 65 years old may have even more years of good health and activity to look forward to.

The years after retirement can be quite enjoyable. This is the time of life when people have time to do many of the things they have always wanted to do. Only one thing is needed besides mental and physical health, and that is money. Where will it come from? Many sources are considered in other chapters — savings, mutual funds, investments in securities or real estate, etc. The sources considered in this chapter are pensions, including Social Security, and annuities.

SOCIAL SECURITY

The foundation of almost everyone's retirement income plan is Social Security. 90 per cent of today's working people are protected by the insurance portion of the Social Security Act, the Old Age, Survivors and Disability Insurance (OASDI). The name of this insurance indicates the three types of benefits that are available: old age, survivors and disability benefits.

Today's OASDI is quite different from the original act passed in 1935. Congress quite regularly changes the law. It has expanded the coverage, increased the dollar benefits, and generally liberalized the entire plan. This chapter is based on the OASDI as amended in 1962.

Is Social Security Insurance?

When the Social Security system first appeared on the American scene, some of those entitled to its benefits were reluctant to accept them. They believed them to be charity. This is not true. Of course, the problem is much less important today as Americans now expect and plan on their Social Security income, and accept it as a pension or insurance program.

Among the many risks every family faces is the risk of the loss of the wage earner's income, due to death, disability or retirement. The old age, survivors and disability insurance program is actually a type of income insurance, as it insures against this particular risk.

In any other program of public assistance, there is a "needs" test. To receive assistance, old-age assistance, aid for those permanently and totally disabled, etc., the applicant must prove the "need" before the assistance can be rendered. This is not true of the Social Security program. Everyone meeting certain basic requirements establishes a right to Social Security. The amount of the benefits is based upon each person's contributions to the program, paid in the form of Social Security taxes.

Social Security taxes are deducted from the first $4,800 of individual, earned income. Table 13–1 presents the schedule of tax rates for the years 1961 through 1968, according to a 1962 government release.

Table 13-1
SCHEDULE OF SOCIAL SECURITY
TAX RATES[1]

Calendar Year	Employee	Employer	Self Employed
1961	3%	3%	4.5%
1962	3⅛%	3⅛%	4.7%
1963–65	3⅝%	3⅝%	5.4%
1966–67	4⅛%	4⅛%	6.2%
1968 and after	4⅝%	4⅝%	6.9%

Notice that the tax rate rises until 1968. In 1968, unless the rates are changed, the amount deducted from the first $4,800 income will be about 28 per cent more than in 1963.

Who is Covered?

Most jobs are covered by the Social Security Act. The easiest way to define covered employment is to consider the employments which are excluded from coverage, or included only under special conditions.

The excluded occupations are:

1. Family employment except when the service is performed in a trade or business by a parent or a child twenty-one years of age or over.
2. Local newsboys under eighteen years of age.
3. Student nurses and interns.
4. Student workers in institutions of learning.
5. Students performing domestic services for college clubs, fraternities and sororities.

---

[1] "Your Social Security," U.S. Department of Health, Education, and Welfare, Social Security Administration, U.S. Government Printing Office, OASI–35a, January 1962, p. 17.

6. Long-service (over ten years) railroad workers.
7. Self-employed physicians.
8. Policemen and firemen covered under an existing retirement system (except in about sixteen states where the situation is similar to that explained below for state and local government employees).
9. Federal government civilian employees covered by a retirement system established by a law of the United States.
10. Some special classifications of federal and state civilian employees.[2]

The occupations included under special conditions are:

1. Self-employment, if the net earnings are $400 or more.
2. Agricultural labor, if the laborer earns $150 or more from any one employer in a calendar year, or if he works for one employer for twenty or more days for cash pay, figured on a time basis rather than a piece-rate basis.
3. Non-farm domestic workers and casual laborers, if they earn $50 or more from one employer per calendar quarter, for sufficient quarters of coverage.
4. Clergymen and members of religious orders, if they earned at least $400 a year, and if they expressed their election to be covered before April 15, 1962.
5. Employees of non-profit organizations, if their employers consent. All new employees are automatically covered, but current employees have a choice. Any employee who elects not to be covered cannot change his mind, unless he acts within twenty-four months after the end of the first month of the calendar quarter in which the coverage for the group becomes effective.
6. State and local government employees not already under a retirement system may be covered, if the state agrees. The employees under a retirement system may be covered, if the state consents and at least half the employees under each separate system agree. In several states, a retirement system can be divided into two parts (those who want coverage and those who do not) to obtain coverage for the members who want it. All new members of the system are automatically covered.[3]

All workers employed in covered employments have a Social Security account number. This is extremely important. The Social

---

[2] For example, the President of the United States.

[3] John G. Turnbull, C. Arthur Williams, Jr., Earl F. Cheit, *Economic and Social Security*, The Ronald Press Company, New York, Second Edition, 1962, pp. 86–87.

Security records contain more than 135 million individual accounts. Many people have identical names, and without account numbers it would be impossible to keep one account from being confused with another. Besides this, the government uses this number to identify taxpayers in its "computerized" income tax record system.

Every employer must report employees' wages for Social Security purposes. Those who are self-employed must report their own earnings each year. The self-employment report is part of a person's individual federal income tax return. This self-employment tax must be paid to the District Director of Internal Revenue, even if a person doesn't have to pay any federal income tax.

Everyone must pay Social Security taxes as long as they work under Social Security. This is true regardless of age, and even if the person is receiving Social Security benefits.

An employer must provide employees with receipts for Social Security taxes deducted from their pay. These must be provided annually, and when the employee leaves. The Social Security Administration provides addressed post card forms for persons wishing to request a statement of their account. This should be done at least every three years, so that any corrections can be made promptly.

CALCULATING BENEFITS

The discussion on the calculating of benefits will be based on Table 13-2. This table is quite complete, but some of the details need more explanation. What do "fully insured" and "currently insured" mean? Who is entitled to certain benefits? How are benefits calculated? Such questions deserve more detailed consideration.

Fully and Currently Insured

Notice that *all* of the benefits presented in the table are available to those classed as "fully insured," but only a few of the survivorship benefits are available to those classed as "currently insured."

Table 13-3 indicates the number of years a person must have worked under covered employment to be fully insured. A worker who retired in 1963 at age 65 (62 for women) would need credit for only three years of work to be considered fully insured. Eventually, by 1991, this is supposed to increase to ten years of work. Anyone under 37 in 1963 would need ten years of coverage at retirement, as he would become 65 in 1991, or later. The same would be true of any woman born later than 1929.

Table 13-2
Social Security — Monthly Benefits[4]

YOUR AVERAGE YEARLY EARNINGS AFTER 1950	MONTHLY SOCIAL SECURITY RETIREMENT AND DISABILITY BENEFITS				MONTHLY SOCIAL SECURITY DEATH BENEFITS FOR THE FAMILY					
	Your Retirement at Age 65 or Disability Benefit	Your Retirement Benefit—Age 62	Wife's Benefit at Age 62 (no child)	Wife's Benefit at Age 65 or With a Child	Widow at Age 62 or 1 Surviving Parent	Widow under 62 With 1 Child or 2 Surviving Children	1 Surviving Child	Widow under 62 With 2 Children	Lump Sum Death Payment	Maximum Family Monthly Benefit
$800 or less	$ 40	$ 32.00	$ 15.00	$ 20.00	$ 40.00	$ 60.00	$ 40.00	$ 60.00	$120	$ 60.00
$1,200	59	47.20	22.20	29.50	48.70	88.50	44.30	88.50	177	88.50
1,800	73	58.40	27.40	36.50	60.30	109.60	54.80	120.00	219	120.00
2,400	84	67.20	31.50	42.00	69.30	126.00	63.00	161.60	252	161.60
3,000	95	76.00	35.70	47.50	78.40	142.60	71.30	202.40	255	202.40
3,600	105	84.00	39.40	52.50	86.70	157.60	78.80	236.40	255	**202.40**
4,200	116	92.80	43.50	58.00	95.70	174.00	87.00	254.00	255	240.00
4,500	121	96.80	45.40	60.50	99.90	181.60	90.80	254.00	255	254.00
4,800	127	101.60	47.70	63.50	104.80	190.60	95.30	254.00	255	254.00

You must be fully insured to get these benefits

You receive these if you are fully OR currently insured

[4] *Your Social Security* (OASI 35) April 1962, p. 9, and *Social Security Benefits* (OAS 1855, leaflet 855), April 1962, U.S. Dept. of Health, Education, and Welfare, Social Security Administration, Washington, D.C.

Table 13-3

FULLY INSURED

Just how much credit you must have to be fully insured depends upon the year you reach 65 if you are a man, or 62 if you are a woman, or upon the date of your death or disability if you die or become disabled before reaching that age.

You are fully insured if you have credit for at least as many years as shown on the appropriate line of the following chart.

A worker who reaches 65 (62 for women) or dies	Will need credit for no more than this much work
In 1957 or earlier	1½ years
1958	1¾
1959	2
1960	2¼
1961	2½
1962	2¾
1963	3
1964	3¼
1965	3½
1966	3¾
1967	4
1968	4¼
1969	4½
1970	4¾
1971	5
1975	6
1979	7
1983	8
1987	9
1991 or later	10

Source: "Your Social Security," U.S. Department of Health, Education, and Welfare, Social Security Administration, U. S. Government Printing Office, OASI-35a, January 1962, p. 2.

This table is easy to read, but it applies only to those retiring due to age. What if you are a male and unable to continue working until you reach 65? If you die, or become disabled before that time (62 for women), you will be fully insured if you have credit for one quarter of a year of work for each year after 1950, up to the year of your death or disability. In counting these years, you omit the year you reached 21 and all previous years. The credit, however, can be earned at any time after 1936. An example might help to clarify this rule.

John will be sixty-five in April of 1970. In 1964, he has a serious accident, permanently disabling him. He earned more than $6,000 per year between January 1, 1956, and December 31, 1961, a period of six years, or 24 quarters. Now count the quarters between 1950 and January, 1964, the year in which he becomes disabled. This period covers fourteen years, or fifty-six quarters. One-fourth of 56 is 14. As John had been credited with more than 14 quarters (between January 1, 1956, and December 31, 1961), he will be fully insured.

Of course, John didn't have to earn $6,000 to be credited for his employment. For most people, a quarter of coverage means each quarter of a year in which they received total wages of $50 or more. Under any circumstances, no one can be fully insured with credit for less than 1½ years of work, and no one needs credit for more than 10 years.

To be currently insured requires much less coverage. A person is currently insured if, within the three years before he dies or retires, he has been credited for at least 1½ years of work.

The words "fully insured" and "currently insured" have nothing to do with the *amount* of benefits a person will receive. They only mean that a person has fulfilled certain requirements which may entitle him to receive benefits.

Old-age and Survivors Benefits

A person who has reached age 62 and is "fully insured," can retire and receive monthly Social Security payments. Certain members of the family also can receive benefits. The question is, should you retire at 62 or wait until you are 65? You will receive larger monthly amounts if you wait until you reach 65, but you will receive payments for a longer period of time if you start at 62.

Benefit payments to a wife and children are based on the benefit payable to the husband at 65, even if he decides to take reduced benefits before reaching 65. If the husband retires, a wife may decide to request benefits when she is between 62 and 65, but her benefits will be reduced if she starts receiving them before reaching 65.

To estimate the amount of benefits, follow these four steps:

1. Determine the number of years between 1955 and up to (not including) the year you reach 65 (62 if a woman). The minimum is 5, so if the answer is less than 5, increase it to 5.

2. Take the number of years found in step one and, starting with 1951, pick the same number, up to the present, in which earnings were the highest. If a person plans to work after 65, these years may be used when the high years are selected.

3. Total the yearly earnings found in step two, and divide the total by the number of years, to get an average.

4. Locate this average at the side of Table 13-2. The column beside this will indicate your benefits.

A few words of additional explanation are needed concerning these steps. Step two says to select the number of years in which earnings were the highest. Actually, the only earnings that count are those used for Social Security purposes. Between 1951 and 1954, the maximum that could be credited by law was $3,600; between 1955 and 1958, $4,200; and $4,800 for 1959 and after. This means that the highest average that can possibly be found in step three will be $4,800, and this will not be very frequent for several years, as those people now retiring will have to include some years in which less than $4,800 was credited to their account.

Let's follow through a brief example, to indicate how this works.

George will be 65 in 1964. He has worked steadily under covered employment since the Social Security system started. His earnings have always been more than the amount that could be credited to Social Security. What would his retirement benefit be?

1. Between 1955 and 1964 (but not including 1964) there are eight years.

2. George selects the eight years in which the earnings credits to Social Security were the highest. He may select the following:

1957	$4,200
1958	4,200
1959	4,800
1960	4,800
1961	4,800
1962	4,800
1963	4,800
1964	4,800

3. These earnings total $37,200. Divided by 8, this is $4,650.

4. Table 13-2 only presents examples of monthly payments. It is very unlikely that anyone's average would be identical to the figure appearing at the side of the table. The Social Security

Administration will, by a very precise formula, determine the specific benefits. However, the examples in the table are numerous enough so that a rough estimate of benefits can be made. It would appear that George would receive about $124 per month.

Disability Payments

To be considered disabled under the Social Security regulations, a person must be unable to "engage in any substantial gainful activity." This doesn't mean just a person's regular work. If a person is unable to do the same work he has done in the past, he still may be able to do other substantial gainful work.

Further, while this may be either a physical or a mental condition, it must be a disability which will show up in medical examinations or tests. The condition must have existed for at least six months, and be expected to continue for an indefinite time.

Not only must a person be fully insured to be entitled to disability payments, but he must have worked in covered employment (received Social Security credit) for at least 5 years of a ten year period ending with the date of disability.

Once it has been determined that a person is entitled to disability benefits, the amount of the benefits can be calculated in the same manner as the old-age and survivors' benefits. The benefits will be exactly the same as a 65 year old person's old-age benefits.

Family Benefits

The families of those receiving Social Security benefits for old-age or disability are also entitled to benefits. As an example, assume that the insured person has average earnings of $4,800, and is entitled to maximum benefits. He would be entitled to $127.00 per month. The benefits along the $4,800 line in Table 13-2 will be used to illustrate the following general rules determining family benefits.

1. a. The child or dependent spouse of a person receiving old-age or disability benefits will receive an amount equal to one-half of the insured person's benefits. In the table, the wife's benefit at 65 would be $63.50.

    b. The benefits will be less for a wife who requests payments before she is 65, unless she is caring for a child who is receiving benefits under her husband's account.

2. If the person receiving old-age or disability benefits dies, his widow, if under 62, and children and parents (if both survive) will each receive an amount equal to ¾ of the insured person's benefits. In the table, the widow's benefit, if she is under 62 and has 1 child, is $190.60. This is calculated as follows:

$$\text{¾ of } \$127.70 = \$95.30 \quad \text{(widow)}$$
$$\text{¾ of } \$127.00 = \underline{95.30} \quad \text{(child)}$$
$$\text{Total} \qquad \$190.60$$

3. If the widow is over 62, or if only one parent survives, the monthly benefit to each is 10 per cent more than the amount calculated in 2 above. Thus, in the table, the widow 62 or over would receive $104.80.

Notice, however, that maximum benefits have been established for a family. Regardless of the number of children, etc., the maximum that may be received by any family is $254.00. If the average yearly earnings amount to less than $4,200, this maximum is less.

A widow with children, or surviving children, are entitled to Social Security benefits if the husband was only currently insured. These, and the lump sum death payment, are the only benefits available if a person is *only* currently insured.

Working After Payments Start

What happens if a person works while receiving old-age or survivors benefits? As long as the income earned is $1,200 or less per year, there will be no reduction in benefits. If the amount earned is over $1,200, then $1 of benefits will be withheld for each $2 earned, from $1,200 to $1,700, and $1 of benefits will be withheld for each $1 earned over $1,700.

Jack is over 65 and receiving old-age benefits. He worked one year, and received an income of $1,800. $350 would be withheld from his benefits. This is one-half of the difference between $1,200 and $1,700 plus all earnings over $1,700.

These rules apply to all employment income, but not to income from pensions, interest, investments, etc.

These rules seem quite simple, but there are several rather fine points which complicate matters. For example, regardless of total annual income, benefits will be paid for any month in which earnings are less than $100, and the person does not perform substantial services in self-employment.

> I am 68 years old, work in a hotel in Florida, and make about $5,000 a year. Each July and August, during the slack season, I travel around the country. Since I do not earn any money in those months, could I receive social security benefits?
>
> Yes, because you are not earning more than $100 in July or August, you can be paid your benefits for those months regardless of your total earnings. You should immediately apply for benefits, if you have not done so.[5]

What happens if a person receiving benefits has a working wife? Will her earnings affect his benefits? The answer is no. The amount earned by a person receiving benefits as a dependent, or survivor, will affect only that person's benefits.

The entire problem is made much easier when a person reaches 72. After 72, any amount may be earned without affecting benefits.

CONCLUSION

This has been a very limited treatment of OASDI and the Social Security program. The rules are actually very precise and rather complicated. Only a few of the most common rules, benefits, etc., have been presented here. Furthermore, the rules and benefits have been changed quite frequently. The Social Security Administration does an excellent job of providing pamphlets which thoroughly explain the rules and benefits. A great deal of the information in this chapter has been obtained from them. The Social Security Administration is the authority on these matters, and if anyone is interested in learning more about Social Security, it is recommended that he request such information from them. Reference to the Administration is, of course, an absolute necessity if a person wants to determine the precise benefits to which he is entitled.

It is anticipated that benefits and rules will be changed in the future.

> Congress amended the Act in 1939, 1946, 1950, 1952, 1954, 1956, 1958, 1960, and 1961. Literally hundreds of bills have been introduced at each session of Congress proposing other changes in social security. Foremost among them in recent years have been those to provide benefits for hospital, nursing home, and medical

---

[5] "For Older People Who Are Working, Questions and Answers About Social Security Payments," U.S. Department of Health, Education, and Welfare, Social Security Administration, Bureau of Old-Age and Survivors Insurance, U.S. Government Printing Office, OASI 23a, October 1961, p. 2.

expenses. Thus, in 25 years, the OASDI program has expanded from coverage of a relatively limited group of workers to embrace all but a few gainfully employed Americans. Originally conceived as a subsistence-level aid to individual old-age security, the program now offers benefits to retired and disabled workers, their wives, widows, and children up to $254 per month. Limited lump-sum death benefits, "waiver-of-premium" provisions in the form of wage-freeze and "drop-out" clauses, and benefits for total and presumably permanent disability benefits have been added. The permissible retirement age has been lowered to age 62. The taxable wage base has been raised from $3,000 per year to $4,800 per year.[6]

PRIVATE PENSION PLANS

What is it that you can't get along with and can't get along without? One possible answer is Social Security. Most of us would find it pretty tough sledding to retire without it, but it isn't sufficient to meet our total needs. Pension plans are one of the answers to this problem.

More than 22 million people are protected under funded private pension plans in the United States with assets totalling more than $44 billion. Over 5 million of these are covered under insured plans with assets amounting to $17½ billion.[7]

This quotation, applying only to "funded" private pension plans, indicates that pension funds are a big business. Most large companies have pension plans for their employees, each with individual features. Unions also have pension funds, which usually are financed by the employers who employ the union members.

Advantages

Pension funds have many advantages. Employees naturally like them, as they give employees money to live on when they retire. Employers like them, because they improve employer-employee relations, build good will, improve public relations, etc. There are also many tax advantages.

---

[6] Edwin J. Faulkner, *Social Security—Another Problem Program*, Proceedings of the Life Insurance Top Management Conference, The University of Arkansas, Arkansas, August 7–8, 1962, Edited by W. A. Guinn, p. 26.

[7] Robert I. Mehr and Emerson Cammack, *Principles of Insurance*, Richard D. Irwin, Inc., Homewood, Illinois, Third Edition, 1961, p. 567.

In a qualified pension or profit sharing program, certain tax benefits are allowed as an incentive for management to inaugurate such programs. They may be summarized as follows:

1. The employer's contributions are currently tax deductible.
2. The employee is taxed only when payments are disbursed or made available to him.
3. The ordinary income and capital gains of the trust fund are tax exempt.
4. If the entire benefit is paid in a lump sum to an employee (at retirement or termination of employment), it is taxed as a long term capital gain, rather than as ordinary income.
5. At an employee's death, distributions which stem from the company's contributions are not includible in his estate for Federal estate tax purposes, provided they are payable to a beneficiary other than the employee's executor.[8]

To be considered qualified for tax purposes there must be a written legally binding agreement that is communicated to the employees, and is for their exclusive benefit. Under such a plan, it must be impossible for the principal or income of the trust to be used for any purpose other than providing benefits for employees, and there must be no discrimination of employees.

Financing

Most pension plans are financed by the employer, although some require employees to share in the cost. "If the plan requires you to contribute, you don't have to join. But it seldom pays to pass it up. Your boss generally puts in two to four times as much as you do. All the income that the money earns during the years until your retirement is tax-free."[9]

Employers have differing opinions on which plan is preferable, one in which the employees pay part of the cost (contributory), or one in which the employer pays everything (non-contributory). There is some feeling that employees appreciate a plan more if they must contribute, and that the total contributions, and therefore the benefits, can be larger. However, all contributions by employers are tax deductible, while contributions by employees are not.

---

[8] "Pension & Profit Sharing Plans," Trust Department, Security First National Bank, Los Angeles, California, p. 2, 1962.

[9] "Your Company Pension Plan," *Changing Times, The Kiplinger Magazine*, The Kiplinger Washington Editors, Inc., Washington, D.C., May 1962, p. 8.

Vesting

Crediting the employer's contributions to the individual employee's account is called vesting. Does an employee who leaves his job before retirement age receive any of the employer's contributions into the fund? Whether or not he may participate in these contributions depends on when, if ever, vesting occurs.

If the plan is contributory, the part contributed by the employee is always immediately vested, and can be withdrawn when the employee leaves. If a fund is completely and immediately vested, it means that the employee has the right to all of the fund's benefits, regardless of when he leaves his job or where he is later employed. Very few funds provide for immediate vesting. Usually employment for some period of years is required, or the employee much reach some specific age. There are a few funds in which vesting doesn't occur until retirement.

There is a very good reason why employers are reluctant to make vesting immediate. If it is deferred, it will tend to hold the employee. An employee is more reluctant to leave his job if it means losing his pension rights. The longer he works for the company, the more beneficial these rights become, and the more reluctant he will be to leave. Conversely, this is also a reason why employees prefer immediate vesting.

Funding

How are the payments of future benefits provided for?

The costs of future benefits can be calculated by actuaries. If a pension fund is funded, these ultimate costs will be provided for in advance. Current funds will be set aside to take care of these future costs. Under this type of plan, a part of the future costs will be met by the interest earned on the money set aside.

Funded pension funds may be insured. In this case, current contributions are paid to an insurance company, and it pays the benefits. If the funded plan is not insured, the funds are placed in the hands of a trustee who invests the money and pays the benefits.

In an unfunded plan, all benefits are paid out of current income. This carries with it an element of risk. If the company suffers reverses, it may be unable to meet its pension plan obligations.

If immediate vesting is the practice, the fund is generally funded. If vesting doesn't occur until retirement, funding is not quite as essential, as many employees will leave the company before retirement, thus reducing the amount of money needed in the fund.

Pensions for Self-Employed

Self-employed persons have to establish their own pension plans entirely out of their own income. Up to 1962, their entire income was taxed, no credit being given to the pension plan contributions. The Self-Employed Individuals' Tax Retirement Act of 1962 changed this.

> In general, this measure permits the professional or business individual or partner to deduct up to $1,250 annually of amounts set aside under a retirement plan. Employees of the professional or business office must also be covered by the plan, and the amounts directed to financing these benefits become deductible in regular course as business expenses.
>
> The taxpayer enjoys considerable leeway in choosing the method of financing his retirement. Securities and other property can be set aside under a trust, with a bank as trustee. Bank custodial accounts are also permitted. Mutual fund shares as well as endowment, annuity and insurance contracts can likewise be purchased to finance the benefits. A new type of U.S. government bond can also be used.[10]

Subsequent to the effective date of this Act, just about everyone has been able to participate in a retirement plan, which permits deferment of the payment of, and a possible reduction in, the federal income tax on this income. This is an added incentive to plan ahead.

ANNUITIES

Both annuities and life insurance are based on mortality tables, but they are quite different. Life insurance is purchased for protection against premature death. An annuity is purchased to provide for extended longevity.

"An annuity is a contract purchased by an individual and sold by an insurance company, in which the company undertakes to pay

---

[10] Reproduced by permission from "New Retirement Tax Benefits for Self-Employed," published by and Copyright 1962, Commerce Clearing House, Inc., Chicago 46, Illinois, Vol. XLV, Number 52, October 15, 1962, p. 2.

a fixed sum periodically for a stated period or, more commonly, for the remaining life of the buyer."[11] Life insurance is a way of building an estate. An annuity can be used to distribute this estate, either over the life of the insured or the life of the beneficiary of the policy. Annuities can be purchased either by investing one single large sum of money or by instalments, regular premiums. These are generally

Chart 13-1

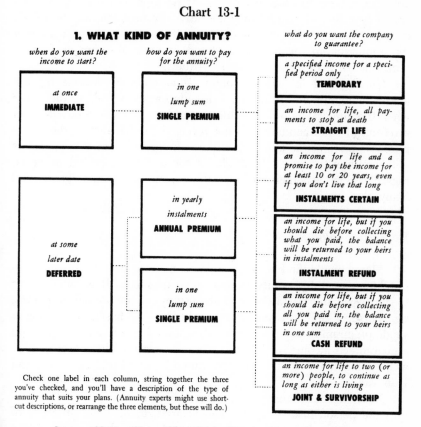

1. WHAT KIND OF ANNUITY?

what do you want the company to guarantee?

when do you want the income to start?

how do you want to pay for the annuity?

at once
IMMEDIATE

in one lump sum
SINGLE PREMIUM

a specified income for a specified period only
TEMPORARY

an income for life, all payments to stop at death
STRAIGHT LIFE

an income for life and a promise to pay the income for at least 10 or 20 years, even if you don't live that long
INSTALMENTS CERTAIN

at some later date
DEFERRED

in yearly instalments
ANNUAL PREMIUM

an income for life, but if you should die before collecting what you paid, the balance will be returned to your heirs in instalments
INSTALMENT REFUND

in one lump sum
SINGLE PREMIUM

an income for life, but if you should die before collecting all you paid in, the balance will be returned to your heirs in one sum
CASH REFUND

Check one label in each column, string together the three you've checked, and you'll have a description of the type of annuity that suits your plans. (Annuity experts might use short-cut descriptions, or rearrange the three elements, but these will do.)

an income for life to two (or more) people, to continue as long as either is living
JOINT & SURVIVORSHIP

Source: *99 New Ideas,* 1954 Edition, *Changing Times, The Kiplinger Magazine,* The Kiplinger Washington Editors, Inc., Washington, D.C., p. 46.

classified as single premium immediate annuities, or as deferred annuities. Many of the variations available are presented in Chart 13-1.

---

[11] Roland I. Robinson (Ed.), Erwin W. Boehmler, Frank H. Gane and Loring C. Farwell, *Financial Institutions,* Richard D. Irwin, Inc., Homewood, Illinois, Third Edition, 1960, p. 488.

Immediate Annuities

Immediate annuities are purchased with a single payment, and are especially attractive to people nearing retirement age. Often, a person finds that his income from Social Security and investments will not be sufficient to meet his needs. If he dips into his capital, and enjoys long life, his capital may not last. The problem may be solved by using the capital to purchase an annuity, as the annuity guarantees the annuitant an income for a stated number of years or for the remainder of his life, whichever he requests.

One type of immediate annuity guarantees an income for the life of the annuitant, but does not provide for any refund to the estate when the annuitant dies. Another guarantees an income for life, and a refund, if the annuitant had not received the benefits of the entire purchase price of the annuity. Still another guarantees that payments will continue to named beneficiaries for a definite period of years, regardless of whether or not the annuitant lives. There are many choices.

Deferred Annuities

Many would find it impossible to acquire a fund sufficient to purchase a sizable annuity in one single payment. It is much easier to start early and buy a deferred annuity by paying annual premiums. Of course, a deferred annuity can also be purchased by paying a single premium in advance. Not only does a deferred annuity promise a guaranteed income for life, but offers the same multitude of choices as an immediate annuity. Deferred annuities also build up a cash and loan value.

Many life insurance policies have a life income option. This permits the person insured, or his beneficiaries, to take the proceeds of the insurance policy as an annuity. In this case, the permanent life insurance policy actually becomes a deferred annuity, purchased by annual premiums.

This is only a brief review of annuities. There are many variations. Industry and union sponsored retirement plans, Social Security, etc., have made annuities less popular, but a person who wishes to increase his retirement income should carefully consider them. For one thing, as indicated by Table 13–4, annuities have definite tax advantages.

Table 13–4

<table>
<tr><td colspan="4">ILLUSTRATION OF INCOME AFTER TAXES
from a CML single premium annuity as compared with income from the same amount of capital invested at various rates of interest.
    Annuity income is composed of portions of the principal as well as interest and is guaranteed for life. Consequently an annuity is taxed differently than other investments, and the difference of its tax treatment is illustrated on the accompanying table.</td></tr>
</table>

Total Annual Income		Portion of Income Subject to Tax	Net After Taxes		
$10,000 (Single Premium Immediate Annuity)*					
			20% Tax Rate	30% Tax Rate	40% Tax Rate
Age 60	$688	$225	$643	$620	$598
Age 65	769	218	725	704	682
Age 70	874	211	832	811	790
$10,000 (Invested to yield annual interest return indicated — any age)					
4%	$400	$400	$320	$280	$240
5%	500	500	400	350	300
6%	600	600	480	420	360
* Male life — instalment refund basis 1961 rates.					

Source: "How you can have the security and peace of mind of a guaranteed income for life . . . through annuities," Connecticut Mutual Life Insurance Company pamphlet, Hartford, Conn., pp. 3-4.

A lifetime annuity will mean that an income is assured regardless of how long you live, but it doesn't build up much of an estate for your heirs. Some other investment may produce a larger estate, but might not provide you with an income for life if you live for many years after retirement. The attractiveness of an annuity, then, depends to a certain degree on what you are most interested in, building an estate for your heirs or making certain of an income for the rest of your life.

VARIABLE ANNUITIES

The so-called variable annuity is similar to a true annuity in that premiums are paid to the issuing company by the annuitant, presumably during his working years, or perhaps even in a lump

sum. At retirement the company makes payments periodically to
the annuitant—generally speaking, over the remaining years of his
life. But there the similarity ends. In the true annuity the amount
of each payment is guaranteed by the insurance company. The
annuitant may well receive more than the guaranteed payment
through dividends, but he will never receive less. However, the
difference, and a vast difference it is, is that in the variable
annuity type of contract the premium payments to the company
are to be invested in equities which to all intents and purposes
means common stocks, and the issuing company makes *no* commitment as to any dollar amount that will be paid to the annuitant
during the period of retirement. The benefits which the annuitant
will receive will fluctuate directly with the rise and fall of the
value of the underlying portfolio of common stock. Here the
annuitant assumes that risk entirely. Under these contracts there
is no substantial guarantee and, practically speaking, no insurance
of a risk by the insurance company.[12]

This statement clearly presents the difference between true annuities and variable annuities. Today, variable annuities are one of
the new forms of investment. They are sold by a very limited number
of companies in only a few states. Some employers, Boeing Airplane,
Bristol-Myers, Chemstrand, etc., have established variable annuity
plans for their employees.

> Proponents of the variable annuity contend that a real need
> exists for a means of saving which will hedge against inflation and
> still have the life annuity feature. They argue that the variable
> annuity will induce systematic savings by individuals who are
> now reluctant to save because of the likelihood that inflation
> will nullify the result of their savings.[13]
> But, there are, however, those who strongly oppose variable
> annuities. They argue that the public is accustomed to thinking
> of the insurance industry in terms of fixed-dollar contracts, and
> that a change to variable payments will undermine confidence in
> insurance company contracts.[14]

There is no certainty as to who will finally win the argument.
Before variable annuities can be sold, there are legal difficulties that

---

[12] *Variable Annuities,* A Statement by Charles G. Dougherty, Vice-President,
Metropolitan Life Insurance Company before the Joint Insurance Committee,
Massachusetts Legislature, Boston, Massachusetts, September 29, 1958, pp. 2–3.
[13] Cedric V. Fricke, *The Variable Annuity—Its Impact on the Savings-
Investment Market,* Bureau of Business Research, School of Business Administration, The University of Michigan, Ann Arbor. Copyright 1959, p. 3.
[14] Ibid., p. 4.

must be solved. The probabilities, however, seem to give the proponents a slight edge. Regardless of which side is "right," the fact remains that life insurance companies in recent years have faced tough competition from mutual funds. In a period when the population seems convinced that inflation is here to stay, variable annuities would seem to be an easily saleable contract and would help insurance companies meet the mutual fund competition. If the various legal problems are solved, variable annuities might very well prove to be one of the most rapidly growing investment media on the market.

For this reason it is necessary to spend some time considering how variable annuities work—not because of their sales volume today but because of their potential sales volume tomorrow.

TIAA — CREF

The first variable annuity plan, the College Retirement Equities Fund (CREF), was established by the Teachers Insurance and Annuity Association of America (TIAA) in 1952. In view of the currently increasing interest in variable annuities on the part of insurance companies, it is worthwhile to examine CREF and appraise its performance.

TIAA, established in 1918, is a non-profit organization, and participation is open only to staff members of colleges, universities, and certain other nonprofit educational and scientific organizations. TIAA has always offered an annuity plan based on fixed income investments. Realizing the problems faced by the individual retiring on such a plan, it established CREF to provide an opportunity for participants to invest in common stocks which would provide some protection against price level fluctuations.

Fixed and Variable Combination

The purpose of the TIAA-CREF plan is to provide a retirement income which is relatively free from extreme fluctuations in amount and from any serious decline in purchasing power due to changes in the price level. An income dependent on fixed income investments may be quite inadequate due to an extreme rise in the price level. This has been the outstanding difficulty of the usual annuity in the past. Twenty years ago a set retirement income of two hundred dollars per month might have been quite satisfactory, but such an income today would be far less satisfactory. On the other hand, an income dependent only on common-stock investments would be subject to such extreme fluctuations that it would not be adequate for the retired person.

Those participating in the combined TIAA-CREF plan may place ¼, ⅓, or ½ of each premium in CREF. Because of the 50 per cent limit, an individual will always have the protection provided by a fixed annuity—the provision of a guaranteed amount of dollar income—as well as the protection against reduced purchasing power offered by equity investments. TIAA and CREF are separate companies, and the TIAA funds and CREF funds can be and are, therefore, completely separate. TIAA, in fact, charges CREF a management fee for operating expenses. By keeping the funds separate, the problem of maintaining a balanced investment portfolio, which would necessitate decisions as to what percentage of the fund should be placed in fixed income investments and what percentage in equity investments, under varying market conditions, is avoided. All funds placed in CREF are invested in common stocks, and all funds placed in TIAA are invested in fixed income securities. A participant will always have at least 50 per cent of his fund invested in fixed income investments. Freed of the responsibility and necessity of maintaining a balanced portfolio, the management of TIAA can then concentrate on selecting the best fixed income investments, and the management of CREF can concentrate on determining which common stock investments are preferable for the long-range objectives of pension funding.

Mechanics

The TIAA-CREF plan is quite simple. The TIAA premium buys retirement income based on a guaranteed rate of interest. This is a fixed annuity. The CREF premiums purchase accumulation units. Under the TIAA plan additional amounts of income are purchased by interest on the accumulating premiums. Under the CREF plan an individual's share of CREF's dividends purchases more accumulation units. The value of an accumulation unit changes monthly with changes in the market prices of the fund's portfolio, and each monthly value represents both the current purchase price for a new accumulation unit and the current dollar value of each previously purchased unit.

Accumulation units are converted to annuity units on retirement and a fixed number of annuity units is paid to the individual for life. The number of units remains fixed but the dollar income to the individual varies each year as the value of the annuity unit changes. The annuity unit is revalued only once a year in order to permit a retired person to plan for a certain amount of income for a year ahead.

Chart 13–2

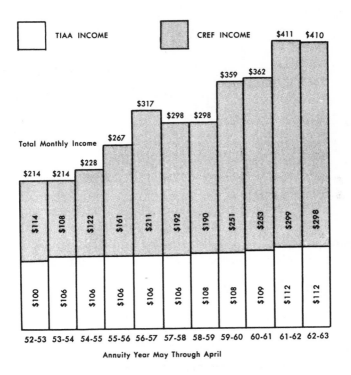

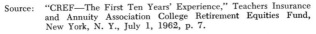

Annuity Year May Through April

Source: "CREF—The First Ten Years' Experience," Teachers Insurance and Annuity Association College Retirement Equities Fund, New York, N. Y., July 1, 1962, p. 7.

Performance

Has the TIAA-CREF plan served the purpose intended—to provide a retirement income relatively free from extreme fluctuations in amount and from any serious decline in purchasing power due to changes in the price level? Chart 13–2 "shows what the annuity income of an educator would have been if he had made a single payment for TIAA-CREF immediate annuities on July 1, 1952, when he was 65 years old. The amount paid to TIAA was assumed to be large enough to purchase an annuity of $100 a month, with the same amount paid to CREF. The total combined monthly income would be com-

Chart 13–3

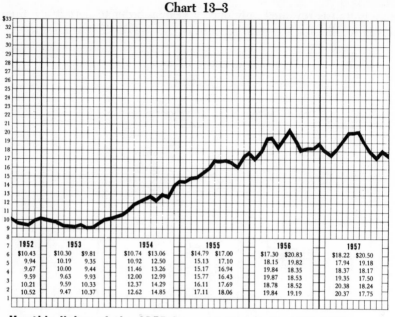

	1952	1953		1954		1955		1956		1957	
6	$10.43	$10.30	$9.81	$10.74	$13.06	$14.79	$17.00	$17.30	$20.83	$18.22	$20.50
5	9.94	10.19	9.35	10.92	12.50	15.13	17.10	18.15	19.82	17.94	19.18
4	9.67	10.00	9.44	11.46	13.26	15.17	16.94	19.84	18.35	18.37	18.17
3	9.59	9.63	9.93	12.00	12.99	15.77	16.43	19.87	18.53	19.35	17.50
2	10.21	9.59	10.33	12.37	14.29	16.11	17.69	18.78	18.52	20.38	18.24
1	10.52	9.47	10.37	12.62	14.85	17.11	18.06	19.84	19.19	20.37	17.75

Monthly Value of the CREF Accumulation Unit, 1952-1962

CREF Annuity Unit Values Since 1952

Annuity Year May through April	Annuity Unit Value
Initial Value	$10.00
1953-54	9.46
1954-55	10.74
1955-56	14.11
1956-57	18.51
1957-58	16.88
1958-59	16.71
1959-60	22.03
1960-61	22.18
1961-62	26.25
1962-63	26.13

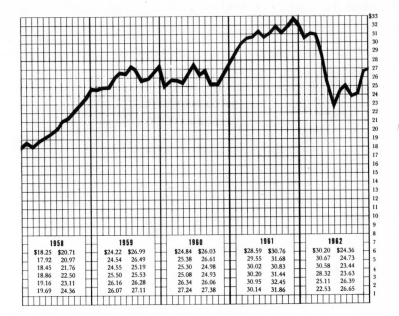

1958		1959		1960		1961		1962	
$18.25	$20.71	$24.22	$26.99	$24.84	$26.03	$28.59	$30.76	$30.20	$24.36
17.92	20.97	24.54	26.49	25.38	26.61	29.55	31.68	30.67	24.73
18.45	21.76	24.55	25.19	25.30	24.98	30.02	30.83	30.58	23.44
18.86	22.50	25.50	25.53	25.08	24.93	30.20	31.44	28.32	23.63
19.16	23.11	26.16	26.28	26.34	26.06	30.95	32.45	25.11	26.39
19.69	24.36	26.07	27.11	27.24	27.38	30.14	31.86	22.53	26.65

Experience of $50 a Month Paid to CREF

YEAR-END DOLLAR VALUES OF CREF ACCUMULATIONS
UNDER FOUR DIFFERENT PERIODS OF PARTICIPATION

This table shows successive year-end CREF accumulations for persons starting a $50 level monthly premium to CREF on four different dates. For example, the person starting January 1, 1957, had a $4,201 year-end accumulation value at the end of 1961 after paying $3,000 in premiums to CREF, and an accumulation of $4,205 at the end of 1962 after paying $600 more in premiums. CREF accumulation amounts are reported to each participant annually on the CREF Yellow Slip.

Date of First $50 Monthly Premium to CREF

Year Ending December 31	July 1, 1952	January 1, 1957	January 1, 1959	January 1, 1961
1952	$ 304			
1953	931			
1954	2,085			
1955	3,261			
1956	4,160			
1957	4,516	$ 552		
1958	7,086	1,488		
1959	8,691	2,316	$ 621	
1960	9,613	3,023	1,272	
1961	12,016	4,201	2,124	$ 616
1962	10,899	4,205	2,426	1,135

Source: "TIAA—CREF," 1962 Annual Report, pp. 22-23.

posed of the fixed TIAA income, TIAA dividends, and the variable CREF income." [15]

It is obvious that total monthly income has grown considerably during the period covered. It is also evident, as would be expected, that the portion derived from CREF has increased much more than the portion derived from TIAA. For the time period covered, TIAA and CREF as a combination more than managed to keep up with cost of living changes. The $410 monthly combined TIAA-CREF income for 1962 was 91 per cent higher than the 1952 income. Consumer prices were approximately 13 per cent higher. The increase was enough to permit a retired person not only to have kept up with changes in the cost of living but also to have improved his standard of living. Thus, the average retired faculty member would have had a rising income corresponding to some degree to the rising salaries paid to faculty members during this period. Chart 13-3 indicates what has happened to CREF since its beginning in 1952.

CONCLUSIONS

The TIAA-CREF combination has seemed to work quite well from the viewpoint of those covered. This does not support variable annuities in general. The variable annuity question is much larger. For this *particular* group, however, this *particular* plan has been and, it seems, will continue to be quite satisfactory. Here, as in every investment program, management is the fundamental determinant of success or failure. The excellence of past and present TIAA-CREF management and the soundness of its policies permit those covered to plan for eventual retirement with confidence.

Would a variable annuity be a good investment for you? It seems quite definite that this should not be your only investment. Remember that TIAA-CREF, for example, is not simply a variable annuity. Participants are only permitted to place a maximum of 50 per cent of each premium in CREF, the equity investment. If an insurance company offered a variable annuity which would invest the entire premium in common stocks, and this was the investor's only retirement income investment, the investor would be at the mercy of the stock market. He would be without the protection of the guaranteed dollar income as provided by a fixed dollar annuity.

Even such a combination is not complete protection. TIAA-CREF's management has been excellent. Another organization's might

---

[15] *CREF—The First Ten Years' Experience,* Teachers Insurance and Annuity Association College Retirement Equities Fund, New York, N.Y., July 1, 1962, p. 7.

not be as good. Remember, too, that the stock market has in general gone up since CREF started in 1952. Common stock prices can also go down. Even with a combination of fixed income and equity investments, the total income to the annuitant could go down over a period of years if the market fell steadily. This could not happen if the entire investment was in a traditional annuity with a guaranteed income. On the other hand, if common stock prices continue to rise, the total income from such an investment would, depending on management, be larger than that from traditional annuity. Management should be carefully investigated. It is extremely important.

Questions

1. How may an individual attain a "fully insured" status under Social Security?

2. Is an individual's monthly check affected if he works while receiving old age and survivors benefits?

3. All Social Security benefits are available to those who are "fully insured." Some are available to those who are "currently insured" but not "fully insured." Does this mean that monthly payments to those who are "fully insured" will be higher than payments to those who are only "currently insured"?

4. You should check regularly on the status of your Social Security Account. Why?

5. Describe four (4) tax advantages of a "qualified" pension plan.

6. What is meant by a "qualified" pension plan?

7. Briefly discuss the "funding" of private pension plans.

8. Abe is receiving $100 a month from an annuity which promises to pay these installments for ten (10) years "certain and continuous." Exactly what does this mean?

9. Investing all of one's savings in a variable annuity is unwise. Discuss.

10. Briefly describe the mechanics of the TIAA-CREF plan.

Problems

1. What is the total annual payment of Social Security taxes for the following:
   a. In 1964—for a self-employed physician earning $15,000.
   b. In 1963—for a male employee earning $5500 from one employer only.
   c. In 1968—a student nurse earning $4200.
   d. In 1965—for an employee earning $6900.

2. A will be 65 in April, 1971. In 1965 he is permanently disabled from an accident. From June 1, 1957 to May 31, 1962, his earnings ranged from $6200 - $7400. Is he fully or currently insured?

3. B is fully insured and is entitled to the maximum Social Security benefits paid. How much monthly income will be paid under the following circumstances:

   a. B dies leaving a wife, who does not work, and 3 children, ages 2, 5, 11.
   b. B dies leaving a wife, who does work, and 3 children, ages 2, 5, 11.
   c. B lives and retires at 65. His wife, age 65, elects to retire at age 65.

4. X, age 68, is married. His wife is age 67. Both are in excellent health and there are no living dependents. X has $24,000 of available cash to invest in an annuity. Which annuity would you recommend and why?

5. Y is eligible to participate in the TIAA - CREF fund. He is debating between this investment media and mutual funds. What would you advise?

Selected Readings

Connecticut Mutual Life Insurance Company, Hartford, Connecticut:
   "Pension Trusts—their advantages to employers and employees"
   "How you can have the security and peace of mind of a guaranteed income for life . . . through annuities"
   "Some Questions & Answers about Profit Sharing Retirement Plans"

"CREF—The First Ten Years' Experience," Teachers Insurance and Annuity Association College Retirement Equities Fund, New York, N.Y., July 1962

Fricke, Cedric V., *The Variable Annuity, Its Impact on the Savings-Investment Market*, Bureau of Business Research, School of Business Administration, The University of Michigan, Ann Arbor, Michigan, 1959

Mehr, Robert I., and Cammack, Emerson, *Principles of Insurance*, Richard D. Irwin, Inc., Homewood, Illinois, 1961

"New Retirement Tax Benefits for Self-Employed," Federal Tax Guide Reports, Commerce Clearing House, Inc., New York, N.Y., Vol. XLV, Number 52, October 15, 1962

"Pension & Profit Sharing Plans," Security First National Bank, Los Angeles, California, 1962

"Your Company Pension Plan," *Changing Times, The Kiplinger Magazine*, Kiplinger Washington Editors, Inc., Washington, D.C., May 1962, p. 7

Turnbull, John G., Williams, Arthur C. Jr., and Cheit, Earl F., *Economic and Social Security*, The Ronald Press Co., New York, N.Y., Second Edition, 1962

Publications of U.S. Department of Health, Education, and Welfare, Social Security Administration, U.S. Government Printing Office, including:
"Your Social Security," OASI 35a, January 1962
"For Older People Who Are Working, Questions and Answers About Social Security Payments," OASI 23a, October 1961
"If You Become Disabled," OASI 29, January 1962
"Your Social Security Earnings Record," OASI 93, August 1961

Chapter **14**

SECURITY MARKETS

Suppose that in our imagination we could compress the total population of the world, about 3 billion people, into one town of 1,000 people. In the imaginary town . . . there would be 60 Americans. The remainder of the world would be represented by 940 persons.

The 60 Americans would receive half the income of the entire town and own half the capital. The other 940 people would divide the other half.

The 60 Americans would have an average life expectancy of
70 years. The other 940, less than 40 years average.

The 60 Americans would have 15 times as many possessions per
person as all the rest of the people.

The lowest income group among the 60 Americans would be
much better off than the average of the rest of the town.[1]

Our capitalistic free enterprise system has outperformed all
others. This was true in 1962. Will it continue to be true in 2062?
Viewed historically, "capitalism" and "free-enterprise" are things to
be proud of.

Whether or not this *will* be true in 2062 cannot be proved, but
it seems clear that this *could* be true then. It is difficult, however, for
any system to be successful unless the people benefiting from it appreciate its value and understand its operation. An understanding of
where the American system obtains the funds for growth, and of the
part *you* play in providing these funds, is essential to an understanding
of the system.

The American capitalistic system is a power plant of mass production. It is geared to producing goods for the mass, the entire
population, and, not for the few. Consider for a moment—do
businesses try to increase their profits by producing items which may
be sold to a few hundred people, or by producing items which may
be sold to millions? Certainly, in the overwhelming majority of cases,
they hope their customers will be in the millions. Of course, some
firms produce items primarily or entirely for the government—rockets,
jet planes, etc. Even here they are producing for a large demand, a
customer larger than millions of us put together. When businesses
produce for consumers, they must produce things that appeal to all
of us, not to just a few. Under our competitive system, even as regulated by the government as it is, these firms attempt to outdo each
other in capturing as large a market as possible for their products.

This system has worked so well that the market keeps growing.
Statistics reveal that the "real income" of the American population has
grown rapidly. While it is true that prices have gone up year after
year, wages have, on the average, gone up even faster; and Americans
have been able to buy more and more products of American business.
This, in turn, has caused American business to continuously expand
and grow.

Added to this growth in purchasing power is the increase in
demand for goods and services brought about by an expanding popu-

[1] Rev. Henry Smith Leiper, Leonia, New Jersey, from a parable "Our World
in Miniature" appearing in Associated Church Press Releases.

lation. Due to the birth rate, better medical care, etc., the population has increased tremendously. The birth rate is increasing, and people live longer. The American population increased by about 19.4% between 1947 and 1957. Assume for the moment that this percentage increase continues, and that the total population will increase by this percentage every ten years. ". . . . under these assumed conditions, the 1947 population of 144 million persons will have doubled before 1987 and will have increased to 10 times its size before 2077."[2] After 2077, the increase in the population each ten years will be larger than the total American population was in 1947.

The American system has had, and will continue to have, problems of growth. More and more machinery and factories will be needed, both to produce goods needed by an expanding population and to employ an ever-increasing number of people so that they may enjoy these products—so that the American standard of living may continue to rise.

FINANCING GROWTH

You, as an individual, are extremely important to this system under which we live. In fact, our present system could not exist in its present form without you.

If the American system is to grow, and this is an absolute necessity, production and employment must increase. Funds must be provided to finance this growth. Where do these funds come from?

If a business needs money for a few weeks, or even a few years, it can borrow from a bank or from a finance company, just as an individual might borrow. However, this method cannot be used to finance long-term growth. General Electric, American Telephone, or any large company, may use short-term borrowing on occasion, but long-term investments are required to finance long-term growth. These long-term funds are available from two sources:

1. Profits made by the business and plowed back into the firm, or
2. Investors

Due to the size and complexity of the jobs that must be done by business firms in the modern world, the corporate form of organization is the most popular. It is increasingly difficult for individual proprietorships and partnerships to acquire the capital needed to competitively produce enough to meet the needs of an expanding and complex

---

[2] From *Statistics as Applied to Economics and Business,* by Robert H. Wessel and Edward R. Willett. Copyright © 1959 by Holt, Rinehart and Winston, Inc., p. 68.

society. Corporations are able to raise sufficient capital because their
owners may number in the thousands or millions. Insurance companies, mutual funds, pensions funds, and other organizations with
large financial resources, own a significant portion of the securities
issued by corporations needing capital. Chart 14–1 indicates, however, that the individual investor is an important source of this
needed capital.

Chart 14–1

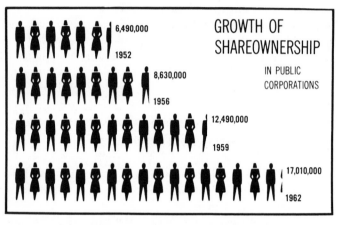

Source: "Understanding the New York Stock Exchange," New York
Stock Exchange, July 1962, p. 43.

THE SECURITIES MARKET

We have been concerned with the nature of the system in which
we live. The question now is, just how do the corporations needing
capital and you, as the individual investor, get together. You obviously do not buy securities from General Motors—you buy automobiles. How, then, does a security travel from General Motors to
you and, in turn, how do your savings get back to General Motors?
All of this takes place in a surprisingly efficient market—the securities market.

The securities market is detailed and complex, but its basic
components can be described and explained rather simply. A brief
explanation will indicate the route securities travel in going from
the corporation to the individual holder, and to give you some understanding of what happens when you buy or sell a share of stock,
or a bond.

Investment Banking

Imagine that a large corporation, American Telephone, General Electric, Westinghouse, Zenith, Ford, any of thousands, decides to issue bonds or common stock to obtain capital. How does it market these securities? There may be millions of individual bonds or shares involved. None of these corporations is organized to sell securities. To attempt to find customers for these securities, and to distribute them, would be an enormous job. Indeed, the cost might easily amount to a sizable part of the money needed by the corporation.

Such a corporation would first contact an investment banker. The investment banker, or a group of investment bankers called a "syndicate," would purchase the securities from the corporation and resell them to the public. The investment banker, or the syndicate, as the case may be, assume the risk and responsibility of marketing the securities. If they do so successfully, they make a profit; if not, they suffer the loss. The corporation's fund-raising effort terminates upon receipt of the money from the investment banker, or syndicate.

There are many investment banking firms. When a giant corporation offers a new issue of securities, these firms will form a syndicate to underwrite the issue, if none of them is large enough to assume the entire issue. Sometimes these syndicates are made up of hundreds of individual investment banking firms.

Investment banking is a risky business. A banker, or a syndicate, might purchase an issue of securities from the most outstanding corporation imaginable; one with an outstanding past record, an untarnished financial reputation, an enviable future, etc. The price paid for the securities would be based upon a careful analysis of the corporation, the market, the state of the economy, and other pertinent factors. The banker, or syndicate, would use techniques derived from long years of experience, and rely upon the advice of expert analysis. Yet, on the day the securities are delivered, the market price may change drastically. A new war threat, a statement by the President of the United States, a strike, etc., might suddenly affect the market. None of these could be predicted by the banker. If they should cause the prices of stocks and bonds—the market—to rise, the banker would profit; if they should cause prices to fall, the banker would lose.

Issues by "new" public corporations will be brought out in the same manner. An aero-space company may become large enough to issue stock to the general public. A family corporation may decide to issue its stock to the general public. In such cases, the stock is sold to an investment banking house, and the investment banker assumes the problems of selling and distribution.

The investment banker is a merchant, a middle man. Such a firm usually is not interested in investing in the securities it underwrites. Its function is to market them. Stocks and bonds are the merchandise it buys and sells, somewhat in the same manner a grocer buys and sells groceries. There is quite a difference, however, in capital requirements. Investment banking involves enormous amounts of capital, highly trained expert personnel, a very small profit margin, and a terrific amount of risk.

Brokers

Investment bankers do not deal directly with the public. Brokers deal with the public. It is true that some firms are so organized that they do many things. Some act as investment bankers and brokers, but the two functions are separate and distinct. It is the broker who does business with the individual buyer or seller of securities. When you place an order to buy or sell, you deal with a broker. Sometimes this broker acts as an *agent;* he buys or sells a security on the instruction of a customer, and has no interest in the securities himself. At other times, the broker may act as a *principal.* If he is a principal, he does have an interest in the securities he sells to a customer. The law requires a broker to tell his customer whether he is acting as an agent or as a principal. In either event, all stock purchased must be paid for within four days after its purchase.

You should select a broker carefully. Brokerage firms, like all businesses, vary in their characteristics. In general, they are honest, well managed, and financially sound, but it has often been said that "there are a few rotten apples in every barrel." An unscrupulous broker, for example, might "churn" your account. This means that he will continuously talk you into letting him buy and sell for your account. Remember, brokers get paid by a commission on purchases and sales. The more often your money is turned over, "churned," the greater his commissions.[3]

---

[3] In a case presented by the SEC in its News Digest in May 1960, the Commission examined four customer accounts handled by a salesman in one of a large brokerage firm's branch offices. The following details were uncovered:

Approx. Investment	Times Turned Over	Approx. Commissions
$57,000	29 times in 46 months	$27,000
66,000	34 times in 56 months	38,000
15,000	27 times in 28 months	8,000
60,000	5.6 times in 16 months	5,500

The customers lost money in all four accounts.

Pseudo-brokers, working out of a "bucket-shop," call potential customers on the telephone. They are, for the most part, fly-by-night operators who are peddling a "hot stock." They will tell you fantastic stories about the profits you can make if you buy a few hundred shares. The stock may be completely worthless, and when you try to find the "broker," he may no longer be available. In his terms, he has taken all the "suckers" (including you) he believes he can take, and has closed shop. This, of course, is illegal, but, like many other illegal things, happens every year. One basic rule is never to buy stock from a broker you don't know.

Brokers are well regulated by law. Most states have state laws regulating their activity. The Securities and Exchange Commission (SEC) regulates them. The National Association of Securities Dealers regulations are at least as strict (in fact many brokers believe more so) as the SEC. Brokerage firms which are members of a stock exchange are also regulated by the rules of the exchange.

Each year, these regulatory bodies penalize brokerage firms which are found guilty of questionable practices. Sometimes these firms are fined, sometimes their operations are temporarily suspended, sometimes they are forced to discontinue operations completely and permanently. Naturally, it would be best to avoid doing business with a broker whose operations are not on the highest possible level.

There is also a vast difference between brokers with respect to the services and advice they offer. Some will do just about anything to be of service. Others will do nothing. Some have expert analysts and personal representatives who offer excellent advice. Others have employees of doubtful ability who offer extremely poor advice.

How do you select a broker who will prove to be honest, and give good service and sound advice? One rule, often suggested, is to deal with a firm which is a member of the New York Stock Exchange. There are several reasons for this rule. One is that the personnel of such a firm must take both the examination given by the National Association of Securities Dealers and the more rigid one given by the New York Stock Exchange. Furthermore, the New York Stock Exchange continually examines and regulates its member firms. As Chart 14–2 indicates, the solvency record of these member firms is outstanding. These are a few of the reasons why a New York Stock Exchange member firm is suggested as a leading candidate, when an individual is searching for a reliable and capable broker.

It would be a disservice to hundreds of other brokers, however, if the choice was limited *only* to member firms. There are many brokerage firms which have excellent reputations and offer excellent service and advice, which are not members of the New York Stock

Chart 14–2
SOLVENCY RECORD

This table compares the solvency record of New York Stock Exchange member organizations with that of all banks in the United States, with national banks, and with commercial companies. The figures represent the proportion of the total number which remained solvent during each year.

Year	NYSE Member Organizations	All U.S. Banks	National Banks	Commercial Companies	Year	NYSE Member Organizations	All U.S. Banks	National Banks	Commercial Companies
1900	98.46%	99.43%	99.87%	99.08%	1930	99.25%	94.33%	97.78%	98.79%
1901	99.43	99.35	99.78	99.10	1931	98.77	89.53	93.99	98.67
1902	99.44	99.49	99.91	99.07	1932	99.68	92.36	95.51	98.47
1903	99.07	99.12	99.74	99.06	1933	99.84	85.10	84.35	98.99
1904	99.45	99.33	99.59	99.08	1934	99.84	99.64	99.98	99.39
1905	99.46	99.52	99.65	99.15	1935	100.00	99.79	99.93	99.38
1906	99.64	99.68	99.90	99.23	1936	100.00	99.72	99.98	99.52
1907	98.58	99.33	99.81	99.17	1937	100.00	99.62	99.92	99.54
1908	98.77	99.16	99.72	98.92	1938	99.85	99.64	99.98	99.39
1909	99.48	99.64	99.88	99.13	1939	100.00	99.72	99.92	99.30
1910	98.97	99.48	99.92	99.16	1940	100.00	99.85	99.98	99.37
1911	99.31	99.56	99.93	99.12	1941	100.00	99.95	99.92	99.45
1912	99.48	99.69	99.92	99.01	1942	100.00	99.94	100.00	99.56
1913	99.83	99.54	99.83	99.01	1943	100.00	99.97	99.96	99.84
1914	98.43	99.21	99.80	98.90	1944	100.00	99.99	100.00	99.93
1915	99.83	99.51	99.74	98.68	1945	100.00	100.00	100.00	99.96
1916	100.00	99.82	99.89	99.00	1946	100.00	100.00	100.00	99.95
1917	99.47	99.85	99.93	99.20	1947	100.00	99.99	100.00	99.86
1918	98.94	99.93	99.97	99.42	1948	100.00	100.00	100.00	99.79
1919	99.47	99.83	99.97	99.62	1949	100.00	99.97	100.00	99.65
1920	99.11	99.61	99.91	99.51	1950	100.00	99.99	100.00	99.66
1921	98.57	98.35	99.36	98.98	1951	100.00	99.98	100.00	99.69
1922	98.39	98.78	99.41	98.81	1952	100.00	99.98	100.00	99.71
1923	99.28	97.83	98.91	99.06	1953	100.00	99.97	100.00	99.67
1924	99.64	97.33	98.49	98.99	1954	100.00	99.98	100.00	99.58
1925	99.82	97.83	98.54	99.00	1955	100.00	99.97	99.96	99.58
1926	100.00	96.50	98.46	98.99	1956	100.00	99.98	99.98	99.52
1927	99.83	97.50	98.83	98.93	1957	100.00	99.98	99.98	99.48
1928	99.83	98.08	99.26	98.92	1958	100.00	99.94	99.98	99.44
1929	99.67	97.38	99.15	98.96	1959	100.00	99.98	100.00	99.48
					1960	99.85	99.99	100.00	99.43
					1961	100.00	99.94	99.96	99.35

The percentage of solvency for all United States banks and national banks was derived, for the period 1900 through 1920, from information obtained from the Comptroller of the Currency and, since 1921, from The Federal Reserve Board. The data for commercial companies was obtained from Dun & Bradstreet.

Source: "New York Stock Exchange Fact Book, 1962," New York Stock Exchange, 1962, p. 37.

Exchange. An individual might do as well with one of these. In such cases, more reliance must be placed on the reputation of the broker with your friends and in the community. Selecting a broker is something like selecting a jeweler when buying a diamond, or selecting a furrier when buying a fur coat. Reputation, trustworthiness, and service, are extremely important considerations. Sharp operators, offering fantastic bargains, must be avoided.

It is easy to open an account with a broker. He will ask you to complete a form similar to the form used by a department store when you wish to establish an account. Once this account is opened, you will not even have to visit your broker's office to transact business. Most transactions can be made by telephone, and the cash and securities transferred by mail. It is unwise, however, *never* to visit your broker. If you plan to entrust him with your investments, especially if they run into thousands of dollars, it would seem both natural and advisable to visit him occasionally, and afford him an opportunity to discuss your account with you.

There are many different instructions which you might give your broker. You might ask him to buy or sell a certain number of securities *at the market*. This means that you would like him to buy or sell these shares at the present market price, regardless of what it may be. You might ask him to buy or sell a certain number of shares at some specific price. Under these circumstances, he would not make the transaction until your specified price could be obtained. A stock broker will supply you with complete information concerning the many variations in orders which you may place with him.

Stock Exchanges

If you call your broker and ask him to buy you 100 shares of American Telephone at the market, the price you pay will be determined by the "double-auction" system. AT&T is listed on the New York Stock Exchange. There are many exchanges. In the United States, the largest is the New York Stock Exchange, which does about 85% of the dollar volume of all stock exchanges in this country. The next largest is the American Stock Exchange, also located in New York City, which does about as much business as all of the other exchanges in the United States combined.

Due to the importance of the New York Stock Exchange, and the fact that transactions on all exchanges are somewhat similar, let us use the New York Stock Exchange as an example. This exchange is a voluntary association of about 1,366 members who have bought mem-

Chart 14-3
MEMBERSHIP PRICES

Year	High	Low	Year	High	Low
1875..........	$ 6,750	$ 4,250	1918..........	$60,000	$45,000
1876..........	5,600	4,000	1919..........	110,000	60,000
1877..........	5,750	4,500	1920..........	115,000	85,000
1878..........	9,500	4,000	1921..........	100,000	77,500
1879..........	16,000	5,100	1922..........	100,000	86,000
1880..........	26,000	14,000	1923..........	100,000	76,000
1881..........	30,000	22,000	1924..........	101,000	76,000
1882..........	32,500	20,000	1925..........	150,000	99,000
1883..........	30,000	23,000	1926..........	175,000	133,000
1884..........	27,000	20,000	1927..........	305,000	170,000
1885..........	34,000	20,000	1928..........	595,000	290,000
1886..........	33,000	23,000	1929*........	625,000	550,000
1887..........	30,000	19,000	1929†........	495,000	350,000
1888..........	24,000	17,000	1930..........	480,000	205,000
1889..........	23,000	19,000	1931..........	322,000	125,000
1890..........	22,500	17,000	1932..........	185,000	68,000
1891..........	24,000	16,000	1933..........	250,000	90,000
1892..........	22,000	17,000	1934..........	190,000	70,000
1893..........	20,000	15,250	1935..........	140,000	65,000
1894..........	21,250	18,000	1936..........	174,000	89,000
1895..........	20,000	17,000	1937..........	134,000	61,000
1896..........	20,000	14,000	1938..........	85,000	51,000
1897..........	22,000	15,500	1939..........	70,000	51,000
1898..........	29,750	19,000	1940..........	60,000	33,000
1899..........	40,000	29,500	1941..........	35,000	19,000
1900..........	47,500	37,500	1942..........	30,000	17,000
1901..........	80,000	48,500	1943..........	48,000	27,000
1902..........	81,000	65,000	1944..........	75,000	40,000
1903..........	82,000	51,000	1945..........	95,000	49,000
1904..........	81,000	57,000	1946..........	97,000	61,000
1905..........	85,000	72,000	1947..........	70,000	50,000
1906..........	95,000	78,000	1948..........	68,000	46,000
1907..........	88,000	51,000	1949..........	49,000	35,000
1908..........	80,000	51,000	1950..........	54,000	46,000
1909..........	94,000	73,000	1951..........	68,000	52,000
1910..........	94,000	65,000	1952..........	55,000	39,000
1911..........	73,000	65,000	1953..........	60,000	38,000
1912..........	74,000	55,000	1954..........	88,000	45,000
1913..........	53,000	37,000	1955..........	90,000	80,000
1914..........	55,000	34,000	1956..........	113,000	75,000
1915..........	74,000	38,000	1957..........	89,000	65,000
1916..........	76,000	60,000	1958..........	127,000	69,000
1917..........	77,000	45,000	1959..........	157,000	110,000
			1960..........	162,000	135,000
* To February 18, 1929.			1961	225,000	147,000
† Ex-Rights.					

Source: "New York Stock Exchange Fact Book, 1962," New York Stock
Exchange, p. 36.

berships (called "seats") on the exchange. As Chart 14–3 indicates, these "seats" are pretty expensive. Most of these members represent brokerage firms, and their primary business is carrying out orders to buy and sell securities. They receive commissions for executing these orders.

More than 1,100 companies have their stock listed on the New York Stock Exchange. Before a company can be listed, it must meet certain rigid requirements and pay certain fees. These requirements are in addition to those which the SEC demands of companies whose stock is to be listed on an exchange, and their purpose is to make certain that these companies meet certain standards of sales, profits, stock distribution, etc.

The stocks of these companies are bought and sold at certain specific positions on the floor of the exchange, called "posts." One of these "posts" is shown in the picture on page 374. American Telephone is traded at one of these. Brokers wishing to buy or sell American Telephone stock for their customers would go to the "post" at which it is located. The buyers and sellers would gather at this post and make "bids" and "offers." It is important to note that there may be many buyers *and* many sellers. This is called a "double-auction." At the usual "country" auction there is one seller, the auctioneer, and many buyers, but on the stock exchange there are many of both. Under this system, when the highest "bid" and the lowest "offer" are equal, a trade takes place. This means that a broker wishing to buy has made a "bid" which equals the amount asked by a broker willing to sell. These "bids" and "offers" must be made in a loud audible voice. No secret transactions are permitted.

Trading on the New York Stock Exchange is in "round lots," units of 100 shares, except for a very few slow moving stocks. "Odd-lots," any number of shares from 1 through 99, are bought and sold through "odd-lot" firms. If you wanted to buy 45 shares of American Telephone, or 145, or 245, 45 shares would be purchased through an "odd-lot" house. Two firms, Carlisle & Jacquelin and DeCoppet & Doremus, do about 99% of all of the "odd-lot" business. When you buy an "odd-lot," your broker will purchase your shares from one of these two firms. Each of these firms maintains inventories of all of the stocks listed on the exchange, and perform many extremely valuable services for brokers. These two firms do not do business with the public. Each of them has representatives located at each post on the exchange. They are there not only to buy and sell round lots for their firm, so that their firm will have an inventory which is neither too large nor too small, but also to determine the price at

Source: New York Stock Exchange.

which your "odd-lot" will be bought or sold. The price of your AT&T stock, even if you only buy or sell a few shares as an "odd-lot," will be determined by a "round-lot" sale on the exchange. There is a fee for "odd-lots" of ⅛ (12½¢) per share for stock selling under $40 per share, and ¼ (25¢) per share for stock selling over $40.

One very important fact, which many people do not realize, is that a stock exchange does not buy, sell, or in any way determine the price of stock. An exchange only performs services, such as providing a "room" in which to trade, operating a "ticker" system throughout the country, etc. So don't blame the stock exchange if your stock goes down.

Over-the-Counter Market

The largest market for securities in the world is the over-the-counter market. The securities of thousands of companies, many times the number traded on exchanges, are traded in this market. This is a negotiated market, not an auction market. Here, business is done by negotiation among security dealers, by telephone rather than on the floor of an exchange. If you ask your broker to buy stock in any of these companies, he will make several telephone calls to other brokers and to dealers who trade only in these over-the-counter issues, and will try to find the broker or dealer offering this stock at the lowest price. Your broker will buy the stock from this firm and sell it to you, adding a commission for his services.

Many people believe that securities sold on the over-the-counter market are speculative, as compared to those sold on exchanges. This is not true. There are many excellent companies traded in the over-the-counter market. Here is the place where most bank and insurance company stocks, U.S. Government bonds, municipal bonds, and the stocks and bonds of many other large reputable companies are traded. True, there are many very speculative securities sold on this market, but not all of the securities listed on stock exchanges are "gilt-edge" investments either.

The reason for the somewhat skeptical opinion of the over-the-counter market held by many, is that the exchanges do have listing requirements. A corporation must meet these requirements in order to be listed. Furthermore, as stated earlier in this chapter, the Securities & Exchange Commission has certain requirements which a corporation must meet before its stock can be listed on an organized exchange. For these reasons, it is obviously much simpler for a corporation to have its stock sold on the over-the-counter market than it is to be listed on an exchange. New companies naturally find that their market is over-the-counter. While over-the-counter securities definitely should not be ruled out by the investor, they should be carefully investigated prior to purchase. This is a good rule to follow at all times. Everyone should investigate before he invests, regardless of the type of investment or where it is made.

Commissions

How much does it cost you to buy or sell stock? Again, the organized exchanges and the over-the-counter market must be separated. Commissions are determined somewhat differently on each.

Using the New York Stock Exchange as the example of an organized exchange, the commission rates presented in Chart 14–4 would apply. It might appear that it is cheaper to buy an odd-lot than a round lot, if you refer to these tables, but remember, there is also an odd-lot fee which must be added to the commission when less than 100 shares are purchased.

Actually these rates are quite reasonable. If you were planning to invest $10,000 in a particular stock selling at $100 per share, you

Chart 14–4

MINIMUM COMMISSION CHARGES ON STOCKS
Effective March 30, 1959

For stock transactions on the New York Stock Exchange involving $100 or more, the minimum commission charge ranges between $6 and $75 per transaction, provided the number of shares involved in the transaction does not exceed 100. Also, within these limits, the minimum charge shall not exceed $1.50 per share. (If the money involved is less than $100, the commission is as mutually agreed upon between the customer and broker.)

Commissions are basically calculated as a per cent of the money involved plus a stated dollar amount per transaction. A simplified method of computing commissions is as follows:

| | MINIMUM COMMISSION PER TRANSACTION | | |
| | | Plus Stated Amount: | |
Money Involved	Per Cent of Money Involved	For 100 Shares	For Less Than 100 Shares
$100 to $400	2%	$3*	$1*
$400 to $2,400	1%	7	5
$2,400 to $5,000	1/2%	19	17
Over $5,000	1/10%	39	37

* Minimum $6

The following examples show how these commission rates may be applied:

Examples

| | COMMISSION PER TRANSACTION OF: | |
Money Involved	100 Shares	Less Than 100 Shares†
$ 100	$6 (minimum)	$6 (minimum)
400	11 ($3+2%)	9 ($1+2%)
2,000	27 ($7+1%)	25 ($5+1%)
4,000	39 ($19+1/2%)	37 ($17+1/2%)
10,000	49 ($39+1/10%)	47 ($37+1/10%)
25,000	64 ($39+1/10%)	62 ($37+1/10%)
50,000	75 (top minimum)	75 (top minimum)

† Subject to the top minimum of $1.50 per share.

For transactions in excess of 100 shares, each 100 shares or fraction thereof is considered separately.

Source: "New York Stock Exchange Fact Book, 1962," New York Stock Exchange, 1962, p. 22.

would be buying exactly 100 shares. The commission on this transaction would be $49. This is .49% (point four nine), less than ½ of 1%. Do you know of anything else which you can purchase at such a low rate?

On the over-the-counter market, your broker buys the stock and then resells it to you at a markup. Usually, it won't be more than 5%, and some firms charge the same rate as on listed (stock exchange) stocks. Generally, it can be said that the more popularly traded securities on the over-the-counter market will cost less to trade, commission-wise, as they are easier for your broker to obtain, and less risky for a dealer to hold in inventory.

Commission charges should be watched, regardless of the market on which securities are traded. An unethical broker might try to overcharge, and even the most legitimate firm can make an honest error. Indeed, considering the volume of paper work, the number of transactions, and the amount of business handled verbally, it is amazing that there aren't more errors.

STOCKS AND BONDS

When you buy securities, you have many decisions to make. One is to decide whether to buy stocks or to buy bonds. Both are traded in the securities market. Both perform vital functions in our economy. But they are quite different. What are they?

Stocks

One method which a business may use to obtain long-term funds from investors is to issue stock. If you own a share of stock you own a share of a corporation. Each share of stock, like the one on page 378, represents part-ownership of a corporation. If there is a total of 100 shares outstanding of a particular corporation's stock, and you own 10, then you own 10% of that company. If there were 1,000 shares, and you owned 10, you would own 1%; 10,000 shares, and you owned 10, you would own .1%; 100,000 shares, and you own 10, you would own .01%, and so forth. Large corporations have millions of shares outstanding. In 1963, AT&T had 243,101,133 shares outstanding, owned by 2,210,000 stockholders.

Being an owner gives you certain advantages and disadvantages. You now have a voice in the management of the company, with the right to vote on particular issues. You vote, for example, in the election of directors. Another advantage is the fact that you share

Source: American Telephone and Telegraph Company, New York, N.Y.

378

in the profits of the company. If profits increase, you benefit—either directly through dividends or indirectly when the company reinvests these earnings in *your* business. You have the opportunity to share in the success of the corporation of which you are part-owner.

The opportunity to share in profit, however, brings with it the risk of sharing losses. Stock dividends are not paid at a fixed rate. If the company makes less profit, you may lose directly by receiving smaller dividends. If the company loses money, you won't get any dividends at all. Another disadvantage is that if the company goes broke, all of the assets may be claimed by the bondholders and other creditors, leaving nothing for you as one of the owners.

The usual type of stock, the kind discussed in the preceding paragraphs, is common stock. This type carries the right to vote and share in profits. Another type is preferred stock. Preferred usually has a claim against the assets of the firm prior to that of the common stock. Usually, its dividend must be paid before any dividend may be paid on common, but there is generally a limit on these dividends. The common stockholder can expect a larger dividend than the preferred would receive if the profits of the company greatly increase.

Bonds

Another method which a business may use to obtain long term funds is to sell bonds. Bonds, like the one on page 380, are similar to promissory notes. If you buy a bond, you are lending money to the company. The company promises to pay you back at a specified maturity date. It also promises to pay you some fixed rate of interest, such as 4% or 5% each year.

Actually, this is an oversimplified description of bonds. They are much more complicated than might be imagined, due to their variety. Maturity dates and interest rates vary. Some bonds, known as mortgage bonds, have specific property of the company pledged as security, while other bonds do not. In some cases, bond interest must be paid under any circumstance, or the company is in default. In other cases, interest must be paid only if the company earns a profit. A person buying a bond must carefully examine the nature of the particular bond being considered, before he decides to buy.

All bonds issued by corporations have one thing in common; they represent a debt of the issuing company. The bondholder is a creditor of the company, not an owner. Being a creditor gives the bondholder certain advantages and certain disadvantages.

N53104

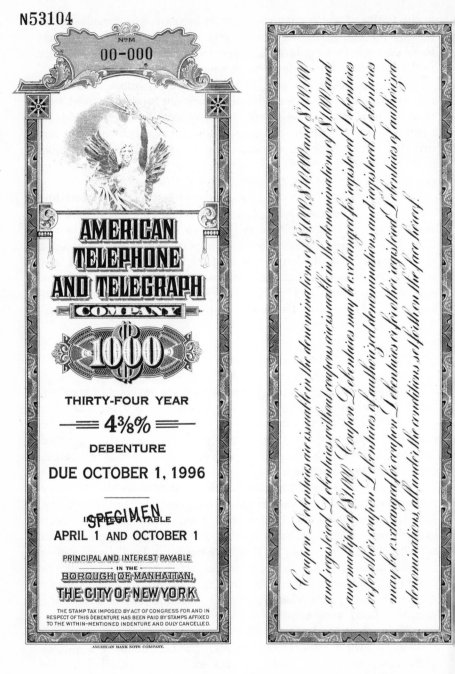

Source: American Telephone and Telegraph Company, New York, N.Y.

If the company goes broke, the bondholder's claim must be satisfied before the owners get a cent. Another advantage is that bond prices are more stable than stock prices, because bonds have a fixed rate of interest. This means that conservative investors, who are willing to take a somewhat smaller return on their money, buy bonds because of the prior claim against the assets of the company, the more stable price, and the fixed rate of return.

There are also disadvantages inherent in bonds. Suppose the company issuing the bond is successful beyond anyone's expectations. Profits are enormous. Under such a situation, you, as a bondholder, might feel quite disappointed that you are not sharing in this success. Great profits do not bring any increase in the bondholder's return; his return is a fixed rate of interest. Another disadvantage of being a bondholder is that you have no part in the management of the company, unless the company defaults. You do not have the right to vote.

Bonds are issued not only by industry but by states, cities and the federal government. Federal government bonds are naturally considered the highest grade investment possible. The reputation and integrity of the nation is behind them, as well as the taxing power of the federal government.

State and city bonds (municipals) pay the lowest rate of return, but are very popular investments. The reason? The federal government does not tax the income you receive from municipals. It does tax the interest you receive on bonds issued by corporations and by the U.S. Government itself. Many states do not levy taxes on the municipals issued in their own states. Under these circumstances, the income is exempt from both state and federal taxes.

Tax exempt bonds are especially attractive to persons in high income brackets. If you have an income of from $10,000 to $15,000 per year, and have some money to invest, municipal bonds are worthy of serious consideration. The higher your annual income, the more worthy these bonds are for consideration.

A little arithmetic will show how valuable this exemption can be to the heavily taxed executive. Let us take a $20,000-a-year New York City executive, who has perhaps $5,000 in deductions. On every additional dollar he earns, he must shell out 30% to Uncle Sam plus 7% (after federal tax credits) to New York State. Total tax bill on the extra dollars: 37%. Let us suppose this $20,000-a-year executive puts $5,000 in a savings bank at 3½%. Of the $175 in interest, Albany and Washington will take $65. Net after-tax return: $110, or 2.2%.

But suppose the same executive invests $5,000 in New York State Power Authority 3¾% bonds at around par. He will get $187.50 in annual interest, free and clear of all state and federal income taxes. To match this "take-home" return on his investment, the $20,000 executive would have to find a pretax yield of close to 7%. As the tax bracket mounts, so does the advantage of owning tax-exempt bonds. An executive earning a taxable income of $32,000 would have to find a pretax yield of close to 8% to come out as well as he would by investing in a tax free bond.[4]

Chart 14–5 illustrates the manner in which tax-exempts become more and more attractive as the person's tax bracket goes up.

Chart 14–5

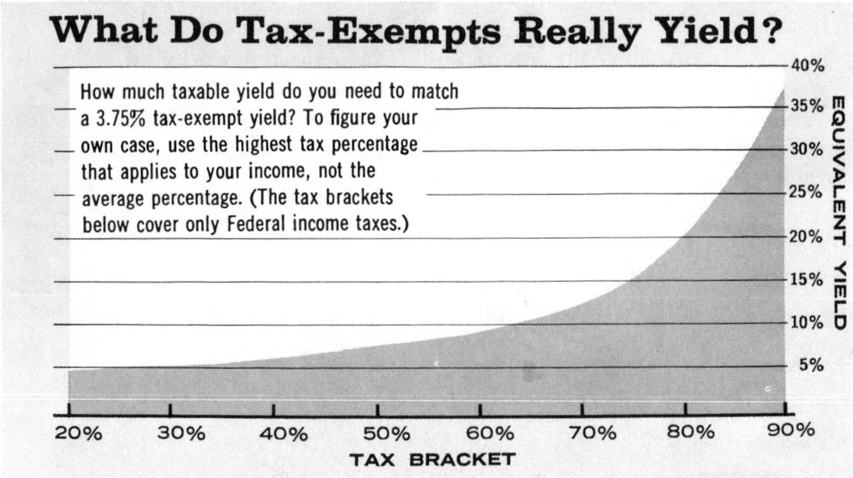

What Do Tax-Exempts Really Yield?

How much taxable yield do you need to match a 3.75% tax-exempt yield? To figure your own case, use the highest tax percentage that applies to your income, not the average percentage. (The tax brackets below cover only Federal income taxes.)

EQUIVALENT YIELD

40%
35%
30%
25%
20%
15%
10%
5%

TAX BRACKET: 20%   30%   40%   50%   60%   70%   80%   90%

Source: "Little Risk-and an 8% Return," *Dun's Review and Modern Industry*, New York, N.Y., August 1961, p. 28.

This might seem to be completely one-sided. It might seem that only wealthy investors are profiting by the laws which permit such securities to be tax-exempt. It must be realized, however, that if this exemption should be removed, it might very possibly cause an increase in the states' and municipalities' costs of borrowing. It is unlikely that investors would purchase these bonds at their present low rate of return, if the return was not tax-exempt. Remember that

---

[4] "Little Risk-and an 8% Return," *Dun's Review and Modern Industry*, New York, N.Y., August 1961, p. 28.

the state raises funds to pay interest charges on bonds it has issued by taxing its citizens. If the interest cost had to be raised, more money would have to be obtained from some source. That source might be you.

Usually, bonds of all kinds are issued in units of $1,000. By custom, the price is generally quoted as a percentage of the face value. If a bond is quoted at 105, it would sell at $1,050. If it is quoted at 98, it would sell at $980.

Additional Securities

Occasionally, a corporation will issue additional securities to raise funds, split the present stock, pay a stock dividend, etc.

In 1961, Mr. Jones received a letter from the American Telephone & Telegraph Co. Mr. Jones was a stockholder in AT&T. He opened the envelope, noted that it did not contain a check, and, because he was a busy man, decided that reading the enclosed literature was a waste of time. He dropped the envelope and its contents into the wastebasket, and in so doing, unwittingly threw away valuable subscription rights to additional stock.

Many people do what Mr. Jones did, every year. Some do not even realize that such rights are worth money.

What are these rights? Chart 14–6 lists thirty-seven companies which offered subscription rights to their stockholders in 1961. According to this list, American Telephone gave its stockholders the right to buy some new stock it had decided to issue, to raise additional capital. According to the chart, AT&T offered its stockholders the right to buy one new share of stock, for $86, for every 20 shares they owned. If a stockholder owned 40 shares at that time, he would have been entitled to buy two new shares at $86 each, or $172. If a stockholder owned less than 20 shares, he could either buy additional rights or sell those he had to someone else.

Notice that the list also indicates that companies sometimes give their stockholders rights to buy bonds, and rights to buy stock in other companies. Thus, in 1961, Canada Dry offered its stockholders the right to buy a new debenture bond if the stockholder owned 33 shares of Canada Dry; and Pacific Tel. & Tel. Co. gave its stockholders the opportunity to purchase shares in Pacific Northwest Bell Tel. Co.

Why are rights worth money? Take the case of AT&T's stock issue again. Why would you, as a stockholder owning 20 shares of AT&T, have been willing to pay $86 for a new share? Obviously

Chart 14–6

RIGHTS OFFERINGS IN 1961

The stockholders of 37 listed companies received last year the right to subscribe to new or additional securities—debentures and common stocks.

In 16 instances, common shares of the company were offered. Sixteen companies offered debentures, and in the remaining 5 cases the offering was in the stock of another company.

16 Common Stock Offerings

Company	Common Shares Needed to Get 1 New Share	Record Date	Subscription Price	Shares Offered
American Tel. & Tel. Co.	20	2/23	$ 86.00	11,176,457
Beckman Instruments, Inc.	20	3/28	114.00	69,933
Certain-teed Products Corp.	15	7/19	34.00	127,632
Consolidated Cigar Corp.	8	5/8	39.00	173,263
Eurofund, Inc.	2	6/20	16.00	551,250
General Public Service Corp.	2	9/12	6.25	3,947,795
Interstate Power Co.	16	5/18	22.00	202,333
Lone Star Gas Co.	10	1/5	40.00	655,733
Northern Natural Gas Co.	20	10/17	35.00	428,981
Pacific Gas & Electric Co.	20	6/13	71.00	896,470
Pittsburgh Steel Co.	1⅓	10/26	9.25	1,189,947
Puget Sound Power & Light Co.	10	2/15	33.75	326,682
Rochester Telephone Corp.	5	3/24	24.25	273,437
Telautograph Corp.	3	2/9	8.75	187,595
Varian Associates	10	6/1	50.00	347,883
Western Union Telegraph Co.	6	9/8	40.00	1,069,451

16 Debenture Offerings

Company	Common Shares Needed to Get $100 Debs. at Par	Record Date	Amount Offered
Allied Stores Corp.	10	9/22	$ 27,006,200
American Distilling Co.	10	10/17	9,551,900
American Machine & Foundry Co.	20	2/28	39,911,100
Armour & Co.	16	8/24	32,648,300
Automatic Canteen Co. of America	32	6/30	20,686,500
Brunswick Corporation	65	1/11	25,634,400
Canada Dry Corp.	33	7/11	7,138,400
Chock Full O'Nuts Corp.	50	7/21	6,938,900
Continental Baking Co.	15	11/16	13,113,200
Crowell-Collier Publishing Co.	25	4/24	11,787,700
Hunt Foods & Industries, Inc.	12	6/28	38,799,500
International Silver Co.	15	6/30	7,822,000
Interstate Department Stores, Inc.	20	8/1	5,859,400
National Airlines, Inc.	18	4/28	10,288,000
Trans World Airlines, Inc. #	6	5/25	111,235,900
United States Freight Co.	7	4/20	15,393,900

and an attached Warrant to purchase common stock.

5 Offerings of Stock in Another Company

Offered by:	Stock in:
Columbia Pictures Corp.	Screen Gems, Inc.
Crescent Petroleum Corp.	Eastern Air Devices, Inc.
Emerson Radio & Phonograph Corp.	Emertron, Inc.
Pacific Tel. & Tel. Co.	Pacific Northwest Bell Tel. Co.
Telautograph Corporation	Hogan Faximile Corp.

Source: "New York Stock Exchange Book, 1962," New York Stock Exchange, 1962, p. 12.

because the market price of AT&T was more than $86. If the market price was, for example, $100, it would be to your advantage to exercise your rights and buy an additional share. But let's assume you were unable, or unwilling, to exercise these rights.

A share of AT&T for $86, when the market price exceeds $86, would be just as good a buy for someone else as it would be for you. Someone else might like to buy some of these new shares for $86, but not have the rights. In that case, your rights would have a sales value.

Rights are bought and sold separately from the stock. They are sent by the company to its present stockholders in the form of subscription warrants, which are quite impressive looking and somewhat resemble stock certificates. Once these warrants have been mailed out, the stock of the corporation is sold "ex-rights." People buying the stock understand that they are not buying any rights when they buy the stock. The rights themselves are now bought and sold separately. For a short period before these warrants are mailed out, the old stock is sold with "rights on," and may command a slightly higher market price as purchasers know they will get the rights with the stock.

How much are rights worth? There are several formulas available for calculating their theoretical value, but they are not too helpful, as rights sell at, above and below this theoretical figure. They also fluctuate. The actual price at any given time is determined by the same forces of supply and demand as determine the price of the stock.

Rights are issued for a specified period of time, and lose all value when they expire. This period of time, during which the stockholder may exercise his rights, or sell them, is generally limited to a few weeks. The point is, that whatever the value of rights may be, *don't throw them in the wastebasket*. Call your broker and find out whether or not they have any value, and how much.

Stock splits and stock dividends are different from a new stock issue; these new shares don't cost you anything.

An example of a stock split is given in the letter presented on page 386, sent by the Transcontinental Gas Pipe Line Corporation to its stockholders on November 26, 1962. Notice that the purpose of the Board of Directors was to improve the marketability of the common stock of the company. This is a quite usual reason. The Transcontinental issue was especially attractive because the Directors, in this letter, also stated their intention to continue to pay the same amount of dividends on the new shares as the company had been paying on the old shares.

TRANSCONTINENTAL GAS PIPE LINE CORPORATION
3100 Travis Street
P. O. Box 296
Houston 1, Texas

November 26,1962

TO THE HOLDERS OF THE COMMON STOCK:

The Board of Directors of your Company has today taken the following action:

(a) Declared a quarterly dividend on Common Stock, in the amount of 25¢ per share, payable February 1, 1963, to stockholders of record at the close of business on January 15, 1963; and

(b) Determined to issue and distribute, on March 1, 1963, to the holders of the Common Stock of the Company of record at the close of business on January 15, 1963, one share of additional Common Stock for each five shares of Common Stock of the Company owned by stockholders of record as of the close of business on January 15, 1963 (cash to be paid in lieu of the issuance of fractional shares).

The Board of Directors of your Company has expressed its present intention to continue to pay dividends at the annual rate of $1.00 per share upon all shares of Common Stock, including those to be outstanding after the distribution. The new rate, since it will not be applicable to the first quarterly dividend of 1963, will, if continued, be equivalent for the year 1963 to $1.15 per share, and to $1.20 per share thereafter, on the shares as presently outstanding. The payment of future dividends will necessarily depend upon the Company's earnings and financial condition and requirements.

The primary purpose of the Board of Directors in deciding to distribute one new share of Common Stock for each five shares outstanding was to improve the marketability of the Common Stock of the Company by increasing the number of outstanding shares and thereby obtaining wider distribution of the outstanding stock.

This announcement of the action of the Board of Directors is sent to you for your information. It is not necessary for you to take any action in order to receive the additional shares of Common Stock and the cash dividend referred to in this letter.

As you undoubtedly are aware, some portion of all cash dividends paid on the Common Stock of the Company from 1957 through 1961 has been excludable from stockholders' dividend income for federal income tax purposes. Through previous letters and reports, stockholders have been advised each year of the percentages so excludable in time to utilize such data in preparing their income tax returns. Pending discussions relating to recent changes in the tax law, it is not possible to determine at this time if any of the cash dividends paid on the Common Stock of the Company for the year 1962 will be so excludable. An exact determination of the excludable amount, if any, cannot be made until the Company's books are closed for 1962 and its 1962 federal income tax return is prepared. It is expected that this will be accomplished in the latter part of February, 1963 at which time stockholders will be notified.

Sincerely yours,

President

Please do not send in your stock certificate(s), as certificate(s) for the additional shares of common stock to which you may be entitled will be mailed to you on March 1, 1963.

Courtesy of Transcontinental Gas Pipe Line Corporation.

Occasionally a company will find itself in a rather awkward position. It has made an excellent net profit, but has very little cash. Now is a good time to emphasize the fact that the two things are different. This will be explained more fully in the discussion of the income statement and balance sheet, in the next chapter. With such large net profits, stockholders will expect dividends, but the company does not have the necessary cash. In such cases, a company will often issue additional stock to its stockholders as a dividend. Quite often, both a cash dividend and a stock dividend are issued at the same time. The company cannot afford to distribute as much of a cash dividend as it would like to, so it gives part cash and part stock.

Insurance companies have followed this practice frequently in the past. While their stockholders' income from cash dividends may not have been very large, the market value of their shares of stock, and the number of shares owned, may have increased over the years so much that their investment proved quite rewarding. Table 14-1 indicates what happened to certain investments in life insurance companies over a period of years. Look at the first company on the list—Aetna Life Insurance Co. According to this table an investment in the stock of this company in 1953 would have increased 358 per cent by 1963. Some of the others on the list are even more spectacular.

Theoretically, of course, stock splits and stock dividends do not give a stockholder anything that he doesn't own without the split or dividend. A two for one split, or a 100 per cent stock dividend, merely subdivides the ownership more than before. His original share of stock represented ownership in the company. The company hasn't increased in value just because it issued more stock. After the split,

Table 14-1 [5]

Name of Company	1953 High Price per share	No. of Shares owned in 1963 per 1953 share	Price Per Share 1963[1]	Total Value	Percent Increase	Amount and year of last stock dividend
Aetna Life	94½	2.67	162	$ 433	358%	33⅓% - 1959
American National	112	33	16	$ 528	371%	10% - 1958
Bankers National	83	9.63	71	$ 684	724%	7½% - 1962
Business Men's Assurance	515	75	75	$5,625	992%	20% - 1962
California Western States	35½	5.84	48	$ 280	689%	10% - 1962
Commonwealth Life	69	12.5	59	$ 738	970%	25% - 1959
Connecticut General	219	9.96	167	$1,663	659%	100% - 1961
Continental Assurance	136	5.6	140	$ 784	476%	20% - 1963
Franklin Life	46	7.53	64	$ 482	948%	5% - 1963
Gulf Life	22	1.32	55	$ 73	232%	10% - 1962
Jefferson Standard	76	3.33	95	$ 316	316%	25% - 1957
Kansas City Life	655	1	3,050	$3,050	366%	300% - 1943
Liberty Life	118	18.75	32	$ 600	409%	25% - 1963
Liberty National	96⅞[b]	12.5	74	$ 925	855%	25% - 1963
Life Insurance of Virginia	68	2.53	126	$ 319	369%	4% - 1963
Lincoln National	193	5	162	$ 810	320%	25% - 1961
Massachusetts Indemnity and Life	a	26.7	55	$1,469	a	33⅓% - 1958
Massachusetts Protective	a	3	123	$ 369	a	50% - 1955
Monumental	52½	2	100	$ 200	281%	25% - 1961
National Life and Accident	61¾	3.6	98	$ 353	472%	20% - 1962
Provident Life and Accident	a	42.2	92	$ 388	a	50% - 1962
Southwestern Life	83	4.4	143	$ 629	658%	10% - 1962
Travelers	841	25	189	$4,725	462%	25% - 1955
United States Life	60	6.6	76	$ 502	737%	20% - 1961

[1] Price per share selected prior to publication in 1963 and not necessarily high or low for year.
a No public market, or practically no market, existed for this stock in 1953.
b 1954 high (1953 not available).

[5] Life Insurance Company Stocks, Eleventh Annual Edition, 1963, The First Boston Corp., New York, New York, pp. 10-11.

or dividend, he still owns the same percentage of the total issued stock as before. If there is a two for one stock split, or a 100 per cent stock dividend, he will own twice as many shares as before, but the company has twice as many shares outstanding.

In practice, however, stock dividends and splits have quite often been of very definite advantage to the stockholder. Stockholders expect higher earnings and dividends in the future. They expect that with more shares out, there will be a lower market price per share, and therefore more buyers. This would make the market price go up. If one share of stock with a market price of $100 becomes two shares, and the market price goes up to $60 on each, then the stockholder is ahead $20. It must be remembered though, that although this is what stockholders expect will happen, it doesn't always work out this way. The fact that you receive more shares of stock doesn't mean that the cash value of your investment is guaranteed to rise. It may not change, or, on the other hand, it may even decline.

SHOULD YOU INVEST?

Now that you know something about the importance of the investor in our economic system, something about the mechanics of the stock market, and something about the nature of stocks and bonds, wouldn't it be nice to triple your money in the market? You read about these things happening.

News stories like this are true, but misleading. They select one small group for special attention. Stories about those "losing their shirts" are less frequently seen. There are also people who win the sweepstakes, or make a fortune at Monte Carlo, but most people don't expect to be as lucky.

The first question everyone should ask is "Should *I* invest in the stock market?" Try to avoid an automatic "yes," as there are many who should not. Due to the waves of speculation which regularly seem to rise to new heights and threaten to completely eliminate sound judgment, it might be worthwhile to remember one sentence:

NOT EVERYBODY SHOULD BUY STOCKS AND BONDS

Before buying stocks and bonds a person should:
1. Be able to meet living expenses—food, clothes, shelter, etc.
2. Have enough savings for possible emergencies.
3. Have enough life insurance to protect his family.

Many would also consider home ownership as a prerequisite.

If a person has these things, then, and only then, should he consider buying stocks and bonds. In fact, at this point he would be making a mistake not to consider their investment possibilities.

Due to the rising standard of living in the United States, more and more people are able to invest in stocks and bonds. The nation's family of stockholders rose from an estimated six and a half million in 1952 to approximately 15 million in 1961.[6]

PLANNING YOUR PORTFOLIO

Your portfolio is your investment program. It refers to your holdings of securities. If you have decided that you are in a position to invest some money in stocks or bonds, just how much should you invest and what objective should you have?

How much money you can afford to put into securities is something only you can decide. Each person will have a different answer. There are certain criteria which are useful, however, in making this decision.

1. Income
    a. Size
    b. Sources
    c. Stability
    d. Permanence or expected duration
    e. Future expectations
2. Number of dependents, degree of dependency, and possibilities
3. Age and health of the investor and members of family
4. Insurance status
5. Tax bracket
6. Ownership of home
7. Retirement or pension plan
8. Accumulated wealth available for investment
9. Unusual expenses expected in the future
10. Temperament of the investor—his willingness to assume risk
11. Knowledge of and skill in handling investments
12. Time available for management of investments
13. Need for preservation of principal
14. Dependence upon investment income
15. Occupation, business, or profession of the investor.[7]

While this seems to be a rather complete list, it could be increased. Each item on the list could be further subdivided, and more

---

[6] G. Keith Funston, President of the New York Stock Exchange, *Sharing the American Dream*, remarks before the Trinity College Alumni Association of Western Connecticut, Cheshier, Connecticut, April 14, 1961, p. 7.

[7] Appearing in *The Stock Market*, Second Edition, by George L. Leffler. Copyright 1957, The Ronald Press Company, pp. 570–71.

could be added. The important point to note is that each individual's circumstances are different. A portfolio must be tailor-made. Only the investor can decide how much he can afford to invest.

Objectives

Why are you investing? Do you need more money for the future, or an income today? Are you worried about inflation? Just why are you investing? There are many possible objectives, but three are outstanding:
1. Growth of capital
2. Income today
3. Safety of principal

Growth of Capital

This is the objective in the minds of most young people. They can look forward to years of productive work and can afford to take some risk. "Young," however, is a relative term. If you do not need the income from your investments and are willing to take some risks, you are young enough to invest in growth. This is why wealthy investors are interested in growth. They can afford to assume some risk to attain possible future growth of their invested capital.

If growth is your objective, your primary interest is that the dollar value of your investment will increase over the years. Income (dividends) from the investment is of secondary importance. There are probably more growth opportunities today than ever before in history. Common stock is the best type of security to buy if your objective is growth. It makes you part-owner of a company, and gives you an opportunity to share in its growing profits.

"A growth stock is by definition a stock in an industry that is growing faster than the average of all industries and in a company that is growing faster than other companies in its industry."[8] Stocks in companies such as this may increase many times in market value over a period of years. Remember though, there is no guarantee that a stock you or anyone else considers to be a growth stock will actually grow.

Income Today

Are you about ready to retire? Do you need an income from your investments to live on? There are many people who must make

---

[8] *How to Invest,* Merrill Lynch, Pierce, Fenner & Smith, June 1962, p. 8.

investments which will give them current income. Such investments are most attractive about the time a person's children go to college.

If immediate income is the objective, growth must be de-emphasized. Growing companies retain their earnings for reinvestment in their business, and usually pay little or nothing in dividends. Your primary consideration is to buy stock which pays good dividends.

Yield is calculated by dividing the annual dividend paid by the corporation by the market price you pay for the stock. If you buy a share of stock for $100, and the annual dividend is $5, then the yield on your investment is 5 per cent. If the dividend stays the same, the yield on your investment stays the same, even though the market price of the stock should change. You invested $100, and as long as the dividend is $5, your yield is 5 per cent. However, if the corporation increases its dividend to $6 per year, the yield on your investment will rise to 6 per cent; if it reduces the dividend to $4, the yield drops to 4 per cent.

Remember that *immediate* income is concerned here. An investment in a growth stock will return less *immediate* yield on your investment, but, because the company is reinvesting its (your) profits and increasing its productive capacity, it may very possibly return a greater yield in the future, on today's investment.

Chart 14–7

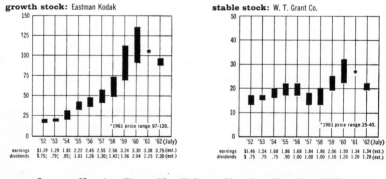

growth stock: Eastman Kodak

*1961 price range 97-120.

'52 '53 '54 '55 '56 '57 '58 '59 '60 '61 '62(July)

| earnings | $1.19 1.29 1.81 2.22 2.45 2.55 2.56 3.24 3.30 3.38 3.75 (est.) |
| dividends | $.75½ .79½ .95½ 1.01 1.26 1.30½ 1.42½ 1.56 2.04 2.25 2.30 (est.) |

stable stock: W. T. Grant Co.

*1961 price range 25-40.

'52 '53 '54 '55 '56 '57 '58 '59 '60 '61 '62(July)

| earnings | $1.46 1.54 1.68 1.86 1.68 1.84 1.86 2.06 1.50 1.34 1.34 (est.) |
| dividends | $ .75 .75 .75 .90 1.00 1.00 1.00 1.10 1.20 1.20 1.20 (est.) |

Source: *Changing Times, The Kiplinger Magazine,* November 1962, p. 15.

Chart 14–7 illustrates the potentially greater yield of a good growth stock. In this case the growth stock, Eastman Kodak, sold at about $20 in 1952, and paid a dividend of $.75½—a yield on your $20 investment of about 3¾ per cent. Your immediate yield would have been greater if you had invested in the stable stock, W. T.

Grant Co. Grant stock sold at about $15 in 1952, and paid $.75—a return of 5 per cent on your $15 investment. $10,000 invested in Eastman Kodak would have returned a little more than $375, while the same amount invested in W. T. Grant Co. would have returned $500.

However, by 1962, the market price of Eastman Kodak had increased to about 4 times its 1952 price, while the market price of W. T. Grant Co. had increased by only one-third. Eastman Kodak was now paying about $2.30 per share as compared to $1.20 by W. T. Grant Co. Your original $20 investment in Eastman Kodak now had a yield of 11½ per cent ($2.30 divided by $20), while W. T. Grant Co. had a yield of only about 8 per cent ($1.20 divided by $15). Your $10,000 in Eastman Kodak would have returned about $1,150, while your $10,000 in W. T. Grant Co. would have returned about $800.

The important point here is that immediate yield should be of primary importance in selecting an investment *only* if you really need the income right now. Otherwise, your long term income might be larger from a good growth stock which is paying out less in dividends today.

Safety of Principal

Are you establishing your investment portfolio with some particular purpose in mind? Are you planning to use these funds to send your children to college or to meet some other specific need? If this is your objective, then you are primarily interested in safety of principal.

The best investment for this purpose is bonds. A $1,000 bond will return $1,000 to you when it matures. If you invest $10,000 in high grade bonds, you are as certain as you can be that your principal —your $10,000—is safe.

You should consider very carefully, however, whether or not you really are interested in safety of principal. "Safety" is not as obvious a term as it might seem. If you have $10,000 to invest, are you primarily interested in making certain that twenty years from now you will still have at least $10,000 in cash, or is $10,000 in purchasing power what you really want? Chart 14-8 illustrates this point. It shows what has happened to bond and stock prices since 1914, adjusted for changes in the purchasing power of the dollar. If you had invested $10,000 in bonds in 1914, and they matured in 1962, they would still pay you $10,000. If, however, you consider that $10,000 would buy a lot more in 1914 than in 1962, you would find that this

Chart 14–8

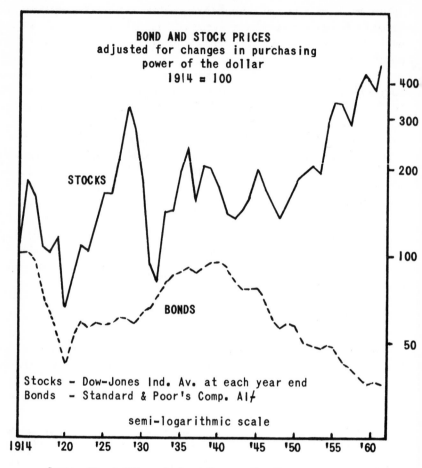

BOND AND STOCK PRICES
adjusted for changes in purchasing
power of the dollar
1914 = 100

STOCKS

BONDS

Stocks – Dow-Jones Ind. Av. at each year end
Bonds – Standard & Poor's Comp. Al

semi-logarithmic scale

1914   '20   '25   '30   '35   '40   '45   '50   '55   '60

Source: "Brevits," Vance, Sanders & Company, Inc., Boston, Mass., Vol.
S–No. 3, Feb. 5, 1962, p. 1.

sum in 1962 would only buy as much as $3,598 would have purchased
in 1914. Stocks went up so much in price during this period that
you would have been better off investing in good stocks. If you had
invested your $10,000 in stocks that performed exactly as well as the
Dow-Jones Industrial Average (discussed in the next chapter), in
1962 your $10,000 would have been worth more than four times its
1914 value, even when the decline in the purchasing power of the
dollar is considered. While the bonds would only buy as much as
$3,598 would have purchased in 1914, the stocks would buy as much
as $44,996 would have purchased then.

Let's suppose that you have $10,000 and a brand new baby. You would like to put this money away to pay your child's college bills when he or she is 18. $10,000, you find, will be enough to pay these costs today, but will it be enough to pay these costs 18 years from today? If tuitions and other costs keep rising, it may be only half enough. Your $10,000, when you think of it in terms of paying future college costs, may be worth only $5,000.

Now this is not to imply that bonds should be overlooked. During deflationary periods—recessions, depressions—bonds do not suffer anywhere near as much as do stocks, in terms of market value. Bonds are good for their relative stability and as protection against the effects of deflation. The important point is that you should not become so enthused with the idea that a particular sum of money is a "lot" of money that you forget the possible effects of inflation. A "big" sum of money today may be a "small" sum tomorrow. "Safety" should be thought of in terms of purchasing power as well as in terms of principal.

Do you expect prices to decline? If you do, then bonds will give you both safety of principal *and* safety in terms of purchasing power. If you expect prices to rise, then you should consider common stocks as a hedge against inflation. In recent years, common stock prices have had a tendency to increase at the same time prices have increased. Common stocks are certainly helpful in counteracting the effect of rising prices, but they are not foolproof. It is certain, however, that bonds cannot possibly be considered as an offset to higher living costs, as bonds have a definite maturity value and will not return more than this amount.

INVESTMENT PRINCIPLES

There are certain guiding principles which should be considered by everyone. One might argue, in fact, as to whether they are principles, philosophies or rules. Three of these are universally considered to be of fundamental importance to the investor.

Investment vs. Speculation

Someone once said that there are two times in a man's life when he should not speculate—when he cannot afford to, and when he can. No one would recommend that a person base his personal financial plan on speculation. Just what is the difference between an investment and a speculation?

"An investment operation is one which, upon thorough analysis, promises safety of principal and a satisfactory return. Operations not meeting these requirements are speculative."[9] This is an extremely conservative definition of investment and speculation. A more common practice is to say that you are investing when you have a specific objective, such as growth, income, or safety, but that you are speculating if your only objective is to make a large quick profit.

Diversification

Putting all of your eggs into one basket has been considered a dangerous practice since the invention of hen houses. It is just as dangerous in the stock market as it is in chicken farming.

How much you need to diversify depends on how much you have to invest. If you have only two eggs to carry back from the hen house, it is rather silly to have two baskets. It is equally true that if you plan to invest only $500, you should not try to split this among ten different securties in order to diversify. With such a small amount of money, you may diversify over the years by investing your present $500 in one security and your next $500 in another. You may also achieve diversification with your present $500 by placing it in the hands of a mutual fund for investment, by buying shares in an investment trust, etc.

If you have a lot of money, you should diversify. The larger the amount, the more your investments may be spread among a number of securities.

There are several methods of diversifying investments. One method is by type of security. A large sum of money should not be in common stocks alone. It should be divided between stocks, bonds and preferred stock. If all of the money is invested in stocks, the value of the portfolio will rise and fall with the market. There will be no stability. If all of the money is in bonds, there is a limit to the income which it may produce, and there is no opportunity to share in the growth of a company. Most people would prefer to divide their investments so that some of the securities (stocks) would permit them to share in a growing economy, while others (bonds) would give them a "cushion," a stable value which could be relied upon in case of adverse economic conditions.

---

[9] From *Security Analysis*, by Benjamin Graham and David L. Dodd, Third Edition. Copyright © 1951, McGraw-Hill Book Company, Inc., New York, N.Y., p. 38. Used by permission.

Consistency

On the average, the most successful investors are the consistent investors. They do not try to "beat" the market by buying when prices are low and selling when prices are high. These investors have a regular and consistent investment program.

Some years ago, the New York Stock Exchange originated a plan called the Monthly Investment Plan (MIP). You may participate in this plan through firms which are members of the exchange. The requirements are easy to meet. The first requirement is that you must be 21; the second is that you must state your intention to invest an amount of money ranging from $40 to $1,000 every month, or every three months. The form you sign to participate in this plan is not a contract, and you may stop whenever you like.

This is an excellent opportunity for a small investor. For a small amount of money an investor may buy shares in some company which he selects. Regular investing is a good habit to adopt, and at the same time you create a reason for taking an interest in a company and in the economy of the country. If you continue to invest regularly, and the company you select is successful, your investment will grow in value over the years. If you make a poor selection, you don't lose your entire life savings, and you can change your selection at any time. While no broker will be willing to make a selection for you,

Table 14-2

Payment	Amount Invested at Odd-Lot Prices	Commission* Amount	Commission* Percent
$ 40	$ 37.74	$ 2.26	6.0
75	70.75	4.25	6.0
100	94.34	5.66	6.0
200	194.00	6.00	3.1
300	293.14	6.86	2.3
500	490.10	9.90	2.0
1,000	985.15	14.85	1.5

*Commission may be less on high-priced stocks, but in all cases the 6% minimum below $100 and the $6 charge above $100 must be maintained.

Source: "Monthly Investment Plan," Merrill Lynch, Pierce, Fenner & Smith, Inc., New York, N.Y., p. 8.

all will be more than happy to provide you with a list of ten or more companies which they consider good investments.

Table 14-2 indicates the cost of this Monthly Investment Plan in terms of commission. As usual, the more you invest, the cheaper it gets. Actually, this is a costly plan for the brokerage firm to handle. Because you are investing a constant amount, let's say $40 per month, you will be buying fractions of shares. Thus if the stock you selected sells for $80 per share, you will buy only ½ a share per month. It is obvious that this creates a detailed bookkeeping problem for the brokerage firms.

Even a large investor will find it to his advantage to invest constant amounts of money at regular intervals, monthly, for example, rather than trying to accumulate a large sum of money to invest all at once.

CONCLUSION

The investor who has been most successful over the years, in the observation of the authors, is one who has followed closely these principles and courses of action:

1. He has had a definite plan and program and has adhered to it faithfully.
2. He has not tried to forecast stock prices nor allowed himself to be influenced by those who think they can do so.
3. He has understood the differences in the characteristics of companies and has invested only in those suited to his long-term objectives.
4. He has bought only those stocks which, at the time of purchase, he could see no reason for ever wanting to sell.
5. He has diversified his holdings among various industries, not by following any mechanical formula, but by analytical selection of those companies and fields of activity most likely to spearhead the long-range expansion of the American economy. That is, he has looked upon diversification not merely as a device for spreading risk but as a means of broadening opportunity for the progress of his investments. And he has avoided scattering his holdings among more companies than he could conscientiously follow.
6. Finally, and perhaps most important of all, he has faced uncertainties in the business or market outlook with equanimity, not allowing himself to be distracted from his prescribed course by ominous predictions or tempting speculations.[10]

---

[10] Thomas E. Babson and David L. Babson, *Investing for a Successful Future,* The Macmillan Company, New York, N.Y., 1959, pp. 257–258.

Here is an excellent set of principles—good sound advice. Some of them, a plan and program and diversification, have been discussed in this chapter. The next chapter will be concerned with methods of selecting a specific investment and of determining when to buy it. The following chapter will be concerned with a special method of investing in the market—mutual funds.

Questions

1. What are the risks involved in investment banking?

2. How does a broker differ from an investment banker?

3. What is a "bucket–shop"?

4. How do you select a good broker?

5. Both the New York Stock Exchange and the Over-the-Counter market are auction markets. Is this true? Why or why not?

6. Must a stock meet listing requirements to be sold in the Over-the-Counter Market?

7. What are the disadvantages to an investor who invests solely in bonds?

8. What are "Rights?"

9. How does a stock split differ from a stock dividend?

10. How can an individual "beat the market" and at the same time be a "consistent" investor?

Problems

1. "C" has $10,000 to invest. He can invest in growth stock "A," yielding 2% or an income stock "B," yielding 6%. He is married, with three children. His primary objective is to acquire sufficient capital to send his 3 children to college. Which investment would you advise? Why?

2. "K" has adopted the following investment plan. He saves $75 per month and deposits this money in a savings bank. After studying the market carefully, he selects a growth industry and then the best company (he thinks) within the industry. When his regular savings is large enough to purchase 100 shares, he withdraws the money from savings to pay for the stock. When asked why he invests in this manner, he replied, "If I bought stock every month, I'd have to buy odd-lots, at a higher commission than round-lots and I'd be paying broker's commissions each month. This way, I pay fewer commissions plus I earn interest on my savings." Do you think this is a good investment plan to follow?

3. "B" has been investing substantial sums of money regularly during the past year, with broker X. He is becoming concerned with the fact that X calls him twice a month, either urging him to sell part of his stock to capture a "paper profit" or to buy a stock which, X says, is selling at its low. After many such transactions "B" feels that he is no further ahead than if he continued his former plan, which was to buy with the intention of holding the stock, rather than buying and then selling. "B" asks your opinion as to which policy is better. What would you advise?

4. "D" earns $40,000 per year. He is in the 40% tax bracket (Federal) and pays 10% tax to the State. He can purchase Corporation "A's" 6% bonds, selling at par, or Corporation "B's" 4% bonds also selling at par. "B" is a Municipal Light Company. "D" has $10,000 to invest. Which bond should he choose? Why?

5. "J" has never exercised any "rights" when they were mailed to him. He tells you that every time the rights are mailed to him, he has no money available to invest, so he merely throws the rights away. Can you show "J" how these rights might prove valuable to him, even if he has no money available to invest?

Selected Readings

"ADR, American Depositary Receipts, BDR, Bearer Depositary Receipts," Morgan Guaranty Trust Company of New York, New York, N.Y.
Publications of the American Stock Exchange, 86 Trinity Place, New York 6, N.Y.

"Business Trends and Progress, a Graphic Picture of Our Economic Travels!,"
published annually by Educational Affairs Department, Ford Motor Co.,
Detroit, Michigan

"History of National Association of Securities Dealers, Inc., Its Activities,
Membership Data, Sanctions Imposed, Members Expelled, Financial
Statements, Liaison and Supervision by SEC from 1936 to November 30,
1958," prepared by National Association of Securities Dealers, Inc.,
Wallace H. Fulton, Executive Director, United States Government
Printing Office, Washington, D.C., 1959

Leffler, George L., Revised by Farwell, Loring, C., *The Stock Market*, The
Ronald Press Co., New York, N.Y., 3rd Edition, 1963

Publications of the New York Stock Exchange, Publications Division,
11 Wall Street, New York 5, N.Y.

"Odd-Lot Manual," Carlisle & Jacquelin, New York, N.Y.

Publications prepared by the various brokerage firms

Chapter **15**

STOCKS: WHAT TO BUY
AND WHEN

No one has ever discovered a foolproof method of stock selection. Those who claim they have, are attempting an obvious ruse. No one can *guarantee* that a particular stock will go either up or down. One bit of advice is simple and definite: If someone in person, in an advertisement, or on the telephone makes such a guarantee, don't buy the recommended security. The person making the statement knows his guarantee is illegal, and the only likely benefit from the transaction will be in his favor. It is obvious that you will be better off financially by not dealing with those who are obviously and knowingly making illegal statements.

There are, however, individuals who make a profession of analyzing stocks and bonds. There are others who carefully study various methods of selection and investment. For the most part, these are people involved in legitimate business, doing their best to perform a valuable service. They will not guarantee that any security will either go up or down, nor will they suggest that their methods will make you a millionaire. They will state that particular stocks and bonds are recommended as good buys — that, on the basis of careful study, they feel the companies they represent seem to have a promising future. They will suggest that some methods of investing have proven to be better than others. These consultants are worth listening to, but you should remember, of course, that some of them are more capable than others. It is still up to you to decide which advice you believe is the best.

Hundreds of books have been written on investment management. Many more have been written on security analysis. Methods of selection number in the dozens, and there are certainly an equal number of methods which might be used to determine how much to invest and when. Obviously, these cannot all be discussed in this chapter, but we will suggest a course of action that is believed to be best for the average person.

If advice is meant for the *average* person, then it is not meant for everyone. The person most nearly meeting the following characteristics are those for whom this chapter is written:

1. An individual who has the prerequisites — savings, life insurance, etc. — presented in the preceding chapter.
2. An individual in a moderate income bracket — one who considers himself to be neither poor nor wealthy.
3. An individual interested in increasing either capital or income or both.
4. An individual who neither is nor has the time or inclination to be an expert security analyst.
5. An individual who, without severe mental strain to himself, is able to invest in securities which might go either up or down.

You might be quite willing to admit that one or more of the first four characteristics prevent you from being *average*, as the word is used here. You might, for example, readily admit that you do not have enough savings or enough income. It is, unfortunately, not as easy to admit that you are not mentally suited for something. In investments, however, this issue must be squarely faced.

As soon as you purchase stock, are you going to start worrying about the price falling? If it does fall, are you going to be unable to eat or sleep properly? There are many people like this. The individual who answers "yes" to these questions shouldn't invest in the stock market. The market will quite definitely go down sometime. No market rises steadily forever, and some individuals will sell through fear when the price of their stock drops. These same people may also lose more in mental anguish than they can possibly gain in monetary profit. If you are this type of person, you should find some investment method better suited to your temperament. Money placed securely in a savings bank, more life insurance, or real estate purchases, may better suit your temperamental needs than stock with less stable tendencies.

WHAT TO BUY

Assuming, then, that you are a person meeting the five characteristics making you an *average* investor, what should you buy? The fact that you meet these characteristics means that likely you are not too interested in a discussion of bonds and preferred stock. Common stock merits the greatest emphasis.

Bonds

If you are interested in bonds, it is quite easy to get a list from which to select those available. Insurance companies and savings banks own high quality bonds. You can find out what they own from their annual reports, or from your broker. Probably the best known sources of information on bonds are Moody's and Standard & Poor's. Two of the oldest, most reputable, and best known financial advisory services, these agencies rate bonds according to quality. "If you confine your holdings to issues rated "A" or better by these services, you're bound to own a good list."[1]

From an investment point of view, bonds have definite advantages in that they are safe, they produce a steady income, they are easy to buy and sell. They also have very definite disadvantages in that they will not offset the effects of inflation on the purchasing power of the

[1] Ira U. Cobleigh, (ed.), *Guide to Success in the Stock Market,* published by Avon Book Division, The Hearst Corporation, Copyright 1961, New York Security Dealers Assoc., p. 30.

dollar, as they cannot grow either in principal value or in interest income. Many investors put their money in bonds when stocks are extremely high and a decline is feared. By doing so, they protect their capital and the profits which they made in the stock market.

Preferred Stocks

Preferred stocks are on a level between common stocks and bonds as an investment. They are not as safe as bonds, and do not offer the possible yield of common stocks. They are, however, safer than common stocks and offer more yield than bonds.

Words like "safer" and "more" are relative terms. A bond issued by a company which is financially unsound is not as "safe" an investment as a share of common stock in a company which is financially sound. The zero yield on common stock in a company operating at a loss is certainly less than the yield on a bond in a company meeting its interest commitments. In *general,* however, bonds are the safest investment, preferred stocks rank next, and common stocks last. In *general,* common stocks offer the possibility of the highest yield, preferred stock may grant the next highest yield, and bonds would be the least profitable.

It is necessary to be more careful in the selection of preferred stock than in the selection of bonds. The interest on bonds *must* be paid by the corporation, while preferred stock dividends depend upon whether or not the company makes a profit. Any preferred stock that you may select should always be issued by a financially sound, large, and well-established company.

Some preferred stocks have special features which occasionally offer the investor the opportunity for extra gain. Some companies, for example, have preferred stock with a cumulative dividend provision. This means that a certain percentage of dividends must be paid to preferred stock holders before common stock holders can receive anything; and each year the preferred dividend is not paid, it cumulates. If you can find such a preferred stock with several years of dividends cumulated, and if you are fortunate enough to purchase it just before these cumulated dividends are paid, you will have made a profitable investment. Not only will the back dividends be paid, but the price of the preferred stock — possibly depressed because of the failure of the company to pay dividends — will undoubtedly rise in value when the dividends are finally paid. All that must be done is to select such a stock. This means you must find a cumulative preferred stock with dividends in arrears. This is easy to do, but the next step is more difficult. You must buy one which will start paying its back dividends; and this must be done before everyone else makes the same discovery and forces the price of the stock up so high that the investment will not be profitable. In general, this type of investment requires more effort, time, and knowledge of security analysis than can be expected of the average person.

Common Stock

The average investor, interested in protecting his principal and earning a rate of return slightly greater than bonds would yield, should seriously consider life insurance. If the investor is willing to assume a greater risk, in the hope that his funds will accumulate more rapidly, he may invest in common stocks.

Common stocks are not a perfect hedge against inflation. They do, however, have a quality that permits them to adjust to a changing price level. On the average, in the United States since 1900, the prices of common stocks have paralleled changes in the price level. In other words, prices of common stocks have tended to rise during a period when the value of the dollar has declined. This has enabled astute investors in common stocks to increase their capital, in terms of dollars, to offset the decline in the value of each dollar. In ten years, a $1,000 bond will still be a $1,000 bond, but $1,000 invested in common stocks may return substantially more, or less, than the original investment. In common stock investment there is at least the hope of counteracting the effects of inflation.

Of course one thing must be decided. Do you expect continued inflation? Is it possible that government spending might decrease, that wages might decline, that our international obligations will be reduced? Economists believe that these things are unlikely — that inflation in the future is the most likely assumption.

Selecting a Common Stock

There has *never* been a time when *all* stocks went up at the same time. Even in the greatest "bull" markets, periods when stock prices are generally rising, many stocks fall in price. Even in the greatest "bear" markets, periods when stock prices are generally falling, many stocks rise in price. Careful selection is always necessary and most students of investment methods believe that the best method for the average investor is to:

1. Select an industry and
2. Select a company in the industry

The idea here is quite simple. At any moment in history, the future appears to be brighter for certain industries than it does for others. It is up to the buyer first to decide which industry or industries he believes have the most promising future, and to select a company in this industry which he believes is a good investment. Even in the most profitable and rapidly growing industries, some companies are better than others. Some even lose money while the industry is rising to new highs. It is, however, easier to select a company which will prove to be a wise and profitable choice in a profitably growing industry than it is to select such a company in an unprofitable and declining industry.

In the 1950's, the word "growth" became extremely popular in the market. When properly used, it is a valuable term and should be considered carefully by investors. In selecting a specific company, two principles are suggested:

1. The first is to consider oneself a part owner of the companies whose stocks he has carefully selected; to plan to retain such ownership as long as he is satisfied they will progress at or above the rate of industry as a whole; and to place his faith in the continuation of this country's dynamic growth, decade to decade.

2. The second of the two principles that past experience shows to be sound, is that one should invest his money in a given company *not* because he thinks stock prices are going up, but because he has faith in the future of the products manufactured or the services performed, the research done and the ability of the management of that specific company as compared with others.[2]

Note that both of these principles concern growth. Obviously, you will want to select investments with this type of growth potential; you will want to invest in a company that manufactures or sells a product which appears to have a future demand, a company whose management you can respect, and a company which recognizes the importance of research.

Product demand and capable management have always commanded attention in investment circles, but research really came into its own as an investment criterion in the past twenty-five years. It increases in importance every year, and there is evidence to indicate that the "pay-off" by research is yet to come. More money has been spent in this area during the past relatively few years than in the

[2] Thomas E. Babson and David L. Babson, *Investing for a Successful Future,* The Macmillan Company, New York, N.Y., 1959, pp. 265–266.

entire history of the human race. It is believed by many that products
of such research will appear at an accelerating rate. Think of the
new developments since 1950; i.e., polio vaccines, jet airliners, earth
satellites, "packaged power," atomic electric power, etc. In 1945, a
trip to the moon was, for the most part, considered to be a dream of
science-fiction dreamers. By 1962, it had become a national project
and a race between two great world powers, the United States and
the Soviet Union.

In the sense in which it is used in the preceding two principles,
"growth" is a valid term which should seriously be considered by
every investor. It is when the word is used in connection with new
companies that danger results. Tremendous profits have obviously
been made by some investors who purchased shares in new companies
when they first appeared. However, only a small percentage of the
companies in a new industry survive more than a few years, and
to select, among many in a new industry, one of the companies which
will survive to become a successful "giant," before other investors
recognize its potential and force the price up, is an almost impossible
task for the average investor.

The investor must find answers to many specific questions in order
to determine whether or not a particular company is a good investment.
For example: Is a particular company financially sound? Where does
it stand in relation to the industry? Does it face much competition?
What have the company's earnings been, historically? Does the management have a good reputation and imagination? Is the present
price of this company's stock high or low, in terms of earnings and
the market?

A considerable amount of information is needed to answer such
questions, but where may it be obtained?

Sources of Information

Opportunities rare
Are not picked from the air
(Though some wonder how they have missed them)
That's why, we suppose
Wise investors are those
Who call on trained minds to assist them.[3]

Our assumption that the average investor neither is nor wants
to be a security analyst means that he will have to rely upon such
trained minds for assistance. With about 4,000 stocks listed on

---

[3] "Investment Parodies," Arthur Weisenberger & Company, New York, N.Y.,
1956, Christmas Edition, p. 14.

exchanges, and an estimated 30,000 more on the over-the-counter market, the average investor needs the help of:

The Broker

A good broker maintains a competent research staff, and offers up to the minute information. His information and advice are given free of charge. He will never tell you which stock to buy, but will suggest a list of securities which he believes are good buys. He will give you some basic information concerning the companies on the list, and extensive information, upon request, concerning any particular company on the list in which you express an interest.

Unfortunately, the broker's advice is not always followed, and the results may be something like this:

Sharp Joe heard from a friend who heard from a friend that the Wonderful Widgit Company has just invented a device which will make refrigerators obsolete. He wants to get in on the ground floor and make his fortune. He goes to a reputable broker and places an order for 1,000 shares at $10 per share. The $10,000 is every cent he can raise and borrow. The brokerage firm's representative calls the firm's research department and is informed that, to their knowledge, Wonderful Widgit is an extremely unprofitable Widgit manufacturer, with no research department and no known device to make refrigerators obsolete. It is somewhat doubtful, in fact, whether they will even be able to continue making Widgits much longer, if present losses continue. Joe decides that his friend's friend is much more reliable than any brokerage firm's research department, and demands that his order for 1,000 shares be filled. Either through this brokerage house or some other, he acquires the stock. The company goes bankrupt, he loses his $10,000, and blames the brokers and the stock market.

A reputable brokerage firm will do its best to suggest investments which competent analysts believe have good possibilities. They are not always right, but their list is an excellent place to start your search for investment opportunities. "There is no substitute for studying the merits of a particular issue, and then deciding, with the help of a reputable broker, whether the stock meets one's personal needs."[4]

---

[4] G. Keith Funston, "Today's Stock Market—The Myths and The Facts," Remarks by G. Keith Funston, President, New York Stock Exchange, at Annual Banquet, Minneapolis Junior Chamber of Commerce, Minneapolis, Minn., Dec. 16, 1958, p. 9.

Advisory Services

There are excellent advisory services available to investors, for a fee. It would be impossible to name all of the reputable ones, but three of the best known are Moody's, Standard & Poor's and Value Line.

Standard & Poor's and Moody's are the oldest services and the most readily available. They also offer the greatest variety of services. Basic corporate information compiled by these firms is available in most libraries. They offer volumes containing corporate statements, corporate backgrounds, bond ratings, lists of stocks and bonds, stock and bond advisory services, and personalized investment services.

Value Line is one of many services which devotes itself primarily to making recommendations concerning a specific list of stocks. Value Line offers two services — its Investment Survey, which regularly analyzes more than 1,100 securities, and its Over-the-Counter Special Situations Service.

Examples of Value Line's, Standard & Poor's, and Moody's analyses of American Telephone & Telegraph Company follow. Note that these analyses were issued on specific dates. Value Line's analysis appeared on September 6, 1963, Standard & Poor's on December 21, 1962, and Moody's on June 25, 1963. Each service carefully analyzed AT&T as of these specific dates. (Each would immediately change its analysis and recommendations to meet new developments from day to day.) Careful reading will indicate that, as of these dates, each service had done a thorough job of analysis.

Circumstances do change from day to day, and it is the job of an efficient advisory service to discover new developments and report them to its customers promptly. If you find that services occasionally misjudge a stock by a wide margin, it is probably due to some completely unexpected development. How many people in 1948 expected a war in Korea? Few had even heard of the country. How many people expected a Russian missile problem to develop in Cuba in the summer of 1962, just a few months before it happened? No one is infallible.

Recommendations made by advisory services, like those made by brokers, afford a sound basis from which to start your search. You still have to decide which of the many favorable recommendations appeal to you, and make a selection.

AMERICAN TELEPHONE NYSE--T

| Recent Price **123** | Yield est'd next 12 mos. **2.9-3.1**% | Next div'd m't'g: about 11/20 Next ex date: about 11/26 | **734** |

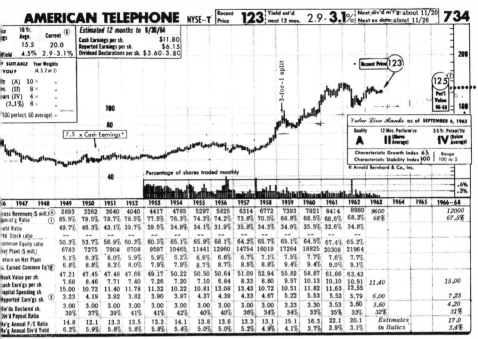

Estimated 12 months to 9/30/64
Cash Earnings per sh. $11.80
Reported Earnings per sh. $6.15
Dividend Declarations per sh. $3.60-3.80

10 Yr. Avg.	Current
15.5	20.0

Yield   4.5%   2.9-3.1%

SUITABLE FOR YOU?   Your Weights (4, 3, 2 or 1)

Quality (A)	10×	=
Business (II)	8×	=
Years (IV)	4×	=
(3.1%)	6×	=
100 perfect, 60 average) =		

7.5 x Cash Earnings*

Percentage of shares traded monthly

Value Line Ranks as of SEPTEMBER 6, 1963

Quality	12 Mos. Perform'ce	3-5 Yr. Potent'ity
A	**II** (Above Average)	**IV** (Below Average)

Characteristic Growth Index 65
Characteristic Stability Index 100   Range 100 to 5

© Arnold Bernhard & Co., Inc.

	1947	1948	1949	1950	1951	1952	1953	1954	1955	1956	1957	1958	1959	1960	1961	1962	1963	1964	1965	1966-68
Gross Revenues ($ mill.)	2893	3262	3640	4040	4417	4785	5297	5825	6314	6772	7393	7921	8414	8980	9600					12000
Operat'g Ratio	85.5%	79.5%	78.7%	78.5%	77.5%	76.3%	74.3%	74.2%	73.8%	70.5%	68.8%	68.5%	68.6%	68.2%	68%					67.5%
Debt Ratio	49.7%	46.3%	43.1%	39.7%	39.5%	34.9%	34.1%	31.9%	35.8%	34.3%	34.9%	35.5%	32.6%	34.8%						
Pfd. Stock ratio	--	--	--	--	--	--	--	--	--	--	--	--	--	--						
Common Equity ratio	50.3%	53.7%	56.9%	60.3%	60.5%	65.1%	65.9%	68.1%	64.2%	65.1%	64.5%	64.5%	67.4%	65.2%						
Net Plant ($ mill.)	6783	7275	7908	8708	9597	10465	11441	12960	14754	16019	17264	18825	20308	21964						
Return on Net Plant	5.1%	6.3%	6.0%	5.9%	5.9%	6.2%	6.6%	6.6%	6.7%	7.1%	7.5%	7.7%	7.6%	7.7%						
% Earned Common Eq'ty	6.8%	8.8%	8.3%	8.0%	7.9%	7.9%	8.7%	8.7%	8.5%	8.8%	9.4%	9.4%	9.0%	9.1%						
Book Value per sh.	47.21	47.45	47.48	47.66	49.17	50.22	50.50	50.64	51.09	52.94	55.82	58.87	61.66	63.43						
Cash Earn'gs per sh.	7.68	8.46	7.71	7.40	7.26	7.20	7.10	6.84	8.33	8.80	9.57	10.13	10.10	10.91	11.40					15.00
Capital Spending sh.	15.00	10.72	11.40	11.78	11.32	10.22	10.81	13.08	13.43	10.72	10.51	11.82	11.63	12.55						
Reported Earn'gs sh.	3.23	4.19	3.92	3.82	3.90	3.97	4.37	4.39	4.33	4.67	5.22	5.53	5.52	5.79	6.00					7.25
Div'ds Declared sh.	3.00	3.00	3.00	3.00	3.00	3.00	3.00	3.00	3.00	3.23	3.30	3.53	3.60	3.60	3.60					4.20
Div'd Payout Ratio	39%	37%	39%	41%	41%	42%	40%	40%	36%	34%	34%	33%	35%	32%						31%
Av'g Annual P/E Ratio	14.8	12.1	13.3	13.5	13.3	14.1	13.8	13.6	13.3	13.1	15.1	16.3	22.1	20.1	*Estimates*					17.0
Av'g Annual Div'd Yield	6.2%	5.9%	5.8%	5.8%	5.8%	5.4%	5.0%	5.0%	5.2%	4.9%	4.1%	3.7%	2.9%	3.1%	*in Italics*					3.4%

CAPITAL STRUCTURE as of 12/31/62
$ 8,224 mill.   Interest $307 mill.

Pfd. Stock none   Div'd none

Common Stock 243,611,000 shares
as 5/31/63

QUARTERLY REVENUES ($ Mill.)				Full Fiscal Year
Feb. 28	May 31	Aug. 31	Nov. 30	
1521.2	1567.0	1584.9	1601.6	6274.7
1631.7	1663.6	1693.7	1730.5	6719.5
1775.3	1836.9	1862.5	1876.6	7351.3
1908.1	1971.3	1991.2	2010.4	7881.0
2028.9	2083.5	2116.2	2150.4	8369.0
2174.1	2242.4	2255.7	2269.4	8941.6
2295.3	2378.0			

QUARTERLY EARNINGS (Per Share)				Full Fiscal Year
Feb. 28	May 31	Aug. 31	Nov. 30	
1.11	1.10	1.07	1.09	4.37
1.07	1.16	1.19	1.21	4.63
1.21	1.32	1.30	1.33	5.16
1.32	1.41	1.40	1.40	5.53
1.36	1.37	1.36	1.40	5.49
1.42	1.47	1.47	1.43	5.79
1.43	1.49			

QUARTERLY DIVIDENDS PAID③				Full Year
Mar. 31	June 30	Sept. 30	Dec. 31	
.75	.75	.75	.75	3.00
.75	.75	.75	.75	3.00
.75	.75	.825	.825	3.15
.825	.825	.825	.825	3.30
.825	.825	.90	.90	3.45
.90	.90	.90	.90	3.60
.90	.90			

Appraisal: We think that the common stock of American Telephone is a worthwhile purchase at present for conservative accounts. This issue, which is of A Quality, has lagged behind the market rise of the past month. It currently ranks high for market action in the coming 12 months. But accounts that stress either generous dividend income or wide price growth over a period of years will find this issue less suitable. Even if Telephone's directors boost the common dividend in the next 12 months, as we expect, the estimated yield would still fall short of the market mean return. In addition, the current price already discounts adequately the gain in earnings and dividends projected for this issue to mid-decade. . .Insiders have bought and sold very few shares of American Telephone so far this year. But a half-dozen more Mutual Funds have taken a position in this issue during the June quarter. At mid-year, 42 of the 70 leading Funds owned 2.3 million Telephone shares, almost 1% of the company's outstanding common.

Analysis: As expected, directors of American Telephone did not avail themselves of the opportunity at their Aug. 21st meeting to boost the common dividend even though the current $3.60 a share annual payment would require only a 60% distribution of this year's estimated profits. This would be one of the lowest payouts of the past decade. With such wide dividend coverage, directors have the wherewithal to raise common payments. Our surmise is that they will do so either at the November dividend meeting or at the subsequent December directors' meeting.

American Telephone's rate of earnings growth in coming years will depend importantly on the amount of equity sold to underwrite future capital expenditures. The more than $3 billion invested each year in new plant and equipment generates increasingly larger depreciation accruals, thus reducing the need for new financing, including the sale of common stock. (The amount of depreciation throw-off is growing faster than annual capital expenditures.) We envision only a modest growth in the equity base in coming years, thus permitting earnings to increase more closely in line with the gain projected for net income than had been the case in the Fifties. The earnings of $7.25 a share that we project to 1966-68 are predicated on 255 million common shares expected to be then outstanding, some 5% more than the number presently issued.   B.M.Z.

BUSINESS: American Telephone and Telegraph Company and subsidiaries operate 66 million phones, about 85% of the nation's total. About 57% of operating revenues are derived from local service. System includes the major telephone companies of the United States. Since 1947-49, revenues have increased 248% (Gross National Product, 121%). Labor costs exceed 50% of revenues. Owns 99.8% of stock of Western Electric Company, maker of telephone apparatus, switchboards, etc. Western in 1962 had sales of $2.8 billion and paid the Bell System $69.8 million in dividends. Since 1956, capital expenditures exceeded $2 billion a year. Has about 11,000 central offices. Employs 728,978; has 2,210,000 stockholders. Directors own less than .1% of outstanding common stock. President: E. J. McNeely. Incorporated: New York. Address: 195 Broadway, New York 7, N. Y.

①-Ratio of operating expenses (including depreciation but excluding income taxes) to revenues. ②-Ratio of operating income (after income taxes but before interest charges) to net plant. ③-Dividend payment dates: Jan. 2, Apr. 2, July 2, Oct. 1. ④-Calendar years. ⑤-All statistics consolidated: earnings based on average shares outstanding. ⑥-Based on current price related to earns. and div'd next 12 months. ⑦-Includes $2 a share of rights. Log Norm. Avg. Value Next 12 Mos.= .800 log (.35 x Earn. + 1.00 x Div.) + 1.421 currently 1.10 *5 yr. moving average of Cash Earnings per share (centered)

Source: Arnold Bernhard & Co., Inc., The Value Line Survey Building, 5 East 44th St., New York 17, N.Y.

T¹   **American Tel. & Tel.**   182

Stock—	Approx. Price	Dividend	Yield
CAPITAL	116⅞	²$3.60	²3.1%

RECOMMENDATION: The company has a dominant position in the communications field, not only through its telephone subsidiaries but also through Western Electric, Bell Telephone Laboratories, and the numerous wire services provided. All aspects of the business have a promising growth potential. The high-grade stock is attractive for secure income and long-term appreciation prospects.

AMERICAN TEL. & TEL.

1951 THRU 1955

425 INDUSTRIALS*

TRADING VOLUME MILLION SHARES

12/21 | 1956 | 1957 | 1958 | 1959 | 1960 | 1961 | 1962

✱ Charted on special comparable scales; values not shown.

⁴OPERATING REVENUES (Million $)

Quarter:	1962	1961	1960	1959	1958
Feb.	2,174	2,029	1,908	1,775	1,632
May........	2,242	2,083	1,971	1,837	1,664
Aug.	2,256	2,106	1,991	1,863	1,694
Nov.		2,150	2,010	1,877	1,731

In the 12 months ended August 31, 1962, total operating revenues for the Bell System rose 7.2% from those of the previous year. Expenses were up less than proportionately, and with the operating ratio reduced to 82.9%, from 83.1%, the advance in operating income was extended to 8.1%. Increased other income offset heavier interest charges and larger minority interest, and net income gained 9%. Earnings per average common share equaled $5.76, against $5.49 on fewer shares.

In the three month period ending August 30, 1962, revenues exceeded those of the same period a year before by 7.1%. Primarily because of higher other income, final net was up 8.1%.

Included in other income is the estimated proportionate interest in net income of Western Electric and other non-consolidated subsidiaries.

³⁵COMMON SHARE EARNINGS ($)

Quarter:	1962	1961	1960	1959	1958	1957
Feb.	1.42	1.36	1.32	1.21	1.07	1.11
May.......	1.47	1.37	1.41	1.32	1.16	1.10
Aug.	1.47	1.36	1.40	1.30	1.19	1.07
Nov.		1.40	1.40	1.33	1.21	1.09

PROSPECTS

Near Term—Earnings for 1962 are estimated at a minimum of $5.80 an average common share, up from $5.52 in 1961. Further moderate improvement is in prospect for 1963. This could pave the way for some increase in the $0.90 quarterly dividend.

Increasing demands for the company's services point to further revenue growth and moderately higher earnings for some time ahead. In the three months ended August 31, 1962, some 600,000 instruments were added to the system, as compared with 550,000 in the 1961 period. Long-distance messages increased about 7.5%, year to year.

Long Term—The outlook for continued growth in all phases of operations is highly promising. In addition to spending large sums for construction ($3 billion in 1962), the important Bell Telephone Laboratories subsidiary plans to spend more than $1 billion on research and development during the next decade. A number of new services under development undoubtedly have very substantial earnings potential. These include communications between business machines over telephone wires, satellite communications, and world-wide television.

RECENT DEVELOPMENTS

Successful launching of AT&T's "Telstar" communications satellite on July 10, 1962, demonstrated the technical practicality of such a communications system. Initial voice and video transmissions, both domestically and between Europe, were highly encouraging. Operation of a permanent system, however, is not in prospect for some time due to various organizational and technical problems yet to be resolved.

Pending completion of product trials, the services available through Data-Phone will be extended to include facsimile transmission.

DIVIDEND DATA

Dividends in the past 12 months were:

Amt. of Divd. $	Date Decl.	Ex-divd. Date	Stock of Record	Payment Date
0.90...	Feb. 14	Feb. 26	Mar. 1	Apr. 2'62
0.90...	May 16	May 28	Jun. 1	Jul. 2'62
0.90...	Aug. 15	Aug. 28	Aug. 31	Oct. 1'62
0.90...	Nov. 21	Nov. 27	Nov. 30	Jan. 2'63

¹Listed N.Y.S.E., Boston, Phila.-Balt.-Wash., Midwest, and Pacific Coast S.Es. and Paris Bourse; also traded Cincinnati, Detroit, and Pitts. S.Es. ²Indicated rate. ³Consolidated; based on average shares outstanding. ⁴Consolidated. ⁵Adjusted for 3-for-1 split in May, 1959.

STANDARD LISTED STOCK REPORTS
STANDARD & POOR'S CORPORATION
Published at Ephrata, Pa. Editorial & Executive Offices, 345 Hudson St., New York 14, N. Y.
Vol. 29, No. 244   Friday, December 21, 1962   Sec. 4

182 AMERICAN TELEPHONE & TELEGRAPH COMPANY

INCOME STATISTICS (Million $) AND PER SHARE ($) DATA

Year Ended Dec. 31	Revenues Local	Revenues Toll	Revenues Gross	[2]Oper. Ratio	% of Gr. Revs. Taxes	% of Gr. Revs. Dep. & Maint.	Net Inc.	[5]Capital Share ($) Data [4]Earns.	Divs. Paid	Price Range
1963--	-----	-----	-----	---	---	---	-----	---	0.90	----------
1962--	-----	-----	-----	---	---	---	-----	---	3.60	136¼ - 98⅛
1961--	4,797.5	3,217.3	8,414.4	83.0	23.4	30.1	1,284.6	5.52	3.45	139⅞ - 103⅛
1960--	4,547.4	2,996.4	7,920.5	83.4	23.3	30.1	1,213.0	5.53	3.30	108½ - 79⅞
1959--	4,250.8	2,786.1	7,393.0	83.4	22.9	30.0	1,113.2	5.22	3.15	89 - 74⅞
1958--	3,944.4	2,490.6	6,771.4	84.4	21.9	30.4	952.3	4.67	3.00	75⅝ - 55⅞
1957--	3,647.6	2,357.7	6,313.8	86.1	20.1	31.2	829.8	4.33	3.00	59⅞ - 53⅜
1956--	3,368.6	2,176.2	5,825.3	86.4	19.8	30.5	755.9	4.39	3.00	62⅜ - 55
1955--	3,086.5	1,959.7	5,297.0	86.4	19.7	30.0	664.2	4.37	3.00	62½ - 57⅝
1954--	2,837.0	1,720.7	4,784.5	87.2	18.5	30.2	549.9	3.97	3.00	59⅜ - 52
1953--	2,642.9	1,571.1	4,416.7	87.9	18.1	29.6	478.5	3.90	3.00	53⅞ - 50¾
1952--	2,397.6	1,407.3	4,039.7	88.2	17.5	30.0	406.7	3.82	3.00	53¾ - 50¼
1939--	744.5	332.4	1,107	80.4	14.1	33.8	190.3	3.26	3.00	57 - 49⅜
1938--	713.1	311.7	1,053	81.9	13.8	34.7	155.5	2.77	3.00	50⅛ - 37
1937--	703.4	321.5	1,051	80.3	12.9	34.7	182.3	3.25	3.00	62⅜ - 46⅝

[1] PERTINENT BALANCE SHEET STATISTICS (Million $)

Dec. 31	Gross Prop.	% Depr. of Gross Prop.	[3]% Earn. on Net Prop.	Net Workg. Cap.	Funded Debt	% Fund. Debt of Net Prop.	% Fund. Debt of Gross Rev.	Total Invest. Cap.	% Earn. on Inv. Cap	Net Inc. per Tel.	[5]($) Book Val. Cap. Sh.
[6] 1962--	26,231	22.0	--	375.2	7,775	38.0	89.6	23,331	--	----	61.59
1961--	25,893	21.6	7.0	351.2	7,271	35.8	86.4	22,299	7.1	20.33	59.82
1960--	24,072	21.8	7.0	128.9	7,232	38.4	91.3	20,452	7.3	19.97	56.50
1959--	22,205	22.2	7.1	271.0	6,432	37.3	87.0	18,832	7.2	19.20	54.48
1958--	20,646	22.4	6.6	372.8	6,042	37.7	89.2	17,651	6.6	17.41	52.57
1957--	19,117	22.8	6.0	27.7	5,688	38.6	90.1	15,945	6.2	15.88	51.24
1956--	17,074	24.1	6.1	497.5	4,618	35.6	79.3	14,487	6.2	15.29	49.87
1955--	15,344	25.4	6.3	524.0	4,376	38.2	82.6	12,844	6.2	14.37	50.14
1954--	14,136	25.9	5.8	266.3	4,001	38.2	83.6	11,485	5.9	12.69	48.87
1953--	13,062	26.5	5.6	320.3	4,189	43.6	94.8	10,632	5.6	11.57	48.22
1952--	11,974	27.3	5.5	223.2	3,790	43.5	93.8	9,558	5.6	10.32	47.42

[1]Consol. [2]After depr. [3]Based on oper. inc. [4]Based on aver. shs. outstg. [5]Adj. for 3-for-1 split in 1959. [6]As of June 30.

Fundamental Position

A holding and operating company, American Telephone & Telegraph, through its operating telephone subsidiaries comprising the Bell System, controls 82% of the 77,000,000 telephones in the United States. Substantial, but not controlling, stock interests are held in other telephone operating companies, including Bell Telephone of Canada, which are not now considered part of the Bell System. The parent company directly operates long distance lines connecting regional units and independent systems. Approximately 59% of system revenues is from local service.

Equipment is purchased largely from the Western Electric Company, 99.8% owned, which has been a substantial contributor to earnings in recent years. Research, development and engineering work is conducted for the company and Western Electric on a nonprofit basis by Bell Telephone Laboratories, a wholly owned subsidiary.

Auxiliary services of the company include teletypewriter exchange service (recently converted to dial operation on a national basis); private line telephone and teletypewriter services; and facilities for transmission of television and radio programs. By means of cable and radio circuits overseas service is provided, and interconnections are maintained between telephone systems in the United States and those in 125 countries and territories.

On August 31, 1962, a law was passed authorizing the establishment of a satellite communications corporation. Through its leadership in this field, AT&T will obviously play an important role in the development of this new company which is to be jointly owned by the public and certain communications companies.

Dividends have been paid each year since 1885. The increase in 1959 was the first since 1922.

Employees: 726,000. Shareholders: over 2,000,000.

Finances

Construction expenditures for 1962 have been budgeted at approximately $3 billion, as compared with $2.7 billion in 1961. To assist in meeting the record high outlays, Bell System companies sold $425 million of debentures in 1962. In addition, the parent sold $300 million of straight debentures in February, 1962 and another $250 million in October.

Parent financing in 1961 consisted of $962 million of stock offered on a 1-for-20 basis to shareholders.

CAPITALIZATION

FUNDED DEBT: Parent...... *$3,499,670,000
Subs. $4,525,000,000

*Includes $9,670,000 4¼% debentures convertible into 3 shares of stock for each $100 debenture and $42 cash.

SUBSIDIARY PFD. STOCKS: $17,904,300
MINORITY INTEREST........ $484,234,000
CAPITAL STOCK: 243,005,002 shares ($33-1/3 par).

Incorporated in N.Y. in 1885. **Office**—195 Broadway, NYC 7. **Pres**—E. J. McNeely. **Secy**—S. W. Landon. **Treas**—L. C. May. **Dirs**—F. R. Kappel (Chrmn), W. C. Bolenius, L. D. Brace, E. B. Hanify, H. T. Heald, J. V. Herd, W. A. Hewitt, J. L. McCaffrey, J. J. McCloy, E. J. McNeely, J. I. Miller, W. B. Murphy, T. F. Patton, M. J. Rathbone, G. F. Smith, J. Taylor, W. White, A. L. M. Wiggins. **Transfer Agents**—Company's offices: 195 Broadway, NYC 7; New England Tel. & Tel. Co., Boston; Illinois Bell Telephone Co., Chicago; Pacific Tel. & Tel., San Francisco. **Registrars**—Bankers Trust Co., NYC; Old Colony Trust Co., Boston; First National Bank, Chicago; Wells Fargo Bank American Trust Co., San Francisco.

Source: Standard & Poor's Corporation, 345 Hudson St., New York 14, N.Y.

AMERICAN TELEPHONE & TELEGRAPH COMPANY common

MOODY'S INVESTORS SERVICE
1962
PRICE RANGE
HIGH 136¼
LOW 98¼
CLOSE .. 116¾

3-for-1

	1946	1947	1948	1949	1950	1951	1952	1953	1954	1955	1956	1957	1958	1959	1960	1961	1962	1963
EARN.	3.37	2.50	3.17	3.07	4.04	3.67	3.48	3.77	3.81	4.09	4.01	4.28	4.50	5.19	5.43	5.44	3.45	3.60
DIV.	3.00	3.00	3.00	3.00	3.00	3.00	3.00	3.00	3.00	3.00	3.00	3.00	3.00	3.15	3.30	3.45	3.60	

CAPITALIZATION:

	(12/31/62)	
	(mill.)	(%)
Debt	$ 8,224.7	34.0
Minority int.	507.3	2.1
Com.& Surp.	15,414.0	63.9
Total	$24,145.6	100.0%
Shs.($33 1/3)-(12/31/62)243,101,133		

LATEST EARNINGS: bc 1963   1962

Period 12 mos.	2/28	
Gross ($ Mill.)	9,062	8,514
Net ($ 000)	1,397.0	1,302.0
Per Share	5.80	5.55
	bc	

INTERIM EARNINGS:

Qu.	Feb.	May	Aug.	Nov.
59	1.21	1.32	1.30	1.33
60	1.32	1.41	1.40	1.40
61	1.36	1.37	1.36	1.40
62	1.42	1.47	1.47	1.43
63	1.43			

DIVIDENDS: 90c qu. 1/10, etc. to stock of record 12/10, etc.

Tax free in Pa.

RECENT PRICE: 121[7]

RANGE: (1963)   126[1] - 114[4]

INDIC. DIV.: $3.60

CURRENT YIELD: 2.9%

INCORPORATED: March 3, 1885

PRINCIPAL OFFICE: 195 Broadway
New York 7, N.Y.

ANNUAL MEETING: 3rd Wednesday in April

SECRETARY: A. G. Barry

LISTED: NYSE

TICKER SYMBOL: T

TRANSFER AGENT: Company
195 Broadway, N.Y.7, N.Y.

REGISTRAR: Bankers Trust Co., N.Y.

MOODY'S INVESTORS SERVICE   99 Church Street, New York 7, N. Y.   June 25, 1963   PRINTED IN U.S.A.

AR-HB-L-100

AMERICAN TELEPHONE & TELEGRAPH COMPANY common

A high grade issue and one of the most popular investment stocks in the country. It is primarily for the conservative investor, but recent developments have provided a new look.

YEAR	GROSS REVS. ($ MILL.)	% OP. INC. TO NET PLT.	GROSS FOR COM. %	NET INCOME ($000)	WORK. CAP. ($ MILL.)	COMMON EQUITY	NO. SHS. OUT. (000)	EARN. PER SH. $	DIV. PER SH. $	DIV. PAY. %	PRICE RANGE	PRICE X EARN.	AVG. YIELD %
52	4,040	5.47	10.0	406.7	223.2	58.4	116,937	3.48	3.00	86	$55^6 - 50^2$	15.0	5.76
53	4,417	5.55	10.8	478.5	320.2	58.8	126,846	3.77	3.00	79	$55^8 - 50^8$	13.8	5.73
54	4,784	5.88	11.4	549.9	266.3	63.3	144,483	3.81	3.00	78	$59^3 - 52$	14.6	5.38
55	5,297	6.30	12.5	664.2	524.0	64.0	162,348	4.09	3.00	73	$62^4 - 57^4$	14.2	5.14
56	5,825	6.10	13.0	755.5	497.5	66.2	188,682	4.01	3.00	75	$62^3 - 55$	14.6	5.11
57	6,314	5.96	13.2	829.8	27.7	62.3	193,944	4.28	3.00	70	$60 - 53^3$	13.2	5.30
58	6,771	6.59	14.1	952.3	372.8	63.6	211,636	4.50	3.00	67	$75^8 - 56$	14.6	4.55
59	7,393	7.08	15.1	1,113.2	271.0	63.8	214,630	5.19	3.15	61	$89 - 74^7$	15.8	3.84
60	7,920	7.00	15.3	1,212.9	128.8	62.6	223,518	5.43	3.30	61	$108^4 - 79^7$	17.3	3.50
61	8,414	7.05	15.3	1,284.5	351.2	65.1	235,929	5.44	3.45	63	$139^7 - 103^1$	22.3	2.83
62	8,980	7.16	15.4	1,388.1	549.1	63.9	243,101	5.71	3.60	63	$136^2 - 98^1$	20.5	3.07

Note: Adj. for 3-for-1 split 4/59. a-Excl. income from nonconsolidated subsidiaries. b-Based on average shares.

BACKGROUND: American Telephone & Telegraph Co. and its subsidiaries comprise the Bell System. They furnish telephone and other services, and own 65.9 mill. or about 82% of the total telephones in the country. Bell Telephone Laboratories, which engages in research, and Western Electric, which manufactures equipment, are wholly owned, but their accounts are not consolidated...

DEVELOPMENTS: Bell System's business continues to grow... The over 2,800,000 telephones added to the system in 1962 represented a gain of 4.4% over 2,443,000 additions in 1961...Station additions in the quarter ended 2/28/63 totaled over 635,000, or a gain of about 6.2%...In April the system inaugurated a flat rate 'after 9 P.M.' long dis-

PROSPECTS: With traffic volume gaining and new customers steadily increasing service demand, the A.T. & T. system is proceeding with a record construction program. It spent about $3 bill. in 1962 and has about $3.1 bill. scheduled for 1963...The outlook is for continued growth

tance telephone rate which should greatly stimulate off hour toll telephone use on a national basis...The report for 12 mos. 2/28/63 showed a mild leveling in rate of earnings gain, related to full 1962...Operating revenues were up 6.5% and net income, 7.3%, with actual shares outstanding earning $5.75.

as the economy develops, with research in space communication and other technologies holding longer term promise...Earnings for full year 1963 could be in the $6.10 range (based on actual shares to be outstanding).

104A

Source: Moody's Investors Service, Inc, 99 Church St, New York 7, N.Y.

An investor should investigate the various advisory services and select one he prefers. They all differ in presentation, amount of detail, stocks surveyed, etc. No one can say just how successful advisory services are in recommending profitable investments, but they are obviously not perfect. ". . . one stock market analyst who did keep check on sixteen services for a period of years found that if an investor had followed all their 7,500 different recommendations, he would have ended up just 1.43% worse than the market averages."[5]

This might sound as though advisory services are not worth the price they charge. This is not true. You don't buy an "average," you buy a stock; and you investigate all of the facts about the company before buying its stock. The advisory services develop and publish these facts. Furthermore, they continuously watch these companies and are able to notify you of new developments immediately. They present complete information in a condensed, easy-to-read style.

Why are they unable to always advise you correctly as to what to buy? Primarily because no one has yet discovered a method of predicting the future with complete accuracy. When advisory services, professional financial advisors, banks, and others, project the future performance of a stock, they are simply expressing an educated opinion. Any number of unforeseeable events can upset their calculations. A court decision may completely change a company's profit picture; anticipated demand for a particular make automobile may fail to materialize, and drastically affect sales; a strike may cut production; or the government may cut back its orders and seriously affect an entire industry.

An advisory service is a good source of information, not a seer. They will recommend many securities as good investments. It would be impossible for you to analyze the thousands of companies which sell stock publicly. An advisory service does this for you.

One thing should be remembered. If you plan to invest a small amount each year, let's say $500, it is not sensible to subscribe to a $200 or $300 advisory service. Examine the field and find a service that best fits your pocketbook. A less expensive service will not give you the same information or service as the more expensive one, but it pays to be practical. Remember, too, that public libraries offer a great deal of information at no expense to you. Subscribe to the service that is commensurate with the value of your proposed investments.

One excellent way of investing a small sum of money is to form or join an investment club. An investment club consists of a small group of people who meet regularly, usually once a month, and pay

---

[5] *How to Buy Stocks*, Copyright 1953, © 1957, 1962 by Louis Engel, by permission of Little, Brown and Company, p. 133.

a small sum, say $20 per month, into the club treasury. Pooling small amounts gives the group a respectable sum to invest regularly. In working together, you are able to share the expenses of acquiring information and analyzing stocks, and can learn a lot about the stock market, stock analysis, and stock selection, at minimum risk.

Financial News

Business conditions affect us all, and should influence your choice of investment from the many suggestions made by your broker or advisory service.

Reading business news daily, at least in your regular newspaper, is a must. Most regular investors subscribe to some financial publication which keeps them informed about particular stocks in which they are interested, as well as to what general business conditions are. Many such financial or business publications are available. Among these are the Wall Street Journal, Barron's, the Commercial and Financial Chronicle, Business Week, Financial World, Forbes, Journal of Commerce, Magazine of Wall Street, the Exchange, etc. Of these, the Wall Street Journal is certainly one of the best known and most widely read.

Besides general financial and business news and analysis, the Wall Street Journal, and many other newspapers, carry tables indicating prices and stock sales on various exchanges. Table 15-1 shows how American Telephone stock appeared in the Wall Street Journal on January 8, 1963. Listed stocks (those sold on exchanges like the New York Stock Exchange) appear in the tables in this manner. Table 15-2 shows how Over-the-Counter stocks are listed.

Table 15-1

1962–63 High	1962–63 Low	Stocks Div.	Sales in 100s	Open	High	Low	Close	Net Chg.
136¼	98⅛	AmTelTel 3.60	292	117¼	117⅜	116	116½	– ⅜

Table 15-2

	Bid	Asked	Prev. Bid
Transco Gas Pl	27⅜	29⅜	27⅞

Notice the difference between these two listings. The information given for listed stocks is definite. AT&T definitely sold at the low and high prices indicated, sometime during the day before publication of the stock tables. It definitely opened and closed at the prices indicated.

Prices on the Over-the-Counter market are not as definite. The Bid and Asked columns do not report the prices at which Transcontinental Gas was bought and sold. These figures represent dealer quotations, and indicate the approximate range within which transactions could have taken place at the time the quotations were obtained.

The figure in the last column in both the AT&T and Transcontinental Gas reports reflects the change that has taken place in these prices since they were last published. Listed stocks show a net change, which indicates whether today's closing price, as reported, is higher or lower than yesterday's. Over-the-Counter stocks show a previous bid, and, by comparison, you can tell whether today's bid is higher or lower.

A great deal of additional information is provided, such as the number of shares traded, the high and low prices for the year, and facts about each company's annual dividend. Occasionally, reference letters will follow the dividend figure, and reference to footnotes which are coded to these reference letters will disclose even more information about a particular stock.

FINANCIAL STATEMENTS

Every reputable company issues annual reports, and many issue reports quarterly. A balance sheet and an income statement are always part of the annual report. Usually, there will also be statistical information covering a period of ten years or more, so that you can see how the company's financial position has changed.

Annual reports can usually be obtained from your broker, from the library, or from the company. These reports are mailed regularly to stockholders.

It would be impossible to present a complete course in bookkeeping, accounting, and financial analysis in this chapter. However, everyone should understand some of the basic information presented in these annual reports. One of the clearest and simplest explanations available is presented by the New York Stock Exchange in its book "How to Understand Financial Statements." Some of this material is presented in the following pages. First, a sample balance sheet, with explanation, is presented on pages 420 and 421. Next, an income statement and explanation is presented on pages 422 and 423.

Notice that the information in these statements covers a period of two years. This enables you to compare the company's condition this year with its condition last year, and to compare the change with that of other companies in the same industry.

Balance Sheet

In comparing a company's balance sheets for two or more years, look for changes which are particularly significant. A change in the cash account, for example, is very important. The corporation needs cash to pay dividends to its stockholders. A decrease in the cash account may indicate that the corporation is facing certain problems. If there is a corresponding increase in accounts receivable, it could mean that the corporation's customers are slowing down in the payment of their bills. Or the corporation may have had to meet unexpected demands upon its cash reserves. Are these continuing demands? The reasons for a change in a company's cash account may significantly affect its future.

An increase in inventories should also be a subject of concern. A large inventory means the corporation is subject to greater risk if prices drop. It might also mean that the corporation has accumulated a lot of unsalable merchandise.

All of the reported liabilities are important in that they represent corporate obligations, but "accounts payable" is of special importance. This represents the money the corporation owes for its everyday bills, for such items as materials, supplies, insurance, etc. If there is a large increase in this account from one year to another, it may indicate that the company is having difficulty meeting its immediate expenses.

The relationship between total current assets and total current liabilities is of more importance than the size of the individual figures by themselves. The preferable relationship of these values to each other varies from industry to industry, but a rough rule of thumb is that current assets should be twice as large as current liabilities. Current assets are those accounts which, roughly speaking, your corporation hopes to convert into cash during a one year period, while current liabilities are those accounts which must be paid within one year. Why then isn't it enough simply to have them balance?

Well, for one thing, a "cushion" is always nice to have as a safeguard. Of greater importance, however, is the fact that a corporation's accounts are like your personal accounts in at least one way— your prospective sources of income are not as certain as the bills you already owe. How much cash will be derived from accounts such as

BALANCE SHEET ("Your Company")

ASSETS, LIABILITIES AND STOCKHOLDERS' EQUITY

ASSETS	Dec. 31 1961	Dec. 31 1960
Current Assets	Million	
Cash	$ 9.0	$ 6.2
U. S. Government securities	—	2.0
Accounts and notes receivable	12.4	11.4
Inventories	27.0	24.6
Total Current Assets	$ 48.4	$ 44.2
Other Assets		
Surrender value of insurance	.2	.2
Investments in subsidiaries	4.7	3.9
Prepaid insurance	.6	.5
Total Other Assets	$ 5.5	$ 4.6
Fixed Assets		
Buildings, machinery and equipment at cost	104.3	92.7
Less accumulated Depreciation	27.6	25.0
	$ 76.7	$ 67.7
Land	.9	.7
Total Fixed Assets	$ 77.6	$ 68.4
Total Assets	$131.5	$117.2

LIABILITIES AND STOCKHOLDERS' EQUITY

Current Liabilities		
Accounts payable	$ 6.1	$ 5.0
Accrued liabilities	3.6	3.3
Current maturity of long term debt	1.0	.8
Federal income and other taxes	9.6	8.4
Dividends payable	1.3	1.1
Total Current Liabilities	$ 21.6	$ 18.6
Reserves	3.6	2.5
Long Term Debt		
5% Sinking Fund Debentures, due July 31, 1980	26.0	20.0
Stockholders' Equity		
5% Cum. Preferred Stock ($100 par)	6.0	6.0
Common Stock ($10 par)	18.3	18.3
Capital Surplus	9.6	9.6
Earned Surplus	46.4	42.2
Total Stockholders' Investment	$ 80.3	$ 76.1
Total Liabilities, and Stockholders' Investment	$131.5	$117.2

EXPLANATION

The Company Owned

Cash and U. S. Government securities the latter generally at either cost or market value, whichever is lower.

Amounts owed the company by its customers and others.

Raw materials, work in process and finished merchandise.

Miscellaneous assets, and advance payments for insurance. Investments in nonconsolidated subsidiary companies.

Land, buildings and equipment and deductions for wear and tear on these properties.

The Company Owed

For materials, supplies, wages and salaries to employees, and such things as dividends declared, real estate, social security and income taxes, etc.

May be either a liability of a more or less definite nature, such as provision for possible inventory losses, or a part of earnings not available for dividends and segregated so as not to be included in surplus available for dividends.

For money borrowed (excluding portion due in next 12 months shown as a current liability).

Amount originally invested in the business by the stockholders. Additional capital received from sale of Capital Stock above par value.

Retained earnings reinvested in the business.

Source: "How to Understand Financial Statements," published by the New York Stock Exchange, New York, N.Y., pp. 6 and 7.

STATEMENT OF INCOME

| | Year Ended December 31 | |
| | 1961 | 1960 |
	— Million —	
SALES	$115.8	$110.0
Less:		
Costs and Expenses:		
Cost of goods sold	74.8	73.2
Selling, general and administrative expenses	14.2	13.0
Depreciation and depletion	4.2	3.5
	$ 93.2	$ 89.7
Operating Profit	$ 22.6	$ 20.3
Interest Charges	1.3	1.0
Earnings before Income Taxes	$ 21.3	$ 19.3
Provision for Federal and State Taxes on Income	11.4	9.8
Net Income for the Year	$ 9.9	$ 9.5
Dividend on Preferred Stock	.3	.3
Balance of Net Income Available for Common Stock	$ 9.6	$ 9.2

STATEMENT OF EARNED SURPLUS

| | Year Ended December 31 | |
| | 1961 | 1960 |
	— Million —	
Balance at beginning of year	$ 42.2	$ 37.6
Add — Net Income for the year	9.9	9.5
	52.1	47.1
Less Dividends Paid on		
Preferred Stock	.3	.3
Common Stock	5.4	4.6
Balance at End of Year	$ 46.4	$ 42.2

EXPLANATION

Amount received or receivable from customers.

Part of income used for wages, salaries, raw materials, fuel and supplies and certain taxes.

Part of income used for salesmen's commissions, advertising, officers' salaries and other general expenses.

Provision from income for the reduction of the service life of machinery and buildings and the use of minerals in mines.

The remainder after deducting the foregoing expenses from sales, but before providing for interest charges and taxes.

Amount required for interest on borrowed funds.

Amount paid or payable for taxes.

This amount was earned for stockholders.

Amount paid to preferred stockholders.

Amount remaining for common stockholders.

Surplus or retained earnings reinvested in the business. Usually not all of the year's earnings can be paid out in dividends, a part being retained in the business for expansion or other purposes.

Source: "How to Understand Financial Statements," published by the New York Stock Exchange, New York, N.Y., pp. 8 and 9.

423

accounts receivable and inventories depends upon how well customers pay their bills, and upon the price at which the inventory can be sold. The amounts under current liabilities, which the corporation now owes, such as accounts payable, taxes, etc. are fixed. A "cushion," then, is a necessity.

The difference between current assets and current liabilities is a company's net working capital. This is the money it has to grow on, the surplus it may use to buy more materials and supplies to make more products and increase sales, and make next year an even better year than this one. If the net working capital declines from one year to another, and continues to do this for three or four years, you might seriously consider selling your stock.

Statement of Income

Now let's glance at the Statement of Income. The first item reported is sales. It has often been said, and correctly so, that sales are the lifeblood of business. All of the company's expenses, as well as returns to stockholders, must be paid out of the proceeds of sales. An increase in sales from year to year is something every investor should hope for, as it indicates his company is growing. On the other hand, increasing sales cannot be considered alone. A company with fantastically increasing sales over a short period, is not necessarily a good investment. Increasing sales are of no value if the company is losing money. Of course, such a loss may be temporary, but if sales continue to increase, and losses also continue, the corporation is certainly not improving its financial condition from the investor's viewpoint.

Notice that in 1961, this corporation had Earnings Before Income Taxes of $21.3 million. Referring back to the balance sheet, you will notice that the corporation had a cash account of $9.0 milllion. It is extremely important to remember that cash and profits are two quite different things. People ask questions like, "Why can't that corporation increase wages or dividends? Look at the profits it made"; or "Why should this corporation have any problem paying its income tax? After all, it made a tremendous profit." Tremendous profits do not mean ready cash. Profits may be tied up in accounts receivable, buildings, other assets which are not immediately convertible into cash. If you had to pay your entire personal federal income tax in one lump each year (no withholding), wouldn't you have a problem? Most people would. Why? You must have made the income, or you wouldn't be faced with the tax. The reason is, that by tax payment time your income is no longer cash. It may now be in the form of food, a house, an automobile, anything. Remember, too, that the corporation's federal income tax on a profit of $9.0 million in 1961 was 52%, or $4.68 million dollars.

A shortage of cash is one reason why a corporation occasionally may issue a stock dividend. It knows that when it makes a profit, stockholders expect a return. A stock dividend conserves its cash account, and still gives the stockholders some satisfaction.

You can also understand why, when the government permits a corporation to increase its depreciation allowance, the action is regarded with delight by the corporation and its stockholders. Notice that, according to this Statement of Income, if depreciation and depletion allowances in 1961 could have been 5.0 million instead of 4.2 (a difference of about 20 per cent), earnings before taxes would have been only $20.5 million (21.3 – .8). $800,000 less earnings, at a 52 per cent tax rate, would have meant a reduction in federal taxes of $416,000. This is money the corporation would have retained, and could have used for other things.

This is a very simplified explanation of just one of the ways in which increased depreciation allowances benefit business, but it should indicate how such allowances can benefit the stockholders. The fact that they reduce earnings might seem to indicate that they would reduce profits. As dividends are paid out of profits, you might feel that this would be contrary to the stockholders' interests. However, by reducing income taxes, the corporation's cash position may be improved to the extent that it will be better able to pay cash dividends. It must also be recognized that any allowance which provides a corporation with increased ability to replace equipment more rapidly encourages more rapid growth, and this is certainly in the interest of the investor.

Leverage

As you can see by further examining the Income Statement, the tax treatment of interest and dividends is quite different. Interest payments are deducted from profit before taxes are calculated. Dividends are not deductible. From the government's point of view, interest is an expense and dividends are not. From the corporation's point of view, this is an attractive feature of bonds. Its interest payments to bondholders will reduce its taxes, while dividend payments to stockholders will not.

A stockholder should be aware of the effects of "leverage" when investing in a company which has issued bonds as part of its capital structure. Let's assume that two corporations each have a total of $10 million in capital. In corporation "A," the entire $10 million is in common stock, while in corporation "B," half is in common stock and the other half in 5 per cent bonds. The capital structures of the two would be:

	Corporation A	Corporation B
Common Stock	$10,000,000	$ 5,000,000
Bonds (5%)	0	5,000,000
Total Capital	$10,000,000	$10,000,000

The interest on the bonds must be paid before any dividends can be paid to the stockholders so Corporation "B" must plan on paying $250,000 (5 per cent on $5,000,000 bonds) to its bondholders before paying any dividends. If both corporations made an annual profit of 5 per cent, the common stock holders in both corporations would earn 5% on their stock. However, if both corporations earned 7 per cent, this is what would happen:

	Corporation A		Corporation B	
	Dollar Earnings	Per Cent Earned	Dollar Earnings	Per Cent Earned
Common Stock	$700,000	7%	$450,000	9%
Bonds (5%)	0	0	250,000	5%
Total Capital	$700,000	7%	$700,000	7%

You can see that the percentage return to stockholders in corporation "B" is greater than in corporation "A." This is known as leverage. Note, though, that leverage also works in reverse. In this example, if the total return on capital had been 2.5 per cent, the stockholders in corporation "A" would have had a 2.5 per cent return, but the stockholders in corporation "B" would have had no return. There are situations more complicated than the example given. The degree to which leverage affects returns to stockholders depends upon the ratio of bonds to stock The greater the amount of borrowed money (bonds) in relation to equity money (stock), the greater the effect of leverage.

The basic idea of leverage is an old one. If a corporation can earn a greater return on borrowed money than the cost of borrowing, the borrowing is profitable. In a growing, profitable company with a promising future, leverage should be considered as an advantage to the stockholder. If the company suffers reverses, leverage becomes a disadvantage to the stockholder.

It is generally believed that the industrial companies with the smaller bond issues are better for the average investor. Conversely, the larger bond issues of more stable companies, such as utilities, are an attractive investment because there is less possibility of the earnings of these companies declining to a point where it would be difficult for them to pay the bond interest.

Ratios

The Balance Sheet and Income Statement are the sources of many ratios which are important in security analysis. Only a few of those most significant from the viewpoint of the common stockholder will be taken up here.

One of the most basic ratios is the earnings per share. This is found simply by dividing the corporation's net income by the number of shares of stock outstanding.

$$\frac{\text{Net Income}}{\text{Number of Shares}} = \text{Earnings Per Share}$$

The corporation we have been considering in the sample Balance Sheet and Income Statement had net earnings of $9.6 million in 1961, and 1,830,000 shares of stock outstanding. Its Earnings Per Share ratio would be:

$$\frac{\$9,600,000}{1,830,000} = \$5.24.$$

By comparing this ratio with those of previous years, you can tell whether or not the amount earned per share of stock is increasing or decreasing. You will also be interested in comparing the ratio which exists in your company with ratios in other companies, to find out whether your company is doing as good a job as others in making profits for its stockholders.

Another significant ratio is Dividends Per Share. This is found by dividing the dividends paid on the common stock by the number of shares. This corporation paid dividends on common stock of $5,490,000 in 1961.

$$\text{Dividends Per-Share} = \frac{\text{Dividends Paid}}{\text{Number of Shares}} = \frac{\$5,490,000}{1,830,000} = \$3.00.$$

Again, by comparing this figure with that of other years and with those of other companies, you can determine how well your corporation is treating its stockholders.

High dividends per share, however, isn't the only value to consider. If two companies both paid a dividend of $5 per share, but one company had earnings per share of $10 and the other $5, then a stockholder would be a lot better off in the one with earnings of $10. Reinvested earnings work to the advantage of the investor, and may very possibly increase long range earnings. Is the corporation paying all of its earnings out in dividends or reinvesting them? The Dividend Payout Ratio indicates the percentage of earnings on the common stock actually paid in dividends. It is calculated by dividing the dividend paid per share by the earnings per share. The ratio in 1961 for this company would be:

$$\text{Dividend Payout Ratio} = \frac{\text{Dividends Per Share}}{\text{Earnings Per Share}} = \frac{\$3.00}{\$5.24} = 57\%$$

Investors are interested in the relationship between dividends paid by the corporation and the price of its stock. What percentage return does a particular dividend produce? The Dividend Yield on your investment is found by dividing the annual dividend per share by the price of the stock. If this stock was selling at $60 per share, the Dividend Yield would be:

$$\text{Dividend Yield} = \frac{\text{Dividends Per Share}}{\text{Market Price Per Share}} = \frac{\$3.00}{\$60} = 5\%$$

If the stock was selling for $79 per share the Dividend Yield would be:

$$\frac{\$3.00}{\$79} = 3.8\%$$

How important Dividend Yield is, depends to a considerable degree on how important income is to you. If you have purchased the stock for immediate income, Dividend Yield is of great importance. If you have purchased the stock for capital appreciation, Dividend Yield is of only secondary importance.

One of the most frequent ratios referred to in investment publications is the Price-Earnings Ratio. If the market price of this stock was $60 per share, the Price-Earnings Ratio would be:

$$\text{PE Ratio} = \frac{\text{Market Price Per Share}}{\text{Earnings Per Share}} = \frac{\$60}{\$5.24} = 11.4.$$

If the market price was $79 the PE Ratio would be about 15 times earnings.

$$PE = \frac{\$79}{\$5.24} = 15$$

The PE Ratio is widely used to assist in determining the value of a share of stock, and this ratio will be discussed more fully, later in this chapter. Comparing the last two ratios—the Dividend Yield Ratio and the Price-Earnings Ratio—you will notice that if the dividend per share remains the same, the PE Ratio will rise as the market price of the stock increases, while the dividend yield ratio will fall. A stock selling at a high PE Ratio has a low dividend yield. People are not buying it for immediate dividend income, but because they hope that this is a growing company and that the market price of the stock will rise. A stock selling at a high Dividend Yield Ratio, with a low PE Ratio, will attract those interested in immediate income.

HOW MUCH IS STOCK WORTH?

The answer to this question depends upon your definition of the word "worth." It can be defined in terms of par value, book value, or market value.

Par Value

Par value is the nominal value of securities. It has nothing to do with market value, liquidating value, or anything else that might be of interest to the investor. Many companies issue stock using a stated value—no par stock.

Book Value

The book value of a share of stock is the sum of the par value plus capital surplus and earned surplus, divided by the total number of shares outstanding. These values are shown on the Balance Sheet on pages 420–21 as:

Common stock	$18.3 million
Capital surplus	9.6 "
Earned surplus	46.4 "
Total	$74.3 million

$$\text{Book value} = \frac{\$74,300,000}{1,830,000} = \$40.60 \text{ per share.}$$

This value presumably is the amount of money each share of stock would be worth if the company liquidated its assets and settled all of its liabilities. However, a large part of an industrial company's assets is its plant and equipment, and the market value of these physical assets has little or no relationship either to their cost or to their value to the company's operations. For example, a blast furnace has a definite measurable value to the company while in operation, but would have a very questionable value if offered for sale in the open market as a second-hand blast furnace. Whether or not the common stockholders would actually receive $74.3 million would depend entirely upon what the company's assets might be sold for. The only asset that has a fixed value is cash.

How much will the inventory bring at a liquidation sale? What percentage of the accounts receivable will be paid? How much can the land and buildings be sold for? All of these questions make book value a rather unsatisfactory answer to the question, "How much is stock worth?," from the stockholder's point of view.

One significant point, however, is that an increase in book value indicates an increase in earning power, by virtue of additions to the company's productive facilities, and increased financial strength.

The book value of bank, insurance company, and investment company stocks is much more important to the average investor. Their assets are of a type which can more readily be converted into cash. It is also important in connection with public utilities, as the law gives them the right to earn a certain return on their investment. As their investment is primarily in fixed assets, their rates and earnings are, to a considerable degree, determined by the value of their plant and equipment.

Book value, however, leaves out something in which you, as an investor, are primarily interested. The real value of a corporation should be measured by the earnings which the company can make with its assets, rather than being measured by the value of the assets. Management, location, and many other things, play a part in determining the value of a company, and none of these can be calculated in book value.

"Real" value

How much is a share of stock really worth? "Bluntly, it's only worth what somebody else is willing to pay for it when you want to sell it."[6] This is a fundamental truth. It will do you no good to argue

---

[6] *How to Buy Stocks*, Copyright 1953, © 1957, 1962 by Louis Engel, by permission of Little, Brown and Company, p. 8.

that American Telephone stock is worth more than its market value at a particular time. If you want to sell your shares, you will get the market value and no more.

But is there some way you can determine a stock's "real" value, below which you would buy because you think it is selling for less than its true value, and above which you would sell because you think it is too high?

"Conceptually, the intrinsic value of common stock is the present value of all future dividend payments expected to be made."[7] If you could calculate what the corporation will pay out in dividends many years into the future and discount these dividends to the present, you could find the "real" value of a share of common stock. This would not necessarily establish its price. Other buyers in the market might not agree with your calculations, and a war, depression, strike, or other major occurrence, would radically affect the market. Secondly, it is impossible to successfully project dividend payments far enough into the future to establish a realistic current-day value.

A practical approach to the determination of the "real" value of stock is the Price-Earnings approach. While this method is not as theoretically accurate as discounting future dividends, it is more realistic. Investment analysts use it frequently.

We calculated a PE Ratio of 11.4, earlier in this chapter, on the basis of company earnings of $5.24 per share and a market price of $60 $\frac{P}{E}$. Is $60 a proper price for this stock? This would depend on the past average levels reached by this ratio, and by what you expect the earnings might be in coming years.

The PE Ratio will vary considerably between industries and between companies in each industry. Stock in a successful company in a rapidly growing industry will sell at a high PE Ratio, while the stock in a company whose earnings are uncertain, and which is in a declining industry, will sell at a low PE Ratio. Growth industries usually sell at extremely high ratios.

You must investigate the industry in which your company is located, find out what the average PE Ratio has been in the past, then examine the history of your company, and the relationship of its average PE Ratio to that of the industry. Is today's PE Ratio out of line with the historical ratio?

The relationship between today's PE Ratio in this particular company and the historical ratio is an extremely helpful guide. Referring again to the earlier example, if this company's current PE Ratio of 11.4 is low in relation to historical ratios in the industry and in the

---

[7] Dr. William C. Freund and Dr. Murray G. Lee, *Investment Fundamentals*, by permission of The American Bankers Association, New York, N.Y., 1960, p. 99.

company itself, the price of $60 per share would appear to be reasonable; if the PE Ratio is comparatively high, the $60 market price would appear to be too high.

WHEN TO BUY AND SELL

Buying low and selling high is an obvious method of making money in the market, if you can do it consistently. That is a big "if." Experts state that they know of no firm or individual investor who has been successful in predicting the market even as much as 50 per cent of the time.[8]

Hindsight is a wonderful way to make terrific imaginary profits. It's obvious, now, that everyone should have purchased stocks in 1942 when they were quite low. But the United States seemed to be losing World War II in 1942. Pearl Harbor had seriously weakened our sea power. Hitler seemed to have no serious obstacles to a conquest of Europe. Fuel oil rations were being cut. American youth was either enlisting or being drafted into the armed forces as rapidly as possible. This obviously was not a favorable atmosphere for investment.

A more recent example of the advantages of hindsight can be found in 1958. The Dow-Jones Industrial Average had dropped about 100 points in late 1957 and early 1958. Obviously, stocks were quite low. Obviously, they have since climbed to relatively fantastic heights. Again, however, the word "obviously" is only true on the basis of hindsight. In 1958, there was a general belief that the United States was facing the most serious recession since World War II. Few people were optimistic. A cautious investment policy was recommended by many advisory services. It was not a favorable atmosphere for investment.

Investors, in general, are more likely to invest during boom periods than during periods of decline or recession. During booms, they have money to invest. Business news is favorable, and everyone exudes confidence. The opposite is true in periods of recession. The reports are gloomy, pessimistic. Business news is discouraging, and everybody lacks confidence.

"Most individuals contemplating investments in common stocks would be well advised to ignore market predictions in their investment decisions."[9] On the average, the most consistent investors have

---

[8] Thomas E. Babson and David L. Babson, *Investing for a Successful Future,* The Macmillan Company, New York, N.Y., 1960, p. 263.

[9] Douglas A. Hayes, *Investments: Analysis and Management,* The Macmillan Company, New York, N.Y., 1961, p. 75. Reprinted with permission.

been the most successful investors. They do not try to "beat" the
market by buying when prices are low and selling when prices are
high. These investors have a regular and consistent investment program.

Dollar-Cost-Averaging

There are many formulas which are supposed to increase your
chances of success when you invest in the market. Many of them are
quite mathematical and complicated. An interesting fact, however, is
that, over the years, one of the simplest has proved to be one of the
most successful. It is called "dollar-cost-averaging."

All that this system requires is a periodic investment of a fixed
number of dollars in the same stock. Suppose you decide to invest
$100 each month in a particular stock. If the market price is $50 per
share, you buy 2 shares; if it rises to $100, you buy 1 share, and if it
falls to $25, you buy 4 shares. But you buy each month.

Now this doesn't assure success. If you start to buy at the highest
price and prices continuously fall, you will lose money. However, even
under these circumstances you would lose less than if you invested all
of your funds at the highest price. In recent years, many excellent
companies have been able to grow fairly consistently, and the market
price of their stock has gone up with their growth. Between 1952 and
1962, dollar-cost-averaging in companies like International Business
Machines, Corning Glass, Chas. Pfizer & Co., Eastman Kodak, etc.,
would have been extremely profitable. The prices of these stocks did
not always go up from year to year, but they *usually* did. If you had
started to invest in 1952, the market value of your stock would have
gone up considerably by 1962, even though 1962 prices went down
late in the year.

The point is that while dollar-cost-averaging will not produce
profits if the price of a stock steadily declines, it will produce profits
when the price goes down and then comes back up again. This is true
even if the final price is lower than the original price. Let's assume,
for example, you had bought stocks making up the Dow Jones Industrial Average at the 1929 high, and had continued to invest $1,000 a
year during the great depression, for a ten year period from 1929
through 1938.

At the end of the ten years, the market value was worth less
than half, only 43% of its original value, but the mathematics of
dollar-cost-averaging had actually resulted in a profit of about 6%.
In addition to the market profit, $2,503 or 25% had been received

in dividends. In other words, capital appreciation of 6% and dividend income of 25% of the total investment cost, resulted in an investment increment of 31% in a market that had lost 57% of its original value. This would have been the result of the mathematics of dollar-cost-averaging of the Dow Jones Industrial Stocks during the worst crash of securities' prices in the history of our markets.[10]

Chart 15–1 illustrates that buying a fixed number of shares at regular intervals is not as rewarding as putting in a fixed number of dollars at regular intervals. Even though both investors bought stock

Chart 15–1

How to acquire stock at a reasonable cost

See how investor B, who decides to put a fixed number of dollars into stock regularly, will do better than investor A, who decides to buy a fixed number of shares regularly.

date	price per share	Investor A's program			Investor B's program		
		number of shares bought	cumulative total cost	cumulative cost per share	number of shares bought	cumulative total cost	cumulative cost per share
12/31/57	100	10	$1,000	$100.00	10.0	$1,000	$100.00
12/31/58	75	10	1,750	87.50	13.3	2,000	86.00
12/31/59	50	10	2,250	75.00	20.0	3,000	69.30
12/31/60	25	10	2,500	62.50	40.0	4,000	48.00
12/31/61	75	10	3,250	65.00	13.3	5,000	51.80
12/31/62	125	10	4,500	75.00	8.0	6,000	57.40
12/31/63	150	10	6,000	85.80	6.7	7,000	62.90
12/31/64	200	10	8,000	100.00	5.0	8,000	68.75
totals		80	$8,000	$100.00	116.3	$8,000	$68.75

Source: "Family Success Book," by the Editors of *Changing Times, The Kiplinger Magazine*, 1959 Edition p. 67.

at the same time and at the same price, the results are quite different. Both investors would have invested the same total amount of money, but Investor "B" — the dollar averager — would have more shares and a lower average cost per share.

While investing a fixed amount in dollars does not insure success, it has proved to be an excellent system, and should be just as good in the future. Of course, if you expect that the future is bleak, that the United States is facing many years of falling prices, then dollar averaging will not produce profits; but if you think the future is going to be like the past, a period of ups and downs with a long term upward trend, then dollar-cost-averaging is a tried and true method.[11]

---

[10] Hugh A. Johnson, *Johnson's Investment Company Charts, 1962*, Fourteenth Annual Edition, Copyright by Hugh A. Johnson & Company, Inc., Buffalo, New York, p. XVIII.

[11] The small investor interested in dollar averaging should refer to the Monthly Investment Plan described on page 397 in the preceding chapter.

Chart 15-2

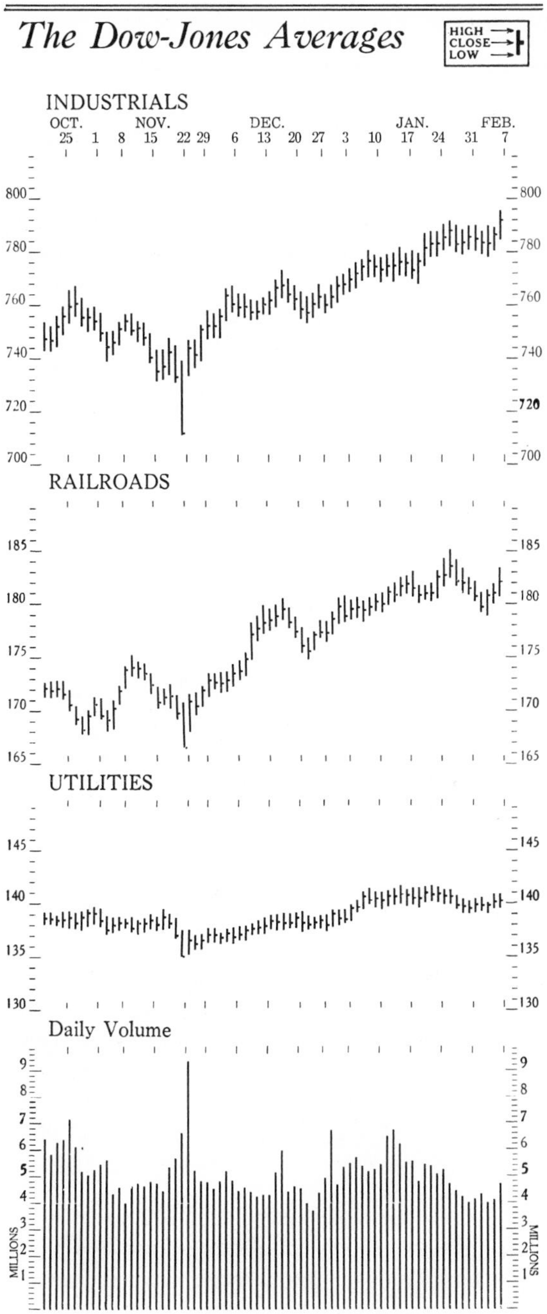

The Dow-Jones Averages

INDUSTRIALS

RAILROADS

UTILITIES

Daily Volume

Source: The Wall Street Journal, 44 Broad St., New York 4, N.Y.

Averages

Advising the average investor to be consistent, and to invest
for the long term, does not mean that any time is a good time to buy,
nor does it mean that stocks should never be sold. Some judgment
must be exercised. One of the many guides that should be considered
is a stock market average.

The best known averages are the Dow-Jones and Standard &
Poor's. While the Standard & Poor's is considered by many to be
superior (it covers more stocks, for example), the Dow-Jones Average
is most widely quoted. One reason might be that the company origi-
nating it, Dow-Jones & Company, publishes the Wall Street Journal.

Actually, there is not just one Dow-Jones Average, but four —
industrial, rails, utilities, and a composite of all three. The industrial
average is based upon just 30 industrial stocks, the rails average on
20 rail stocks, the utilities average on 15 utility stocks, and the composite average on the total of these 65 stocks.

Chart 15–3

PRICE-PERFORMANCE OF COMMON STOCKS* vs. DOW-JONES AVERAGE SINCE 1946
*(The 650 Stocks which were listed on the New York Stock Exchange in 1946 and were also listed in 1961)

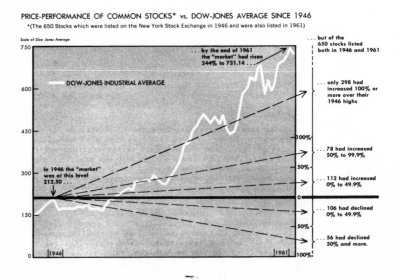

These averages are widely publicized and freely available, and
indicate what is happening in the market. The averages are given in
terms of points. If, for example, the composite average was 700 at the

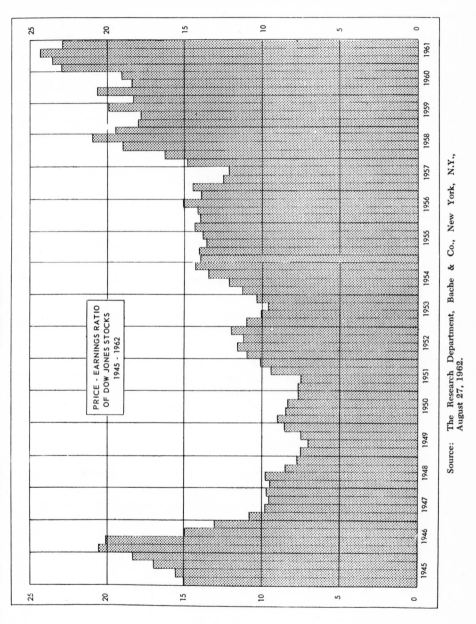

PRICE - EARNINGS RATIO
OF DOW JONES STOCKS
1945 - 1962

Source: The Research Department, Bache & Co., New York, N.Y.,
August 27, 1962.

437

close of the market yesterday, and rose to 710 at the close of the market today, it would indicate prices were up 1.4% — not $10.

Chart 15–2 shows the Dow-Jones Averages. Chart 15–3 shows the relationship between the industrial average (based as it is on 30 selected industrial stocks) and the price performance of the 650 common stocks listed on the New York Stock Exchange, for the period 1946 to 1961 inclusive. While the average indicated the market trend, the movement of most of these stocks did not correspond to the movement of the average.

The market is never predictable. There are, however, certain guides which have proven to be quite helpful. The two most frequently used are:

1. Price–Earnings Ratio.
2. Relative yields on stocks and bonds.

Chart 15–4 shows the price-earnings ratio of the Dow-Jones Industrials from 1945 through 1961. From 1952 through 1961, the Dow-Jones Industrial Average showed a mean PE Ratio of about 15.8. In December, 1961, this ratio reached a historic peak of 25. Later, after the market break of May, 1962, it dropped back to about 15.

Since 1926, the PE Ratio of *all* stocks, as measured by Standard and Poor, has averaged around 14.

Now it again must be emphasized that no one can say that a Price-Earnings Ratio of 20 is too high or that a Price-Earnings Ratio of 15 is just right. Since 1952, the market average has varied from 10 to 25. It would seem reasonable to make a *general* statement that 10 is extremely low, that anything above 20 seems too high, and that 15 seems to be a sound middle position.

These Price-Earnings Ratios are for the *market* and are used to indicate whether or not the *market* is abnormally high or low. Whether or not the Price-Earnings Ratio of the company in which you are interested is high or low depends upon the usual Price-Earnings Ratio for that company and for that industry. However, buying any stock when the market appears abnormally high, is risky business.

Chart 15–5 indicates the yield comparison between stocks and bonds.

A second suggested guide to a determination as to whether the market is high or low is the relative yield on stocks and bonds. Historically, and logically, the yield on stocks has been higher than the yield on bonds. Bonds represent a funded indebtedness, and are less risky than stocks, which represent ownership. An investor should expect a higher return from stocks, the more risky investment.

As the chart indicates, stock yields dropped below corporate bond yields in 1957 for the first time since 1938. Historically, the stock

Chart 15-5

A·YIELD COMPARISON - MUNICIPAL BONDS - CORPORATE BONDS - INDUSTRIAL COMMON STOCKS

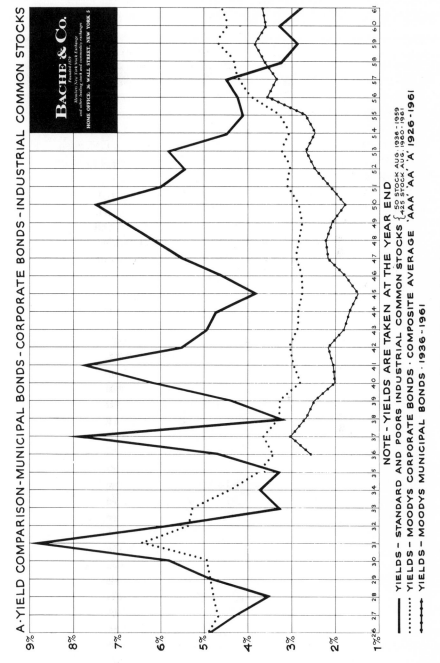

NOTE - YIELDS ARE TAKEN AT THE YEAR END

——— YIELDS - STANDARD AND POORS INDUSTRIAL COMMON STOCKS { 50 STOCK AUG. 1936 - 1959
425 STOCK AUG. 1960 - 1961

········· YIELDS - MOODYS CORPORATE BONDS · COMPOSITE AVERAGE 'AAA' 'AA' 'A' 1926 - 1961

➤➤➤ YIELDS - MOODYS MUNICIPAL BONDS · 1936 - 1961

Source: Bache & Co., New York, N.Y.

439

market has always been high when the yield on corporate stocks has dropped below the yield on high grade corporate bonds. This isn't definite proof of a high market, but it is an indicative guide.

In the past, whenever stock yields fell below bond yields, it was considered to be a danger signal. Many now believe that this is no longer true; that holding a fixed dollar investment such as bonds has become more risky than holding an equity investment such as stocks, due to the dangers of inflation. For this reason, stock yields could now *usually* be below bond yields. Whether or not this reasoning is correct remains to be seen. It is obvious, though, that even if it does prove to be true, a significant drop in stock yields below bond yields will indicate that the market is too high.

There are other guides that could be suggested, but these two are the easiest to follow. The best time to buy stock is when the Price-Earnings Ratio for the market, according to the Dow-Jones Average, is around its average position or below, and when yields on common stocks are above or near yields on high grade bonds.

Buying on Margin

On Wednesday, October 23, 1929, the stock market started to crash. Then came days known as Black Thursday, October 24, and Black Friday, October 25. Investors lost fortunes. Radio Corporation stock fell from $115 per share to $3, General Motors from $92 to $7, American Telephone from $310 to $70, etc. This débacle led to many corrective changes. The management of the stock exchanges were completely reorganized, regulations were stiffened, stringent rules were instated against manipulation, and more information was required to be made public by corporations.

One drastic change was the margin requirement. In the late 1920's, you could purchase stock with a down payment of 10 per cent or 20 per cent. You can still buy a house, an automobile, a deep freeze, almost anything, with little or no down payment; but the down payment (margin) requirement on stock purchases has been increased. Table 15–3 indicates the "initial margin" — the amount which the customer must now put down when he buys stock. This is a definite percentage, which is regulated by the Federal Reserve Board.

Let's use a 70 per cent margin as an example. Under such a margin, a purchaser of stock must put down 70 per cent of the market price. Thus, if a stock is purchased which has a market price of $100 per share, the buyer would have to put up at least $70

Table 15–3

MARGIN REQUIREMENTS[12]
(Per cent of market value)

Regulation	Effective Date		
	Oct. 16, 1958	July 28, 1960	July 10, 1962
Regulation T:			
For extensions of credit by brokers and dealers on listed securities	90	70	50
For Short Sales	90	70	50
Regulation U:			
For loans by banks on stocks	90	70	50

Note.—Regulations T and U, prescribed in accordance with Securities Exchange Act of 1934, limit the amount of credit that may be extended on a security by prescribing a maximum loan value, which is a specified percentage of its market value at the time of extension: margin requirements are the difference between the market value (100%) and the maximum loan value.

per share. He can buy only $30 per share on credit. The increased margin requirement by the Federal Reserve Board should discourage speculation and stabilize stock market activities. If speculative trading tends to become excessive, the Board can increase the margin requirement, which, of course, would immediately reduce credit buying. If market activity becomes depressed, the Board can reduce the margin requirement as an inducement to investors to buy more stock. This could be enough to spark a market recovery.

Margin restrictions apply only to securities traded on an exchange. Securities of the United States Government, state and municipal bonds, and other similar securities, are known as "exempt" securities and are not subject to margin restrictions. Other securities, such as stocks and bonds dealt in on the over-the-counter market, cannot be purchased except on a 100 per cent cash basis.

Margin buying is usually used to buy and sell within short periods of time for quick profits (trading), and is recommended only for the large investor. Most brokerage houses require a large minimum deposit before a margin account may be opened. The best policy for the small investor to follow is to buy high quality stocks in companies which appear to have a good future, and hold them for yield and long-term gain.

[12] Federal Reserve Bulletin, 1/62, p. 1643.

Selling Short

Another practice, which is not recommended for the small investor, is "selling short." This is selling stock you don't own, with the expectation that it will go down in price.

Suppose you believe the price of a particular stock is due to go down. You sell 100 shares at the current market price, $100 per share. The rules require that you deliver this stock to the broker within four days. This means that you will have to buy this stock for delivery. If within the next four days the price falls to $90, you will be able to buy the 100 shares for $9,000. As you have already sold this stock for $10,000, you have made $1,000 profit (minus commissions, of course). However, if the price goes up to $110 per share instead of dropping to $90, you will have to pay $11,000 for 100 shares, and, as you have already sold it for $10,000, you will suffer a $1,000 loss.

One of the great dangers of selling short is overconfidence. A person is so certain the price will go down that he doesn't worry about having the necessary cash to buy the stock for delivery if the price should rise. If the price does rise, he is in that unhappy situation described by a famous market manipulator, Daniel Drew, in a poem which he composed:

> "He who sells what isn't his'n,
> Must buy it back or go to prison."[13]

WHEN TO SELL

While the best system for the average investor to follow seems to be a buy and hold technique, it can be carried to extremes. If, for example, you make a bad selection, you should get rid of it as soon as the mistake becomes apparent. It is obviously poor judgment to keep it just because you intend to follow a buy and hold system.

Even if you are right, and your stock is a good selection, buy and hold doesn't mean forever. A company may be a "blue-chip" in one era and decline drastically, or go out of business, at a later date.

You should give some consideration to selling when:
1. The whole market appears too high. This condition is most apparent at the top of a long bull market when the Dow-Jones average is within 15% of its historic high.
2. A particular industry (in which you hold stock) displays a flattening out of earnings or long term downward earnings trend. The oil industry in late 1956 is a good illustration.

---

[13] Appearing in George L. Leffler, *The Stock Market,* Second Edition, The Ronald Press Co., New York, N.Y., 1957, p. 336.

Though the stock market as a whole advanced for the three following years, the major oils declined.

3. A particular stock shows an adverse earnings trend.
4. An industry, or certain stocks in it, get "over-glamorized" and sell at a times/earnings ratio that discounts the millenium. Uranium shares in 1955, air line stocks in 1946, and certain electronics in 1959 illustrate this overvaluation.
5. You need money. This can occur regardless of the height of the market, or the trend of earnings. The point to remember here is to sell the weaker issues, and (usually) those that show a loss, first. Most people do it the other way around, selling the best issues and ones showing a good profit.
6. The stock you bought has attained the market objective for which you purchased it and you are satisfied to take your profit and pay the tax.
7. For tax reasons. To establish a loss, offset loss with gain, anticipate inheritance taxes, achieve a loss "carry-over," or for many other tax reasons, selling may be both appropriate and effective. Get the guidance of a good accountant on such matters, however. In any event, don't stubbornly hang on to a stock that should be sold, just because you hate to pay the capital gains tax. Your market profit may melt away.[14]

It is up to you to determine which of these factors you consider most important. While trading is not a good technique for the average investor, stocks have to be sold sometime. These factors will help you determine the best time for you.

Investors who lose the most by selling are those who are completely emotional. A statement by the President of the United States, a statement by a Russian leader, a Presidential heart attack, the announcement of an investigation into security markets by the Securities and Exchange Commission, can cause a decline in the market. Such events cause many investors to panic and sell securities in outstanding companies at a loss. Avoid such emotional decisions. Sell only for the reasons given in the above list.

CONCLUSION

This chapter has covered a lot of territory in trying to help you decide what to buy and when to buy it. These were the conclusions reached:

---

[14] *Guide to Success in the Stock Market,* Edited by Ira U. Cobleigh, published by Avon Book Division, The Hearst Corporation, N.Y., Copyright New York Security Dealers Association, N.Y., 1961, pp. 110–111.

1. Common stocks are a very desirable investment medium for the average investor who is trying to accumulate money for the future.
2. First select an industry, then select a particular company in that industry.
3. Plan to invest in a company because you have faith in its future, and retain your ownership as long as you are satisfied with its progress.
4. Acquire a "recommended" list from your broker or advisory service to use as a starting point from which to make your particular selection.
5. Keep up to date by faithfully reading business and financial news.
6. Examine your company's balance sheet and income statement each year to see what changes have taken place.
7. The most practical method of determining what a share of stock is worth is to use the Price-Earnings Ratio approach.
8. Don't try to "beat the market." Invest regularly, and give serious consideration to the inherent possibilities of "dollar-cost-averaging."
9. Price-Earnings Ratios and relative yields on stocks and bonds are the two easiest guides to follow in trying to determine the market level.
10. Pay for what you buy and own what you sell. Neither margin buying nor short selling is recommended for the average investor.
11. Sell only after careful consideration; do not be moved by emotion.

Adherence to these rules does not guarantee success in the market. No person, or set of rules, or system, can make this guarantee. Awareness of these rules, however, will help you avoid some of the most frequent mistakes made by small investors in the past.

Questions

1. One of the large investment advisory services has consistently stated that the stock of a large electronics firm is not recommended as an investment and that the stock is worth much less than the market price.

Yet the market price of the stock continues to steadily rise. Does this mean that a subscriber to this service is wasting his money?

2. Compare the information appearing in the newspaper stock quotation columns for listed securities with that appearing for over-the-counter securities.

3. "The relationship between total current assets and total current liabilities is of more importance than the size of the individual figures by themselves." Discuss.

4. If the government permits a corporation to increase it depreciation allowance it may mean both a reduction in net profits and improvement in the stockholder's position. How can this be true?

5. What is the basic idea of "leverage?"

6. Compare par value, book value, and market value.

7. What is the "real value" of a share of stock?

8. How does "dollar-cost-averaging" work?

9. a. Why historically have bond yields been lower than stock yields?
   b. Why might this relationship be reversed in the future?

10. The Federal Reserve Board might raise the margin requirement if the stock market seemed extremely high. Why?

Problems

1. The "X" corporation is in the 52% tax bracket. Its net profit before taxes was $507,000 in 1962 and $480,000 in 1963. Would the fact that this corporation increased its annual depreciation allowance from $25,000 to $100,000 indicate the reason for the decline in net profits? Explain.

2. "B" has been investing regularly using the dollar-cost-averaging method. He recently reads that "business appears uncertain this week—there is neither an upward nor a downward trend in the stock market." Contrast B's reaction to this article with that of an individual not investing under a dollar-cost-averaging plan.

3. In comparing two stocks, "X" finds that AC Corporation has a Price Earnings Ratio of 15 to 1 while KO Corporation has a Price-Earnings Ratio of 32 to 1. "X" decides to buy the KO stock. Can you justify his decision?

4. "C" has been doing business with the same stock broker for a period
of 5 years. During the past 3 months, "B" has been buying a stock
regularly because its price has been steadily rising. He has not bought
on margin as of yet. The current margin requirement is 70%. One
day "C's" broker calls him and states that it is rumored the Federal
Reserve Board will raise its margin requirement to 90%. Should "C"
   a. Do nothing, ignore the rumor.
   b. Start buying more of this particular stock while the margin requirement is 70%.
   c. Wait until the margin requirement changes to 90%, then buy on
   margin.
   d. Sell this particular stock.
   What action should "C" take and why?

5. A Stock has the following values:
   a. Par Value $100
   b. Market Value $42
   c. Book Value $85
   Which value would you rely upon, if you were investing in this
   company?

Selected Readings

Babson, Thomas E., and Babson, David L., *Investing for a Successful
Future,* The Macmillan Company, New York, N.Y., 1959

Engel, Louis, *How to Buy Stocks,* Little, Brown & Co., Boston, Mass., 1962

Freund, William C., and Lee, Murray G., *Investment Fundamentals,* The
American Bankers Association, New York, N.Y., 1960

Guide to Success in the Stock Market, edited by Cobleigh, Ira U., published
by Avon Book Division, The Hearst Corporation, New York, N.Y., copyright New York Security Dealers Association, New York, N.Y., 1962

Hayes, Douglas A., *Investments: Analysis and Management,* The Macmillan
Company, New York, N.Y., 1961

How to Understand Financial Statements, New York Stock Exchange, Publications Division, 11 Wall Street, New York 5, N.Y.

Publications of the various brokerage firms

Chapter 16

MUTUAL FUNDS

Mr. Dan Raustis would like to invest in securities. He has an adequate reserve for emergencies, life insurance, etc. and has a modest surplus remaining. He wants to put this surplus money to work. He has read some material on the stock market but he is still worried. Even if he does follow all of the suggestions made, he realizes that certain problems would remain.

1. Is he able to do the research necessary to select "good" securities?
2. Does he have enough to invest to be able to spread his investment around, or will all of his "eggs be in one basket?"

3. After he selects securities, will he have the time to continuously supervise them?

Many people, and Mr. Raustis may be one of them, believe that investing directly in securities is not for them. Take the matter of time for example. ". . . several years ago, it was estimated by the New York Stock Exchange that investment dealers annually issue a total of 30,700 market letters running to 46,800 pages, plus 15,500 pieces of sales literature totaling 37,300 pages. The Exchange's survey went on to comment that 'in a single pile, these 84,100 pages of literature would stack 35 feet high; weigh more than 900 pounds. Such a pile would, incidentally, exclude 1,800 special reports by the same firms, amounting to 7,000 additional pages.'

"A little calculating indicates to us that to wade through this mass of material would be equivalent to reading a 250-page book each day for 365 days a year."[1]

There are several different routes an investor may follow to obtain professional management of his investments. The three most commonly followed today are, investing in an "open-end" investment fund, a "closed-end" investment fund, or in a small business investment company. There are other methods, such as buying shares in insurance companies or banks, which have many securities in their portfolios; by investing in a real estate trust, or by buying a variable annuity, but they are quite different. The investment funds and the small business investment companies (SBIC) are in the money managing business. Insurance companies and banks do invest in securities, but are primarily engaged in either insurance or banking. Real estate trusts seem to be a little too specialized for the taste of the average investor, and variable annuities, while they might someday be the most attractive of the lot, still have certain regulatory problems to overcome before their attractiveness can be fully appraised.

INVESTMENT COMPANIES

"Open-end" investment funds, "closed-end" investment funds, and small business investment companies are all in the *business of managing* an investor's money.

> Investment companies are designed to provide you with three major advantages and services:
> 1. Professional management of your invested money.
> 2. Diversification: they reduce the risk by spreading your investment among many different securities.

---

[1] "Brevits," Vance, Sanders & Company, Inc., Boston, Mass., Vol. R—No. 12, June 5, 1961, p. 2.

3. Convenience: a ready market for your shares if you wish to sell them.[2]

"Closed-end" Funds

The basic difference between the "open-end" and "closed-end" company is that the "closed-end" has a fixed number of shares outstanding. The price of its shares is determined by the value of the securities in which it has invested and by the demand for its own stock on the market.

When a person buys or sells shares in a "closed-end" company, he does business with a broker or dealer, and pays the same commissions as he would pay to buy shares in an industrial corporation.

"Closed-end" investment companies obtain their investment funds in the same way an ordinary business corporation obtains capital to finance its production and distribution. It determines how much money it wants to manage, and offers securities for sale in that amount to the general public.[3]

The Boston Personal Property Trust, originally organized in 1893, is the oldest American trust still in operation. Its shares are listed on the Boston Stock Exchange.

Small Business Investment Companies

Small business investment companies — S.B.I.C.'s — are similar, from the investor's viewpoint, to the closed-end investment company. They offer the investor the advantages of professional management, diversification, and convenience, while investing in new, small business enterprises.

The Small Business Investment Act was passed by Congress to help small businesses obtain equity capital and long-term financing. In the past, most small businesses could obtain only short-term loans from banks, with the exception of mortgage loans on their real estate. Insurance companies and other institutional investors were not interested in investing in small privately held firms. Public sale of stock by most small businesses was not

---

[2] *Investing Made Easy,* Newest Edition, Investment Company Institute, New York, N.Y., p. 5.

[3] Leo M. Loll, Jr., and Julian G. Buckley, *The Over-the-Counter Securities Markets: A Review Guide,* Copyright 1961, Prentice-Hall, Inc., Englewood Cliffs, N.J., p. 212.

practical because of the high cost involved and the size of the
business which made for a very high degree of risk.[4]

Many of these S.B.I.C.'s have made public stock offerings, and by
doing so become similar to a closed-end fund. The risks of investing
in S.B.I.C.'s are great. They are in business to supply venture capital
to small firms. Experience, so far, indicates that an investor must
regard S.B.I.C.'s in general as an investment involving considerable risk.

Open-end Funds

"When Massachusetts Investors Trust was organized in 1924, the
managers of the fund stated that it would continuously offer new
shares, and redeem outstanding ones upon demand. This was the
start of the open-end investment company, now known as a mutual
fund."[5] Today the open-end fund is by far the most common.

The open-end fund doesn't have a fixed number of shares outstanding. It will sell new shares or buy back old ones at any time.
To buy a share in a closed-end fund, you buy, through a broker,
shares owned by another person. To buy a share in an open-end
fund, you may do business with a broker, but you buy from the fund.
When you want to sell the share, you sell it to the fund.

How do open-end funds and closed-end funds compare? "As to
performance, studies tend to show that the closed-end funds have
done the best for the investor over the past 20 years."[6] Yet open-end
funds have increased in size and number much more rapidly (see
Chart 16–1). Why should this be true? One outstanding reason is
the mutual fund salesman. The sales commission on mutual funds
is usually about 8% of the net asset value. On a closed-end fund,
the commissions are the same as for any other stock, depending on
the size of the transaction. There is an understandable reason why
salesmen have been more interested in selling open-end funds.

Another reason for the more rapid growth of open-end funds is
the unlimited number of shares they may issue. A closed-end fund
with 500,000 shares outstanding will always have 500,000 shares out-

---

[4] Thomas M. O'Donnell, analyst, "Small Business Investment Companies,"
Industry Review, Saunders, Stiver & Co., Cleveland, Ohio, 1962, p. 1.

[5] Stuart B. Mead, *Mutual Fund and Investment Company Performance in the
Fifties,* Occasional Paper No. 9, Bureau of Business and Economic Research,
Graduate School of Business Administration, Michigan State Univ., East Lansing,
Michigan, 1961, p. 4.

[6] Kiplinger, "99 New Ideas on Your Money, Job and Living," *Changing
Times Family Success Book,* 1963 Edition, Washington, D.C., p. 21.

Chart 16–1

GROWTH OF INVESTMENT COMPANY ASSETS
SINCE 1940

Year	Open-End	Closed-End†	Total
1961	$22,788,812.00	$3,205,277,000	$25,994,089,000
1960	17,025,684,000	2,083,898,000	19,109,582,000
1958	13,242,388,000	1,931,402,000	15,173,790,000
1956	9,046,431,000	1,525,748,000	10,572,179,000
1954	6,109,390,000	1,246,351,000	7,355,741,000
1952	3,931,407,000	1,011,089,000	4,942,496,000
1950	2,530,563,000	871,962,000	3,402,525,000
1948	1,505,762,000	767,028,000	2,272,790,000
1946	1,311,108,000	851,409,000	2,162,517,000
1944	882,191,000	739,021,000	1,621,212,000
1942	486,850,000	557,264,000	1,044,114,000
1940	447,959,000	613,589,000	1,061,548,000

† Including funded debt and bank loans.

Sources: Open-End—Investment Company Institute.
Closed-End—Investment Company Institute 1940-1946.
Arthur Weisenberger & Company 1947-1961.

Source: Arthur Weisenberger, *Investment Companies*, 1962
Edition, New York, N.Y., p. 26.

standing, regardless of investor interest. An open-end fund, however, has an increase in the number of outstanding shares corresponding to an increase in investor demands. Both funds acquire more capital through their own investment operations—capital appreciation, dividends, etc.—but only the open-end fund will continuously receive new money from investors. Theoretically, of course, more shares could be sold than bought, and the size of an open-end fund could decrease. In practice, though, this just hasn't happened, and it seems quite unlikely that it will happen.

"Load" and "No-load" Funds

"Load" is the name given to the selling cost charged by a mutual fund. Funds which do not charge a selling cost are called "no-load" funds. If $500 is invested in a fund with a "load," the average charge is about 8%.

Why are some funds able to operate without any selling charge? Primarily because they don't have any salesmen. It is up to the investor to take the initiative and buy, rather than to wait for someone to sell to him.

Now it is commonly known that no one does business for nothing. All funds, whether they have a "load" or not, charge a management fee. Typically, this is about one-half of 1 per cent each year of the total amount of capital managed by the fund, or about $5,000 for every $1,000,000 managed. Usually, these managers are in the investment counseling business. To them, the costs involved in managing the mutual fund are not entirely added costs. To use one decision in two places does not cost any more than to use the decision in just one place. This isn't to say that some added expenses aren't involved in handling the mutual fund, but certainly a great deal of the research, analysis, and decision making is already being done for other reasons. The management fee is an additional source of income.

There are certainly good buys in "no-load" funds, and yet "load" funds sell much faster. The reason, again, is the salesman. It seems obvious that even the proverbial "better mousetrap" would never sell successfully without a sales force promoting it to the public; and salesmen are always especially interested in selling what is most profitable to them.

Is Selling Mutual Funds Profitable?

Of the 8% commission, or loading charge, the dealer who sells the funds gets about 6%. Is it any wonder that mutual funds are so popular today with security dealers and many member firms of the New York Stock Exchange? On a $2000 order a broker makes $120. In contrast, on a $2000 odd-lot order for a listed stock he makes a standard commission of only $25.[7]

Many people refuse to buy anything, even if they need it, until someone sells it to them. There is, however, another group which carries things to the other extreme. They resent every selling charge, and always try to avoid paying such a charge. Thus the "no-load" funds appeal to them. There are many excellent "no-load" funds which should certainly be considered by investors of all groups. However, a "no-load" fund shouldn't be purchased just because it has no "load."

One thing that must be remembered is that there are many more funds with a "load" than without. This means that an investor has a great deal more choice in "load" funds. The fund which best suits his particular needs might not exist in the "no-load" group.

Another point has to do with performance. Let's imagine that ten years ago you could have invested $1,000 in either "Load Fund A" or "No-Load Fund B." Both funds were supposedly similar in terms of their goals and investment policies. Obviously, if "Load Fund A" is now worth $4,000 and "No-Load Fund B" is only worth $3,000, the selling costs on "Load Fund A" were well worth paying.

---

[7] Louis Engel, *How to Buy Stocks*, Little, Brown & Co., Copyright 1953, © 1957, 1962 by Louis Engel, p. 154. By permission of Little, Brown and Company.

VARIETIES OF FUNDS

Chart 16–2 indicates the wide variety of investment companies on the market today, and their comparative size. This breakdown includes both open and closed-end funds.

Chart 16–2

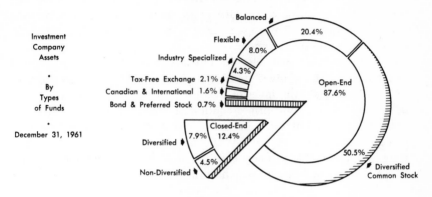

Source: Arthur Weisenberger, *Investment Companies*, 1962 Edition, New York, N. Y., p. 42.

Mutual funds can generally be classified as:

Common Stock Fund—Investments, primarily common stocks, diversified throughout many companies in several different industries.

Balanced Fund—Diversified investments of bonds, preferred, and common stocks in several companies in different industries.

Bond Fund—Diversified bond investments of various kinds in different companies of a particular industry, or of several different industries.

Preferred Stock Fund—Diversified preferred stock investments in several companies of different industries.

Specialty Fund—Diversified investments of one or more kinds of securities, generally common stocks, in general companies in one particular industry.[8]

SELECTING A FUND

How do you decide which fund to buy, out of the hundreds available? Three questions should be asked:

[8] Hugh A. Johnson, *Johnson's Investment Company Charts*, Buffalo, N.Y., 1962, p. IV.

1. What is your goal?
2. Which type of mutual fund is most likely to meet your needs?
3. How effective is management?

Your Goal

Differences in investment objectives were discussed in Chapter 14. Some people are interested in investing so that their money will grow over a period of years. Others are most interested in preserving a specific sum of capital for a specific need. Still others are primarily interested in current income.

The particular goal selected depends primarily on the individual circumstances of the investor, his age, income, etc., and also depends to some degree on the investor's estimate of the future of the society in which he lives. Will prices continue to rise? Will the average life span increase? Will there be more leisure time? Is the attempt to conquer space to continue? While an investor's individual circumstances must receive primary consideration, he must consider himself in relation to the world in which he lives.

WHICH TYPE OF FUND

There is a mutual fund for just about every need imaginable. Once the investor determines his goal and needs, in other words, how he would invest his own money, he must find a mutual fund which will do this particular job for him. Let's take the three primary objectives: growth of capital; immediate income; and safety of principal.

If an investor wants growth of capital, he will be interested in the common stock funds which, in their prospectus, state that their objective is capital appreciation. These funds will invest in common stocks which they believe have the greatest potential for an increase in value, and will be only secondarily interested in dividends, etc.

There is need for careful selection even within a category. In examining the various common stock funds, the investor will find that some of them invest only in real "blue-chip" investments, while others specialize in more speculative investments in newer and smaller firms.

Growth of capital might also be achieved by purchasing one of the so-called specialty funds. These are funds specializing in life insurance, atomics, petroleum, electronics, or any one of many other specific industries. It is generally believed that more diversified common stock funds are preferable for the average investor, as they give him greater diversification and do not depend solely upon conditions in one segment of the economy.

If an investor wants income today, he should select one of the funds which state that their objective is income. Any kind of fund might have this objective. It might be common stock, balanced, bond, preferred stock, or specialty. Again, the investor must read the prospectus to determine the objective of the particular fund being considered. Funds having income as their objective will invest primarily in securities returning a high current income.

For safety of principal, an investor would turn to a bond, preferred stock, or balanced, fund. Here the investor would purchase a fund which stated in its prospectus that stability of principal was its primary objective.

True balanced funds try to give an investor a little of everything, some growth, current income, and stability. They do this by investing in common and preferred stocks, and bonds. In general, they will not do any of these things as well as a fund which specializes toward just one objective, but they are preferred by many investors. A balanced fund should not rise as fast as a growth fund when the stock market is rising, but it should fall less when the market is going down.

Effectiveness of Management

Chart 16–3 presents Johnson's Stock Fund Average of 67 different stock funds. An investment of $10,000 in this average on January 1, 1952, would have returned $32,499, including dividends, if the fund had been liquidated on December 31, 1961. This is 225 per cent more than the original investment.

"During the same period, the best individual performer in this group of stock funds would, if liquidated, have returned 397% more than invested, while the poorest performer would have returned 113% more."[9]

No one can state that differences such as this are entirely due to management. Different funds have different policies and objectives, and quite different results are expected. If, however, two funds have the same objectives and the same policies, then differences in performance become significant, and indicate possible differences in the effectiveness of management.

---

[9] Hugh A. Johnson, *Johnson's Investment Company Charts,* Buffalo, N.Y., 1962, p. XII.

Chart 16–3

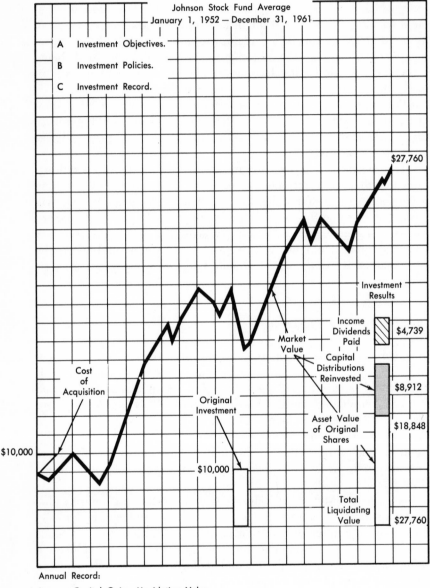

Johnson Stock Fund Average
January 1, 1952 — December 31, 1961

A   Investment Objectives.

B   Investment Policies.

C   Investment Record.

$27,760

Investment
Results

Income
Dividends
Paid $4,739

Market
Value

Capital
Distributions
Reinvested $8,912

Cost
of
Acquisition

Asset Value
of Original
Shares $18,848

Original
Investment

$10,000

$10,000

Total
Liquidating
Value $27,760

Annual Record:

Income, Capital Gains, Liquidating Value

Source: Hugh A. Johnson, *Johnson's Investment Company Charts,*
Buffalo, N.Y., 1962, p. XXII.

Many attempts are made to rate management. One of the easiest for the average investor to read and understand is presented each year in Forbes. Forbes is also more readily available than many of the others. It attempts to rate funds according to performance ratings and management results.

Table 16–1 can be used to illustrate the method used. Forbes compares the performance of fund averages and individual funds to Standard & Poor's 500 Stock Average. This average appears at the top of the table.

The two columns headed "Forbes Performance Rating" are supposed to measure the ability of management to match the performance of Standard & Poor's index. "They measure a management's ability to match the S&P average over a long period of time and under a wide variety of circumstances. Three periods of rising markets were chosen, three of sharply declining ones.* A plus score shows that a fund has tended to outrun the averages; a minus score that it has generally fallen behind the averages."[10]

The last two columns, headed "Management Results," show what would have happened to $100 worth of each fund's net asset value over the 1953–61 bull market and in 1962's declining market.[11]

Table 16–1 does not use individual funds as examples, as such treatment might be misleading. Those interested in this comparison should refer to Forbes' latest ratings. Under the S&P Average is Forbes' average for 10 top stock funds in 1962, and then Forbes' average for 10 top balanced funds. Below these averages are the results Forbes obtained by applying the methods described to the twenty most widely owned U. S. stocks in 1962.

Notice that the —1 Performance Rating, appearing for Forbes' Average for 10 Top Stock Funds, indicates that this average did not perform as well as the S&P average during the three periods of rising markets, and the same relationship was true for the three periods of declining markets. On the other hand, the —18 rating of Socony Mobil indicates that the stock fund average did much better than Socony in rising markets; and the +54 rating of IBM indicates that the stock fund average did not do as well as IBM. In declining markets, the stock fund average did better than U. S. Steel (—16) but not as well as Consolidated Edison (+14).

---

* The three periods of rising markets: 1) Sept. 30, 1953 to June 30, 1956; 2) Oct. 25, 1957 to Dec. 31, 1959; 3) Sept. 30, 1960 to Dec. 31, 1961. The three periods of declining markets: 1) June 30, 1957 to Oct. 25, 1957; 2) Dec. 31, 1959 to Sept. 30, 1960; 3) Jan. 1, 1962 to June 30, 1962.

[10] Forbes, "Annual Mutual Fund Survey: 1962," *Forbes Business & Finance*, Forbes, Inc., New York, N.Y., August 15, 1962, pp. 29–35.

[11] *Ibid.*, p. 28.

Table 16–1

	FORBES PERFORMANCE RATING		MANAGEMENT RESULTS	
	In Rising Markets	In Declining Markets	In the 1953–1961 Bull Market	In the 1962 Market Decline
			\$100 Ended as . . .	
Standard & Poor's 500 Stock Average			\$ 306.42	\$76.51
Forbes' Average for 10 Top Stock Funds	— 1	— 1	296.68	75.83
Forbes' Average for 10 Top Balanced Funds	—14	+ 6	209.83	83.58
American Telephone & Tel.	—10	+12	264.33	76.21
Bank of America	— 6	+ 2	226.31	74.10
Bethlehem Steel	+10	— 5	366.67	80.06
Cities Service	— 8	+ 5	213.89	88.98
Columbia Gas System	—15	+11	220.95	89.22
Consolidated Edison	—16	+14	205.31	85.08
du Pont*	+ 3	— 4	239.13	80.60
Ford Motor	....	—13	....	68.02
General Electric	+ 4	— 4	308.72	79.07
General Motors	+ 5	+ 1	306.04	84.87
General Telephone & Elec.	+47	+ 3	878.78	68.62
International Business Mach.	+54	+ 3	1,945.56	58.60
Sears, Roebuck	+18	+ 6	485.86	71.47
Socony Mobil	—18	+ 8	158.69	95.38
Sperry Rand	....	—12	....	60.43
Standard Oil (Calif.)	— 6	+ 8	254.88	97.62
Standard Oil (N.J.)	— 7	+ 5	220.65	98.52
Texaco	+15	+ 2	482.35	84.66
U.S. Steel	+22	—16	448.57	56.21
Westinghouse Electric	—17	— 2	177.16	68.29

* Prices adjusted for distribution of one-half share of General Motors stock.

Source: Forbes, "Annual Mutual Fund Survey: 1962," *Forbes Business & Finance,* Forbes, Inc., New York, N.Y., August 15, 1962, pp. 29-35.

$100 invested in the stock fund average in the 1953–1961 bull market would have grown to $296.68—not as good as the S&P average. $100 invested in IBM would have grown to $1,945.56 during this period, but only to $158.69 if invested in Socony. During the 1962 market decline, $100 worth of assets in the stock fund average would have declined to $75.83, a little more than the S&P average, but the same $100 in United States Steel would have dropped to $56.21. On the other hand, $100 in Standard Oil (N. J.) would have declined only to $98.52.

These figures will change from year to year, and as specific numbers they are only important for the year 1962. They should, however, convince a mutual fund investor that *any* mutual fund is not the answer to his investment problems. Johnson's comparative measurements of ten years' performance certainly indicate that some funds did much better than the average fund, and some much worse. Forbes' figures indicate that some individual stocks did much better than the average mutual fund, and some did much worse. Selection is still essential to success. When policies and objectives are the same, this selection must be based on the effectiveness of management to a considerable degree.

Chart 16–4 illustrates the structure of a management organization. Note its complexity and thoroughness. In a mutual fund, all of this talent is devoted to managing the investor's money. The best managements make errors, but it seems quite reasonable to believe that a competent staff will select investments much more wisely than the average investor.

> It is sensible, therefore, to think about the past record of the company—and the people in the company—upon whom you will be depending for future results. Who are they? What do you know about them? What have they done to warrant your confidence? How good are they, specifically, at selecting worthwhile stocks? [12]

FUND OPERATIONS

To understand mutual funds, the investor should have some basic knowledge of how they do business. How do they sell their shares? What can cause your shares to increase or decrease in value?

How Shares are Sold

When you purchase shares in a "load" fund, you must pay the net asset value for each share, plus a loading charge. When you buy shares in a "no-load" fund you pay the net asset value. What is the net asset value?

---

[12] Eugene E. Glardon, American Investors Fund, Inc., Letter to Investors, Larchmont, New York.

Chart 16–4

How the National Securities Series of Mutual Funds are Managed

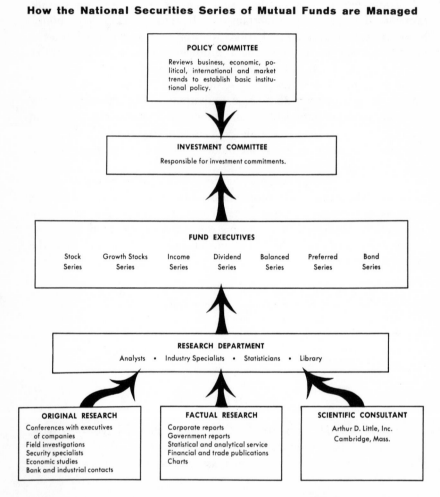

National Securities & Research Corporation is responsible for managing more than 210,000 shareowner accounts in the National Securities Series of mutual funds with total assets of over $535,000,000. Shareowners include individuals, trust funds, colleges and universities, banks and pension and profit-sharing plans.

Source: National Securities & Research Corp., New York, N.Y.

Net asset value is found by a simple procedure:

Value of Portfolio — Liabilities = Net Asset Value

Net Asset Value ÷ Number of Shares Outstanding = Net Asset
Value Per Share

Most mutual funds determine the value of the securities in their portfolio twice each day. If you take this market value (minus liabilities, if there are any) and divide by the total number of the mutual funds' own outstanding shares, you find the net asset value per share. In a "no-load" fund, this is what you pay when you buy a share.

The shares of closed-end funds are traded on the over-the-counter market or exchanges, just like other stocks. For this reason they may sell for more or less than the net asset value per share—at a premium or at a discount—depending on the number of buyers and sellers interested in these shares, the condition of the stock market that day, etc. Open-end funds (mutual funds), on the other hand, always have a price based on the net asset value per share.

Price ranges for mutual funds are published daily in the Wall Street Journal and in other newspapers. Bid and asked prices are presented for each fund listed. In the case of "no-load" funds, the bid and asked prices will be exactly the same. (Except for those few funds which charge a slight redemption fee and add this fee to the asked price.) There is, however, a difference between the bid and asked prices for "load" funds. This is due to the "loading," or sales charge.

"In most cases the load charge is based on the ask price, which is the bid price plus the sales commission. This would mean that the per cent of commission quoted by the fund differs from the per cent of commission based on the net asset value of the shares. This is the result of an accounting technique; it is a matter of which figures should be considered to be the base—the bid price or the ask price. To illustrate: a fund which has a quoted load charge of 8 per cent has a bid price (net asset value) on a certain day of $14.49. The ask price would be $14.49 ÷ 92% = $15.75, based on the following accounting concept:

Sales (ask price)	$15.75	100%
Cost (bid price)	14.49	92%
Margin (load price)	$ 1.26	8%

On the other hand, the investor could say that his redemption value, or the value of the assets behind each of his shares, is only

$14.49. Consequently, if he pays a load charge of $1.26, he is paying a commission rate as follows:

$$\$1.26 \div \$14.49 = 8.69\%$$

Both concepts are correct. It is strictly a matter of which figure you believe to be of greater significance, the net asset value or the sales figure."[13]

A few mutual funds charge a small redemption fee when shares are redeemed. In most cases, however, the loading charge is the only charge made when you buy and sell. Remember that when stock is purchased, a commission must be paid, and another commission must be paid when the stock is sold. When a mutual fund is purchased, a "load" must be paid when the fund is purchased, but usually there is no charge when the fund is sold. Many mutual funds have lower loading charges on larger purchases.

Making Money

Most people, other than those interested primarily in immediate income, invest in mutual funds in the hope that their investment will increase in value. How is this increase accomplished? Mutual funds invest the money in securities. Any increase in the value of these securities, or income in the form of interest and dividends, will benefit the mutual fund investor.

The price of mutual fund shares rises when the market price of the securities in the fund's portfolio increases. If the market price of these securities goes down, the price of the fund's shares will also go down.

Mutual fund investors receive two kinds of dividends. They receive dividends from capital gains and from income. Capital gain dividends are distributions of profits which the mutual fund has derived by selling securities in its portfolio. Actually, they do not represent income but are a distribution of capital. When the fund sells securities which have gone up in market value, it converts an unrealized capital gain into a realized gain. It distributes this gain to shareholders. This means that the net asset value of the fund's shares falls; therefore the shareholder is actually no better off.

Most mutual funds make it possible for shareholders to reinvest capital gains dividends. Unless the investor needs cash badly, he

---

[13] Stuart B. Mead, *Mutual Fund and Investment Company Performance in the Fifties*, Occasional Paper No. 9, Bureau of Business and Economic Research, Graduate School of Business Administration, Michigan State University, East Lansing, Michigan, 1961, p. 12.

should take advantage of this opportunity. Reinvestment is made as easy as possible, and usually no sales commission is charged on the additional shares purchased in this manner. Reinvesting dividends of both kinds, capital gains and income, helps an investor to build up his capital more rapidly, and is certainly a good idea. Of course, if his goal is current income, he will probably prefer to accept both distributions in cash.

Taxes

How are capital gains and income distributions taxed? Must both the mutual fund and the investor pay a federal income tax? Most funds distribute all of their income, after expenses, to shareholders. By doing this, they avoid federal income taxes.

A mutual fund shareholder is taxed on realized capital gains and income just as if he had invested directly in the securities which the fund owns. To avoid taxes, an investment company must meet certain requirements and be a "regulated investment company." Otherwise, it will be taxed like an ordinary corporation.

"Regulated investment company" is a rather misleading term, as the regulation involved is not actually supervision by the government. It means only that the investment company has met certain requirements, i.e., it has asked to be a regulated company, it distributes at least 90 per cent of its net income each year, etc.

Most mutual funds are "regulated investment companies." They escape taxes only on the portion of their income which they pay out to shareholders. They must pay a regular income tax on undistributed income, and a regular capital gains tax on any undistributed realized capital gains.

Usually, funds having undistributed capital gains pay the 25 per cent capital gains tax, and notify their shareholders. These shareholders then show this capital gain on their tax statements as if it had been received. They deduct the tax paid by the fund, as a tax credit. If it is greater than the capital gains tax the shareholder should be paying in his tax bracket, he, in effect, receives a refund.[14] Even in this case, the tax is actually paid by the shareholder. Investment companies occasionally use this method to prevent depletion of capital.

Taking dividend or capital gains distributions in additional shares does not mean that the investor avoids taxes. The same taxes must be paid on these distributions as on cash distributions.

---

[14] See Chapter 12 for a discussion of capital gains taxes.

Mutual fund shareholders do receive special treatment of capital gains distributions in one respect; they can consider them as long-term gains even if the fund has held the securities on which it realized the capital gains for only a few days.

State tax regulations on capital gains distributions vary. In some states they are taxed as income, in some as capital gains, in some it depends on whether they are paid in cash or shares, and in some they are not taxed at all. Obviously, taxpayers must consult the tax laws of the state in which they live.

Expenses

It costs mutual funds money to operate, just like other businesses. The biggest expense is management. According to the SEC sponsored Wharton School *Study of Mutual Funds*, the typical fee is ½ of 1% of the average assets per year. This pays for supervision of the fund, research, clerical help, and office space.

Other expenses are trustee's or director's fees, custodian fees, and taxes. The custodian is a bank or trust company that holds the investment company's cash and securities. It has no part in the supervision of the portfolio.

The management fee has come in for special criticism. In some instances such criticism has been justified, but in others it may have been the result of a lack of understanding on the part of the investor. The situation sometimes develops like this:

John Titus purchased shares in a mutual fund. He was told by the salesman, and noted in the prospectus, that the management fee was ½ of 1% of the average assets per year. But this didn't seem very important; in fact, the percentage seemed quite small. After a few years, a study of the fund's annual report made him suddenly realize that the management fee amounted to 25% of the fund's annual income. This shocked him. He had never thought of the expense in relation to income before. He became quite indignant and thought the fee much too high.

Management is important. It is one of the prime reasons why people invest in mutual funds. It performs a service and deserves payment. Its expenses will continue in good years and bad. It is necessary to spend time and money on careful investigation before adding a new security to the fund's portfolio. Supervising the portfolio also is costly. An investor should take an interest in management costs. Some of them *are* too high, but fair management costs are necessary, and must be expected.

Regulation

Investment companies are regulated by both state and federal laws. The most important of these is the Investment Company Act of 1940. The principal provisions of this law are presented in Chart 16-5. An investor should be especially aware of several features of this law. Notice the "musts" in the law for investor protection. It requires that certain things "must" be done with respect to registration, diversification, investment policy, management, dividends, reports, safekeeping, and literature. There is a vast difference between the regulation of investment companies today and in the 1920's. This regulation means greater safety for investors.

On the other hand, an investor should be aware that the various laws do not mean that there is any governmental supervision of the investment policies and practices of management. This is both understandable and desirable. Investment companies must be permitted to be different from one another to meet the varying needs of investors. Investors must realize, however, that it is up to them to select a fund with the policies and management they want.

Chart 16–5

PRINCIPAL PROVISIONS OF THE INVESTMENT COMPANY ACT OF 1940:[15]

REGISTRATION

All investment companies with 100 or more shareholders must register with the Securities and Exchange Commission. A company must have a minimum capital of $100,000 before it may publicly offer securities.

DIVERSIFICATION

The registration statement must clearly define the kind and quality of securities eligible under the investment policy. At least 75% of assets must be in cash or securities, and no individual investment of a diversified company can exceed 5% of its assets or 10% of the controlling stock of any company.

INVESTMENT POLICY

Important investment practices and policies, as well as specific investment objectives, must be detailed in the registration statement and cannot be altered in any way without the approval of a majority of shareholders. The charters of most mutual funds explicitly prohibit such speculative practices as buying securities on margin, selling short, or participating in joint trading accounts with others.

---

[15] Hugh A. Johnson, *Johnson's Investment Company Charts*, Buffalo, N.Y., 1962, p. V.

MANAGEMENT

All contracts with investment advisers must be approved by the shareholders and cannot be altered without the approval of a majority of the shareholders. The board of directors, or trustees as the case may be, is always subject to the approval of shareholders. Investment bankers, brokers, or others connected with the sale of securities must be in the minority. No more than 40% of the board may be officers or employees, or affiliated with the investment advisers of the fund. Directors, officers, trustees, or sponsors cannot sell general market securities to, or buy them from, the fund.

DIVIDENDS

The sources of all distributions must be accurately described to shareholders. Supplement Q of the Revenue Act of 1942 specifically exempts mutual funds from corporate taxes on all income and profits paid to shareholders, provided such payments represent at least 90% of net investment income and security profits.

REPORTS

Full disclosure of all investment activity, financial condition, income, expenses, salaries or fees of management and current status of investments must be reported to shareholders at least twice each year and certified by independent auditors approved annually by shareholders. With few exceptions, these reports are issued quarterly.

SHARES

Each share represents an equal and proportionate claim on all assets, and no security can ever be subsequently issued with a prior claim to assets.

MARKETABILITY

Shares may be redeemed without cost at asset value on any business day. There may be small redemption fees charged, but these are very isolated exceptions. The value of shares upon redemption may, of course, be more or less, than the investor's cost depending upon the market value of all assets.

PROSPECTUS

The prospectus fulfills the purpose of The Securities Act of 1933 and The Investment Company Act of 1940 by making available to prospective investors the information required for an intelligent appraisal of the investment company.

SAFEKEEPING

All assets must be deposited in a bank or trust company, or other company subject to all regulations of the Securities and Exchange Commission. Such bank may also act as dividend disbursing agent and transfer agent of fund shares, but cannot participate in the management policies or practices of an investment company.

REGULATION

While federal and state statutes are extensive and thoroughly designed in the best interests of the public, they do not, however, provide for any governmental supervision of the investment policies and practices of management.

LITERATURE

All sales literature and representations of past investment results must comply with The Securities Act of 1933, The Investment Company Act of 1940, and the Statement of Policy of 1950 (as amended November 5, 1957) and must in no way be deemed to be misleading in an accurate appraisal of a particular company.

Special attention should be given to the regulations in regard to literature. The Statement of Policy of 1950 is quite detailed, and carefully restricts sales presentations so that they do not mislead the investor. The National Association of Securities Dealers (N.A.S.D.) enforces it with respect to its members, and the Securities & Exchange Commission enforces it with respect to others. Some of the features of this Statement of Policy are:

1. Sales literature must not be misleading.
   a. It must not make a statement of a material fact which is not true.
   b. It must not leave out some material fact the exclusion of which would make the literature misleading.
2. All of the following must be stated if an investment company computes the rates of return on its shares, based on dividends in the past 12 months:
   a. Current offering price
   b. Total dividends paid
   c. Change in asset value during the period
   d. A statement disclaiming future results
3. Investment company income and capital distributions cannot be included in one amount.
4. Neither sales literature nor salesmen can even imply that a person investing in an investment company will receive any particular future return.
5. If there is any discussion concerning diversification, appreciation possibilities, protection against loss of purchasing power, etc., the sales presentation must include an explanation of the risk inherent in market fluctuations.
6. There must be no implication that investment company shares are anything like savings accounts, insurance, government bonds, etc.
7. Any discussion of future redemption must include a statement that the future redemption price might be either more or less than the purchase price of the shares.
8. Charts and tables must meet certain standards so that they are not inaccurate or misleading.

9. An investor must be told that there is a sales charge which must be paid when he purchases shares.

10. Sales literature must warn investors that switching from one investment company to another, or from one class of security of a company to another, involves a sales charge.

Now this is only a partial list of the areas covered by the Statement of Policy. It is not intended to be complete, or detailed, but only sufficient to indicate to investors the great lengths to which the Securities and Exchange Commission and The National Association of Securities Dealers go, to try to protect the public from unscrupulous salesmen and advertising. A brief review of this list, before a visit from a fund salesman, should help an investor appraise the propriety of the salesman's presentation.

INVESTMENT METHODS

Mutual funds have attempted to meet the needs of every investor by creating various plans for the purchase of funds. Basically, they permit the investor to invest his money in one lump sum, in small amounts voluntarily invested over a period of time, or in small amounts, by contractual arrangement, over a period of time.

Lump Sum

Buying fund shares by investing a sum of money now on hand is, of course, the simplest method. If a fund with a "load" is purchased, the percentage cost of purchase, or "load," is easily calculated. If, for example, an investor purchases a fund which has a charge of 8% of the asked price of its shares, then $40 would be deducted from a $500 investment for the "load." The net investment in shares of the fund would be $460 (minus a very small federal tax of 4/100 of 1 per cent of the face value). Based on the net investment in fund shares, the "load" charge is about 8.7 per cent ($40 ÷ by $460).

Few investors would object to a $40 "load." However, many would protest an $800 "load" on a $10,000 investment, and most funds reduce the percentage when the amount invested is large. While some funds offer reduced rates starting at $10,000 the majority do not reduce their rates until the minimum investment is $25,000.

One advantage of a lump sum investment is that at no time will the loading charge ever be any more than this percentage—8 per cent in the example. As will be explained shortly, if this investment had been made on a contractual plan, as much as 50 per cent might have been deducted from individual payments at the beginning of the contract. While it is conceivable that, with a rapidly rising market, an investment might rise sufficiently in value over a short period of time (one or two years) to recover the 8 per cent, it is stretching the imagination to hope that a rise in the stock market would result in a recovery of a 50% deduction during any such period.

Another advantage of lump sum investment might seem to be that if an investor buys fund shares when the stock market is extremely low, his investment will rise in value and grow rapidly. Unfortunately, however, the purchase might be made when the market is high, and the investment might subsequently decline in value. In fact, the outstanding disadvantage of lump sum purchases for the average investor is the fact that he does not avail himself of the advantages of dollar-cost-averaging.[16]

Voluntary Accumulation Plans

Instead of investing a sizeable sum of money in one lump, an investor may prefer to invest smaller amounts regularly over a period of time. The purpose of accumulation plans, both voluntary and contractual, is to give an investor the opportunity to build an estate by the continuous investment of small amounts out of current income.

Usually, a voluntary plan permits the investor to make an original investment in some minimum amount, say $100 to $250, and then make subsequent purchases in amounts such as $25 or $50. These amounts vary considerably between funds, but most funds require some minimum initial investment, and establish a minimum amount which can be invested at later dates. If the investor fails to make a payment some month, there is no penalty. Under these voluntary plans, the "load" will be deducted from each payment. If the "load" is 8% of the invested amount, $20 will be deducted from an original investment of $250, and $4 from each subsequent investment of $50.

The voluntary plan gives the purchaser the advantage of the "lump sum" plan in that there is no penalty; the loading charge is based only on the individual payment. Another advantage of this plan, or any accumulation plan involving continuous investments, is the opportunity to dollar-cost-average.

It must be remembered that "dollar-cost-averaging" is not a guaranteed system. An investor can still lose money under this system. It does, however, avoid the difficult problem of "timing" (deciding when the stock market is at the best point to make purchases), and has worked remarkably well, historically.

---

[16] See page 433, Chapter 15 for a complete discussion of dollar-cost-averaging.

Contractual Accumulation Plans

The contractual accumulation plan is similar to the voluntary in that the investor invests a minimum amount at the beginning of the plan, and somewhat smaller amounts regularly over a period of time. There are, however, certain very important differences.

Under the contractual plan, an investor signs a contract and agrees to invest a certain number of dollars at stated intervals over a stated number of years. Usually, this is so much per month, or quarter, for a period of ten or fifteen years. Another very important difference is the fact that there is a penalty involved in a contractual plan. Under these plans, a large part of the total selling costs is deducted from payments into the fund during the first year of the plan, as is true with most types of insurance policies.

The Investment Company Act of 1940 limits selling costs to a maximum of 9 per cent of the total money invested over the life of the plan. It also limits the amount that may be deducted from the first year's installments to 50 per cent. The remainder of the total selling costs must then be spread evenly over the remaining installments. Any capital gain or dividend distributions are usually automatically reinvested into fund shares at their net asset value. This helps to bring about a long-range growth in the value of the plan.

The outstanding disadvantage of the contractual plan is obvious. If 50 per cent of your first year's investment is deducted as a selling cost, then only 50 per cent can possibly remain to be invested. If you invest $1,000 under these circumstances, only $500 is put to work for you. You can stop making payments into the fund at any time. The fund shares which you have purchased are still yours, but, if payments are stopped during the early years of the plan, you are almost certain to have a loss. The possibility of such an investment growing so rapidly that the invested $500 doubles within a year or two, is quite remote.

There are, however, several advantages to contractual plans which should be given serious consideration:

1. If an investor realizes the loss-penalty involved, he has a tremendous incentive to complete the plan. Most people have to be forced to save regularly. Many start a voluntary plan with the best of intentions, then, after a short time, discover that money is not as available as they believed it would be. They skip a payment or two, then decide to discontinue the plan entirely. The loss-penalty is a strong impellent to continue the payments, unless a real financial emergency develops.

2. The "load" charge is often reduced if the total contract is sufficiently large. On a $25,000 contract, for example, the charge might be reduced from 8% to as much as 5½%. This gives the smaller investor the benefit of the lower rates offered on large purchases.

3. Contractual plan investors are often offered services not available under other plans. Some funds, for example, permit an investor to liquidate some of his shares and replace them at a later date, without paying another sales charge.

4. Plan-completion insurance is generally offered. This type of life insurance is quite different from life insurance as the term is usually defined. The "usual" type of life insurance policy guarantees that the beneficiary will receive the face amount of the policy (death benefits) in cash. The plan-completion policy provides that, upon the death of the holder of the plan, the policy will pay the mutual fund the difference between the total of the payments already paid and the face amount of the contract. It insures completion of the contract, and assures the beneficiary receipt of a total number of fund shares. It does not guarantee any fixed amount of cash. The completed plan may have a greater or lesser value than the total amount invested, including the insurance premiums, depending upon market conditions at the time the plan is liquidated. The cost of the insurance is quite reasonable, and the plan is quite worthwhile.

WHAT YOU GET

Just exactly what does a mutual fund do for the investor? What does the investor get for his money? The three basic things the investor gets are management, diversification, and convenience.

Management

There are two points to emphasize in considering management. One is that the management is professional, and the other is that the management is continuous. Not only is the management of a good mutual fund made up of professionals who do their best to select the best investments, but it also continuously manages the investor's money. Even the best investment today may be a poor investment tomorrow. The ordinary investor is faced with problems resulting from a lack of training, and availability of time, in selecting investments. He is faced with the same problems in continuously supervising his investments. A mutual fund can solve these problems for him.

Diversification

Putting all of your eggs in one basket is another problem facing the average investor. With, let's say, $25 a month to invest, an investor is limited to investing in one company. Over a period of years, he may invest in a few shares of several companies, but even then the number of stocks he can buy is severely limited by the limited amount of money he has to invest.

A mutual fund also solves this problem. An investor buying a share in an investment company buys an interest in every one of the investments the investment company has made. This means that the investor's $25 is spread over perhaps 100 or more different companies.

Chart 16-6 illustrates both continuous professional management, and diversification. Notice that a small shareholder has his investment immediately spread over many different industries. The fact that the fund's assets have shifted, percentage wise, over the years indicates that the investments have been continuously supervised.

Convenience

There are many reasons why a mutual fund is a convenient investment for a small investor:
1. Liquidity. Fund shares can be redeemed for cash on any day the New York Stock Exchange is open. The cash value is usually the net asset value at that time, regardless of the number of fund shares owned.
2. All the details of the fund's security transactions are handled by a custodian bank. It holds all of the cash and securities, and regularly remits the capital gain and income distributions to the fund's investors.
3. If the fund has a reinvestment plan, the capital gains and/or income distributions can be automatically reinvested.
4. With an accumulation plan, the investor can invest regularly and in small amounts.
5. If an investor's objective changes—from capital gain to income, for example—many funds permit transferral of capital to another fund at nominal cost. These funds are either different classes of a single fund or one of a "family" of funds. Group Securities, National Securities & Research, Massachusetts Investors' Trust, Keystone, and others, each have several funds with different objectives.

Chart 16–6[17]

DIVERSIFICATION

One of the main services offered by the Fund is diversification of your investment over a list of securities, with the aim of cushioning the effect of the severe losses which can afflict individual issues. For the smaller shareholder, particularly, the Fund's diversification is likely to be much wider than he could otherwise afford.

The chart below illustrates how the Fund's holdings are apportioned through a number of industries. It further shows how the Directors have shifted these holdings over the years, as different industries in turn have shown promise of growth.

It is likely that five years from now, a number of categories will appear that are not included now.

INDUSTRY CLASSIFICATIONS	NOV. 30, 1962 %	NOV. 30, 1957 %	NOV. 30, 1952 %
Aviation	1.0	1.0	—
Automotive	—	1.8	—
Banks and Credit Cos.	4.8	2.2	—
Business Machines	9.2	5.9	2.4
Chemicals	6.7	6.2	10.8
Construction Mat. & Maint.	1.7	3.7	2.8
Containers and Packaging	—	—	4.6
Drugs and Medical	5.4	8.6	6.4
Educational Publishing	3.1	—	—
Electric Utilities	13.4	3.7	—
Electrical and Electronics	9.2	6.0	9.0
Entertainment	1.0	—	—
Insurance	8.5	6.1	3.6
Machinery	—	—	3.7
Natural Gas	3.0	5.1	10.3
Oil Service	0.2	4.2	0.0
Paper Products	2.0	3.2	7.1
Petroleum	15.9	23.3	22.4
Photographic Products	3.5	1.1	—
Retailing and Consumer Goods	4.4	2.0	—
Special Products and Services	5.0	7.6	3.2
Specialty Metals and Mining	2.0	7.2	7.0
Steel	—	1.1	2.0
Synthetic Fibers	—	—	4.7
	100.0	100.0	100.0

6. There are many withdrawal arrangements which may be made so that, for example, money might be paid by the fund every month.

7. It is usually possible to file a Declaration of Trust, so that beneficiaries may obtain the fund shares after the investor's death without waiting for the outcome of probate proceedings.

---

[17] "Massachusetts Investor's Growth Stock Fund, Annual Report," Massachusetts Investors Growth Stock Fund, Inc., Boston, Mass., 1962, p. 13.

8. According to law, funds must furnish complete reports to share-holders twice a year. Most do so quarterly. It is easy for an investor to get up-to-date information about his investment.

Even this isn't a complete list, but it should be sufficient to indicate that mutual funds do offer a convenient method of investing, for the average investor.

WHAT YOU DON'T GET

An investor gets a lot from a mutual fund investment, but not everything. Every investor should be aware of the fact that he is not guaranteed that the fund's shares will increase in value. An investor could lose all of his investment. Any investment involving common stocks must be considered as a risk investment. Funds specializing in bonds and preferred stocks, of course, reduce this type of risk considerably, but, in turn, sacrifice the growth possibilities inherent in common stocks.

There are certain other things which many investors seem to think they get in a mutual fund which they do not. Mutual fund investors often consider a fund to be a substitute for life insurance. This is not true. Many others believe that they have completely eliminated the problem of selection if they buy a fund. This is not true.

Not an Insurance Substitute

A life insurance contract assures the purchaser of specific per-formance under all conditions. Regardless of what happens to the stock market, or the economy, a $10,000 life insurance contract is a $10,000 contract. Mutual funds, or any investment involving equity investments, cannot guarantee the final value of the investment.

Furthermore, life insurance contracts offer certain features which are rarely available when you invest in a fund. For example, a per-manent insurance contract offers many other things:

1. A guaranteed rate of return for a long term.
2. Specific amounts of money you may borrow.
3. No current income tax on accruing interest, or on the annual increase in cash value.
4. Almost always exemption from State Inheritance taxes.
5. No probate or administration costs.

Usually, a mutual fund does not offer these advantages, and can-not guarantee a specific rate of return. On the other hand, if the stock market soars, insurance cannot provide the capital appreciation that might possibly be obtained by a mutual fund investment. Because of these differences it is often suggested that an investor buy term insurance (which is cheaper than straight life) rather than straight life, and invest the difference.

There have been many studies of this combination. One of the clearest of these appeared in Kiplinger's *Changing Times*. Referring to the chart presented as Chart 16-7, Kiplinger reached the following conclusions:

1. If the insured died before reaching age 65:
   a. Death proceeds would almost certainly be greater, perhaps by a wide margin, under the term-to-65 approach than if he bought straight life.
   b. Straight life would probably yield somewhat higher death proceeds than the decreasing term program if the insured died in the early years. Stock investments might not climb fast enough, at first, to offset the yearly drop in insurance in force. They might even decline over a short haul. After about 15 years or so, though, the decreasing term plus the increasing investment fund would start to produce more death benefits than straight life.
   c. The term-to-65 plan is likely to produce more death benefits than the decreasing term.
2. If the insured lived and cashed in his program:
   a. By age 65, either of the term-and-invest programs could amass a nest egg much bigger than the values and accumulated dividends of straight life. True, an income tax would have to be paid on the stock dividends and capital gains. (Life insurance cash values build up tax-free.) But unless the insured's tax bracket was quite high, say over 50%, he'd still come out far ahead. Since the decreasing term plan provides more money for investment, it should produce a bigger kitty than the term-to-65 program.
   b. If the insured quits much before 65, however, the advantage of term-and-invest plans isn't nearly so great.[18]

Kiplinger carefully points out in his article that, actually, the problem isn't quite so simple. Several assumptions are made in the chart. There is no way of predicting how fast the stock market will rise. Your particular mutual fund may not rise rapidly, even if the market does. At the time you or your heirs need cash, the stock market might be quite low. This would not affect your life insurance policy, but it would affect your mutual fund.

[18] "Buy Term Insurance and Invest the Difference?," *Changing Times, The Kiplinger Magazine,* Washington, D.C., October 1962, pp. 9 and 11.

Chart 16-7

Straight life vs. term-and-invest

The buyer is a man just turned 35. In case A he buys a $10,000 straight life policy at an annual premium of $237 and leaves dividends with the company to gather interest. In B he buys $10,000 of 30-year decreasing term (premium of $76 for 24 years and no charge thereafter). In C he buys term-to-65 (annual premium of $120). In both B and C he regularly invests the difference in premiums in an investment trust that charges an 8% sales commission. Dividends and distributions of capital gains are reinvested in the fund.

It's assumed the investment fund will increase in value, over a given period, at a rate equal to 10% compounded annually. Obviously, the fund won't gain exactly 10% each year and may even decrease.

Mutual fund values, of course, are not guaranteed, whereas life insurance cash values are.

Note: No allowance has been made for income taxes on dividends and capital gains on the investment fund. For an extremely rough idea of the tax load, use this rule of thumb: In the 20% tax bracket, you'd pay one-eighth of the difference between the total you invested and its accumulated value at any given point. In the 30% bracket, about one-fifth. In the 43% bracket, one-fourth. (In practice, if taxes were paid out of investment earnings, it would slow down the growth of the fund. If, as is more likely, you paid taxes out of other income, it would run the total cost of programs B and C somewhat above what is shown.)

	A straight life	if he drops policy at end of year he gets . . .		B 30-year decreasing term plus mutual fund investment				C term-to-65 plus mutual fund investm[ent]			
his age at start of year	premiums paid to date	this cash value	plus these accumulated dividends	premiums paid to date	amount invested to date	insurance in force	savings to date if accumulated at 10%	premiums paid to date	amount invested to date	cash value of policy	savings to date if accumu[lated] at 10[%]
35	$ 237	0	0	$ 76	$ 161	$10,000	$ 163	$ 120	$ 117	0	$ 1
36	474	$ 200	$ 26	152	322	9,667	342	240	234	0	2
37	711	400	56	228	483	9,333	539	360	351	0	3
38	948	600	89	304	644	9,000	756	480	468	$ 20	5
39	1,185	810	127	380	805	8,667	994	600	585	90	7
40	1,422	1,020	169	456	966	8,333	1,256	720	702	150	9
41	1,659	1,230	216	532	1,127	8,000	1,545	840	819	220	1,1
42	1,896	1,420	267	608	1,288	7,667	1,862	960	936	290	1,3
43	2,133	1,600	323	684	1,449	7,333	2,211	1,080	1,053	350	1,6
44	2,370	1,790	383	760	1,610	7,000	2,595	1,200	1,170	420	1,8
45	2,607	1,980	449	836	1,771	6,667	3,017	1,320	1,287	480	2,2
46	2,844	2,170	521	912	1,932	6,333	3,481	1,440	1,404	540	2,5
47	3,081	2,360	599	988	2,093	6,000	3,992	1,560	1,521	600	2,9
48	3,318	2,550	684	1,064	2,254	5,667	4,554	1,680	1,638	650	3,3
49	3,555	2,740	775	1,140	2,415	5,333	5,173	1,800	1,755	700	3,7
50	3,792	2,940	923	1,216	2,576	5,000	5,853	1,920	1,872	740	4,2
51	4,029	3,130	1,039	1,292	2,737	4,667	6,601	2,040	1,989	780	4,8
52	4,266	3,320	1,172	1,368	2,898	4,333	7,424	2,160	2,106	810	5,4
53	4,503	3,520	1,328	1,444	3,059	4,000	8,329	2,280	2,223	840	6,0
54	4,740	3,710	1,492	1,520	3,220	3,667	9,324	2,400	2,340	860	6,8
55	4,977	3,910	1,638	1,596	3,381	3,333	10,420	2,520	2,457	850	7,6
56	5,214	4,100	1,789	1,672	3,542	3,000	11,624	2,640	2,574	830	8,4
57	5,451	4,290	1,946	1,748	3,703	2,667	12,950	2,760	2,691	800	9,4
58	5,688	4,480	2,110	1,824	3,864	2,333	14,407	2,880	2,808	750	10,5
59	5,925	4,670	2,281	1,824	4,101	2,000	16,088	3,000	2,925	690	11,6
60	6,162	4,860	2,459	1,824	4,338	1,667	17,937	3,120	3,042	610	12,9
61	6,399	5,050	2,645	1,824	4,575	1,333	19,970	3,240	3,159	500	14,3
62	6,636	5,240	2,839	1,824	4,812	1,000	22,206	3,360	3,276	370	15,9
63	6,873	5,420	3,041	1,824	5,049	667	24,667	3,480	3,393	200	17,6
64	7,110	5,600	3,253	1,824	5,286	333	27,374	3,600	3,510	0	19,5

RESULTS AT 65:

total outlay	$7,110	$7,110	$7,110
insurance in force if premiums continued*	$10,000	—	—
insurance in force if premiums stopped*	$10,000 for 15 years or $7,330 for life	—	—
cash if insurance surrendered	$8,853	cash-in value of mutual fund $27,374	cash-in value of mutual fund $19,542

*plus $3,253 in cash from accumulated dividends

Source: *Changing Times, The Kiplinger Magazine, October 1962, p. 10.*

There have been unscrupulous salesmen who have tried to persuade people to cash in their straight life policies and follow the term-plus-fund route. Remember that insurance can do many things which funds cannot do. Furthermore, remember that a sales commission was paid when the straight life policy was purchased. Another sales charge would now have to be paid if the old policy is to be replaced by a new one.

Selection Still Important

It seems that very little need be said about the problem of selection. It has been emphasized in this chapter that investment companies differ drastically in objectives and performance. Not only must an investor find a fund which has policies corresponding to his particular goals, but he must also find a fund which past performance indicates has good management. Because there are several hundred investment companies, and because performance varies widely, selection is still quite a problem.

CONCLUSIONS

Mutual funds are well worth considering. If you expect costs to rise in the future as rapidly as they have in the past, then education for your children, and retirement, will present special problems which a fund could help to meet. In 1940, $50 per week might have been enough to retire on quite comfortably, but could you be comfortable on this amount today? You may have gone to a fine college, but if college costs double or triple before your children reach college age, will you be able to send them?

After a person has the necessary prerequisites—emergency fund, insurance, etc.,—equity investments should be a part of his savings program. Mutual funds are one way of investing in the stock market which you, as an investor, might prefer.

Mutual funds are also quite attractive for certain special purposes. Churches, wealthy people, pension funds, and others, find them especially useful. Services offered by mutual funds are just as advantageous to such groups, sometimes more so, as they are to small investors.

There are many criticisms concerning the fact that the average mutual fund has performed only about as well as the Dow-Jones Average. This is true, but misleading. How many people buy, or can afford to buy, all of the stocks in the Dow-Jones Average? ". . . nearly one Big Board stock in every four collapsed a terrifying 50 per cent or more from its 1961 highs to its 1962 lows."[19] During this period, the Forbes mutual fund average dropped 28 per cent. Averages of any kind are misleading. The real question is whether or not, in your opinion, funds can outperform *your* record in the market.

Are mutual fund costs too high? A rate of 7, 8, or 9 per cent may seem to be high, but selling costs on many other items are even higher. On door-to-door items, you may pay 33⅓ per cent for commissions; on life insurance, it may be 5 per cent to 10 per cent; and on auto insurance, 15 per cent to 25 per cent. By comparison, the mutual fund "load" doesn't seem quite so high. Furthermore, it may be lower than the total commissions you pay when you buy and sell stocks directly. The "load" charge on funds is paid only when you buy; the commission on stock is paid when you buy and when you sell. As very few stock investments will be satisfactory over a period of ten or fifteen years, you may have to buy and sell several times. Paying a commission each time could mean that the total sum paid in commissions could be much more than 8 or 9 per cent at the end of 10 or 15 years.

Management costs vary. An investor should make certain that the management costs in the fund he is considering are reasonable. The usual fee is about one-half of 1 per cent of the fund's average assets. If you think this is high, try an experiment. Assume that you would have to spend one hour each day managing your investment. How much do you make per hour at work? Multiply this by 365 days. This is the total amount it would cost if you managed your own money. Is the portion of the fund's management cost which is devoted to managing your investment more or less than this? If your fund investment is $12,000, one-half of 1 per cent would be $60.

Unfortunately, the mutual fund field has proved extremely attractive to high pressure salesmen with questionable arguments and often very inadequate training. In buying a mutual fund, find a salesman who is reputable, who sells a reputable fund, and who is trained so that he may offer sound financial advice.

It is up to the investor to investigate before buying a fund. It is unbelievable how many people will sign a contract to invest ten or twenty thousand dollars, over a period of years, on the advice of a completely untrained salesman, and without the slightest investigation. Information is available in almost every library. It would seem only sensible that a person would do a little investigating before buying a fund, and make certain that he is investing in a well

---

[19] Forbes, "Annual Mutual Fund Survey: 1962," *Forbes Business & Finance,* Forbes, Inc., New York, N.Y., August 15, 1962, p. 27.

managed company and, if the fund is sold through brokers, buying through a reputable brokerage firm.

Questions

1. What are the prerequisites that should be met before investing in securities?

2. Distinguish between a closed-end and an open-end investment fund.

3. What is a "balanced" fund?

4. Discuss the advantages and disadvantages of a "load" and a "no-load" fund.

5. Discuss taxation of a mutual fund.

6. What general conclusions can be made of a mutual fund made up mostly of common stock?

7. How may leverage aid a closed-end investment company in providing a larger return to its stockholders?

8. What is the best way to measure the performance of a mutual fund?

9. Justify the management fee charged by a mutual fund.

10. Under what method of purchasing a mutual fund may an individual obtain the advantages of dollar-cost-averaging?

Problems

1. Ted King purchased 10 shares of stock about three years ago. When he tried to sell these shares recently, he could find no buyer willing to pay even the net asset value of these shares. If this was stock sold by an investment company, what type of company might it be? Give reasons for your answer.

2. Frank Murray has a large accumulated estate. His home is valued at $40,000, he owns $120,000 of life insurance, and has a $10,000 savings account, which he uses as an emergency fund. He has surplus earned income of $5,000 per year, which he hopes to invest at a good rate of return. Should he buy shares of stock outright in a few "blue-chips" stock or would it be better for him to invest in a mutual fund? Discuss.

3. Jack Katz, a 27 year old single man, earns $15,000 a year as a salesman. He can save $2500 annually and desires to invest in a mutual fund. He is undecided as to what type of fund will give him the best growth. He must decide between investing the $2500 per year in a contractual fund or a non-contractual fund. Which would you advise and why?

4. The following information is taken from the financial records of the XYZ mutual fund. Compute the Net Asset Value per share.
   a. Total Assets—$3,400,000
   b. Current Assets $560,000
   c. Net Income for Year $1,632,000
   d. Current Liabilities $221,500
   e. Total Liabilities $821,000
   f. No. of Shares Outstanding 800,000

5. John Carberry is married and has 3 children. He is earning $5000 per year and is just about able to make ends meet. He has just been informed that his brother has died and left him a trust fund, which will provide $500 per year, with no right to withdraw the principal. John has not been able to accumulate much of an estate. He has a $10,000 G.I. term insurance policy and $200 in savings. He knows he needs more life insurance, but he would also like to see his savings grow. He is contemplating one of the following:
   a. Deposit $500 in his savings account yearly
   b. Use the $500 to buy a contractual mutual fund plan
   c. Buy a sufficient amount of term insurance and invest the difference in a mutual fund
   d. Purchase a $25,000 Ordinary Life Insurance policy
   Which method would you recommend and why?

Selected Readings

"Buy Term Insurance and Invest the Difference?" *Changing Times, The Kiplinger Magazine,* The Kiplinger Washington Editors, Inc., Washington, D.C., October, 1962

Forbes, "Annual Mutual Fund Survey: 1962," *Forbes Business & Finance*, Forbes, Inc., New York, N.Y.

Investing Made Easy, Investment Company Institute, New York, N.Y.

Loll, Leo M., Jr., and Buckley, Julian G., *The Over-the-Counter Securities Markets*, Prentice-Hall, Inc., Englewood Cliffs, New Jersey, 1961

Mead, Stuart B., *Mutual Fund and Investment Company Performance in the Fifties*, Occasional Paper No. 9, Bureau of Business and Economic Research, Graduate School of Business Administration, Michigan State Univ., East Lansing, Michigan, 1961

Publications of:

Johnson, Hugh A., Buffalo, New York

Weisenberger, Arthur, New York, N.Y.

Various brokerage firms

Chapter **17**

STARTING YOUR OWN
BUSINESS

A large percentage of the total businesses in this country are small business firms. Only 5 per cent of them are worth over $125,000; 50 per cent of them are worth less than $10,000. There are about 2,000 new businesses started every day, and about 1,800 withdrawals. This proves that while it is still easy to start your own business in the United States, success isn't assured.[1]

---

[1] These statistics from two Dun & Bradstreet, Inc. publications: *The Pitfalls in Managing a Small Business*, 1956, and *Profitable Management for Main Street*, 1959.

The great majority of all businesses are retail and service establishments. The Small Business Administration defines a small business as one with annual sales of less than $1 million. About 19 out of every 20 retail firms are in this category. For these reasons, most of the discussion in this chapter will concentrate on the problems of this type of business.

The mortality of these small businesses is high. Many fail. Others are voluntarily liquidated. Many others barely struggle along. A few become extremely successful.

In November, 1946, Mr. Ralph D. Tedeschi started a grocery business — Tedeschi's Supermarket — in Rockland, Massachusetts. Tedeschi's was typical of hundreds of grocery stores starting business during November of 1946. It started like these others, with limited capital and high hopes. The first year, total sales volume was less than $200,000.

By 1961, Mr. Tedeschi had a chain of stores with an annual sales volume of about $30,000,000. In April of 1961, he sold his stores to Stop & Shop for several million dollars. Very few of the people who started their own grocery business in 1946 did as well. Mr. Tedeschi's success took a combination of initiative, hard work, and ability which is extremely rare.

THE QUESTION

Should you or should you not start your own business? What do you need? What are the problems?

According to studies made by the U.S. Department of Commerce, wholesale firms, financial, real estate, construction, and manufacturing businesses survive better than the average. Service and retail establishments, the majority of all businesses, have a below-average survival rate. About 50 per cent of new firms are sold or liquidated within two years, and the chances are only about 1 in 5 that a new firm will live 10 years.

Many of these withdrawals are due to voluntary reasons such as health, changes in family situations, the appearance of what seems to be a better opportunity elsewhere, or some other similar reason. The really important discontinuances to consider, however, are the involuntary ones—the failures.

But there are two kinds of failures. There is the failure that ends up in court or with loss to creditors. There are very few of those in the United States. In 1961, there were only about 17,000 such failures. These are the "formal" failures.

The other kind of failure is the more important—the failure where the man puts his savings into a business and losses wipe out his savings. Creditors don't suffer; the businessman uses his *own* invested capital to absorb losses and to pay off what he owes. He packs up, closes the door, and says, "That's the last time I ever try starting a business of my own."[2]

Sometimes the only way to find out whether a personal business venture will or will not be successful is to try it. However, in many instances, careful thought and investigation before starting would have avoided heartache and financial loss.

Your Personality

Some people are simply not suited to operating a business of their own. Emotionally and psychologically, they are unable to assume the responsibilities and risks. Working for someone else gives them a sense of security. This is especially true in today's world of fringe benefits, where employees receive life insurance, medical insurance, pension funds, etc. Furthermore, some people operate only on emotion, and are unable to analyze the facts of a situation and be influenced only by the facts.

The loss of the security that might be gained by working for someone else is not the only loss that is risked when a person starts his own business. There is also a financial risk involved. This usually involves both a person's savings and credit. Many people are psychologically incapable of taking this kind of risk. To them, every minor setback becomes a catastrophe, and for the sake of their health, peace of mind, and future happiness, this type of person would be far better off not starting his own business.

Conversely, other people are emotionally and psychologically unable to work for someone else. They cherish independence and are happy only with responsibilities and risks. They are able both to see and to recognize opportunities to make a profit. They are able to analyze a situation, and proceed on the basis of the facts. These are the persons who should start their own business. While success can never be guaranteed, these persons are the most likely to succeed.

Experience

The most basic requirement probably is experience. This is the one thing most experts agree is essential for success in starting a

---

[2] W. H. Kuehn, *The Pitfalls in Managing a Small Business,* Dun & Bradstreet, Inc., Copyright 1956, pp. 5–6.

business. Furthermore, it has to be general experience, not specific. Take, for example, a person thinking about starting his own television sales and service business. If he has been repairing television sets for many years, he has had a specific type of experience. This would not be considered sufficient to start his own business. His chances of success will be greater if he has had general experience, such as an opportunity to take part in negotiating agreements with parts and set distributors, arranging financing with the bank, selling, handling customer credit problems, etc.

No one can say that certain specific qualities are essential to success, or that lack of them inevitably leads to failure. However, the personality traits mentioned in the preceding paragraphs, a thorough general experience, and sufficient education, are usually essential.

Education helps too. How much is needed depends, of course, upon the type of business. Every business man should be able to handle certain basic requirements such as figuring discounts, maintaining adequate records, and handling correspondence.

Advantages of Your Own Business

The first advantage of having your own business is independence. You are your own boss. You can do what you please, when you please, and in the manner you please. There is no possibility of being fired. New ideas can be initiated immediately and dropped if they don't work.

Another advantage is pride of ownership. The development of a successful business is just as creative as a work of art, or a novel. It takes initiative and imagination to start it, hard work and perseverance to nurture and guide it, and a constant attention to details to make it grow. Pride of ownership is a natural human trait and, within limits, must be recognized as an impelling force underlying new business starts.

A third advantage is the possibility of great profit. If the business is successful, it will be a valuable investment. It will mean security and a greater opportunity for the businessman and his family to enjoy life.

Disadvantages of Your Own Business

It is not a bed of roses, however. There are just as many, if not more, disadvantages. The greatest is the amount of work involved. No one works harder than a man who owns his own business and really tries to make it successful. The employees may work from nine to five, but the owner—at least at the beginning—will work longer hours than anyone.

Secondly, there is the constant pressure of financial needs. If a person works for someone else, he is not concerned with where the money comes from to provide him with a paycheck, to pay the firm's rent, or to buy goods and materials. The owner must meet these needs as they arise. Each payday, cash must be available to pay the employees. Cash must be available to pay the rent. Cash must be available to pay for goods and materials.

A third disadvantage is the weight of general responsibility. Many of the factors affecting the future of the business are completely beyond the owner's control. What if the country goes into a period of depression? What if a competitor opens next door? What if the state builds a new highway and the traffic that the business relies upon disappears? Wrong judgment will affect not only the owner, but his family, his employees, his creditors and his customers.

In a sense, the owner of a business really isn't his own boss. He must meet the demands of his customers. Without them, the business can't exist. He must satisfy his creditors. His operation is dictated, to a degree, by his competitors. He must maintain amicable employer-employee relationships if he is to retain the loyalty of his employees. He must be careful to conform to the various laws and regulations applying to his business.

STARTING THE BUSINESS

Problems of starting a business fall into three general areas: first, determining what business to enter—selecting the field; second, going through the preliminary steps necessary to enter the selected field; and third, selecting the form of organization.

SELECTING THE FIELD

This selection is often determined by a person's experience. A barber, for example, would undoubtedly select barbering, hair styling, a beauty shop operation, or some business related to these fields. He would do best to choose what he does best.

Sometimes a person has a new idea he wants to commercialize. In this case, background experience is non-existent, and reliance must be placed upon experience in other fields. A new idea is often born from activities in other fields, and the experiences which lead to the conception of the idea may be drawn upon to project it into a business enterprise.

Occasionally, someone simply decides that he wants to be his own boss. If this is his only reason, his chances of success are slim. Whatever the reason for going into business, a person should carefully study the market and seek out the most opportune openings. A wealth of experience in the buggy whip business wouldn't be enough to assure the success of that type of business in today's market. A brilliant new idea with little probability of public acceptance is of negligible value as the foundation of a business. A person simply wanting to be in business for himself will have little chance of success if he picks a field for which there is little or no public demand.

How does a person decide which fields are promising? The answer to that lies in the analysis of information concerning specific fields and information concerning certain basic factors about the economy.

General Information

Information concerning the national economy will be very helpful in determining which lines of business show the most promise. No one has ever discovered a foolproof method of forecasting business trends, but generally, almost all forecasts are in general agreement with respect to the business climate and the general business trend. They are available from many of the larger banks, mutual funds, brokerage houses, investment advisory services, and other financial institutions.

Information concerning the current availability of money and credit is usually included in these forecasts. The Federal Reserve System is an excellent source of such information, and its publications merit attention. If financing is going to be needed, and most new businesses need working capital, it will be helpful to know whether money and credit are "tight" or readily available.

Such general information is important, and indicates the general prospects for all kinds of business, but cannot, of itself, lead to any conclusion as to which fields hold the greatest promise of success. Other sources must be found which will contribute more specific data as to which fields afford the more optimistic opportunities for new business enterprises.

One of these sources is the growth of the population. While forecasting the number of people who will be living in the United States in ten years is not an exact science, it is much more precise than even short term forecasts of the state of the economy. Present birth rates indicate that the American population will continue to grow; and, if the annual percentage of increase does not decline, the population growth will include an increase in the number of new babies arriving on the American scene each year. This means a market for baby products, including baby furniture, baby food, diaper services, and nursery products.

An increase in the population is naturally important. It means more people to be housed, to wear clothes, to eat food, and to drive automobiles. Of equal importance is the forecasted composition of the population—the relative sizes of the various age groups. This is a factor that can be determined with reasonable accuracy. The number of 65-year-olds who will be alive ten years from now can be estimated by gathering statistics as to the number of 55-year-olds alive today, and reducing their number by amounts indicated by mortality tables. Such information is important because it indicates the items that will be most in demand. If, for example, an increase in the proportion of the "65 and over" age group is indicated, it will indicate an increase in the demand for services and products that will most appeal to that group.

The general direction of the movement of real income is another important source of information. For some time, this has been upward. Money incomes have increased faster than prices. This has meant an increase in purchasing power. As real incomes increase, the pattern of spending changes. More money, for example, is available for recreation and services.

The education level of the population is still another important source, for two reasons. As the general level of education increases, product-demand changes to a demand for new and different products. More education means not only an increase in the demand for text-books and such "educational" products, but also an increase in the demand for products of higher quality. A second effect of more education is an increase in the discovery rate. More education means an increasing number of able researchers. The increased emphasis placed upon research by business means that there will be more new products and new inventions. This, in turn, means many new opportunities for those who wish to start their own business.

The change that has taken place in recent years in hours of work is also important. The tendency has been for hours of work to be steadily reduced. This has meant an increase in leisure time, and this increase will probably continue. More leisure time means more opportunity for entertainment and travel, and consequently an increase in the demand for such services.

Specific Information

Information concerning specific fields seems to be a rather obvious need. Due to the tremendous number of business fields, it is impossible to consider each in detail. About all that can be done is to emphasize the importance of such information and to make several recommendations.

One general recommendation is never to overlook the information made available by the federal government. The Small Business Administration, Department of Commerce, and others, provide a considerable amount of information. In its Occupational Outlook Handbook, for example, the Department of Labor not only predicts the age composition of the American population during the decade of the "sixties," but also the industries expected to increase most rapidly during this period, and those expected to decline. Other available sources of such information are state and local development companies, commercial banks, investment banking houses, professional consulting firms, manufacturers, and trade associations.

At this point, the information needed must be quite specific. There must be an estimate of the demand for the product or services to be offered; the extent and nature of the competition; the amount of capital needed; the quantity and quality of personnel needed; the availability of financing, etc. Today, more and more reliance is being placed on market research by new firms. Long appreciated by established larger firms, it is now realized that such services are extremely valuable to those interested in establishing a new business.

PRELIMINARY STEPS

After a decision has been made as to the best field to enter, certain preliminary steps are necessary before actually starting business. One of these is to decide whether to start a new firm, or buy an existing one. Others are: selecting a location, estimating the amount of capital needed, and estimating the financing needed.

New or Old?

Should you try to start a completely new business, or buy an old one that is up for sale? Both methods have their advantages and disadvantages. If a completely new business is started, the physical plant can be planned to meet the specific desires of the owner; there is no inheritance of the gripes and complaints of past customers; and there is no question as to whether or not the previous owner will start a new business across the street, as a competitor.

On the other hand, it may be possible to buy an existing business for less money than the amount needed to establish a comparable new business. The original owner may have been overly optimistic, and have invested so heavily in equipment, buildings, and other overhead items that he could not make a satisfactory profit on the investment. He may be selling it for less than he paid for it, and a new owner with a lower initial cost might find it a profitable enterprise.

In the early 1960's, a group started a large amusement park. They installed boat rides, amusements, refreshment stands, and all of the usual facilities. They purchased enough deep freeze and kitchen equipment to take care of many times the number of people that could be expected to visit the park at any one time. Some of the money was borrowed and, due to the over-investment in equipment, the park could not earn a rate of return sufficient even to pay the interest on the borrowed money. The park was sold to a new group of owners at a fraction of its original cost. The new owners sold off the excess equipment. The net result was an extremely reduced investment which could reasonably be expected to yield a satisfactory return.

If the existing business is well managed, it is well stocked and ready to go, and may have built up considerable good-will among its customers. One question that must be carefully considered, of course, is why the present owner is selling. Perhaps the business is unprofitable, or is facing new competition. There are innumerable reasons for selling. The value of a going business must be thoroughly investigated. It is folly to rely upon the seller's figures and other volunteered information without careful checking. After all, he wants to sell and naturally will do everything to place his best foot forward.

Where to Locate

There are many factors that influence the selection of a location. Naturally, everyone wants to locate in the spot where the most business is. The only problem is finding it.

Some of the factors which should be considered in selecting a location are:

1. Population trends—is the area growing or declining?
2. Composition of the population—availability of customers and employees.
3. Zoning regulations.
4. Nature of merchandise—jewelry stores, for example, do best in a main shopping center, while drug stores do well in smaller, neighborhood centers.
5. Seasonality of industries—an area relying principally on summer beach trade, for example, will be a poor location for a business that needs customers the year around.
6. Traffic—the number of people and/or automobiles passing the location each day.

There are, of course, many other factors. Today, with the development of suburban shopping centers and the general tendency to decentralize, the problem of location for a retail store has become even more puzzling, and requires a thorough location survey. Wholesalers, manufacturers, and federal, state, and local governments provide a considerable amount of helpful information. Here is one area where professional market research is especially helpful. While a small firm cannot afford to engage in the extensive market research which a large company might undertake, there are many market research firms and consultants today offering such services at reasonable cost.

Estimating Capital Needed

Another potential that must be estimated is income. Here, again, the market researcher can provide a valuable service. It is obviously senseless to go into a business where income will be insufficient to cover expenses. Conversely, if estimated income is extremely large, budgeting more for rent, furnishings, and fixtures, might well be justified.

In establishing a business, it is not too difficult to figure the amount of capital needed. Here are the steps:

(1) You first figure the EXPENSES carefully. Calculate how much for rent, light, advertising, as examples, and add a salary for yourself. There you have your basic minimum expenses. Then arbitrarily add 25%, maybe 50%. The expenses always seem to run more than expected. Don't ask why that happens. Business people tell us that no matter how you figure the expenses, they seem to run higher.

(2)   Now, the next question is what SALES do you have to have to cover those expenses? Suppose you have a gross profit margin of one-third. If you do $6,000 a month, you'll get a gross profit of $2,000 on which you will just break even if your basic expenses are $2,000. There's no profit involved; you'll just cover your expenses.

(3)   Now, when you know that your sales must equal $6,000 a month or $72,000 a year to break even, then and then only can you begin to ask yourself, "What merchandise do I need, to do this volume? What receivables must I carry if I am to sell on credit? What fixtures do I need?" In other words, what capital is needed to produce the sales, which in turn will give the gross profit to cover expenses and a reasonable living?

These calculations should be written out on a piece of paper very, very carefully before you ever sign anything.[3]

Estimating Necessary Financing

Once income, expenses, and costs have been estimated, the need for financing can be estimated. This can be done by listing each of the financial requirements in detail. The list should include the funds needed for inventory, customer credit, equipment, fixtures, land, buildings, etc. In making up such a list, care must be taken not to omit a cash surplus as one of the financial needs.

When all items have been listed and totalled, the cash resources of the person or persons who propose to establish the business should be listed and totalled. If the financial requirements exceed the cash resources, the difference is the amount that must be financed through outside sources. This financing can be done by borrowing, incorporating and selling stock, entering into a partnership with others who would provide the additional capital, or in other ways. Other sources of funds will be discussed in some detail later. Now, let us consider the various forms of business organization, and the problem of selecting the one most appropriate to the needs of the entrepreneur.

SELECTING THE FORM OF ORGANIZATION

One of the first problems in establishing a new business is determining what form of organization to use. There are many different forms, but the three most commonly used are the sole proprietorship, the partnership, and the corporation. To determine which would be

---

[3] W. H. Kuehn, *The Pitfalls in Managing a Small Business,* Dun & Bradstreet, Inc., 1956, pp. 8–9.

best for a particular business would require a much more detailed study than can be presented here. Special attention should be given to the particular laws affecting each form of business organization in the state in which the business is to be located.

Definitions

The sole proprietorship is a business owned by a single person who assumes all of the responsibilities of the business, receives all of the profits, and assumes all of the risks. Everyone else working for the business is an employee. There are no officers. The sole proprietorship is the easiest type of business to establish. Few legal formalities are necessary.

A partnership is "an association of two or more persons to carry on, as co-owners, a business for profit," according to the Uniform Partnership Act. All partnership agreements should be written, but the relationship may be written, oral, or implied. In a general partnership, each partner is responsible for all of the debts and business contracts of the firm. In a limited partnership, partners are not liable for the debts of the firm in excess of their capital contribution, but the limited partners must be careful not to actively participate in the conduct of the business, or they will be held liable as general partners.

The corporation is an artificial person created by law. The law gives it some of the privileges and rights of natural persons. To exist, a corporation needs a charter from the state in which it is organized. Except as limited by this charter, it has the right to buy and sell, own and hold property, make contracts, sue and be sued, and to exercise many other rights and responsibilities of natural persons.

Comparison

In some types of business, only a particular form of organization is permitted. Commercial banks, for example, must be incorporated, while incorporation is forbidden in the professions of law, medicine, dentistry, etc. Generally speaking, however, a person starting his own business can select the form he prefers. It must again be emphasized that careful study is necessary, but we can briefly list some of the differences between these three forms.

1. Efficiency
   a. Individual proprietorship and corporation have the advantage of centralized management.

b. A partnership requires the unanimous agreement of the partners, making it somewhat less efficient.

2. Continuity of existence
   a. Proprietorship ends with the death of the owner.
   b. A partnership is dissolved by the death of a partner.
   c. A corporation is not terminated by the death of its officers or stockholders.

3. Liability of owners
   a. A proprietor assumes unlimited personal liability for all of the debts and obligations of the business.
   b. Partners in a general partnership also assume unlimited personal liability, as far as third parties are concerned.
   c. Owners of a corporation are not personally liable for its debts. It is a separate legal entity, and responsible for its own debts.

4. Transferability of ownership
   a. A proprietor must sell the entire business.
   b. A partner cannot sell his interest. He can sell only by dissolving the existing partnership and then disposing of his share of the liquidated value.
   c. Corporate ownership is divided into shares of stock, which may be sold by the owners as they wish.

5. Ability to raise capital
   a. A proprietor must rely upon his own funds and credit.
   b. More funds are available to a partnership because of the multiple ownership, but borrowing is limited by the reluctance of the individual owners to assume unlimited personal liability for the entire debt.
   c. A corporation can raise large amounts of capital through the sale of stocks, bonds, and debentures.

6. Taxes and regulations
   a. A proprietor has fewer tax problems and regulations to cope with.
   b. A partnership has about the same number of tax problems and regulations as a sole proprietorship.
   c. A corporation has numerous special taxes and regulations.

7. Ease and cost of starting
   a. A sole proprietorship is the easiest to start.
   b. A partnership is simple to organize, but a written contract should be drawn up between the partners.

c. A corporation is the most expensive and legally complicated of all to start.

This is a very brief outline of certain of the characteristics of the three types of organization most frequently considered by those starting their own business. These must be considered carefully, and attention given to the peculiarities of the particular business about to be started. One of the reasons the corporate form is so popular is that it protects a business from being affected by the owner's personal financial losses and, as is more frequently the case, protects the owner's personal assets from business losses. This definite advantage of limited liability encompasses a disadvantage in that creditors may be unwilling to advance as much credit to the corporation as it might to the owner.

There are many arrangements that may be made to give one form of organization some of the advantages of another. The use of limited partnership agreements, "buy and sell" stock agreements, preferred or non-voting stock issues—all may be used for such a purpose. Each person starting his own business should carefully discuss the choice of form with a lawyer, or other expert, to make certain that he is selecting the form best suited to his special circumstances.

MANAGEMENT

Experts agree that inadequate and inefficient management is the outstanding cause of business failures. Good management requires skillful buying and pricing, ability to sell, adequate record keeping, etc. Let's consider some of these problems in detail.

Adequate Record Keeping

A simple but adequate bookkeeping system is an absolute necessity for any business. Many businesses fail because they actually do not know what it is costing them to do business, or the amount of credit outstanding, or their general financial condition.

An adequate system should include basic information on sales, inventory, accounts payable, accounts receivable, and expenses. These will enable the businessman to continuously check the condition of his business, keep it from getting into difficulty, and take immediate remedial action when it is necessary.

Besides this, at least a balance sheet and income statement are necessary, and specific information is needed for this purpose. The type of information required is indicated in the sample balance sheet and income statement presented on pages 420–423 in Chapter 15. As you can see, the preparation of such statements require complete factual data on assets and liabilities, and income and expense, such as cash, accounts receivable, sales, accounts payable, taxes, expenses, debts, etc. Not only is such information necessary for tax reporting but, if used properly, will be extremely helpful to management. Comparing, for example, this year's liability figure on the balance sheet with the same figure for past years will clearly indicate whether debt is being reduced or increased.

Budgets and cash-flow statements are also especially helpful. A business budget, like a personal budget, provides a goal to shoot for—a guide. The very act of creating a budget impels the owner of the business to think, and plan for the future.

A cash-flow statement is prepared by estimating anticipated periodic cash income and the cash payments that it must cover. There may be times of the year when borrowing becomes necessary because anticipated cash income may be less than the bills that must be paid. Careful estimates of cash flow will indicate the amount that may have to be borrowed, when it should be borrowed, and how long it may be needed. Such a statement will be especially helpful when the businessman applies to his banker for the necessary loan.

Ratios are important, and are often overlooked. Dun & Bradstreet issues annual data covering 14 important financial ratios in 72 lines of retail, wholesale, and manufacturing business. An application of the ratios pertinent to a person's own business will enable him to spot certain danger signs. Comparing them with the same ratios in similar firms will help him judge the efficiency of the firm's operation.

> There is strong evidence that the companies which use ratio analysis as a management tool are more successful and profitable than those which do not.[4]

Of course, a business man can overdo the task of record keeping. Records must be adequate but not excessive. It is advisable to employ an accountant to set up a bookkeeping system most appropriate to the business; and if keeping the books should subsequently become a problem, it is also advisable to have them kept by an accountant or accounting firm.

---

[4] Albert Slavin and Seth Avakian Armen, *Small Business Accounting in Massachusetts–Practices and Problems,* prepared by The Bureau of Business and Economic Research, Northeastern University, Boston, Mass., under the Small Business Administration Management Research Grant Program, 1962, p. 8.

Credit Practices

A common management error is to extend credit unwisely, and to have a poor system of credit control in general. It is surprising how many businessmen become so enthused about "sales" that they completely disregard the fact that sales are unprofitable if the customers don't pay. If the business plans to extend credit, someone must assume the responsibility of collecting. Large companies which extend customer credit investigate customers before granting credit, and establish methods and procedures for collecting the amounts due. While this doesn't always work, it does keep credit losses to a minimum. To grant credit without proper investigation, and to carry accounts receivable without making consistent efforts to collect them, is to court failure.

Most small businessmen are anxious to be accepted by the community. They want to be liked, and many, even after their business is fairly well established, are unable to adopt the realistic attitude that overdue bills must be collected. They feel this is "hard-hearted." It isn't. It is common sense. Manufacturers demand payment from wholesalers, and refuse to ship merchandise if payment is not received. Wholesalers must make the same demand of retailers in order to pay the manufacturer. Obviously, retailers must adopt a firm credit policy in order to pay their suppliers, or they will soon be out of business. Actually, consumers seem to respect a firm, fair, credit system. Failure to pay a debt when due is caused by adverse circumstances, oversight, neglect, or just plain indifference. The debt can be extended in hardship cases; a notice will correct the oversight; a second, firmer notice, or demand, should overcome the neglect; and legal action should move the indifferent to act.

In 1958, a television and radio parts wholesale company in New England found a number of overdue accounts on its books. Its customers were retail stores that serviced television and radio receivers. They usually made the consumer pay cash before delivering the serviced receiver. Theoretically, the cost of the parts should have been deducted from the bill and used to pay the wholesaler. Most of these retailers paid promptly. Regular credit terms were 30 days. Upon visiting those that were 90 days or more overdue, an officer of the wholesale firm was given the following reasons for non-payment:

1. My husband isn't here. He can't pay you yet. He became so tired that he just had to go on a three week hunting trip to Maine.
2. I haven't got the money. I'll pay next month. No special reason.

3. Business has been slow and I have to pay for my new truck.

4. My wife just had a baby last month.

5. I needed a new car.

These are only a few of the answers given. Out of twelve retailers visited, only one had a legitimate reason for not paying. This was because of serious illness, and the wholesaler agreed not to press for payment. The others evidenced neither intent to pay nor concern over the fact that payment was overdue. Reasons given were found to be only excuses, without any legitimate foundation.

Every businessman must realize that it takes money to extend credit. If selling terms are 30 days, it is usually estimated that a businessman must have additional capital equal to about 45 days credit sales (1½ months). If a business expects to do about $5,000 worth of business a month on credit, it will usually be found that accounts receivable will average about $7,000 to $7,500, even if the customers pay promptly.

Salesman Expense

Many retail businesses require the employment of one or more sales persons. Let's assume, for example, that an ambitious teacher of organ and piano decides to open a retail store and sell musical instruments. He plans to continue giving lessons, to maintain his regular income until the store can pay for itself, and because he believes some of the pupils may buy an organ or piano. To do both, he must hire a salesman or saleswoman to run the store while he is giving lessons. Other businesses, such as a small department store, require more sales personnnel. A store selling appliances would likely need a salesman and a repair man. Occasionally, someone believes he can start a business and have others do most of the work. Generally, it doesn't work.

Estimates of anticipated business volume should be made before any personnel is hired, and then only those needed to handle that estimate should be employed. Subsequently, a constant check should be made to make certain the employees are doing the jobs they were hired to do, and only essential personnel should be retained.

Chart 17-1 is useful in measuring the cost of a salesman. As an example, let's assume that the owner of a new business estimates anticipated sales volume at $500 per week, and believes he can afford to allocate 16 per cent of sales for a salesman. This is obviously $80 per week. Now let's assume that sales are only $375. Find this figure at the side of the table and follow along the horizontal column until 16.0 is found. Then follow the vertical column in which this 16.0 is found up to the top of the page. Here you will find a weekly salary figure of $60. According to the chart, and our assumption that 16 per cent of sales is a fair salary cost percentage for this particular business, this salesman is earning only $60 per week instead of the $80 he is being paid.

This is not necessarily a reflection on the salesman's effort or ability. The owner may have over-estimated his sales potential. However, whatever the reason, the volume of sales produced will not support both the business and an $80 a week salesman. Either sales performance will have to be improved or the salary reduced to $60. The value of each salesman in an organization, large or small, can be measured in this way.

The same analysis must be made of salaries of other employees. A business cannot afford to pay an employee more than he produces, and be successful. This analysis is much easier to apply to some types of jobs than to others. Clerical help is certainly essential, but the amount such employees produce each week for the firm is not easily determined.

Margin and Markup

Another problem faced by the owner of a new business is pricing his goods. The price must be sufficient to cover all costs, including overhead, and leave something for profit. The table and explanation on page 503 indicate the error that is sometimes made in pricing, and the method that should be used to obtain a proper price.

The problem is that margin is always figured on selling price, and markup may be computed on either cost or selling price. The easiest, and least confusing method is to consider markup as a percentage of cost.

Let's assume that an article which costs $1.05 is sold for $1.50. The margin here, $.45, is 30 per cent of the selling price. It may be that in the business being considered, a 30% margin is necessary. According to the table, a 42.9 per cent markup of cost would produce the needed 30% margin. A *markup* of only 30% of cost would give a retail price of 1.365, and, according to the table, a margin of only 23.1%. The difference between this margin and the required 30% margin could mean the difference between success and failure.

Chart 17-1

HOW MUCH A SALESPERSON SHOULD SELL

WEEKLY SALARIES ▶	$15.00	$17.50	$18.00	$19.00	$20.00	$21.00	$22.00	$23.00	$24.00	$25.00	$27.50	$29.00	$30.00	$32.50	$35.00	$37.50	$40.00	$42.50	$45.00	$47.50	$50.00
									SALARY	COST	PERCENTAGES										
$ 150	10.0	11.7	12.0	12.7	13.3	14.0	14.7	15.3	16.0	16.7	18.3	19.3	20.0	21.7	23.3	25.0	26.7	28.3	30.0	31.7	33.3
160	9.4	10.9	11.3	11.9	12.5	13.1	13.8	14.4	15.0	15.6	17.2	18.1	18.8	20.3	21.9	23.4	25.0	26.6	28.1	29.7	31.3
170	8.8	10.3	10.6	11.2	11.8	12.4	12.9	13.5	14.1	14.7	16.2	17.1	17.6	19.1	20.6	22.1	23.5	25.0	26.5	27.9	29.4
180	8.3	9.7	10.0	10.6	11.1	11.7	12.2	12.8	13.3	13.9	15.3	16.1	16.7	18.1	19.4	20.8	22.2	23.6	25.0	26.4	27.8
190	7.9	9.2	9.5	10.0	10.5	11.1	11.6	12.1	12.6	13.2	14.5	15.3	15.8	17.1	18.4	19.7	21.1	22.4	23.7	25.0	26.3
200	7.5	8.8	9.0	9.5	10.0	10.5	11.0	11.5	12.0	12.5	13.8	14.5	15.0	16.3	17.5	18.8	20.0	21.3	22.5	23.8	25.0
210	7.1	8.3	8.6	9.0	9.5	10.0	10.5	11.0	11.4	11.9	13.1	13.8	14.3	15.5	16.7	17.9	19.0	20.2	21.4	22.6	23.8
220	6.8	8.0	8.2	8.6	9.1	9.5	10.0	10.5	10.9	11.4	12.5	13.2	13.6	14.8	15.9	17.0	18.2	19.3	20.5	21.6	22.7
230	6.5	7.6	7.8	8.3	8.7	9.1	9.6	10.0	10.4	10.9	12.0	12.6	13.0	14.1	15.2	16.3	17.4	18.5	19.6	20.7	21.7
240	6.3	7.3	7.5	7.9	8.3	8.8	9.2	9.6	10.0	10.4	11.5	12.1	12.5	13.5	14.6	15.6	16.7	17.7	18.7	19.8	20.8
250	6.0	7.0	7.2	7.6	8.0	8.4	8.8	9.2	9.6	10.0	11.0	11.6	12.0	13.0	14.0	15.0	16.0	17.0	18.0	19.0	20.0
260	5.8	6.7	6.9	7.3	7.7	8.1	8.5	8.8	9.2	9.6	10.6	11.2	11.5	12.5	13.5	14.4	15.4	16.3	17.3	18.3	19.2
270	5.6	6.5	6.7	7.0	7.4	7.8	8.1	8.5	8.9	9.3	10.2	10.7	11.1	12.0	13.0	13.9	14.8	15.7	16.7	17.6	18.5
280	5.4	6.2	6.4	6.8	7.1	7.5	7.9	8.2	8.6	8.9	9.8	10.4	10.7	11.6	12.5	13.4	14.3	15.2	16.1	17.0	17.9
290	5.2	6.0	6.2	6.6	6.9	7.2	7.6	7.9	8.3	8.6	9.5	10.0	10.3	11.2	12.1	12.9	13.8	14.7	15.5	16.4	17.2
300	5.0	5.8	6.0	6.3	6.7	7.0	7.3	7.7	8.0	8.3	9.2	9.7	10.0	10.8	11.7	12.5	13.3	14.2	15.0	15.8	16.7
325	4.6	5.4	5.5	5.8	6.2	6.5	6.8	7.1	7.4	7.7	8.5	8.9	9.2	10.0	10.8	11.5	12.3	13.1	13.8	14.6	15.4
350	4.3	5.0	5.1	5.4	5.7	6.0	6.3	6.6	6.9	7.1	7.9	8.3	8.6	9.3	10.0	10.7	11.4	12.1	12.9	13.6	14.3
375	4.0	4.7	4.8	5.1	5.3	5.6	5.9	6.1	6.4	6.7	7.3	7.7	8.0	8.7	9.3	10.0	10.7	11.3	12.0	12.7	13.3
400	3.8	4.4	4.5	4.8	5.0	5.3	5.5	5.8	6.0	6.3	6.9	7.3	7.5	8.1	8.8	9.4	10.0	10.6	11.3	11.9	12.5
425	3.5	4.1	4.2	4.5	4.7	4.9	5.2	5.4	5.6	5.9	6.5	6.8	7.1	7.6	8.2	8.8	9.4	10.0	10.6	11.2	11.8
450	3.3	3.9	4.0	4.2	4.4	4.7	4.9	5.1	5.3	5.6	6.1	6.4	6.7	7.2	7.8	8.3	8.9	9.4	10.0	10.6	11.1
475	3.2	3.7	3.8	4.0	4.2	4.4	4.6	4.8	5.1	5.3	5.8	6.1	6.3	6.8	7.4	7.9	8.4	8.9	9.5	10.0	10.5
500	3.0	3.5	3.6	3.8	4.0	4.2	4.4	4.6	4.8	5.0	5.5	5.8	6.0	6.5	7.0	7.5	8.0	8.5	9.0	9.5	10.0
525	2.9	3.3	3.4	3.6	3.8	4.0	4.2	4.4	4.6	4.8	5.2	5.5	5.7	6.2	6.7	7.1	7.6	8.1	8.6	9.0	9.5
550	2.7	3.2	3.3	3.5	3.6	3.8	4.0	4.2	4.4	4.5	5.0	5.3	5.5	5.9	6.4	6.8	7.3	7.7	8.2	8.6	9.1
575	2.6	3.0	3.1	3.3	3.5	3.7	3.8	4.0	4.2	4.3	4.8	5.0	5.2	5.7	6.1	6.5	7.0	7.4	7.8	8.3	8.7
600	2.5	2.9	3.0	3.2	3.3	3.5	3.7	3.8	4.0	4.2	4.6	4.8	5.0	5.4	5.8	6.2	6.7	7.1	7.5	7.9	8.3
625	2.4	2.8	2.9	3.0	3.2	3.4	3.5	3.7	3.8	4.0	4.4	4.6	4.8	5.2	5.6	6.0	6.4	6.8	7.2	7.6	8.0
650	2.3	2.7	2.8	2.9	3.1	3.2	3.4	3.5	3.7	3.8	4.2	4.5	4.6	5.0	5.4	5.8	6.2	6.5	6.9	7.3	7.7
675	2.2	2.6	2.7	2.8	3.0	3.1	3.2	3.4	3.5	3.7	4.1	4.3	4.4	4.8	5.2	5.6	5.9	6.3	6.7	7.0	7.4
700	2.1	2.5	2.6	2.7	2.9	3.0	3.1	3.3	3.4	3.6	3.9	4.1	4.3	4.6	5.0	5.3	5.7	6.1	6.4	6.8	7.1
725	2.1	2.4	2.5	2.6	2.7	2.9	3.0	3.2	3.3	3.4	3.8	4.0	4.1	4.5	4.8	5.2	5.5	5.9	6.2	6.5	6.9
750	2.0	2.3	2.4	2.5	2.7	2.8	2.9	3.1	3.2	3.3	3.7	3.9	4.0	4.3	4.7	5.0	5.3	5.7	6.0	6.3	6.7
775	1.9	2.2	2.3	2.4	2.6	2.7	2.8	3.0	3.1	3.2	3.5	3.7	3.9	4.2	4.5	4.8	5.2	5.5	5.8	6.1	6.4
800	1.9	2.2	2.2	2.4	2.5	2.6	2.7	2.9	3.0	3.1	3.4	3.6	3.7	4.1	4.4	4.7	5.0	5.3	5.6	5.9	6.2
825	1.8	2.1	2.2	2.3	2.4	2.5	2.7	2.8	2.9	3.0	3.3	3.5	3.6	3.9	4.2	4.5	4.8	5.1	5.4	5.7	6.1
850	1.8	2.1	2.1	2.2	2.3	2.5	2.6	2.7	2.8	2.9	3.2	3.4	3.5	3.8	4.1	4.4	4.7	5.0	5.3	5.6	5.9
875	1.7	2.0	2.0	2.2	2.3	2.4	2.5	2.6	2.7	2.8	3.1	3.3	3.4	3.7	4.0	4.3	4.6	4.8	5.1	5.4	5.7
900	1.7	1.9	2.0	2.1	2.2	2.3	2.4	2.5	2.7	2.8	3.1	3.2	3.3	3.6	3.9	4.2	4.4	4.7	5.0	5.3	5.5
925	1.6	1.9	1.9	2.0	2.2	2.3	2.4	2.5	2.6	2.7	3.0	3.1	3.2	3.5	3.8	4.0	4.3	4.6	4.9	5.1	5.4
950	1.6	1.8	1.9	2.0	2.1	2.2	2.3	2.4	2.5	2.6	2.9	3.0	3.1	3.4	3.7	3.9	4.2	4.5	4.7	5.0	5.3
975	1.5	1.8	1.8	1.9	2.0	2.1	2.2	2.3	2.5	2.6	2.8	3.0	3.1	3.3	3.6	3.8	4.1	4.3	4.6	4.9	5.1
1000	1.5	1.7	1.8	1.9	2.0	2.1	2.2	2.3	2.4	2.5	2.7	2.9	3.0	3.2	3.5	3.7	4.0	4.2	4.5	4.7	5.0

Left row label reading vertically: A M O U N T   O F   W E E K L Y   S A L E S

The figures in the top line of the table represent weekly salaries. Those in the extreme left and right columns are the weekly sales required to justify the salaries according to salary cost percentages.

To determine how much a salesperson should sell, select the column headed with the weekly salary of the salesperson. Follow this column down to the salary cost percentage nearest that of your store. The dollar figures on the same line in the AMOUNT OF WEEKLY SALES column (extreme left or right) show what the salesperson should sell each week to earn his salary.

Example: A salesperson receives $75.00 per week in a hardware store having annual sales of $300,000 in a county with a population of over 2,000,000. The salary cost percentage for stores in this classification is 14.9%, as shown on page 15. Under the column marked $75.00, locate this salary percentage or the one closest to it. In this case the

$52.50	$55.00	$57.50	$60.00	$62.50	$65.00	$67.50	$70.00	$72.50	$75.00	$77.50	$80.00	$82.50	$85.00	$87.50	$90.00	$92.50	$95.00	$97.50	$100.00	WEEKLY SALARIES / AMOUNT OF WEEKLY SALES
35.0	36.7	38.3	40.0	41.7	43.3	45.0	46.7	48.3	50.0	51.7	53.3	55.0	56.7	58.3	60.0	61.7	63.3	65.0	66.7	$150
32.8	34.4	35.9	37.5	39.1	40.6	42.2	43.8	45.3	46.9	48.4	50.0	51.6	53.1	54.7	56.3	57.8	59.4	60.9	62.5	160
30.9	32.4	33.8	35.3	36.8	38.2	39.7	41.2	42.6	44.1	45.6	47.1	48.5	50.0	51.5	52.9	54.4	55.9	57.4	58.8	170
29.2	30.6	31.9	33.3	34.7	36.1	37.5	38.9	40.3	41.7	43.0	44.4	45.8	47.2	48.6	50.0	51.4	52.8	54.2	55.6	180
27.6	28.9	30.3	31.6	32.9	34.2	35.5	36.8	38.1	39.5	40.8	42.1	43.4	44.7	46.1	47.4	48.7	50.0	51.3	52.6	190
26.2	27.5	28.7	30.0	31.2	32.5	33.7	35.0	36.2	37.5	38.7	40.0	41.3	42.5	43.8	45.0	46.3	47.5	48.8	50.0	200
25.0	26.2	27.4	28.6	29.8	31.0	32.1	33.3	34.5	35.7	36.9	38.1	39.3	40.5	41.7	42.9	44.0	45.2	46.4	47.6	210
23.9	25.0	26.1	27.3	28.4	29.5	30.7	31.8	32.9	34.1	35.2	36.4	37.5	38.6	39.8	40.9	42.0	43.2	44.3	45.5	220
22.8	23.9	25.0	26.1	27.2	28.3	29.3	30.4	31.5	32.6	33.7	34.8	35.9	37.0	38.0	39.1	40.2	41.3	42.4	43.5	230
21.9	22.9	23.9	25.0	26.0	27.1	28.1	29.2	30.2	31.2	32.3	33.3	34.4	35.4	36.5	37.5	38.5	39.6	40.6	41.7	240
21.0	22.0	23.0	24.0	25.0	26.0	27.0	28.0	29.0	30.0	31.0	32.0	33.0	34.0	35.0	36.0	37.0	38.0	39.0	40.0	250
20.2	21.2	22.1	23.1	24.0	25.0	26.0	26.9	27.9	28.8	29.8	30.8	31.7	32.7	33.7	34.6	35.6	36.5	37.5	38.5	260
19.4	20.4	21.3	22.2	23.1	24.1	25.0	25.9	26.8	27.8	28.7	29.6	30.6	31.5	32.4	33.3	34.3	35.2	36.1	37.0	270
18.7	19.6	20.5	21.4	22.3	23.2	24.1	25.0	25.9	26.8	27.7	28.6	29.5	30.4	31.3	32.1	33.0	33.9	34.8	35.7	280
18.1	19.0	19.8	20.7	21.5	22.4	23.3	24.1	25.0	25.9	26.7	27.6	28.4	29.3	30.2	31.0	31.9	32.8	33.6	34.5	290
17.5	18.3	19.2	20.0	20.8	21.7	22.5	23.3	24.2	25.0	25.8	26.7	27.5	28.3	29.2	30.0	30.8	31.7	32.5	33.4	300
16.1	16.9	17.7	18.5	19.2	20.0	20.8	21.5	22.3	23.1	23.8	24.6	25.4	26.2	26.9	27.7	28.5	29.2	30.0	30.8	325
15.0	15.7	16.4	17.1	17.8	18.6	19.3	20.0	20.7	21.4	22.1	22.9	23.6	24.3	25.0	25.7	26.4	27.1	27.9	28.6	350
14.0	14.7	15.3	16.0	16.7	17.3	18.0	18.7	19.3	20.0	20.7	21.3	22.0	22.7	23.3	24.0	24.7	25.3	26.0	26.7	375
13.1	13.8	14.4	15.0	15.6	16.3	16.9	17.5	18.1	18.8	19.4	20.0	20.6	21.3	21.9	22.5	23.1	23.8	24.4	25.0	400
12.3	12.9	13.5	14.1	14.7	15.3	15.9	16.5	17.0	17.6	18.2	18.8	19.4	20.0	20.6	21.2	21.8	22.4	22.9	23.5	425
11.7	12.2	12.8	13.3	13.9	14.4	15.0	15.6	16.1	16.7	17.2	17.8	18.3	18.9	19.4	20.0	20.6	21.1	21.7	22.2	450
11.0	11.6	12.1	12.6	13.1	13.7	14.2	14.7	15.3	15.8	16.3	16.8	17.4	17.9	18.4	18.9	19.5	20.0	20.5	21.1	475
10.5	11.0	11.5	12.0	12.5	13.0	13.5	14.0	14.5	15.0	15.5	16.0	16.5	17.0	17.5	18.0	18.5	19.0	19.5	20.0	500
10.0	10.5	10.9	11.4	11.9	12.4	12.8	13.3	13.8	14.3	14.8	15.2	15.7	16.2	16.7	17.1	17.6	18.1	18.6	19.0	525
9.5	10.0	10.4	10.9	11.4	11.8	12.3	12.7	13.2	13.6	14.1	14.5	15.0	15.5	15.9	16.4	16.8	17.3	17.7	18.2	550
9.1	9.6	10.0	10.4	10.9	11.3	11.7	12.2	12.6	13.0	13.5	13.9	14.3	14.8	15.2	15.7	16.1	16.5	17.0	17.4	575
8.7	9.2	9.6	10.0	10.4	10.8	11.2	11.7	12.1	12.5	12.9	13.3	13.8	14.2	14.6	15.0	15.4	15.8	16.3	16.7	600
8.4	8.8	9.2	9.6	10.0	10.4	10.8	11.2	11.6	12.0	12.4	12.8	13.2	13.6	14.0	14.4	14.8	15.2	15.6	16.0	625
8.1	8.5	8.8	9.2	9.6	10.0	10.4	10.8	11.1	11.5	11.9	12.3	12.7	13.1	13.5	13.8	14.2	14.6	15.0	15.4	650
7.8	8.1	8.5	8.9	9.2	9.6	10.0	10.4	10.7	11.1	11.5	11.8	12.2	12.6	13.0	13.3	13.7	14.1	14.4	14.8	675
7.5	7.9	8.2	8.6	8.9	9.3	9.6	10.0	10.4	10.7	11.1	11.4	11.8	12.1	12.5	12.9	13.2	13.6	13.9	14.3	700
7.2	7.6	7.9	8.3	8.6	9.0	9.3	9.6	10.0	10.3	10.7	11.0	11.4	11.7	12.1	12.4	12.8	13.1	13.4	13.8	725
7.0	7.3	7.7	8.0	8.3	8.7	9.0	9.3	9.7	10.0	10.3	10.7	11.0	11.3	11.7	12.0	12.3	12.7	13.0	13.3	750
6.8	7.1	7.4	7.7	8.1	8.4	8.7	9.0	9.3	9.7	10.0	10.3	10.6	11.0	11.3	11.6	11.9	12.3	12.6	12.9	775
6.6	6.9	7.2	7.5	7.8	8.1	8.4	8.7	9.1	9.4	9.7	10.0	10.3	10.6	10.9	11.3	11.6	11.9	12.2	12.5	800
6.4	6.7	7.0	7.3	7.6	7.9	8.2	8.5	8.8	9.1	9.4	9.7	10.0	10.3	10.6	10.9	11.2	11.5	11.8	12.1	825
6.2	6.5	6.8	7.1	7.3	7.6	7.9	8.2	8.5	8.8	9.1	9.4	9.7	10.0	10.3	10.6	10.9	11.2	11.5	11.8	850
6.0	6.3	6.6	6.8	7.1	7.4	7.7	8.0	8.3	8.6	8.9	9.1	9.4	9.7	10.0	10.3	10.6	10.9	11.1	11.4	875
5.8	6.1	6.4	6.7	6.9	7.2	7.5	7.8	8.0	8.3	8.6	8.9	9.2	9.4	9.7	10.0	10.3	10.6	10.8	11.1	900
5.7	5.9	6.2	6.5	6.7	7.0	7.3	7.6	7.8	8.1	8.4	8.6	8.9	9.2	9.5	9.7	10.0	10.3	10.5	10.8	925
5.5	5.8	6.0	6.3	6.6	6.8	7.1	7.4	7.6	7.9	8.1	8.4	8.7	8.9	9.2	9.5	9.7	10.0	10.3	10.5	950
5.4	5.6	5.9	6.1	6.4	6.7	6.9	7.2	7.4	7.7	7.9	8.2	8.5	8.7	9.0	9.2	9.5	9.7	10.0	10.3	975
5.2	5.5	5.7	6.0	6.2	6.5	6.7	7.0	7.2	7.5	7.7	8.0	8.3	8.5	8.8	9.0	9.3	9.5	9.8	10.0	1000

nearest figure is 15.0%. The amount in the AMOUNT OF WEEKLY SALES column opposite 15.0% is $500. This is the average amount of merchandise the salesperson should sell each week to earn his salary of $75.00.

If you know the average weekly sales of your salespeople, you can determine which ones deserve salary increases with this table. Find the salesperson's amount of weekly sales and follow that row across to your salary cost percentage. The weekly salary at the top of that column is what your salesperson is actually earning. If you're paying him less than the table indicates he should be paid, he may be entitled to a raise. But if you're paying him more, the difference is coming directly out of your profit.

(Continued on Page 45)

MERCHANTS SERVICE, THE NATIONAL CASH REGISTER COMPANY
Dayton 9, Ohio

Source: *Expenses in Retail Businesses,* Merchants Service, The National Cash Register Company, Dayton, Ohio, pp. 24-25.

COMPUTING MARGIN AND MARKUP[5]

Many a business fails to make an expected profit because its owner figures his percentage of margin on the cost of goods. He assumes that the percentages of margin and markup on cost are the same. This confusion is not strange, because margin and markup in dollars are identical. The percentages, however, are different. Both represent the difference between cost of merchandise and selling price.

Selling price covers the cost of merchandise plus all expenses of operation and net profit. The selling price is always 100% because it is the total amount of money we are going to get from the sale.

Margin is always figured on the selling price. It is a *percentage of sales.*

> Example: Suppose we buy an article for $1.20 and sell it for $1.60. The margin would be 40¢, which is ¼ or 25% of the selling price. Therefore, our margin on this article would be 25%.

Markup can be computed either as a *percentage of cost or of selling price.* Although many consider markup a percentage of the selling price, retailing authorities point out that figuring markup on the cost price is easier and less confusing in everyday pricing. The important thing to keep in mind is that when markup is figured on the selling price, a different markup percentage must be used than when figuring the markup on the cost price. Otherwise, the anticipated margin will not be attained.

> Example: Suppose we buy an article for $1.20 and wish to sell it on a markup of 25%. What must the selling price be? The markup of 25% times the cost, 1.20, equals 30¢. Add 30¢ to the cost price of $1.20 and we have a selling price of $1.50 with a margin of 30¢, or 20%. However, if we want to mark up the article so that we have a 25% margin, we must first determine the percentage that will yield the desired margin when applied to the cost price. Looking at the Markup Table below, we see that a 25% margin is equivalent to a 33⅓% markup on cost. Multiplying 33⅓% times the cost, $1.20, equals 40¢. Adding 40¢ to the cost price gives us a selling price of $1.60, and a margin of 40¢, or 25%.

We can readily see from these two examples that on an item costing $1.20 a *margin* of 25% gives a selling price of $1.60,

> BUT

> a *markup on cost* of 25% gives a selling price of $1.50.

Therefore, if we must have a margin of 25% to cover the cost of operation and net profit, we would be losing money by pricing merchandise on the basis of a 25% markup on cost! To realize a 25% margin, we would have to use a markup of 33⅓% on the cost price.

---

[5] *Expenses in Retail Businesses,* Merchants Service, The National Cash Register Company, Dayton, Ohio, p. 44.

MARKUP TABLE

The following table shows what the markup on cost must be to give the desired margin in a number of more common cases. To use this table, find your margin or gross profit percentage in the left-hand column. Multiply the cost of the article by the corresponding percentage in the right-hand or markup column. The result added to the cost gives the correct selling price.

Margin Per Cent of Selling Price	Markup Per Cent of Cost	Margin Per Cent of Selling Price	Markup Per Cent of Cost
4.8	5.0	25.0	33.3
5.0	5.3	26.0	35.0
6.0	6.4	27.0	37.0
7.0	7.5	27.3	37.5
8.0	8.7	28.0	39.0
9.0	10.0	28.5	40.0
10.0	11.1	29.0	40.9
10.7	12.0	30.0	42.9
11.0	12.4	31.0	45.0
11.1	12.5	32.0	47.1
12.0	13.6	33.3	50.0
12.5	14.3	34.0	51.5
13.0	15.0	35.0	53.9
14.0	16.3	35.5	55.0
15.0	17.7	36.0	56.3
16.0	19.1	37.0	58.8
16.7	20.0	37.5	60.0
17.0	20.5	38.0	61.3
17.5	21.2	39.0	64.0
18.0	22.0	39.5	65.5
18.5	22.7	40.0	66.7
19.0	23.5	41.0	70.0
20.0	25.0	42.0	72.4
21.0	26.6	42.8	75.0
22.0	28.2	44.4	80.0
22.5	29.0	46.1	85.0
23.0	29.9	47.5	90.0
23.1	30.0	48.7	95.0
24.0	31.6	50.0	100.0

Firms occasionally get so thoroughly enthused about "volume" that costs and proper pricing are overlooked. During the 1950's, a particular firm enjoyed a tremendous sales volume in the field of wholesale television parts. Within a period of two or three years, it had risen from its start to one of the top wholesalers in the area, in terms of sales. The primary reason was that it sold products at much cheaper prices than the same products were sold by competing wholesalers. A comparison of its sales volume from one year to another would have indicated a fantastic growth rate. But they were selling below cost, earned nothing, and finally went bankrupt. Increasing sales are of no value if the company is losing money. Of course, such a loss may be temporary, but if the losses continue, the company is certain to fail.

WHERE TO GET FUNDS

There may have been a time when a business could operate without borrowing money, but this is almost impossible today. Very rarely is it possible to start a business with total capital of only one or two thousand dollars. In many fields, the minimum size of a firm has to be relatively large in order to have a chance for success. As a business grows, additional funds are needed to finance the growth. In fact, rapid growth is a frequent cause of financial difficulty. It would seem that a growing business is a successful business (assuming sales are profitable), but as the firm grows, more money is needed to maintain a larger inventory, a larger sales force, a larger manufacturing plant, more clerical help, etc. If growth is essential to its existence, a lack of funds could cause it to fail. At best, the lack of funds with which to grow will keep it small, and perhaps defeat its opportunity to be an outstanding success.

Unfortunately, firms occasionally get into financial difficulty, not because funds are not available, but because the company doesn't know where to look.

Sometimes the availability of capital can be increased by changing the form of organization under which the business operates. A sole proprietorship might take in partners with capital, or a proprietorship or partnership might incorporate and sell stock. Such moves are usually in the best interests of the business, but generally result in a surrender, or dilution, of ownership. Partners, for example, will restrict the independence enjoyed by the proprietor. Incorporation is complicated and means that ownership is shared. Each of these moves must be considered in the light of the statements made earlier in this chapter, concerning the choice of a form of organization.

Trade Credit

Trade credit is an important source of short term credit. Inventories and equipment purchases, especially, are financed in this manner. The supplier extends the credit, permitting the purchaser to pay for merchandise and equipment over a period of time. While this is an important source of financing, it is primarily of a short-term nature, and limited in its extent. One inherent problem of such credit is that the supplier's salesman may tend to over-sell, and overload the firm to the extent that it cannot pay its bills.

Banks

The bank is the loan source most businessmen think of when they need money. Commercial banks do offer both money and sound advice. An experienced banker can be of great assistance to a small businessman in solving financial problems.

Businessmen are often surprised to find that business loans are considered more risky than personal loans, loans made to finance an automobile, or the mortgage on a home. Business loans are usually made at a higher interest rate and for shorter periods of time. Frequently, assets must be pledged as security.

Banks usually discount a business loan (subtract the interest from the amount loaned at the time the loan is made), and maturity is usually 30, 60 or 90 days. A business may or may not be permitted to renew the loan at maturity.

A loan application should be made in a thoroughly businesslike manner, and only after careful preparation. Any source, including commercial banks, is favorably impressed by a carefully laid out plan. The applicant should be prepared to submit a balance sheet, income statement, cash flow analysis, and an explanation of the need for and planned use of the money requested.

Despite the slightly higher risk classification, and perhaps because of the higher interest rate, banks are quite interested in making business loans. Besides the familiar 30-60-90 day type of loan, other loan plans have been developed to meet business needs. Some of these plans are extremely flexible, and provide relatively large sums of money for periods of from two to three years. A businessman should investigate the plans offered by his local bank.[6]

Government Sources

While bank loans may be made for longer terms than trade credit, and made available under circumstances where trade credit is not, they are still limited to maximum terms of just a few years, in most cases. What about long term credit? Surprisingly enough, in a day when the government is a common subject of conversation, it is often overlooked as a source of credit for small business. The chart on pages 507 through 510 indicates the various loan plans made available by the

---

[6] For a more complete list of bank loans available to business see page 93 in Chapter 4, "Using Your Bank."

Small Business Administration (SBA). While time does not permit the discussion of each of these plans in detail, the general features of Small Business Administration business loans can be briefly described.

>In SBA's financial assistance program, the agency counsels small firms on their financial problems, helps them obtain loans from private sources, and provides financing in participation with banks. When private financing is not available on reasonable terms, SBA makes loans to qualified small businesses.

>As a further aid to economic growth and expansion of job opportunities, SBA stimulates the flow of funds to small firms from privately-owned small business investment companies and from State and local development companies.

>In times of natural disasters, the agency provides low interest, long term loans to rehabilitate or replace damaged business and homes. SBA also makes loans to assist small firms that have suffered economic injury from drought or excessive rainfall, or from displacement by federally-aided construction programs.[7]

SBA makes loans to small manufacturers, wholesalers, retailers, service concerns and other business. These loans are available to qualified firms, providing these firms cannot obtain private financing on reasonable terms and are not eligible for financing from other government agencies. Loans are made for business construction, conversion, or expansion; purchase of equipment, facilities, machinery, supplies, or materials; and for working capital.

There are two types of SBA loans: "participating" and "direct." If the loan is a participating loan, the SBA joins in making it with a bank or some other private lending institution. The direct loan is made solely by the SBA directly to the borrower. The agency is not permitted by law to make a direct loan if a participation loan can be arranged.

To be considered for an SBA loan, a business must qualify as a small business and must meet the agency's credit requirements. The general definition of a "small business" is one that is independently owned and operated and nondominant in its field, and that meets more detailed standards developed by the SBA. These standards and credit requirements are generally as follows:

1. Size of the business
   a. Manufacturing concerns are considered small if average employment in preceding four calendar quarters was 250 or less, and large if average employment was more than 1,000.

---

[7] John E. Horne, "A Message from the Administrator, SBA Loans at Work," Office of Information Services, Small Business Administration, Washington, D.C., U.S. Government Printing Office: 1962 O—655923, 1962, p. 1.

SMALL BUSINESS ADMINISTRATION
John E. Horne, Administrator
Washington 25, D. C.

Key Features of SBA's Principal Lending Programs

BUSINESS LOANS

	REGULAR BUSINESS	LIMITED LOAN PARTICIPATION PLAN	SIMPLIFIED BANK PARTICIPATION PLAN	SIMPLIFIED EARLY MATURITY PLAN
WHO IS ELIGIBLE?	Most businesses that are independently owned and operated and non-dominant in their fields; that cannot obtain private financing on reasonable terms and are not eligible for financing from other Government agencies, and that qualify as "small" under SBA's size standards, which generally are based on dollar volume of business or number of employees.	Any business that meets criteria stated under Regular Business Loan Plan. However, Limited Loan Participation Plan is of special interest to small retail, wholesale and service concerns.	Any business that meets criteria stated under Regular Business Loan Plan. However, this plan, under which the businessman deals entirely with his bank, is intended to assist the "stronger credits."	Same as under Simplified Bank Participation Plan. Major distinction between this plan and Simplified Bank Participation Plan is that bank provides at least 50% of loan and is repaid before SBA.
LOAN PURPOSES	Business construction, conversion or expansion; purchase of equipment, facilities, machinery, supplies or materials; and working capital.	Same as under Regular Business Loan Plan.	Same as under Regular Business Loan Plan.	Same as under Regular Business Loan Plan.
MAXIMUM AMOUNT	$350,000 to any one borrower. This is maximum SBA share of "participation loan" - - one made jointly by SBA and private lending institution - - and maximum SBA "direct loan" - - one made entirely by Agency.	Maximum SBA share of $25,000 or 75% of total loan, whichever is lesser; private lending institution's share must equal any outstanding loan to be repaid to it with part of participation loan or must be 25% of participation loan, whichever is larger.	$350,000 to any one borrower, as SBA share of participation loan or SBA direct loan.	Same as under Simplified Bank Participation Plan.
INTEREST RATE	Maximum of 5½% per annum on SBA share of "immediate participation loan" (where SBA and private lending institution each put up part of loan funds immediately) and on SBA direct loan. 1/ Where SBA "defers" providing its share of participation loan until asked by lending institution to do so, institution may set "reasonable and legal" rate on entire loan. However, if SBA later provides its share of "deferred participation loan," rate on SBA share then is maximum of 5½%. 1/	Maximum of 5½% per annum on SBA share of loan where Agency puts up its share immediately or where Agency has provided its share of deferred participation loan at request of participating institution. 1/ Participating institution may set "legal and reasonable" rate on its share of loan and on SBA share of deferred participation loan until SBA provides its share.	Same as under Limited Loan Participation Plan.	Same as under Limited Loan Participation Plan, but on immediate participation basis only.
MATURITY	Maximum of 10 years as a rule. However, working capital loans generally are limited to 5 years, while construction loans may have maximum of 10 years plus estimated time required to complete construction.	Maximum of 5 years.	Same as under Regular Business Loan Plan.	Same as under Regular Business Loan Plan.
TYPE OF COLLATERAL	Real estate or chattel mortgage; assignment of warehouse receipts for marketable merchandise; assignment of certain types of contracts; guarantees or personal endorsements; in some instances assignment of current receivables, and inventories stored in bonded or otherwise acceptable warehouse.	Real estate or chattel mortgage; assignment of accounts receivable or funds due on contracts; pledges of warehouse receipts; negative pledge agreements, and corporate guarantees or personal endorsements.	Same as under Regular Business Loan Plan.	Same as under Regular Business Loan Plan, except that collateral must be of a type not subject to rapid depreciation or obsolescence.

MARCH 1963   1/ 4% interest charged in areas classified by Federal Government as having substantial unemployment.

SBA's Lending Programs *(Cont.)*

STATE AND LOCAL DEVELOPMENT COMPANY LOANS

	STATE DEVELOPMENT COMPANIES	LOCAL DEVELOPMENT COMPANIES
WHO IS ELIGIBLE?	Any corporation organized under or pursuant to a special State legislative act, with authority to operate Statewide and to assist the growth and development of business concerns, including small businesses, in its area.	Any corporation which (a) is formed by public-spirited citizens with at least 75% ownership and control held by persons living or doing business in the community, (b) has been incorporated under laws of the State in which it expects to do business, and (c) is authorized to promote and assist growth and development of small businesses in its area.
LOAN PURPOSES	To help development company provide equity capital and long-term loans to small business (SBA loans under Section 501 of Small Business Investment Act); to help company buy land and build a new factory, acquire machinery and equipment, expand or convert an existing plant, or construct shopping center space, provided project will help a specific small business (SBA loans under Section 502 of Act).	To help a development company buy land and build a new factory, acquire machinery and equipment, expand or convert an existing plant or construct shopping center space, provided the project will assist a specific small business.
MAXIMUM AMOUNT	Under Section 501, as much as development company's total outstanding borrowings from all other sources; under Section 502, $350,000 for each identifiable small business to be assisted--as a prerequisite to obtaining SBA financing, development corporation to provide up to 20% of the cost of the project in funds raised by sale of equity (and if necessary debt) security, or in cash equivalent (e.g., land).	$350,000 for each identifiable small business to be assisted--as a prerequisite to obtaining SBA financing, development corporation to provide up to 20% of the cost of the project in funds raised by sale of equity (and if necessary debt) security, or in cash equivalent (e.g., land).
INTEREST RATE	On Section 501 loans, 5% per annum [2]; on Sec. 502 loans maximum of 5½% per annum on SBA's share of immediate participation loan, on SBA's share of deferred participation loan after providing its share, and on SBA direct loan.[3] Participating lending institution may set reasonable interest rate on its share of 502 loan, and on SBA's share of deferred participation loan until SBA has provided its share.	5½% per annum on SBA's share of immediate participation loan, on SBA's share of deferred participation loan after it has provided its share, and on SBA direct loan. [3] Participating lending institution may set interest rate on its share of loan and on SBA's share of deferred participation loan until Agency provides its share.
MATURITY	On Section 501 loans, maximum of 20 years; on Section 502 loans, maximum of 25 years plus estimated time required to complete plant construction, conversion or expansion. SBA also may extend a Section 502 loan for as much as 10 more years if this will aid in orderly liquidation.	Maximum maturity of 25 years plus estimated time required to complete construction, conversion or expansion; however, SBA may extend a loan for as long as 10 years beyond stated maturity if this will aid in orderly liquidation.
TYPE OF COLLATERAL	For Section 501 financing, securing of SBA loan on an equal basis with funds borrowed by development company from any other sources after August 21, 1958 (SBA funds may be secured on a ratable basis with other funds); for Section 502 loans, security of such nature that repayment is reasonably assured - - for example, a first lien on project to be financed.	Collateral that will reasonably assure repayment; for example, a first lien on the project.

[2] 4% where development company will use funds for long-term loans in areas of substantial unemployment.

[3] 4% where loan will be used to help a small business in an area of substantial unemployment.

SBA's Lending Programs *(Cont.)*

SMALL BUSINESS INVESTMENT COMPANY LOANS

	LOANS TO HELP MEET STARTING CAPITAL REQUIREMENTS	LOANS FOR OPERATING CAPITAL PURPOSES
WHO IS ELIGIBLE?	Any company licensed by SBA under the Small Business Investment Act to provide equity capital and long-term loans to small business concerns.	Same as under loans for starting capital requirements.
LOAN PURPOSES	To enable a company that otherwise is qualified under the Act and SBA regulations to meet initial capital requirements for licensees, as well as growth capital requirements.	To provide a company operating capital for use in financing small businesses.
MAXIMUM AMOUNT	Up to $150,000 in the case of a company which plans to start with the minimum required capital of $300,000, and in the same ratio for companies planning greater starting capital. However, the maximum loan to any one company is $400,000.	Loans totaling 50 percent of company's statutory paid-in capital and surplus, with a maximum of $4 million of loans to any one company.
INTEREST RATE	5% per annum.	5% per annum.
MATURITY	Maximum of 20 years.	Maximum of 20 years, but maturity may be extended at SBA's discretion.
SECURITY	Loan secured by the general credit of the company but subordinate to all other debts of the company.	Small business securities held by investment company and earmarked against SBA loan.

SBA's Lending Programs *(Cont.)*

DISASTER LOANS

	STORMS, FLOODS, ETC.	DROUGHT AND EXCESSIVE RAINFALL	DISPLACED BUSINESSES
WHO IS ELIGIBLE?	Individuals, business concerns, nonprofit organizations such as churches provided (a) they have suffered tangible property loss from a disaster and (b) SBA has declared their area a disaster area for purposes of financial assistance.	Any small business located in area of drought or excessive rainfall provided (a) it has suffered substantial economic injury because of drought or excessive rainfall, and (b) the President or Secretary of Agriculture has declared its area a major disaster area.	Any small business which has been displaced or is about to be displaced by a Federally-aided construction project provided the business was established or acquired by loan applicant prior to approval of project. Nonprofit, charitable and religious institutions are not eligible.
LOAN PURPOSES	To restore a home, business, or nonprofit institution as nearly as possible to its pre-disaster condition; loans may be used for real estate repair and replacement and for repair and replacement of furnishings, equipment, fixtures and inventory.	Working capital, replenishment of normal inventories, and payment of financial obligations (except bank loans) which the small business would have been able to meet had it not suffered loss of revenue because of the disaster conditions.	To help firm relocate under circumstances comparable to those which it previously occupied. Funds may be used for purchase of land and buildings, moving expenses, replacement of machinery and equipment, increased rent, inventory, working capital, etc. A reasonable upgrading is permitted. Renters, lessees, or nonowners of real estate are not eligible for funds to purchase land, construct buildings, or acquire realty.
MAXIMUM AMOUNT	Actual tangible loss suffered as a result of the disaster, less any insurance proceeds or funds obtained from other sources such as American Red Cross.	Determined by the economic loss suffered by applicant as a result of the disaster.	No fixed dollar limit. Amount of loan is based on a reasonable estimate of cost of reestablishing the business consistent with economic injury suffered by displacement. Loan cannot exceed estimated cost of reestablishment, less net funds received as damages, moving expenses or condemnation.
INTEREST RATE	3% per annum on SBA's share of loan made in participation with a private lending institution and on SBA direct loan. Private lender participating in a loan for home repair or construction may charge maximum of 3% per annum on its share of loan; on other disaster loans it may set reasonable rate on its share.	3% per annum on SBA's share of immediate participation loan, on SBA's share of deferred participation loan after it has provided its share, and on SBA direct loan. Private lending institution participating in a loan may set reasonable interest rate on its share and on entire deferred participation loan until SBA provides its share.	3½% per annum on SBA's share of loans made in participation with private lender and on SBA direct loans made between July 1, 1962 and June 30, 1963. Private lending institution may set reasonable interest rate on its share of loan.
MATURITY	Based on borrower's ability to repay, but may not exceed 20 years.	Based on borrower's ability to repay, but may not exceed 20 years.	Based on borrower's ability to repay, but may not exceed 20 years.
TYPE OF COLLATERAL	No specific collateral requirements; however, applicants must pledge whatever collateral they can provide.	No specific collateral requirements; however, applicants must pledge whatever collateral they can provide.	No specific collateral requirements; however, applicants must pledge whatever collateral they can provide.

PREPARED AND ISSUED BY OFFICE OF INFORMATION SERVICES   ☆ U.S. GOVERNMENT PRINTING OFFICE : 1963 O—677836

Source: "SBA Loans at Work," Small Business Administration, Office of Information Services, U.S. Govt. Printing Office: 1963, O—677836.

In between these numbers, its classification will depend upon the employment size standard the SBA has developed for the particular industry.

   b. Wholesale concerns are considered small if their yearly sales are $5 million or less.

   c. Retail businesses and service trades are considered small if their annual receipts are not more than $1 million.

2. Credit requirements

   a. Applicant must be of good character.

   b. There must be evidence that he has the ability to operate his business successfully.

   c. He must have sufficient capital to operate on a sound financial basis with the SBA loan assistance.

   d. The proposed loan must be of such sound value, or must be so secured, that repayment will be reasonably assured.

   e. Past earnings and future prospects must indicate ability to repay loan out of business income.

   f. In the case of a new business venture, the applicant is expected to provide funds about equal to the desired loan.

These are general standards and credit requirements, and a business desiring such loan should ask the SBA for more specific details. In some instances, specific standards have been developed for particular types of businesses.

There are also certain circumstances under which the agency will not consider applications for loans. Loans, for example, will not be granted if the funds are otherwise available on reasonable terms; or if the purpose is to pay off creditors, or to distribute funds to owners, etc.[8]

The maximum amount the agency may have outstanding to any one borrower is $350,000, or less. Loans are usually repayable in monthly installments, including interest on the unpaid balance. The maximum maturity is generally 10 years, although the maximum may vary from 6 to 20 years depending upon the purpose of the loan. The maximum interest rate charged by the SBA is 5½ per cent. Terms and conditions of loan depend upon the particular circumstances. The agency specifies the type of collateral that will be accepted.

The Small Business Administration also indirectly provides small business with funds through Small Business Investment Companies (SBIC's) and through loans to state and local development companies.

---

[8] See "SBA Business Loans for Small Firms," Small Business Administration, Washington, D.C., U.S. Government Printing Office: O—654992, 1962.

SBIC's include both privately and publicly owned small business investment companies. The SBA licenses these companies to operate in accordance with the Small Business Investment Act of 1958, furnishes them with funds which they may require under the Act, and regulates their activities. SBIC's should be investigated as a possible source of money, for they are licensed to provide funds through long-term loans, the purchase of convertible debentures, the purchase of capital stocks, etc. There are also many benefits in forming SBIC's, including the special tax exemptions granted by Congress.

State and local development companies are formed to assist in financing small firms in their areas. The SBA makes loans to such companies. The idea is to aid community business growth through the process pictured on page 513.

These are only a few of the types of credit made available through the SBA. Refer again to the chart for a more complete picture.

Many other agencies of the federal government have programs beneficial to small business firms. Among these are the General Services Administration, Department of Defense, Department of Commerce, Department of Labor, Department of the Interior, Department of Agriculture, etc. One excellent source of such information is the pamphlet *Federal Handbook for Small Business*,[9] frequently updated and republished.

CONCLUSION

Starting your own business may still be relatively easy in these United States, but success still requires a combination of intelligence, experience, a sense of responsibility, a willingness to take a chance, and just plain old-fashioned work.

And how does the future look?

LOOKING AHEAD

. . . we are a nation of small businesses. As we look into the future, will we remain so? There is every likelihood that we will. The very large businesses will continue to grow, but the number of units in the small business category will steadily advance. Some estimate that in twenty years the number of small businesses in operation will increase by 1,000,000.

---

[9] Sponsored by Select Committee on Small Business, United States Senate, Select Committee on Small Business, United States House of Representatives, White House Committee on Small Business, and the Small Business Administration.

HOW SBA LOCAL DEVELOPMENT LOANS HELP COMMUNITIES

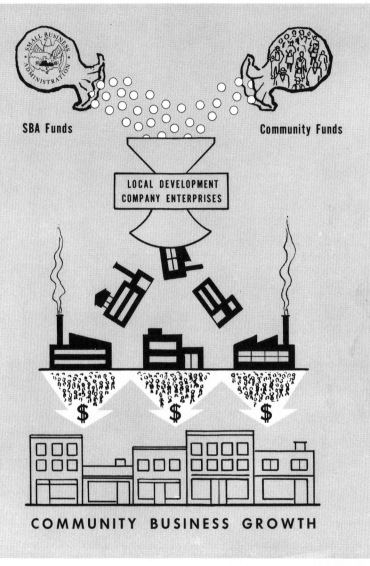

Source: "SBA Loans at Work," Small Business Administration, Office
of Information Services, U. S. Govt. Printing Office: 1962
O—655923, p. 11.

The population growth will call for many new services. Technological development will bring into being thousands of small units. There will be many men in new businesses dealing in products that do not even exist today.

Human nature being what it is and the normal trading risks being what they are, there will still be obstacles to success, even in the bright future. But we can learn the basic rules from those predecessors who have faced the pitfalls and who know how to avoid them.[10]

Questions

1. People differ. Some are suited to the problems of operating their own business while others are not. Discuss.

2. Present two advantages and two disadvantages of having your own business.

3. List five (5) factors that should be considered in selecting a location for a business.

4. How do you calculate the amount of capital needed to start a business?

5. Compare the proprietorship, partnership and corporation as forms of business organization.

6. "The greater the volume of sales the more successful the business." Discuss.

7. What is the difference between margin and markup?

8. Describe the sources of funds available to business firms.

9. Differentiate between "participating" and "direct" SBA loans.

10. What is a Small Business Investment Company?

Problems

1. John Hemingway has for many years been a cook in a fine restaurant. One day he becomes "fed up." He gets a good salary but sees the owner of the business making a large profit and enjoying a high

---

[10] W. H. Kuehn, *The Pitfalls in Managing a Small Business,* Dun & Bradstreet, Inc., 1956, p. 23.

standard of living. John reasons that it is his cooking which attracts customers. Therefore he should start his own restaurant and make a lot more money because he will get the profits. After all, if he has worked in a restaurant for many years, he has certainly had plenty of experience. What do you think of John's idea?

2. Bill Sampson plans to start his own garage business. He has a choice. Should he build his own garage and acquire new equipment or should he buy an existing garage, which the present owner wants to sell as he can't make a go of it? Bill doubts that the existing garage would be a good buy. After all, even if it is stocked with all of the necessary supplies and equipment, if the old owner couldn't make a profit there must be something wrong with the garage or the location. What do you think?

3. Andrew Levering is starting his own business. He knows very little about the characteristics of the different forms of business organization, but he has heard that the corporation has the advantage of limited liability. Therefore, according to Andrew, everyone starting his own business should incorporate. What do you think?

4. Using the chart "How Much Should a Salesperson Sell" calculate:
   a. The amount a salesman must sell to justify his salary of $70 a week if his salary is supposed to amount to 8.0% of sales.
   b. The salary actually earned by the salesman if his salary is supposed to be 12.5% of sales and his weekly sales are $400.

5. Sara Mathews owns a gift shop. She figures that to operate at a profit she must have a margin of 30%. Therefore, when she buys an article for $5.00 she sells it for $6.50. Is she correct?

Selected Readings

Expenses in Retail Businesses, Merchants Service, The National Cash Register Company, Dayton, Ohio

Federal Handbook for Small Business, Sponsored by Select Committee on Small Business, United States Senate, Select Committee on Small Business, United States House of Representatives, White House Comm ttee on Small Business, Small Business Administration, 1962 (frequently updated)

Kuehn, W. H., The Pitfalls in Managing a Small Business, Dun & Bradstreet, Inc., New York, New York, Sixth Printing 1961, Copyright 1956

Profitable Management for Main Street, Dun & Bradstreet, Inc., Public Relations Division, 99 Church St., New York 8, New York, 1959

Slavin, Albert and Armen, Seth Avakian, *Small Business Accounting in Massachusetts—Practices and Problems,* Prepared by The Bureau of Business and Economic Research, Northeastern University, Boston, Mass., under the Small Business Administration Management Research Grant Program, 1962

Small Business Administration; Office of Information Services, Washington, D.C.

Horne, John E., "A Message from the Administrator, SBA Loans at Work," U.S. Government Printing Office, O—655923, 1962

"Key Features of SBA's Principal Lending Programs," U.S. Government Printing Office, O—677836, March, 1963

"SBA Business Loans for Small Firms," U.S. Government Printing Office, O–654992, 1962

Johnson, Robert W., *Financial Management,* Allyn and Bacon, Inc., Boston, Mass., 1962, Second Edition

Corley, Robert N., and Black, Robert L., *The Legal Environment of Business,* McGraw-Hill Book Company, Inc., New York, N.Y., 1963

Chapter 18

ESTATE PLANNING

Some fine but unfortunate person will die during the time it takes to read this paragraph. He can be described as a "fine" individual because his life has been well spent. He worked hard, went to church regularly, was an excellent family man, and had all the attributes of a good citizen. He can be described as "unfortunate" in the sense that at death his assets were unnecessarily depleted by taxes, and those individuals whom he loved the most did not receive the amount from his assets which he would have wished them to receive.

These things happened because this individual did not include estate planning in his thoughts of the future. Obviously, since his assets did not go where he would have wished, he did not leave a will, an essential instrument in estate planning.

Should young people be worried about such problems? The answer is a very definite "yes." In fact, if any one group was selected as *the* group that should be most concerned, young married couples—especially those with children—would be well in the running. In this group the heir is often a young widow and the estate is small. Every possible protection is needed.

While no accurate figure is available, it is often estimated that at least half of the property owners in this country die without leaving a will. This means that their estate, everything they have worked for, may not be distributed as they would have wished. Other results of a lack of estate planning during life may be unnecessarily high taxes, an inadequate total estate, and other related problems.

If you own anything at the time you die, you have an estate. The best time to begin the building of an estate is while you are relatively young. One of the most important considerations is whether or not the estate is going to be large enough. If you believe that your wife and children will need a larger estate than will be provided, the time to consider ways to increase its size is just as early in life as possible. You may even find that your estate is too large, though, of course, this will not be a too common discovery. It is possible, however, that after taking inventory, the real total value of your estate may be larger than you anticipated. You may prefer to use a part of it now rather than leave it all in the total inheritance to come.

Another problem concerns who will share in the estate. A series of questions should be asked in determining this. Who will receive the benefits of your hard work? More important, who do *you* want to receive these benefits? What protection can be provided to make certain that these benefits are not unwisely used by those whom you wish to protect?

There are many objectives, goals, and legal technicalities, which must be considered. A consideration of all of these problems is called "Estate Planning." Estate planning is a personal problem in which you have different problems and goals regarding your estate than your next door neighbor has with his estate. Both of you, however, should be aware of the fact that "Estate Planning" should be considered *now* instead of being put aside for a more convenient time. Furthermore, this is not a "do it yourself" project. The services of a good lawyer, banker, accountant, life insurance agent, or other qualified expert, are absolutely necessary.

THE ESTATE PLAN

The development of an estate plan involves several questions:

1. Whom is the plan for?
2. What are the objectives of the plan?
3. When should the estate be divided?
4. What does the estate consist of?
5. What methods are to be used?

Whom is the Plan for?

Your plan must be good, not only for those who come after you, but for you during your lifetime. The primary reason for making a plan, however, is to benefit certain other persons. A wife and children are usually the first to be considered. There often are others: a daughter-in-law, loyal employees, or charities, for example.

The important point at this time concerns procedure. It is wrong to determine what you have and then decide who should receive it. The better way is to identify the individuals involved, to analyze these individuals, and to plan for them the greatest benefit. A wise plan for one individual may not be a wise plan for another. Individuals vary in terms of personality, education, health, needs, and many other ways. To plan wisely you must plan for a *person*—not a name.

For example, the following characteristics might be applied to a wife:

young	strong
middle aged	weak
old	healthy
financially astute	delicate
financially inept	invalid
employable	"remarriageable"
unemployable	not "remarriageable"
extravagant	good mother
frugal	poor mother
stingy	good judge of character
desirable relatives	poor judge of character
greedy relatives	strong willed
generous relatives	easily led

All of these characteristics, and many more, could be used to describe wives in general (or husbands for that matter), but only certain of them can be used to describe any one specific wife. A recognition of these characteristics is essential in the construction of an estate plan.

In some states the law requires you to take care of certain members of your family. Your spouse, for example, *must* share in your estate under the laws of many states. Your plan might be subject to such legal limitations.

What are the Objectives of the Plan?

What are you trying to accomplish by your plan? What do you really want for specific heirs? Are you interested in providing a home? Education? Family support? Capital for emergencies? Protection against incompetency?

> Here are some of the objectives which could come to your mind in planning for your wife's future happiness and security:
> To provide her with an adequate and convenient home;
> To provide her with satisfactory income;
> To assure her a reasonable amount of luxury if she wishes it;
> To protect her against the partial incompetence which may come with senility;
> To protect her against evil influences;
> To protect her against her own improvidence;
> To give her complete financial management;
> To arrange for competent financial advice or management;
> To give her financial protection only until her remarriage;
> To enable her to continue your own business;
> To enable her to start a business of her own;
> To cause your business to be managed so that she will reap its benefits;
> To give her complete control of the children's eventual share of your wealth;
> To limit that control;
> To make sure that she cannot interfere with the children's independence.[1]

Beneficiaries differ, and for this reason each should receive special treatment. Treating all beneficiaries alike may be just as unfair to them as not planning at all.

When should the Estate be Divided?

If you owned a business and wanted your son to run it after you were gone, would you plan to leave it to him by will, or would

---

[1] From the book, *Wormser's Guide to Estate Planning* by René A. Wormser © 1958 by Prentice Hall, Inc., Englewood Cliffs, New Jersey, pp. 35–36.

it be better to give him an interest in it, by gift or in trust, during your lifetime?

If you wanted to provide for others out of the income from the business, would you rely wholly upon your son's judgment as to who should get what, or would you prefer to establish the provisions you want others to enjoy?

If you keep your son waiting too long, he may develop his own interests, and lose all interest in perpetuating your business or its income. The business may be lost, or sold at a sacrifice, and the income lost to those for whom you hoped to provide. Consider his interests and abilities, and plan your estate accordingly. Consider the needs of others, and gratify these needs when your help can be most appreciated. In other words, plan to give when the giving does the most good.

What does the Estate Consist of?

To determine how much you are worth, list all of your assets and liabilities, and subtract. The difference is your net worth.

Examine this net worth carefully. Of what does it consist? Is there enough cash to cover estate taxes and expenses, or might a business have to be liquidated, or real estate sold, to raise the necessary cash? Such forced sales would almost certainly reduce the value of your estate, and the size of your bequests. They might even deprive your son of a livelihood, or your widow of a home.

Take good account of what you have before you start to plan. Then plan to have enough. A satisfactory estate plan must provide sufficient cash to pay the inheritance tax and meet the many expenses that must be paid out of the estate. Chart 18–1 illustrates how much average estate settlement costs are.

What Methods are to be Used?

There are five ways in which property may be passed on to heirs:
1. By gift;
2. By will;
3. By right of inheritance (no valid will);
4. By joint ownership;
5. By naming a beneficiary in a contract.

Each of these methods can be used in estate planning. Each can be subdivided. A gift, for example, might be either a simple gift or a trust. In the absence of a will, state laws prevail and these vary

Chart 18–1

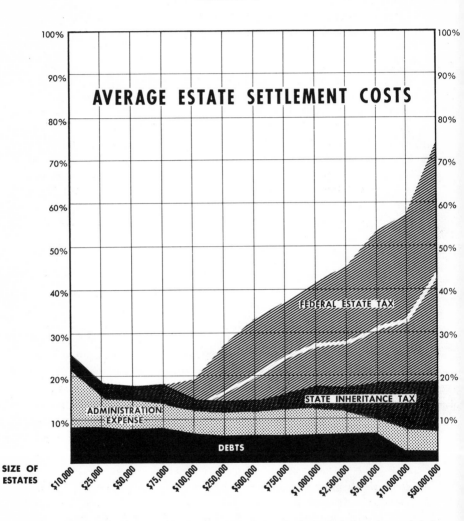

This graph was prepared by the Estate Recording Company, an independent statistical organization, from a survey of the court records of over 10,000 estates probated in all parts of the United States. "Debts" comprise mortgages payable, income and real estate taxes, and everything else the decedent owed; "Administration Expense" includes funeral costs, fees, court costs, and miscellaneous charges; "State Inheritance Tax" is the average found as a result of this study.

The broken line indicates the extent of the Federal Estate Tax in those estates where the full marital deduction was taken but in those estates where no marital deduction was taken the complete Federal Estate Tax applied.

Source: Estate Recording Company, San Diego 5, Calif. Copyright, Estate Recording Company.

between states. Contracts include life insurance policies, annuities, and pension plans, which name a specific beneficiary.

These methods are the tools of estate planning and careful attention should be given to each. Their proper use will benefit everyone.

WILLS

Many people avoid the subject of "Wills" because it is associated with dying. Others are indifferent to it because they believe it to be something with which only the wealthy are concerned. Neither viewpoint is a legitimate reason for failure to have a will. First, mortal existence is just that—mortal—and inevitably ends. Second, those with extremely few assets need a will, in some respects, more than persons of considerable wealth. If an estate is large enough, it is unlikely that a casual attitude toward estate planning will leave any of the heirs destitute, but if the estate is small, the heirs need all the financial protection possible.

Intestacy

A person who dies without leaving a will is said to have died "intestate." In such a situation, state laws determine the division of the estate. Imagine a quite common situation. Mr. Bacon dies and leaves, as his heirs, a loyal wife (sixty years old) and two adult children. The children have been successful, and are financially quite well off. Neither has relied upon the parents for many years, and neither has maintained a "close" relationship. Mr. Bacon's wife has only his estate to live on, after his death. Mr. Bacon's estate amounts to $75,000, and he assumes that this will be sufficient to support his wife for the remainder of her life.

Under the laws of many states, and in the absence of a will, Mr. Bacon's wife would receive only one-third of his estate and his children would receive two-thirds. His children do not need the money; his wife does. The children might take care of her, but she is now dependent upon their charity. If she lives for another ten years, her share of the estate would amount to $2,500 per year ($25,000 divided by 10). Of course, this money would probably earn interest during this period, but she obviously will live far less comfortably than she would have if she had received the total estate, or $7,500 per year ($75,000 divided by 10). If Mr. Bacon had made a will, the estate would have been left the way he wished it.

When a person dies intestate, the court appoints someone to settle the estate. This may work out satisfactorily, but, in some instances, the task is placed in the hands of a stranger. Not only is it more difficult to deal with a stranger than with a friend under trying circumstances, but the court appointee is limited by the letter of the law, and does not have the freedom of action that can be given to an executor. The "executor" is a person named in a will to carry out the terms of the will. The person selected by the court to administer an estate when no valid will exists, is an "administrator." A person selected by the court to manage an estate if the heir is either a minor or an incompetent adult, is a "guardian."

Most people would certainly prefer to have their estate handled by a friend, rather than to leave the task to a court appointee. This can be done only if an executor is specified in a will.

Some other undesirable results of intestacy are: (1) the estate must be distributed immediately, even though some planned division over a period of years might be far more advantageous for the heirs; (2) settlement costs and taxes may be heavier; and (3) questions concerning a clear title to real estate may exist. Everyone should have a will.

It is sometimes thought that having property jointly owned eliminates the need of a will. This is erroneous. Bank accounts, securities, and other investments, jointly owned, are still subject to inheritance taxes, unless the heir can prove that he or she actually contributed the funds involved. Joint ownership does not avoid inheritance taxes and cannot be considered as a substitute for a will.[2]

Advantages of a Will

To summarize, the advantages of making a will are:

1. You distribute your estate the way you wish. The law will restrict you very little. You can provide for those you care about, and leave gifts for the charities important to you.
2. You choose the executor best suited to settle your estate and deal with your family. You can give this executor broad powers to sell or lease property, to continue your business or sell it under the right conditions.
3. You can avoid unnecessary taxes.
4. You leave your beneficiary a clear title to real estate. Along with the title, you give power to sell.

---

[2] "Joint Ownership—right for you?," *Changing Times, The Kiplinger Magazine,* The Kiplinger Washington Editors, Inc., Washington, D.C., June 1962, pp. 33–36.

5. A carefully drawn Will prevents the controversy that sometimes arises among heirs.
6. By adding a few important sections to your Will you can create a trust, or trusts, designed to protect your family throughout their lives.[3]

Contents of a Will

"A will is a person's declaration of what is to be done after his death, which declaration is (1) revocable during his lifetime, (2) operative for no purpose until his death, and (3) applicable to the situation which exists at his death. Usually a will relates to the disposition of the maker's property."[4]

This is the definition of a will. What does this instrument contain, in order to meet all of these characteristics? While wills differ from person to person and estate to estate, there are five elements which generally exist in all wills.[5]

1. Opening recitations—these state the name of the person making the Will, his address, the fact that the following is his Will, the fact that he is competent and the cancellation of all previous Wills.
2. Dispositive clauses—these tell how and to whom your estate is to be divided. Usually they begin with specific items (family heirlooms etc.), next more general bequests (usually cash) and finally bequests disposing of the "residual" amount of the estate.
3. Administrative clauses—these set up the procedure to be followed in carrying out the instructions stipulated in the Will. They include the naming of an executor (or executors), trustees and guardians for children, and the specific powers which each of these is to have.
4. Testimonium clause—this states that the individual making the Will has actually done so and that on a certain date his name has been signed as witness to this fact.
5. Attestation clause—this clause is signed by witnesses who testify to the fact that the maker of the Will told them that this was his Will and signed it in their presence.

[3] "When there's a Will . . .," Old Colony Trust Company, Boston, Mass., p. 4.
[4] Thomas E. Atkinson, *Handbook of the Law of Wills*, West Publishing Co., St. Paul, Minn., 1953, p. 1. Permission to reprint granted by the copyright holder, West Publishing Company.
[5] "What's in a Will—and Why," 99 *New Ideas, Changing Times, The Kiplinger Magazine*, 1954, pp. 68–71.

The simplicity of these clauses is misleading. Even lawyers are advised to hire other lawyers when making out their wills. One tremendous problem concerns the wide variation in state laws. This alone would require a lawyer. In addition, even the simplest provisions of a will should be carefully stated in proper legal language and form. The address of the person making the will, for example, is quite important in that it will help to determine which state will have jurisdiction over the estate. This is important for inheritance tax purposes.

Another legal problem is the situation where the maker of the will intends to bar a child from sharing in the estate; a ne'er-do-well son, for example, who has led a wasteful life and has earned a reputation as a spendthrift. The father wants to leave his estate to his wife and his other child, a hardworking, highly regarded offspring. Usually, the mere omission of the spendthrift son's name will not serve to prevent him from sharing in the estate, as statutes in most states will assume that the father did not wish to disinherit his son. At the very least, it is necessary to specifically state the son's name in the will, and the fact that he is not to receive any portion of the estate. In addition to this statement, some states further require that the property involved be specifically given to someone else.

These few examples should indicate that making a will necessitates hiring a lawyer. The service performed is quite definitely worth the cost.

Selecting an executor, trustee, or guardian, deserves much more consideration than it often receives. The duties of an executor, especially when a large estate is involved, are quite numerous and complicated. This is indicated in Chart 18–2, pages 536 and 537. Examination of this chart should also emphasize the distinct advantage of naming a competent executor in a will, rather than leaving such responsibilities to an administrator, trustee, or guardian, selected by the probate court.

Another clause that should be in most wills is a "Common Disaster Clause." If a husband and wife are fatally injured in an automobile accident, it is often extremely difficult to determine which one died first. This is quite important, as it may determine which heir or heirs will inherit the estate. If the wife dies first, the husband would inherit from her, and his heirs would inherit from him. If the husband dies first, the wife would inherit from him, and her heirs would inherit from her. An example of a "Common Disaster Clause" is:

If any beneficiary named or referred to in this, my Will, and I shall die under such circumstances that it is difficult or impossible to determine who predeceased the other, then I direct that the terms and provisions of this my Will shall be construed as though I had survived such beneficiary and that my estate shall be administered and distributed in all respects accordingly.[6]

A Wife's Will

It is often incorrectly assumed that only the man in the family need make a will. A wife's will is important because:

If a wife *dies first*, her will disposes of her estate. Here, the wife's prior death can easily have an adverse effect on the husband's estate plan unless she has a carefully prepared will.

If a wife *survives her husband*, her will not only controls any separate property that she may have owned but also all property that she acquired upon the death of her husband. Here, in many instances, the wife's will is the final word that controls the distribution of a large part of the family's estate.[7]

Tax considerations also make it important for a wife to have a will. The important factor about a wife's will is that it be coordinated with that of her husband. Evidently, marriage requires a joint effort to the very end.

In a way, emphasizing the importance of a wife's will is merely stating again something which cannot be repeated too often, "Everyone should have a will." "Everyone" means everyone legally competent. While this excludes minors and insane persons, it certainly includes wives, who, today, control a sizeable share of the nation's wealth.

TRUSTS

One very important tool of estate planning is the "trust." This is especially useful in the case of larger estates. ". . . . a person's gross estate should be at least $100,000 before a trust would be of much

---

[6] *Suggestions for the Preparations of Wills and Trust Agreements*, Morgan Guaranty Trust Company of New York, 1963, p. 20.

[7] "The Importance of a Wife's Will," *Taxes and Estates*, Lowe & McKenney, New York, N.Y., May 1958, p. 2.

value taxwise."[8] There are, however, possible reasons for establishing a trust other than for tax purposes, and for this reason trusts should be considered by everyone concerned with estate planning.

Purposes of a Trust

There are two fundamental purposes in the mind of a person creating a trust:

1. To provide experienced, continuous supervision for a portion, or all, of his or her capital for the benefit of a specified person or persons (often minors, or adults unfamiliar with the many complexities of managing money). In some cases, the beneficiary is a charitable organization, or an institution, such as a college or a church.
2. To assure that the income, and eventually the principal, shall be distributed as desired.[9]

The brief parenthetical phrase in number one above, referring to those persons unfamiliar with the complexities of managing money, includes a large group of people. It sometimes seems that the great majority of the population could be placed in this general category, but there are certain specific groups which quite definitely deserve this classification. They are young children, adults considered legally incompetent (insane persons for example), and all of those wives, children, and heirs, who, due either to a lack of aptitude, training, or both, are unable to manage money successfully.

Types of Trusts

There are basically two kinds of trusts, the "testamentary trust" and the "living" or "voluntary trust." The difference is in the way they are established. The "testamentary trust" is established in a will, while the "living" or "voluntary trust" is created by a simple contract.

A "living trust" can be further subdivided into "revocable" and "irrevocable." If the desire is to create a trust which will avoid the inheritance tax, an "irrevocable living trust" will be created in such a manner that the person establishing the trust will have no interest

---

[8] "Estate Planning," *Changing Times, The Kiplinger Magazine*, The Kiplinger Washington Editors, Inc., Washington, D.C., Sept. 1960, p. 9.

[9] *Personal Trusts for Practical People*, First National City Bank, New York, N.Y., p. 4.

in it. Under such circumstances, the funds in trust are subject to a gift tax, but not to an inheritance tax.

A more usual situation is that of a couple now reaching retirement age, who wish to establish a trust in such a manner that they will receive the income from the trust as long as they live, but that after the death of both, the income from the trust will go to their children. Under such circumstances, a "revocable living trust" will be created. Since this is a "revocable" trust, it may be canceled or altered at any time prior to the death of the person creating it, and it will be subject to inheritance taxes rather than gift taxes.

The Trustee

Usually, trusts involve rather sizeable sums of money, but even in the case of relatively small trusts it is hoped that the funds will be carefully managed. This means that a trustee must be selected who will have the ability to manage the trust during its entire life.

> The ideal Trustee should be always available and never incapacitated by age, illness or death; should have unquestioned integrity and ample financial responsibility; and should maintain the closest and most friendly relations with the beneficiaries of the Trust.[10]

It can be safely stated that no single individual can meet all of these requirements. There are instances when some one person is selected as a trustee and, due to certain special circumstances, completely satisfies the needs of the trust. It can be easily understood, however, after considering the requirements of the trustee, why a bank is frequently selected to perform this function.

A bank, or some other institution, is especially necessary when a trust is created with an extremely long life. All states have rules against "perpetual" trusts, and state laws vary as to the length of time for which a trust may be created. In some states, a trust can be created only for a period ending when some presently living person dies, while in others it may be continued after the death of persons now alive. It would be possible, under either of these laws, to create a trust which would last for at least fifty or more years, and it would be quite as impossible to select an individual, believed to be a "competent" trustee, who will guarantee to remain either alive or

---

[10] *Wills and Trusts*, Old Colony Trust Company, Boston, Mass., August 1957, p. 16.

Table 18–1

FEDERAL ESTATE TAX
(1954 Code Sec. 2001)

Taxable Estate
(After deducting the $60,000
exemption)*

From	To	Tax = **	+ %	Of Excess Over
$ 0	$ 5,000	$ 0	3	$ 0
5,000	10,000	150	7	5,000
10,000	20,000	500	11	10,000
20,000	30,000	1,600	14	20,000
30,000	40,000	3,000	18	30,000
40,000	50,000	4,800	22	40,000
50,000	60,000	7,000	25	50,000
60,000	100,000	9,500	28	60,000
100,000	250,000	20,700	30	100,000
250,000	500,000	65,700	32	250,000
500,000	750,000	145,700	35	500,000
750,000	1,000,000	233,200	37	750,000
1,000,000	1,250,000	325,700	39	1,000,000
1,250,000	1,500,000	423,200	42	1,250,000
1,500,000	2,000,000	528,200	45	1,500,000
5,000,000	6,000,000	2,468,200	67	5,000,000
10,000,000	....	6,088,200	77	10,000,000

* If one half of taxable estate is transferred to a surviving spouse the federal estate tax does not become effective until the taxable estate is $120,000.

** The ultimate tax is computed at these rates less a credit for state taxes amounting to the figure indicated in a "State Death Tax Credit" table or the amount of state taxes, whichever is smaller.

competent for this period of time. A reputable bank, however, can be expected to be here for centuries.

TAXES

The two most important taxes affecting estate planning are inheritance taxes and gift taxes. They must be considered together, as it is quite often possible to reduce the tax burden on an estate by making gifts during one's lifetime.

Inheritance Taxes

Both federal and state governments levy a tax on estates. State taxes vary considerably, and make any specific discussion of state inheritance taxes impractical. Yet they are certainly important, especially to those persons with relatively small estates.

Imagine, for example, the case of a man living in Massachusetts, who died in 1962 and left his wife their home, and $20,000 in securities, bank accounts, and other assets. In Massachusetts, the home itself, or the proceeds from its sale, would not be subject to an inheritance tax, but the $20,000 would be. In 1962, the tax was 1.23 per cent on the first $10,000 and 2.46 per cent on the second, or a total of $369. The federal tax on this size estate would be zero. Now $369 may not seem like an extremely large sum of money, but to a widow looking forward to possibly another fifteen or twenty years of life, this $369 is a very real burden. While state inheritance taxes are not as high on large estates as the federal tax, they are the only tax, and therefore the most important tax, on relatively small estates.

How large is "relatively small?" Table 18–1 indicates the Federal Estate Tax on estates of various sizes. Notice, first, that the first $60,000 of an estate is tax exempt. Next, notice that a man and wife are each assumed to own half of their property. Under the Federal Estate Tax, 50 per cent of the entire estate would be considered as belonging to the surviving wife and therefore would not be taxed. There is, then, the $60,000 exemption that may be deducted from the remainder. This means that a wife could be left an estate of $120,000, exempt from any Federal Estate Tax.

Adjusted Gross Estate (after administrative expenses) Less marital deduction of 50%	$120,000 − 60,000
Balance Less $60,000 exemption	$ 60,000 − 60,000
Taxable estate	0

Now from the point of view of those levying taxes, $120,000 may be a "relatively small" amount, but from the point of view of most people, $120,000 is a considerable amount of money. Only the state inheritance tax would apply to the estate of a widow up to this amount.

The Federal Estate Tax is progressive in that it increases in percentage as the size of the estate increases, but, except for the marital deduction provision, all estates are subject to the same tax, regardless of who the beneficiary might be. In certain states, however, the state inheritance taxes are not only progressive, depending upon the size of the estate, but also vary depending upon the relationship between the deceased and the beneficiary. Under such laws, estates going to beneficiaries such as nephews and nieces will be subject to a higher rate of tax than those going to a wife or children.

One common misconception is that life insurance is not subject to inheritance taxes. Federal law requires that the face value of an insurance policy be included in a person's gross estate. In many states, life insurance payable to named beneficiaries is exempt from the state inheritance tax, but state laws vary, and must be considered individually.

Gift Taxes

Any reduction in inheritance taxes would be a boon to a person's heirs. The provision of adequate cash to meet the requirements of the tax collector, and the keeping of the tax burden to a minimum, are two of the functions that are performed by estate planning.

The principal method now available to reduce estate taxes is to reduce the estate by making gifts. Table 18–2 presents the Federal Gift Tax rates. Note that these rates are somewhat lower than those of the Federal Estate Tax. There are rarely any state gift taxes.

Table 18–2

FEDERAL GIFT TAX
(1954 Code Sec. 2502)

Taxable Gifts*

From	To	Tax =	+ %	Of Excess Over
....	$ 5,000	0	2¼	....
$ 5,000	10,000	112.50	5¼	$ 5,000
10,000	20,000	375	8¼	10,000
20,000	30,000	1,200	10½	20,000
30,000	40,000	2,250	13½	30,000
40,000	50,000	3,600	16½	40,000
50,000	60,000	5,250	18¾	50,000
60,000	100,000	7,125	21	60,000
100,000	250,000	15,525	22½	100,000
250,000	500,000	49,275	24	250,000
500,000	750,000	109,275	26¼	500,000
750,000	1,000,000	174,900	27¾	750,000
1,000,000	1,250,000	244,275	20¼	1,000,000

* "Taxable gifts" are amounts after deduction of $30,000 exemption. If a gift is to one's spouse, one-half may be deducted as a marital deduction.

If you wait until your last breath to give away part of your estate, you will be too late. Under such circumstances, a gift will be held to be "in contemplation of death" and taxable as part of the estate. In fact, any gift made within three years prior to death will be held as "made in contemplation," and will be taxed as part of the estate, unless the estate can prove that death was not contemplated. On the other hand, no gift made more than three years prior to death will be held to be "in contemplation."

The principal advantage of the use of gifts in estate planning is the exemptions which can be realized. In the first place, there is a total lifetime exemption of $30,000 before any gift taxes must be paid. In addition, $3,000 can be given to each of any number of people each year, without being taxed. These annual exemptions are in addition to the $30,000 lifetime exemption.

There is also a marital exemption in gift taxes. A wife is assumed to own half of any gift made to her by her husband. This means that $60,000 may be given to a wife (double the lifetime exemption of $30,000) under the lifetime exemption, and $6,000 (double the annual exemption) annually, without a gift tax. Furthermore, with the spouse's permission, this extra exemption may be used in making gifts to third persons. Mr. Jones might wish to give his son a sizeable gift. With his wife's permission, he may give his son $66,000 in one year (his wife's lifetime exemption of $60,000 plus her annual exemption of $6,000), or $6,000 per year for any number of years, without having the gifts subject to any gift tax.

Tax laws are extremely complicated. Even gift taxes are not quite as simple and definite as they might seem. Sometimes a gift may create an income tax saving. Sometimes an action may be considered taxable as a gift without the possibility having been considered. Some gifts should be made in the form of a trust. In our present society, it is necessary to consult a lawyer even when making a gift, to make certain that federal and state tax laws are properly understood.

It must also be remembered that tax laws change. States may or may not have a gift tax. Those who do not have them today may very well enact them tomorrow. Both federal and state rates will undoubtedly be changed, both on gifts and on estates. This is another reason why an expert must be consulted; to make certain that information is up-to-date.

Gifts should not be made indiscriminately, just to avoid the inheritance tax. The goals of the particular estate plan should always be considered. Quite often, however, when a large estate is involved, the problem is not one of making too many gifts but one of making too few.

Must you wait until both you and your wife are dead before the children get anything? It should certainly be a major objective to make sure that your wife is sufficiently protected for life; but you might consider carefully whether or not you wish to be certain also that your children will have some benefits from your wealth while they are still young enough to use it constructively.[11]

ADMINISTERING AN ESTATE

There are many special problems involved in estate planning. Only the most common, and to some degree the simplest, have been dealt with in this chapter, but these affect every estate. Another problem common to all estates is the final settlement.

Settlement of Estates

The settlement of an estate includes the paying of the deceased person's debts and the distributing of the remainder of the estate to his heirs and beneficiaries. The following steps must be followed in this settlement:

A. Prepare and present a petition to the Probate Court asking that a particular person be appointed the legal representative of the decedent's estate. If there is a will, it should accompany the petition. The legal representative in a will is known as an executor, or executrix if a woman. If no will, the legal representative is known as the administrator, or administratrix if a woman. The petition must contain the names and addresses of all the decedent's next-of-kin.
B. Obtain written consent to the petition from all the next-of-kin, or notify them as directed by the Court.
C. Publish legal notice in the newspaper for the benefit of creditors and next-of-kin who may have been omitted from the petition.
D. File a bond, with or without sureties as the case may be, with the Court.

---

[11] René A. Wormser, "The Story of Family Estate Planning," Boston Safe Deposit and Trust Company, Boston, Mass., Copyright 1957, Koster-Dana Corp., Stamford, Conn., pp. 78–79.

E. Obtain the appointment of the executor or administrator from the Court.

F. Obtain the appointment of an appraiser. Complete the appraisal of all assets of the estate and submit a copy to the Court.

G. Pay the bills, including income taxes, as soon as the legal representative is certain that the estate is solvent.

H. Pay estate and inheritance taxes and obtain receipts or waivers and file or record them.

I. Distribute the assets to the beneficiaries named in the will, or in accordance with the law if there is no will.

J. Prepare, file and obtain approval from the court, of all accounts and acts of the legal representative.[12]

While these steps apply specifically to the Commonwealth of Massachusetts, they are typical of the steps required in all states. Note that all of these steps require time, effort and knowledge. Some of them (H for example) concern tax forms which are extremely complicated. None of these steps can be taken in leisurely fashion. Not only do particular heirs need the use of some of the estate immediately, a widow for example, but some of the assets, such as a business, may require constant attention. Furthermore, state and federal laws establish specific time limits.

Chart 18–2 indicates all of the things that an executor "can" do. These do not all enter into the settlement of every estate, but a careful examination of this chart should indicate why, especially in large estates, a bank is frequently selected as the executor of an estate. Everyone should ask, "How many of these duties will the executor of my estate have to perform?," and base his selection of a competent executor on the answer.

LOOSE-ENDS

Good estate planning requires careful attention to small details. Chart 18–3 indicates most of the details that should be considered. Many of these are quite simple *today*, such as stock certificates, discharge papers, etc., but may be extremely troublesome for your heirs after your death. Many of these are complicated, such as making a will, and require the services of a lawyer. All must be considered carefully.

---

[12] Bruce G. Brown, *Settlement of Estates*, Cooperative Extension Service, University of Massachusetts, Amherst, Mass., 1961, p. 4.

Chart 18–2

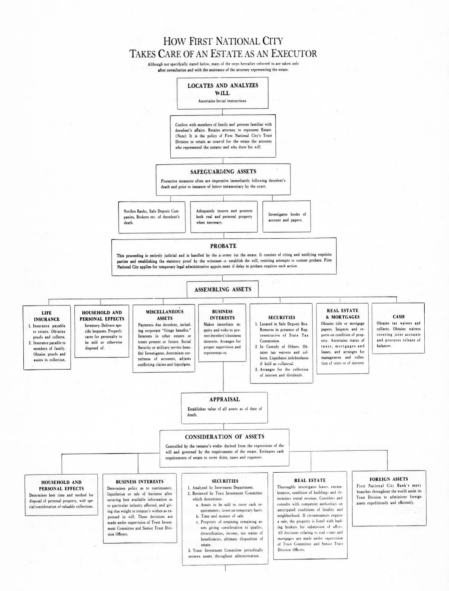

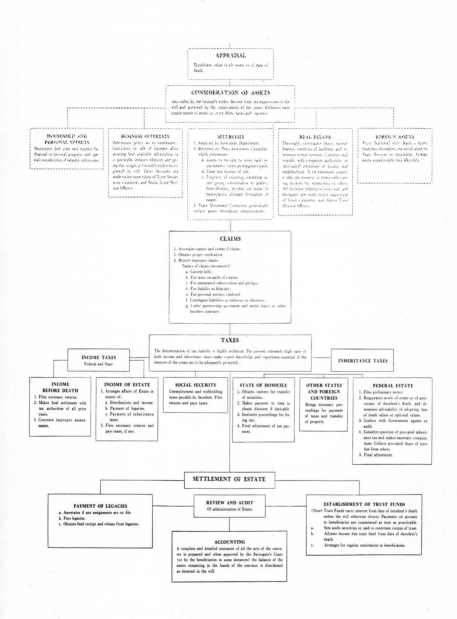

Source: First National City Bank, New York, N.Y.

Chart 18–3

YOUR CHECK LISTS[13]
Are your affairs in order?
Use these to find out.

1. Are your records in order?

	yes	no	needs more work
will	☐	☐	☐
insurance policies	☐	☐	☐
real estate deeds	☐	☐	☐
stock certificates	☐	☐	☐
bonds	☐	☐	☐
notes receivable	☐	☐	☐
bank books	☐	☐	☐
safe-deposit key	☐	☐	☐
income tax returns for prior years	☐	☐	☐
marriage certificate	☐	☐	☐
divorce papers	☐	☐	☐
family birth certificates	☐	☐	☐
list of close relatives with addresses and dates of birth	☐	☐	☐
veteran's discharge paper or certificate	☐	☐	☐
social security card or record of number	☐	☐	☐
list of your assets	☐	☐	☐
burial instructions	☐	☐	☐
general instructions to wife, including list of advisers	☐	☐	☐

2. What is the value of your estate?

assets:
savings   _____
securities   _____
real estate   _____
life insurance face value   _____
other assets   _____

total assets _____

_____
[13] "How to Help Your Widow," *99 New Ideas,* The Kiplinger Magazine, The Kiplinger Washington Editors, Inc., Washington, D.C., 1963, p. 34.

estimated liabilities:
debts
burial expense
estate and inheritance taxes
income taxes due
administration expense

total liabilities ————————————
net estate ————————————

3. What would your wife's income be?

source: monthly income
life insurance
social security
veteran's pension
income from securities (Figure 3½% annual
return on amounts to be invested. Omit value
of home if wife is to occupy it.)
income from trust funds
any income wife might have of her own such
as salary, if she would be working, help from
relatives, etc.

total ————————————

What would your wife's minimum expenses be?
food
shelter
clothing, medical, miscellaneous
education

total ————————————

4. List of advisers   (1st, 2nd, 3rd choice)
lawyer   1 ———————————————
                                2 ———————————————
                                3 ———————————————

bank officer
or businessman   1 ———————————————
                                2 ———————————————
                                3 ———————————————

investment adviser   1_____
                                     2_____
                                     3_____

insurance adviser   1_____
                                     2_____
                                     3_____

_____

5. Planning

	yes	no
Have you made an over-all plan for your estate?	☐	☐
Have you a will?	☐	☐
Has your wife a will?	☐	☐
Are your beneficiary arrangements up to date in insurance policies and pension plans?	☐	☐
Have you made provision for children's guardian?	☐	☐
Have you left burial instructions?	☐	☐
Have you minimized taxes and administration costs?	☐	☐
Have you gone over these matters recently with a lawyer?	☐	☐

Mr. Adam might be used as an example of what can happen when estates are not planned. When he died, the undertaker wanted to know the names of his grandparents, but his children didn't remember them. His wife's income was inadequate, and she was forced to live with her daughter. He left no instructions as to place of burial, and his heirs argued about it. His sister and brother fought over heirlooms which both claimed had been promised to them. What a sorry condition in which to leave a person's affairs.

If the purpose of an estate plan is to take care of your loved ones, then you should make their job as easy as possible when your problems and your estate become theirs.

Questions

1. Why is a will an essential instrument in estate planning?

2. Name five (5) objectives of a typical estate plan.

3. Would you prefer your estate to be handled by an administrator or an executor? Discuss.

4. Joint ownership solves the problems of estate planning. Discuss.

5. What limitations are imposed by the Internal Revenue in the use of gifts to reduce a person's taxable estate?

6. Dying "intestate" is sometimes better than dying under the terms of a will. Discuss.

7. Distinguish between a dispositive clause and a testimonium clause in a will.

8. In recent years, the "living" trust has gained popularity in estate planning. What are the characteristics of this form of trust?

9. How does a person qualify for the marital deduction?

10. Must a bond always be filed (with the court) by an executor in the settlement of an estate?

Problems

1. A has been studying "estate planning" in great detail, particularly in (attempting to reduce) administration costs of his estate. He is a married man with four (4) young children ranging in age from 2 to 15. He is a traveling manufacturer's representative for a large chemical company. He lives in New York but also maintains a summer cottage in Connecticut and a hunting cabin in Maine. Most of his assets are in real estate. He has named his brother-in-law as his estate executor. What suggestions would you advise to aid A in reducing administration costs?

2. C owns $80,000 of life insurance, $10,000 in savings, a home held jointly with his wife for $40,000, and stock worth $4,000 based on current market value. He has been told by his life insurance agent that a widow receives lump sum life insurance proceeds tax free. He has also been told by a close friend that jointly owned property is exempt from inheritance taxes. In estimating what federal estate tax must be paid in the event of his death, he ignores the $80,000 of insurance and his $40,000 home. Explain the fallacies of his reasoning.

3. *X* has recently drawn a will, leaving everything he owns to his wife. He has included the common disaster provision, named primary and contingent guardians and is satisfied that if he should die his wife would receive his entire $100,000 estate with but a small amount being paid to the State for inheritance taxes. What factors may he have overlooked that could account for the fact that Mrs. *X* may receive considerably *less* than the $100,000?

4. *B* is considering establishing a trust fund of $30,000 for the college education of his son, age 10. He wants his son to receive $6000 per year and then $6000 as a graduation present. If he establishes an irrevocable 15 year trust, what possible problems might arise?

5. Referring to Table 18–1 in the chapter, compute the federal estate tax for an estate of $106,000 assuming:
   a. No marital deduction
   b. Full marital deduction

Selected Readings

Brown, Bruce G., *Settlement of Estates,* Cooperative Extension Service, University of Massachusetts, Amherst, Mass., Publication No. 368, 1961

How to Choose Your Executor, First National City Bank, New York, N.Y., 1961

How to Safeguard Your Estate, The Connecticut Mutual Life Insurance Co., Hartford, Connecticut

Personal Trusts for Practical People, First National City Bank, Trust Division, New York, N.Y., 1962

Suggestions for the Preparation of Wills and Trust Agreements, Morgan Guaranty Trust Company of New York, New York, N.Y., 1963

Wills and Trusts, Old Colony Trust Co., Boston, Mass.

Wormser, René A., *Wormser's Guide to Estate Planning,* Prentice-Hall, Inc., Englewood Cliffs, N.J., 1958, Second Printing 1959

Index